Microsoft® Word 6.0

For Windows™

Katie Layman
Gavilan College, Gilroy, California

and

LaVaughn Hart
Chabot College, Hayward, California

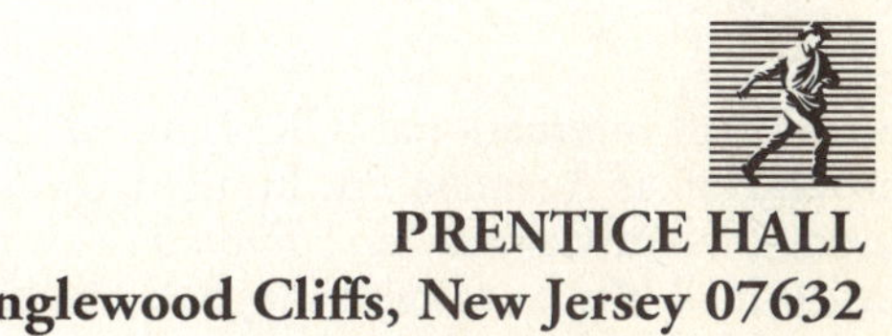

PRENTICE HALL
Englewood Cliffs, New Jersey 07632

Library of Congress Cataloging-in-Publication Data

Layman, Katie
Microsoft Word 6.0 for Windows / Katie Layman and LaVaughn Hart.
p. cm.
Includes index.
ISBN 0-13-124868-5
1. Microsoft Word for Windows. 2. Word processing. I. Hart, LaVaughn. II. Title.
Z52.5.M523L37 1995
652.5'536--dc20 95-12903
CIP

Acquisition editor: *Carolyn Henderson*
Editorial/production supervision: *Elaine Lynch*
Buyer: *Paul Smolenski*
Cover design: *Maureen Eide*
Editorial assistant: *Jane Avery*

Printed in the United States of America

10 9 8 7 6 5 4 3

ISBN 0-13-124868-5

Prentice-Hall International (UK) Limited, *London*
Prentice-Hall of Australia Pty. Limited, *Sydney*
Prentice-Hall of Canada Inc., *Toronto*
Prentice-Hall Hispanoamericana, S.A., *Mexico*
Prentice-Hall of India Private Limited, *New Delhi*
Prentice-Hall of Japan, Inc., *Tokyo*
Simon & Schuster Asia Pte. Ltd., *Singapore*
Editora Prentice-Hall do Brasil, Ltda., *Rio de Janeiro*

CONTENTS

Part 4—A Step Ahead: Advanced Documents and Features

Chapter 13: Create a Letterhead, Flier, and Newsletter 305

Chapter 14: Create Documents with Special Features 333

Chapter 15: Create Documents Using Special Functions 353

Chapter 16: Managing Document Windows and Files 377

Appendices

PREFACE

Introduction

The purpose of this textbook is to provide students with simple step-by-step instructions to quickly master Word 6.0 for Windows. Numerous hands-on activities and easy-to-follow instruction lists within the text's chapters allow students to learn by doing. All of these carefully guided walk-thoroughs are accompanied by thorough, precise explanations of each Word function being introduced, making *Microsoft® Word 6.0 for Windows*™ appropriate for use in individualized instruction programs as well as for use in traditional classrooms.

By focusing on the *tasks* students need to perform along with the help from Word functions, ***Microsoft® Word 6.0 for Windows*** aids instructors in their efforts to assist students in acquiring the work-ready skills needed to succeed in today's job market. But the book's commitment to students' acquisition of these skills does not stop here.

As students work through the text's activities, they are introduced to the proper format for various business documents (e.g., memorandums, letters, reports, résumés, and newsletters). What's more, all of the text's activities are based on authentic, real-world documents—"just what students will encounter in everyday life on the job," according to one reviewer. And because students can never have too much training in or reinforcement of their basic English and grammar skills, each chapter includes an *Enriching Language Arts Skills* section and activity.

Finally, the end-of-chapter and end-of-part sections—*The Next Step* and *Checking Your Step* sections, respectively—are designed to fulfill the competencies and basic skill requirements that have been identified by Tech Prep and the Secretary's Commission on Achieving Necessary Skills (SCANS), U. S. Department of Labor. *The Next Step* and *Checking Your Step* activities reinforce students' reading, writing, thinking, and decision-making skills. SCANS icons are placed within the text so that instructors and students can quickly identify the activities that build **SCANS/Tech Prep** competencies.

Content Highlights

Above all else, ***Microsoft® Word 6.0 for Windows*** is committed to providing students with the work-ready skills they need to excel. The book's pedagogical system and the features described in the following section have been carefully crafted to achieve this end. Some of the key components of this performance-based system are as follows:

The chapter opening *Features Covered* sections identify the Word functions introduced in the chapter and provide students with a clear road map of precisely what is to come.

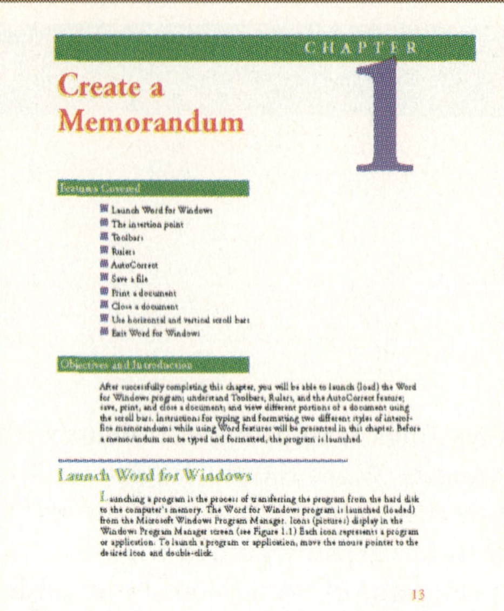
CHAPTER 1

Create a Memorandum

Features Covered

- Launch Word for Windows
- The insertion point
- Toolbars
- Rulers
- AutoCorrect
- Save a file
- Print a document
- Close a document
- Use horizontal and vertical scroll bars
- Exit Word for Windows

Objectives and Introduction

After successfully completing this chapter, you will be able to launch (load) the Word for Windows program; understand Toolbars, Rulers, and the AutoCorrect feature; save, print, and close a document; and view different portions of a document using the scroll bars. Instructions for typing and formatting two different styles of interoffice memorandums while using Word features will be presented in this chapter. Before a memorandum can be typed and formatted, the program is launched.

Launch Word for Windows

Launching a program is the process of transferring the program from the hard disk to the computer's memory. The Word for Windows program is launched (loaded) from the Microsoft Windows Program Manager. Icons (pictures) display in the Windows Program Manager screen (see Figure 1.1) Each icon represents a program or application. To launch a program or application, move the mouse pointer to the desired icon and double-click.

13

Objectives and Introduction preview chapter material in terms of the actual tasks students will perform as they work through the chapter and provide a narrative overview of the chapter material.

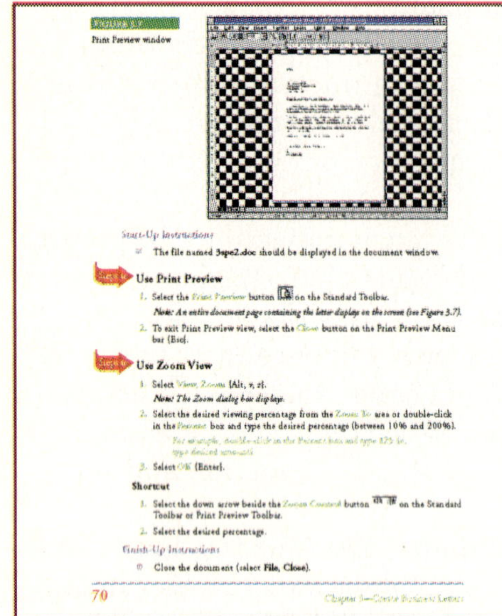
Print Preview window

Start-Up Instructions

- The file named **3spe2.doc** should be displayed in the document window.

Use Print Preview

1. Select the Print Preview button on the Standard Toolbar.
   ***Note:** An entire document page containing the letter displays on the screen (see Figure 3.7).*
2. To exit Print Preview view, select the Close button on the Print Preview Menu bar (Esc).

Use Zoom View

1. Select View, Zoom (Alt, v, z).
   ***Note:** The Zoom dialog box displays.*
2. Select the desired viewing percentage from the Zoom To area or double-click in the Percent box and type the desired percentage (between 10% and 200%).
3. Select OK (Enter).

Shortcut

1. Select the down arrow beside the Zoom Control button on the Standard Toolbar or Print Preview Toolbar.
2. Select the desired percentage.

Finish-Up Instructions

- Close the document (select **File, Close**).

70

Numerous screen captures clarify concepts and instructions for students as they proceed through each chapter.

Careful step-by-step instruction lists are provided in the body of the chapter and are accompanied by a *Steps to* icon in the margin to make them easy for students to find when referring back to the text later.

In addition to the step-by-step instruction lists, activity-specific *Start-Up Instructions* and *Finish-Up Instructions* are clearly identified and provide information necessary to the completion of in-chapter activities. These, coupled with the *Steps to* icon, give students the best of both worlds—detailed, enumerated step-by-step tutorials now and easy-to-locate generic instruction lists later, when the text needs to function as a reference manual.

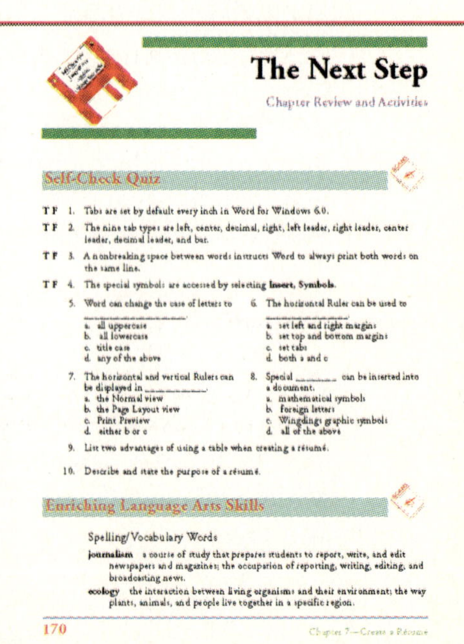
The Next Step

Chapter Review and Activities

Self-Check Quiz

T F 1. Tabs are set by default every inch in Word for Windows 6.0.

T F 2. The nine tab types are left, center, decimal, right, left leader, right leader, center leader, decimal leader, and bar.

T F 3. A nonbreaking space between words instructs Word to always print both words on the same line.

T F 4. The special symbols are accessed by selecting **Insert, Symbols**.

5. Word can change the case of letters to ____________.
   a. all uppercase
   b. all lowercase
   c. title case
   d. any of the above
6. The horizontal Ruler can be used to ____________.
   a. set left and right margins
   b. set top and bottom margins
   c. set tabs
   d. both a and c
7. The horizontal and vertical Rulers can be displayed in ____________.
   a. the Normal view
   b. the Page Layout view
   c. Print Preview
   d. either b or c
8. Special ________ can be inserted into a document.
   a. mathematical symbols
   b. foreign letters
   c. Wingdings graphic symbols
   d. all of the above
9. List two advantages of using a table when creating a résumé.
10. Describe and state the purpose of a résumé.

Enriching Language Arts Skills

Spelling/Vocabulary Words

journalism a course of study that prepares students to report, write, and edit newspapers and magazines; the occupation of reporting, writing, editing, and broadcasting news.

ecology the interaction between living organisms and their environment; the way plants, animals, and people live together in a specific region.

170 Chapter 7—Create a Résumé

Each end-of-chapter *Self-Check Quiz* includes true/false, multiple choice, and short answer questions, enabling students to check their understanding of key chapter concepts and procedures. (Answers are provided at the back of the book.)

A unique *Enriching Language Arts Skills* section at the end of each chapter reinforces students' spelling and grammar skills—skills the student is called on to use in the chapter's final hands-on activity.

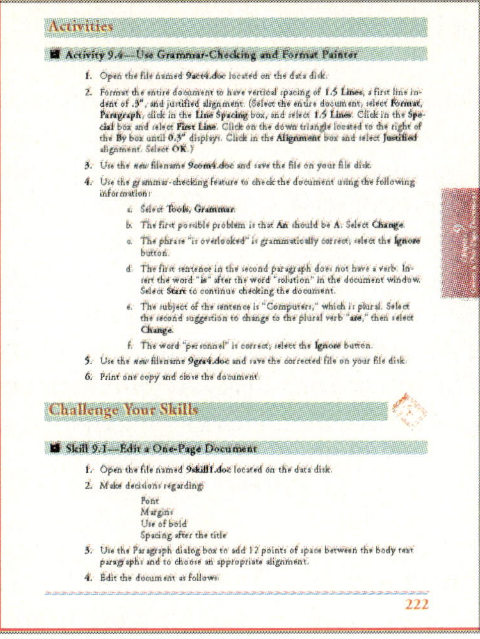

Activities

Activity 9.4—Use Grammar-Checking and Format Painter

1. Open the file named **9act4.doc** located on the data disk.
2. Format the entire document to have vertical spacing of **1.5 Lines**, a first line indent of .3", and justified alignment. (Select the entire document, select **Format, Paragraph**, click in the **Line Spacing** box, and select **1.5 Lines**. Click in the **Special** box and select **First Line**. Click on the down triangle located to the right of the **By** box until 0.3" displays. Click in the **Alignment** box and select **Justified** alignment. Select **OK**.)
3. Use the *new* filename **9com4.doc** and save the file on your file disk.
4. Use the grammar-checking feature to check the document using the following information:
   a. Select **Tools, Grammar**.
   b. The first possible problem is that **An** should be A. Select **Change**.
   c. The phrase "is overlooked" is grammatically correct; select the **Ignore** button.
   d. The first sentence in the second paragraph does not have a verb. Insert the word "**is**" after the word "solution" in the document window. Select **Start** to continue checking the document.
   e. The subject of the sentence is "Computers," which is plural. Select the second suggestion to change to the plural verb "**are**," then select **Change**.
   f. The word "personnel" is correct; select the **Ignore** button.
5. Use the *new* filename **9gra4.doc** and save the corrected file on your file disk.
6. Print one copy and close the document.

Challenge Your Skills

Skill 9.1—Edit a One-Page Document

1. Open the file named **9skill1.doc** located on the data disk.
2. Make decisions regarding:

   Font
   Margins
   Use of bold
   Spacing after the title
3. Use the Paragraph dialog box to add 12 points of space between the body text paragraphs and to choose an appropriate alignment.
4. Edit the document as follows:

222

Many guided, hands-on *Activities* at the close of each chapter let students practice—in a structured, unintimidating environment—what they've learned in the chapter.

Independent *Challenge Your Skills* activities at the close of each chapter give students ample practice to apply what they have learned without the help of guided instructions.

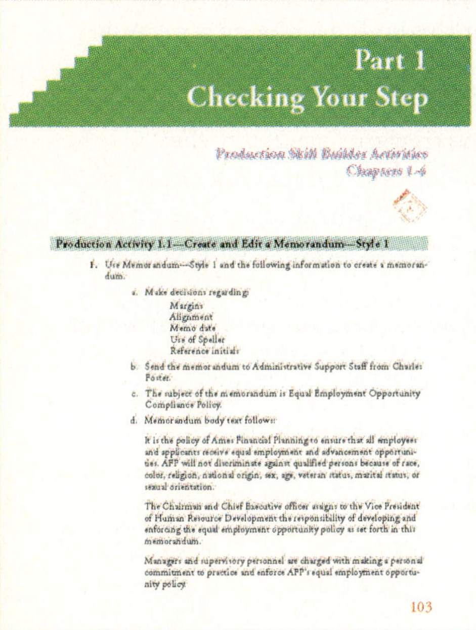

Part 1 Checking Your Step

Production Skill Builder Activities
Chapters 1-4

Production Activity 1.1—Create and Edit a Memorandum—Style 1

1. Use Memorandum—Style 1 and the following information to create a memorandum.
   a. Make decisions regarding:

      Margins
      Alignment
      Memo date
      Use of Speller
      Reference initials
   b. Send the memorandum to Administrative Support Staff from Charles Foster.
   c. The subject of the memorandum is Equal Employment Opportunity Compliance Policy.
   d. Memorandum body text follows:

      It is the policy of Ames Financial Planning to ensure that all employees and applicants receive equal employment and advancement opportunities. AFP will not discriminate against qualified persons because of race, color, religion, national origin, sex, age, veteran status, marital status, or sexual orientation.

      The Chairman and Chief Executive officer assigns to the Vice President of Human Resource Development the responsibility of developing and enforcing the equal employment opportunity policy as set forth in this memorandum.

      Managers and supervisory personnel are charged with making a personal commitment to practice and enforce AFP's equal employment opportunity policy.

103

End-of-part *Checking Your Step* production skill builder activities allow students to stretch their mastery of the program and to develop their decision-making and critical-thinking skills. The production skill builder activities can be used for testing, hands-on projects, or as brief office simulation exercises.

QUICKCLICKS

Quick Reference for Microsoft Word 6.0 for Windows

Layman and Hart — Prentice Hall

Alignment		
Change Alignment	Select the text that is to be changed. Click once on the desired alignment button (**Align Left, Center, Align Right**, or **Justify**) on the Formatting Toolbar.	60
Center Alignment (Horizontal Centering)	Position the insertion point to the left side of the screen and type the words to be centered. Select the **Center** alignment button on the Formatting Toolbar. Press **Enter** once. Select the **Align Left** button on the Formatting Toolbar to return to the left side of the screen.	18
AutoFormats		
Apply Auto Format	Place the insertion point at any location in the document or with the desired text selected, select the **AutoFormat** button on the Standard Toolbar. See also **Tables, Auto Format**.	357
AutoText		
Create an AutoText Entry	Select the desired text. Select the **Edit AutoText** button on the Standard Toolbar. Type a name for the AutoText entry in the Name box. Select **Add**.	338
Delete an AutoText Entry	Select the **Edit** menu and choose **AutoText**. Highlight the name of the AutoText entry to be deleted. Select the **Delete** button. Select **Close**.	339
Insert and AutoText Entry	Place the insertion point at the desired location. Type the AutoText name and then select the **Insert AutoText** button.	339
Bold Text		
	Select the desired text. Select the **Bold** button on the Formatting Toolbar.	61

Microsoft Word 6.0 for Windows QuickClicks—1

An excellent reference source is the *QuickClicks* booklet provided with each copy of the text. The *QuickClicks* booklet lists all the Word functions presented and includes page references should the student want to go back to a chapter for additional information.

Instructor Support Materials

A comprehensive *Instructor's Resource Manual* is available which contains solutions for the end-of-chapter short-answer questions and *all* practice activities, end-of-chapter activities, challenge activities, and skill-builder production activities. The manual includes a chapter overview, student objectives, lecture notes, teaching suggestions, and one or more additional activities for each chapter. Also provided are production and theory tests. Included with the *Instructor's Resource Manual* are a student data disk and instructor's disks. The student data disk includes unformatted files for practice activities, end-of-chapter activities, challenge activities, and production activities. The instructor's disks contain formatted files for the practice activities, end-of-chapter activities, challenge activities, and production and theory tests.

To the Student

Every chapter is divided into several sections with each section explaining a different Word function. An overview of each function is provided followed by Start-Up Instructions which present information or actions to be taken in order to prepare you for a hands-on practice activity. Following the Start-Up Instructions are numbered step-by-step instructions which guide you through each action necessary to perform the feature being learned. These are identified by the Steps to icon. Finish-Up Instructions follow each set of step-by-step instructions and indicate what should be performed in order to complete the practice activity.

The text for many chapter activities is provided on the data disk supplied to your instructor. You will see this icon in the text to indicate that the data (text) is available on disk. This saved text is necessary in order to perform the activity identified by the disk icon.

Answer the Self-Check Quiz questions and check your answers with the answer key provided at the back of the book. If desired, study the vocabulary words, punctuation, capitalization, or typing rule provided in the Enriching Language Arts section. Many of these vocabulary words and punctuation rules are used in the last activity of the Challenge Your Skills section at the end of each chapter and in the final Production Skill Builder Activity that is provided in each Part.

ACKNOWLEDGMENTS

A sincere thank you to our editor, Carolyn Henderson, for her avid support and constant attention to our business *and* personal needs. Using your superb editorial skills, you guided us through every detail needed to improve our book(s). Thank you! Your willingness to work with us seven days a week is very much appreciated. We prize your ideas, energy, and enthusiasm that you give to us and our projects!

Thank you, Jeanette Hart, for your assistance in writing the *Microsoft Word 6.0 for Windows* manuscript. Your presentation of material and explanations were most valuable. Many thanks too, for writing a comprehensive ***Instructor's Resource Manual*** and for creating the student and instructor disks. And thank you again for developing excellent teacher and student resources.

A tremendous thank you is extended to Judith Johnson, DeAnza College, for assisting in researching and writing information that made our job of finalizing material much easier and quicker to prepare.

Cheryl Dukarich, your assistance in preparing material for the table chapters was an immense help. Thank you, too, for your promptness and thoroughness in preparing the chapter content and instructions.

Thank you, Betsy Pollick, Gavilan College, for joining our team and assisting with the manuscript writing.

Kathy Ponti, College of San Mateo, your keystroke testing skills are outstanding. Thank you for providing us with questions and suggestions that assisted in creating accurate instructions, activities, and function explanations.

Alana Zdinak and Elaine Lynch, thank you for your production assistance. We appreciate you keeping us on schedule!

A huge thank you to the sales representatives and support staff at Prentice Hall, Inc. who have contributed and continue to contribute outstanding support for the success of the series.

To Nancy Evans, our marketing manager, we very much appreciate your interest in marketing our books. Thank you for personally meeting with us and for responding promptly to our requests.

Natacha St. Hill, marketing assistant, thank you for **all** your excellent assistance. We always know we can count on you to promptly process our book requests!

Again we send a special salute to Jane Avery for assisting with our many phone calls, swiftly processing contract agreements, and promptly responding to our numerous requests. Your expert clerical skills and amiable service are highly praised and very much appreciated.

Paul Smolenski, we are most grateful to you for always "going to bat" for our projects! Your support is always appreciated.

Deborah Leighton at Maine Proofreading service, you are the best! We appreciate your superb copyediting skills and your quick turn-around time. Your queries and comments assisted us in making many improvements to our manuscript.

Kathy Englehart, Courier, thank you for keeping us up-to-date on all the details (and challenges) associated with printing our books. Thank you for always being available for our frantic phone calls on weekends and after work hours.

Helen LeFevre, Courier Epic, your constant assistance with the many challenges of printing this book is tremendously appreciated! Thank you for your support.

To the participants at the Focus Group in Boston, Massachusetts, we extend our biggest thank you for sharing your teaching ideas and specific suggestions for enhancing the appearance and content of the book. Thank you, Susan McGowan, Caroleann Bready-Lyons, and Marilyn Sherry of Massasoit Community College; Eileen Zisk of the Community College of Rhode Island–Lincoln; Mary Belluardo and Jack Szeredy of Quinsigamond Community College; Barbara Cotoia and Roberta Neuschatz of Mt. Wachusett Community College; and Hannah Darling of the Computer Learning Center, Somerville, Massachusetts.

An enormous to the instructors and their students who worked with the first copies of the *Microsoft Word 6.0 for Windows* book and data disk. Thank you, Laura Fraser, Susan Jaderstrom, and Joyce Moreira. Joyce, we greatly appreciated your questions and suggestions, which assisted in the creation for a quality book.

Word 6.0 for Windows Toolbars

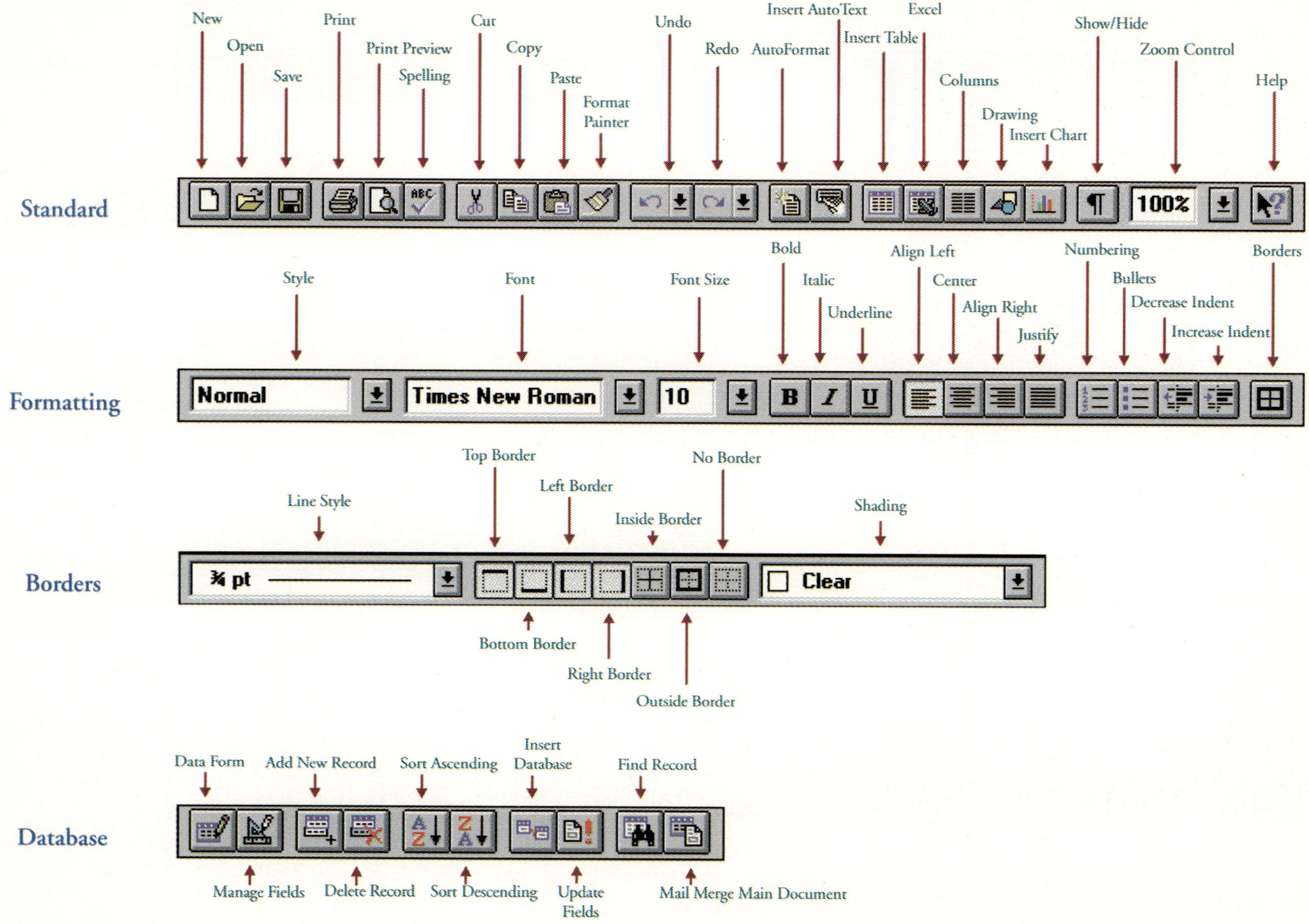

Standard

New, Open, Save, Print, Print Preview, Spelling, Cut, Copy, Paste, Format Painter, Undo, Redo, AutoFormat, Insert AutoText, Insert Table, Excel, Columns, Drawing, Insert Chart, Show/Hide, Zoom Control, Help

100%

Formatting

Style, Font, Font Size, Bold, Italic, Underline, Align Left, Center, Align Right, Justify, Numbering, Bullets, Decrease Indent, Increase Indent, Borders

Normal

Times New Roman

10

Borders

Line Style, Top Border, Bottom Border, Left Border, Right Border, Inside Border, Outside Border, No Border, Shading

¾ pt

Clear

Database

Data Form, Manage Fields, Add New Record, Delete Record, Sort Ascending, Sort Descending, Insert Database, Update Fields, Find Record, Mail Merge Main Document

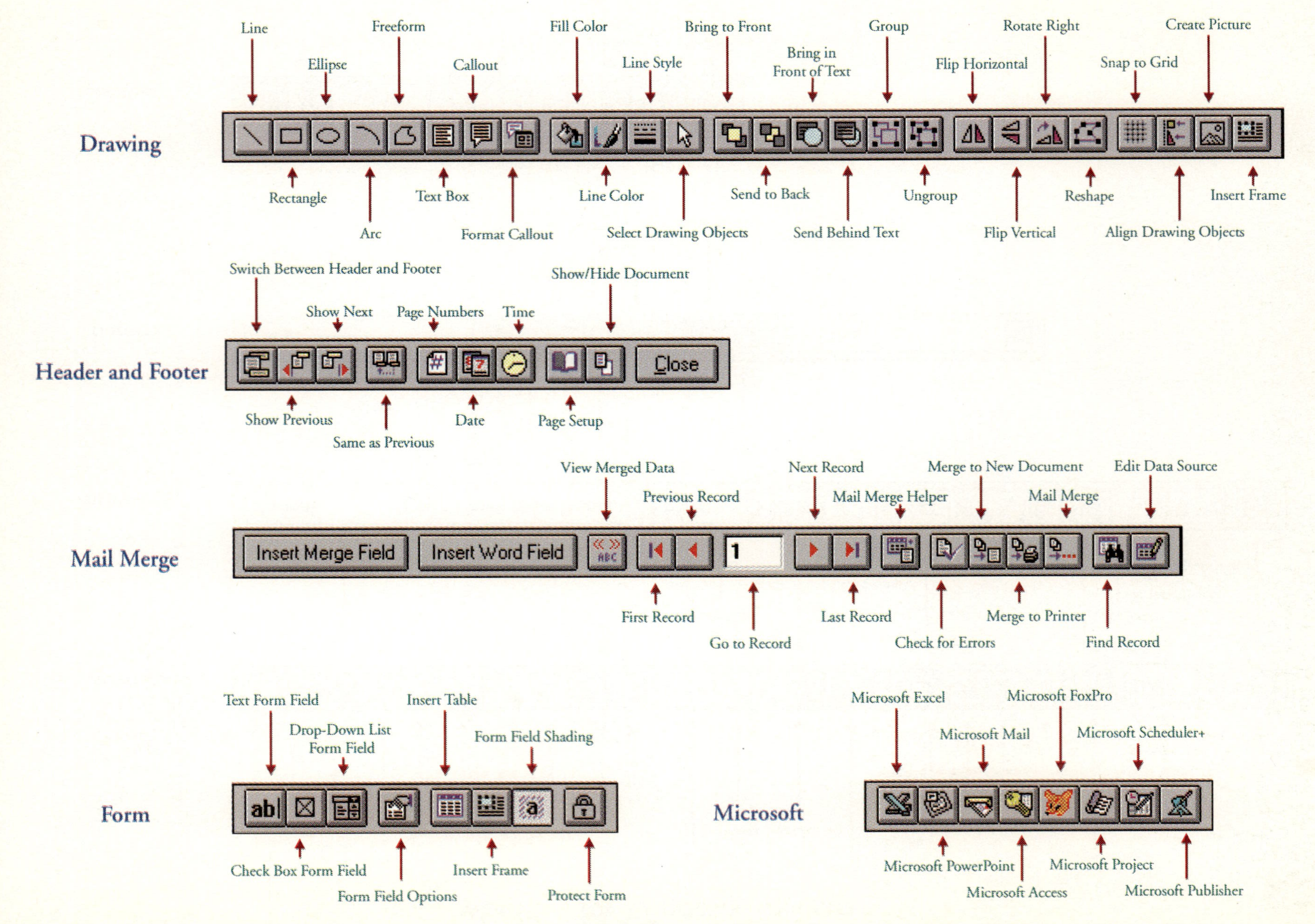
Drawing
Line
Ellipse
Freeform
Callout
Fill Color
Line Style
Bring to Front
Bring in Front of Text
Group
Flip Horizontal
Rotate Right
Snap to Grid
Create Picture
Rectangle
Arc
Text Box
Format Callout
Line Color
Select Drawing Objects
Send to Back
Send Behind Text
Ungroup
Flip Vertical
Reshape
Align Drawing Objects
Insert Frame
Header and Footer
Switch Between Header and Footer
Show Next
Page Numbers
Time
Show/Hide Document
Close
Show Previous
Same as Previous
Date
Page Setup
Mail Merge
View Merged Data
Previous Record
Next Record
Mail Merge Helper
Merge to New Document
Mail Merge
Edit Data Source
Insert Merge Field
Insert Word Field
First Record
Go to Record
Last Record
Check for Errors
Merge to Printer
Find Record
Form
Text Form Field
Drop-Down List Form Field
Insert Table
Form Field Shading
Check Box Form Field
Form Field Options
Insert Frame
Protect Form
Microsoft
Microsoft Excel
Microsoft Mail
Microsoft FoxPro
Microsoft Scheduler+
Microsoft PowerPoint
Microsoft Access
Microsoft Project
Microsoft Publisher

What Is a Microcomputer System?

A *microcomputer system* is a small computer system designed to provide methods for creating, processing, storing, and printing data. A small computer system normally includes the computer, keyboard, mouse, monitor, printer, and software programs. Many microcomputer systems today, however, include internal fax modems, sound boards, CD ROM players, and stereo speakers, and are referred to as *multimedia* systems.

The microcomputer system consists of two basic elements: hardware and software. The physical components of the microcomputer system are called hardware; the programs that instruct the computer to perform functions are called software.

Hardware

The microcomputer hardware includes the monitor (TV-like screen), keyboard, mouse, computer unit, disk drives, and printer. The hardware can be seen, felt, and touched. The IBM PC and compatible computers enclose the disk drive(s) with the computer. The monitor, keyboard, mouse, and printer are attached to the computer via cables (see Figure I.1). The computer unit and the attached hardware make up a microcomputer system.

The computer unit holds the electronic circuitry where the main memory and central processing unit (CPU) reside. The CPU processes and controls information by storing data, performing operations, and transferring information from one location to another. The CPU is often referred to as the "brains" of the computer.

Software

Software programs are lists of instructions that tell the computer what to do. The master program is the disk operating system (DOS). DOS directs the basic operation of the microcomputer system and carries out procedures within application programs. Application programs are more advanced software designed to perform specific tasks. Common applications are word processing, spreadsheet, database, communications, graphics, drawing, and desktop publishing programs.

DOS and application programs are stored on master disks. A copy of DOS and an application program can be transferred to the computer's memory when the computer is turned on. Transferring a copy of a program to the computer's memory is called "loading the program." The disk is being "read" when a copy of a program or other information is transferred from the disk into the computer's memory.

FIGURE I.1

The PC hardware

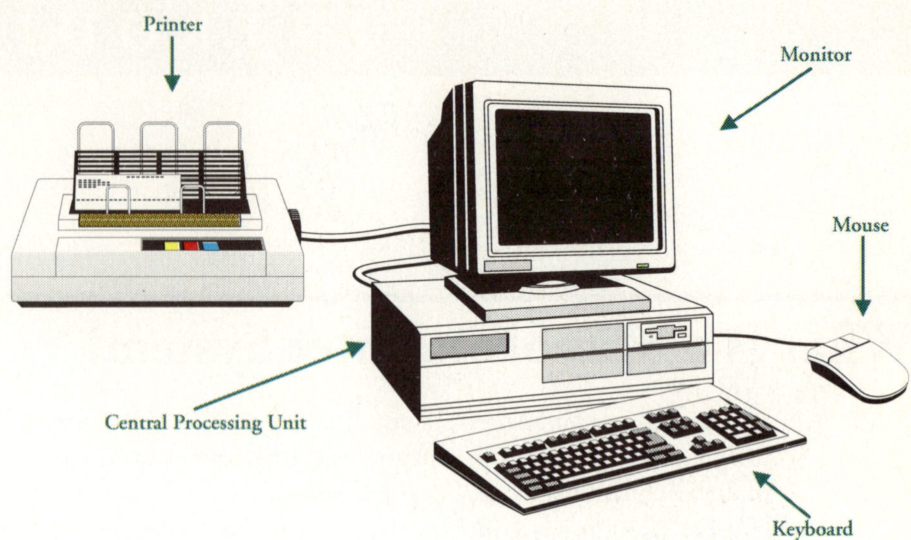

System Requirements and Recommendations for Word 6.0 for Windows

Minimum System Requirements*	Recommended System Requirements
286 IBM PC or compatible with 1.2M or greater capacity floppy disk drive	386 (or higher) IBM PC or compatible with 1.2M or greater capacity floppy disk drive
4M RAM	8M (or more) RAM
24M hard disk space	24-30M hard disk space free
Windows 3.1 or later	Windows 3.1 or later
EGA graphics adapter and monitor	SVGA graphics adapter and monitor
Mouse or other pointer device	Mouse or other pointer device

What Are Disks?

Disks are storage devices. Information that is processed and used by a computer must be stored on either a hard or floppy disk. Because the computer's memory is temporary, all programs and data are erased when the computer is turned off. Therefore, disks are used to store programs and data.

The rigid hard disk usually resides inside the computer and is not removed by the user. Programs are normally stored on a hard disk. However, removable hard disks, contained in plastic cartridges, are also available. A floppy disk, contained in a plastic cartridge or paper jacket, is flexible and can be handled by the user. Floppy disks are generally used to store data or files. The most commonly used disk sizes are 5.25" and 3.5" (see Figure I.2).

FIGURE 1.2

Hard disk and floppy disks

Information that has been created is saved on either a floppy disk or a hard disk. A floppy disk is referred to as a *file disk* or *data disk*. If information, such as a letter, memorandum, or statistical data, is not saved on a disk, the information will be lost from the computer's temporary memory when the computer is turned off. When a copy of the information is transferred from the computer's memory to a disk, the process is called *saving*. Saving information to a disk is also called "writing" to a disk.

Care for Floppy Disks

Floppy disks should be labeled using a felt-tip pen. Store disks in a dry, protected location. Avoid dust, smoke, bending, and extreme temperatures. (Keep disks out of the sun and away from beverage containers!) Any magnet or magnetized object can damage the data on a disk; therefore, avoid using a paper clip on a disk, especially a paper clip that has been stored in a holder with a magnetized ring at the top.

Formatting a Floppy Disk

Before information can be saved on a disk, the disk must be formatted (prepared) with electronic instructions to partition the disk into storage areas, to create a directory, to check for disk defects, etc.

The formatting process is usually performed only once. If a disk is formatted a second time, all information previously saved on the disk is erased.

Steps to Format a File Disk Using Windows' File Manager

1. If necessary, turn on the computer and load Windows.
2. Double-click on the **File Manager** icon usually located in the Window's Main group.

3. Select **Disk, Format Disk**.
4. Select the down arrow button in the **Disk In** option box; select the disk drive letter where the disk to be formatted is located (e.g., select Drive A: or Drive B:).
5. Generally, the Capacity option box displays the appropriate disk capacity. If necessary, however, select the down arrow button in the **Capacity** option box and select the correct disk capacity.
6. Select **OK**.

   Note: *The message, "Formatting will erase ALL data from your disk...," displays.*

7. Select **Yes**.

   Note: *A "Formatting disk" message displays with various messages indicating the formatting progress.*

8. When the Format Complete dialog box displays, select **Yes** or **No** to indicate whether you want to format another disk (e.g., select No).
9. Select **File, Exit**.

What Is DOS?

DOS is the disk operating system for IBM PC and compatible microcomputers. DOS is a collection of related programs that controls and manages the computer's operations. DOS is necessary to handle the temporary storage and processing of information and to direct the orderly transfer or sharing of information between the computer unit and the disk, monitor, keyboard, printer, etc. In order for the computer to operate, the DOS programs must be accessible when the computer is turned on. Generally, DOS programs are stored on the hard disk.

What is Windows?

Windows is a program that works in conjunction with DOS to enable a user to perform computer tasks more easily. Windows provides a structure within which many programs can operate. Windows programs have a common way of accomplishing tasks. For example, the procedure for saving a file is the same when working with most Windows programs. In addition, data can be easily transferred from one Windows program to another. For example, a graph created in a Windows spreadsheet program can be easily transferred to a Windows word processing program.

The Windows program allows the user to complete tasks such as launching (loading) programs, copying files, formatting disks, and deleting files. When performing traditional DOS tasks such as copying files, formatting a disk, etc., using a mouse and the Window's drop down menus is usually much easier than remembering and typing DOS commands.

When Windows is loaded, the Program Manager window displays on the screen (see Figure 1.1 on page 14). The Windows program is often referred to as a graphical user interface because icons (pictures) display on the screen to represent each program. The user can launch a program simply by placing the mouse pointer on the program icon and pressing the left mouse button twice rapidly. This is called double-clicking (see page 7).

Windows allows multiple programs to run at the same time. Each program is placed in a separate *window*. The windows for each application program share common elements. For example, the Title bar, Menu bar, scroll bars, and control boxes are elements common to each application program. These common elements provide a standard method for accomplishing tasks. For example, the File, Print option is used in any Windows application to print a document. As more and more application programs are written to operate in Windows, the more common the elements will become to simplify the learning of additional Windows programs.

Windows programs are also compatible with each other (i.e., the information in each program can be transferred and shared easily between programs). For example, a spreadsheet file can be transferred to a WordPerfect document window. A *link* is established between the spreadsheet and WordPerfect files so that any changes made in the spreadsheet file are automatically changed in the linked file.

What are Directories and Paths?

A *directory* is a named location on a disk where a group of files is stored. A directory is used to keep files organized in separate areas on the disk under different directory names. Application programs such as word processing, spreadsheet, and database programs are usually stored on the computer's hard disk. The files for each application program can be kept together in one directory location. For example, all the Word program files are stored in a directory named *winword* or *winword6*.

Other directories can be created and grouped together in the winword directory. Any directories created in the winword directory are called subdirectories. For example, if the subdirectory named memos was created, memos would be a subdirectory of the *winword* directory.

A path is a route from a disk drive letter (root directory) to the location of a file or subdirectory. For example, the path for a file named *mem3* that is located in the subdirectory named memos that is in the winword directory is: *c:\winword\memos\mem3*. When using Word 6.0 for Windows, the various directories and subdirectories can be chosen in the Directories boxes that are available in the Open and Save As dialog boxes (see Chapter 1, page 21).

Filenames

Every file to be saved is assigned a filename. Filenames can contain one to eight characters and, if desired, a filename extension of one to three characters. The filename extension is separated from the first 1–8 characters by a period. For example, *morris.doc* or *martin.doc* are valid filenames. However, *morganstern.doc* is not a valid filename because there are more than eight characters before the filename extension.

Any letter (a to z) or number (0–9) and most symbols can be used in a filename. A filename cannot contain spaces, commas, backslashes, asterisks, or a second period.

A filename should represent the information and/or person's name contained in the file. For example, a letter written to Gerry Anderson concerning a tax assessment could be assigned the name *g-andsn.doc* or *andsn-tx.doc.*

What Is Word 6.0 for Windows?

The Word program is one of the most prevalent word processing programs in the world. Word 6.0 for Windows is the latest version of Word for the Windows environment. The Word program is one component of the popular Microsoft Office package. The Microsoft Office (standard) package includes the following programs: Word (word processing), PowerPoint (presentation), Excel (spreadsheet), and Mail (electronic mail).These Microsoft programs can be purchased as part of the Microsoft Office package or can be individually purchased.

The Mouse (Pointer Device)

There are various types of pointer devices. The mouse pointer device and the trackball are presently the most popular. The mouse is a hand-held device used to move an arrow or rectangular symbol (pointer symbol) on the screen. The mouse pointer is moved over the screen area until the pointer symbol touches the item or items to be selected. The left button on the mouse device is pressed to initiate the desired action, such as selecting options, sizing windows, formatting text, or creating objects.

Generally, the mouse is held between the thumb and little or ring finger. The index finger or middle finger is used to press the mouse buttons. To maintain consistent control of the mouse, hold the mouse motionless when pressing the mouse buttons.

When the mouse is moved over a flat surface, the pointer symbol moves in the same direction on the screen. When the mouse reaches the edge of the flat surface, hold the mouse firmly, lift, and relocate. Also, alternating between a short rubbing stroke and lifting the mouse slightly using wrist movement can be very helpful when the mouse reaches the flat surface edge.

The track-ball pointer device is stationary; the "ball" is moved by a finger or the palm of the hand. The track-ball can be built into the keyboard, or it can be connected to the computer via a cable.

The pointer symbol changes shape depending on the location on the screen where the pointer is positioned. For example, the pointer symbol changes to a two-headed arrow when sizing graphic images or document windows and to a four-headed arrow when moving graphic images or document windows (see chapter 13 and 16). The mouse pointer shapes are shown in Figure I.3.

Different techniques are used to initiate an action with the pointer device. The following list shows the basic actions:

	Used to select buttons, menu commands, and graphic images.		A down selection arrow is used to select table columns.
	Insertion point	+	Displays when a frame or graphic item is being created
	I-beam mouse pointer. Used to locate the insertion point in text.		Indicates that a frame, graphic image, or window can be moved.
	Displays when the Help button is selected.	↔	Indicates that a frame, graphic image, or window can be sized.

FIGURE I.3
Mouse pointer shapes

Click	Press the left button once and release.
Double-click	Press the left button twice rapidly.
Drag	Press and hold down the left mouse button while moving the mouse or trackball.
Point	Move the mouse pointer to a specific position on the screen.

The Word Document Window

The Word document window displays after the program is launched (loaded). The window is displayed in full size (maximized). (See Chapter 16 for changing the window size.) Each part of the window is shown in Figure I.4.

The *Title bar* displays at the top of the window and contains the application name and document title. The Control box displays on the left side of the Title bar and when selected provides keyboard users the capability to size, move, close, or switch to another program. The Minimize and Restore buttons are displayed on the right side of the title bar and are used to change the size of the application window. When the *Minimize* button is selected, the application is reduced to a small icon and the Program Manager or another application window is displayed. To return the program to the screen, double-click on the Microsoft Word icon. If the Microsoft Word icon cannot be seen on the screen, press **Ctrl** and **Esc** to display the Task List and double-click on Microsoft Word. (See Chapter 16 for additional information on managing document windows.)

The *Menu bar* displays directly below the Title bar. Each menu in the Menu bar contains commands that are used to instruct Word to perform specific functions. To view the menu commands, click to select the Menu. The menu "drops down" and a list of the menu commands displays with the first item highlighted. When a menu command is highlighted, a brief description of that command displays at the bottom of the screen.

FIGURE 1.4

Word 6.0 for Windows document window

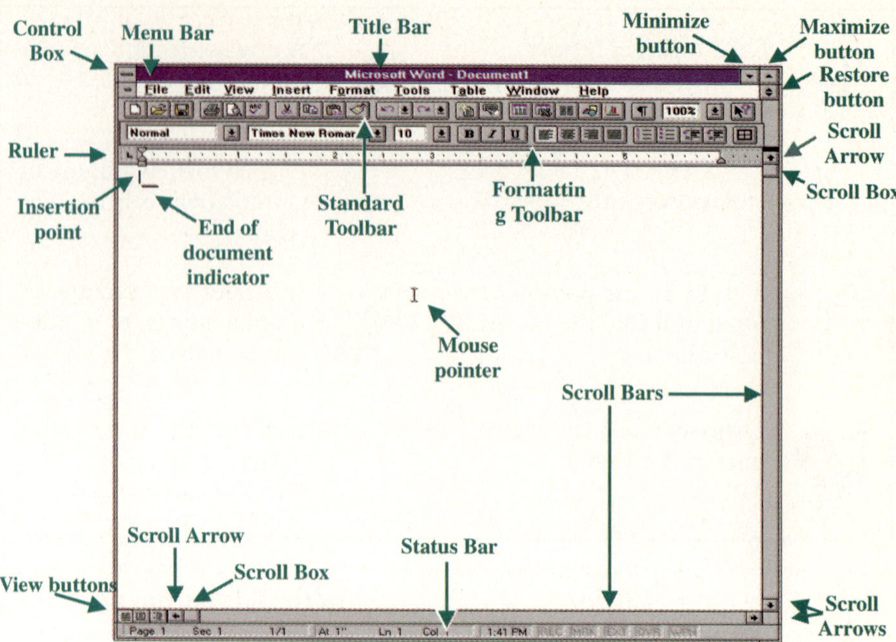

Each drop-down menu has a list of menu commands that are accessed easily by pointing and clicking the mouse or by pressing a designated letter from the keyboard. The first item listed in a drop-down menu is highlighted. An underline displays beneath one letter in each menu command that can be typed to select the desired option. Listed beside some of the commands are keystrokes that can be used to activate a command. For example, in the File menu, **Ctrl + s** display next to the Save command and **Ctrl + p** display next to the Print command. Some menu commands are followed by three periods (Save As...) to indicate that, if selected, a dialog box will display.

A Toolbar can be displayed and used to quickly activate frequently used Word functions. After the mouse pointer has touched a button for a couple of seconds, a *ToolTip* displays. The ToolTip is a brief description of a button's function.

The Standard Toolbar and the Formatting Toolbar are defaulted (preset) to display on the screen. By selecting the **Toolbar** option in the **View** menu, however, the user can choose to display none or any of the listed Toolbars. When the Toolbar dialog box displays, an X beside the Toolbar name indicates that the Toolbar is displayed. If desired, the Toolbars can be removed from the screen in order to see more text in the document window.

The Standard Toolbar contains a variety of buttons that are used for document creation (creating tables, columns and charts) and for saving, printing, and opening documents. The Standard Toolbar also contains buttons for rearranging text (cut, copy, and paste), obtaining Help, and changing the size of the display of text.

The Formatting Toolbar contains buttons that are used to quickly format text such as fonts, point sizes, indents, and alignment. The Formatting Toolbar also contains buttons that are used to create bullets, numbering, and borders.

A horizontal ruler displays below the Toolbar(s) and contains a measurement scale that shows the placement of tabs, column margins, and left and right margins. A vertical ruler displays on the left side of the document window (in Page Layout view only) and also contains a measurement scale. The rulers can be used to change margin settings without accessing a menu. The horizontal and vertical rulers can be removed from the document window by selecting **View**, **Ruler**.

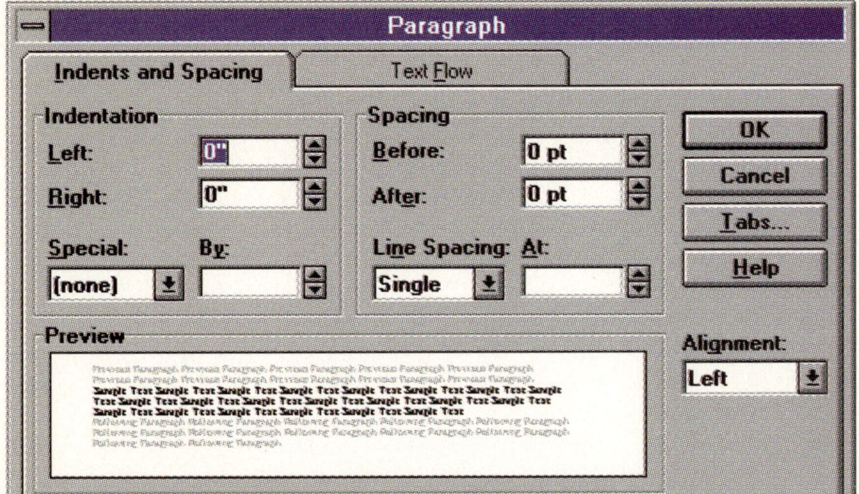

FIGURE I.5

Paragraph dialog box

Dialog Boxes

Dialog boxes provide additional Word commands. The dialog boxes display after menu commands are selected. For example, when the **Format**, **Paragraph** command is selected, the Paragraph dialog box displays (see Figure I.5).

In a dialog box, instructions are supplied to the program by selecting from a list of options and/or by typing information. Often a dialog box contains commands followed by three periods (...). When these commands are selected, a second dialog box with additional options displays. The second dialog box allows the user to provide more specific information on how the chosen command is to be accomplished.

In many dialog boxes, two or more tabs display. For example, in the Paragraph dialog box shown in Figure I.5, two tabs display, i.e., Indents and Spacing and Text Flow. When a tab is selected, a card with options displays. For example, in the Paragraph dialog box shown in Figure I.5, the Indents and Spacing card is displayed and contains indentation and spacing options. The Text Flow options could be displayed by moving the mouse pointer to the Text Flow tab and clicking once.

Information about the options in a dialog box can be obtained by selecting the **Help** button. When Help is selected, a window displays containing a description of each option.

Part 1
The Beginning Step

Create and Edit Business Documents

Chapters 1-4

- Launch Word for Windows
- The Toolbars and Rulers
- AutoCorrect
- Center alignment
- Save a file
- Print a document
- Close a document
- Obtain a new document window
- Scroll bars
- Move the insertion point
- Exit Word for Windows
- Open a document
- Select text
- Delete and insert text
- Undo and Redo
- Use Help
- Use the automatic date feature
- Change alignment
- Bold, underline, and italic text attributes
- Change margins
- Font changes
- Check spelling
- Print Preview and Zoom
- Move and copy text
- Find and replace text
- Indent paragraphs
- Numbered and bulleted lists
- Print selected text

CHAPTER

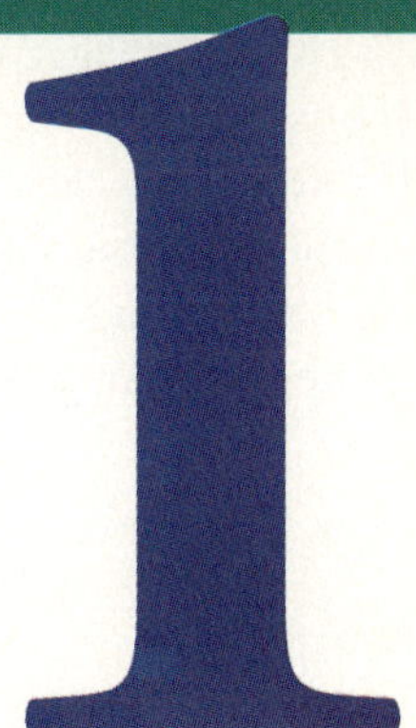

Create a Memorandum

Features Covered

- Launch Word for Windows
- The insertion point
- Toolbars
- Rulers
- AutoCorrect
- Save a file
- Print a document
- Close a document
- Use horizontal and vertical scroll bars
- Exit Word for Windows

Objectives and Introduction

After successfully completing this chapter, you will be able to launch (load) the Word for Windows program; understand Toolbars, Rulers, and the AutoCorrect feature; save, print, and close a document; and view different portions of a document using the scroll bars. Instructions for typing and formatting two different styles of interoffice memorandums while using Word features will be presented in this chapter. Before a memorandum can be typed and formatted, the program is launched.

Launch Word for Windows

Launching a program is the process of transferring the program from the hard disk to the computer's memory. The Word for Windows program is launched (loaded) from the Microsoft Windows Program Manager. Icons (pictures) display in the Windows Program Manager screen (see Figure 1.1) Each icon represents a program or application. To launch a program or application, move the mouse pointer to the desired icon and double-click.

FIGURE 1.1

Sample of the Windows Program Manager screen. (Icons may be arranged differently on each computer because icons can be rearranged easily in the Program Manager.)

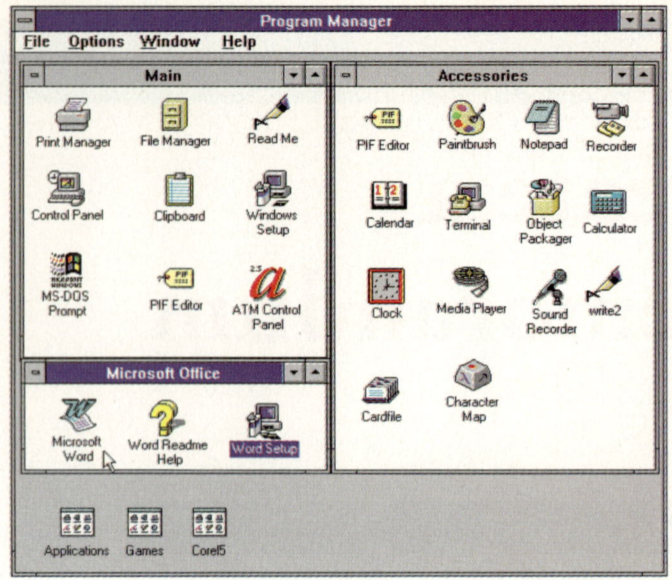

When the Word for Windows program is launched, the Word document window displays with a Title bar, Menu bar, a Standard Toolbar, a Formatting Toolbar, and a Ruler at the top of the screen and a Status bar at the bottom of the screen (see Figure 1.2).

Note: *The first set of instructions in each step-by-step instruction in this textbook uses the mouse/trackball device. Place the mouse pointer on the option desired; click the left mouse button once to select. The instructions for using the keyboard keys immediately follow the instructions for using the mouse and are indicated in braces { }, e.g., {Alt, f, c* **or** *Ctrl and F4}.*

Start-Up Instructions

- The computer and monitor should be turned on and the Windows Program Manager displayed on the screen. If necessary, see your instructor and write down the steps needed to display the Program Manager on your screen.

  ____

  ____

- Place a formatted file disk in drive A or B.

Launch (Load) the Word for Windows Program

1. Move the mouse pointer to the **Microsoft Word** icon; press the left mouse button twice quickly (double-click).

   Note: *An hourglass displays on the screen to indicate that the program is being launched. Keys pressed while the hourglass is present are ignored by the program. The copyright screen displays briefly, then the Word document window displays (see Figure 1.2).*

   If a different method is used to launch (load) Word for Windows on your computer, see your instructor or instructional assistant and write the steps needed on the following lines.

   ____

   ____

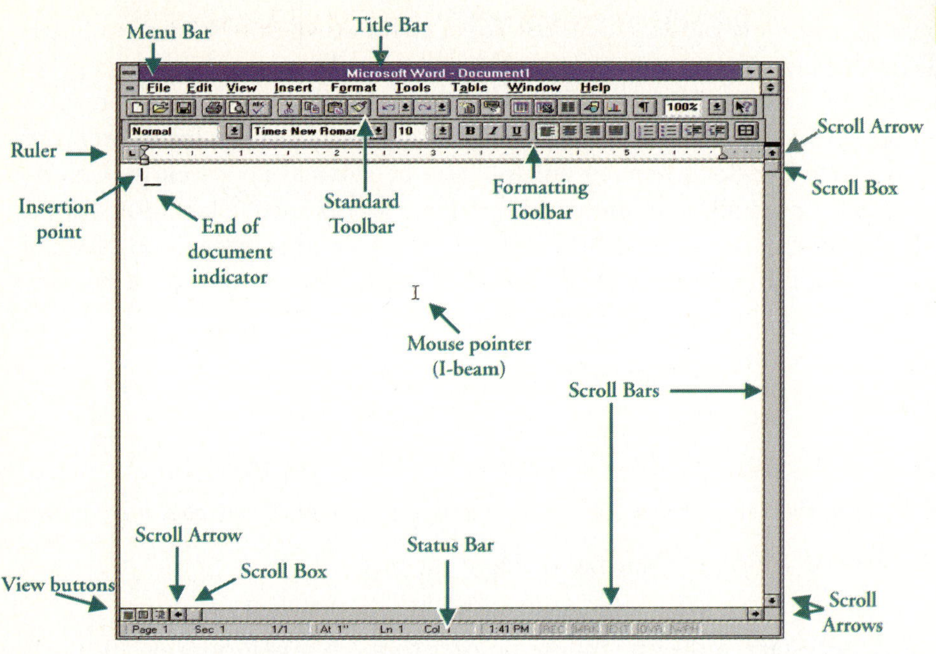

FIGURE 1.2

Word 6.0 for Windows document window

The Insertion Point and Mouse Pointer

The insertion point indicates the location where the next action takes place and displays as a bold, blinking vertical line. The insertion point will move to characters and lines that have been typed. However, the insertion point will not move into blank space unless the **Enter** key or **Spacebar** is pressed. As the **Enter** key or **Spacebar** is pressed or text is typed, the insertion point moves. See also Steps to Move the Insertion Point Quickly, page 26.

The mouse pointer symbol moves around the screen as the mouse is moved on the desktop. The shape of the mouse pointer changes depending on the location of the mouse pointer on the screen. For example, the mouse pointer is an I-beam when located in the text area, but usually changes to an arrow when the mouse pointer is out of the text area. See the Introduction, Figure I.3, for a list of the various mouse pointer shapes.

The mouse device can be used to move the insertion point by placing the pointer symbol at the desired location and pressing (clicking) the left mouse button once. Also, when *Num Lock* is turned off, the direction (arrow) keys on the 10-key numeric keypad can be used to move the insertion point up, down, left, or right one character or line at a time. On many keyboards, a duplicate set of arrow keys is provided on separate keys.

View Modes

Word for Windows has several ways of presenting a document on the screen. For creating and editing documents, two view modes may be used. In the Normal view mode, a simplified picture of the screen is displayed. This reduces the amount of memory needed so the program works faster and is the best mode to use for keying text. The Page Layout view mode is a WYSIWYG (wizz-ee-wig or What You See Is What You Get) display. All the elements on the page are shown in the proper relation to one another. The Page Layout view mode is useful when formatting text and for checking the page arrangement before printing, but it uses a lot of memory and scrolling through the document or editing may be slower. To check that Normal view mode is selected, choose **View** in the Menu bar. A small black dot should display beside the Normal option. If necessary, move the mouse pointer to Normal and click. To select a different view from the View menu, move the mouse pointer to the desired view and click the left mouse button once.

Steps to Change Views

1. Move the mouse pointer to the **View** menu and click once {Alt, v}.

   Note: A list of options displays. A dot displays beside the currently selected view option.

2. Select the desired view, i.e., **Normal** or **Page Layout**.

   For example, check that a dot displays beside the **Normal** option. If necessary, move the mouse pointer to the **Normal** option and click once.

Shortcut

1. Move the mouse button to the **Normal View** or **Page Layout View** button located at the bottom left of the document window and click once.

Toolbars

Word provides an easy way to access frequently used commands via the *Toolbars* (see Figure 1.3). The Standard Toolbar and the Formatting Toolbar are two rows of buttons that display below the Menu bar. A mouse must be used to select a button on a Toolbar. When the mouse pointer is placed on a button in a Toolbar, the name of the button appears under the button and a brief description of the purpose of the button displays in the Status bar.

The Standard Toolbar and the Formatting Toolbar are the preset (default) Toolbars because they contain options for working quickly with commonly used Word features. Other Toolbars can be accessed by moving the mouse pointer to any button in either Toolbar and clicking the *right* mouse button once to display a list of available Toolbars. For example, in an office where many Microsoft programs are available, the Microsoft Toolbar can be displayed with buttons to switch to other Microsoft program(s), such as Excel, a spreadsheet program, and/or Access, a database program.

FIGURE 1.3

The Toolbars

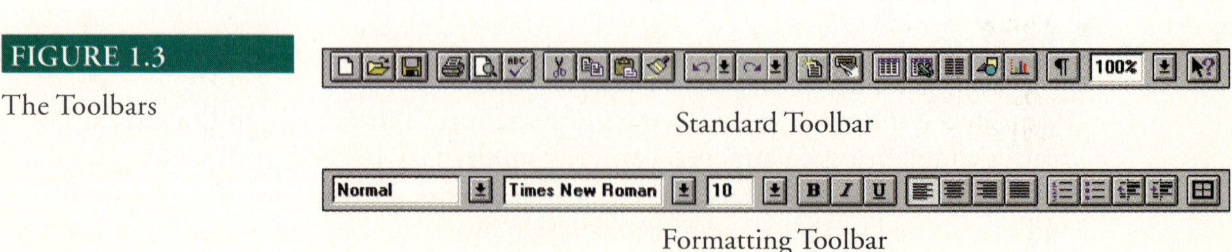

If Toolbars are not displayed on the screen, select **View**, **Toolbars**, then select the Toolbar(s) to be displayed by moving the mouse pointer to the name and clicking the left mouse button once. An X displays in the box in front of each Toolbar name that will display in the document window. When each desired Toolbar has been selected, choose **OK** or press the **Enter** key.

Toolbars can be created and customized by adding and removing buttons. Also, some specialized Toolbars, such as the Outline Toolbar, will appear when you use certain features. More information on creating and customizing Toolbars is available in Appendix A.

The Rulers

The Horizontal Ruler is a bar that displays under the Standard and Formatting Toolbars and contains a measurement scale showing the placement of tabs, column margins, and left and right margins. The Ruler is used to change tabs and margin settings without accessing a menu. Also, a Vertical Ruler displays at the left of the document window when the Page Layout view or Print Preview is active. The Horizontal Ruler is preset to display after the Word program is launched. If the Horizontal Ruler does not appear on the screen, select **View**, **Ruler** to display the ruler. Also, the Ruler(s) can be removed from the screen by selecting **View**, **Ruler**. (See Steps to Display or Remove Rulers in Chapter 7.)

Display Nonprinting Characters

In Word for Windows, nonprinting characters, such as the end of paragraph marker, tabs, and spaces, normally do not appear on the screen. However, when editing, it may be useful to see the location of nonprinting characters on the screen. If the nonprinting characters are not displaying on the screen, select the **Show/Hide** button ¶ on the Standard Toolbar. Select the **Show/Hide** button ¶ again to turn the display of nonprinting characters off. A button that is used to turn a feature on and off is referred to as a *toggle* button. *Toggling* is the term used when a feature is turned off and on by selecting the same button.

The AutoCorrect Feature

The AutoCorrect feature automatically corrects common typing and spelling errors. When a commonly misspelled word is typed incorrectly followed by pressing the **Spacebar**, **Tab**, or **Enter** key, the correct word is immediately displayed in the document window. For example, if the characters "teh" are typed followed by a space, Word will automatically display the correct word "the." Also, if two uppercase letters are typed followed by other lowercase letters and a space, Word will change the second uppercase letter to a lowercase letter. Word has prerecorded ten commonly misspelled words. These prerecorded words can be deleted and/or additional words can be included in the list of commonly misspelled words.

Formatting

Formatting is the process of determining the placement and arrangement of a document when it is printed on a page. The arrangement of a document includes the amount of blank space in the left, right, top, and bottom margins. Formatting also includes alignment, underline/bold text, capitalization, and the number of vertical and horizontal spaces used between words and lines.

The purpose of formatting is to arrange text in a manner that is attractive and easy to read. This textbook includes information on formatting memorandums, letters, tables, reports, mailing labels, newsletters, reports, etc.

In this chapter, formatting using different justification options will be introduced to create memorandum styles. The Center and Left alignment options will be discussed as well as the format for the paragraphs of a memorandum. The alignment options and text format options will be used when creating many documents in this book.

Word Wrap

One automatic formatting feature of word processing programs is word wrap. As you type text, the **Enter** key is pressed only at the end of a paragraph or short line. When text reaches the right margin, the insertion point automatically returns to the beginning of the next line. This automatic return feature is called *word wrap*.

Word wrap automatically formats the document paragraph to adjust to the left and right margins. If words are inserted or deleted from the paragraph, text automatically readjusts to the margins.

Memorandum—Style 1

There are many acceptable formats for memorandums. In a traditional memorandum, a heading, such as *Memorandum*, *Memo*, or *Interoffice Correspondence*, is typed or preprinted at the top of the page. The memorandum heading is followed by the recipient's name, author's name, date, and subject. The words *To:*, *From:*, *Date:*, and *Subject:* usually precede the recipient's name, author's name, the date and subject and are called "lead words." The lead words can be typed in the memorandum or preprinted.

The main text of the memorandum (body text) is typed using word wrap within each paragraph to automatically begin new lines. The **Enter** key is pressed twice after each paragraph. Each paragraph begins at the left margin. After the final paragraph, the **Enter** key is pressed twice followed by the initials of the person typing the memorandum.

Start-Up Instructions

❖ Use the following information to begin creating the memorandum shown in Figure 1.4.

Use Center Alignment (Horizontal Centering)

1. The insertion point should be located on the left side of the screen.

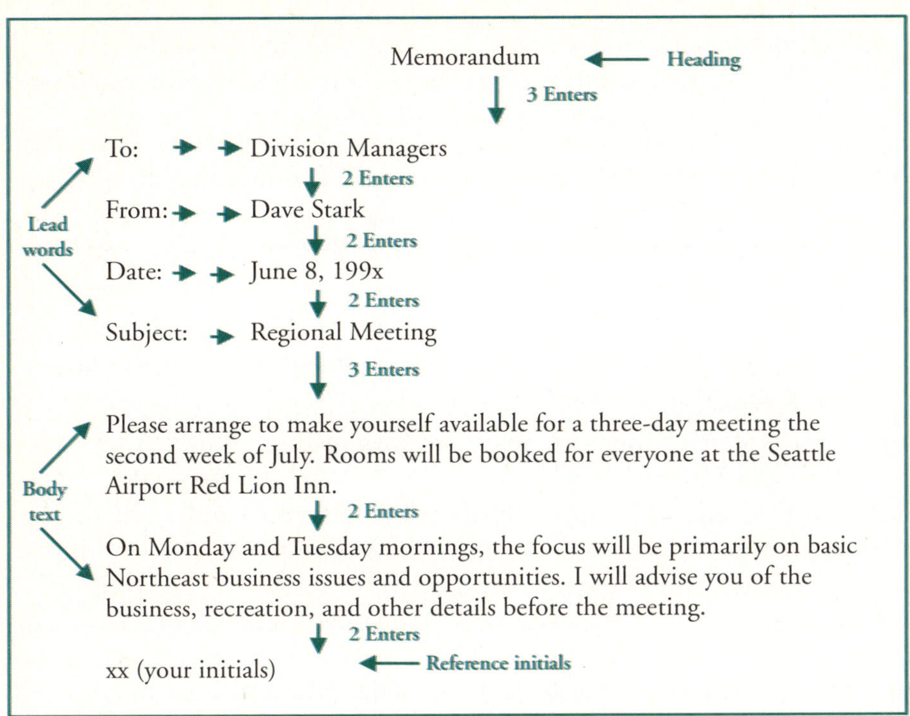

FIGURE 1.4

Memorandum—Style 1

2. Type the word(s) to be centered.

   For example, type **Memorandum.**

3. Select the **Center** alignment button on the Formatting Toolbar {Ctrl and e}.

   Note: *The word Memorandum is horizontally centered in the document window.*

4. Press **Enter** once.

5. Select the **Align Left** alignment button on the Formatting Toolbar to return the insertion point to the left side of the screen.

   Note: *The word(s) are now horizontally centered on the screen and the insertion point is located at the left margin, one line below the heading.*

Start-Up Instructions

- Press the **Enter** key two more times to create two blank lines after the heading.
- Backspace to correct errors made while typing. For now, ignore any errors noticed after the memorandum is typed.
- Use word wrap when typing the body text paragraphs.

  Note: *The paragraph lines may not end with the same words as shown in Figure 1.4.*

Steps to Create a Memorandum

1. Press the **Tab** key twice after the lead words.

   Note: *The* **Tab** *key is pressed once or twice after the lead words in order to align the heading information and to provide space after the lead words and before the information that follows. Visually check that the information following the lead words is aligned.*

2. Press the **Enter** key three times after the subject line and two times after each paragraph.

3. With the insertion point at the left margin, begin typing the text of the first paragraph. When the insertion point reaches the right margin, continue typing. Word wrap will automatically return the insertion point to the left margin.

4. Press **Enter** twice after the last paragraph; type your initials in lowercase letters.

Save a File

After a document is created, it must be saved to the computer's hard disk or to a floppy disk. Saving is the process of transferring the document from the computer's temporary memory to permanent memory on a hard disk or floppy disk. A saved document is referred to as a *file* or *data file.*

When a document is saved, a filename is assigned. A filename can be one to eight characters with no spaces. If desired, a period and a one- to three-letter filename extension can be added (see Filenames on page 5). If a filename extension is not typed, Word automatically adds the extension *.doc* to the filename when a document is saved.

Before a named document is saved, the location of the disk where the file is to be saved must be selected. For example, if a file is to be saved to a disk that is located in the A drive, Word must be instructed to access the A drive.

Files can also be saved to different directories on the computer's hard disk or to floppy disks. For example, a memo file could be saved to a directory named *c:\memos* (see What Are Directories and Paths? on page 5.)

Once a document has been saved, the filename and location display in the Title bar. If a saved document is changed, selecting the **Save** button on the Standard Toolbar or choosing **File**, **Save** will save the edited file immediately using the filename displayed in the Title bar. To save the edited file with a new filename, see Steps to Use Save As to Rename a File on page 40.

Start-Up Instructions

- A file disk should be placed in the A or B disk drive.

Save a New File

1. Select the **Save** button on the Standard Toolbar {Alt, f, s *or* Ctrl and s}.

   Note: *The Save As dialog box displays because the file has not been previously saved. (See Figure 1.5.) The current drive and directory display below the words "Directories" at the top center of the dialog box, e.g., a:\ or c:\winword. The insertion point is located in the File Name box.*

2. In the File Name box, type a filename with eight characters or less (no spaces).

   For example, type **1drill1**. (Do not type the period.)

   Note: *Check the accuracy of the filename before continuing. If necessary, use the* **Backspace** *key to erase an incorrect filename and type the correct filename.*

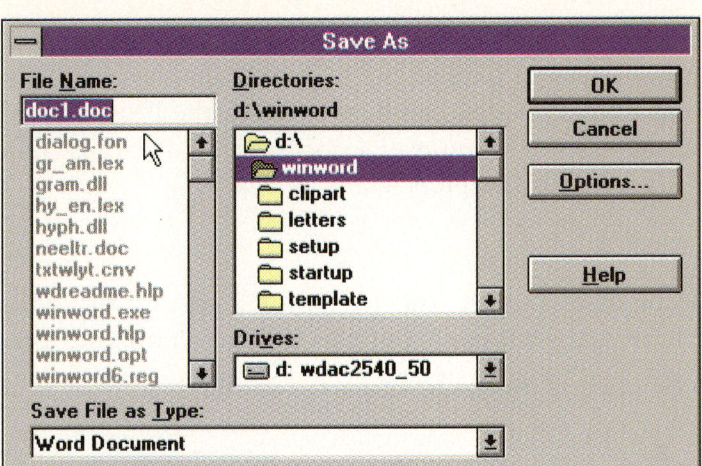

FIGURE 1.5

Save As dialog box

To Select a Different Drive

3. Move the mouse pointer to the box below the word "Drives" and click the left mouse button once {Alt and v}.

   Note: A list of available drives displays.

4. Move the mouse pointer to the desired drive letter and click once {press the up or down arrow key to highlight the desired drive letter, press Tab}.

   For example, move the mouse pointer to the drive letter containing your file disk, i.e., a: or b:, and click once.

   Note: The newly selected drive displays below the word "Directories" at the top center of the dialog box.

To Complete the Save Process

5. Select OK {press Enter}.

   Note: The document is saved on the file disk that is located in the selected disk drive and the document name is displayed in the Title bar of the document window, e.g., 1DRILL1.DOC. The three letter extension .doc is added automatically to the filename when the file is saved.

Select a Different Directory

Note: The following steps are provided for your information.

1. In the Directories box, double-click on the root directory symbol, e.g., c:\.

   Note: A list of available directories displays in the Directories box.

2. Move the mouse pointer to the desired directory name and double-click.

   Note: A list of available subdirectories displays in the Directories box.

Print a Document

A document can be printed using two methods. When the Print button on the Standard Toolbar is selected, the entire file prints immediately, using the default (preset) settings for the Print dialog box. Selecting the **File, Print** command or using the shortcut keystrokes **Ctrl** and **p** displays the Print dialog box and printing starts after **OK** is selected. Other options can be selected in the Print dialog box, such as printing individual pages or sections of a document. Additional information concerning printing is discussed in Chapters 4 and 10.

Start-Up Instructions

- The printer should be turned on. If you are sharing a printer, check that the switch box or local area network (LAN) printer is selected for your printer.
- The document to be printed should be displayed in the document window.

Print a Document Using the Print Button

1. Select the **Print** button on the Standard Toolbar.

   Note: If there is more than one printer available to the computer, use the ***File, Print*** *command to initiate printing to ensure that the correct printer is selected.*

Print a Document Using the File, Print Command

1. Select **File, Print** {Ctrl and p *or* Alt, f, p}.
2. Check that the desired options are selected and that the correct printer is selected. If necessary, see your instructor or instructional aide for assistance.
3. Select **OK** to start printing

Close a Document

Once a document has been typed, saved, and printed, the document is usually cleared from the document window before a new document is begun. However, more than one document window can be displayed on the screen at one time. (See Chapter 16, The Windows in Word.) Closing a document is often referred to as *clearing a document* from the screen. After a document is closed, a blank document window displays and a new document can be typed or an existing document can be opened. If more than one document has been opened, you may need to close another document window or select **File, New** to obtain a clear document window.

Close a Document

1. Select **File, Close** {Alt, f, c}. The document will be removed from the document window.

   Note: If a message displays, "Do you want to save changes to [filename]?," select ***No*** *{press n} to close without saving changes. Repeat Step 1 if more than one window is open. When there are no more documents in the document window, only the File and Help menus display in the Menu bar. Also, several of the buttons on the Standard Toolbar and Formatting Toolbar are empty.*

Memorandum—Style 2

Memorandum—Style 2, shown in Figure 1.6, illustrates a second acceptable memo format. The lead words and body text format are the same as Memorandum—Style 1. However, the heading "Interoffice Correspondence" is used and placed on two lines, and the lead words are arranged in a different order.

In either Memorandum style, the lead word "To:" may be followed by the recipient's name or by a name that identifies a group of individuals, e.g., sales representatives, district managers, etc. When the memorandum is sent to a group, a distribution list can be typed after the reference initials identifying the individuals who are part of the group. If copies of the memo are to be sent to other individuals, the notation "c:" is typed below the distribution list and followed by the name(s) of a person(s) to whom copies are to be sent.

Obtain a New Document Window

An empty document window displays each time the Word program is launched. After a document has been created in the first document window, a new, empty document window must be obtained to create another document. An empty document window can be obtained by selecting the **New** button on the Standard Toolbar.

Obtain a New Document Window

1. Select the **New** button on the Standard Toolbar {Alt, f, n, Enter}.

Finish-Up Instructions

- Type the memorandum as shown in Figure 1.6.
- The memorandum heading, **Interoffice Correspondence**, is typed on the left. Press **Enter** after typing **Interoffice**. Press the **Enter** key three times after typing **Correspondence**.
- Backspace to correct errors made while typing. Use word wrap.

  Note: The lines may not end exactly as shown in Figure 1.6.
- Continue to type the memorandum with the spacing indicated in Figure 1.6.
- Save the memorandum on your file disk; use the filename **1drill2** (Chapter 1, drill 2). (Select the **Save** button on the Standard Toolbar; type the filename in the File Name box; if necessary, click in the Drives box and click on the drive letter where your file disk is located; select **OK**.)
- Print one copy (select **File, Print**; choose **OK**).

FIGURE 1.6

Memorandum—Style 2

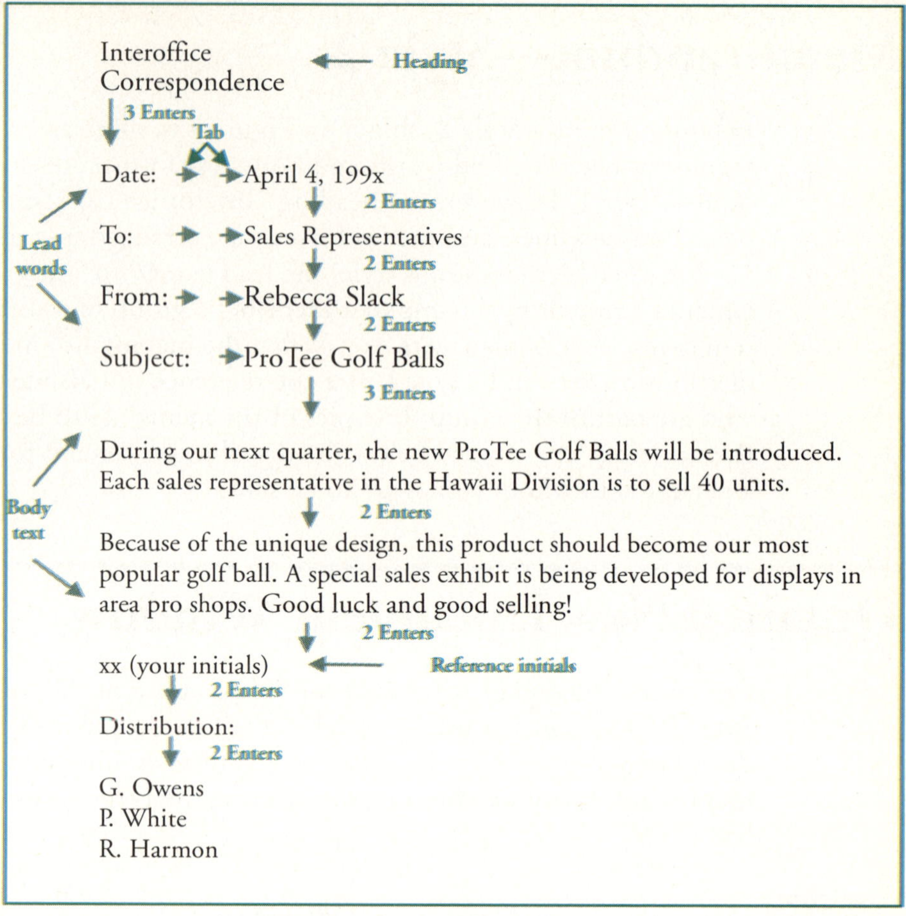

Scroll Horizontally and Vertically

Scrolling is the process of moving text quickly up, down, left, or right in order to view parts of the document not displayed in the document window. A vertical scroll bar displays at the right of the screen and a horizontal scroll bar displays at the bottom of the screen. Each scroll bar contains a scroll box and scroll arrows (controlled by the mouse) that can be used to view various parts of a document. See Figure 1.7. In the Page Layout view, the **Previous Page** and **Next Page** buttons located at the bottom of the vertical scroll bar can be used to scroll quickly from page to page in a multiple-page document.

Start-Up Instructions

- With the file named **1DRILL2.DOC** displayed in the document window, use the following steps to practice vertical and horizontal scrolling.

Use the Mouse for Vertical or Horizontal Scrolling

1. Place the mouse pointer on the scroll box in the *vertical scroll bar* on the right side of the document window; press and hold the left mouse button, then drag the scroll box up or down to scroll. Release the mouse button.

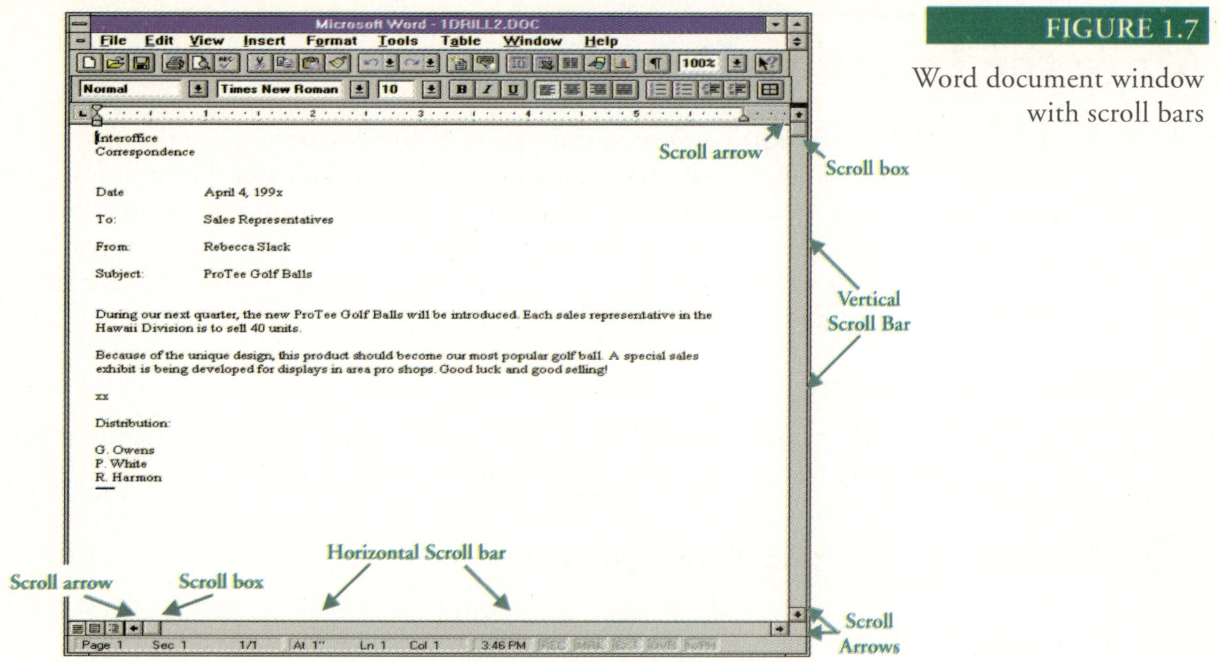

FIGURE 1.7

Word document window with scroll bars

For example, move the mouse pointer to the vertical scroll box; press and hold the left mouse button while dragging the box down; release the mouse button.

Note: *The text on the screen scrolls. However, the insertion point does not change location in the text. To change the location of the insertion point, see the Steps to Move the Insertion Point Quickly on page 26.*

2. Place the mouse pointer on the up scroll arrow located at the top of the vertical scroll bar or the down scroll arrow located at the bottom of the vertical scroll bar and click the left mouse button once to scroll the text down or up a single line.

   For example, place the mouse pointer on the down scroll arrow located at the bottom of the scroll bar and click once or twice.

   Note: *Holding down the left mouse button while pointing to the up or down scroll arrows will cause the text to move continuously up or down.*

3. Place the mouse pointer on the scroll box in the *horizontal scroll bar* at the bottom of the document window; press and hold the left mouse button and drag the scroll box to the left or right. Release the mouse button.

   For example, move the mouse pointer to the scroll box in the horizontal scroll bar; press and hold the left mouse button while dragging the box to the right. Release the mouse button.

Finish-Up Instructions

- Move the scroll box in the horizontal scroll bar to the far left of the scroll bar. If desired, move the scroll box in the vertical scroll bar to the top of the scroll bar.

Move the Insertion Point

To relocate the insertion point to various parts of the document, use the arrow keys or move the mouse pointer and click on the desired location. For example, the mouse can be used to relocate the insertion point to any position in the document by pointing on the desired position and clicking once. The up, down, left, and right arrow keys as well as the **Page Up** (**PgUp**), **Page Down** (**PgDn**), **Home**, and **End** keys can also be used to relocate the insertion point.

Start-Up Instructions

❖ With the file named 1DRILL2.DOC displayed in the document window, use the following steps to practice moving the insertion point.

Move the Insertion Point Quickly

Using the Mouse

1. Move the mouse pointer to any location in the document and click. The insertion point moves to that location.

   Note: If the desired location is not visible in the document window, scroll the text to display the desired location. (See Steps to Use the Mouse for Vertical or Horizontal Scrolling on page 24.)

2. To move the insertion point to a different page, move the mouse pointer to any location on the left side of the Status bar and double-click to display the Go To dialog box. Type the page number desired, and select **OK**. When the selected page appears, select **Close** to exit the dialog box.

Using the Keyboard

*Note: The WordPerfect Help feature should be turned off. When the WordPerfect help feature is turned on, the WP(H or N) flag in the Status Bar displays in black. If desired, double-click on the WP(H or N) flag, select **Options**, deselect the Help for WordPerfect Users and/or Navigation Keys for WordPerfect options. Select **OK**, choose **Close**. If necessary, see your instructor or instructional aide for assistance.*

1. To move the insertion point to the beginning of the current line, press the **Home** key.
2. To move the insertion point to the end of the current line, press the **End** key.
3. To move the insertion point to the beginning of the document, press and hold the **Ctrl** key and tap the **Home** key once (**Ctrl** and **Home**).
4. To move the insertion point to the last character in the document, press and hold the **Ctrl** key and tap the **End** key once (**Ctrl** and **End**).
5. To move the insertion point to the left one word, press the **Ctrl** and **left arrow** keys.
6. To move the insertion point to the right one word, press the **Ctrl** and **right arrow** keys.

7. To move the insertion point to the top of the previous screen, press the **Page Up** key.

8. To move the insertion point to the top of the next screen, press the **Page Down** key.

9. To move the insertion point to the previous page, hold down the **Alt** and **Ctrl** keys while pressing the **Page Up** key once.

10. To move the insertion point to the next page, hold down the **Alt** and **Ctrl** keys while pressing the **Page Down** key once.

11. To move the insertion point to a different page, press **F5** or **Ctrl** and **g** to display the Go To dialog box. Type the page number desired, then press **Enter**. When the selected page appears, press **Esc** to remove the Go To dialog box from the screen.

Exit Word for Windows

After completing your work, the Word for Windows program is exited and the Windows Program Manager screen displays. If desired, Windows can be closed and the cursor returned to the system prompt, e.g., C:\. Remember to always save your files before exiting the Word program.

Exit Word

Note: If necessary, save your file before exiting the Word program using the Steps to Save a New File on page 20.

1. Select **File, Exit** {Alt, f, x *or* Alt and F4}.

   *Note: If a message displays, "Do you want to save changes to . . . ?", select **Yes** to save changes, **No** to abandon changes, or **Cancel** to return to the document window.*

The Next Step

Chapter Review and Activities

Self-Check Quiz

T F 1. Launching is the process of transferring the Word program from a hard disk to the computer's memory.

T F 2. Formatting is the process of determining the placement and arrangement of a document when it is printed on a page.

T F 3. To center a line of text, type the text, then select the **Center** alignment button on the Formatting Toolbar.

T F 4. To print all the text in a file, select **File**, **Print**, **Close**.

T F 5. A document can be saved to a floppy disk only.

6. To display the list of available Toolbars, _______________.
   a. move the mouse pointer to any button in the current Toolbar and click the right mouse button once
   b. select **Tools**, **Toolbars**
   c. select **File**, **Toolbars**

7. The Standard Toolbar___________.
   a. is the same as the Formatting Toolbar
   b. can be removed from the screen by selecting **View**, **Toolbar**
   c. has buttons that can be accessed using keystrokes

8. Press the **Enter** key to_________.
   a. begin a new paragraph
   b. end a short line
   c. both a and b

9. What is the difference between the insertion point and the mouse pointer?

10. Explain two ways to return to and place the insertion point at the top of a document.

Enriching Language Arts Skills

Each chapter contains vocabulary/spelling words and basic rules for punctuation, capitalization, or grammar. The last *Challenge Your Skills* activity in each chapter is identified by the ➾ symbol and has mistakes in spelling, punctuation, capitalization, and/or grammar that are to be corrected. These activities should be proofread and corrected to produce a document that is grammatically accurate and ready for distribution.

Spelling/Vocabulary Words

recipient one who receives something.
efficient producing the desired result with a minimum of effort or expense.
comply to act in accordance with a request or order.

Introductory Adverbs and Phrases

A comma often follows an introductory adverb or phrase because the word or phrase provides a transition from the previous sentence. Some common introductory adverbs/phrases are: *however, for example, also, consequently, in other words.*

Examples:

A decision was made yesterday to postpone the approval of the budget. Consequently, the purchase order for the new desks will be delayed.

The post office requested that we use the new extended zip code. In other words, use the current 5-digit zip code followed by the new 4-digit extension.

Activities

Activity 1.1—Create a Memorandum—Style 1

1. If necessary, launch (load) the Word program (see page 14) or choose the **New** button on the Standard Toolbar.
2. If errors are made while typing, use the **Backspace** key to delete. For this chapter, ignore any errors noticed *after* the memo is typed.
3. Use Memorandum—Style 1 (see page 19) and type the following memorandum.

Memorandum

To: Al Edwards

From: Phyllis Falls

Date: (Use current date)

Subject: Safeguard Security Program

The newest version of the Safeguard Security program is currently available.

An information bulletin is being sent to all consultants informing them that the program documentation is now available at all our regional offices. Old versions of Safeguard

Security diskettes and manual contents can be destroyed. The binders can be reused with the new material, and the diskettes can be recycled.

xx (your initials)

---

4. Save the file on your file disk; use the filename **1act1** (Chapter 1, activity 1). (Select the **Save** button on the Standard Toolbar; type the filename; if necessary, click in the Drives box and click on the drive letter where your file disk is located; select **OK**.)
5. Print one copy (select **File, Print**; choose **OK**).
6. Close the document to clear the document window (select **File, Close**).

Activity 1.2—Create a Memorandum—Style 1

1. If necessary, launch (load) the Word program (see page 14) or select the **New** button on the Standard Toolbar.
2. If errors are made while typing, use the **Backspace** key to delete. For this chapter, ignore any errors noticed *after* the memo is typed.
3. Use Memorandum—Style 1(see page 19) and type the following memorandum.

Memorandum

To: All Insurance Agents

From: Dennis Rausch, Field Services Manager

Date: (Use current date)

Subject: Exchange Procedures for Multiple Contracts

The purpose of this memorandum is to clarify the procedure for processing exchanges when more than one contract is involved. The correct procedure is to list each company name along with the policy number for each policy that will be relinquished for the purpose of exchange.

At policy delivery, the policyowner will sign both of the contract forms. Return the forms and policies to the Contract Revision Department. If you have questions, please feel free to contact us in Field Services.

xx (your initials)

---

4. Save the file on your file disk; use the filename **1act2** (Chapter 1, activity 2). (Select the **Save** button on the Standard Toolbar; type the filename; if necessary, click in the Drives box and click on the drive letter where your file disk is located; select **OK**.)

5. Print one copy (select **File, Print**; choose **OK**).
6. Close the document to clear the document window (select **File, Close**).

Activity 1.3—Create a Memorandum—Style 2

1. If necessary, launch (load) the Word program (see page 14) or select the **New** button on the Standard Toolbar.
2. If errors are made while typing, use the **Backspace** key to delete. For this chapter, ignore any errors noticed *after* the memo is typed.
3. Use Memorandum—Style 2 (refer to page 24) and type the following memorandum.

Interoffice
Correspondence

Date: (Use current date)

To: See Distribution Below

From: Roger Parker

Subject: Reimbursement Guidelines

All offices have been provided with the new travel reimbursement guidelines that should be placed into effect immediately. Each office will photocopy a set of the guidelines and forward the guideline sheets to all area representatives.

You will notice that seasonal adjustments have been added to the hotel and airline guidelines. These should reflect appropriate price fluctuations for on and off-season travel.

If air travel or gasoline prices decline this fall, revised guidelines will be published and sent to you promptly.

xx (your initials)

Distribution:

Denice Bennett
John Devine
George Watkins

---

4. Save the file on your file disk; use the filename **1act3** (Chapter 1, activity 3). (Select the **Save** button on the Standard Toolbar; type the filename; if necessary, click in the Drives box and click on the drive letter where the file disk is located; select **OK**.)
5. Print one copy (select **File**, **Print**, choose **OK**).

6. Close the document to clear the document window (select **File, Close**).

Challenge Your Skills

The *Challenge Your Skills* section at the end of each chapter contains a group of activities that will reinforce your understanding of the chapter's concepts. The activities require decision-making and critical thinking skills. The *Challenge Your Skills* activities should be completed only after completing appropriate chapter drills and activities.

Skill 1.1—Create a Memorandum—Style 1

1. If necessary, launch the Word program or select the **New** button.
2. If errors are made while typing, use the **Backspace** key to delete. For this chapter, ignore any errors noticed *after* the memo is typed.
3. Use Memorandum—Style 1 and the following information:
   a. Send the memorandum to All Employees from John Armstrong. The subject of the memorandum is Recycling Disks.
   b. Use the current date; include your reference initials.

A question has been raised about the best method for recycling disks that contain information that is no longer needed. I would suggest reformatting the disks and reusing them. In some cases, people may end up with far more disks than they can reuse, so we will set aside a bin in the storage area for used disks. Please indicate on the disk label whether it is single-density or double-density and whether it has been formatted for low- or high-density use.

If you need disks for internal use other than backups, please check the recycling bins first and use these before opening new packages. It would, however, be safer to use new diskettes for backups and for any disks you are sending to clients.

---

4. Save the file on your file disk; use the filename **1skill1** (Chapter 1, skill 1).
5. Print one copy and close the document to clear the document window.

Skill 1.2—Create a Memorandum—Style 2

1. If necessary, launch the Word program or select the **New** button.
2. If errors are made while typing, use the **Backspace** key to delete. For this chapter, ignore any errors noticed *after* the memo is typed.
3. Use Memorandum—Style 2 and the following information:
   a. Send the memorandum to GIM Agents from Marjorie Cuson. The subject of the memorandum is Purchase of Portfolios.
   b. Use the current date; include your reference initials.

c. The memo is to be distributed to the following: Jody Carbajal, Sarah Gutekunst, Mark Pinkerton, Sateesh Rowse, and Lois Waymon.

Global Investment Management (GIM) will soon acquire the investment portfolios of Monterey Financial Consultants (MFC). MFC is a small mutual fund investment consulting firm that has experienced financial difficulty and is being liquidated.

As part of the liquidation process, GIM has agreed to purchase MFC's client investment portfolios. This will ensure that the investment programs continue without loss to the investors.

We think that the acquisition of MFC's portfolios will help us control our unit expenses, which is certainly in everyone's best interest. If you have any questions on the acquisition, please contact my assistant, Janice Krueck.

---

4. Save the file on your file disk; use the filename **1skill2** (Chapter 1, skill 2).
5. Print one copy and close the document to clear the document window.

Skill 1.3—Create a Memorandum—Style 2; Language Arts

1. If necessary, launch the Word program or select the **New** button.
2. If errors are made while typing, use the **Backspace** key to delete. For this chapter, ignore any typing errors noticed *after* the memo is typed.
3. Use Memorandum—Style 2 and the following information:
    a. Send the memorandum to Global Express Corporate Card Recipients from Gerald B. Rovella, Controller. The subject of the memo is Global Express Corporate Card Program.
    b. Use the current date; include your reference initials.
    c. The memo is to be distributed to the following: A. Hackley; L. Laney; M. Dominguez; S. Stelter; J. Anderson; and T. Marshall.
    d. While typing, correct three spelling errors and one punctuation error.

Perry & Russ is pleased to announce that we have implemented the Global Express Corporate Card (GEX) Program as a tool which will make you a more effeciant employee and provide the company with better management of our travel and entertainment expenses. You have been identified as an employee who requires a Corporate Card. Consequently you will be receiving a card within the next two weeks, directly from Global Express.

The program provides key benefits to both recipeents and the company. Recipient benefits include travel and accident insurance, baggage insurance, and personal check cashing privileges at any Global Express office and at most hotels. In other words, utilization of the Global Express Card eliminates the need for carrying large amounts of cash by providing you with worldwide card acceptance and 24-hour customer service.

Company benefits include improved expense documentation and detailed information on the travel and entertainment spending of employees.

A copy of the corporate Charge Card Program Policy will be sent to you next week. Please review the policy and commply with the requirements. If you have any questions, call Melanie Abbott, Director of Technical Accounting Services, at Extension 2065.

---

4. Save the file on your file disk; use the filename **1skill3** (Chapter 1, skill 3).
5. Print one copy.
6. If you have completed your work, exit Word (select **File**, **Exit**).

CHAPTER 2

Edit a Memorandum

Features Covered

- Open a document
- Select text
- Delete text
- Insert text
- Replace text using the Typeover mode
- Save and rename a document file
- Undo and Redo features
- Use the Help feature

Objectives and Introduction

After successfully completing this chapter, you will be able to open a previously created document; select, delete, insert, and replace text; and save a document with a new filename. You will also be able to use the Undo, Redo, and Help features. After a memorandum has been created, authors often make revisions to the document. Revisions can include information to be deleted, inserted, or replaced.

Open a Document

Before a file can be edited, the saved document must be opened and displayed in the document window. Opening a document is the process of transferring a document file from a disk to the computer's memory. When a file is opened, the document displays in a new document window. Several files can be opened (in memory) at the same time (see Chapters 9 and 16). To open a file, select the **Open** button on the Standard Toolbar, choose the desired drive/directory, and double-click on the filename.

The last four to nine files that have been opened are listed at the bottom of the File menu. To open one of the listed files, move the mouse pointer to the filename and click once. If Word cannot locate the selected file, a message displays "Word cannot open [path/filename]."

FIGURE 2.1

Open dialog box

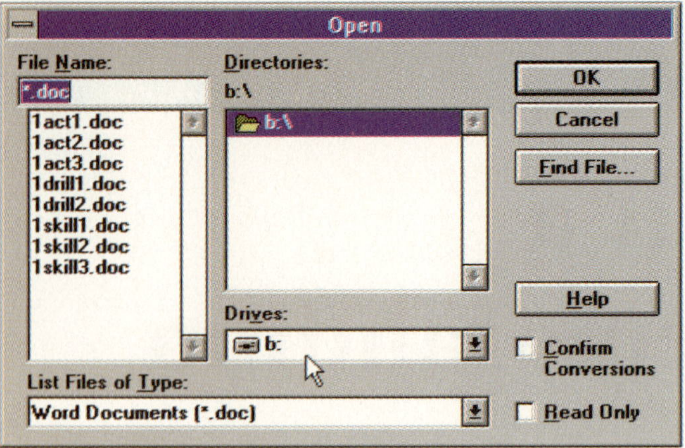

Open a File

1. Select the **Open** button on the Standard Toolbar {Alt, f, o *or* Ctrl and o}.

   Note: *The Open dialog box displays (see Figure 2.1).*

2. To display the files stored on a different drive, move the mouse pointer to the Drives box and and click once. Move the mouse pointer to the desired drive letter and click once {Alt and v, press the down arrow key, press the up or down arrow key to highlight desired drive letter, press Enter}.

3. Move the mouse pointer to the desired filename and double-click {Alt and n, press the Tab key once, press the down arrow key to highlight the desired filename, press Enter}.

   For example, double-click on the file named **1drill1.doc**.

   Note: *Wait a moment for the selected file to display in the document window.*

Delete and Insert Text

Text can be deleted by using the **Backspace** key or the **Delete** (Del) key. When the Backspace key is pressed, the character or space to the left of the insertion point is erased. When the Delete key is pressed, the character or space to the right of the insertion point is erased. Text deleted by using the **Backspace** or **Delete** keys can be returned to the screen by using the Edit, Undo command or the Undo button on the Standard Toolbar (see the Undo Feature, page 41).

Selected text can be erased and replaced without using either the **Delete** or **Backspace** key. The text to be deleted is selected. When the first character of the new text is typed, the selected text is deleted.

Text can also be selected and then deleted. A character, word, sentence, line, paragraph, or entire document can be selected and deleted. After text is selected and the **Delete** or **Backspace** key is pressed, the deleted text is placed in the Clipboard. The Clipboard is temporary memory that holds the deleted text. When additional text is selected and deleted, the original text held in the Clipboard is erased and replaced with the text deleted last.

Text is inserted by placing the insertion point at the location where the new characters are to be typed and typing the characters. As the inserted text is typed, the characters to the right of the insertion point move over and provide space for the new text. Changing text by deleting and inserting is often referred to as editing text.

Select Text

- *Using the Mouse Drag method*: To select any quantity of text, move the mouse pointer (I-beam) to the beginning of the text to be selected; press and hold the left mouse button while dragging the mouse to highlight the desired text. Release the mouse button.
- *Extended Selection method*: To select any quantity of text, move the mouse pointer (I-beam) to the left of the first character to be selected and click the left mouse button once. Move the mouse pointer to the light gray EXT flag in the Status bar and double-click the left mouse button. Move the mouse pointer (I-beam) to the right of the last character to be selected and click the left mouse button once.
- *Shift and Click method:* To select any quantity of text, move the mouse pointer (I-beam) to the left of the first character to be selected and click the left mouse button once. Move the mouse pointer (I-beam) to the right of the last character to be selected. Press and hold the **Shift** key and click the left mouse button once. Release the **Shift** key.
- *To select a word,* move the mouse pointer to any character in the desired word and double-click.
- *To select a line,* move the mouse pointer into the left margin beside the desired line until a right arrow displays; click the left mouse button once.
- *To select a paragraph,* move the mouse pointer to any location within the paragraph and click three times, or move the mouse pointer into the left margin beside the desired paragraph until a right arrow displays and double-click.
- *To select the entire document,* select **Edit, Select All** or move the mouse pointer into the left margin until the right arrow displays and triple-click.

Using Keystrokes

- *To select the entire document,* press **Ctrl** and **a** or **Ctrl** and **Numeric Keypad 5**.
- To select any quantity of text, place the insertion point to the left of the character at the beginning of the text to be selected. Press **F8** or hold down the **Shift** key, then use any of the following keystrokes:
    - *To select one character* to the right or left, press the **right arrow** or **left arrow** key.
    - *To select one line* up or down, press the **up** or **down arrow** key.
    - *To select to the end of the line,* press the **End** key.
    - *To select to the beginning of the line,* press the **Home** key.
    - *To select to the beginning of the document,* press the **Ctrl** and **Home** keys.
    - *To select to the end of the document,* press the **Ctrl** and **End** keys.
    - *To select to the top of the previous screen,* press **Page Up** (PgUp).

- *To select to the top of the next screen,* press **Page Down** (PgDn).
- *To select one word to the right or left,* press **Ctrl** and the **left** or **right arrow** key.
- *To select one paragraph up or down,* press **Ctrl** and the **up** or **down arrow** key.

- Place the insertion point at the beginning of the desired text; press **F8**; then use either of the following keystrokes:
  - *To select to the end of the sentence,* press the key corresponding to the punctuation mark at the end of the sentence.
  - *To select to the next instance of any specific letter or number,* press the key corresponding to that letter or number, e.g., press g to select through the next occurrence of a word ending in g.

Turn Off Select

1. To turn off select and remove the highlight from text, click once {Esc, then press any arrow key}.

Delete Text

1. Once the desired text has been selected, press the **Delete** (Del) key.

Shortcut for Deleting Text Without Selecting Text

1. To delete an entire word, position the insertion point to the right of the final character in the word to be deleted and press **Ctrl** and **Backspace**.

Insert Text or Spaces

1. Place the insertion point to the left of the character or space that will follow the inserted text or space.
2. Type the text or space to be inserted.

   Note: *If text is erased as new text is typed, press the* ***Insert*** *(Ins) key once to turn off the Typeover mode. See Replace Text Using the Typeover Mode.*

Replace Text Using the Typeover Mode

When text is replaced using the Typeover mode, the original character(s) are deleted and new characters are substituted. For example, if the insertion point is located to the left of the character *b* in the word *band* and the character *s* is typed, the *b* is deleted and the character *s* displays on the screen, changing the word to *sand.* Replacing text using the Typeover mode is accomplished by first pressing the **Insert** (Ins) key or by double-clicking on the **OVR** flag in the Status bar, then typing the new character(s). When the Typeover mode is turned on, the OVR flag in the

Status bar darkens. The Typeover mode is turned off by pressing the **Insert** key again or double-clicking on the **OVR** flag again. When the Typeover mode is off, the OVR flag dims (becomes light gray) in the Status bar.

Steps to Replace Text

1. Place the insertion point to the left of the first character of the text to be replaced.
2. Double-click on the **OVR** flag in the Status bar {press the Insert (Ins) key}.

   Note: *The OVR flag in the Status bar darkens.*
3. Type the new character(s).
4. When you have finished replacing the text, double-click on the **OVR** flag again to turn (toggle) Typeover mode off {press Ins again}.

   Note: *To restore the replaced text, see the Undo Feature.*

Start-Up Instructions

- The file named **1drill1.doc** typed in Chapter 1 (Figure 1.4) should be opened and displayed in the document window. (If necessary, select the **Open** button on the Standard Toolbar; click in the Drives box and click on the drive letter where the file disk is located; double-click on the desired filename.)
- Review the steps to select and/or delete text and the steps to replace text using the Typeover mode. Make the changes shown in Figure 2.2.

Memorandum

To: Division Managers

From: Dave Stark (handwritten: id R. ... Regional Manager)

Date: June 8, 199x

Subject: (handwritten: Northwestern) Regional Meeting

Please arrange to make yourself available for a three-day meeting the second week of July. Rooms will be booked for everyone at the Seattle Airport Red Lion Inn. (handwritten: for three days and two nights.)

(handwritten: Tuesday Wednesday)
On ~~Monday~~ and ~~Tuesday~~ mornings, the focus will be primarily on basic Northeast business issues and opportunities. I will advise you of the business, recreation, and other details before the meeting. (handwritten: On Thursday we will join Kathy Barton's group to discuss the new marketing promotion.)

(handwritten: ¶ Casual attire will be appropriate for Tuesday and Wednesday. Thursday's attire will be announced pending the determination of the meeting location.)

xx

FIGURE 2.2

Changes for Memorandum—Style 1

❖ Continue with the Steps to Use Save As to Rename a File.

Save and Rename a File

Once a document (file) has been edited, the changed file can be saved using a new filename. By using a different filename, the original file is not changed and the edited file is saved under a new filename. If the edited file is saved with the original filename, the original file is erased and replaced by the changed file.

Start-Up Instructions

❖ The file named **1drill1.doc** should be displayed in the document window.

Use Save As to Rename a File

1. With the document displayed in the document window, select **File, Save As** {Alt, f, a}.
2. Type the new filename. (If necessary, select the drive where the file disk is located by clicking in the Drives box and selecting the desired drive letter, or type the drive letter followed by a colon and the filename).

   For example, type **a:2drill1r**. (Do not type the period.)
3. Select **OK** {press Enter}.

Finish-Up Instructions

❖ Print one copy (select **File**, **Print**; choose **OK**).

❖ If additional changes are made to the document, select the **Save** button on the Standard Toolbar to save and not rename the document. If no changes are made to the document after printing, clear the screen (select **File**, **Close**).

The Undo Feature

Text that has been selected and deleted with the Delete or Backspace keys can be recalled (or put back) into the document. When text is recalled, the deleted text is retrieved to the screen. Recalling text into a document on the screen is referred to as *undo*.

In addition to recalling text, the **Undo** command can reverse many editing actions. Word will undo remembered actions one at a time working from the most recent to the earliest action each time the **Edit**, **Undo** command or the **Undo** button is selected. Word remembers up to 128 previous actions. When the arrow next to the **Undo** button is selected, a list of remembered actions displays. Selecting an item on the list will reverse all changes back to that original action. For example, three sentences are deleted one after the other. The Undo list is displayed and the third item is selected. All three deleted sentences will return to the document screen.

Text that has been recalled using Undo can be deleted again by selecting the **Edit**, **Redo** command or the **Redo** button. If the Edit menu is selected, the exact

The Association rules have been updated. The updated rules will be placed in your mailbox over the weekend. The revised rules are easy to read and comprehend.

FIGURE 2.3

Practice paragraph to use with Undo and Redo commands

wording of the Undo and Redo commands will vary depending on the last action taken. For example, if text has been deleted, the Undo command will read **Undo Clear**. When deleted text has been restored, the Redo command will read **Redo Clear**.

Start-Up Instructions

- Select the **New** button on the Standard Toolbar. Type the paragraph shown in Figure 2.3.
- Select and delete the *first* sentence.
- Select and delete the *last* sentence.

Undo Deleted Text

1. After the text has been selected and deleted, select the **Undo** button on the Standard Toolbar {Alt, e, u *or* Ctrl and z}.

   For example, select the **Undo** button to redisplay the last sentence in the paragraph.

   Note: The last sentence deleted returns to the screen and displays highlighted in its original location.

2. Select the **Undo** button again to reverse the next to the last action.

   For example, select the **Undo** button again to redisplay the first sentence in the paragraph.

Start-Up Instructions

- Click once to deselect the highlighted sentence.
- The paragraph typed previously from Figure 2.3 should be displaying in the document window.

Redo Deleted Text

1. After the deleted text is reinserted, select the **Redo** button to delete it again {Alt, e, r *or* Ctrl and y}.

   For example, select the **Redo** button to delete the first sentence in the paragraph again.

2. Select the **Redo** button again to reverse the next previous "undo" action {Alt, e, r *or* Ctrl and y}.

   For example, select the **Redo** button to delete the last sentence in the paragraph again.

Finish-Up Instructions

- Close and do not save the document (select **File**, **Close**, **No**).

Use Help

Word has a Help feature that provides detailed information about program topics and specific instructions for performing commands. The Help feature can be accessed at any time through the Help menu or from any dialog box or menu.

The Help feature can be accessed in several ways. One method is to select the **Help** menu and choose the **Contents** or the **Index** option. A list of topics displays. The Contents option displays a list of general areas covered in Word Help. One of the general areas can then be selected to display another, more detailed list of topics. This is repeated, narrowing the focus of the topic until the information desired is displayed (see Figure 2.4). When the **Index** option is selected, an alphabetical list of all topics covered by Word Help displays.

The Contents option is most useful when the general type of help desired is known but the exact terminology used by Word is not known. When the terminology used by Word is known, using the Index option may be faster.

If the information desired is listed under several topics, the **Search for Help on** option in the **Help** menu can be selected. When the **Search** option is selected, all Help topics are reviewed to find the specified text. The topics where the specified text is found are displayed, and the desired topic is then selected.

When a topic is selected, additional information can be viewed by selecting the "jump terms" or "glossary terms" icon. A word(s) that is displayed with an underline is referred to as a jump term(s). When a jump term is selected, a new Word Help window displays with information on the related topic. A words(s) that displays with a dotted underline is referred to as a glossary term(s). When a glossary term is selected, additional information displays on the screen. To remove glossary information from the screen, click the mouse button once outside of the glossary box or press **Esc**.

Help can also be accessed by selecting a menu command or by displaying a dialog box and pressing **F1**. Help information displays for the menu command or for each option shown in the dialog box. To display Help information about buttons on a Toolbar or other areas of the document window, access the context-sensitive Help by selecting the **Help** button on the Standard Toolbar or by pressing the **Shift** and **F1** keys, then moving the mouse pointer to the item, and clicking the mouse button once.

Word also provides an **Examples and Demos** option that lists the steps necessary to complete a task.

Start-Up Instructions

- While performing the following "Steps to. . ." instructions, a clear document screen or a document can be displayed in the document window.

Access Help Using the Contents Option

1. Select the **Help** menu {Alt, h}.
2. Select **Contents** {c}.
3. Move the mouse pointer to the desired topic and click once {press the Tab key repeatedly until the desired topic is highlighted, press Enter}.

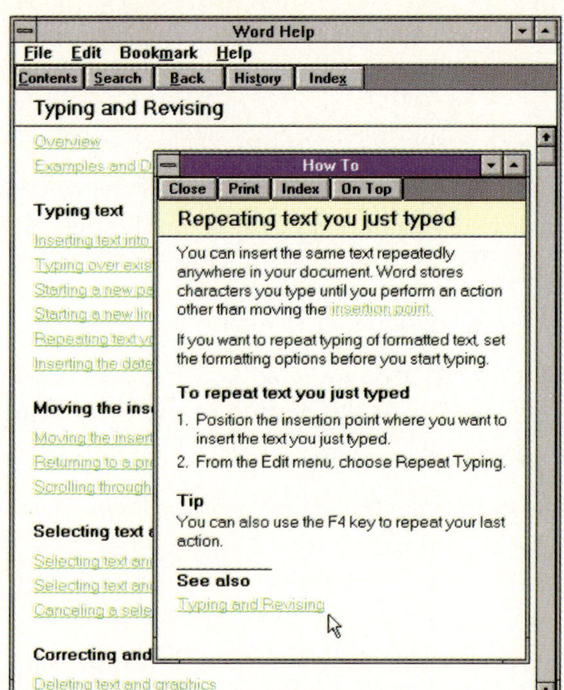

FIGURE 2.4

Word Help and How To windows

For example, select **Using Word.**

Note: A list of topics associated with using Word displays.

4. Select the desired topic.

   For example, select the **Typing and Revising** topic that is listed below the Typing and Editing heading.

   Note: A second list of topics displays.

5. Select the next desired topic.

   For example, select the ***Repeating text you just typed*** *topic listed below the Typing text heading.*

   Note: The How To window containing information on the selected topic displays (see Figure 2.4). Continue with Steps to Print a Help Topic in a How To Window.

Steps to Print a Help Topic in a How To Window

Note: *A mouse is needed to perform the following steps.*

1. Display the desired Help topic in the How To window.

   For example, the **Repeating text you just typed** Help topic should be displaying in the How To window.

2. Select the **Print** button in the How To window.

Steps to Exit the Help Feature

1. Select the **Close** button in the How To window {Alt and F4}.
2. Select **File, Exit** in the Help window {Alt and F4}.

Access Help Using the Index Option

1. Select **Help, Index** {Alt, h, i}.
2. Move the mouse pointer to the desired letter at the top of the window and click once {press the Tab key repeatedly to highlight the desired letter, press Enter}.

   For example, select **N.**

   Note: *A list of topics beginning with the letter N displays.*
3. Move the mouse pointer to the desired topic and click once {press the Tab key repeatedly to move through the list to the desired topic, press Enter}.

   For example, select **naming documents.**

   Note: *The How To window containing the information on saving a new unnamed document displays.*

Finish-Up Instructions

- Exit the Help window and return to the document window (select **Close**, choose **File, Exit** in the Help window {press Alt and F4 twice}.

Start-Up Instructions

- While performing the following "Steps to . . ." instructions, a clear document screen or a document can be displayed in the document window.

Access the Help Feature for a Menu Command or Dialog Box

1. Highlight the menu command desired or display the desired dialog box.

   For example, select the **Open** button on the Standard Toolbar to display the Open dialog box {Alt, f, o}.
2. Press **F1**.

   Note: *The Word Help window explaining the Open command (File menu) displays. Additional information can be obtained by selecting a word(s) that has a solid or dotted underline.*
3. If necessary, select the desired related topic(s) that is listed under the "See Also" heading.

   For example, scroll down to the bottom of the information displayed and double-click on the related topic, **Opening, Saving, and Protecting Documents.**

   Note: *Only some Help windows contain a related topic(s) that displays at the bottom of the help information.*
4. Select **File, Exit** {Alt and F4}.

   Note: *The dialog box for the option selected displays again on the screen.*

Finish-Up Instructions

- If desired, complete any actions necessary using the options in the dialog box or select **Cancel** to return to the document window.

Start-Up Instructions

- While performing the following "Steps to . . ." instructions, a clear document screen or a document can be displayed in the document window.

Steps to Access the Context-Sensitive Help Feature

Note: A mouse must be used to perform the following steps.

1. Select the **Help** button on the Standard Toolbar or press the **Shift** and **F1** keys.

   Note: A question mark is added to the mouse pointer.

2. Move the mouse pointer to the item where information is desired and click once.

   For example, move the mouse pointer to the **Undo** button on the Standard Toolbar and click once.

   Note: A Word Help window displays containing information on the Undo feature. Continue with Steps to Print a Help Topic in a Word Help window.

Steps to Print a Help Topic in a Word Help Window

1. Display the desired Help topic in the Word Help window.

   For example, the **Undo command** Help topic should be displaying in the Word Help window.

2. Select **File, Print Topic** in the Word Help window {Alt and f, p}.

   Note: A printing message displays briefly, and the topic information goes directly to the printer for printing.

Finish-Up Instructions

- Exit the Help window and return to the document window (choose **File, Exit** in the Help window {press Alt and F4}.

The Next Step

Chapter Review and Activities

Self-Check Quiz

T F 1. Once text has been selected and deleted, the text cannot be recalled into the document.

T F 2. A file can be opened by selecting the **Open** button on the Standard Toolbar, clicking in the Drives box and selecting the drive letter where the file disk is located, and then double-clicking on the desired filename.

T F 3. Place the insertion point to the left of a character and press the **Delete** key once to delete the character.

T F 4. The **Backspace** key is used to delete characters to the left of the insertion point.

T F 5. When text is replaced, the original characters are deleted and new characters are substituted.

6. Typeover is turned off and on by __________.
   a. double-clicking on the **OVR** flag in the Status Bar
   b. pressing the up arrow key
   c. pressing the **Insert** key
   d. either a or c

7. To select the entire document, __________.
   a. press **Ctrl** and **a**
   b. select **View**, **Document**
   c. select **Edit**, **Document**
   d. select **Tools**, **Select All**

8. The Help feature can be used by __________.
   a. selecting **Help**, **Contents**
   b. pressing **F1**
   c. selecting **Help**, **Index**
   d. all of the above

9. Explain two ways to select a paragraph.

10. List the three steps to save and rename a file.

Enriching Language Arts Skills

Spelling/Vocabulary Words

passive offering no resistance, taking no action to cause or prevent.

environment surroundings; all the surroundings and conditions affecting the development of an organism.

compliance agreement with, willingness to act in accordance with rules.

Introductory (Dependent) Clauses

A comma should follow a dependent clause. (A dependent clause has both a subject and a verb but cannot stand alone as a sentence.) An introductory dependent clause often begins with if, in, when, since, or as.

Example:

As you prepare your expense report, remember to use the updated gasoline rate schedule.

Activities

Activity 2.1—Open a File and Edit a Memorandum

1. If necessary, launch the Word program.
2. Open the file named **1act1.doc** that was typed in Chapter 1, page 29. (Select the **Open** button on the Standard Toolbar; if necessary, click in the Drives box and click on the drive letter where the file disk is located; double-click on the desired filename.)
3. Make the revisions shown.

Memorandum

To: Al Edwards

From Phyllis ~~Falls~~ Langa, Consultant Manager

Date: (Use current date)

Subject: Safeguard Security Program

The newest version of the Safeguard Security program (Version 6.0) is currently available.

An information bulletin is being sent to all consultants informing them that the program documentation is now available at all our regional offices. Old versions of Safeguard Security Plan diskettes and manual contents can be destroyed. The binders can be reused with the new material, and the diskettes can be recycled. If you have binders, please either send them to my assistant, Gary, or let us know the number of binders you have, and we will send you the newest contents.

xx ¶ To install the program on a PC, insert disk 1 in drive A and type A:INSTALSP.

4. Proofread and correct any errors.
5. Use the *new* filename **2act1r** (Chapter 2, activity 1, revised) and save the revised file. (Select **File, Save As**; type the new filename; if necessary, click in the Drives box and click on the drive letter where your file disk is located; select **OK.**)
6. Print one copy (select **File, Print**; choose **OK**).
7. Close the document to clear the document window (select **File, Close**).

Activity 2.2—View and Open a File; Edit a Memorandum

1. If necessary, launch the Word program.
2. Open the file named **1act3.doc** that was typed in Chapter 1, page 31. (Select the **Open** button on the Standard Toolbar; if necessary, click in the Drives box and click on the drive letter where your file disk is located; double-click on the desired filename.)
3. Make the revisions shown.

Interoffice
Correspondence

Date: (Use current date)

To: See Distribution Below

From: Roger Parker

Subject: Reimbursement Guidelines

All offices have been provided with the new travel reimbursement guidelines that should be placed into effect immediately. We are requesting that each division office will photocopy a set of the guidelines and forward the guideline sheets to all area representatives.

¶ Also, the sales office has been provided with the guidelines for all area offices under their authority. Please forward the ~~You will notice that seasonal adjustments have been added to the hotel and airline guidelines. These should reflect appropriate price fluctuations for on and off-season travel.~~ reimbursement guidelines to your area operations manager.

If air travel or gasoline prices decline this fall, revised guidelines will be published and sent to you promptly.

xx (your initials)

Distribution:

Denice Bennett
John Devine
George Watkins
Warren Happ
Agusto Moreno

4. Proofread and correct any errors.
5. Use the *new* filename **2act2r** (Chapter 2, activity 2, revised) and save the revised file. (Select **File**, **Save As**; type the new filename; if necessary, click in the Drives box and click on the drive letter where the file disk is located; select **OK**.)
6. Print one copy (select **File**, **Print**; choose **OK**).
7. Close the document to clear the document window (select **File**, **Close**).

Activity 2.3—Create and Edit a Memorandum

1. If necessary, launch the Word program or select the **New** button.
2. Type the following memorandum. Use Memorandum—Style 1 (see Chapter 1, Figure 1.4).

Memorandum

To: See Distribution Below

From: R.L. Cannizzaro

Date: (Use current date)

Subject: Staff Update

At the end of this month, Rubin Turner will be leaving BTS. He will, however, be available to work on projects as an independent contractor.

Rosada Garcia will be promoted to take over Rubin's duties effective immediately.

On behalf of BTS, I want publicly to wish Rubin the best of luck in his new life. By next month, his first book, SURVIVING LANS, will be available in bookstores.

xx (your initials)

Distribution:

Jin Choi
Sarina Laxague
William Nunez
Lena Tully

3. Save the file as **2act3** (Chapter 2, activity 3). (Select the **Save** button on the Standard Toolbar; type the filename; if necessary, click in the Drives box and click on the drive letter where the file disk is located; select **OK**.)
4. Make the revisions shown.

To: See Distribution Below

From: R. L. Cannizzaro [Handwritten: onald; Human Resources Director]

Date: (Use current date)

Subject: Staff Update

At the end of this month, Rubin Turner will be leaving BTS. He will, however, be available to work on projects as an independent contractor.

Rosada Garcia will be promoted to take over Rubin's duties effective immediately. [Handwritten: If you have training or graphics needs, please direct your request to Rosada.]

On behalf of BTS, I want publicly to wish Rubin the best of luck in his new life. By next month, his first book, SURVIVING LANS, will be available in bookstores.

[Handwritten: ¶ Rubin's work at BTS contributed toward professional-looking course materials and sales presentations and to more knowledgeable coworkers on Word for Windows and CorelDraw. Thank you, Rubin.]

xx (your initials)

Distribution:

Jin Choi
Sarina Laxague
William Nunez
Lena Tully

---

5. Proofread and correct any errors.
6. Use the *new* filename **2act3r** (Chapter 2, activity 3, revised) and save the revised file. (Select **File**, **Save As**; type the new filename; if necessary, click in the Drives box and click on the drive letter where the file disk is located; select **OK**.)
7. Print one copy (select **File**, **Print**, choose **OK**).
8. Close the document to clear the document window (select **File**, **Close**).

Challenge Your Skills

Skill 2.1—Create and Edit a Memorandum

1. If necessary, launch the Word program or select the **New** button.
2. Use Memorandum—Style 1 (see Chapter 1, Figure 1.4) and the following information:
   a. Send the memorandum to All Smithers Distributing Employees from S. Eliason. The subject of the memorandum is Promotion Announcement.
   b. Use the current date; include your reference initials.

It is my pleasure to announce the appointment of Helen Vanaken-Doner to the position of Vice President of Operations for the Consumer Group Division.

In her new role, Helen's primary responsibility will be the management of the Akron warehouse, which recently became a part of the Consumer Group family. In this capacity, Helen will be exploring new ways to increase the efficiency of our order cycle, improve the accuracy of our shipping department, and enhance our image with our customers.

Please join me in welcoming Helen to the Consumer Group and congratulating her on her promotion. I am sure this will be an exciting time for her and for the employees who are privileged to work with her.

---

3. Save the file; use the filename **2skill1** (Chapter 2, skill 1).
4. Use the following information to edit the memorandum:
   a. Change the S. in the From line to Stanley and add his title, Personnel Manager.
   b. Delete the last sentence in the third paragraph that begins "I am sure . . ."
   c. Insert the following new paragraph between the last two paragraphs:
      Helen will be located at the Akron warehouse and can be reached at (216) 555-0531, extension 218.
   d. Add the following sentence at the end of the fourth paragraph:
      The Washington office will sponsor a Promotion/Transfer Lunch for Helen next Tuesday from 1-3 p.m. at the Bombay Bicycle Club. If you would like to join the celebration, let Marsha Napier at e-mail stop 522 know by close of business Monday.
5. Proofread and correct any errors.
6. Use the *new* filename **2skill1r** (Chapter 2, skill 1, revised) and save the file.
7. Print one copy of the memo.
8. Close the document.

Skill 2.2—Create and Edit a Memorandum

1. If necessary, launch the Word program or select the **New** button.
2. Use Memorandum—Style 2 (see Chapter 1, Figure 1.6) and the following information:
   a. Send the memorandum to Manuel Bettencourt, Director of Nursing, from Jane Johnson, Administrator. The subject of the memorandum is East Coast Regional Conference.
   b. Use the current date; include your reference initials.

This year's East Coast NAMM Conference will be held April 12-16, 199x, in Boston. The theme of the conference is "The Body-Mind Connection," and it will focus on the various ways in which the body and mind interact in the healing process. A complete list of the seminars and workshops will be e-mailed to all nurses as soon as it is available.

Please let me know as soon as possible the names of the nurses and other staff members who are interested in attending. The hospital has a limited budget for travel and expenses, but if a sufficient number of people are interested, we may be able to charter a bus and arrange for hotel discounts.

---

3. Save the file; use the filename **2skill2** (Chapter 2, skill 2).
4. Use the following information to edit the memorandum:
   a. Change the subject of the memo to NAMM Annual Conference.
   b. In the first paragraph, change the date of the conference to May 12-18, 199x.
   c. Insert the following paragraph between the two paragraphs:
      I would particularly like to see the Nursing Department heavily represented at Monday and Tuesday's workshops. My understanding is that these workshops will focus on enlisting the mind to assist in healing the body using a variety of techniques.
   d. In the third paragraph, change "as soon as possible" to "before next Friday."
   e. Two returns after your reference initials, use the following format to indicate that a copy of the memo will be sent to the following person.
      c: Jaimi Cornejo, Medical Director
5. Proofread and correct any errors.
6. Use the *new* filename **2skill2r** (Chapter 2, skill 2, revised) and save the file.
7. Print one copy of the memo.
8. Close the document.

Skill 2.3—Create and Edit a Memorandum; Language Arts

1. If necessary, launch the Word program or select the **New** button.
2. Use Memorandum—Style 2 (Chapter 1, Figure 1.6) and the following information.
   a. Send the memorandum to All CTA Employees from Jane Avery, Personnel Director. The subject of the memo is Smoking in the Workplace.
   b. Use the current date; include your reference initials.
   c. The memo is to be distributed to the following (alphabetize by last name): Tamis, D.; Kerdasha, P.; Metzger, A.; DuBois, R.; Pham, N.; Giovanetti, M.; and Haslam, E.
   d. Correct three spelling words and two punctuation errors. Remember to check for the spelling words and grammar rules discussed in both Chapters 1 and 2.

To address the increasing concerns of non-smokers regarding the effects of pasive exposure to cigarette, cigar, and pipe smoke, and to provide a safer working environment for all employees, CTA is encouraging employees not to smoke during office hours.

CTA recognizes that the decision to smoke or not to smoke is a personal one. However, it is the company's policy to limit smoking during work hours to breaks and lunch periods. Smokers may smoke only in the DESIGNATED SMOKING AREA of the employee cafeteria or outside the building. Smoking in all other areas of the invironment is prohibited.

The Security Department will monitor the building to ensure complience with company policy. Security guards will request employees who are violating the smoking policy to extinguish their cigarettes, cigars, or pipes. We require all employees to comply with the requests of the security guards.

If you have questions regarding the Smoking Policy please call your Human Resources representative. The Internal Complaint Procedure may be utilized to resolve disputes under the revised Smoking Policy and to protect employees from retaliatory action for reporting co-workers who are not complying with the policy.

---

3. Save the file; use the filename **2skill3** (Chapter 2, skill 3).
4. Use the following information to edit the memorandum:
   a. Delete the second sentence of the third paragraph.
   b. Insert the following sentence at the end of the third paragraph:
      Employees who do not comply with the requests of the security guards will be subject to disciplinary action in accordance with the policy stated in Section 1.2 of the Employee Handbook.
   c. Insert the following new paragraph after the last paragraph:

Any employee who wants to stop smoking is encouraged to contact John Madison at Ext. 4425 for a list of programs in the area and for a pamphlet explaining how to apply for reimbursement of any costs associated with such programs. John also has materials on how to discuss smoking with children and teenagers, and has contacts with several groups who sponsor school programs to encourage students to say no to smoking.

5. Proofread and correct any errors.
6. Use the *new* filename **2skill3r** (Chapter 2, skill 3, revised) and save the file.
7. Print one copy and close the document.
8. If you have completed your work, exit Word (select **File**, **Exit**).

CHAPTER 3

Create Business Letters

Features Covered

- Use the automatic date feature
- Change alignment
- Use bold, underline, and italic text attributes
- Change margins
- Change fonts
- Use the Spelling command
- Use Print Preview and Zoom view

Objectives and Introduction

After successfully completing this chapter, you will be able to use the automatic date feature, change alignment, use text attributes such as bold, italic, and underline, and change margins and fonts to create attractive business letters. In addition, this chapter covers convenient features such as Spelling, Print Preview, and Zoom view that make it easier to prepare documents.

Business Letters

A letter is formal written communication used to convey information from one business to another or from one individual to another. Business letters are one of the most important types of written communications.

Traditionally, letters have followed one of two styles: a modified block or block style. With the development of word processing equipment and programs, the block style has become the most frequently used letter style. With the block style, all lines of the letter begin at the left margin (see Figure 3.1).

Another style of letter that is now being used is the AMS (Administrative Management Society) simplified letter style. The AMS simplified style omits the salutation and complimentary closing. A subject line and the typewritten signature are

FIGURE 3.1

Traditional style letter

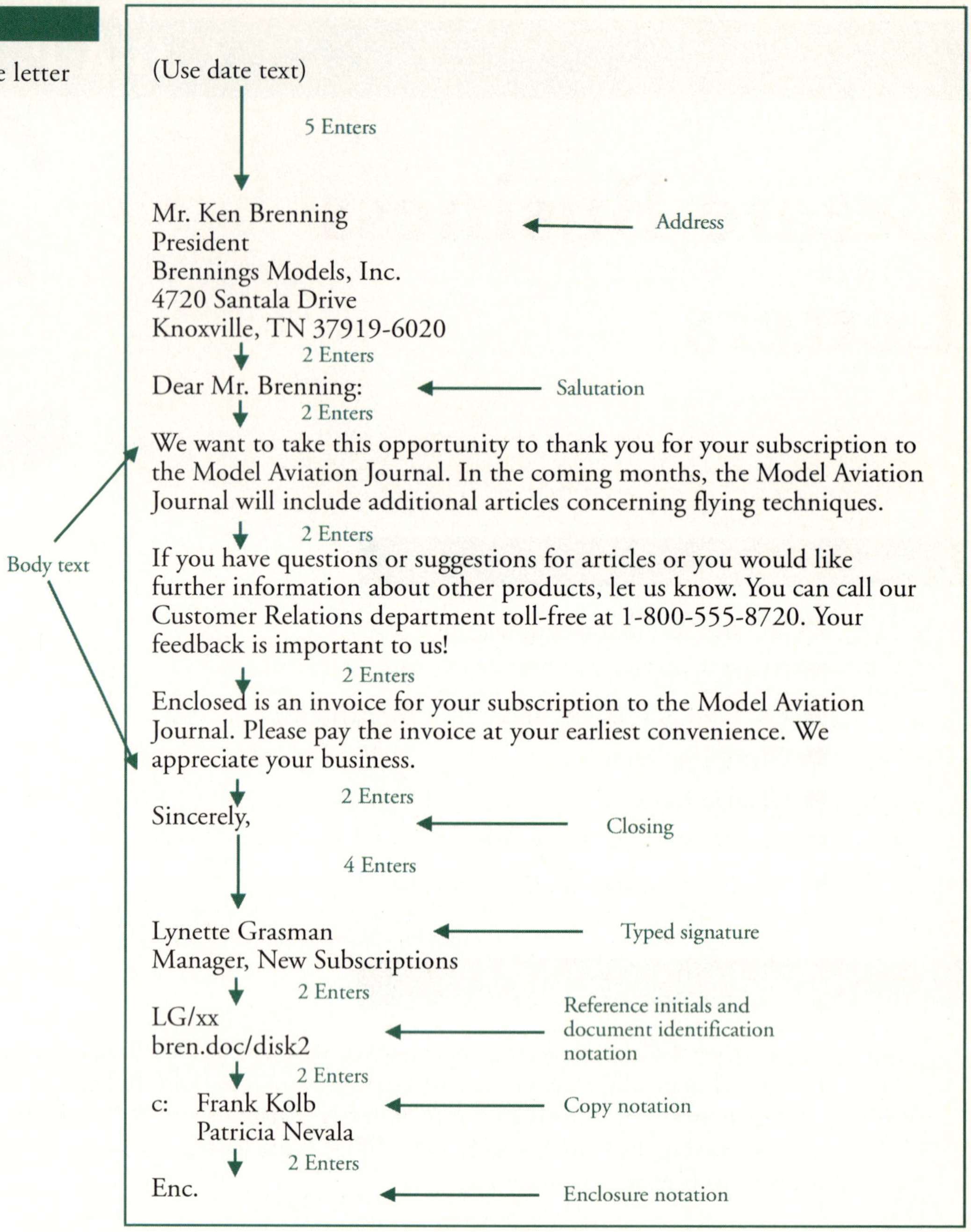

(Use date text)

5 Enters

Mr. Ken Brenning
President
Brennings Models, Inc.
4720 Santala Drive
Knoxville, TN 37919-6020 ← Address

2 Enters

Dear Mr. Brenning: ← Salutation

2 Enters

We want to take this opportunity to thank you for your subscription to the Model Aviation Journal. In the coming months, the Model Aviation Journal will include additional articles concerning flying techniques.

2 Enters

If you have questions or suggestions for articles or you would like further information about other products, let us know. You can call our Customer Relations department toll-free at 1-800-555-8720. Your feedback is important to us!

2 Enters

Enclosed is an invoice for your subscription to the Model Aviation Journal. Please pay the invoice at your earliest convenience. We appreciate your business.

Body text

2 Enters

Sincerely, ← Closing

4 Enters

Lynette Grasman ← Typed signature
Manager, New Subscriptions

2 Enters

LG/xx
bren.doc/disk2 ← Reference initials and document identification notation

2 Enters

c: Frank Kolb ← Copy notation
Patricia Nevala

2 Enters

Enc. ← Enclosure notation

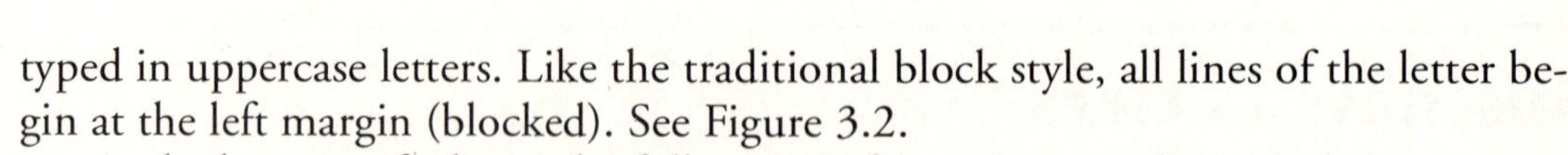

typed in uppercase letters. Like the traditional block style, all lines of the letter begin at the left margin (blocked). See Figure 3.2.

At the bottom of a letter the following information may be included:

- ☐ The author's initials in capital letters and the typist's initials in lowercase letters, e.g., LG/xx. The x's indicate where you type your initials. If desired, the author's initials can be omitted and only the typist initials used.
- ☐ A document identification notation showing the filename and location of the document, e.g., *bren.doc/disk2.*
- ☐ If a photocopy of the letter is to be sent to another person(s), a copy notation is typed. Generally, a photocopy is indicated by a lowercase

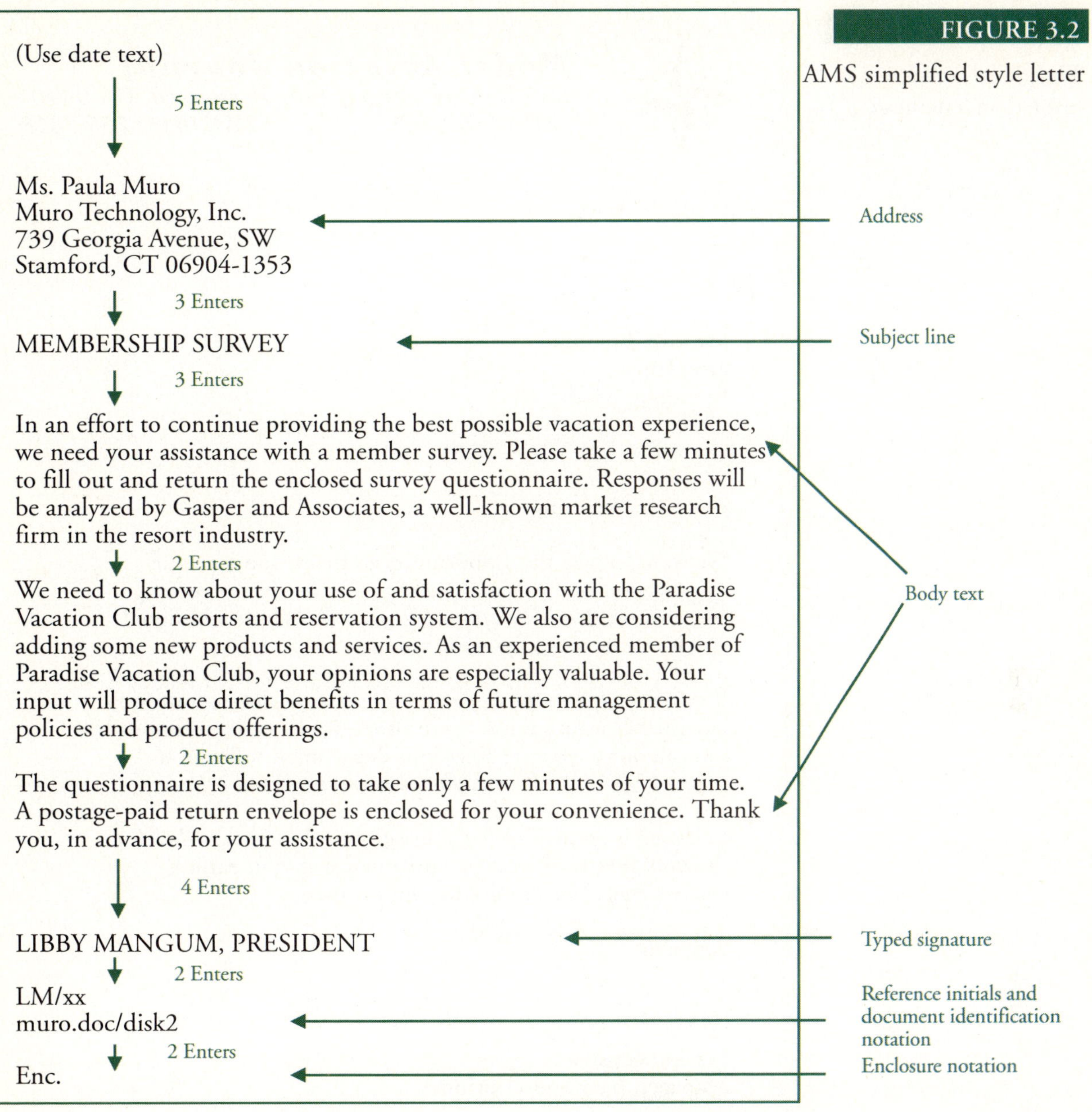
(Use date text)

Ms. Paula Muro
Muro Technology, Inc.
739 Georgia Avenue, SW
Stamford, CT 06904-1353

MEMBERSHIP SURVEY

In an effort to continue providing the best possible vacation experience, we need your assistance with a member survey. Please take a few minutes to fill out and return the enclosed survey questionnaire. Responses will be analyzed by Gasper and Associates, a well-known market research firm in the resort industry.

We need to know about your use of and satisfaction with the Paradise Vacation Club resorts and reservation system. We also are considering adding some new products and services. As an experienced member of Paradise Vacation Club, your opinions are especially valuable. Your input will produce direct benefits in terms of future management policies and product offerings.

The questionnaire is designed to take only a few minutes of your time. A postage-paid return envelope is enclosed for your convenience. Thank you, in advance, for your assistance.

LIBBY MANGUM, PRESIDENT

LM/xx
muro.doc/disk2

Enc.

FIGURE 3.2

AMS simplified style letter

"c" followed by a colon, e.g., c:. Press the **Tab** key once and type the name; press **Enter**.

Note: *Always press the **Tab** key before each listed name; otherwise the names may not align when fonts are changed.*

- ☐ If the letter contains a statement that an item(s) is being enclosed, type an enclosure notation two **Enters** below the document identification notation or two **Enters** below a copy notation, e.g., type **Enc.**

After a business letter has been typed, formatted, reviewed, and proofread, a final copy is printed. A final letter is customarily printed on letterhead stationery. The letterhead information usually includes the company name, address, phone number, and fax number. Typically, the letterhead information is preprinted on company stationery. Today, however, many individuals who use word processing and desktop publishing programs create their own letterheads. In Chapter 13, a letterhead will be created. A letter printed on company letterhead in final form will look similar to Figure 3.3.

FIGURE 3.3

Traditional style letter printed on letterhead

Model Aviation Journal
580 Deharo Street, San Francisco, CA 94107
(415) 555-8303 FAX (415) 555-8318

(Use date text)

Mr. Ken Brenning
President
Brennings Models, Inc.
4720 Santala Drive
Knoxville, TN 37919-6020

Dear Mr. Brenning:

We want to take this opportunity to thank you for your subscription to the *Model Aviation Journal.* In the coming months, the *Model Aviation Journal* will include additional articles concerning flying techniques.

If you have questions or suggestions for articles or you would like further information about other products, let us know. You can call our Customer Relations department toll-free at 1-800-555-8720. ***Your feedback is important to us!***

Enclosed is an invoice for your subscription to the *Model Aviation Journal.* Please pay the invoice at your earliest convenience. We appreciate your business.

Sincerely,

Lynette Grasman
Manager, New Subscriptions

LG/xx
bren.doc/disk2

c: Frank Kolb
Patricia Nevala

Enc.

Automatic Date Feature

Word provides two methods for automatically inserting the current date into a document: date text and date field. In order for the current date to be inserted by Word, the date must be stored in the computer's memory.

When inserting the date as text, the current date is placed automatically in the document by Word. If the document is opened on a different date, the date will not change unless edited manually.

When inserting the date as a field, a special code is inserted by Word (see Date Field in Chapter 11). If the document is opened and printed at a later date, the date is automatically changed to the current date.

After selecting the **Insert, Date and Time** option, a Date and Time dialog box displays. Various formats are listed for the date. For example, the day can be displayed followed by the month and year (14 July, 1995).

Start-Up Instructions

- An empty document window should be displayed on the screen. If necessary, select the **New** button on the Standard Toolbar.

Insert the Date as Text

1. Select **Insert, Date and Time** {Alt, i, t}.

   Note: The Date and Time dialog box displays.

2. Click once on the desired date format {press the up or down arrow keys to highlight the desired format}.

   For example, click once on the fourth format that displays the month, day, and year (August 2, 199x).

3. Select **OK** {Enter}.

   Note: The current date is inserted at the location of the insertion point. If necessary, the date can be changed.

Finish-Up Instructions

- Type the traditional block style letter shown in Figure 3.1 on page 56 using the spacing shown. Use word wrap to type the body text paragraphs of the letter.
- After typing the letter, use the filename **3drill1** and save the file on your file disk (select the **Save** button on the Standard Toolbar; type the filename; if necessary, click in the Drives box and click on the drive letter where the file disk is located; select **OK**).
- Print one copy (select the **Print** button).

Alignment

The term *alignment* is used to describe the relationship of text to the left and right margins. Four different types of alignment are available as buttons on the Formatting Toolbar: Align Left, Center, Align Right, and Justify (see Figure 3.4). With left alignment, text is aligned at the left margin and is not aligned at the right margin (ragged right). Left alignment is the default (preset) setting for Word 6.0. Right alignment is the opposite of left alignment, i.e., text is aligned at the right margin, not at the left margin (ragged left). Center alignment positions text so that an equal amount of blank space displays to the left and right of the centered text. Justify

FIGURE 3.4

The four types of alignment

This is an example of left alignment (Align Left). The text is aligned at the left margin.

This is an example of Right alignment (Align Right). The text is aligned at the right margin.

This is an example of center alignment. An equal amount of blank space displays to the left and right of the centered text.

This is an example of justify alignment. Text begins and ends exactly at the left and right margin, except for the last line of the paragraph.

To justify the last line of a paragraph or a short line, select Justify alignment. Then move the insertion point to the end of the paragraph and press the **Shift** and **Enter** keys.

alignment adjusts lines to begin and end exactly at the left and right margins. Generally, justified alignment does not, however, align the last line of a paragraph (see Figure 3.4).

With justify alignment, additional spaces are placed between words to align the text at both the left and right margins. The extra spaces between words may make the text difficult to read and visually unattractive. Therefore, left alignment is used for most business correspondence and justify alignment is used primarily for narrow columns and formal documents.

Start-Up Instructions

❖ The file named **3drill1.doc** should be displayed in the document window.

Change Alignment

1. Select the text for which alignment is to be changed. (If necessary, see Chapter 2, page 37 for information on selecting text.)

   For example, select all the paragraphs in the body text of the letter.

2. Move the mouse pointer to the **Justify** alignment button on the Formatting Toolbar and click once {Ctrl and j}.

Finish-Up Instructions

❖ Click once to deselect the letter paragraphs.

❖ Use the *new* filename **3full.doc** and save the file on your file disk (select **File, Save As**; type the new filename; if necessary, click in the Drives box and click on the drive letter where the file disk is located; select **OK**).

❖ Print one copy (select the **Print** button).

Text Attributes

Emphasis can be added to word(s) by using text attributes such as bold, underline, and italic. Some text attributes can be set in the Font dialog box by selecting the desired attribute(s). More frequently, text attributes are set by using the **Bold**, **Underline**, and **Italic** options on the Formatting Toolbar or by using the corresponding keystrokes. More than one text attribute can be applied to the same text characters, e.g., **<u>bold and underline</u>**.

The bold text attribute prints words darker on the page as compared to other printed words. Text to be printed in bold will be displayed darker than the other characters on the screen.

Words are underlined in printed text to show emphasis. Once the text to be underlined is selected and the underline feature is used, the text displays underlined in the document window. Traditionally, underlining was used in the place of italic because many typewriters were unable to create italic text. Because most printers now support italic, the trend is to replace underlining with italic or bold to add emphasis.

The italic text attribute prints text somewhat slanted to the right. However, there are some dot matrix printers that do not print italicized text. Once the text to be italicized is selected and the italic attribute is applied, the text displays slightly slanted on the screen.

Start-Up Instructions

- The file named **3ful1.doc** should be displayed in the document window.

Bold Text

1. Select the text to be printed in bold. (If necessary, see Chapter 2, page 37 for information on selecting text.)

   For example, select the last sentence in the second paragraph, beginning **Your feedback is . . .**

2. Select the **Bold** button **B** on the Formatting Toolbar {Ctrl and b}.

Underline Text

1. Select the text to be underlined. (If necessary, see Chapter 2, page 37 for information on selecting text.)

   For example, select the phone number **1-800-555-8720** located in the second paragraph

2. Select the **Underline** button **U** on the Formatting Toolbar {Ctrl and u}.

Italicize Text

1. Select the text to be italicized. (If necessary, see Chapter 2, page 37 for information on selecting text.)

   For example, select the first occurrence of the words **Model Aviation Journal** in the first paragraph.

2. Select the **Italic** button [I] on the Formatting Toolbar {Ctrl and i}.

Finish-Up Instructions

- Select the second occurrence of the words **Model Aviation Journal** in the first paragraph and italicize the text.
- Select the words **Model Aviation Journal** in the third paragraph and italicize the text.
- Select the final sentence in the second paragraph and italicize the text. This sentence will be both bold and italic.
- Use the *new* filename **3att1.doc** and save the file on your file disk (select **File, Save As**; type the new filename; if necessary, click in the Drives box and click on the drive letter where the file disk is located; select **OK**).

Remove Bold, Underline, or Italic Text Attributes

Note: The following are for your information.

1. Select the desired text.
2. Select the **Bold, Underline,** or **Italic** button on the Formatting Toolbar {Ctrl and b, Ctrl and u, *or* Ctrl and i}.

Change Margins

Generally, Word's default (preset) margins are used to print a final letter. If a letter is unusually short or long, however, it may be desirable to change the document's margins. Margins can be changed in the Page Setup dialog box or by using the Ruler bar (see Chapter 7, page 162). In this chapter, the Page Setup dialog box will be used to set margins.

The top and bottom margins are preset to 1 inch. When using a standard size $8^1/_2$- x 11-inch paper and a combined top and bottom margin of 2 inches, 9 inches remain for typed lines on a page. Depending on the information preprinted in a letterhead, the top margin can vary between 2 and $2^1/_2$ inches. The bottom margin on an average length letter generally remains unchanged. The left and right document margins are preset for 1.25 inches. With these settings, 6 inches are available across the page.

When margins are changed using Page Setup and no text is selected, the changes affect the entire document. If text is selected before margins are changed, the changes affect only the selected text, which Word places within a separate "section" of the document (see Chapter 8, page 180).

The margins can be changed in the document at any time, i.e., before or after the document is typed. Changing the margins is best accomplished after the document is completed, because a decision can more easily be made as to whether margins should be changed depending on the length of the document. A letter should be printed on the page with the space around the edges of the letter evenly balanced. After a letter is typed, estimate the desired placement of the document on the page.

The number of words in the letter body text and the depth of the letterhead are used to make decisions regarding margin changes. The following are some suggested margin settings for letters:

	Top Margin	**Left and Right Margins**
Short letter (under 100 words*)	2.5"	2.0"
Average letter (100-200 words)	2.0"	1.5"
Long letter (over 200 words)	1.75"	1.0"

*See Word Count, Chapter 9, page 209.

Before printing the final letter, preview the entire document on the screen by selecting the **Print Preview** button on the Standard Toolbar (see Print Preview later in this chapter).

Start-Up Instructions

- The file named **3att1.doc** should be displayed in the document window.
- The insertion point can be located at any position in the document.

Change Margins

1. Select **File, Page Setup** {Alt, f, u}.

Note: The Page Setup dialog box appears. The Page Setup dialog box contains separate sections for changing Margins, Page Size, Paper Source, and Layout. These sections are designed to look like index cards, with tabs at the top of the card. Only the options on the top card (the active card) can be changed. To activate a card, select its tab {press Alt and the underlined letter on the tab} (see Figure 3.5).

2. Choose the desired tab.

For example, check that the **Margins** tab is selected. If necessary, move the mouse pointer to the **Margins** tab and click once {Alt and m}.

3. *To change the top margin,* if necessary, double-click in the **Top** box to highlight the figure and type the desired margin in inches {Alt and t, type desired margin}.

For example, type **1.5**. (Do not type the last period.)

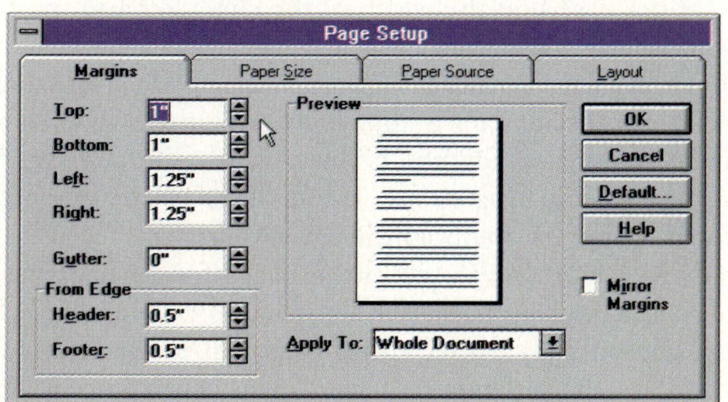

FIGURE 3.5

Page Setup dialog box with Margins options activated

Note: With the current margin figure highlighted in a margin box, the new amount is typed, automatically replacing the existing figure(s). If the insertion point displays in the margin box and the amount is not highlighted, delete the original amount and type the new amount. Typing a final zero or the quotation mark is unnecessary.

To change the bottom margin, double-click in the **Bottom** box to highlight the figure and type the desired margin in inches {Alt and b, type desired margin}.

For example, check that 1" displays.

To change the left margin, double-click in the **Left** box to highlight the figure and type the desired margin in inches {Alt and f, type desired margin}.

For example, type **1.5**. (Do not type the last period.)

To change the right margin, double-click in the **Right** box to highlight the figure and type the desired margin in inches {Alt and g, type desired margin}.

For example, type **1.5**. (Do not type the last period.)

4. Select **OK** {press Enter}.

Finish-Up Instructions

- Use the *new* filename **3mar1.doc** and save the file on your file disk (select **File**, **Save As**; type the new filename; if necessary, click in the Drives box and click on the drive letter where the file disk is located; select **OK**).
- Print one copy (select the **Print** button).

Font Changes

By using a variety of typefaces (fonts) and sizes, the appearance of letters, reports, résumés, or other business documents can be enhanced. A typeface is a specific design of type (shape), such as Arial or Times New Roman. A font includes all the letters, numbers, symbols, and punctuation marks for a given typeface in one size and style. For example, Arial 14-point bold is one font and Times New Roman 10-point italic is another font.

Each printer has one or more built-in fonts. Many built-in fonts, such as Courier, are monospaced and fixed-pitch (i.e., each character is allocated the same amount of horizontal space).

TrueType fonts are the most common fonts used with the Word for Windows program. These fonts are proportional and scaleable (i.e., the horizontal space allocated for each character varies based on the width of the character and the characters can be printed in almost any size).

Scaleable/proportional fonts are measured in points. There are approximately 72 points in an inch. A 24-point character is approximately one-third inch tall. A ruler at the back of this book shows the letter "E" in various point sizes and can be used to determine appropriate point sizes to use. Generally, a 10- to 12-point font is used for the text of business letters, memorandums, and reports.

Traditionally when using a typewriter with monospaced fonts, the Spacebar was pressed twice after a final punctuation mark. When using proportional spaced fonts, the Spacebar is pressed only once after a final punctuation mark, because a single space is sufficient to visually separate sentences. Also, when initials are used for both the first and middle names, such as E.R. Gilbert, the space may be omitted between the two initials. Additional information on letter and word spacing is available in Chapter 14, page 336-339.

Font characteristics such as font name, font size, and appearance (bold, underline, italics) can be changed by selecting the **Font** option on the Format menu. In addition, the font can be changed by selecting the down arrow beside the **Font** button on the Formatting Toolbar; the font size can be changed by selecting the down arrow beside the **Font Size** button on the Formatting Toolbar; and the appearance of text can be changed by selecting the **Bold**, **Underline**, or **Italic** buttons on the Formatting Toolbar. When the down arrow beside the **Font** button is selected, the last four fonts used are displayed at the top of the Font list.

Font changes take effect at the insertion point and any text typed from that point forward in the document will reflect the different font characteristics. However, existing text before or after the insertion point will not pick up the new formatting. To apply the font changes to specific text, select the text before choosing the desired font options.

Start-Up Instructions

- The file named **3mar1.doc** should be displayed in the document window.

Change Font, Size, and/or Appearance

Note: *Using the mouse is the most efficient way to change fonts. A mouse is needed to perform the following steps.*

1. Select the text to which the new font is to be applied.

   For example, select the entire document.

2. Move the mouse pointer to the down arrow located beside the **Font** button Times New Roman on the Formatting Toolbar and click once.

   Note: *A list of available fonts displays.*

3. Move the mouse pointer to the desired font name and click once.

   For example, select **Bookman Old Style** or **make a decision of your own.**

   Note: *The text is changed to display the new font.*

4. With the text selected, move the mouse pointer to the down arrow beside the **Font Size** button 10 on the Formatting Toolbar and click once.

   Note: *A list of available sizes displays.*

5. Move the mouse pointer to the desired size and click once.

   For example, select **11**.

To Make Multiple Changes at One Time

6. Select the desired text.

   For example, select the enclosure notation (**Enc.**).

7. Select **Format, Font**.

   Note: *The Font dialog box displays containing two tabs, Font and Character Spacing.*

8. If necessary, select the **Font** tab.

Note: The Font options, such as font names, font sizes, and other text attributes, are displayed.

9. Move the mouse pointer to the desired font size and click once.

For example, select **10** in the Size box or **make a decision of your own.**

10. Move the mouse pointer to the desired text attribute in the Font Style box and click once.

For example, select **Bold Italic.**

Note: Word displays a sample of the chosen font name, size, and appearance in the Preview box located in the lower right corner. The displayed sample is only an approximate size and style.

11. Select **OK**.

To Change Font Size Only

12. Select the desired text.

For example, select the document notation (**bren.doc/disk2**).

13. Move the mouse pointer to the down arrow located beside the **Font Size** button [10 ▾] on the Formatting Toolbar and click once.

14. Move the mouse pointer to the desired size and click once.

For example, select **10**.

Finish-Up Instructions

- ❖ A final letter printed on letterhead is shown in Figure 3.3. If desired, practice changing fonts, font sizes, text attributes, margins, and alignment.
- ❖ Use the *new* filename **3fon1.doc** and save the file on your file disk (select **File, Save As**; type the new filename; if necessary, click in the Drives box and click on the drive letter where the file disk is located; select **OK**).
- ❖ Print one copy (select the **Print** button).
- ❖ Close the document (select **File**, **Close**).

Check Spelling

The Spelling command checks the spelling of each word and identifies duplicate words and irregular capitalization in a document. When a word is found that is not in one of Word's dictionaries, a list of words similar to the unrecognized word is displayed on the screen. If the correctly spelled word is displayed in the list of words, it can be selected. If the correctly spelled word is not displayed in the list, the word can be added to one of the Word dictionaries or the misspelled word and correct word can be added to the AutoCorrect list

Word has two types of dictionaries: a main dictionary and custom dictionaries. The main dictionary is used to check the spelling of words for all documents. Custom dictionaries are created by individual users and contain terms that an individual uses frequently. For example, a medical secretary might create a custom dictionary that contains medical terms. An unlimited number of custom dictionaries can be created.

If an entire document is to be checked for spelling accuracy, the insertion point can be located anywhere in the document. If only part of the document or a single word is to be checked, the desired portion of the document or the individual word is selected.

If the same word is typed twice, the Spelling command will identify the duplicated word. The duplicated word can be removed by selecting **Delete**. To leave both occurrences of the duplicated word, **Ignore** is selected.

The Spelling command will also identify words that contain irregular capitalization, such as tHe or THe. When a word with irregular capitalization is identified, the various capitalization options will be presented along with other possible words.

Not all errors in a document are discovered when using the spelling feature. For example, words easily misspelled or mistyped, such as there/their, form/from, she/he, are not identified as incorrect words. Therefore, once the document is checked for spelling, it should also be carefully proofread for accurate meaning.

Start-Up Instructions

Note: *The icon indicates that the data (text) is available on disk. The data disk is supplied to your instructor.*

- Open the file named **3drill2.doc** that is located on the data disk (select the **Open** button on the Standard Toolbar; if necessary, click in the Drives box and click on the drive letter where the data disk is located; double-click on the filename).
- Use the following steps and spell-check the file named **3drill2.doc**. After spell-checking the document, be sure to proofread the document carefully for the meaning of words and sentences.

Use the Spelling Command

1. Select the **Spelling** button on the Standard Toolbar {Alt, t, s *or* F7}.

   Note: *The Spelling dialog box displays (see Figure 3.6). The main dictionary being used, English (US), displays in the Title bar of the dialog box. The first unrecognized word is highlighted in the document and displays to the right of the words "Not in Dictionary" in the Spelling dialog box. Word displays the word that most closely matches the spelling of the unrecognized word in the **Change To** box and the word is also highlighted at the top of the list of suggestions.*

2. *To accept the highlighted word*, select **Change** {Alt and c}.

   For example, select the **Change** button to accept the suggested word "being."

   Note: *The identified word is corrected on the screen and the spell check continues.*

   To choose a word from the Suggestions list, select the word and select **Change** {press the down arrow key to highlight the word, Alt and c}.

3. *To delete one occurrence of a duplicated word*, select **Delete** {Alt and d}.

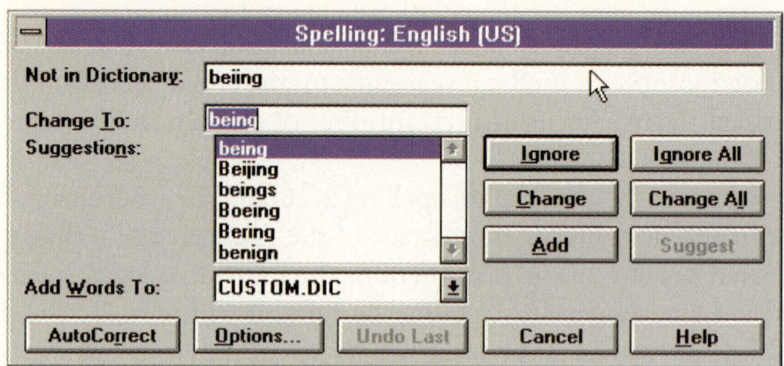

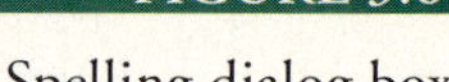

Spelling dialog box

For example, select **Delete** to delete one occurrence of the word "of."

Note: To retain both occurrences of a duplicated word, select **Ignore** *{Alt and i}.*

4. T*o correct irregular capitalization*, select the desired suggestion and choose **Change** {Alt and c}.

   For example, "and" should display in the Change To box. Select **Change.**

5. If the correct spelling of a word is not on the list, other options can be selected.

   a. Select **Ignore** to ignore the current instance of the word {Alt and i}.

      For example, select **Ignore** to ignore the reference initials "PJM." Select **Ignore** to ignore your initials, the document name, and file location.

   b. Select **Ignore All** to ignore the word throughout the remainder of the document {Alt and g}.

   c. Select **Change All** to change to the word in the Change To box for all occurrences in the document {Alt and L}.

   d. Select **Add** to add the word to a custom dictionary {Alt and a}. The word will be added to the default custom dictionary. *To choose a different custom dictionary*, choose **Add Words To** and select the desired dictionary {Alt and w}.

   e. To correct a word that is not found in any of Word's directories, click in the Change To box and type the correctly spelled word. Select **Change** {Alt and t, type the correction, Alt and c}.

      Note: To discontinue spell-checking before completion, select ***Close*** *{Esc}.*

6. When the entire document has been checked, the message "The spelling check is complete." displays. Select **OK** {press Enter}.

Finish-Up Instructions

- Use the *new* filename **3spe2.doc** and save the file on your file disk (select **File, Save As**; type the new filename; if necessary, click in the Drives box and click on the drive letter where the file disk is located; select **OK**).
- Print one copy (select the **Print** button).

Print Preview and Zoom

A full document page can be displayed by selecting either the **Print Preview** button on the Standard Toolbar, or by selecting **View, Zoom** and choosing a percentage that allows the full page to be displayed. Displaying a document page assists in making decisions on the alignment of text and the amount of blank space in the margins.

When the Print Preview button is selected, the Print Preview window displays. The Standard and Formatting Toolbars are removed from the screen and the Print Preview Toolbar displays. The Print Preview Toolbar buttons are used to change how the document is displayed and to print the document (see Figure 3.7 for a description of the Print Preview Toolbar buttons). A horizontal ruler and a vertical ruler can be displayed at the top and left of the preview window (if necessary, select **View, Ruler** to display the rulers). The horizontal and vertical rulers can be used to change the top, bottom, left, and right margins and to set paragraph indents (for additional information, see Chapter 7, Use the Rulers to Change Margins and Set Indents).

When the mouse pointer is moved into the page area of the Preview window, the pointer resembles a magnifying glass. To enlarge a portion of the page, move the mouse pointer to the desired area and click once. The area is enlarged so that the text can be read and edited if desired. To return the display to a full page, click the mouse button again.

The Zoom view feature has the capability of magnifying or reducing the display of text. The percentage of magnification or reduction can be selected or specified in the Zoom dialog box. The Zoom dialog box contains Zoom To options and a Preview box. Preset percentages or a specific percentage between 10% and 200% can

FIGURE 3.7

Description of Print Preview Toolbar buttons

Button	Name	Description
	Print	Print the displayed document.
	Magnifier	Magnify a portion of the page displayed in the Print Preview window.
	One Page	Display a single page of a multiple-page document.
	Multiple Pages	Display several pages of a multiple page document.
42%	Zoom Control	Enlarge or reduce the display size.
	View Ruler	Show (or hide) the horizontal and vertical rulers.
	Shrink to Fit	Reduce the font size of text so that the text will fit on fewer pages.
	Full Screen	Hide the Title bar, Menu bar, Ruler bars, Scroll bars, and Status bar and enlarge the page area. To return the Menu bar to the screen and reduce the page area, select the **Full Screen** button again.
Close	Close	Exit the Print Preview window.
	Help	Obtain help information.

FIGURE 3.8

Print Preview window

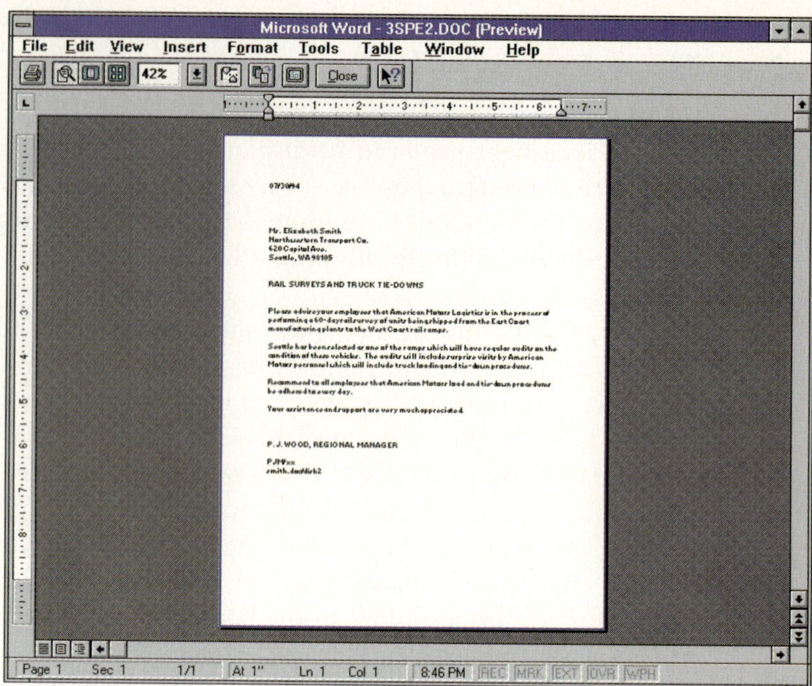

be selected. The preset Zoom options are also available by selecting the **Zoom Control** button on the Standard Toolbar or the Print Preview Toolbar.

Start-Up Instructions

- The file named **3spe2.doc** should be displayed in the document window.

Use Print Preview

1. Select the **Print Preview** button on the Standard Toolbar.

   Note: An entire document page containing the letter displays on the screen (see Figure 3.8).

2. To exit Print Preview view, select the **Close** button on the Print Preview Menu bar {Esc}.

Use Zoom View

1. Select **View, Zoom** {Alt, v, z}.

   Note: The Zoom dialog box displays.

2. Select the desired viewing percentage from the **Zoom To** area or double-click in the **Percent** box and type the desired percentage (between 10% and 200%).

   For example, double-click in the Percent box and type 125 {e, type desired amount}.

3. Select **OK** {Enter}.

Shortcut

1. Select the down arrow beside the **Zoom Control** button on the Standard Toolbar or Print Preview Toolbar.
2. Select the desired percentage.

Finish-Up Instructions

- ❖ Close the document (select **File**, **Close**).

Start-Up Instructions

- ❖ Optional. Type the AMS simplified style letter shown in Figure 3.2 (select the **New** button to obtain a new document window).
- ❖ Use the Speller to review the document for spelling errors. After using the Speller, be sure to proofread the document. Use the filename **3drill3** and save the file.
- ❖ Print one copy (select **File**, **Print**; choose **OK**).
- ❖ Close the document (select **File**, **Close**).

The Next Step

Chapter Review and Activities

Self-Check Quiz

T F 1. When a font change is made for selected text, the changed font affects the selected text only.

T F 2. When using the Spelling command, you can correct a word that is not found in any of Word's dictionaries.

T F 3. The document identification notation is typed above the reference initials.

T F 4. In the traditional letter style, the **Enter** key is pressed four times after typing the last paragraph.

5. The ______ button is selected to view an entire page in the document window.
   a. **Open**
   b. **Print Preview**
   c. **Print**

6. Word's default margins are ____________.
   a. 1" top and bottom; 1.25" left and right
   b. 1" left and right; 1.25" top and bottom
   c. 1" left, right, top and bottom

7. To bold a paragraph, first select the paragraph, then select ____________.
   a. **View, Bold, OK**
   b. the **Bold** button on the Standard Toolbar
   c. the **Bold** button on the Formatting Toolbar
8. List the top, left, and right margins that are suggested for an average letter (100-200 words).
9. List the four different types of alignment.
10. State one reason for using Print Preview to view a document before printing.

Enriching Language Arts Skills

Spelling/Vocabulary Words

prospectus a statement of the features of a new work or enterprise.
minimum the smallest quantity or number possible.
redeem (stock) to turn in for cash or other stock.
in accordance with in compliance or agreement with rules, guidelines or orders.

Appositives

Appositives are words that immediately follow a noun and further identify the noun but usually are not necessary to the meaning of the sentence. Appositives are set off by commas.

Example:

Ester Tam, a copyeditor for eight years, will be our new senior editor.

Activities

Activity 3.1—Create a Traditional Style Letter; Use the Bold Text Attribute

1. Launch Word or select the **New** button.
2. Type the following letter using the traditional style letter (see Figure 3.1 on page 56).

(Use date text)

Donald and Judie Waite
101 East Avenue
St. Paul, MN 55102-1718

Dear Donald and Judie:

Recently you visited Pine Cone Park on White Bear Lake. You have experienced the panoramic views and the quiet country setting. And you have seen the large, family-oriented floor plans.

Now we have some exciting news! Pine Cone Park is releasing a small number of sites for sale. We invite you to revisit our sales office to choose from the home sites now available.

The moment you have been waiting for is NOW! It is time to own your own home at Pine Cone Park.

Cordially,

Carolyn Inouye
Sales Manager

CI/xx
waite.doc/d1

3. Bold each occurrence of the words **Pine Cone Park** (select the text; select the **Bold** button on the Formatting Toolbar).
4. Save the file on your file disk; use the filename **3act1** (Chapter 3, activity 1). (Select the **Save** button on the Standard Toolbar; type the filename; if necessary, click in the Drives box and click on the drive letter where the file disk is located; select **OK**.)
5. Print one copy (select the **Print** button).
6. Close the document (select **File**, **Close**).

Activity 3.2—Create a Traditional Style Letter; Use Justified Alignment; Change Margins and Font

1. Launch Word or select the **New** button.
2. Type the following letter using the traditional style letter (see Figure 3.1 on page 56).

(Use date text)

Ms. Leslie Vachon
President
Sentinel Peak Industries
850 W. Natanes Road
Tucson, AZ 85716-4134

Dear Leslie:

Thank you for taking the time to speak with me yesterday. Please find enclosed a copy of our Value-Added Seminar brochure.

As we discussed, Bottom Line Consulting (BLC) will be holding Value-Added Seminars at the end of next month. I highly recommend that you and several of your team members plan to attend the Las Vegas seminar.

If BLC can be of any other service to Sentinel Peak Industries, please do not hesitate to give us a call.

Regards,

Henry Loret
Seminar Coordinator

HL/xx
vachon.doc/d2

c: J.E. Huskey

Enc.

3. Change the left, right, and top margins to **1.5"** (place the insertion point at any location in the document; select **File, Page Setup**, **Margins**; double-click in the margins boxes and type the desired margins; select **OK**).
4. Change to **Justify** alignment (select all body text paragraphs, move the mouse pointer to the **Justify** alignment button on the Formatting Toolbar and click once).
5. Change the font to **Footlight MT Light** or make a choice of your own (select all the text; select the down arrow beside the **Font** button on the Formatting Toolbar; select the desired font).
6. Save the file on your file disk; use the filename **3act2** (Chapter 3, activity 2). (Select the **Save** button on the Standard Toolbar; type the filename; if necessary,

click in the Drives box and click on the drive letter where the file disk is located; select **OK**.)

7. Print one copy (select the **Print** button).
8. Close the document (select **File**, **Close**).

Activity 3.3—Create an AMS Simplified Style Letter; Use Bold and Italic; Change Margins and Font Size; Use the Spelling Command; Print Preview

1. Launch Word or select the **New** button.
2. Type the following letter using the AMS simplified style letter (see Figure 3.2 on page 57). Use the bold and italic text attributes as shown.

(Use date text)

Mr. Carl LoVerde
68439 Thorton Avenue
Newark, CA 94560-2062

SPRING MEMBERSHIP PROMOTION

As you are well aware, in the past year *Eden Point Fitness Center* has made a great deal of progress in managing, rebuilding, and improving its facility and equipment.

With our spring membership promotion, you will receive **FREE** a beautiful, deluxe bathrobe and three months added to your present membership, compliments of *Eden Point Fitness Center.* All you have to do is introduce two new members to the club during the next two months.

We are looking forward to your participation in this program!

MARIZE LOCKHARDT, PRESIDENT

ML/xx
loverde.doc/disk3

---

3. Change the left and right margins to 2" and the top margin to 1.75" (place the insertion point anywhere in the document; select **File**, **Page Setup**, **Margins**; double-click in the margin boxes and type the desired margins; select **OK**).
4. Select the words **SPRING MEMBERSHIP PROMOTION** and change the font size to 14 point (select the down arrow beside the **Font Size** button on the Formatting Toolbar; select **14**).

5. Use the Spelling command to find and correct misspelled words. (Select the **Spelling** button on the Standard Toolbar. When the spell check is complete, select **OK**.)
6. Use the Print Preview feature to display the entire document in the document window (select the **Print Preview** button on the Standard Toolbar; select **Close**).
7. Save the file on your file disk; use the filename **3act3** (Chapter 3, activity 3). (Select the **Save** button on the Standard Toolbar; type the filename; if necessary, click in the Drives box and click on the drive letter where the file disk is located; select **OK**.)
8. Print one copy (select the **Print** button).
9. Close the document (select **File**, **Close**).

Challenge Your Skills

Skill 3.1—Create and Edit a Traditional Style Letter

1. Use the traditional style letter and the following information:
   a. Use the current date.
   b. Send the letter to George Kozusko, 242 Appleton Road, Blacksburg, VA 20460-2604.
   c. Use Dear George for the salutation.
   d. Use an appropriate complimentary closing.
   e. The letter is from Eileen Ciccantell, Corporate Training Program Manager.
   f. Include your reference initials and document identification notation.
   g. A copy will be sent to D.B. Zisk.
   h. Make decisions regarding:

      Alignment
      Margins
      Fonts
      Use of bold, italic, and underline text attributes
   i. The letter body text follows:

      Congratulations. You have been selected to participate in the Group Dynamics and Management Training Seminar. This seminar will be held at the Doubletree Hotel, Greensboro, North Carolina, beginning on the last Monday of next month.

      Reservations have been made in your name for Monday and Tuesday evening. Your airfare and lodging costs will be reimbursed; however, you are responsible for all meals and other expenses. Please contact the corporate travel office immediately to arrange for airline tickets.

There will be important materials to review Monday night, so plan to arrive rested and ready to work. A seminar orientation meeting will be held at 6:30 p.m. Attendance at the orientation meeting is mandatory.

Attire throughout the seminar will be business dress. The seminar will end by 6 p.m. Wednesday.

Again, congratulations. You have been recognized for your current performance and future potential and are joining a select group of management people.

2. Save the file on your file disk; use the filename **3skill1** and print one copy.
3. Use the following information to change the letter:
   a. Change the hotel to the Marriot Hotel.
   b. Delete the last sentence in the third paragraph beginning "Attendance at the orientation . . ."
   c. Delete the last paragraph.
4. Use the Spelling command to find and correct any misspelled words; also carefully proofread for accurate meaning.
5. Use the new filename **3skill1r** and save the file on your file disk.
6. Print one copy and close the document.

Skill 3.2—Create and Edit an AMS Simplified Style Letter

1. Use the AMS simplified style letter and the following information:
   a. Use the current date.
   b. Send the letter to George and Hillary Barstow, 444 Winton Avenue, Hayward, CA 94542.
   c. The subject of the letter is CLASS OF 1980 REUNION.
   d. The letter is from J.M. Moore, Coordinator for the 1980 Class Reunion.
   e. Include your reference initials, document identification notation, and enclosure notation.
   f. Make decisions regarding:

      Alignment
      Margins
      Fonts
      Use of bold, italic, and underline text attributes
   g. The letter body text follows:

   It's time for our yearly class reunion, and I can't wait to see you all again. This year we have decided on a picnic format and have reserved the Walden Pond Pavilion at the Lake Chabot Picnic Grounds. There will be plenty of games and refreshments during the afternoon, dancing to Buddy's Swinging Singles in the evening, and fireworks, courtesy of Jake's Pyro-Mania Company to round out the evening.

In addition, our own Class of 1980 celebrity, Jeannie Fontaine, has promised to put in an appearance at the picnic, flying to us straight from the set of her latest movie, Hot Kisses in a Cold World. I know you are all as eager as I am to have a chance to talk to Jeannie and find out whether she's the same sweet kid who was voted Miss Popularity at the Senior Ball.

So get your reservation in now. We have made arrangements for a special discount rate at the Lake Chabot Sheraton, and they will also have baby-sitters available in the evening for children under age 10.

2. Use the filename **3skill2** and save the file on your file disk.
3. Use the following information to change the letter:
    a. Insert the following paragraph above the last paragraph.

       If you have addresses for any of the following people, please let me know so we can send them invitations: George Rembrant, Rochelle Jaye, Murray Rose, Michelle Bazaar.
4. Use the Spelling command to find and correct any misspelled words; also carefully proofread for accurate meaning.
5. Use the new filename **3skill2r** and save the file on your file disk.
6. Print one copy and close the document.

Skill 3.3—Create and Edit a Traditional Style Letter; Language Arts

1. Use the traditional style letter and the following information.
    a. Use the current date.
    b. Send the letter to Mr. Joseph Nakomura, 18023 Shawsheen St., Hyannis, MA 02601-1086.
    c. The letter is from Jeremy P. Lupone, Customer Services Manager.
    d. Include your reference initials, document identification notation, and enclosure notation.
    e. Make decisions regarding:

       Appropriate salutation
       Alignment
       Margins
       Fonts
       Use of bold, italic, and underline text attributes
       Appropriate complimentary closing
    f. Correct three spelling and two punctuation errors.
    g. The letter body text follows:

A recent review of shareholder accounts indicates that your Lighthouse Money Market Reserves account balance is below the Fund's minimum total investment of $1,000 as required in the Fund prospectus. A current statement of your account is enclosed for your reference.

Lighthouse established the minnimum account balance because the expense of maintaining smaller accounts raises the Fund's operating expenses. We hope you will want to bring your balance up to at least the $1,000 minimum. If you wish to make an additional investment an Invest-by-Mail form (found at the bottom of your account statement) and a postage-free envelope are enclosed for your convenience. Of course, you also have the option of redeeming your account.

Your Lighthouse Money Market Reserves account will be reviewed in approximately 60 days to see if the balance has increased to the $1,000 minimum or if the shares have been redeamed. If the balance remains below the minimum, the account will be closed in accordence with the procedures outlined in the Fund prospectus, and a check for the account balance will be mailed to you.

We trust you understand our ongoing objective of keeping Fund costs as low as possible. If you have any questions, please call Doreen McMahon, my assistant at 1-800-555-2739.

2. Use the Spelling command to find and correct any misspelled words; also proofread carefully for accurate meaning.
3. Save the file on your file disk; use the filename **3skill3**.
4. Print one copy.
5. If you have completed your work, exit Word (select **File**, **Exit**).

CHAPTER

Editing and Enhancing Documents

Features Covered

- Move text
- Copy text
- Find text
- Replace text
- Indent text
- Create numbered and bulleted text
- Print selected text

Objectives and Introduction

After successfully completing this chapter, you will be able to rearrange text using the Move and Copy features, search for specified text, and replace text automatically. You will also be able to create enumerated and bulleted lists using the Bullets and Numbering feature as well as indent paragraphs from the left margin.

Move Text

Moving text is the process of relocating text. For example, a paragraph in the middle of a letter can be moved to the end of the letter. Paragraphs, sentences, or lines can be moved. Generally, once text has been typed, retyping should be unnecessary.

The text to be moved must first be selected. Once the text is selected, Word provides several methods for moving the text. Two methods for moving text are described in the following Steps to Move Text Using the Cut and Paste Commands and in the Steps to Move Text Using the Drag and Drop Text Feature.

Start-Up Instructions

❖ Open the file named **4drill1.doc** located on the data disk (select the **Open** button on the Standard Toolbar; if necessary, click in the Drives box and click on the drive letter where the data disk is located; double-click on the filename).

Move Text Using the Cut and Paste Commands

1. Select the desired text.

   For example, move the mouse pointer to the left of the first character in the second paragraph, press and hold the mouse button and drag downward to select the paragraph and the following blank line.

2. Select the **Cut** button on the Standard Toolbar {Alt, e, t *or* Ctrl and x}.

   Note: The text is deleted (cut) from the original location and placed in the Clipboard. The Clipboard is temporary memory that holds deleted or copied text.

3. Place the insertion point to the left of the first character or space that will follow the moved text.

   For example, move the insertion point to the left of the first character in the first paragraph.

4. Select the **Paste** button on the Standard Toolbar to insert the text at the new location {Alt, e, p *or* Ctrl and v}.

   Note: The second paragraph is now the first paragraph. A copy of the moved text remains in the Clipboard (temporary memory) until replaced by other cut, deleted, or copied text or until Windows is exited.

Finish-Up Instructions

- Use the *new* filename **4capl1.doc** and save the file on your file disk (select **File**, **Save As**; type the filename; if necessary, click in the Drives box and click on the drive letter where the file disk is located; select **OK**).
- Print one copy (select **File**, **Print**; choose **OK**).
- Close the document (select **File**, **Close**).

Start-Up Instructions

- Open the file named **4drill1.doc** located on the data disk (select the **Open** button on the Standard Toolbar; if necessary, click in the Drives box and click on the drive letter where the data disk is located; double-click on the filename).

Move Text Using the Drag and Drop Text Feature

Note: A mouse must be used to perform the following steps.

1. Select the desired text.

   For example, move the mouse pointer to the left of the first character in the second paragraph, press and hold the mouse button and drag downward to select the paragraph and the following blank line.

2. Move the mouse pointer into the selected (highlighted) text.
3. Press and hold the left mouse button while dragging the mouse pointer and insertion point to the new location.

   For example, while holding the mouse button, drag the mouse pointer and insertion point to the left of the first character of the first paragraph.

   Note: An outline of a square displays at the bottom of the mouse pointer and the insertion point is a dotted vertical line.

4. Release the mouse button.

   Note: The paragraph is moved to the new location.

Finish-Up Instructions

- ❖ If desired, click the left mouse button once to deselect the text.
- ❖ Use the *new* filename **4dad1.doc** and save the file on your file disk (select **File**, **Save As**; type the filename; if necessary, click in the Drives box and click on the drive letter where your file disk is located; select **OK**).
- ❖ Print one copy (select **File**, **Print**, choose **OK**).
- ❖ Close the document (select **File**, **Close**).

Copy Text

Copying text is the process of duplicating text. For example, a document, sentence, name, or paragraph may need to appear again on the page, in another part of the current document, or in a different document. Text can be copied from the original location and repeated in a second location. The text to be copied must first be selected. Once the text has been selected, Word provides several methods for copying text. Two methods for copying text are described in the following Steps to Copy Text Using the Copy and Paste Commands and in the Steps to Copy Text Using the Drag and Drop Text Feature.

Start-Up Instructions

- ❖ Open the file named **1drill2.doc** typed in Chapter 1, page 23 (select the **Open** button on the Standard Toolbar; if necessary, click in the Drives box and click on the drive letter where the file disk is located; double-click on the filename).
- ❖ The following steps will be used to make a copy of all the memorandum text in the file named **1drill2.doc**. Both copies will appear on the same page.

Copy Text Using the Copy and Paste Commands

1. Select the text to be copied.

   For example, select the existing text by choosing **Edit, Select All** {Alt, e, L *or* Ctrl and a}.

2. Select the **Copy** button on the Standard Toolbar {Alt, e, c *or* Ctrl and c}.

Note: A copy of the selected text is placed in the Clipboard. The Clipboard is temporary memory that holds deleted or copied text.

3. Place the insertion point to the left of the first character or space that will follow the copied text.

   For example, move the insertion point to the right of the last name in the distribution list and press the **Enter** key three times.

4. Select the **Paste** button on the Standard Toolbar to insert the copied text into the document {Alt, e, p *or* Ctrl and v}.

   Note: When the copied text is inserted, the insertion point is located at the end of the copied text. Use the up arrow key to move up through the document to see the copied text. The copied text remains in the original location and a duplicate is displayed in the new location. A copy of the copied (or deleted) text also remains in the Clipboard (temporary memory) until replaced by other copied (or deleted) text or until Windows is exited.

Finish-Up Instructions

- Use the *new* filename **4dup2.doc** and save the file on your file disk (select **File, Save As**; type the filename; if necessary, click in the Drives box and click on the drive letter where your file disk is located; select **OK**).
- Print one copy (select **File, Print**; choose **OK**).
- Close the document (select **File, Close**).

Start-Up Instructions

- Open the file named **1drill2.doc** typed in Chapter 1, page 23 (select the **Open** button on the Standard Toolbar; if necessary, click in the Drives box and click on the drive letter where the file disk is located; double-click on the filename).
- Move the insertion point to the bottom of the document (**Ctrl** and **End**) and press **Enter** twice.
- The following steps will be used to make a copy of all the memorandum text. Both copies will appear on the same page.

Copy Text Using the Drag and Drop Text Feature

Note: A mouse must be used to perform the following steps.

1. Select the desired text.

   For example, select the existing text by choosing **Edit, Select All.**

2. Move the mouse pointer to any location in the selected (highlighted) text.

3. Press and hold the left mouse button while dragging the mouse pointer and insertion point to the new location.

   For example, while holding the mouse button, drag the mouse pointer and insertion point to the second blank line below the last name in the distribution list.

   Note: An outline of a square displays at the bottom of the mouse pointer and the insertion point is a dotted vertical line.

4. Press and hold the **Ctrl** key.

   Note: A plus (+) symbol displays above the mouse pointer.

5. Release the mouse button and then release the **Ctrl** key.

   Note: The memo displays in the original location and a duplicate displays in the new location. Use the up and down arrow keys to view the copied memo and the original memo.

Finish-Up Instructions

- ❖ If necessary, click the left mouse button once to deselect the text.
- ❖ Use the *new* filename **4cop2.doc** and save the file on your file disk (select **File, Save As**; type the filename; if necessary, click in the Drives box and click on the drive letter where the file disk is located; select **OK**).
- ❖ Print one copy (select **File, Print**; choose **OK**).
- ❖ Close the document (select **File, Close**).

Find Text

The Find command is used to locate a word or group of words in a document. The Find command can also be used to locate codes, such as margins and justification. When the Find command is accessed, the Find dialog box displays. Options in the Find dialog box are used to give Word more information on how to perform the find operation. See Figure 4.2 for information on each Find option. Find is also referred to as *search*.

Start-Up Instructions

- ❖ Open the file named **4drill3.doc** located on the data disk (select the **Open** button on the Standard Toolbar; if necessary, click in the Drives box and click on the drive letter where the data disk is located; double-click on the filename).

Steps to Find Text

1. Select **Edit, Find** {Alt, e, f *or* Ctrl and f}.

   Note: The Find dialog box displays. The insertion point is located in the Find What box (see Figure 4.1).

2. Type the word or words to be found in the Find What box.

FIGURE 4.1

Find dialog box

For example, type **DF** in the Find What box.

3. Select the desired options below the Find What box. An X displays in the box next to the selected option. To turn (toggle) the selection on or off, click once on the box next to the option {press Alt and the underlined letter in the option}.

   For example, select **Find Whole Words Only** {Alt and w}.

4. Select the desired search direction by clicking on the arrow next to the Search box and clicking once on the desired direction {Alt and s, use the up or down arrow to highlight the desired direction}.

   For example, to search the entire document, check that **All** displays in the Search box.

5. Select the **Find Next** button {Alt and f}.

   Note: *The first occurrence of the specified text is highlighted in the document window.*

6. The text can be edited by moving the mouse pointer to the location in the document where editing is to occur and clicking once to relocate the insertion point {Ctrl and Tab}.

   a. Edit by deleting, inserting, or replacing.

      For example, move the mouse pointer to the highlighted text in the document window and click once. Delete **DF**

FIGURE 4.2

Find dialog box and Replace dialog box options

Find Whole Words Only	Locates the next occurrence of matching text that is a word by itself.
Match Case	Locates words that exactly match the case of the text typed in the Find What box. When selected in the Replace dialog box, text is replaced with capitalization matching that in the Replace With box, rather than that of the original text.
Use Pattern Matching	Allows searches using wildcard characters for some letters or numbers. This is useful when words may not be spelled in exactly the same way. For example, the pattern *sa?e* would find sale, same, sane, and sake.
Sounds Like	Allows searches for words that sound like the text in the Find What box. For example, if night is typed in the Find What box and the Sounds Like option is selected, knight or nite would be found as matches. This option is useful for people who tend to spell phonetically.
Search	
All	The All setting will search through all text for a match. It is the default setting whenever there is no block of text selected before the Find command is activated.
Down	Text is searched from the position of the insertion point to the end of the document.
Up	Text is searched from the position of the insertion point to the beginning of the document.
Format	A drop-down list of formatting options will appear when this button is selected. The formatting options can be used to find or replace text.
Special	A drop-down list of special characters will appear. Select one of these characters to add it to the text in the Find What box or the Replace With box.

and type **DIRECT FLIGHTS** {Ctrl and Tab; edit the text}.

b. To continue to search for the next occurrence of the same text, select the **Find Next** button in the Find dialog box {Ctrl and Tab, Alt and f}.

For example, continue the Find process and change all occurrences of **DF** to **Direct Flights**.

Note: *When Word cannot find any additional occurrences of the specified text, the message displays, "Word has finished searching the document. The search item was not found."*

7. Select **OK** {Enter}.

8. Select **Cancel** {Esc}.

Finish-Up Instructions

- When the entire text has been searched, use the *new* filename **4drill3.fin** and save the file on your file disk (select **File**, **Save As**; type the filename; if necessary, click in the Drives box and click on the drive letter where the file disk is located; select **OK**).
- Print one copy (select **File**, **Print**; choose **OK**).
- Close the document (select **File**, **Close**).

Replace Text Automatically

Replacing text automatically is the process of locating and deleting specific text or codes and inserting new text or codes. The document is searched for a specific word/code or group of words/codes. Each occurrence of the specified text can be replaced automatically with new text.

When the Replace command is accessed, the Replace dialog box displays. Options in the Replace dialog box are used to give Word more information about the text to be replaced. The options available are the same as those in the Find dialog box, but there may be slight differences in the functions when used in the Replace dialog box. For example, if the **Match Case** option is selected, Word replaces the text with capitalization matching the capitalization of the word(s) that are in the Replace With box, rather than using the capitalization of the text being replaced.

Undo Replaced Text

Because Word replaces all occurrences of specified text rapidly, it may be necessary to undo the replaced text if word(s) are found that should not have been changed. Select the **Cancel** button in the Replace dialog box to exit and to return the insertion point to the document window. Select the **Undo** button one or more times until the desired word(s) displays in the document.

Start-Up Instructions

- Open the file named **4drill3.doc** located on the data disk (select the **Open** button on the Standard Toolbar; if necessary, click in the Drives box and click on the drive letter where the data disk is located; double-click on the filename).

FIGURE 4.3

Replace dialog box

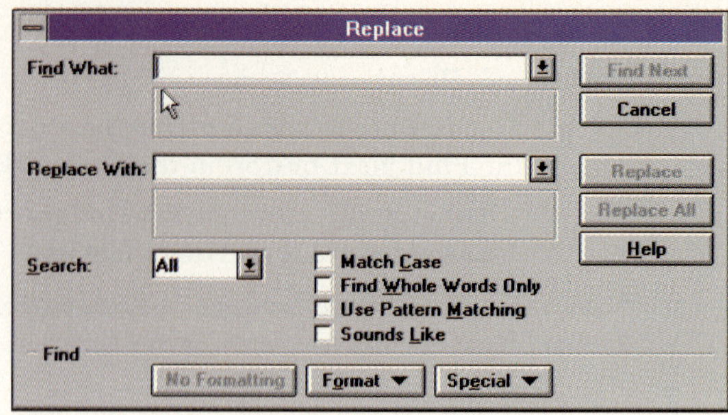

Steps to Replace Text Automatically

1. Select **Edit, Replace** {Alt, e, e *or* Ctrl and h}.

   Note: The Replace dialog box displays. The insertion point is located in the Find What box (see Figure 4.3).

2. In the Find What box, type the text to be replaced.

   For example, type **DF** in the Find What box.

3. Click in the **Replace With** box {Tab}.

4. Type the new text in the Replace With box.

   For example, type **Destination First**. (Do not type the period.)

5. Select the desired options below the Replace With box. An X displays in the box next to the selected option. To turn (toggle) the selection on or off, click once on the box next to the option {press Alt and the underlined letter in the option}.

   For example, select or check that **Find Whole Words Only** is chosen {Alt and w}.

6. Select the desired search direction by clicking on the arrow next to the Search box and clicking once on the desired direction {Alt and s, use the up or down arrow to highlight the desired direction}.

   For example, make sure **All** appears in the Search box to search the entire document.

7. Select the **Replace All** button {Alt and a}.

   Note: Word quickly replaces the specified text. The message displays, "Word has finished searching the document. [#] replacements were made."

8. Select **OK** and **Close** to return to the document window {Enter, Esc}.

Finish-Up Instructions

- Use the *new* filename **4rep3.doc** and save the file on your file disk (select **File, Save As**; type the filename; if necessary, click in the Drives box and click on the drive letter where the file disk is located; select **OK**).
- Print one copy (select the **Print** button).
- Close the document (select **File, Close**).

Create Text Using the Bullets, Numbers, and Indent Features

Text can be indented to improve readability and to enhance the document's appearance. If the Indent feature is used, all lines of a paragraph are indented from the left margin. The first time the **Increase Indent** button is selected, the insertion point or text moves to the first preset tab and all text is indented at that position. If the **Increase Indent** button is selected a second time, the insertion point or text moves to the second preset tab that is used to indent the text. Select the **Decrease Indent** button to reduce the amount text is indented from the left margin.

Numbers, letters, or bullets (special characters placed at the left of a paragraph) can be inserted into a document to provide extra emphasis or to improve readability. The desired number, letter, or bullet style is chosen from a list of available styles displayed in the Bullets and Numbering dialog box. Various number styles are available such as 1., 2., 3., or I., II., III. Uppercase and lowercase letter styles are also available, such as A., B., C., or a), b), c). Some of the bullet styles available are small or large circles (• or ●) or a diamond (♦).

Numbers, letters, or bullets can be inserted as text is typed or after the text has been typed.

Start-Up Instructions

- Open the file named **4drill4.doc** located on the data disk (select the **Open** button on the Standard Toolbar; if necessary, click in the drives box and click on the drive letter where the data disk is located; double-click on the filename).

Create Paragraphs Using the Indent Feature

1. With the paragraph(s) to be indented displayed in the document window, place the insertion point anywhere in the paragraph to be indented.

   For example, place the insertion point to the left of the **R** in the paragraph that begins Results-Oriented.

2. Select the **Increase Indent** button on the Formatting Toolbar {Ctrl and m}.

   Note: All lines of the paragraph are indented.

Finish-Up Instructions

- Repeat steps 1 and 2 and indent the last three paragraphs of the document.
- Use the *new* filename **4obj4.doc** and save the file on your file disk (select **File, Save As**; type the filename; if necessary, click in the Drives box and click on the drive letter where your file disk is located; select **OK**).
- Print one copy (select **File, Print**; choose **OK**).
- Close the document (select **File, Close**).

FIGURE 4.4

Bullets & Numbering dialog box with Numbered card activated

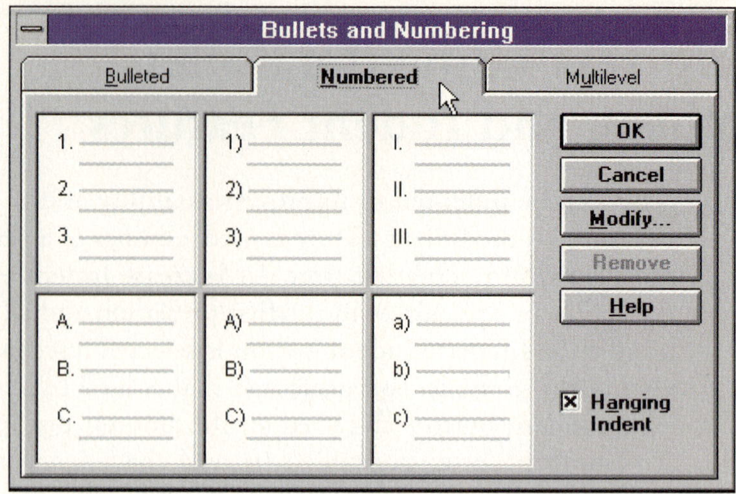

Start-Up Instructions

- Open the file named **4drill4.doc** located on the data disk (select the **Open** button on the Standard Toolbar; if necessary, click in the drives box and click on the drive letter where the data disk is located; double-click on the filename).

Create a Numbered or Bulleted List

1. Select the paragraphs to be numbered or bulleted.

   For example, select the last four paragraphs.

2. Select **Format, Bullets and Numbering** {Alt, o, n}.

   Note: The Bullets and Numbering dialog box displays. The options for each type of bullet are on a card designed to look like an index card in a file. A card must be "active" before numbering or bullet options can be selected. The top card is active (see Figure 4.4).

3. To activate the desired card, move the mouse pointer to its tab and click once {Alt and the underlined letter in the desired tab}.

   For example, select the **Numbered** tab {Alt and n}.

   Note: The Numbered card displays in front of the other cards and is now the "active" card. Samples of the various numbering formats available are displayed.

4. Select the desired bullets or numbering option by moving the mouse pointer to the sample and clicking the left mouse button once {press Tab until a dark outline shows around the first sample on the left, then press the right or left arrow keys to highlight the desired sample}.

   For example, select the **first sample on the left** showing the numbers as 1., 2., etc.

5. Select **OK** {Enter}.

   Note: The selected paragraphs are numbered and remain highlighted. Your document should look similar to Figure 4.5. If items in the numbered list are moved, the items are automatically renumbered.

Developing Objectives

An objective is a statement of intent. An objective states what you are expected to accomplish, how well, and by when.

Quality objectives typically have the following characteristics:

1. Results-Oriented--Aimed at achieving results. Results can be the outcome of activities or they can be tangible products.

2. Traceable--Related to the unit goal as determined by your manager.

3. Specific--Written in specific terms. Each objective should state the result that you intend to achieve.

4. Measurable--Include a means for measuring your performance. This measurement can be based on the quantity and/or the quality of results.

FIGURE 4.5

Numbered paragraphs

Shortcut

To use the same type of bullets or numbering style previously used, select the text, then select the **Bullets** button or the **Numbering** button on the Formatting Toolbar. The text will be formatted immediately with the options that were set the last time the Bullets and Numbering dialog box was accessed.

Finish-Up Instructions

- If desired, click once to deselect the numbered list.
- Use the *new* filename **4num5.doc** and save the file on your file disk (select **File, Save As**; type the filename; if necessary, click in the Drives box and click on the drive letter where the file disk is located; select **OK**).
- Print one copy (select the **Print** button).
- Change the numbered list to a bulleted list (select all numbered paragraphs; select **Format, Bullets and Numbering**; select the **Bulleted** tab; select the **Stars** style; select **OK**).

  Note: *When the numbered or bulleted list is selected, the number or bullet character will not be highlighted. That's OK.*
- If desired, click once to deselect the bulleted list.
- Use the *new* filename **4star5.doc** and save the file on your file disk (select **File, Save As**; type the filename; if necessary, click in the Drives box and click on the drive letter where the file disk is located; select **OK**).
- Print one copy (select the **Print** button).
- Close the document (select **File, Close**).

Print Selected Text

Once a document has been typed, a part of the text can be printed if desired. For example, a single paragraph from a document containing several paragraphs can be printed. First, the portion of text to be printed is selected. Then the **File, Print** command is selected and the **Selection** option is chosen. The selected text prints starting at the top of the printed page.

Start-Up Instructions

❖ Open the file named **4num5.doc** located on your file disk (select the **Open** button on the Standard Toolbar; if necessary, click in the Drives box and click on the drive letter where the file disk is located; double-click on the filename).

Print Selected Text

1. Select the text to be printed.

    For example, select all the numbered paragraphs.

2. Select **File, Print** {Alt, f, p *or* Ctrl and p}.
3. Choose the **Selection** option {Alt and n}.

    Note: A black dot displays beside the Selection option.

4. Select **OK** to print the selected text {Enter}.

Finish-Up Instructions

❖ Close the document (select **File**, **Close**).

The Next Step

Chapter Review and Activities

Self-Check Quiz

T F 1. The Find command is used to locate a word or group of words in a document.

T F 2. Moving text is the process of duplicating text.

T F 3. Before text can be copied or moved, the text is selected.

T F 4. To begin the Replace function, select **Edit**, **Replace**.

T F 5. A single paragraph from a document containing multiple paragraphs cannot be selected and printed.

6. Bullet characters can be inserted to the left of selected paragraphs by choosing ______________.
   a. **Format, Bullets and Numbering**
   b. **Tools, Bullets**
   c. **Edit, Bullets and Numbering**

7. When using the drag and drop method to move text, ______________.
   a. the text must be selected
   b. a mouse must be used
   c. keystrokes can be used
   d. both a and b

8. When the **Increase Indent** button is selected ______________.
   a. the text is indented from both the left and right margins
   b. a bullet character is inserted at the left of the selected paragraphs
   c. all lines of a paragraph are indented from the left margin until the **Enter** key is pressed

9. Which option in the Replace dialog box should be selected in order to instruct Word to find only the whole word(s) typed in the Find What box?

10. What is the difference between selecting **Format**, **Bullets and Numbering** and selecting the **Bullets** button on the Formatting Toolbar?

Enriching Language Arts Skills

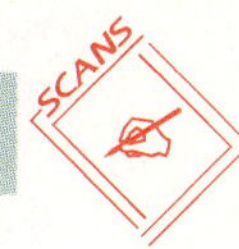

Spelling/Vocabulary Words

appreciate to recognize gratefully.
legislation the making of laws; the laws made.
qualify to make legally capable; to make fit for a job.

Compound Adjectives and Coordinating Conjunctions

Hyphenate two words that precede and describe a noun and function as a single adjective.

Example:

Senior management will be in a high-level conference all day Thursday.

A comma is placed before a coordinating conjunction (e.g., *and, but, or*) that joins two independent clauses (i.e., clauses that are complete sentences). No comma is placed before a coordinating conjunction if *one* or both clauses are dependent.

Example:

Clarence will arrive in Portland at noon, and Judy will arrive at 3:30 p.m. (Two independent clauses.)

*We mailed 400 surveys yesterday **and** expect to obtain a 3 percent response by the end of May.* (One independent and one dependent clause.)

Activities

Activity 4.1—Create a Numbered List and Move Text

1. Launch Word or select the **New** button.
2. Type the following paragraphs using the spacing shown.

Features of Word 6.0 for Windows

Drag and drop text and graphics across windows--even across applications. The drag and drop feature is no longer limited to moving or copying text within the same document. Now you can drag and drop into any window or Windows program.

Wizards simplify production of documents--With Wizards, you answer a few questions, and Word sets up the basic formatting and layout. This can give you a big head start in creating business letters, memos, and reports. There is even a Table Wizard that allows you to select the look you want and automatically adjusts the column widths.

AutoCorrect--The AutoCorrect feature fixes common typing mistakes as you work.

AutoFormat--With the AutoFormat feature, Word can analyze and format a document for you based on previous styles and templates.

Multi-Level Undo--Now the Undo feature remembers many previous actions and can reverse your changes, even if you have edited or deleted other text in the interim.

---

3. Number all paragraphs except the title using standard numbers (1., 2., 3., etc.) (select all paragraphs to be numbered, select **Format, Bullets and Numbering,** select the **Numbered** tab, select the 1., 2., 3., Numbering style sample, select **OK**).
4. Save the file on your file disk; use the filename **4act1.doc** (select the **Save** button; type the filename; if necessary, click in the Drives box and click on the drive letter where the file disk is located; select **OK**).
5. Print one copy (select the **Print** button).
6. Move the items as shown.

Features of Word 6.0 for Windows

1. Drag and drop text and graphics across windows--even across applications. The drag and drop feature is no longer limited to moving or copying text within the same document. Now you can drag and drop into any window or Windows program.

2. Wizards simplify production of documents--With Wizards, you answer a few questions, and Word sets up the basic formatting and layout. This can give you a big head start in creating business letters, memos, and reports. There is even a Table Wizard that allows you to select the look you want and automatically adjusts the column widths.

3. AutoCorrect--The AutoCorrect feature fixes common typing mistakes as you work.

4. AutoFormat--With the AutoFormat feature, Word can analyze and format a document for you based on previous styles and templates.

5. Multi-Level Undo--Now the Undo feature remembers many previous actions and can reverse your changes, even if you have edited or deleted other text in the interim.

---

7. Use the *new* filename **4rev1.doc** and save the file on your file disk (select **File, Save As**; type the filename; if necessary, click in the Drives box and click on the drive letter where the file disk is located; select **OK**).
8. Print one copy (select the **Print** button).
9. Close the document (select **File, Close**).

Activity 4.2—Create a Bulleted List and Replace Text Automatically

1. Launch Word or select the **New** button.
2. Use the traditional style and type the following letter as shown.

(Use current date)

Mr. Austin Elsass
55 Johnston Rd., #8
Schenectady, NY 12304-6204

Dear Mr. Elsass:

Enclosed is a copy of the GTA Constant Traveler newsletter highlighting our expanded world of service and membership benefits.

Our latest expansion opens new corners of the globe to you for mileage building and award opportunities. Wherever you fly on GTA, you will earn our minimum of 1,500 miles per flight segment. No airline offers more.

In addition to our expanded service, the newsletter highlights:

New fares for GTA business-class fliers.

Triple mileage for selected GTA intercontinental routes.

Special "GTA Partners Program" holiday promotion.

To increase your flexibility when traveling within North America, GTA has introduced upgrade awards for our business fliers. Also, members may continue to purchase a GTA First Class seat at reduced rates any time before departure through our paid upgrade program.

We at GTA thank you for flying with us and look forward to serving your air travel needs.

Sincerely,

Anna R. Irvine
Senior Vice President

ARI/xx
elsass.ltr/disk4

Enc.

---

3. Select the three sentences that follow the third paragraph, which begins "In addition to our expanded . . ." and create a bulleted list (select **Format, Bullets and Numbering**; select the **Bulleted** tab; select the **Small Circle** style; select **OK**). Click once to deselect the list.
4. Save the file on your file disk; use the filename **4act2.doc** (select the **Save** button; type the filename; if necessary, click in the Drives box and click on the drive letter where the file disk is located; select **OK**).
5. Print one copy (select the **Print** button).
6. Replace all occurrences of GTA with Global Trans Airline (place the insertion point at the top of the document, select **Edit, Replace**; type **GTA** in the Find What box; type **Global Trans Airline** in the Replace With box; if necessary, select **Find Whole Words Only**; select **Match Case**; select **Replace All**).
7. Use the *new* filename **4rep2.doc** and save the file on your file disk (select **File, Save As**; type the filename; if necessary, click in the Drives box and click on the drive letter where the file disk is located; select **OK**).
8. Print one copy (select the **Print** button).
9. Close the document (select **File, Close**).

Activity 4.3—Copy, Edit, and Print Selected Text

1. Open the file named **4num5.doc** or type the document shown on page 91 (Figure 4.5).
2. Change the numbered list to a bulleted list (select the numbered items, select **Format, Bullets and Numbering**, select the **Bulleted** tab, select the **Diamond** style bullet; select **OK**). Click once to deselect the list.
3. Add three **Enters** at the bottom of the document.
4. Select the entire document.
5. Copy the entire document by selecting **Edit, Copy**.
6. Move the insertion point to the blank line at the bottom of the document and select **Edit, Paste** to insert a copy of the document.
7. Make the following changes to the pasted copy. (Do not change the line spacing.)

Developing Objectives

An objective is a statement of intent [and purpose]. An objective states what you are expected to accomplish, how well, and by when.

Quality objectives typically [include] ~~have~~ the following [ideas:] ~~characteristics:~~

◆ Results-Oriented--Aimed at achieving results. Results can be the outcome of activities or they can be tangible products.

◆ Traceable--Related to [one or more] ~~the~~ unit goal[(s)] as determined by your manager.

◆ Specific--Written in specific terms. Each objective should state the [end] result [desired.] ~~that you intend to achieve.~~

◆ Measurable--Include a means for measuring your performance. This measurement can be based on the quantity and/or the quality of results.

[◆ Documented--A table should be created that lists each objective, the result desired, and how the performance will be measured.]

---

8. Use the filename **4app3.doc** and save the file on your file disk (select **File, Save As**; type the filename; if necessary, click in the Drives box and click on the drive letter where the file disk is located; select **OK**).
9. Select the edited copy and print one copy of the selected text (select **File, Print**; choose the **Selection** option, and select **OK**).
10. Close the document (select **File, Close**).

Activity 4.4—Create Paragraphs Using the Indent Feature

1. Launch Word or select the **New** button.

2. Use the traditional block style and type the following letter. Use the Indent feature to indent the second and third paragraphs from the left margin as shown (select the **Increase Indent** button on the Formatting Toolbar).

   Hint: After the ***Enter*** *key is pressed following the second indented paragraph, select the* ***Decrease Indent*** *button to return the insertion point to the left margin.*

(Use current date)

Mr. Phil Emerson
P. O. Box 7526
Ashville, NC 28801-9945

Dear Mr. Emerson:

We have great news for you! Your application for a ValueCard account has been preliminarily approved. However, before we can send you your new card, we need your assistance in verifying all income.

> Please send us a copy of your last two paycheck stubs issued within the last thirty (30) days. If you have listed other income, please provide verification.
>
> If we receive the requested information within thirty (30) days, we will be able to complete your evaluation.

We certainly hope to hear from you so that we can complete our approval process, and you can begin to enjoy the many advantages that a ValueCard has to offer.

Sincerely,

Carol Schofield
Credit Card Director

CS/xx
emerson.ltr/d2

---

3. Save the file on your file disk; use the filename **4pem4.doc** (select the **Save** button; type the filename; if necessary, click in the Drives box and click on the drive letter where the file disk is located; select **OK**).
4. Print one copy (select **File, Print**; choose **OK**).
5. Close the document (select **File, Close**).

Challenge Your Skills

Skill 4.1—Create a Numbered List; Move and Edit Text

1. Use Memorandum—Style 1 and the following information:
   a. Send the memo to Sales Associates from Carole Pemberton, Division Manager.
   b. Use the current date; include your reference initials.
   c. The subject of the memo is Current Sales Promotion.
   d. Send copies to J. Laucella and G. Hurst.
   e. The unformatted memorandum body text follows:

      Enclosed are photographs to assist in building your current sales promotion displays.

      Please note the following:

      Wingits have been discontinued and Chocwiz quantities reduced in order to incorporate Ultimate Almonds and expand on the successful Cheesecake Minis. Chocwiz should be placed next to snack crackers for a common price point. Ultimate Almonds should be placed in the space previously occupied by Chocwiz.

      Order quantities will be communicated through the central ordering office and will be processed automatically. Sales associates will not key in any orders.

      Orders reflect only the quantities necessary to build displays. Make plans to order refill quantities when necessary.

      Stores will require extra service calls during this promotion. Let your stores know when you will be visiting their sites.

      Announcement to the stores of this promotion has already been distributed. Orders will now be processed electronically. The new electronic order processing will ensure accurate and timely delivery of products.

      Remember—proper point of sale, displays, and shelf!

2. Select and number the third, fourth, fifth, and sixth paragraphs.
3. Use the filename **4skill1.doc** and save the file on your file disk.
4. Move items 3 and 4 above item number 2.
5. Delete the last paragraph and insert the following two paragraphs:

   Advise stores now of their upcoming shipment, and make plans to build displays. Stores resisting this promotion should be advised to call Leonard Koenig or Laura Gonzales (department buyers) at 555-3422.

6. Use the *new* filename **4skill1r.doc** and save the file on your file disk.
7. Print one copy and close the document.

Skill 4.2—Copy and Edit Text

1. Create the following form using the format and spacing shown:

   Hint: *Press the **Tab** button four or five times to align the items in the second column.*

Preliminary Sales Inventory Report
Sales Associate: Jacqueline Villegas
Store #: 286

(3 Enters)

Item Name	**Purchased**
(2 Enters)	
Cheesecake Minis	12 gross
(2 Enters)	
Chocwiz	10 gross
(2 Enters)	
Ultimate Almonds	20 gross
(3 Enters)	

---

2. Use the filename **4skill2.doc** and save the file on your file disk.
3. Copy the form below the original form. Change the data in the copied form as follows:

   Sales Associate: David Kane
   Store #: 235
   Cheesecake Minis: 10 gross
   Chocwiz: 15 gross
   Ultimate Almonds: 22 gross

4. Copy the original form again and place it below the second form. Change the data in the copied form as follows:

   Sales Associate: Monie Lampert
   Store #: 182
   Cheesecake Minis: 15 gross
   Chocwiz: 12 gross
   Ultimate Almonds: 18 gross

5. Save the file again using the same filename, **4skill2.doc**.
6. Print one copy and close the document.

Skill 4.3—Replace Text Automatically; Language Arts

1. Use Memorandum—Style 1 and the following information:

a. Change both the left and right margins to **1.25"** and the top margin to **1.5"**.

b. Send the memo to Concord Life Insurance Field Force from Juan Vincent, Vice President.

c. Use the current date; include your reference initials.

d. The subject of the memo is UAI Membership.

e. Correct three spelling and four punctuation errors.

In order to qualifie for the National Quality Awards, your UAI membership dues must be current. If you have been a member of UAI under another company's name please write a letter to UAI National Headquarters and ask that your affiliation be changed to Concord Life Insurance.

Your UAI membership is important because of the awards or honors it can bring you personally. In addition UAI has a long and distinguished history in representing professional agents in the Life, Health, and Financial Services industry. The benefits far outweigh the membership dues. UAI provides information for agents to learn from each other and share sales ideas and it serves as a platform for defending your interests in relation to state and federal legisllation.

For us to fight legislative efforts to control the insurance industry, we need your help by renewing or beginning your membership with UAI and by maintaining an active relationship with your local government representatives.

Concord Life Insurance takes great pride in the number of long term agents who are members of the UAI and the distinguished service rendered by members of our field force. We here at Concord Life Insurance appreceate your services and applaud your outstanding accomplishments. If you are not a member of UAI, please give this serious consideration.

---

2. Use the filename **4skill3.doc** and save the file on your file disk.
3. Automatically replace all occurrences of UAI with Underwriters Associated Insurers.
4. Automatically replace all occurrences of Concord Life Insurance with CLI.

   Hint: Remember to select the Match Case option.
5. Save the file again using the same filename, **4skill3.doc**.
6. Print one copy.
7. If you have completed your work, exit Word (select **File**, **Exit**).

Part 1
Checking Your Step

Production Skill Builder Activities
Chapters 1-4

Production Activity 1.1—Create and Edit a Memorandum—Style 1

1. Use Memorandum—Style 1 and the following information to create a memorandum.

   a. Make decisions regarding:

      Margins
      Alignment
      Memo date
      Use of Speller
      Reference initials

   b. Send the memorandum to Administrative Support Staff from Charles Foster.

   c. The subject of the memorandum is Equal Employment Opportunity Compliance Policy.

   d. Memorandum body text follows:

      It is the policy of Ames Financial Planning to ensure that all employees and applicants receive equal employment and advancement opportunities. AFP will not discriminate against qualified persons because of race, color, religion, national origin, sex, age, veteran status, marital status, or sexual orientation.

      The Chairman and Chief Executive officer assigns to the Vice President of Human Resource Development the responsibility of developing and enforcing the equal employment opportunity policy as set forth in this memorandum.

      Managers and supervisory personnel are charged with making a personal commitment to practice and enforce AFP's equal employment opportunity policy.

2. Save the file; use the filename **1pact1.doc**.
3. Revise the memorandum as shown:

with regard to human resource matters, including but not limited to recruitment, hiring, placement, compensation, benefits, and training

It is the policy of Ames Financial Planning to ensure that all employees and applicants receive equal employment and advancement opportunities. AFP will not discriminate against qualified persons because of race, color, religion, national origin, sex, age, veteran status, marital status, or sexual orientation.

citizenship, disability

The Chairman and Chief Executive officer assigns to the Vice President of Human Resource Development the responsibility of developing and enforcing the equal employment opportunity policy as set forth in this memorandum.

communicating,

¶ Senior management is responsible for providing the direction and control required to make the equal employment opportunity program effective and successful.

Managers and supervisory personnel ~~are charged with~~ making a personal commitment to practice and enforce AFP's equal employment opportunity policy.

will

¶ If you have any questions regarding AFP's equal employment opportunity program, please contact Efrain Valderama, Manager, EEO, 804-555-1424.

4. Use the *new* filename **1pact1r.doc** and save the file on your file disk.
5. Print one copy and close the document.

Production Activity 1.2—Create a Numbered List and Copy Text

1. Type the following information and use center, bold, and italic as shown.
2. Press **Enter** three times after the last item.

Marjorie Quatro
Mortgage Broker
602-555-4200

Licensed Real Estate Mortgage Broker with over 25 years' experience in the Real Estate industry.

Funded in excess of $30 million in 1994.

Expert knowledge of the mortgage market accompanied by a current awareness of secondary market guideline changes.

Creative and professional service for each client.

Member of the Association of Professional Mortgage Women, Association of Executive Saleswomen, and Chandler Board of Realtors.

Graduate of CSUF, majoring in business/communications.

Believes the customer deserves the best!

---

3. Select all paragraphs except the first three lines and create a bulleted list using the Bullet and Numbering feature. Select a bullet character of your choice.
4. Select a font of your choice with a point size of 12 to 14 for the entire document.
5. Save the file; use the filename **1quatro2.doc**.
6. Print one copy.
7. Select and copy the entire document and place the copied text below the original copy.

   Note: *Three Enters should follow the last item. Both the copy and the original will be on the same page. If a second page is created, delete the extra Enters below the copied paragraphs. Also, change the margins and/or reduce the font size so that both copies fit on one page.*
8. Save the file again using the same filename, **1quatro2.doc**.
9. Print one copy and close the document.

Production Activity 1.3—Create a Numbered List and Replace Text

1. Use Memorandum—Style 1 and the following information to create a memorandum.
   a. Make decisions regarding:

      Margins
      Alignment
      Fonts
      Memo date
      Reference initials
      Indention

   b. Send the memorandum to Kevin R. Masterson.

   c. The memorandum is from Patrick W. Coltron.

   d. The subject of the memorandum is Registration of Power Story Materials for Copyright.

   e. Memorandum body text follows:

      Pursuant to our recent discussion, the following is a summary of the PS materials that need to be registered for copyright immediately:

PS show number 635 broadcast on October 28. This show contained two (2) segments on Gil VanBuren, including a surveillance video of Mr. VanBuren speaking to Darla Clifton. The Gil VanBuren surveillance tape, which is included in this broadcast, was obtained by PS and is owned by Capital. Accordingly, we would also like this surveillance video separately registered for copyright (see paragraph 4 below).

PS show number 640 broadcast on November 4. This show contained a segment entitled "New Life" on the Milton Dutra Radio Show, a segment on a new book concerning the British Royal Family, and a segment on Kelly Dillon and her divorce trial.

PS show number 714 broadcast on December 16. This show contained a segment on Milton Dutra's "Funeral" for Los Angeles disc jockey's "Jon and Jo" and an exchange between PS reporters Elaine Parsons and Milton Dutra.

A surveillance tape of Gil VanBuren talking to Darla Clifton, which was obtained by PS and is owned by Capital. This surveillance tape was first broadcast on PS show number 635 on October 28.

The above materials should be registered for copyright to ensure preservation of all statutory remedies for unauthorized use of materials. Please forward copies of all registration applications and verifications of registration to me as soon as completed or received.

2. Select the second, third, fourth, and fifth paragraphs and create a numbered list using the Bullets and Numbering feature.
3. Replace **PS** with **Power Story**.
4. Save the file; use the filename **1pact3.doc**.
5. Print one copy and close the document.

Production Activity 1.4—Edit, Move, Use Spelling Command, and Bullets and Numbering Feature

1. Open the file named **1pact4.doc** located on the data disk.
2. Change the font to **Arial** or **make a choice of your own**. Change the font size to **12 point**.
3. Revise the text as shown.

Ames Financial Planning
Equal Employment Opportunity Policy

AFP pledges to:

Base decisions on employment so as to further the principles of equal employment opportunity.

Recruit, hire, train, and promote for all job classifications regardless of race, color, religion, national origin, sex, age, citizenship, disability, veteran status, marital status, or sexual orientation.

Ensure that the work environment is void of any verbal or physical abuse, intimidation or harassment against any employee.

Ensure that all personnel actions, such as compensation, benefits, company-sponsored training, education, tuition assistance, and social and recreational programs, will be administered regardless of race, color, religion, national origin, sex, age, citizenship, disability, veteran status, marital status, or sexual orientation.

Ensure that promotion decisions are in accord with principles of equal employment opportunity by imposing only appropriate requirements for promotional opportunities.

---

4. Select five paragraphs starting with the paragraph that begins "Recruit, hire, train . . ." Use the Bullets and Numbering feature to create a numbered list.
5. Use the Spelling command to find and correct any misspelled words; also proofread carefully for accurate meaning.
6. Use the *new* filename **1ames4.doc** and save the file on your file disk.
7. Print one copy and close the document.

Production Activity 1.5—Create and Edit an AMS Simplified Style Letter; Language Arts Skills

1. Use the AMS simplified style letter and the following information to create a letter.

   a. Make decisions regarding:

      Margins
      Alignment
      Fonts
      Subject line
      Text attributes (bold, underline, italic)
      Use of Spelling command
      Reference initials
      Documentation identification
      Enclosure notation

b. Correct five spelling and two punctuation errors.

c. The letter should be sent to Leroy and Nadine Kirkland, 2288 Millpark Court, Honolulu, HI 96815-1998.

d. The letter is from Sean Tennyson, Vice President.

e. The letter body text follows:

You have undoubtedly read and heard a lot recently about the problems of the nation's financial institutions, including some insurance companies. Therefore, we are pleased to send you a copy of last year's annual report for World-Wide Life Insurance (WWL) and a prospectis for the planned merger with United Insurers.

The proposed merger promises many advantages for both companies, including the ability to merge our recycling programs to the advantage of the enfironment. In addition all of our stockholders will have the option to reedeem their Preferred Class A Stock for cash or common stock.

This merger is part of an overall plan to react aggressively, rather than passevely, to the market conditions surrounding us and to make our operations more efficeint. If you need additional insurance or seek a high return on an individual annuity we hope you will contact your WWL agent. Our company has been in existence for more than 90 years, and you can count on WWL being there when you need us.

2. Save the file; use the filename **1pact5.doc**.

3. Use the following information to revise the letter.

   a. In the second paragraph change the words "proposed merger" to "merger of WWL and United."

   b. Add this sentence to the end of the first paragraph. "The combined revenues of WWL and United are estimated at $900 million for next year."

   c. Delete the last sentence of the third paragraph and insert the following sentences:

   Based on the company's financial condition and operating performance, WWL continues to earn a superior rating. We have had a top rating recommendation since 1955.

   d. Insert the following paragraph above the third paragraph:

   Of course, the financial strength of the company really rests on the quality of our invested assets, and we believe that our invested assets are first-rate.

4. Use the *new* filename **1pact5r.doc** and save the file again.

5. Print one copy and close the document.

6. If you have completed your work, exit Word (select **File**, **Exit**).

Part 2
A Step Further

Work with Special Features

Chapters 5-8

- Create a table
- Insert table rows and columns
- Change column widths
- Merge cells
- Change table row height
- Center a table horizontally
- Convert tabbed text to a table
- Apply AutoFormats to tables
- Center a table or text vertically
- Move and delete a row or column
- Copy and delete a table
- Calculate column/row totals
- Customize table borders and shading
- Use single and double underlines
- Insert special symbols
- Change the case of characters
- Nonbreaking space
- Use the Rulers to change margins and set indents
- Set tabs
- Create newspaper-style columns
- Create customized columns
- Change column definition
- Insert a column break
- Use hyphenation
- Format Painter
- Create side-by-side columns

CHAPTER 5

Create a Table

Features Covered

- Create a table
- Insert a row
- Insert a column
- Change column widths
- Merge cells
- Change alignment of cell contents
- Set row height
- Center a table horizontally and vertically
- Convert tabbed text to a table
- Apply AutoFormats to tables

Objectives and Introduction

After successfully completing this chapter, you will be able to create a table, increase and decrease column widths, insert columns and rows, and merge table cells. In addition, you will be able to change row height, center a table horizontally and vertically, and create a table using existing text. Traditionally, a table has been created by calculating the location of column tabs so that when the table is printed it will be centered horizontally on the page. Tables in this book will be created using the Tables feature, which will determine the column widths and row height automatically.

The Tables feature is used to organize information into columns and rows without using tab settings. A sample table containing information is shown in Figure 5.1. Table information can include either text or numbers or both.

Create a Table

A table can be easily created using the **Insert Table** button on the Standard Toolbar or the **Insert Table** command in the **Table** menu. Also, text typed in col-

FIGURE 5.1

Sample table with nonprinting gridlines and ruler

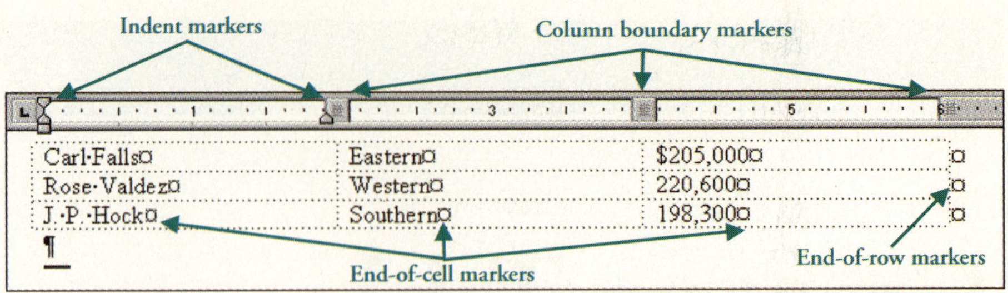

umns can be converted to a table by using either the **Insert Table** button or the **Convert Text to Table** command in the **Table** menu. Once the number of table columns and rows are specified, table gridlines display in the document window. (The table gridlines display on the screen but do not print.) However, borders can be printed if desired (see Chapter 6). If the table gridlines do not display, select **Table, Gridlines**.

The table gridlines form columns and rows. The intersection of each column and row is called a cell. Cells are generally identified by a cell address, such as A5 or C29. The cell address specifies the column and row in which the insertion point is located. Imagine that the columns are labeled from left to right, A, B, C, etc., and that the rows are numbered down the left side of the table beginning with row 1.

Column boundary markers display on the Ruler and indicate the left and right sides of the columns. When the insertion point is located in a column cell, the Ruler shows indent markers to indicate the current column (see Figure 5.1). If non-printing symbols are turned on, end-of-cells markers and end-of row markers display.

The **Tab** key, **Shift** and **Tab** keys, or an arrow key can be used to move the insertion point from cell to cell. After text is typed in one cell, the **Tab** key or the right arrow key is used to move the insertion point to the next cell. To return to the previous cell, press **Shift** and **Tab** or press the left arrow key.

Text typed in each table cell wraps around in the cell. If the **Enter** key is pressed in a cell, the cell automatically increases in height. If text within a cell is to be indented, press the **Ctrl** and **Tab** keys.

Start-Up Instructions

❖ A empty document window should be displayed. If necessary, select the **New** button.

Create a Table

1. Move the mouse pointer to the **Insert Table** button on the Standard Toolbar. Click the mouse button once {Alt, a, I}.

   Note: A miniature grid displays at the location of the Insert Table button (see Figure 5.2).

FIGURE 5.2

Miniature table grid

2. Press and hold the left mouse button while dragging to highlight the desired number of columns and rows. Release the mouse button {type the number of columns, press Tab, type the number of rows, press Enter}.

   For example, drag to highlight a 3 x 3 table; release the mouse button.

Finish-Up Instructions

- To type the unformatted information in each cell, press the **Tab** key or the arrow keys to move from cell to cell and row to row. Type the unformatted information shown in Figure 5.1. Type the dollar sign and commas when entering the numbers in the third column.

  *Note: If the **Enter** key is mistakenly pressed while typing information in a table cell, press the **Backspace** key to delete the unwanted return. If the **Tab** key is pressed after the last cell entry, check that the insertion point is located in any cell in the last row. Select **Table, Cells, Delete Entire Row,** then choose **OK**.*

- Use the filename **5ptable1.doc** and save the file on your file disk (select the **Save** button; type the filename; if necessary, click in the Drives box and click on the drive letter where the file disk is located; select **OK**).
- Optional. Print one unformatted copy.

Format and Modify a Table

Formatting a table is the process of completing such tasks as increasing or decreasing the column widths, merging table cells, changing the alignment of cell contents, and centering the table horizontally on the page. The primary goals of formatting a table are to present a pleasing appearance and to make reading easier. To produce a table that is formatted for an appealing appearance, visually adjust the width and height of cells and the alignment of text within the cells. (If desired, the ruler provided in the back of this book can be used to assist in measuring a column width.)

When the insertion point is located in any table cell, the ToolTip for the Insert Table button changes to *Insert Rows*. When a table column is selected, the ToolTip changes to *Insert Columns*. If one or more cells are selected, the ToolTip changes to *Insert Cell*. Use the **Insert Table** button to insert one or more rows *above* the cell containing the insertion point or to insert one or more columns to the *left* of the column containing the insertion point.

Modifying a table can also include changing row height. Row height is the amount of space between the top and bottom cell lines. When row height is increased, the cell text will be placed at the top of the cell and the additional space will be added between the text and the bottom cell line. Three row height options are available: **Auto, At Least**, and **Exactly**. Auto is the default row height setting. Row height is changed in the Cell Height and Width dialog box.

When the **Auto** option is selected, Word increases or decreases the row height automatically to accommodate any amount and size of text typed in the cells. When the **At Least** option is selected, a minimum amount of space is specified for each row. If text is added, the row height will be increased to accommodate the new text. If text is deleted, the row height will not be decreased to less than the minimum amount specified. When the **Exactly** option is selected, a specific row height amount can be set for each row. When the **Exactly** option is selected and text is added or deleted, the row height will not adjust automatically. If desired, however, a new row height amount can be entered.

Two or more cells in a row can be merged (joined) to provide space for information that relates to more than one cell or column. Also, some or all of the cells in the column can be merged.

Word provides shortcut menus for easy access to options related to a specific feature. The right mouse button is pressed to obtain a shortcut menu. For example, if several cells are selected and the right mouse button is pressed, the shortcut menu displays with various options such as **Cut**, **Copy**, **Paste**, **Insert Columns**, **Delete Columns**, **Table AutoFormat**.

Start-Up Instructions

- The file named **5ptable1.doc** should be displayed in the document window.
- The Normal view should be selected. If necessary, select **View**, **Normal**.

Insert Table Rows

1. To select the number of rows to be inserted, place the mouse pointer to the left side of the row that will be located below the inserted rows. When the right-pointing arrow displays, press and hold the left mouse button while dragging the mouse downward to highlight the desired row(s) (see Figure 5.3) {place the insertion point in the first cell in the first row to be selected, press F8, press the right and down arrow keys repeatedly until the desired rows are selected; or, to select a single row, press Alt, a, r}.

   For example, obtain the right-pointing arrow beside row 1 and drag downward to select rows 1 and 2.

   Note: To insert a single row, place the insertion point in the row below where the new row will be inserted. It is not necessary to highlight the row below where the new row will be inserted.

2. Place the mouse pointer on the **Insert Table** button on the Standard Toolbar {Alt, a}.

   *Note: The ToolTip displays **Insert Rows**.*

3. Click once on the **Insert Table** button {i, r, Enter}.

   *Note: To insert a row at the end of a table, move the insertion point to the last table cell, and press the **Tab** key.*

FIGURE 5.3

Table row selection arrow

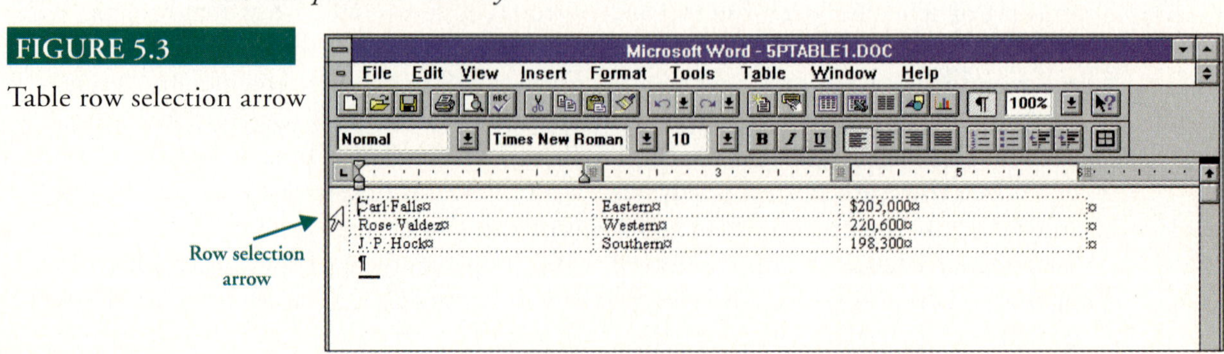

Finish-Up Instructions

- Click once to deselect the new table rows.
- Place the insertion point in the first table cell.
- Use the **Tab** key or arrow keys to move from cell to cell and type the following text into the new cells as shown.

Annual Sales		
Employee	Division	Sales

- Use the *new* filename **5ptable2.doc** and save the file on your file disk (select **File**, **Save As**; type the new filename; if necessary, click in the Drives box and click on the drive letter where the file disk is located; select **OK**).

Start-Up Instructions

- The file named **5ptable2.doc** should be displayed in the document window.

Steps to Insert Table Column(s)

1. *To insert a single column,* select the column to the right of where the new column will be inserted by moving the mouse pointer to the top border of the desired column until a down arrow displays; click once (see Figure 5.4) {place the insertion point in the top cell of the desired column, press F8, press Alt and PgDn *or* press Alt, a, c, then press the right arrow key to select the column(s) to the right}.

For example, select the third column.

To insert a column to the right of the last table column, move the mouse pointer to the top of the end-of-row markers until a down arrow displays; click once.

To insert multiple columns, move the mouse pointer to the top border of the first column until a down arrow displays and drag right to select the number of columns desired {press the right arrow key to select column(s) to the right}.

2. Place the mouse pointer on the **Insert Table** button on the Standard Toolbar {Alt and a}.

Note: The ToolTip displays ***Insert Columns.***

3. Click once on the **Insert Table** button {i}.

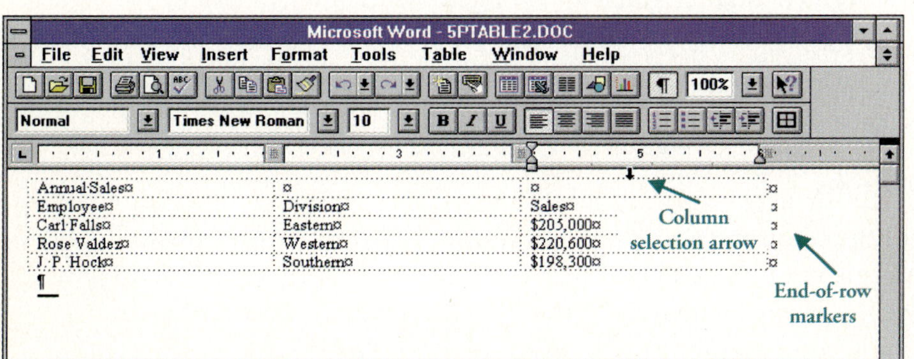

FIGURE 5.4

Selecting columns

Note: The new column is highlighted and the previously selected column is moved to the right of the document window.

Finish-Up Instructions

- ❖ If desired, scroll to the right to view the fourth column. Then, scroll the screen left to view the first three columns.
- ❖ Type the following information into the new column.

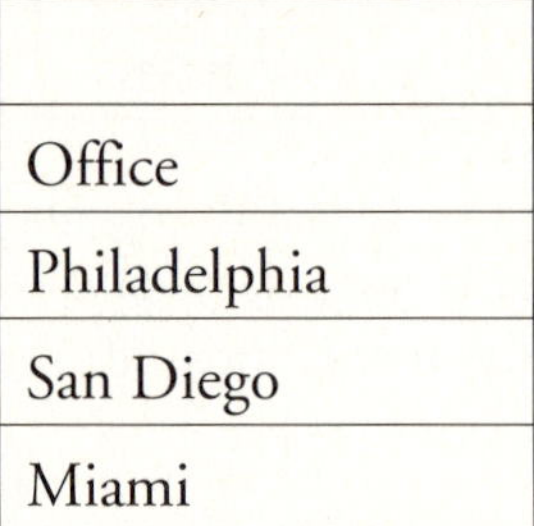

Office
Philadelphia
San Diego
Miami

- ❖ Use the *new* filename **5ptable3.doc** and save the file again on your file disk (select **File**, **Save As**; type the new filename; if necessary, click in the Drives box and click on the drive letter where the file disk is located; select **OK**).

Start-Up Instructions

- ❖ The file named **5ptable3.doc** should be displayed in the document window.

Change Column Widths

1. Move the mouse pointer to a table column border until a double-headed arrow displays {place the insertion point in any cell in the column to be changed}.

For example, point to the table column border between the first and second columns until the double-headed arrow displays {locate the insertion point in any cell in column one}.

2. *To decrease a column width,* press and hold the left mouse button while dragging the mouse to the left {Alt, a, w; Alt and c, press Tab, type the width desired, press Enter once}.

To increase a column width, press and hold the left mouse button while dragging the mouse to the right.

For example, visually estimate and drag the mouse pointer approximately .5 inch to the left until the column marker on the Ruler is located at approximately 1.5 inches {Alt, a, w, Alt and c, type 1.50, press Enter once}.

Note: The column width changes; the table width does not change. See Figure 5.5 for column width change options.

Finish-Up Instructions

- ❖ Move the mouse pointer to the column border between the second and third columns. Visually estimate and drag the column border to the left until the column marker is approximately at the $2^3/_4$ inch mark on the Ruler (the width of the second column is approximately $1^1/_4$ inches).

Procedure	Column Change	Table Change
Press and hold the **Shift** key. Obtain the two-headed arrow between two columns and drag the mouse to the desired column width.	Adjusts current column and one column to the right.	Table width does not change.
Press and hold the **Ctrl** key. Obtain the two-headed arrow between two columns and drag the mouse to the desired column width.	Adjusts current column and all columns to the right are equal width.	Table width does not change.
Press and hold the **Ctrl** and **Shift** keys. Obtain the two-headed arrow between two columns and drag the mouse to the desired column width.	Adjusts current column and no other columns widths are changed.	Table width changes.

FIGURE 5.5

Column width change options

- Repeat steps 1 and 2 of the Steps to Change Column Widths to decrease the widths in the third and fourth columns. Drag the column border between the third and fourth columns to the left so that the column marker is located at approximately 4 inches.
- Scroll to the right to view the right column border. Drag the column border at the right of the fourth column to the left so that the column marker is located at approximately $5^1/_4$ inches.
- Use the *new* filename **5ptable4.doc** and save the file on your file disk (select **File, Save As**; type the new filename; if necessary, click in the Drives box and click on the drive letter where the file disk is located; select **OK**).

Start-Up Instructions

- The file named **5ptable4.doc** should be displayed in the document window.

Steps to Merge Table Cells

1. *To select cells to be merged,* move the mouse pointer inside the left cell border until the right-pointing arrow displays. Press and hold the left mouse button while dragging the mouse to select the desired cells {place the insertion point in the first and/or left cell to be selected, press F8, press the arrow keys to select the desired cells}.

   To select an entire row to be merged, move the mouse pointer outside the gridline to the left side of the desired row until the right-pointing arrow displays; click once {place the insertion point in the first cell in the desired row, press F8, press Alt and End}.

   For example, select the cells in row 1.

2. Select **Table, Merge Cells** {Alt, a, m}.

   Note: An extra blank line appears in the row. Place the insertion point to the left of the paragraph (¶) symbol and press ***Delete****. If necessary, select the* ***Show/Hide*** *button on the Standard Toolbar to display the paragraph symbol.*

Finish-Up Instructions

- ❖ Use the same filename, **5ptable4.doc**, and save the file again (select the **Save** button).
- ❖ Continue with the Steps to Change Alignment of Cell Contents.

Start-Up Instructions

- ❖ The table named **5ptable4.doc** should be displayed in the document window.

Change Alignment of Cell Contents

1. Select the cells where justification is to be changed. (If necessary see step 1 in the Steps to Merge Table Cells on page 117}.

   For example, select all cells in rows 1 and 2.

2. Select the desired alignment button on the Formatting Toolbar {Alt, o, p; Alt and g, press the down arrow key to highlight the desired option, press Enter}.

   For example, select the **Center** alignment button.

Finish-Up Instructions

- ❖ If necessary, click once to deselect the table cells.
- ❖ Select the last three cells in the fourth column, which contain the sales amounts; select the **Align Right** button on the Formatting Toolbar.

  Note: *Your table should look similar to the following table:*

Annual Sales			
Employee	Division	Office	Sales
Carl Falls	Eastern	Philadelphia	$205,000
Rose Valdez	Western	San Diego	220,600
J. P. Hock	Southern	Miami	198,300

- ❖ Use the same filename, **5ptable4.doc**, and save the file again (select the **Save** button).

Start-Up Instructions

- ❖ The file named **5ptable4.doc** should be displayed in the document window.

Change Table Row Height

1. Select the row(s) where the row height is to be changed. (If necessary, see step 1 of the Steps to Merge Table Cells on page 117.)

   For example, select rows 1 and 2.

2. Select **Table, Cell Height and Width** {Alt a, w}.

   Note: *The Cell Height and Width dialog box displays (see Figure 5.6).*

3. Select the desired tab.

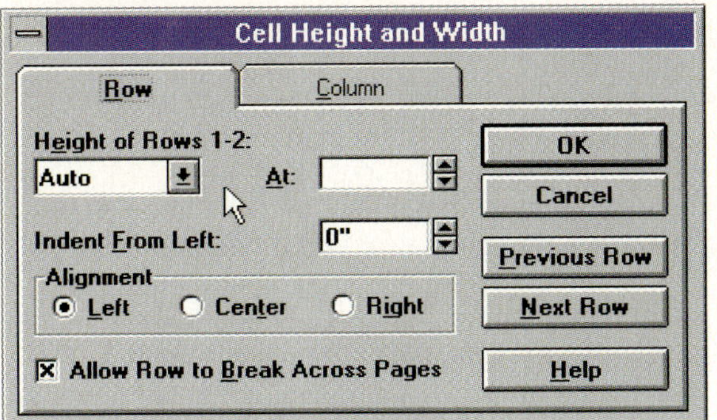

FIGURE 5.6

Cell Height and Width dialog box

For example, check that **Row** tab is selected. (If necessary, select the **Row** tab {Alt and r}.)

4. Move the mouse pointer to the down arrow below the Height of Rows option; click once {Alt and e}.
5. Select the desired height option.

   For example, select **At Least** {press the down arrow key}.
6. Change the setting in the **At** box either by clicking on the up/down arrows to increase/decrease the current setting or double-click on the figure in the At option box and type the desired setting {Alt and a, type desired setting}.

   For example, double-click on the figure in the **At** option and type **18.**

   Note: Typing the abbreviation pt. is unnecessary.
7. Select **OK** {press Enter once}.

   Note: Rows 1 and 2 are increased in height.

Finish-Up Instructions

- Click once to deselect the table rows.
- Use the *new* filename **5ptable5.doc** and save the file on your file disk (select **File**, **Save As**; type the new filename; if necessary, click in the Drives box and click on the drive letter where the file disk is located; select **OK**).

Start-Up Instructions

- The file named **5ptable5.doc** should be displayed in the document window.

Center a Table Horizontally

1. Place the insertion point in any cell in the table.
2. Select **Table, Cell Height and Width** {Alt, a, w}.

   Note: The Cell Height and Width dialog box displays and the Row tab should be selected (see Figure 5.6).
3. Select the desired option in the Alignment option box {Alt and L, t, or i to select the desired alignment option}.

   For example, select the **Center** option {Alt and t}.

4. Select **OK** {press Enter}.

   Note: The table displays horizontally centered in the document window.

Finish-Up Instructions

- Use the same filename, **5ptable5.doc**, and save the file again (select the **Save** button).
- Print one copy (select the **Print** button).
- Close the document (select **File**, **Close**).

Convert Tabbed Text to a Table

Text that is separated by tabs and hard returns can be easily converted to a table. Once the tabbed text is typed, select the columns, select the **Insert Table** button, or choose the **Convert Text to Table** option in the **Table** menu.

Once text is converted to a table, the information is contained in individual cells and surrounded by table gridlines. The information in the cells can be formatted and the structure of the table modified by using the buttons on the Formatting Toolbar (such as alignment, bold, italics, underline) or by selecting the desired options from the **Table** menu.

Start-Up Instructions

- Select the **New** button on the Standard Toolbar to create a new document.
- Type the text to be converted to a table. Press the **Tab** key once between each item and press the **Enter** key at the end of the first two lines. Do not press the **Enter** key after typing the last line.
- Type the information shown in Figure 5.7. (The columns may not appear aligned on the screen. That's OK.)

Steps to Convert Tabbed Text to a Table

1. Select all lines of the desired tabbed text.

   For example, select all four lines of text {Ctrl and a}.

2. Select the **Insert Table** button on the Standard Toolbar {Alt, a, v; i; check that the Tabs option is selected; if necessary, press Alt and t; press Enter}.

Finish-Up Instructions

- Change the widths in each column to approximately 1 inch. (If necessary, see the Steps to Change Column Widths on page 116.)

FIGURE 5.7

Tabbed text to be converted to a table

Tabs

```
AA     →SF  →  1086 →10:30 a.m.   Press Enter.
UA     →LA  →  2062 →8:20 a.m.    Press Enter.
Delta  →NY  →  234F →4:34 p.m.    Press Enter.
Alaska →LA  →  1282 →12:01 p.m.   Do not press Enter.
```

- Center the table horizontally (select **Table, Cell Height and Width, Row, Center, OK**).
- Use the filename **5ptable6.doc** and save the file on your file disk (select the **Save** button; type the filename; if necessary, click in the Drives box and select the drive letter where the file disk is located; select **OK**).

Apply Table AutoFormats

The cell and table gridlines that display in the document window will not print; the gridlines are displayed on the screen to assist you when entering and editing table text in a table. The gridlines can be turned on and off by choosing **Table, Gridlines.** Generally, you will find it helpful to turn on the gridlines when working with a table.

A variety of cell and table border styles can be added to a table. In addition, cells or groups of cells can be shaded or filled with a particular pattern. Word comes with a number of pre-formatted table styles that contain preset borders and fill patterns. Word refers to the pre-formatted table styles as Table AutoFormats. Using the Table AutoFormat feature is a very efficient method for formatting a table quickly.

Each Table AutoFormat can contain borders, shading, fonts, and colors. If desired, you can choose to apply only specific formats. For example, you might choose to apply only the borders and shading formats contained in a specific AutoFormat. When a Table AutoFormat is selected, the **AutoFit** option will adjust the widths of the columns to accommodate the column text. If table cells have been merged, deselect the **AutoFit** option before applying a Table AutoFormat.

Start-Up Instructions

- The file named **5ptable6.doc** should be displayed in the document window.

Apply a Table AutoFormat

1. Place the insertion point in any table cell.
2. Select **Table, Table AutoFormat** {Alt, a, f}.

   Note: The Table AutoFormat dialog box displays (see Figure 5.8).

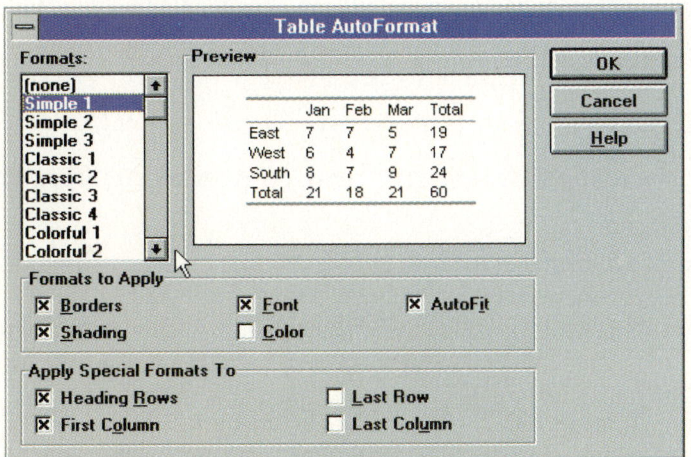

FIGURE 5.8

The Table AutoFormat dialog box

3. Select the desired format in the Formats list box {Alt and t, press the down arrow key to select the desired format}.

For example, scroll down the list and click on the **List 7** format.

Note: A sample of the format appears in the Preview box.

4. Choose **OK** {press Enter once}.

Finish-Up Instructions

- Notice that the text in the first column and row are bolded and that the rows are shaded. Bold all cell text. (If necessary, refer back to step 1 in the Steps to Merge Table Cells on page 117 for selecting cells.)
- Use the *new* filename **5ptable7.doc** and save the file on your file disk (select **File, Save As**; type the new filename; if necessary, click in the Drives box and click on the drive letter where the file disk is located; select **OK**).
- Optional. Print a copy of the file.

Start-Up Instructions

- The file named **5ptable7.doc** should be displayed in the document window.

Edit the Table AutoFormats

1. Place the insertion point anywhere within the table.
2. Select **Table, Table AutoFormat** {Alt, a, f}.

   Note: The Table AutoFormat dialog box displays (see Figure 5.8).

3. Select the desired format in the Formats list box {Alt and t, press the up or down arrow key to select the desired format}.

   For example, scroll through the list and select the **Colorful 2** format.

   Note: A sample of the format appears in the Preview box.

4. Select (or deselect) the desired formats in the Formats to Apply box {press Alt and b to deselect Borders; Alt and f to deselect Font; Alt and s to deselect Shading, etc.}.

   For example, deselect **Font**.

   Note: The italic and bold attributes disappear from the sample table in the Preview box.

5. Select **OK** {press Enter once}.

Finish-Up Instructions

- Insert a new row above the first row. (If necessary, refer to the Steps to Insert Table Rows on page 114).
- Type the following text in the new row.

Airline	City	Flight No.	Arrival Time

- Select the cells in the first row and change the point size to **14 points**. (If necessary, refer to step 1 in the Steps to Merge Table Cells on page 117 for selecting a row.)
- Adjust the column widths as necessary so that the contents of each cell are on a single line. (If necessary, refer to the Steps to Change Column Widths on page 116).
- Format the table using the List 4 AutoFormat and deselect the Shading option (select **Table**, **Table AutoFormat**, select **List 4** in the Formats list box, deselect **Shading**, and choose **OK**).
- Use the same filename, **5ptable7.doc**, and save the file (select the **Save** button).
- Print a copy of the table (select the **Print** button).

Chapter 5
Create a Table

Start-Up Instructions

- The file named **5ptable7.doc** should be displayed in the document window.

Steps to Remove a Table AutoFormat

1. Place the insertion point anywhere within the table.
2. Select **Table, Table AutoFormat** {Alt, a, f}.

   Note: The Table AutoFormat dialog box displays.
3. Select **(none)** at the top of the Formats list box {Alt and t, press the up arrow key to select (none)}.
4. Select **OK** {press Enter}.

Finish-Up Instructions

- Format the table again, using your choice of an **AutoFormat** option.
- Center the table horizontally (see the Steps to Center a Table Horizontally on page 119).
- Use the same filename, **5ptable7.doc**, and save the file (select the **Save** button).
- Optional. Print a copy of the file (select the **Print** button).

Center a Table or Text Vertically

Table rows or lines of text can be centered vertically on a page between the top and bottom margins. On an $8^1/_2$- by 11-inch sheet of paper, approximately 66 lines (6 lines per inch) or approximately 50 table rows (4.5 rows per inch) can be printed. Text that occupies fewer than 54 lines (66 – 12 = 2 inch top/bottom margins) and tables that occupy fewer than 45 rows will usually display more attractively on a page if the lines/rows are centered between the top and bottom margins. The tables typed in this book will be fewer than 20 rows; therefore, vertical centering will be useful.

Start-Up Instructions

- ❖ The file named **5ptable7.doc** should be displayed in the document window.

Center a Table or Text Vertically

1. With the insertion point located in any table cell, select **File, Page Setup** {Alt, f, u}.

   Note: The Page Setup dialog box displays.

2. Select the **Layout** tab {Alt and L}.
3. Move the mouse pointer to the down arrow next to the **Vertical Alignment** box and click the left mouse button once to display the list {Alt and v}.
4. Select the desired alignment option, then select **OK** {press the down arrow key to select the desired alignment option, then press Enter}.

   For example, select the **Center** vertical alignment option.

5. Select **OK** {Enter}.

   *Note: Select the **Print Preview** button on the Standard Toolbar to view the table centered vertically on the page. Select **Close** to return to the normal document view.*

Finish-Up Instructions

- ❖ Save the file again using the same filename, **5ptable7.doc** (select the **Save** button).
- ❖ Print one copy (select the **Print** button). Close the document (select **File, Close**).

The Next Step

Chapter Review and Activities

Self-Check Quiz

T F 1. A table can be created by selecting the **Insert Table** button on the Standard Toolbar.

T F 2. The intersection of each column and row is called a cell.

T F 3. The **Enter** key is pressed in the last row cell to insert a new table row.

T F 4. Formatting a table can include increasing or decreasing the table column widths.

T F 5. Text that is separated by tabs and hard returns can be converted to a table.

6. To indent text in a cell, press ______________.
   a. **Tab**
   b. **Shift** and **Tab**
   c. **Ctrl** and **Tab**
   d. either a or c

7. A table or text can be centered vertically on a page by selecting ____________.
   a. **Table, Cell Height and Width**
   b. **Table, Alignment**
   c. **Table, Table AutoFormat**
   d. none of the above

8. To select a table row, move the mouse pointer ______________.
   a. inside the first row of cell
   b. to the left of the row, outside the left table gridline
   c. to any row cell
   d. none of the above

9. State the primary purpose for formatting a table.

10. Give one reason for merging table cells.

Enriching Language Arts Skills

SCANS

Spelling/Vocabulary Words

initiative readiness to begin action.

strategic pertaining to the importance of accomplishing a plan.

alliances a joining together to meet a common goal.

Dollar Amount Formats

Use a comma to separate the number digits into groups of thousands. No space is placed between a number and the dollar sign. If even numbers are used in the body of a document or if a column of numbers has even dollar amounts, the zeros are omitted. Even dollar amounts should be right justified; if the numbers include decimal points, the numbers should be right aligned or a decimal tab should be set to align the numbers properly.

Example:

$28,655,342
1,389
10,843

Activities

Activity 5.1—Create and Format a Table and Align Numbers

1. In a new document window, create a table with 4 rows and 3 columns (select the **Insert Table** button on the Standard Toolbar, press and hold the mouse button while dragging to highlight a 4 x 3 table, release the mouse button).

2. Type the unformatted text as shown.

Abbey Growth Shares	Yearly increase	$2,303.50
FTI Growth Trust	Bi-annual increase	710.89
Noble Fidelity	Quarterly increase	515.26
Global Affiliates	Yearly increase	2,204.75

3. Use the filename **5atable1.doc** and save the file on your file disk (select the **Save** button; type the filename; if necessary, click in the Drives box and click on the drive letter where your file disk is located; select **OK**).
4. Use the following information to format the table:
    a. Change the alignment of the text in the third column to **Right** (select the third column and select the **Align Right** button on the Formatting Toolbar; click once to deselect the cells).
    b. Change the alignment of the text in the second column to **Center** (select the second column and select the **Center** alignment button on the Formatting Toolbar; click once to deselect the cells).
    c. Visually estimate and change the width of the third column to approximately 1 inch. (Place the mouse pointer on the column border at the right side of the table until the double-headed arrow displays; press and hold the mouse button while dragging the border to the left until the column marker on the Ruler is located at approximately 5 inches. Release the mouse button.)
    d. Select all table rows and select 12-point font size.
    e. Center the table horizontally on the page. (Place the insertion point in any table cell, select **Table, Cell Height and Width, Row** tab, **Center**).
    Note: Your table should look similar to the following table:

Abbey Growth Shares	Yearly increase	$2,303.50
FTI Growth Trust	Bi-annual increase	710.89
Noble Fidelity	Quarterly increase	515.26
Global Affiliates	Yearly increase	2,204.75

5. Use the same filename, **5atable1.doc**, and save the file again (select the **Save** button).
6. Print one copy (select the **Print** button).
7. Close the document (select **File, Close**).

Activity 5.2—Create and Format a Table, Insert Rows, Merge Cells, Change Row Height

1. In a new document window, create a table with 5 rows and 2 columns (select the **Insert Table** button on the Standard Toolbar, press and hold the mouse button while dragging to highlight a 5 x 2 table, release the mouse button).
2. Type the unformatted text as shown.

Arkansas	2,986,000
Kentucky	3,995,000
Nevada	1,200,000
North Carolina	6,481,350
Oregon	3,106,110

3. Use the filename **5atable2.doc** and save the file on your file disk (select the **Save** button; type the filename; if necessary, click in the Drives box and click on the drive letter where your file disk is located; select **OK**).
4. Change the alignment of the second column to **Right** (select the second column, select the **Align Right** button).
5. Insert three rows above the first row (select the first three rows, then select the **Insert Table** button on the Standard Toolbar).
6. Merge the cells in the first row (select the first row, select **Table**, **Merge Cells**).
7. Merge the cells in the second row (select the second row, select **Table**, **Merge Cells**).
8. Center all cells in the first three rows. (Select the first three rows, select the **Center** alignment button on the Formatting Toolbar.)
9. Change the row height for the first two rows to **24 points**. (Select the first two rows, select **Table**, **Cell Height and Width**, **Row** tab, click on the down arrow below the **Height of Rows 1-2** option, select **Exactly**, double-click on the number in the At box, type **24**, select **OK**.)
10. Locate the insertion point in row 1 and type the title **State Populations**. Notice that the text is centered.
11. Locate the insertion point in row 2 and type the subtitle (Approximately).
12. In row three, type the column heading **State** in the first cell and the heading **Population** in the second cell.
13. Visually estimate and change the width of each column to approximately 2 inches. (Place the mouse pointer on the column gridline between the columns until the double-headed arrow displays; press and hold the mouse button while dragging the gridline to the left until the column marker on the Ruler is located at approximately 2 inches. Release the mouse button. Locate the right column gridline at approximately 4 inches.)
14. Select the text in row 1 and change the font size to **18 point**. Select the text in row 2 and change the font size to **14 point**. (Select the row, select the down arrow beside the **Font Size** button, and choose the desired font size.)

15. Select and bold the text in row 3 (select row 3, select the **Bold** button).

Note: Your table should look similar to the following table:

State Populations	
(Approximately)	
State	**Population**
Arkansas	2,986,000
Kentucky	3,995,000
Nevada	1,200,000
North Carolina	6,481,350
Oregon	3,106,110

16. Center the table horizontally on the page (place the insertion point in any table cell, select **Table**, **Cell Height and Width**, **Row** tab, **Center**, **OK**).
17. Use the same filename, **5atable2.doc**, and save the file again.
18. Print one copy (select the **Print** button).
19. Close the document (select **File**, **Close**).

Activity 5.3—Create and Format a Table, Insert a Column, Apply AutoFormats, Center a Table Vertically

1. In a new document window, create a table with 5 rows and 2 columns (select the **Insert Table** button on the Standard Toolbar, press and hold the mouse button while dragging to highlight a 5 x 2 table, release the mouse button).
2. Type the unformatted text as shown.

Mortgage Affordability	
Annual Income	Mortgage Amount
$30,000	$60,000
50,000	120,000
70,000	171,000

3. Use the filename **5atable3.doc** and save the file on your file disk (select the **Save** button; type the filename; if necessary, click in the Drives box and click on the drive letter where your file disk is located; select **OK**).
4. Use the following information to format the table:

a. Insert a new column between the two columns in the table. (Select the second column, select the **Insert Table** button on the Standard Toolbar.)

b. Type the following information into the new column cells:

Home Prices
$75,000
141,700
215,000

Chapter 5 Create a Table

c. Merge the cells in the first row (select the first row, select **Table, Merge Cells**, click once to deselect the row, delete the paragraph symbol).

d. Center the title and column headings in the first two rows (select the first two rows, select the **Center** alignment button on the Formatting Toolbar, click once to deselect the rows).

e. Right align the dollar amounts in the last three rows (select the last three rows, select the **Align Right** button).

f. Visually estimate and change the width of the second and third columns to approximately 1½ inches. (Place the mouse pointer on the column gridline until the double-headed arrow displays; press and hold the mouse button while dragging the gridline left to the desired position. Release the mouse button. The column markers on the Ruler will be located at approximately 3½ inches and 5 inches.)

g. Apply the **Grid 8** AutoFormat to the table and deselect **AutoFit**. (With the insertion point in any table cell, select **Table, Table AutoFormat**, select **Grid 8**, deselect **AutoFit, OK.**)

*Note: If a mistake is made and AutoFit is not deselected, the width of the first row will change. If necessary, select **Edit, Undo AutoFormat** and complete step 4g again.*

h. Select and bold the text in the second row. (Select the second row, select the **Bold** button on the Formatting Toolbar, click once to deselect the row.)

Note: Your table should look similar to the following:

Mortgage Affordability		
Annual Income	**Home Prices**	**Mortgage Amount**
$30,000	$75,000	$60,000
50,000	141,700	120,000
70,000	215,000	171,000

5. Center the table horizontally on the page (place the insertion point in any table cell, select **Table, Cell Height and Width, Row** tab, **Center, OK**).

6. Center the table vertically on the page (place the insertion point in any table cell, select **File**, **Page Setup**, **Layout**, click on the down arrow next to the **Vertical Alignment** box, select **Center**, select **OK**).
7. Use the same filename, **5atable3.doc**, and save the file again.
8. Print one copy (select the **Print** button).
9. Close the document (select **File**, **Close**).

Activity 5.4—Create and Format a Table; Apply Table AutoFormat

1. In a new document window, create a table with 6 rows and 4 columns (select the **Insert Table** button, press and hold the mouse button while dragging to highlight a 6 x 4 table, release the mouse button).
2. Type the unformatted text as shown:

Daily Summary of Sales Calls			
October 19	General	Agency	Total
Calls answered	6,958	1,307	8,265
Calls lost	135	17	152
Inquiries	1,964	913	2,877
Bookings	725	306	1,031

3. Use the filename **5atable4.doc** and save the file on your file disk (select the **Save** button; type the filename; if necessary, click in the Drives box and click on the drive letter where your file disk is located; select **OK**).
4. Use the following information to format the table:
   a. Select the last three columns and change to **Right** alignment (select the **Align Right** button).
   b. Visually estimate and decrease the width of the second, third, and fourth columns to approximately 1 inch. (Place the mouse pointer on the desired column gridline until the double-headed arrow displays. Press and hold the mouse button while dragging the gridline left to the desired position. Release the mouse button. The column markers on the Ruler will be located at approximately $2^1/_2$, $3^1/_2$, and $4^1/_2$ inches.)
   c. Merge the cells in the first row (select row 1, select **Table**, **Merge Cells**, click once to deselect the row, delete any extra paragraph symbols).
   d. Center the title in row 1 (select row 1, select the **Center** alignment button).
   e. Change the row height for the last five rows to **22 points**; change the row height for row one to **30** point.s (Select the desired row(s), select **Table**, **Cell Height and Width**, **Row** tab, click on the down arrow below the Height of Rows option, select **At Least**, double-click on the number in the At box, type the desired size, select **OK**.)

f. Apply the **List 6** AutoFormat to the table and deselect **AutoFit**. (With the insertion point in any table cell, select **Table**, **Table AutoFormat**, select **List 6**, deselect **AutoFit**, select **OK**.)

Note: If a mistake is made and AutoFit is not deselected, the width of the first row will change. If necessary, select ***Edit, Undo AutoFormat*** *and complete step f again.*

5. Center the table horizontally on the page (place the insertion point in any table cell, select **Table**, **Cell Height and Width**, **Row**, **Center**, **OK**).

Note: Your table should look similar to the following:

Daily Summary of Sales Calls			
October 19	General	Agency	Total
Calls answered	6,958	1,307	8,265
Calls lost	135	17	152
Inquiries	1,964	913	2,877
Bookings	725	306	1,031

6. Center the table vertically on the page (place the insertion point in any table cell, select **File**, **Page Setup**, **Layout**, click on the down arrow next to the **Vertical Alignment** box, select **Center**, select **OK**).
7. Use the same filename, **5atable4.doc**, and save the file again.
8. Print one copy (select the **Print** button).
9. Close the document (select **File**, Close).

Challenge Your Skills

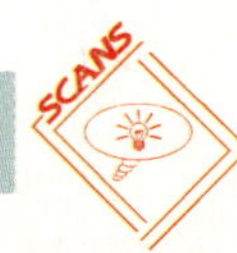

Skill 5.1—Create and Format a Table, Insert a Column, Change Row Height, and Apply Table AutoFormat

1. Create a table with 12 rows and 3 columns.
2. Type the information shown below in the table.

Parts List		
Item	Description	Part No.
A	Left upright	2307-8
B	Right upright	2308-3
C	Top shelf	2310-7
D	Rail	2311-5
E	Bottom shelf	2314-1

Chapter 5 Create a Table

F	Adjustable shelf	3400-5
G	Kick panel	3415-9
H	Back panel	3418-4
I	Screw	4420-3
J	Dowel	4425-9

3. Use the following information to format the table:

    a. Insert a new column between the second and third columns.

    b. Change the alignment for the new column to Center.

    c. Type the text as shown into the new column.

Quantity
1
2
1
4
1
3
1
1
9
14

    d. Change the alignment for the last column to Right.

    e. Change the font for the entire table to Bookman Old Style, 11 point.

    f. Adjust the widths of the columns so that the table information is appealing and easy to read.

    g. Merge the cells in row one.

    h. Change the alignment of row one to center.

    i. Change the height of the first row to a size larger than 18 point.

    j. Use a table AutoFormat of your choice.

4. Center the table horizontally and vertically.
5. Use the filename **5stable1.doc** and save the file.
6. Print one copy and close the document.

Skill 5.2—Create and Format a Table and Insert Rows and a Column

1. Create a table with 8 rows and 2 columns.
2. Type the unformatted text as shown:

Cost/Expense Items	Amount Budgeted
Salaries, program testers	$97,000
Salaries, system designers	157,000
Salaries, computer programmers	198,000
Salary, division manager	73,500
Computer supplies	41,000
Miscellaneous expenses	6,200
Insurance expenses	14,950

3. Use the following information to format the table:
   a. Insert a row at the top of the table. Set the row height for the new row to **24 points**.
   b. Insert a row above the item "Miscellaneous expenses."
   c. Type the following information into the new row:

      Computer equipment: 59,300
   d. Insert a column between the two columns.
   e. Type the following information into the new column cells, beginning in the second row. (Do not type the semicolons.)

      Actual Amount Spent; $98,125.60; 87,329.42; 134,216.75; 76,855.40; 47,320.55; 68,500.00; 6,125.50; 15,166.75
   f. Adjust the column widths so that the information appears attractive and easy to read.
   g. Merge the cells in row 1 and type the title **Pablo Consulting Services** in this row; use Center alignment.
   h. Make decisions regarding aligning the table information so that it appears attractive and easy to read.
   i. Use a Table AutoFormat of your choice. Modify the Table AutoFormat if desired.
4. Use the filename **5stable2.doc** and save the file.
5. Print one copy and close the document.

Skill 5.3—Create and Format a Memorandum with a Table; Language Arts

1. Use Memorandum—Style 1 and the following information:
   a. The memo should be sent to Ahmanson Food Supply Corp. from Eduardo Saucedo.
   b. The subject of the memo is New Vice President
   c. Use the current date; include your reference initials.
   d. Correct three spelling errors, one punctuation error, and one dollar amount format error.

e. After creating the table, format the cells as desired (e.g., increase or decrease column widths, change the alignment of column headings and dollar amounts, and choose the appropriate AutoFormat to apply).

f. The memorandum body text follows:

Terry Fitzgerald has been appointed to the position of Vice President, Marketing Development—Grocer, Sales & Integrated Logistics Division.

The role of Marketing Development continues to grow in importance as the foundation of Sales & Integrated Logistics' initative to pursue strategic customer aliances. In this new position Mr. Fitzgerald will be responsible for developing and directing startegic programs and partnership alliances with national and regional account grocery customers. He will report to Cathleen Cassel, Senior Vice President, Sales & Integrated Logistics Division, Ahmanson Food Supply Corp.

Reporting to Mr. Fitzgerald are:

Name	Accounts	Account Value
Ernest Garcia	Marketing Development & National Accounts	$494,000
Lyla Granado	Marketing Development & Eastern Region	215,000
Roger Hurtado	Marketing Development & Midwestern Region	97,000
Jackie Feldman	Marketing Development & Southern Region	89,000.00

Mr. Fitzgerald assumes his new responsibilities from the position of Regional Vice President, Broker Sales, Central Region. His office is located at 182 Bunsen Street, Hazelwood, MO 63042, and the telephone number is (314) 555-6202.

2. Use the filename **5stable3.doc** and save the file.
3. Print one copy.
4. Close the document.
5. If you have completed your work, exit Word.

CHAPTER 6

Edit a Table

Features Covered

- Move a row and column
- Delete a row and column
- Copy a table
- Delete a table
- Calculate column and row totals
- Customize table borders and shading
- Print double underlines

Objectives and Introduction

After successfully completing this chapter, you will be able to move and delete a table row and column and copy and delete a table. You will also be able to calculate a column or row total, customize table borders and shading, and use double underlines.

Once a table has been typed and printed, the table information can be edited. Changes can include moving or deleting columns and rows, customizing table borders and shading, using formulas to total a column or row, as well as copying or deleting an entire table.

Move a Table Column or Row

A table column or row can be moved to another column or row location within a table. When a column or row is moved, the column or row is deleted from the original location and relocated. When a column or row is copied, the column or row displays in the original location *and* in the new location.

The column or row to be moved must be selected before the move process can be performed. The selected row or column can also be moved by using the drag and drop or the cut and paste features (see Chapter 4).

FIGURE 6.1

Move a column using the drag and drop feature

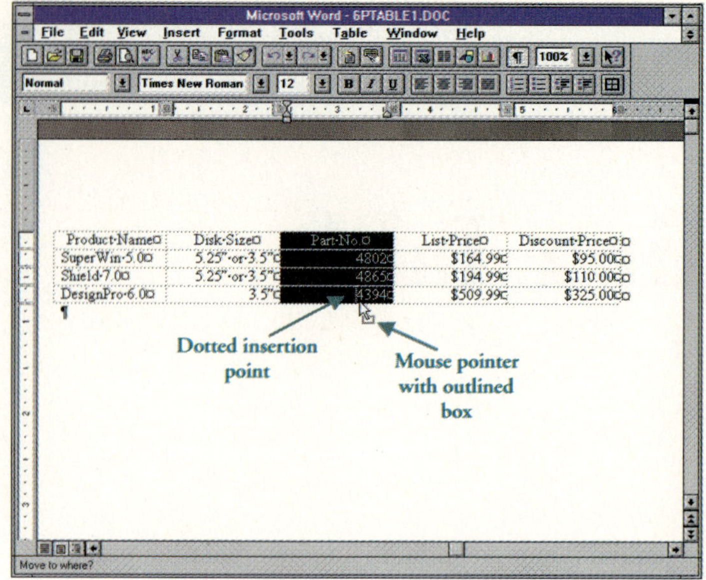

When using the cut and paste feature to move a column or row, the insertion point must be placed in the correct column or row before the **Paste** button is chosen. Before inserting a cut column, the insertion point is placed in any cell in the column that will be located to the right of the moved column. Before inserting a cut row, the insertion point is placed in any cell in the row that will be located below the moved row.

Start-Up Instructions

-  Open the file named **6ptable1.doc** located on the data disk.

  Note: If the table gridlines do not appear on the screen, select ***Table, Gridlines*** *{Alt, a, L}.*

- The nonprinting characters should be displayed. If necessary, select the **Show/Hide** ¶ button.

Steps to Move a Table Column

1. Select the column to be moved by moving the mouse pointer to the gridline at the top of the column until a down arrow displays. Click once to select and highlight the column {place the insertion point in the first cell in the column to be moved, press F8, press Alt and PgDn}.

   For example, move the mouse pointer to the gridline at the top of column 3 and click the mouse button once.

2. Move the mouse pointer into the selected column until the left-pointing arrow displays. Press and hold the mouse button until an outlined box displays at the bottom of the mouse pointer and a dotted insertion point appears (see Figure 6.1). Drag the dotted insertion point to the column that will appear to the right of the moved column. Release the mouse button {Ctrl and x, move the insertion point to the first column cell that will appear to the right of the moved column, press Ctrl and v}.

   For example, move the mouse pointer into the selected column until the left-pointing arrow displays, press and hold the mouse button and drag the dotted insertion point to column 2. Release the mouse button.

Note: Column 3 is moved to the left of column 2. A column can also be moved by using the ***Cut*** *and* ***Paste*** *buttons on the Standard Toolbar.*

3. Click once to deselect the column {press an arrow key}.

Finish-Up Instructions

- Use the *new* filename **6colmove.doc** and save the file on your file disk.
- Print one copy.

Start-Up Instructions

- The file named **6colmove.doc** should be displayed in the document window.
- If necessary, display the table gridlines (select **Table**, **Gridlines**).

Chapter 6 Edit a Table

Move a Table Row

1. Select the row to be moved by placing the mouse pointer outside the gridline to the left of the desired row until a right arrow displays and clicking once {place the insertion point at the left of the text in the first cell of the row to be moved, press F8, press the right arrow key repeatedly until all row cells are highlighted}.

    For example, move the mouse pointer outside the gridline to the left of row 3 and click once.

2. Move the mouse pointer into the selected row until the left-pointing arrow displays. Press and hold the mouse button until an outlined box displays at the bottom of the mouse pointer and a dotted insertion point appears. Drag the dotted insertion point to the first cell in the row that will be located below the moved row. Release the mouse button {Ctrl and x, move the insertion point to the first row cell that will display below the moved row, press Ctrl and v}.

    For example, move the mouse pointer into the selected row until the left-pointing arrow displays, press and hold the mouse button while dragging the dotted insertion point to the first cell in row 2. Release the mouse button.

    Note: Row 3 is moved above row 2. The row can also be moved by using the ***Cut*** *and* ***Paste*** *buttons on the Standard Toolbar.*

3. Click once to deselect the row {press an arrow key}.

Finish-Up Instructions

- With the insertion point in any table cell, select **Table**, **Table AutoFormat**, click on the **Classic 2** format. Select **OK**.

    Note: Your table should look similar to the following:

Product Name	Part No.	Disk Size	List Price	Discount Price
Shield 7.0	4865	5.25" or 3.5"	$194.99	$110.00
SuperWin	4802	5.25" or 3.5"	$164.99	$95.00
Design Pro 6.0	4894	3.5"	$509.00	$325.00

- Use the *new* filename **6rowmove.doc** and save the file on your file disk.
- Print one copy.

Delete a Table Column or Row

When editing a table, a column or row can be deleted. A column or row is deleted by first selecting the column or row to be deleted and then selecting the **Delete Columns** or **Delete Rows** option in the **Table** menu. The Delete option in the **Table** menu changes depending on the selected cells. If a row is selected, the Delete option displays **Delete Rows** and if a column is selected, the Delete option displays **Delete Columns**. When a portion of a column or row is selected, the Delete option displays **Delete Cells**. A column or row can also be deleted by selecting the row or column and then selecting the **Cut** button on the Standard Toolbar.

If a column or row is deleted by mistake, **Edit**, **Undo** can be selected (or select the **Undo** button on the Standard Toolbar) to retrieve and display the deleted column or row. If other actions have been performed after the column or row was deleted, select **Edit**, **Undo** (or the **Undo** button) repeatedly until the correct row or column displays.

Start-Up Instructions

- The file named **6rowmove.doc** should be displayed in the document window.

Delete a Table Column

1. Select the column to be deleted. (If necessary, refer to step 1 in the Steps to Move a Table Column on page 136).

   For example, select column 2.

2. Select **Table, Delete Columns** {Alt, a, d}.

   Note: *The second column is deleted and the columns on the right move to the left. If a table column is deleted by mistake, select the* ***Undo*** *button to retrieve the deleted column.*

Finish-Up Instructions

- Center the table horizontally (with the insertion point in any table cell, select **Table**, **Cell Height and Width**, **Row**, choose **Center** alignment, **OK**).

❖ Use the *new* filename **6delete.doc** and save the file on your file disk.

❖ Print one copy (select the **Print** button).

Start-Up Instructions

❖ The file named **6delete.doc** should be displayed in the document window.

Delete a Table Row

1. Select the row to be deleted. (If necessary, refer to step 1 in the Steps to Move a Table Row on page 137.)

For example, select row 2.

2. Select **Table, Delete Rows** {Alt, a, d}.

Note: *Row 2 is deleted. If a table row is deleted by mistake, select the* ***Undo*** *button to retrieve the deleted row.*

Finish-Up Instructions

❖ Insert a new row above the first row (place the insertion point in any first row cell, select the **Insert Table** button).

❖ Merge the cells in the first row (with row 1 selected, choose **Table, Merge Cells**, click once to deselect the row).

❖ With the insertion point in row 1, type the title **Product List**.

❖ Use the *new* filename **6delrow.doc** and save the file on your file disk.

Chapter 6 Edit a Table

Copy a Table

An entire table can be copied to another window or to another location within the current document window. A table can be copied for many reasons including:

- making changes to the copied table without changing the original table
- saving paper by placing two items on a page or
- using the table information in another letter, memorandum, or report

Start-Up Instructions

❖ The file named **6delrow.doc** should be displayed in the document window.

Copy a Table

1. Select the entire table by obtaining the right-pointing arrow outside the gridline to the left of the first row, pressing and holding the mouse button and dragging downward to select all rows of the table {place the insertion point anywhere within the table; with NumLock off, press Alt and numeric keypad 5}.

2. Select the **Copy** button on the Standard Toolbar {Alt, e, c *or* Ctrl and c}.

3. Locate the insertion point at the desired position.

For example, locate the insertion point below the table and press **Enter** twice to insert blank lines.

4. Select the **Paste** button on the Standard Toolbar {Alt, e, p *or* Ctrl and v}.

   Note: *A copy of the table is inserted at the location of the insertion point.*

Finish-Up Instructions

- Use the *new* filename **6tcopy.doc** and save the file on your file disk.
- Continue with the Steps to Delete a Table or close the document.

Delete a Table

A table can be deleted by selecting the entire table and using the **Delete Rows** option in the **Table** menu. If a table is deleted by mistake, select the **Undo** button on the Standard Toolbar to retrieve and redisplay the deleted table.

Start-Up Instructions

- The file named **6tcopy.doc** should be displayed in the document window.

Delete a Table

1. Select the table to be deleted. (If necessary, refer to step 1 in the Steps to Copy a Table).

   For example, select the first table on the screen.

2. Select **Table, Delete Rows** {Alt, a, d}.

Finish-Up Instructions

- Close the document and do not save the file.

Calculate a Column or Row Total

Table cells containing numbers (values) can be calculated by using formulas to add, subtract, multiply, or divide. A value is a number used to obtain a mathematical result. A text number is a number that will not be used to compute a result. Examples of text numbers are a social security number or a year (e.g., 1995).

Columns and rows are totaled by using a table formula. Table formulas are easily created in the Formula dialog box. The insertion point is first placed in the cell that will contain the column or row calculation and then the **Formula** option is selected from the **Table** menu. The Formula dialog box displays, and the appropriate formula is typed or constructed by choosing a function(s).

When the Formula dialog box displays, the SUM formula appears in the Formula box. (Word assumes the cells are to be added.) If the cells are not to be added, a different formula can be typed or options can be selected from the Functions box to create the desired formula.

The results of the formula are inserted into the cell as a field. The field contains special codes that instruct Word to insert information into the table cell. The result of the field displays in the table cell and is shaded gray when the I-beam is moved to the result value and the mouse button is clicked. When the formula result displays in gray, the field codes can be turned on or off by moving the mouse pointer to the center of the formula result, pressing the *right* mouse button, and selecting the Toggle Field Codes option. The field code replaces the gray result, e.g., { =SUM(ABOVE) }. If field codes are turned on in Normal view, only the field code in the gray cell displays. If field codes are turned on in Page Layout view, all cells containing formulas display field codes.

A formula is deleted by selecting and highlighting the cell that contains the formula and either pressing **Delete**, selecting the **Cut** button on the Standard Toolbar, or selecting the **Cut** option in the **Edit** menu. The cell must be selected by pointing the mouse to the bottom of the cell until the right arrow displays and then clicking the mouse button once.

If numbers (values) are changed in the table cells, the cells that contain formula results will need to be recalculated. The **Formula** option in the **Table** menu is used to recalculate existing formulas. The formula result can also be updated by selecting the **Update Field** option on the shortcut menu.

The number format used in the formula results will be the same as the highlighted values. For example, if the formula =SUM(ABOVE) is used to calculate the sum of the cells in column 3 and those cells all contain dollar signs, Word will include a dollar sign in the total amount. If desired, the number format for the formula results can be changed in the Formula dialog box.

Start-Up Instructions

- Open the file named **6calc.doc** located on the data disk.
- The nonprinting characters should be displayed. If necessary, select the **Show/Hide ¶ button.**

Use a Formula to Calculate the Sum of a Column

1. Select the cell that will contain the formula results.

   For example, select the last cell of column 2.

2. Select **Table, Formula** {Alt, a, o}.

   Note: The Formula dialog box displays as shown in Figure 6.2

3. Create the appropriate formula in the Formula box either by typing the formula or by selecting a **Paste Function** option {Alt and u} and then completing the formula by typing the necessary information in the Formula box.

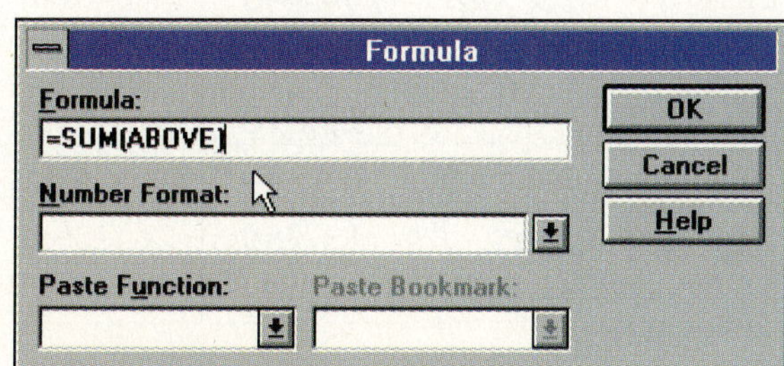

FIGURE 6.2

Formula dialog box

For example, check that the formula =*SUM(ABOVE)* displays in the Formula box. (If necessary, type **=SUM(ABOVE)** in the Formula box.)

4. In the Number Format box, type the desired format or select the down arrow beside the Number Format box and choose a format {Alt and n).

   For example, click in the Number Format box and type **$#,###**. (Do not type the period.)

   Note: If no number format is specified, Word attempts to apply a format by using the same format as the numbers in the cells being totaled.

5. Select **OK** {press Enter}.

   *Note: The figure **$133,074** displays in the last cell of column 2.*

Finish-Up Instructions

- Calculate the sum of column 3 (select the last cell of column 3 and repeat steps 2–5 in the Steps to Use a Formula to Calculate the Sum of a Column).
- Use the *new* filename **6calcexp.doc** and save the file on your file disk.

Start-Up Instructions

- The file named **6calcexp.doc** should be displayed in the document window.
- Edit the table as shown in Figure 6.3.

Steps to Edit Table Figures and Recalculate

1. After the table figures are changed, highlight the formula results by placing the I-beam pointer in the desired figure and clicking once {press Tab to move the insertion point to the desired cell}.

   For example, highlight the formula result in the last cell of column 2.

   Note: A highlighted formula result appears a shaded gray. Check that only the figure is shaded gray. (Do not highlight the entire cell.)

2. Select **Table, Formula** {Alt, a, o}.

   Note: The Formula dialog box displays.

FIGURE 6.3

Edited table

Expense Category	Eastern Division	Western Division
Indirect labor	62,140 $~~59,850~~	$65,815
Materials	17,455	19,630 ~~20,250~~
Supplies	19,610	23,430
Utilities	21,907 ~~22,379~~	23,710 ~~25,670~~
Insurance	13,780	15,875
TOTALS	$133,074	$151,040

Recalculate totals

3. Verify that the formula in the Formula text box is correct and that the Number Format is correct, then select **OK** {press Enter}.

   Note: The original formula results are replaced with the recalculated formula results.

Shortcut

1. Move the I-beam to the figure in the cell containing a formula.
2. Click the *right* mouse button once.
3. Select **Update Field**.

Finish-Up Instructions

- Recalculate the formula result in the last cell in column 3 (highlight the formula result in the last cell of column 3, repeat steps 2 and 3 in the Steps to Edit Table Figures and Recalculate).
- Use the same filename, **6calcexp.doc**, and save the file again.
- Print one copy.

Start-Up Instructions

- The file named **6calcexp.doc** should be displayed in the document window.
- The nonprinting characters should be displayed. If necessary, select the **Show/Hide ¶** button.
- Insert one table column after column 3 (move the mouse pointer to the top of the end-of-row markers until the down arrow displays and click once to highlight the end-of-row markers. Select the **Insert Table** button on the Standard Toolbar).
- Type the column heading **Total Expenses** in the first cell of column 4.

Steps to Total a Row

1. Select the cell where the new total is to be inserted.

   For example, select the second cell in the last column.

2. Select **Table, Formula** {Alt, a, o}.

   Note: The Formula dialog box displays.

3. Create the appropriate formula in the Formula box either by typing the formula or by selecting a Paste Function option {Alt and u} and then completing the formula by typing the necessary information in the Formula box.

   For example, check that the formula **=SUM(LEFT)** displays in the Formula box. (If necessary, type **=SUM(LEFT)** in the Formula box.)

4. In the Number Format box, type the desired format or select the down arrow beside the Number Format box and choose a format {Alt and n).

   For example, click in the Number Format box and type **$#,###**. (Do not type the period.)

5. Select **OK** {press Enter}.

Note: The figure $127,955 displays.

Finish-Up Instructions

- Calculate the total of rows 3 through 7 by repeating steps 2–5 in the Steps to Total a Row.

  Note: When the formula =SUM(ABOVE) displays, change the word Above to Left, i.e., =SUM(LEFT).

- Insert a new row above the first row in the table (place the insertion point in any cell in row 1, select the **Insert Table** button).
- Merge the cells in row 1 (select row 1, choose **Table, Merge Cells**).
- Type the title **Division Expenses** in the top row of the table. Check that all headings are centered.

  Note: Your table should look similar to the following table:

Division Expenses			
Expense Category	Eastern Division	Western Division	Total Expenses
Indirect labor	$62,140	$65,815	$127,995
Materials	17,455	19,630	37,085
Supplies	19,610	23,430	43,040
Utilities	21,907	23,710	45,617
Insurance	13,780	15,875	29,655
TOTALS	$134,892	$148,460	$283,352

- Use the *new* filename **6recalc.doc** and save the file on your file disk.
- Print one copy.

Customize Table Borders and Shading

In Chapter 5, instructions for applying autoformats to tables were discussed. In this chapter, applying individual borders and shading options is discussed. Rather than choosing from various pre-formatted combinations of borders and shades for an entire table, individual borders and shades can be applied to a table. For example, borders can be placed around a single cell, a group of cells, or the entire table. Or, only row borders (horizontal lines) or column borders (vertical lines) can be added. The style of the borders can vary from solid lines of varied thickness to double or dashed lines.

In addition to adding borders, cells can be shaded (filled) with a variety of shades or fill patterns. Shades (or gradients) generally refer to a certain shaded percentage of a color. For example, a 10% shade appears as a light gray. Customized borders and shades are often used to draw attention to certain parts of a table, such as row or column total or a grand total.

Borders and shading are applied by using either the Borders Toolbar or the **Borders and Shading** option in the **Format** menu. After selecting the desired cells, click on the **Borders** button on the Formatting Toolbar to display the Borders Toolbar (see Figure 6.4). The buttons on the Borders Toolbar are used to specify the width and position of borders and the type of shading to apply. When the mouse pointer is placed on any button in the Borders Toolbar, a ToolTip (description of the button) displays. Select the **Borders** button again to turn off the Borders Toolbar.

To remove borders, display the Borders Toolbar and select the **No Border** button. *To remove individual borders,* select the cells to which the border has been applied, display the Borders Toolbar, and click to deselect the highlighted border button(s). *To remove shading,* select the cells to which the shading has been applied, display the Borders Toolbar, and click on the down arrow next to the **Shading** box, then select **Clear**.

Start-Up Instructions

- The file named **6recalc.doc** should be displayed in the document window.
- The table gridlines should be displayed. (If necessary, select **Table**, **Gridlines**.)
- Increase the row height of the first two rows to **24 point** (select the first two rows, select **Table**, **Cell Height and Width**, **Row**, **Height of Rows 1-2**, **Exactly**, select the figure in the At box, type **24**, select **OK**).
- Select the remaining rows and increase the row height to **18** point.

Steps to Apply Borders to All Cells in a Table

1. Select the entire table by obtaining the right arrow outside the gridline to the left of row 1, drag the mouse downward to select all rows {place the insertion point in any table cell; with NumLock off, press Alt and numeric keypad 5}.
2. Select the **Borders** button on the Formatting Toolbar {Alt, o, b}.

   *Note: The Borders Toolbar displays below the Formatting Toolbar (see Figure 6.4). (If the **Borders and Shading** option in the **Format** menu is selected, the Table Borders and Shading dialog box displays.)*
3. To place a border around all cells, select the **Inside Border** button on the Borders Toolbar, then select the **Outside Border** button {Alt and g, Enter}.
4. Click once to deselect the table cells {press an arrow key}.

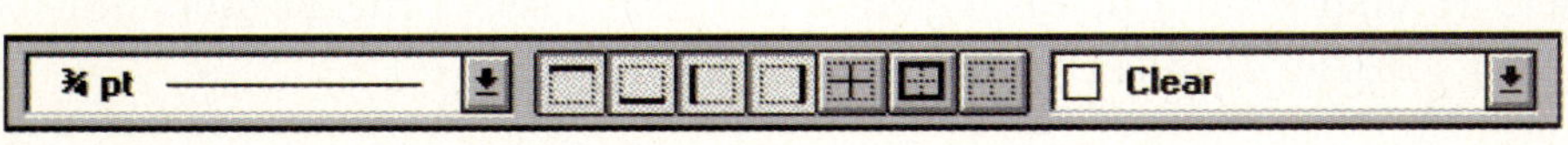

FIGURE 6.4

Borders Toolbar

FIGURE 6.5

Line Style options

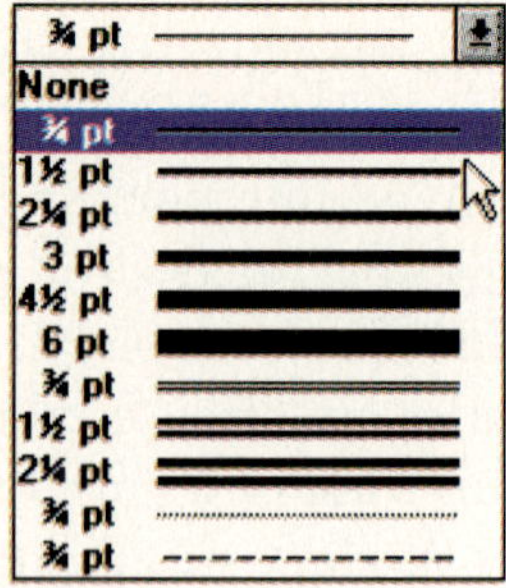

Note: Borders display around all table cells.

Finish-Up Instructions

- Use the *new* filename **6border.doc** and save the file on your file disk.

Start-Up Instructions

- The file named **6border.doc** should be displayed in the document window.
- The Borders Toolbar should be displayed. If necessary, select the **Borders** button on the Formatting Toolbar.

Modify a Row Border

Note: A mouse must be used to perform the following steps.

1. Select the row to be modified.

   For example, select row 1.

2. Click on the down arrow next to the **Line Style** box on the Borders Toolbar (see Figure 6.5) and select the desired style or thickness.

   For example, select the **4½ pt** line style.

3. Select the desired border button on the Borders Toolbar (Top Border, Bottom Border, Left Border, or Right Border).

   For example, select the **Bottom Border** button.

4. Click once to deselect the row.

   Note: The line style for the bottom of row 1 displays as 4½ point line.

Finish-Up Instructions

- Select row 2 in the table and change the bottom border of row two to the 2¼ pt line style (select row 2 and repeat steps 2–4 in the Steps to Modify a Row Border).
- Use the *new* filename **6modbord.doc** and save the file on your file disk.

Start-Up Instructions

- The file named **6modbord.doc** should be displayed in the document window.
- The Borders Toolbar should be displayed. If necessary, select the **Borders** button on the Formatting Toolbar.

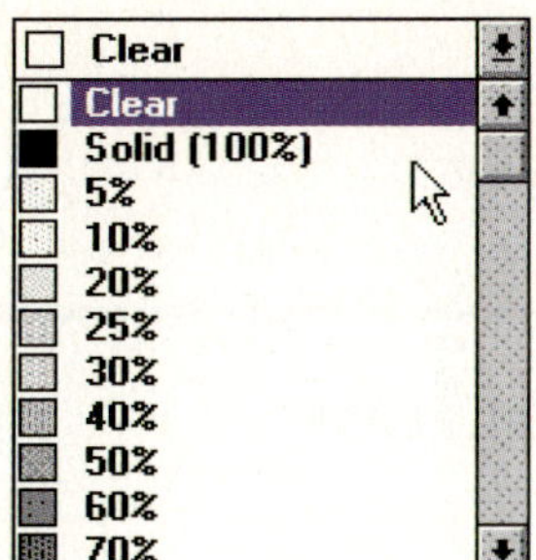

FIGURE 6.6

Shading options

Apply Shading to Table Cells

1. Select the cell or cells to be shaded.

   For example, select all cells in column 4 that contain the total expense figures, including the column heading.

2. Click the down arrow beside the Shading box on the Borders Toolbar to display the drop-down list of available fills (see Figure 6.6). Select the desired shade {Alt, o, b; Alt and s to display the Shading tab: Alt and d, press the down arrow key to select the desired shade, Enter}.

   For example, select **20%**.

3. Click once to deselect the cells {press an arrow key}.

   Note: A 20% shade displays on the screen in column 4.

Finish-Up Instructions

- Select the last table row and apply a **20%** shade (repeat steps 2 and 3 of the Steps to Apply Shading to Table Cells).
- Select rows 1 and 2, then select the **Bold** button on the Formatting Toolbar.
- Use the same filename **6modbord.doc** and save the file again.
- Print one copy.

  Note: Your table should look similar to the following:

Division Expenses			
Expense Category	**Eastern Division**	**Western Division**	**Total Expenses**
Indirect labor	$62,140	$65,815	$127,955
Materials	17,455	19,630	37,085
Supplies	19,610	23,430	43,040
Utilities	21,907	23,710	45,617
Insurance	13,780	15,875	29,655
TOTALS	$134,892	$148,460	$283,352

- Close the document.
- Remove the Borders Toolbar from the screen (select the **Borders** button).

Print Double Underlines Below the Total Amount

Double underlines are placed under a column total amount in order to emphasize the total. If double underlines are used, table borders generally are not printed. When a column is totaled, a single underline is used to separate the last column amount from the total amount. The single underline traditionally is formatted to extend the width of the total amount. Therefore, one or more spaces are placed to the left of the last column number to extend the underline.

Traditionally, the dollar sign ($) in the first figure and the last figure of a column have been formatted to align. Since there is often an additional digit in the total amount, extra space is needed between the dollar sign and the first digit in the first column entry. Placing a space in the Number Format box when typing the desired format will provide the extra space to ensure the alignment of the dollar signs.

Once the column total has been calculated, the amount is selected and the **Font** option in the **Format** menu is chosen. In the Font dialog box that displays, the underline style is changed to double.

Start-Up Instructions

- Open the file named **6underl.doc** located on the data disk.
- Place the insertion point between the dollar sign and the first digit of the figure in row 3, column 2. Press the **Spacebar** three times. Repeat for the figures in row 3, columns 3 and 4.
- Underline the cells in row 4 that contain figures (select the cells containing the figures, select the **Underline** button).
- Extend the underline below the last column amount in each cell of row 4 (place the insertion point to the left of the first digit in the cell and press the **Spacebar** repeatedly until the underline extends the length of the total amount including the dollar sign).
- Click once to deselect the cells {press an arrow key}.

Print Double Underlines

1. Select the desired cells.

   For example, select the cells in row 5 that contain total amounts.

2. Select **Format, Font** {Alt, o, f}.

   Note: *The Font dialog box displays.*

3. Select the the desired tab.

   For example, check that the Font tab is selected. (If necessary, select the **Font** tab {Alt and n}.)

4. Click the down arrow to the left of the **Underline** box to display the list of available underline styles {Alt and u}.
5. Select **Double** {press the down arrow key to select Double}.
6. Select **OK** {Enter}.
7. Click once to deselect the cells {press an arrow key}.

Finish-Up Instructions

- Use the *new* filename **6double.doc** and save the file on your file disk.
- Print one copy.
- Close the document.

The Next Step

Chapter Review and Activities

Self-Check Quiz

T F 1. A table row or column can be moved.

T F 2. To delete a table column, select the column and press **Delete**.

T F 3. An entire table can be copied to another document window or to another location in the current document window.

T F 4. If values in table cells are changed, the column or row totals can be recalculated by selecting the **Recalculate** option in the **Table** menu.

5. A row can be deleted by selecting the ___________ option in the **Table** menu.
   a. **Delete Table**
   b. **Delete Row**
   c. **Delete Formatting**
   d. none of the above

6. A moved column is deleted from the original location and ___________ a new location.
   a. duplicated in
   b. copied to
   c. relocated to
   d. reproduced in

7. The _____________ Toolbar is used to apply borders and shading to table cells.
   a. Formatting
   b. Rows and Columns
   c. Borders
   d. Standard

8. To print double underlines, the ___________ dialog box must be displayed.
   a. Character Format
   b. Paragraph Format
   c. Style
   d. none of the above

9. Write down the formula to sum the contents of cells in a table row.

10. Give one reason for adding borders and/or shading to a table.

Enriching Language Arts Skills

Spelling/Vocabulary Words

adversely having an unfavorable effect.

per diem an amount allowed for daily expenses.

reimbursement money repaid for expenses incurred.

Single and Double Underlines for Dollar Amounts

Place a single underline between the last column amount and the total amount. Traditionally, the single underline extends the width of the amount with the most characters, including the dollar sign. Add spaces before the digits in the last column amount to extend the underline. In a table without borders, a total amount is usually emphasized by placing double underlines beneath the total amount.

Example:

```
$110,550
   3,600
   2,820
$116,970
```

Activities

Activity 6.1—Calculate the Total of the Columns and Row

1. In a new document window, create a table with 4 columns and 6 rows.
2. Type the unformatted information as shown:

   ***Remember:** Text will automatically wrap around in cells.*

General Fund Disbursements			
Fund	June	July	Totals
Equipment replacement	$86,000	$28,900	
Maintenance	72,000	29,750	
Interfund transfers	53,400	15,210	
Totals			

3. Use the following information to format the table:
   a. Center and bold the title and column headings in the first two rows (select the rows, select the **Center** alignment button and the **Bold** buttons).
   b. Right align the cells containing amounts and the cells that will contain the totals. It's OK that some of the cells are currently empty (select the desired cells and choose the **Align Right** button).
   c. Calculate the sum for columns 2 and 3 (select the last cell of column 2, select **Table, Formula**; the Formula box displays *=SUM(ABOVE),* click in the Number Format box, type **$#,###**, select **OK**). Select the last cell in column 3 and repeat these instructions.
   d. Calculate the total for row three, column four (select the desired cell, select **Table, Formula**; the Formula box displays *=SUM(LEFT),* click in the Number Format box, type **$#,###**, select **OK**).
   e. Follow the instruction in step 3d and calculate the row totals for rows 4–6. Change the formula to read *=SUM(LEFT)* in rows 4 and 5 and do not include the dollar sign. Include the dollar sign when typing the Number Format for the last cell in row 6.
   f. Insert two spaces between the dollar sign and the first digit in row three, column 2 to align the dollar sign with the column totals.
   g. If necessary, visually estimate and adjust the column widths so that the columns containing figures are approximately the same width.
   h. Merge the cells in row 1 (select row 1, select **Table, Merge Cells**, delete the paragraph symbol).
4. Center the table horizontally (place the insertion point in any cell, select **Table, Cell Height and Width, Row** tab, **Center, OK**).
5. Add inside and outside borders to the table, using the **3/4 pt** line style (select the entire table, select the **Borders** button, check that 3/4 pt displays in the Line Style box, select the **Inside Border** and the **Outside Border** buttons).

   Note: *Your table should look similar to the following table:*

General Fund Disbursements			
Fund	**June**	**July**	**Totals**
Equipment replacement	$ 86,000	$28,900	$114,900
Maintenance	72,000	29,750	101,750
Interfund transfers	53,400	15,210	68,610
Totals	$211,400	$73,860	$285,260

6. Use the filename **6atable1.doc** and save the file on your file disk.
7. Print one copy and close the document.

Activity 6.2—Move Columns and Rows, Copy and Delete a Table, Apply Borders and Shading

1. In a new document window, create a table with 4 columns and 7 rows.
2. Type the unformatted information as shown:

   Remember: *Text will automatically wrap around in cells.*

Kidwell Products			
Annual Conference Costs			
Item	1993	1994	1995
Promotional materials	$10,950	$12,430	$11,738
Registration fees	3,400	3,600	3,600
Accommodations and meals	59,600	60,120	60,930
Travel	38,200	37,350	39,000

3. Move the columns and rows as described in the following instructions:
   a. Move column 4 (the 1995 information) between columns 1 and 2 (select column 4, move the mouse pointer into the selected column until a left pointing arrow displays, press and hold the mouse button while dragging the dotted insertion point to column 2, release the mouse button).
   b. Move the now column 4 (the 1994 information) between columns 2 and 3 (see step 3a, if necessary).
   c. Move row 6 (Accommodations and meals) above row 5 (Registration fees) (select row 6, move the mouse pointer into the selected row cell until a left pointing arrow displays, press and hold the mouse button

while dragging the dotted insertion point to row 5, release the mouse button).

4. Use the following instructions to format the table:

    a. Increase the width of the first column so that the text displays on one line. If necessary, visually estimate and adjust the widths of the remaining columns so that those columns are smaller than the first column.

    b. Right align the cells containing the years and dollar amounts.

    c. Merge the cells in row 1 (select row 1, select **Table**, **Merge Cells**, delete the paragraph symbol). Repeat to merge the cells in row 2.

    d. Center and bold the title and subtitle in rows 1 and 2 (select rows 1 and 2, select the **Center** alignment button and the **Bold** button).

    e. Select the entire table and change the row height to **24 point** (select **Table**, **Cell Height and Width**, **Row** tab, **Height of Rows**, **Exactly**, **At**, type 24, **OK**).

    f. Select cells 3–7 in column 1 and use a **10%** shade (select the cells, click the **Borders** button, select the down arrow beside the **Shading** box, select **10%**). Repeat to use a 20% shade for rows 1 and 2.

    g. Add inside and outside table borders, using the **$^3/_4$ pt** line style (select the entire table; select the **Inside Border** button, then select the **Outside Border** button).

    h. Center the table horizontally (place the insertion point in any table cell, select **Table**, **Cell Height and Width**, **Row** tab, **Center**, **OK**).

    i. Change the bottom border of row 2 to the **$1^1/_2$ pt** line style (select row 2, click on the down arrow next to the Line Style box, select **$1^1/_2$ pt.**, choose the **Bottom Border** button). Repeat to change the right border of rows 3–7 in column 1 to the $1^1/_2$ pt line style (select rows 3–7 in column 1, choose the **Right Border** button).

5. Copy the entire table (select the entire table and select the **Copy** button).

6. Move the insertion point to the end of the document below the table, and press **Enter** twice to insert two new blank lines. Select the **Paste** button to insert a copy of the table.

7. Use the filename **6ctable2.doc** and save the file on your file disk.

8. Print one copy.

9. Delete the first table (select the entire table and choose **Table**, **Delete Rows**).

10. Optional. Print the table.

11. Close the document (do not save the modified file).

Activity 6.3—Calculate Column Totals, Delete a Row and Column, Delete Borders and Shading, and Print Double Underlines

1. Open the file named **6table3.doc** located on the data disk.

2. Calculate the sum of column two (select the last cell of column 2, select **Table**, **Formula**, check that the formula *=SUM(ABOVE)* displays, select the down arrow beside the Number Format box, select the **$#,##0.00;($#,##0.00)** format, select **OK**). Repeat to calculate the sum of columns 3 and 4.
3. Use the new filename **6cost3.doc** and save the file on your file disk.
4. Edit the table as follows:
    a. Delete row eight that contains the Deck repairs information (select the row, select **Table**, **Delete Rows**).
    b. Recalculate the total in column two (move the I-beam to column 3 and click once to display the gray shading, click the *right* mouse button, and select **Update Field**). Repeat to recalculate the totals in columns 3 and 4.
    c. Delete column 4 (the October information). (Select column 4, select **Table**, **Delete Columns**.)
5. Finalize the table as follows:
    a. Merge the cells in row one (select row 1, select **Table**, **Merge Cells**, delete the paragraph symbol). Repeat to merge the cells in row 2.
    b. Select columns 2 and 3 in row 8 (Tennis Courts). Select the **Underline** button.
    c. Select columns 2 and 3 in row 9 (Totals). Place a double underline below the total amounts (select **Format**, **Font**, the **Font** tab should be selected, **Underline**, **Double**, **OK**).
    d. Center the table horizontally (place the insertion point in any table cell, select **Table**, **Cell Height and Width**, check that **Row** displays, **Center**, **OK**).
    e. Select the column headings in row 3 and choose the **Underline** button.
    f. Remove the table borders (select the entire table, select the **Borders** button to display the Borders Toolbar, select the **No Border** button).
    g. Remove the shading from rows 3 and 9 (select the desired row, select the down arrow beside the **Shading** box, scroll up to display and select **Clear**).
6. Use the *new* filename **6costr.doc** and save the file on your file disk.
7. Print one copy and close the document.

Challenge Your Skills

Skill 6.1—Create a Table and a Formula

1. Create a two-column table using the following information:
    a. The title of the table is TOTAL MINI-BLIND WASH

b. The price of the Mini-Blind Wash is $1,698.99.

c. The price of the Soap Solution is $152.54.

d. The price of the Hi-Dri Powder is $125.83.

e. Shipping and handling will be $56.80.

f. The charge for Express Delivery is $38.64.

g. Calculate the total amount due.

2. Make decisions regarding:

   Alignment of table contents
   Row height
   Column widths
   Placement of the table on the page (vertically and horizontally)
   Borders
   Shading
   Number format and dollar sign placement

3. Use the filename **6stable1.doc** and save the file.

4. Print one copy and close the document.

Skill 6.2—Calculate Column Totals; Language Arts Skills

1. Use the traditional style letter and the following information:

   a. Send the letter to Ms. Paula Toskan, Branch Manager, Grossman Enterprises, 8261 Orange Grove Street, Irvine, CA 92714.

   b. The letter is from Marla T. Abmed, District Manager.

   c. Make decisions regarding:

      Margins
      Alignment
      Date
      Salutation
      Closing
      Alignment of table contents
      Formulas and number formats
      Column widths
      Table borders and shading
      Reference initials
      Document identification

   d. Correct three spelling and two punctuation errorrs, and one dollar amount format errors.

   e. Letter body text follows:

   Changes in our corporate travel reimbursement rates are necessary because of increased capital expenditures. The current travel rates remain in effect until the first of next month.

   The following table shows the current and new rates.

Per Diem Amounts		
Items	Current Rate	New Rate
Accommodations	$99.00	$108.00
Meals	56.80	$53.50
Parking	20.00	18.80
Car rental	45.60	41.00
Total Per Deim		

As you will note while the amount allowed for accommodations has been increased by $ 9, the amount allowed for meals, parking, and car rental has decreased. Please let me know by the first of the month if you feel that these changes will adverseily affect your personnel.

Please remind all employees that receipts for every item must be submitted before a reinbursement check can be written. As of the first of the month, no out-of-pocket expenses will be reimbursed unless preapproved by a branch manager.

If you have any questions regarding these rate changes please call me.

2. Use the filename **6stable2.doc** and save the file.
3. Print one copy.
4. If you have completed your work, exit Word.

CHAPTER

Create a Résumé

Features Covered

- Insert special symbols
- Change case
- Use a nonbreaking space
- Change margins and set indents using the Rulers
- Set tabs

Objectives and Introduction

After successfully completing this chapter, you will be able to insert special characters; change the case for characters to all lowercase, all uppercase, sentence case, or title case; use a nonbreaking space to keep words on the same line; change margins using the Rulers; and set tabs to format an attractive, easy-to-read résumé.

A résumé is a document that summarizes a person's education, work experience, and work skills. A résumé is submitted to a prospective employer when applying for a job. Because a résumé serves as a person's introduction to a prospective employer, it is important that the résumé be attractive and easy to read. A résumé may be formatted using the Tab and Indent features or the Tables feature.

Tab settings can be changed so that paragraphs can be indented in an attractive manner. Emphasis can be added to text by using text attributes such as bold, underline, and italic. Special symbols, such as the accent marks in résumé, can be inserted easily into a document. In addition, emphasis can be given by placing special symbols (bullets) in front of desired paragraphs (see Figure 7.1).

Insert Special Symbols

Special text symbols, such as the é's in résumé, and graphic symbols, such as ❖ and ✰, can be inserted into a document by accessing Word's special symbols. Special

FIGURE 7.1

Completed résumé

Résumé
Shu-Ting Lee Swanson
3589 Hackamore Drive
Hayward, CA 94541
(510) 555-7701

EDUCATIONAL BACKGROUND

A.A. Paralegal, Chabot Community College 6/94
❖ Studied Paralegalism, the Justice System, and all aspects of American and California Law.

Certificate, De Anza Community College 6/93
❖ Earned a Certificate in Electronic Publishing.

Graduate, U.S. Air Force NCO Academy 12/91

EMPLOYMENT EXPERIENCE

U.S. Air Force--4 years
Have experience as a crew member of the C141 StarMaster, also worked in Maintenance and Civil Engineering.

Exploratorium--1 year
Worked as an Explainer giving laser beam and electricity demonstrations and assisting visitors with exhibits.

Mountain High Ski Rental
Fitted customers with skis, maintained inventory, and handled customer relations in supervisor's absence.

REFERENCES

Available upon request.

symbols, such as mathematical symbols, foreign letters, and graphic symbols, are not on the computer keyboard.

The text symbols, such as é, ©, or ö, can be selected from most of the fonts available on your system. If a text symbol is selected using a specific font, the symbol font will not change when the font in the document window is changed. To change the symbol font when the font in the document window changes, select the (**normal text**) font option in the Symbol dialog box. In other words, if the (normal text) font is selected in the Symbol dialog box, the font of the chosen special symbol will automatically be changed when the font of the text in the document window is changed. The Wingdings font provides many graphic symbols such as ✰, ❖, ✈, and 🖰. The Symbols font provides many mathematical and scientific symbols, such as Σ, ÷, ↔, and π.

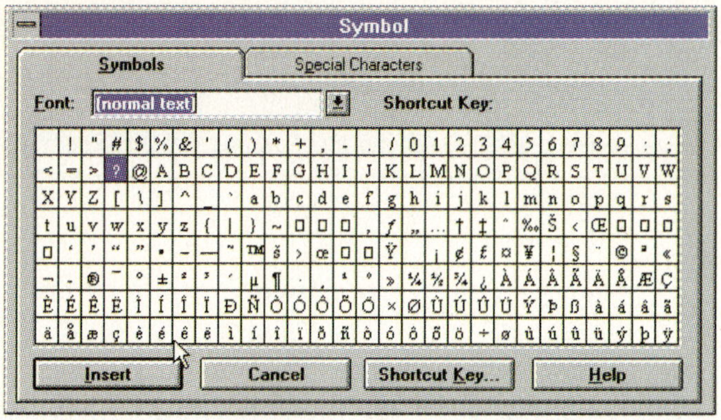

FIGURE 7.2

Symbol dialog box

Start-Up Instructions

- The nonprinting symbols should be displayed. If necessary, select the **Show/Hide** button ¶ .
- Type an **R** (to begin typing the word Résumé).

Steps to Insert Special Symbols

1. Place the insertion point at the location where the special symbol should be inserted.

   For example, the insertion point should be located immediately following the letter *R*.

2. Select **Insert, Symbol** {Alt, i, s}.

   Note: The Symbol dialog box displays (see Figure 7.2). Check that the Symbols tab is selected.

3. Move the mouse pointer to the down arrow located to the right of the Font box and click once {Alt and f}.

4. Move the mouse pointer to the desired font and click once. If necessary, scroll up or down the list of available fonts to display the desired font {press the down or up arrow key until the desired font is highlighted, Tab}.

   For example, scroll up the list of fonts until **(normal text)** displays. Move the mouse pointer to **(normal text)** and click once.

5. Move the mouse pointer to the desired symbol. Click once to highlight and enlarge the symbol {use the arrow keys to locate the desired symbol}.

   For example, move the mouse pointer to the é symbol (bottom row, sixth symbol and click once.

   Note: The symbol is highlighted and enlarged.

6. Select **Insert** to copy the selected symbol into the document at the location of the insertion point {Alt and i}.

   Note: The Symbol dialog box remains on the screen.

7. Click in the document window at the desired location and type the additional text.

   For example, move the mouse pointer to the right of the é characters and click once. Type **sum**. (Do not type the final period.)

FIGURE 7.3

Selecting a special character in text

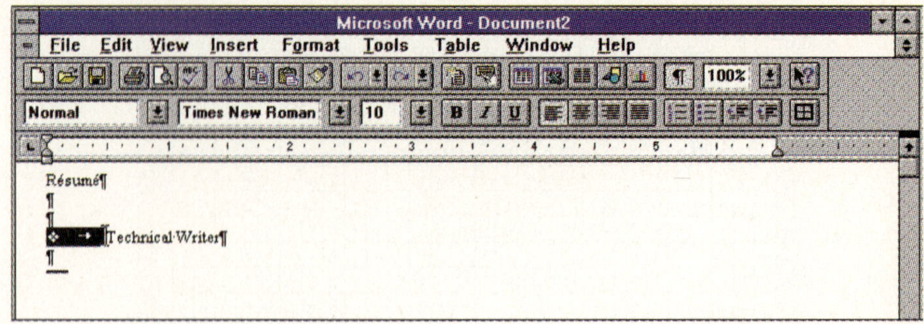

8. To insert the selected symbol again, select the **Insert** button in the Symbols dialog box {Alt, i, s; Alt and i}.

    For example, check that the **é** is highlighted in the Symbols dialog box and select **Insert**.

9. When all needed symbols have been inserted into the document, select **Close** in the Symbol dialog box {Esc}.

    For example, select **Close** to remove the Symbol dialog box from the screen.

Finish-Up Instructions

- Press the **Enter** key several times to insert some blank lines below the word Résumé.
- Repeat steps 2–4 in the Steps to Insert Special Symbols to display the Symbol dialog box and to select the **Wingdings** font.
- Locate the ❖ character (row four, third symbol). Click on the ❖ symbol and choose **Insert**. Select **Close** to remove the Symbols dialog box from the screen.
- Press the **Tab** key and type **Technical Writer**. Press **Enter**.
- To copy the symbol, select the ❖ symbol and the blank space (the Tab) before the letter *T* (see Figure 7.3).
- Select the **Copy** button.
- Move the insertion point to the location where the ❖ symbol should be inserted, e.g., place the insertion point in the blank line below the words Technical Writer.
- Select the **Paste** button.
- Type the words **Copyeditor** and press **Enter** once.
- Select the **Paste** button again to insert the ❖ symbol.
- Type the words **Assistant Copyeditor** and press **Enter** once.
- Use the filename 7**drill1.doc** and save the file on your file disk.

Change the Case of Text

After text has been typed, Word can automatically change the case of the text to all uppercase characters, all lowercase characters, sentence case (capitalizes the first letter of the first word at the beginning of a sentence or the first letter of the first word after a sentence), and title case (capitalizes the first letter of each selected word). In addition, the toggle case option changes the case of selected text from uppercase to lowercase and lowercase to uppercase. When using the Change Case feature, the text to be changed is selected. Choose **Format, Change Case**, and select the desired case option. Also, the case of selected text can be changed by pressing the **Shift** and **F3** keys until the text displays in the desired case. The case of a letter(s) can only be changed to all uppercase, all lowercase, or sentence case when using the **Shift** and **F3** method.

Start-Up Instructions

- The file named **7drill1.doc** should be displayed in the document window.

Change the Case of Characters

1. Select the desired text.

   For example, select the words **Technical Writer**.

2. Select **Format, Change Case** {Alt, o, e}.

3. Choose the desired option.

   For example, select **UPPERCASE** to convert all selected text to uppercase characters {u}.

4. Select **OK** {Enter}.

5. Click once to deselect the text.

Finish-Up Instructions

- Select the word **Copyeditor**. Repeat steps 2–5 in the Steps to Change the Case of Characters and change the characters to UPPERCASE.
- Select the words **Assistant Copyeditor**. Repeat steps 2–5 in the Steps to Change the Case of Characters and change the characters to UPPERCASE.
- Use the same filename, **7drill1.doc**, and save the file again.

Nonbreaking Space

Sometimes two words, such as dates or a person's first and last names, are dependent on each other to be a complete thought and should be printed on the same line. A nonbreaking space can be inserted between the dependent words to instruct Word to always print the word(s) on the same line. For example, the date September 25, 199x, should print on the same line; therefore, a nonbreaking space is placed between September and 25 and between the comma and 199x. A nonbreaking space is also referred to as a hard space.

Start-Up Instructions

- The file named **7drill1.doc** should be displayed in the document window.
- Place the insertion point at the end of the document (**Ctrl** and **End**).

- Type the following information on a new line:

  Assisted with the copyediting of the company newsletter, sales brochures, annual report, and procedures manuals. After eighteen months as an Assistant Copyeditor, I received a promotion to Copyeditor on May 1, 1993.

Insert a Nonbreaking Space

1. Move the insertion point to the location where the nonbreaking space should be inserted.

   For example, place the insertion point immediately after the **y** in **May**.

2. Press the **Delete** (Del) key once to delete the space between characters.
3. Press and hold the **Ctrl** and **Shift** keys and then press the **Spacebar** once (Ctrl and Shift and Spacebar) to insert a nonbreaking space.

   Note: *The nonbreaking space symbol (°) is inserted to represent the nonbreaking space. (If necessary, click on the* ***Show/Hide*** *button ¶ to display the nonprinting symbols, e.g., paragraph, tab, and space symbols.)*

Finish-Up Instructions

- Place the insertion point immediately after the comma that follows the number 1. Repeat steps 2 and 3 to insert a nonbreaking space.
- Use the same filename, **7drill1.doc**, and save the file again.
- Continue with the Steps to Display or Remove the Ruler on page 163.

Use Rulers to Change Margins and to Set Indents

A horizontal Ruler containing margin, paragraph, indent, and tab markers can be displayed below the Formatting Toolbar. Also, in Page Layout view, a vertical Ruler displays at the left side of the document window. The Rulers show measurement in inches (see Figure 7.4). The left and right margins, paragraph indents, and tab locations can be set by using the mouse to move the appropriate markers on the horizontal Ruler. The vertical Ruler can be used to set the top and bottom margins of a document and to check the placement of text on the page. The Page Layout view or Print Preview must be selected to change margins using the horizontal and vertical Rulers.

The margin amounts and line length (in inches) can be displayed by pressing the **Alt** key while moving the left or right margin boundary marker. The top or bottom margin amount can be viewed by pressing the **Alt** key while moving the top or bottom margin boundary marker.

The horizontal Ruler can be used to set four types of paragraph indents: first line indent, hanging indent, left indent, and right indent. To set any of the four indent types, move the mouse pointer to the appropriate indent marker on the horizontal Ruler, press and hold the mouse button, and drag the indent marker to the

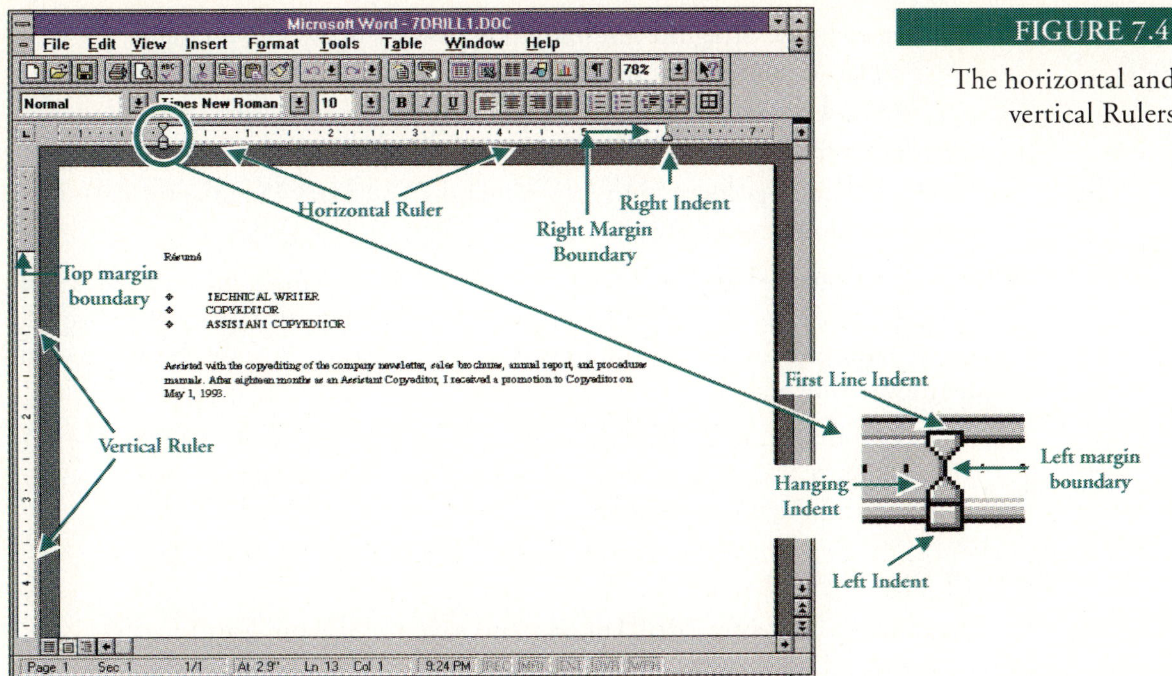

FIGURE 7.4

The horizontal and vertical Rulers

desired location. The indent markers are identified in Figure 7.4. A sample of each indent type is shown in Figure 7.5. Paragraph indents can also be created by selecting **Format**, **Paragraph**, **Indents and Spacing** tab and using the **Left**, **Right**, and **Special** (First Line and Hanging) indentation options.

Start-Up Instructions

- The file named **7drill1.doc** should be displayed in the document window.
- If necessary, select the Page Layout view (select the **Page Layout View** button at the bottom left of the document window).

Steps to Display or Remove the Ruler

1. Select **View, Ruler** {Alt, v, r}.

   *Note: The horizontal Ruler displays below the Formatting Toolbar. A vertical Ruler displays in Print Preview or Page Layout view. If the Ruler(s) is displayed, selecting **View, Ruler** will remove the Ruler(s) from the screen.*

Steps to Change the Left and Right Margins Using the Ruler

Note: A mouse must be used to change margins using the Ruler.

1. Select the down arrow beside the **Zoom Control** button and choose **Page Width** so that the left and right edges of the page display.
2. Move the mouse pointer to the left margin boundary (see Figure 7.4) until a double-headed arrow displays.
3. Press and hold the **Alt** key. Press and hold the mouse button to display a dotted vertical line. Drag the left margin boundary until the desired left margin amount displays at the left side of the Ruler. Release the **Alt** key and the mouse button.

For example, drag the left margin boundary marker to the right until 1.5" displays at the left side of the Ruler. Release the **Alt** key and the mouse button.

Note: The text moves to the new left margin.

4. Move the mouse pointer to the right margin boundary (See Figure 7.4) until a double-headed arrow displays.
5. Press and hold the **Alt** key. Press and hold the mouse button to display a dotted vertical line. Drag the right margin boundary marker until the desired right margin amount displays at the right side of the Ruler. Release the **Alt** key and the mouse button.

   For example, drag the right margin boundary marker to the left until 1.5" displays at the right side of the Ruler. Release the **Alt** key and the mouse button.

Finish-Up Instructions

- Use the *new* filename **7drill1m.doc** and save the file on your file disk.

Start-Up Instructions

- The file named **7drill1m.doc** should be displayed in the document window.
- If necessary, select the Page Layout view (select the **Page Layout View** button at the bottom left of the document window).
- The horizontal and vertical rulers should be displayed on the screen. If necessary, select **View**, **Ruler**.

Change the Top and Bottom Margins Using the Ruler

Note: A mouse must be used to change the top or bottom margins using the Ruler.

1. *If changing the top margin,* scroll up the document window so that the top edge of the page is displayed.

   If changing the bottom margin, scroll down the document window so that the bottom edge of the page is visible.

   For example, if necessary, scroll up the document window so that the top edge of the page is visible.
2. Move the mouse pointer to the top or bottom margin boundary until a double-headed arrow displays.

   For example, move the mouse pointer to the top margin boundary (see Figure 7.4) until the double-headed arrow displays.

   Note: The margin boundaries are the thin horizontal lines that separates the dark gray areas of the vertical Ruler from the white areas.
3. Press and hold the **Alt** key. Press and hold the mouse button to display a dotted horizontal line. Drag the top or bottom margin boundary marker until the desired margin amount displays. Release the **Alt** key and mouse button.

For example, drag the top margin boundary down until **1.5"** displays at the top of the vertical Ruler. Release the **Alt** key and the mouse button.

Finish-Up Instructions

- Use the same filename, **7drill1m.doc**, and save the file again.
- Continue with the Steps to Indent Paragraphs Using the Ruler.

Chapter 7 Create a Résumé

Start-Up Instructions

- The file named **7drill1m.doc** should be displayed in the document window.
- If necessary, select the Page Layout view (select the **Page Layout View** button at the bottom left of the document window).
- The horizontal and vertical rulers should be displayed on the screen. If necessary, select **View**, **Ruler**.
- Move the insertion point to the bottom of the document (**Ctrl** and **End**) and press the **Enter** key three times.
- Select **Insert**, **Symbol**, choose the **Wingdings** font, click on the ♦ character (fourth row, second character). Select **Insert**, **Close**.
- Press the **Tab** key and type the following sentence:

  Studied Paralegalism, the Justice System, and all aspects of American and California Law.

Indent Paragraphs Using the Ruler

1. Place the insertion point in the desired paragraph, or select the paragraphs to be indented.

   For example, place the insertion point anywhere in the sentence that was just typed.

2. Move the mouse pointer to the desired indent marker.

   For example, move the mouse pointer to the **hanging indent** marker (see Figure 7.4).

3. Press and hold the mouse button and drag the indent marker to the desired location on the horizontal Ruler.

   For example, drag the hanging indent marker to .5" on the horizontal Ruler.

   Note: *When the hanging indent marker is selected, the hanging indent marker and the left indent marker move as one unit and the first line indent marker remains at the left margin. If the left indent marker is selected, the left indent marker, hanging indent marker, and the first line indent marker move as one unit. If the first line indent marker is selected, the first line indent marker moves and the left indent marker and hanging indent marker remain at the left margin.*

4. Release the mouse button.

   Note: *The bullet symbol remains at the left margin and the remaining text is indented .5" from the left margin.*

FIGURE 7.5

Sample indented paragraphs

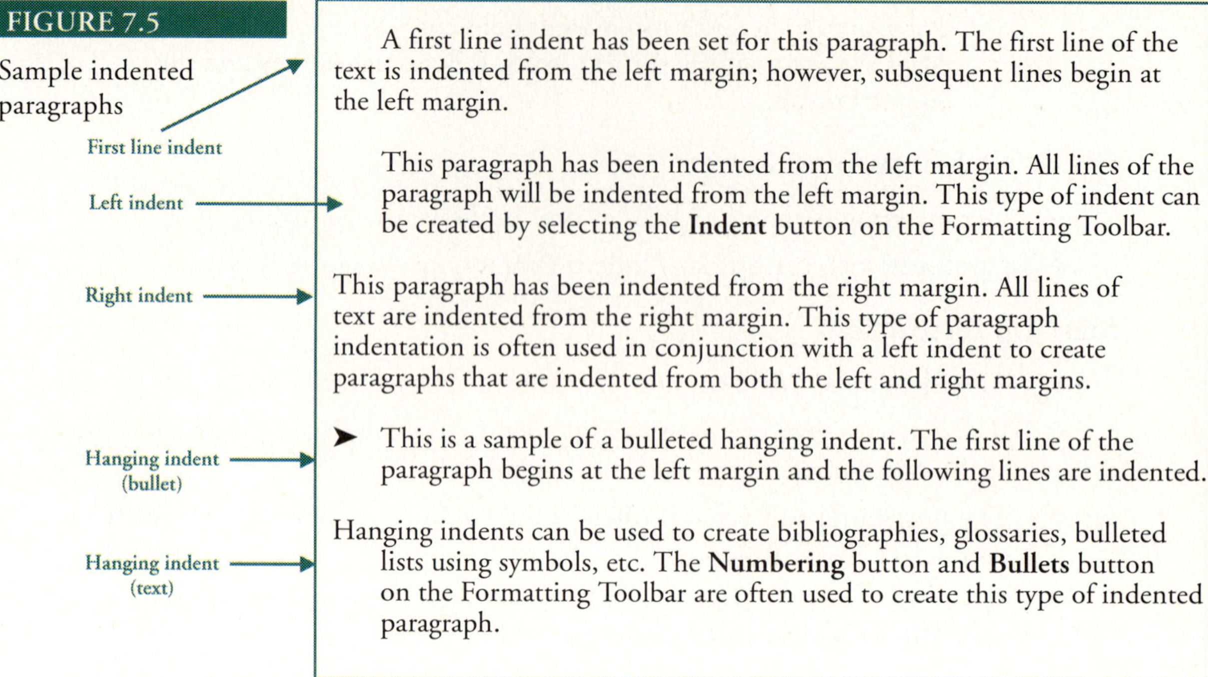

Finish-Up Instructions

- Use the same filename, **7drill1m.doc**, and save the file again.
- Continue with the Steps to Set Tabs Using the Tab Dialog Box on page 167.

Set Tabs

By default, tabs are set every one-half inch. Small, light gray marks are placed at each one-half inch mark at the bottom of the Ruler. If desired, tabs can be changed to indent information at a position other than the preset tabs. There are nine types of tabs available: left, center, right, decimal, left leader, right leader, center leader, decimal leader, and bar. Bar tabs place a vertical bar (|) at the tab stop. Leader tabs contain dots, dashes, or underlines that display between tabbed information. All nine types of tabs can be set using the Tabs dialog box (see Figure 7.6). Left, center, right, and decimal tabs can also be set by choosing the desired location on the horizontal Ruler.

When tabs are set using the Ruler, the **Tab Alignment** button displayed at the left of the Ruler (see Figure 7.8) is selected to choose the desired tab type. Each time you click on the **Tab Alignment** button a different tab alignment symbol displays. The four tab alignment symbols are shown in Figure 7.8.

When creating a document, type the text and press the **Tab** key once between each section (column) of information. Once all the text is typed, tab settings can be adjusted to create a more readable and attractive presentation. Also, the Word Tables feature can be used to type and format each column of information. (See Chapter 5 for information on converting existing tabbed text into a table.)

When a new tab is set, the default tab(s) to the left of the new tab are automatically cleared. If necessary, all tab settings can be deleted to return to the default tab settings.

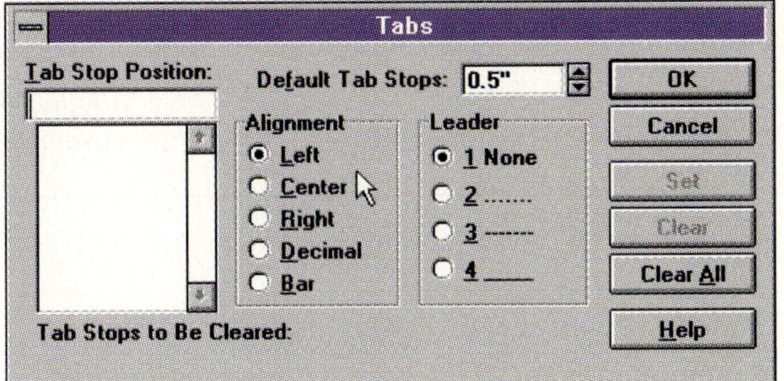

FIGURE 7.6

Tabs dialog box

Start-Up Instructions

- The file named **7drillm1.doc** should be displayed in the document window.
- The horizontal ruler should be displayed on the screen. If necessary, select **View, Ruler**.

Set Tabs Using the Tabs Dialog Box

1. Place the insertion point at the location where the tabs are to be set, or select the text for which tabs are to be set.

   For example, select the three bulleted items, **TECHNICAL WRITER, COPYEDITOR,** and **ASSISTANT COPYEDITOR.**

2. Select **Format, Tabs** {Alt, o, t}.

   Note: *The Tabs dialog box displays (see Figure 7.6). Your insertion point is located in the Tab Stop Position box.*

3. To set a tab, type the desired tab location in the Tab Stop Position box.

   For example, type **.25**. (Do not type the final period.)

4. Select **Set** {Alt and s}.

5. Repeat step 2 and type the desired tab location in the Tab Stop Position box.

   For example, type **5.25**. (Do not type the final period.)

6. To select a different tab alignment, move the mouse pointer to the Alignment box and click on the desired type.

   For example, select **Right** {Alt and r}.

Insert Leader Characters

7. In the Leaders area, select the desired leader character.

   For example, select the **dot leader** character (**number 2**) {Alt and 2}.

8. Select **Set** {Alt and s}.

9. When all needed tabs have been set, select **OK** {Enter}.

   Note: *A left tab symbol displays on the Ruler at .25" and a right tab symbol displays on the Ruler at 5.25". Continue with the following Finish-Up Instructions to complete the typed information.*

FIGURE 7.7

Document with dot leader characters

❖ TECHNICAL WRITER . . . . June 199x
❖ COPYEDITOR . . . . May 1994
❖ ASSISTANT COPYEDITOR . . . . . November 1992

Finish-Up Instructions

- Place the insertion point to the right of the last character in the word **WRITER**. Press the **Tab** key once.

  Note: Leader characters display from the end of the word WRITER to the tab stop at 5.25".
- Type **June 199x**.
- Move the insertion point to the right of the last character in the next line, **COPYEDITOR**. Press the **Tab** key once and type **May 1994**.
- Move the insertion point to the right of the last character in the final line, **ASSISTANT COPYEDITOR**. Press the **Tab** key once and type **November 1992**.
- The bulleted lines of your document should look similar to Figure 7.7.
- Use the new filename **7drill1t.doc** and save the file on your file disk.
- Close the document.

Create Evenly Spaced Tabs

Note: *The following Steps to Create Evenly Spaced Tabs are for your information only.*

1. Place the insertion point at the location where the evenly spaced tabs are to be set or select the text for which evenly spaced tabs are to be set.
2. Select **Format, Tabs** {Alt, o, t}.
3. If other tabs have been set, select **Clear All** to delete the existing tabs {Alt and a}.
4. Click on the up or down arrow located beside the **Default Tab Stops** box until the desired spacing displays or double-click in the **Default Tab Stops** box and type the desired spacing {Alt and f, type desired spacing}.
5. Select **OK** {Enter}.

Start-Up Instructions

- Open the file named **7drill2.doc** located on the data disk.
- The text is not aligned in columns at this time. That's OK. The following Steps to Set Tabs Using the Ruler will be used to align the tabbed text in four columns.

Set Tabs Using the Ruler

Note: *A mouse must be used to set tabs using the Ruler.*

1. Place the insertion point at the location where tabs are to be set or select the text for which tabs are to be set.

   For example, select all four lines of text.

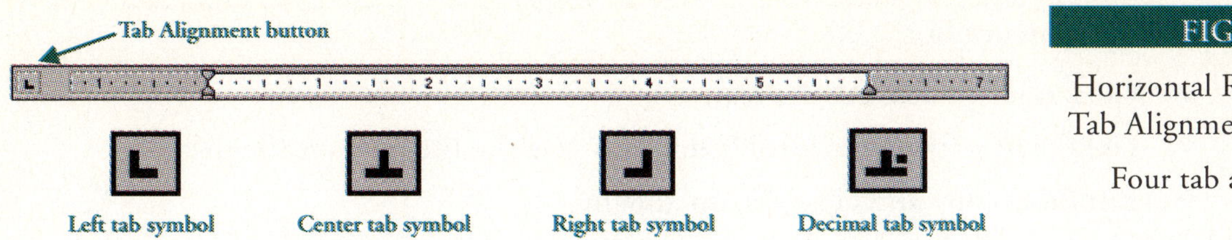

FIGURE 7.8

Horizontal Ruler with Tab Alignment button

Four tab alignment symbols

2. Check that the desired tab alignment symbol displays at the left of the horizontal Ruler. If necessary, click on the **Tab Alignment** button until the desired tab alignment symbol displays.

   For example, check that the **Left Tab** symbol displays. (If necessary, click on the **Tab Alignment** button until the **Left** tab symbol displays.)

   Note: *The four tab alignment symbols available for setting tabs using the horizontal Ruler are shown in Figure 7.8.*

3. Move the mouse pointer to the desired position on the Ruler and click to set the tab location.

   For example, move the mouse pointer to approximately **.25"** on the Ruler and click.

   Note: *A Left tab symbol is placed on the Ruler at .25".*

4. Click on the **Tab Alignment** button to display the desired tab alignment symbol.

   For example, click on the **Tab Alignment** button until the **Center** tab symbol displays.

5. Repeat step 3 and click at the desired tab location on the Ruler.

   For example, move the mouse pointer to approximately **2.5"** on the Ruler and click.

   Note: *A Center tab symbol is placed on the Ruler at 2.5" and the default tabs to the left of the center tab are deleted.*

6. Repeat step 4 to display the desired tab alignment symbol.

   For example, click on the **Tab Alignment** button until the **Right** tab symbol displays.

7. Repeat step 3 and click at the desired tab location on the Ruler.

   For example, move the mouse pointer to approximately **4.5"** on the Ruler and click.

   Note: *A Right tab symbol is placed on the Ruler at 4.5".*

8. Repeat step 4 to display the desired tab alignment symbol.

   For example, click on the **Tab Alignment** button until the **Decimal** tab symbol displays.

9. Repeat step 3 and click at the desired table location on the Ruler.

   For example, move the mouse pointer to approximately **5.25"** on the Ruler and click.

   Note: *A decimal tab symbol is placed on the Ruler at 5.25". The text is now aligned in four columns.*

Finish-Up Instructions

- ❖ Click once to deselect the text.
- ❖ Use the *new* filename **7drill2t.doc** and save the file on your file disk.
- ❖ Print one copy and close the document.

Remove a Tab from the Ruler

Note: *The following steps are for your information only.*

1. Move the mouse pointer to the desired tab symbol on the Ruler.
2. Press and hold the mouse button and drag the tab symbol off the Ruler. Release the mouse button.

Create a Résumé

- ❖ Use the following information to create the résumé shown in Figure 7.1 on page 158.
- ❖ Change the font to **Bookman Old Style, 11 point** or **make a font choice of your own**. Use bold and underline text attributes as shown.
- ❖ Use the horizontal Ruler to change the left and right margins to **1.5"**.
- ❖ Use the vertical Ruler to change the top margin to **1.5"**.
- ❖ Set a left tab at **.25"** and a right tab with dot leaders at **5.25"**.
- ❖ Use special text and bullet symbols as shown. The é is found in the (normal text) font and the ❖ is found in the Wingdings font.
- ❖ Use the ruler to set a hanging indent at **.25"** for the paragraphs that begin with the ❖ symbol.
- ❖ Use the **Increase Indent** button to indent the paragraphs below each job listing.
- ❖ Use the filename **7swa.doc** and save the file on your file disk.
- ❖ Print one copy and close the document.

Create a Résumé Using the Tables Feature

A résumé can also be created using the Tables feature to format the information in two columns. Sideheads, such as Employment Experience, Educational Background, Honors, and References, can be typed in the first column and related information can be placed in the second column. The widths of the table columns can be adjusted to accommodate headings and text. Some of the advantages of using a table to format a résumé are ease of setup and formatting, ease of reading, and visual attractiveness.

Create a Résumé Using the Tables Feature

- ❖ Use the following information to create the résumé shown in Figure 7.9.
- ❖ Change the font to **Bookman Old Style, 12-point** or **make a font choice of your own**. Use bold and italic text attributes as shown.
- ❖ Use the horizontal Ruler and change the left and right margins to **1.5"**. Use the vertical Ruler and change the top margin to **1.5"**.
- ❖ Type and center the heading information.

  Note: *The capital* ***É*** *for the word* ***RÉSUMÉ*** *is found in the (normal text) font.*
- ❖ Create a table with two columns and six rows. Decrease the width of column 1 and increase the width of column 2. (If necessary, see Chapters 5 and 6 for information on changing the width of table columns.) To create spacing between the paragraphs in column 2, press the **Enter** key *once* after each paragraph.
- ❖ Use the filename **7wen.doc** and save the file on your file disk.
- ❖ Print one copy and close the document.

FIGURE 7.9

Résumé created using the Tables feature

RÉSUMÉ
THOMAS B. WENDELL
7482 Kincaid Road
Cincinnati, OH 45213-1416
(513) 555-7744

Employment Experience	*Autohaus European Automobile Repair,* Cincinnati, OH. Full-time technician specializing in 4-stroke cycle gas and diesel engine repair. December 1990 to present.	Enter
	American RV Sales and Repair, Toledo, OH. Part-time mechanic for recreational vehicles. Repaired electrical systems and electronic chassis controls. September 1987 to December 1990.	Enter
Educational Background	Toledo Technical/Vocational Institute, Toledo, OH. A.A. Automotive Technology, specialized in electrical and mechanical automotive mechanisms.	Enter
	High School Diploma, Toledo Senior High School, Toledo, OH.	Enter
Honors	Automotive Service Excellence certificate— Highest Honors	Enter
	Automotive Technician Internship Program—Outstanding Graduate	Enter
References	Available upon request.	Enter

The Next Step

Chapter Review and Activities

Self-Check Quiz

T F 1. Tabs are set by default every inch in Word for Windows 6.0.

T F 2. The nine tab types are left, center, decimal, right, left leader, right leader, center leader, decimal leader, and bar.

T F 3. A nonbreaking space between words instructs Word to always print both words on the same line.

T F 4. The special symbols are accessed by selecting **Insert, Symbols**.

5. Word can change the case of letters to ____________________.
   a. all uppercase
   b. all lowercase
   c. title case
   d. any of the above

6. The horizontal Ruler can be used to ________________.
   a. set left and right margins
   b. set top and bottom margins
   c. set tabs
   d. both a and c

7. The horizontal and vertical Rulers can be displayed in ____________.
   a. the Normal view
   b. the Page Layout view
   c. Print Preview
   d. either b or c

8. Special ________ can be inserted into a document.
   a. mathematical symbols
   b. foreign letters
   c. Wingdings graphic symbols
   d. all of the above

9. List two advantages of using a table when creating a résumé.

10. Describe and state the purpose of a résumé.

Enriching Language Arts Skills

Spelling/Vocabulary Words

journalism a course of study that prepares students to report, write, and edit newspapers and magazines; the occupation of reporting, writing, editing, and broadcasting news.

ecology the interaction between living organisms and their environment; the way plants, animals, and people live together in a specific region.

specifically precisely, exactly.

Commas Used in a Series

Words and/or ideas listed in a series are separated by commas.

Example:

The mailing list was sent to Karen Smith, Georgia Cain, and Perry Arnston.

Activities

Activity 7.1—Create a Résumé, Set Tabs, and Insert Special Symbols

1. Use the following information to create the résumé shown.
   a. Use the Rulers to change the top, left, and right margins to 1.5". (If necessary, select the **Page Layout View** button. Move the mouse pointer to the margin boundary, press and hold the **Alt** key, press the mouse button, and drag the margin boundary marker to the desired location. Release the **Alt** key and mouse button.)
   b. Set a left tab at .3" and .75" and a right tab with dot leaders at 5.25".
   c. Change the font to **Bookman Old Style, 11 point** or **make a font choice of your own**. Use bold and italic text attributes as shown.
   d. Use special symbols for the é's in Résumé and the ♦ symbols (select **Insert, Symbols**). The é is found in the (normal text) symbols font and the ♦ is found in the Wingdings symbols font.

Résumé
Wendy Norman
8504 Zyle Road
Austin, TX 78737
(512) 555-4927

Educational Background

B.A. Education, University of Texas, Austin 6/94
♦ Major courses: Computer-Aided Instruction, Word Processing, Spreadsheets, Databases, and Electronic Publishing.

G.E.D., Blanco, Texas 1991

Special Skills

Typing: 85 words per minute. Experienced with Microsoft Word for Windows and WordPerfect on an IBM PC, Microsoft Word and Excel on a Macintosh.

Employment Experience

Teach for America, Austin, Texas

◆ Elementary School Math Teacher 6/94-Present

Teach third-grade mathematics to inner-city students using computer-aided instruction to reinforce basic skills in problem solving. Responsibilities include developing curriculum and lesson plans, maintaining student records, and counseling students and parents.

Wendy's Tutorial Service, Blanco, Texas

◆ Elementary School Tutor 9/89-6/91

Tutored elementary students in computer and math skills. Responsibilities included preparing individualized lesson plans for each child, reporting progress to parents, maintaining records, managing business checking account, and paying state and federal taxes on income from business.

References

Available upon request.

---

2. Use the filename **7norman1.doc** and save the file.
3. Print one copy and close the document.

Activity 7.2—Create and Edit a Résumé Using the Tables Feature

1. Use the Tables feature and the following information to type the résumé shown.
   a. Use the horizontal ruler to change the left and right margins to **1** inch.
   b. Use bold and italic text attributes as shown.
   c. Select a font of your own choice in a point size of 10 or 12.
   d. Use a special text character for the É's in RÉSUMÉ. The É is found in the (normal text) symbols font.

RÉSUMÉ
SHIRLEY H. KINGSTON
8055 ARBOR LANE
STURGIS, KY 42459

Education	Webster University, St. Louis, Missouri B.A. in Business Administration, Minor in Office Administration Studied Behavioral Science in Business, Business Law, Office Administration and Communications, Economics and Management, and Accounting. 5/92

Experience	*Management World Magazine*, Trevose, PA. Full-time editor/reporter. Responsible for covering statewide meetings on management and office technology and developing feature articles. Submit all work electronically. June 1992 to present.
	Professional Secretaries International, Kansas City, Missouri. Part-time reporter. Responsibilities include reporting on meetings of Association of Information System Professionals, National Association of Legal Secretaries, and the Administrative Management Society. Submit all work electronically. 9/88 to present.
	Webster University, St. Louis, Missouri. Part-time office assistant in Admissions and Records department. Answered telephones, researched student records, distributed inter-office mail, and ordered supplies. 9/87 to 6/92.
Activities	Recording secretary for Kentucky state chapter of *National Association of Legal Secretaries*, member of Kentucky Horseback Club, and volunteer in the newborn nursery at County General Hospital.
References	Available upon request.

2. Use the filename **7king2.doc** and save the file.
3. Use the following information and edit the résumé.
   a. Change the sideheads to all uppercase letters.
   b. Insert and center the phone number (502) 555-2438 beneath the city, state, and zip code.
   c. Delete the words "Available upon request" that follow the References sidehead.
   d. Insert the following two references:

      Linh Nguyen, Supervisor, Registrar's Office
      Webster University
      390 University Avenue, Room 450
      St. Louis, MO 63001
      (314) 555-8901

      Reuben Sisneros, Senior Editor
      Management World Magazine
      4622 Street Road
      Trevose, PA 19047
      (717) 555-2249
4. Use the filename **7king2r.doc** and save the file.
5. Print one copy and close the document.

Chapter 7
Create a Résumé

Activity 7.3—Create Your Own Résumé

1. Create your own résumé using Figure 7.1 or Figure 7.9 as a guide.
2. If necessary, change margins to increase or decrease the amount of text that will fit on a page. For example, if your résumé is short, it may be desirable to increase the left, right, and top margins. If your résumé is long, decrease the left, right, top, and bottom margins.
3. Remember to insert special characters for the é's in the word résumé.
4. Use one or two fonts to enhance the appearance of your résumé. Also, use bold, italic, or underline text attributes as desired.
5. Use the Speller and proofread carefully.
6. Use the filename **7myresum.doc** and save the file.
7. Print one copy and close the document.

Challenge Your Skills

Skill 7.1—Create a Résumé, Set Tabs, and Insert Special Characters

1. Use the following information to create the résumé shown.
   a. Change the top margin to .75" and the bottom margin to .5"; reduce the left and right margins to 1".
   b. Select a font of your choice in a 10- or 12-point size.
   c. Set a left tab at .4" and 8" and set a right tab with dot leaders at the right margin.
   d. Use the bold and italic text attributes as shown.
   e. Select a symbol of your choice from the Wingdings symbols font. Insert the chosen symbol in front of each job title.

Résumé
Jamal Carter
782 Bahama Drive
Rio Rancho, NM 87124
(505) 555-5941

EDUCATIONAL BACKGROUND

New Mexico State University, Las Cruces, New Mexico 6/92
Candidate for Masters of Physics degree. Concentration in astronomy and astrophysics. Member of Chamber of Commerce and Planetary Society of New Mexico.

B.S. Physics, University of New Mexico, Albuquerque, New Mexico 6/90
NAACP Scholar, Toastmasters Scholarship recipient, Dean's List.
President of Astrophysics Club, *Optical Illusions*.

EMPLOYMENT EXPERIENCE

National Radio Astronomy Observatory, Socorro, New Mexico
* *Astronomer* 6/92-Present
Review and analyze data gathered by very large Array telescopes. Present and submit reports of findings to senior management, manage budget for department.

University of New Mexico, Albuquerque, New Mexico
* *Computer Lab Assistant* 9/88-6/90
Assisted computer programming and computer applications students with assignments. Supervised work study students. Maintained hardware and software.

Carter's Telescopes, Rio Rancho, New Mexico
* *Sales Assistant* 6/86-9/88
Sold telescopes for business and home use. Maintained inventory of telescopes and supplies.

REFERENCES

Ms. Delia Jimenez, Computer Lab Manager
University of New Mexico
1724 Central Avenue, #204
Albuquerque, NM 87131
(505) 555-2774

Celeste Johnson, Ph.D., Director
National Radio Astronomy Observatory
94 Galileo Circle
Socorro, NM 85149
(505) 555-9258

---

2. Use the filename **7carter.doc** and save the file.
3. Print one copy and close the document.

Skill 7.2—Create a Résumé with Special Characters; Language Arts

1. Create a résumé for Charlotte Quemado using the following information.
   a. Make decisions regarding:
      Résumé format
      Margins
      Tab settings and indentions

Fonts
Hard spaces
Uppercase and lowercase headings
Bold and italic text attributes
Special symbols
References

b. Correct three spelling errors and one punctuation error.

c. Charlotte lives at 887 Seascape Dr., Mt. Pleasant, SC 29447, (803)555-2994.

d. Charlotte graduated in 1987 with a B.S. in English from the University of South Carolina, Columbia, SC. She is currently a master's degree candidate in Environmental Journalsm at the University of Charleston, Charleston, SC.

e. Charlotte's work experience is as follows:

   Marine Habitat, Pawley's Island, SC
   Director of Communications
   6/90-Present

   Job responsibilities include: writing proposals, reports and articles for publication regarding the marine animals, plants, and ekology of South Carolina wetlands.

   Piedmont Publications, Columbia, SC
   Reviewer
   6/87-5/90

   Job responsibilities included reviewing manuscripts for publication in the area of secondary and post-secondary biology education. Specificaly, manuscripts were assessed and editing suggestions were made regarding content and reading level.

   University of South Carolina, Columbia, SC
   Newspaper Editor
   9/86-6/87

   Job responsibilities included overseeing the publication of a daily newspaper for a campus of 3,000 faculty and students.

f. Charlotte's references are:

   George L. Washington, Ph.D., Director, Marine Habitat, 17 Ocean Avenue, Pawley's Island, SC 29477, (803)555-2898

   Mary Susan Hutsell, Senior Editor, Piedmont Publications, 1275 Maple Avenue., Columbia, SC 29301, (803)555-1002

2. Use the filename **7quemado.doc** and save the file.

3. Print one copy.

4. If you have completed your work, exit Word.

CHAPTER

8

Create Newspaper and Side-by-Side Columns

Features Covered

- Newspaper-style columns
- The Columns button
- Change views
- Column breaks
- Change column definitions
- Hyphenation
- Format Painter button
- Side-by-side columns (Parallel columns)

Objectives and Introduction

After successfully completing this chapter, you will be able to use the Columns button and the Columns dialog box to format text in newspaper-style columns and to use the Tables feature to create side-by-side columns (parallel columns). In addition, you will also learn how to control the flow of text in newspaper columns using section and column breaks and how to use the Hyphenation and Format Painter features to improve the look and readability of columnar text.

Columns of text can be arranged in newspaper or side-by-side styles. Text in newspaper columns wraps around from line to line, column to column, and page to page (see Figure 8.2). Paragraphs of related text can be arranged in side-by-side columns so that information can be read from left to right. The Hyphenation feature can be used to improve the readability of columnar text by reducing the amount of space at the end of lines and avoiding large gaps of space between words in a line. Sideheads or subheads are often bolded or put in a different font or font size for emphasis. Formatting, such as bold and font size, can be quickly applied to multiple items using the Format Painter feature.

Newspaper Columns

Newspaper columns are created by formatting text as columns, either before or after the text is typed. The simplest method for creating columns is to first type the text and then create the column format.

When printing newspaper columns, the title is often centered on the page and the remainder of the text is divided into multiple columns. To create more than one column format, the document must be divided into more than one section. Each section can have distinctive document formatting such as a one- or two-column layout and different margins. There are four types of section breaks: **Next Page** that begins the next section on the following page; **Continuous** that begins the next section on the same page; **Even Page** that begins the next section on the following even page of the document; and **Odd Page** that begins the next section on the following odd page of the document.

A quick way to create columns is to select the **Columns** button on the Standard Toolbar and choose the desired number of columns. Word automatically places a continuous section break in a document when text is selected and multiple columns are created using the **Columns** button. Also, equal column widths are calculated based on the page margins, and a .5-inch gutter (blank space between columns) is inserted between columns.

If different column settings are desired, use the Columns dialog box. Also, the number of columns, space between columns, and column widths can be specified in the Columns dialog box (see Figure 8.1).

In the Columns dialog box, the *Number of Columns* box is used to specify the number of desired columns (the default is 1). Once the number of columns is specified, Word automatically calculates equal widths for each column and determines the left and right margins for each column. The width of each column and the distance between each column displays in the *Width and Spacing* boxes. If the number of columns or distance between columns is changed, the column widths are automatically recalculated when the insertion point is moved to another option or when **OK** is selected.

The *Width and Spacing* boxes in the Columns dialog box are used to specify the width of each column and the amount of space (in inches) to be placed between the columns. The default spacing between columns (.5 inches) is often changed if there are more than two columns on the page.

If the *Equal Column Width* option is selected (turned on), only the column width and spacing for the first column need to be entered. Word will automatically adjust the columns to be the same width and distance apart. When the *Equal Column Width* option is turned off, column width and spacing can be entered for each column. The column widths and spacing between columns can also be changed by dragging the column marker on the horizontal ruler.

A line can be placed between columns by selecting the *Line Between* option. Other types of lines and borders can be placed around a column using the **Format, Borders and Shading** command (see Chapter 6).

The *Apply To* options are used to specify the text to be affected by the settings selected in the Columns dialog box. For example, the *This Point Forward* option in the Apply To box is selected to apply column settings from the location of the insertion point forward in the document.

Depending on the view selected, Word displays the text in different column formats. In Normal view, only one column is displayed at a time. To see the columns across the page, select **View, Page Layout**. The text can be displayed in any size by selecting **View, Zoom**, then selecting the desired size or entering a percentage.

Text in newspaper columns automatically flows from the bottom of one column to the top of the next column and from the bottom of one page to the top left column of the next page (see Figure 8.2). The term *snaking* is often used to describe columnar text that flows from column to column and page to page.

The text flow of newspaper columns can be controlled by inserting a column break to force text to the next column or page. A column break is inserted by selecting **Insert, Break, Column Break**. A column break moves the insertion point and any text that follows the insertion point to the top of the next column. However, the text is forced to the top left column of the next page if the insertion point is located in the final column of the page.

After newspaper columns are typed, extra space may display at the end of lines, making the columnar information difficult to read. Hyphenation can be used to avoid extra end-of-line space and to improve the appearance and readability of the columnar text by aligning words more evenly at the margin.

Start-Up Instructions

- Open the file named **8drill1.doc** located on the data disk.
- Use the Normal view (if necessary, select the **Normal View** button at the bottom left of the document window).
- Display nonprinting symbols (if necessary, select the **Show/Hide** ¶ button).

Create Newspaper Columns

1. Select the text to be placed in columns.

   For example, place the I-beam to the left of the first word in the body text (The). Press and hold the mouse button and drag downward to select all the paragraphs prior to the sidehead *Products* (including the blank line before the Products sidehead).

2. Select the **Columns** button on the Standard Toolbar {Alt, o, c}.
3. Move the mouse pointer to the desired number of columns and click the mouse button once {type th desired number of columns, Enter}.

   For example, select the second column from the left to create a two-column layout.

   Note: *In Normal view, the text is displayed in one column on the left side of the document window. Click once to deselect the text and scroll up to view the top of the document. Below the title, a section break displays with a double-dotted line and the words "End of Section" that indicate the end of a section. If the insertion point is located below the section break, the words Sec 2 display on the left side of the Status bar.*

Finish-Up Instructions

- Use the Page Layout view to display the text in two columns in the document window (select the **Page Layout View** button at the bottom left of the document window).

  Note: The title of the report displays centered at the top of the document and the highlighted text displays in two columns.

- Use the *new* filename **8new1.doc** and save the file on your file disk.

Start-Up Instructions

- The file named **8new1.doc** should be displayed in the document window.
- Move the insertion point to the left of the "P" in "Products" and press **Enter** twice to include two additional blank lines.

Create Customized Columns

1. Select the text where the customized columns are to begin (or anywhere in the document if the customized columns are to affect the entire section).

   For example, select the sidehead **Products** and the paragraphs that follow to the end of the document.

2. Select **Format, Columns** {Alt, o, c}.

   Note: The Columns dialog box displays (see Figure 8.1).

3. In the Number of Columns box, type the number of columns.

   For example, type 3.

4. Click once in the Width box in the Width and Spacing area.

   Note: This action requires Word to calculate the column widths based on the new number typed in the Number of Columns box; the program will then allow the spacing between columns to be changed.

5. Double-click in the **Spacing** box in the first row and type the amount of spacing to be placed between columns or click on the up or down triangle located to the right of the **Spacing** box until the desired spacing amount displays {Alt and s, type the desired spacing amount}.

FIGURE 8.1

Columns dialog box

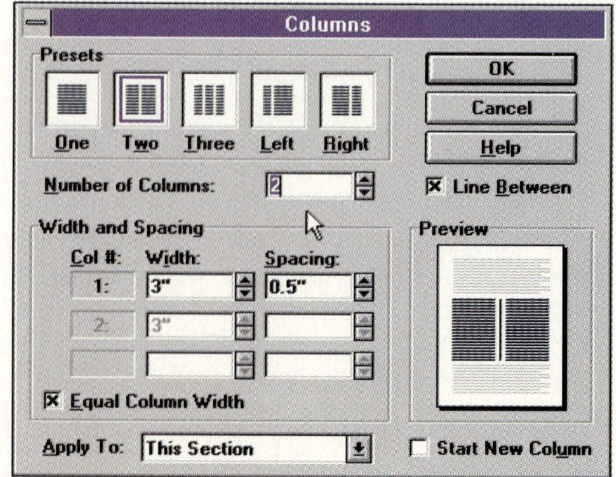

FIGURE 8.2

Text formatted in multiple columns

Example of a one-column format (first section)

SAVING AND INVESTING TRENDS

Example of a two-column format (second section)

The pattern for saving and investing money during the next ten years will be drastically different than in the years past. Several changes are predicted for the next decade.

Healthy Savings Attitudes

Americans' attitudes towards saving and investment are improving. During the past few years, the average savings rate for Americans was 5% of after-tax income--far less than the previous decade. However, last year Americans had a healthy increase in savings to 6.5%.

Demographics

The Baby Boom generation is fast approaching middle age. They are planning for their children's education, their own retirement, and their own leisure activities. In addition, Americans have increased their wealth dramatically and are recognizing the need to save and invest wisely.

Example of a three-column format with vertical lines between columns (third section)

Products

During the past decade, Americans began to achieve their savings goals by investing in nontraditional products. For example, mutual funds, money market funds, and annuities were selected for investments because they provided an opportunity for higher returns with limited risks. In the next decade, the demand will continue to move away from the traditional investment in bonds to investments in the more unconventional markets such as mutual funds and annuities.

Demand for Change

The American people are telling financial institutions that they want more products, more security, and honest advisors. Such requests are driving financial institutions to re-evaluate their philosophies in order to make major changes in the way business is conducted.

Financial Institutions

Traditionally, individuals have used Savings and Loan associations for their savings needs and turned to brokerage firms for investments. People are seeking the most secure place for their savings.

For example, double-click in the **Spacing** box in the Width and Spacing area and type **.3**. (Do not type the final period.)

Note: *If the spacing amount is not highlighted, delete the amount before typing the new spacing amount.*

6. Select the **Line Between** option box to place a line between the columns {Alt and b}.

Note: *An X should display beside the Line Between option. The Preview box displays an example of a three-column format with vertical lines.*

7. Check that the **Equal Column Width** option is turned on (i.e., an X displays in the option box).

    For example, check that an X displays beside the **Equal Column Width** option. If necessary, click on the box once to turn it on {Alt and e}.

8. Choose the desired Apply To option.

    For example, check that the **Selected Text** option displays.

9. Select **OK** {Enter}.

    *Note: Click once to deselect the text. Turn off nonprinting symbols (select the **Show/Hide ¶** button). Your document should look similar to Figure 8.2. Click on the down arrow beside the **Zoom Control** button and choose **Whole Page** to view the entire page; click on the down arrow beside the **Zoom Control** button and choose **100%** to return to the normal size.*

Finish-Up Instructions

- Use the *new* filename **8col3.doc** and save the file on your file disk.
- Print one copy.

Start-Up Instructions

- The file named **8col3.doc** should be displayed in the document window.

Change the Column Definition

1. Place the insertion point at any location in the section to be affected by the column change.

    For example, place the insertion point in the section where the two columns are displayed. (*Sec 2* displays in the Status bar). If necessary, scroll up to display the section of the document that contains two columns.

2. Select **Format, Columns** {Alt, o, c}.

3. Make any desired changes to the number of columns, spacing, or other options.

    For example, click once on the Line Between box to place a line between the columns.

4. Select **OK** {Enter}.

    Note: A line displays between the columns in the two-column section of the document.

Finish-Up Instructions

- Insert two blank lines after the last column entry (press **Ctrl** and **End** to move the insertion point to the end of the document; press **Enter** once).
- Select the **Columns** button on the Standard Toolbar and click on **1 column**.
- Press **Enter** once before typing and centering the following sentence:

    START YOUR SAVINGS PLAN TODAY!

*Note: Select the down arrow beside the **Zoom Control** button and choose **Whole Page**. Notice that the one-column format is in effect for the last line. The three-column section has been "balanced" across the page, with each column having the same number of lines. This balanced effect was created when the section break was inserted to change the number of columns to one.*

- ❖ Use the *new* filename **8fin1.doc** and save the file on your file disk.
- ❖ Print one copy and close the document.

Start-Up Instructions

- ❖ Open the file named **8drill2.doc** located on the data disk.
- ❖ Select the body text (move the I-beam to the left of the *G* in the word *Gerald* in the first paragraph, press and hold the mouse button and drag downward to select all paragraphs to the end of the document).
- ❖ Create two newspaper columns (select the **Columns** button, select the second column).
- ❖ If desired, click once to deselect the text.
- ❖ If necessary, change to Page Layout view {select the **Page Layout View** button at the bottom left of the document window}.
- ❖ Select the down arrow beside the **Zoom Control** button and choose 75%.

Insert a Column Break to Control the Flow of Columnar Text

1. Locate the insertion point to the left of the first character of text to be placed in another column.

   For example, place the insertion point at the beginning of the third paragraph to the left of the **B** in the word *Before.*

2. Select **Insert, Break, Column Break, OK** {press Ctrl and Shift and Enter}.

   Note: The text following the insertion point is moved to the second column.

Finish-Up Instructions

- ❖ Center the text vertically on the page (select all text; select **File**, **Page Setup**, **Layout**, **Vertical Alignment**, **Center**, **OK**).
- ❖ If desired, select the down arrow beside the **Zoom Control** button and choose **Whole Page** to display the vertically centered columns. Select the down arrow beside the **Zoom Control** button and choose **100%** to return to the normal size.
- ❖ Use the *new* filename **8fred2.doc** and save the file on your file disk.
- ❖ Print one copy and close the document.

Hyphenation

Hyphenation is the process of dividing a word at the right margin so that the first part of the word prints at the end of the line and the remainder of the word prints at the beginning of the next line. Hyphenating words is used to make line endings at the right margin look more even (less ragged) or to avoid large gaps of space between words in a line with justified alignment. Word has two hyphenation features that are available through the **Tools, Hyphenation** command. The fully automatic hyphenation feature will insert hyphens in a document without asking for approval. The manual hyphenation feature finds locations where a word could be hyphenated, then prompts you to accept, reject, or change the position for each hyphen it proposes.

When text is typed, regular, nonbreaking, and optional hyphens can be inserted. A *regular hyphen* breaks compound words at the right margin when necessary. For example, the hyphenated word *well-defined* will divide after the hyphen if the hyphen is at the right margin.

A *nonbreaking hyphen*, such as the hyphen in the compound name *Jones-Meyer*, is inserted between words that should always appear on the same line of text. A nonbreaking hyphen is inserted by pressing and holding the **Ctrl** and **Shift** keys while tapping the **hyphen** (-) key once. The nonbreaking hyphen is also referred to as a required hyphen.

An *optional hyphen* can be inserted by placing the insertion point to the left of the character that will follow the hyphen and pressing the **Ctrl** and **hyphen** (-) keys. When a word that contains an optional hyphen does not break at the end of line, the hyphen is hidden. In other words, an optional hyphen will only display in the document window and print if the hyphenated word breaks at the end of the line.

Word uses a hyphenation zone to determine if words need to be hyphenated. The hyphenation zone is an allowable distance between the right margin and the end of the line. When the zone is small, the right margin will be less ragged, but more words may need to be hyphenated. A larger hyphenation zone will reduce the number of hyphenated words, but will produce a more ragged edge. Generally, the default hyphenation zone will produce a visually acceptable hyphenation area.

After a document has been proofread, edited, and is being prepared for final form, view the document and observe if there are gaps of space between words or if there are large spaces at the right margins. If the gaps or spaces are visually unattractive, hyphenation may be desirable.

Start-Up Instructions

- Open the file named **8fin1.doc** created earlier in this chapter.

Automatically Hyphenate Text

1. Place the insertion point at the beginning of the document (if necessary, press **Ctrl** and **Home**).
2. Select **Tools, Hyphenation** {Alt, t, h}.

   ***Note:** The Hyphenation dialog box displays (see Figure 8.3).*

FIGURE 8.3

Hyphenation dialog box

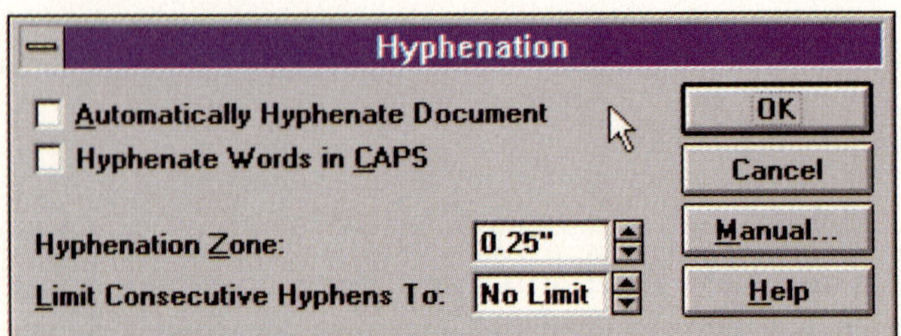

3. Select the desired Hyphenation option.

   For example, select the **Automatically Hyphenate Document** option {Alt and a}.

   Note: An X should display in the Automatically Hyphenate Document box. Check that the Hyphenate Words in CAPS option is not selected (no X displays beside the Hyphenate Words in CAPS option). When this option is selected, words in all caps will be hyphenated, and during automatic hyphenation Word might hyphenate acronyms such as IRS or USA.

4. Select **OK** {Enter}.

5. When the entire document has been reviewed for possible words to be hyphenated, any words that were hyphenated display with a hyphen at the end of the text line(s).

   Note: Scroll through the document to observe any hyphenated words. Depending on the selected font and point size (see Chapter 3), the hyphenation zone setting, and the words used in the document, there may not be any words hyphenated.

Finish-Up Instructions

- Place the insertion point below the final paragraph in the two-column section. Press the **Enter** key several times until a blank line displays at the top of the three-column section.
- Use the *new* filename **8hyp3.doc** and save the file on your file disk.
- Print one copy and close the document.

Start-Up Instructions

- Open the file named **8fred2.doc** created earlier in this chapter.
- Place the insertion point at the beginning of the document.

Manually Hyphenate Text

1. Read the following guidelines for correct word division before proceeding to step 2.

   a. Hyphenate only between syllables. Use a dictionary, if necessary.

   b. Avoid hyphenating words of five characters or less, e.g., *often*.

   c. Hyphenate a word so that at least three characters remain on the line, e.g., *in-* or *ly.*, but not *i-* or *ly* without the period.

   d. Place a hyphen after a vowel, e.g., *initi-ate*.

   e. Place a hyphen between double consonants, e.g., *accom-modate*.

   f. Do not hyphenate the last word of a paragraph; do not hyphenate the last word on a page.

   g. Avoid hyphenating words at the end of two consecutive lines.

   h. Do not hyphenate proper nouns, e.g., Apprenticeship Council.

   Note: When Word has checked a document for possible words to be hyphenated, there may not be any words hyphenated.

2. Select **Tools, Hyphenation** {Alt, t, h}.
3. Select **Manual** {m}.

   Note: The Manual Hyphenation dialog box displays with the first word to be hyphenated in the Hyphenate At box.

4. Use the the guidelines for hyphenation listed in step 1, and select one of the following options for each word:
   - To skip the word, select **No** {Alt and n}.
   - To hyphenate the word where Word has placed the blinking cursor, select **Yes** {Enter}.
   - To hyphenate the word at a different location, move the mouse pointer to the desired location and click once, then select **Yes** {use the left or right arrow key to move the blinking cursor to the desired point, then press Enter}.

     Note: The thin, nonblinking vertical line shows the maximum number of characters that can fit in the line. Select a hyphenation point to the left of this line.

5. When Word cannot find any more words to hyphenate, the message "Hyphenation is complete." displays. Select **Yes** to return to the document window {press Enter}.

Finish-Up Instructions

- Scroll down to view the hyphenated text. If necessary, correct any errors in hyphenation by deleting the hyphen. To insert an optional hyphen, press **Ctrl** and **hyphen** (-). Use optional hyphens when manually hyphenating text.
- Use the *new* filename **8hyp4.doc** and save the file on your file disk.
- Print one copy and close the document.

Format Painter

Different font styles and font sizes are often used to enhance and emphasize text such as sideheads. When using different fonts and sizes for a sidehead, a uniform appearance can result if the format for each sidehead is the same. The Format Painter feature can be used to quickly copy the format from one text item to another.

The text that contains the desired format is selected. If the format is to be copied to multiple paragraphs, double-click on the **Format Painter** button (located on the Standard Toolbar. If the format is to be copied to a single paragraph, click once on the **Format Painter** button. After clicking on the **Format Painter** button, the paragraph(s) where the format is to be copied is selected. When the mouse button is released, the format is immediately copied to the selected text.

If the **Format Painter** button was selected by clicking once, the **Format Painter** feature is turned off when the mouse button is released. If the **Format Painter** button was selected by double-clicking, the Format Painter feature remains in effect until the **Format Painter** button is selected again.

Start-Up Instructions

❖ Open the file named **8fin1.doc** created earlier in this chapter.

Copy Formats Using the Format Painter Button

Note: A mouse must be used to perform the following steps.

1. Select and format the text from which the format is to be copied.

   For example, select the title **SAVING AND INVESTING TRENDS.** Click on the **Font** button and select the **Brittanic Bold** font or **make a font choice of your own.** Click on the **Size** button and select **14.**

2. With the formatted text selected, double-click on the **Format Painter** button on the Standard Toolbar.

   Note: The format will be immediately copied from the selected text. The mouse pointer changes to a paintbrush with an I-beam when the pointer is moved into the document window.

3. Select the text where the formatting is to be copied.

   For example, select the next sidehead **Healthy Savings Attitudes.**

   Note: The copied format will be immediately applied to the selected text.

4. Repeat step 3 to copy the format to the desired paragraphs.

   For example, copy the format to all remaining sideheads in the document and to the centered paragraph at the bottom of the document.

5. When the format has been copied to all desired paragraphs, click on the **Format Painter** button once to turn off the Format Painter feature.

Finish-Up Instructions

❖ Use the *new* filename **8drill5.doc** and save the file on your file disk.

❖ Print one copy and close the document.

Side-by-Side Columns

Side-by-side columns are blocks of related information that are placed next to each other so that information can be read easily from left to right. Text in side-by-side columns wraps within each column. When using side-by-side columns, the information in the first column and the related information in the second column may vary in length. For example, the information in the first column could include only one or two lines of text while the related information in the second column includes three or more lines of text. Side-by-side columns are also referred to as parallel columns.

Side-by-side columns are created in Word using the Tables feature. To create a table with the desired number of columns and rows, see Chapter 5. When typing, text automatically wraps around within each table cell.

Start-Up Instructions

- The text shown in Figure 8.4 will be used to create side-by-side columns using the Tables feature.
- A new document window should be displayed. If necessary, select the **New** button.
- Type and center the title **COMPUTER TERMINOLOGY**. Press **Enter** three times.

Create Side-by-Side Columns Using the Tables Feature

1. Move the mouse pointer to the **Insert Table** button on the Standard Toolbar. Highlight the desired number of columns and rows.

   For example, highlight a **4 x 2** table.

2. Type the text for column A.

   For example, type **ASCII** (see Figure 8.4).

3. Press the **Tab** key to move the insertion point to column 2.

4. Type the text for the first paragraph in column 2.

   For example, type the paragraph beginning **The acronym ASCII stands for . . .** After the last character in the paragraph, press **Enter** once.

   Note: *The text wraps around within each cell.*

5. Press the **Tab** key to move the insertion point back to column A.

Finish-Up Instructions

- Repeat steps 2–5 to type the remaining information in Figure 8.4.
- Use the filename **8drill6.doc** and save the file on your file disk.
- Print one copy and close the document.

COMPUTER TERMINOLOGY	
ASCII	The acronym ASCII stands for American Standard Code for Information Interchange (pronounced *ask-kee*). This standard code enables computers to convert keyboard symbols, such as letters, numbers, and punctuation, into binary code. Enter
BUG	An error or problem that prevents the proper execution of a computer task. A bug can be a hardware or software error. Enter
COMPUTER GRAPHICS	Pictures that are created by using a computer with graphics software. Today, graphics software is capable of producing movies, animation, color illustrations, and three-dimensional drawings. Enter
DOWN	A computer that is "down" is not operating, usually because of software or hardware failure. Enter

FIGURE 8.4

Side-by-side columns created using the Tables feature

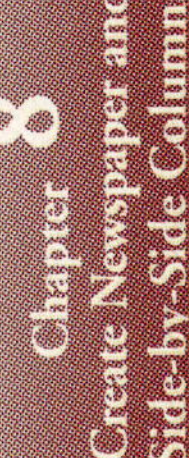

The Next Step

Chapter Review and Activities

Self-Check Quiz

T F 1. When typing newspaper columns, select **Insert**, **Break**, **Column Break**, **OK** to insert a column break.

T F 2. The **Format Painter** button is a quick method for adding pictures to a document.

T F 3. Newspaper-style columns can be created before *or* after text is typed.

T F 4. The amount of blank space between newspaper columns cannot be changed.

T F 5. The Tables feature is used to create side-by-side columns.

6. A vertical line can be added between columns by selecting the _______ option in the Columns dialog box.
   a. **Spacing**
   b. **Line Between**
   c. **Width**
   d. **Vertical Line**

7. Which of the following guidelines should be remembered when hyphenating text?
   a. Avoid hyphenating words of fewer than five characters.
   b. Place hyphens between double consonants.
   c. Hyphenate between syllables.
   d. All of the above.

8. What are the default settings Word uses when the **Columns** button is selected to create columns?

9. When and why should hyphenation be used?

10. Show the correct hyphenation points for the following words.

opportunity seminar thoroughly

Enriching Language Arts Skills

Spelling/Vocabulary Words

opportunity a good chance; a combination of circumstances favorable for the purpose.

seminar a course of study.

thoroughly done in a complete, exact, or absolute manner.

Using the Abbreviations *e.g.* and *i.e.*

The abbreviation *e.g.* is used in place of "for example" and is often used when there are many possible examples and only a few are listed. The abbreviation *i.e.* is used in place of "that is" and is used when all potential conditions are listed. A period follows each initial with no space between the period and the initials. The final period is followed by a comma.

Examples:

There are many word processing programs that include desktop publishing features, e.g., WordPerfect, Microsoft Word, and AmiPro.

When the president's name is typed in the signature line, use the first name initial and include Sr., i.e., J. Thomas-Meyers, Sr.

Activities

Activity 8.1—Create Balanced Newspaper Columns; Use Format Painter

1. Open the file named **8act1.doc** on the data disk.
2. Create newspaper columns:
   a. Move the I-beam to the left of the **R** in the first word of the first sidehead, Report. Press and hold the mouse button and drag downward to select all paragraphs.
   b. Select the **Columns** button on the Standard Toolbar. Select **2 columns.**
3. Use the **Format Painter** button to format the sideheads:
   a. Format the first sidehead. Choose a different font and make the sidehead bold and larger than the body text.
   b. With the first sidehead selected (highlighted), double-click on the **Format Painter** button on the Standard Toolbar.
   c. Select the second sidehead.
   d. Repeat step 3c until all the sideheads are formatted.
   e. Click once on the **Format Painter** button to turn off the Format Painter feature.
4. Use the *new* filename **8for1.doc** and save the file on your file disk.
5. Print one copy.
6. Close the document.

Activity 8.2—Create Parallel Columns Using the Tables Feature

1. Type, center, and bold the title, **PEOPLE IN THE NEWS**. Press **Enter** three times.
2. Create and keyboard the following side-by-side columns:
   a. Select the **Insert Table** button on the Standard Toolbar.
   b. Drag the mouse pointer to select a **3 x 2 table**.
   c. With the insertion point in the first table cell, type each entry from left to right.

      Hint: *Press the* **Enter** *key after the short lines in the first column but let text wrap around in the cells in the second column. Use the* ***Tab*** *key to move from cell to cell. Press the* **Enter** *key once after each paragraph in the second column.*

PEOPLE IN THE NEWS

Nancy Wright Personnel Manager King City, Oregon	Nancy received the 1994 Woman of Achievement Award. North Bay United Bank nominated her for the award because of her exceptional leadership and community activities.
Donald Marks Quality Assurance Representative Eugene, Oregon	Donald raised $2,400 selling T-shirts at the Jet Fan Fly Air Show. The proceeds from the sale were used to provide grocery gift certificates for homeless families in the Eugene area.
Barnard Daniels Director of Foreign Currency Portland, Oregon	The Foreign Currency Department has been created to handle all aspects of wholesale trading of foreign currency for corporations, hotels, and travel agencies. Formerly part of the International Division, growing corporate overseas marketing and travel now require a full-time director and staff. Barnard's time will be divided between currency trading and overseas business development.

3. Use the filename **8act2.doc** and save the file on your file disk.
4. Print one copy.
5. Close the document.

Activity 8.3—Create Newspaper Columns; Insert Column Breaks; Change Column Definition

1. Open the file named **8act3.doc** located on the data disk.
2. Select all the body text (do not select the blank space above the first paragraph). Format the body text into **three** columns with .3" spacing between columns (select **Format, Columns;** set Number of Columns to 3; check that the **Equal Columns Width** option is selected; click once in the Width box; double-click in the Spacing box in the first row, type .3; select **OK**).
3. Use the *new* filename **8trend3.doc** and save the file on your file disk.
4. Print one copy.
5. Change the number of columns to 2 with .4" spacing and a line between the columns. (Place the insertion point anywhere in the three-column section; select **Format, Columns;** set the Number of Columns to 2; check that the **Equal**

Column Width option is selected; double-click in the first **Spacing** box, then type .4; select **Line Between**; select **OK**.)

6. Use the *new* filename **8trend3r.doc** and save the file on your file disk.
7. Print one copy.
8. Close the document.

Challenge Your Skills

Skill 8.1—Create Newspaper Columns

1. Open the file named **8skill1.doc** located on the data disk.
2. Change the top, bottom, left, and right margins to .5 inches.
3. Change the body text to a two-column newspaper format and make decisions regarding:

   Space between columns
   Line between columns
   Alignment
   Appropriate use of bold, underline, and spacing for title and sidehead(s)
   Fonts
   Hyphenation

4. Use the *new* filename **8loan1.doc** and save the file on your file disk.
5. Print one copy.
6. Close the document.

Skill 8.2—Create Newspaper Columns with Multiple Sections; Use Format Painter; Hyphenation

1. Open the file named **8skill2.doc** located on the data disk and make decisions regarding:

   Margins
   Fonts
   Font size
   Alignment

2. Center the title and format it, using bold and an 18-point font size.
3. The first news item, "Quake-Proof Your Home," should be divided into **three** columns with a .2" spacing between columns.
4. The second news item, "Henry W. Coe State Park," should be divided into a two-column format.
5. Format the first news item's heading with a different font, a 14-point font size, and bold.

6. Use the Format Painter and apply the heading format to the second news item's heading.
7. Format the first sidehead in the first article as desired. Use the Format Painter and apply the sidehead format to the other sideheads in both articles.
8. Hyphenate the entire document.
9. Use the *new* filename **8quake2.doc** and save the file on your file disk.
10. Print one copy.
11. Close the document.

Skill 8.3—Create Parallel Columns; Language Arts

1. Open the file named **8skill3.doc** located on the data disk.
2. Format the document creatively and attractively using multiple columns. Make your own decisions regarding:

   Margins
   Alignment
   Fonts
   Format for title and sideheads
   Use of Format Painter
   Use of text attributes, such as bold, italic, and underline
   Number of columns and whether to use a different number of columns for part of the document
   Amount of space between columns
   Line between columns
   Hyphenation
3. Correct three spelling errors and two punctuation errors.
4. Use the *new* filename **8desk3.doc** and save the file on your file disk.
5. Print one copy.
6. If you have completed your work, exit Word.

Part 2
Checking Your Step

Production Skill Builder Activities
Chapters 5-8

Production Activity 2.1—Create Formulas, Insert a Row, and Recalculate

1. Create the table shown. Type the following unformatted information into the table cells.

   Note: The text may wrap around in the cells differently than shown because of the fonts and point sizes selected on your computer.

AUCTION SALES			
First Quarter			
Item	Current Owner's Purchase Price	Appraised Value	Price Realized
Louis XIV chair	30,000	45,000	42,500
Wedgewood stove	350	2,500	3,000
Spode tea set	13,000	14,700	13,525
Brass bed frame	200	350	275
Totals			

2. Select and merge the cells in row 1. Also merge the cells in row 2.
3. Make decisions regarding:

   Alignment for title, subtitle, and column heading cells
   Alignment for columns containing dollar amounts
   Table lines
   Shading for cells
   Column widths

4. Create formulas to calculate the column totals.
5. Insert a row between rows 6 and 7. Type the following information into the new row table cells:150-volume library; 4,000; 6,000; 2,500. Recalculate the table column totals.

6. Use the filename **2pact1.doc** and save the file on your file disk.
7. Print one copy and close the document.

Production Activity 2.2—Create a Résumé, Set Tabs, and Insert Special Symbols

1. Use the following information to type the résumé shown.
    a. Change the top margin to .75" and the bottom margin to .5"; change the left and right margins to 1".
    b. Set left tabs at .5 and .75 and set a right tab with dot leaders at **6**.
    c. Make decisions on the use of bold, underline, and italic text attributes.
    d. Select a font of your own choice in a point size of 12.
    e. Use special symbols to create the é's in Résumé.
    f. Choose an appropriate bullet symbol to replace the asterisks shown.
    g. Use the **Format Painter** button to copy the sidehead format from the first sidehead to other sideheads.

Résumé
Katrina Martinez
756 Allen Ave.
Paterson, NJ 07509
(201) 555-8552

EMPLOYMENT EXPERIENCE

Darwin Communication Systems, Wyckoff, New Jersey
* Technical Writer 8/93-Present
Write and review technical journals and procedure manuals for computer systems and applications; train new writers; assist marketing department with product literature.

Academia Computers, Boston, Massachusetts
* Editor 5/88-7/93
Handled all aspects of production of technical manuals for hardware and instruction manuals for software applications.

* Assistant Editor 8/84-5/88
Assisted with the production of technical and instruction manuals and handled production of company newsletters, internal procedure manuals, and some advertising information. Promoted to Editor on May 1, 1988.

Newark Medical Group, Newark, New Jersey
* Receptionist and Clerical Assistant (part-time) 1/82-5/84
Duties included scheduling appointments, routing incoming phone calls, typing, photocopying, faxing, and mail distribution.

EDUCATIONAL BACKGROUND

Rutgers University, Newark, New Jersey (part-time) 2/91-Present
A.A. English, Montgomery Jr. College, Takoma Park, Maryland 7/81-5/83
High School Diploma, Denbigh High School, Denbigh, Virginia 6/81

REFERENCES

Maggie Halter, Supervisor
Academia Computers
390 Fallones St., Suite 55
Boston, MA 02110
(617) 555-4523

Tom Yim, MD
7630 Mission Ave.
Takoma Park, MD 20912
(301) 555-4890

---

2. Use the filename **2pact2.doc** and save the file on your file disk.
3. Print one copy and close the document.

Production Activity 2.3—Create Side-by-Side Columns

1. Create the following document using a table to format side-by-side columns. Make decisions regarding:

   Margins
   Alignment
   Fonts
   Font Size
   Width of columns
   Bold/underline/capitalization of title, subtitle, and sideheads
   Hyphenation
   Use of Table AutoFormats and/or Format Painter features

Property inspection report
3555 South Grand
August 25, 199x

general	The property is known as 3555 South Grand and is located on the south side of South Grand.
construction	The building was built in 1950 under the new building application NB-19244. It is constructed of wood floors and roof beams of masonry bearing and is classified as Class 3, non-fireproof construction, under the Minneapolis Administrative Building Code.

occupancy	The building is classified as a Class A single dwelling. The occupancy, room, and residency counts have not changed since the building was constructed.
street	The front of the building abuts South Grand, which is a publicly owned and maintained street with a single sidewalk on the north side of the street. The street is paved with asphalt and is in fair condition.
utilities	Water is supplied to the building from a Minneapolis City water main in the bed of South Grand from a curb box at the edge of the sidewalk at the south property line. Gas for domestic cooking ranges is supplied from a main in the bed of South Grand maintained by the Consolidated Gas Co. Electricity is supplied from a main line in the bed of South Grand maintained by Union Electric Co.

---

2. Use the filename **2pact3.doc** and save the file on your file disk.
3. Print one copy and close the document.

Production Activity 2.4—Create Newspaper Columns; Language Arts

1. Open the file named **2pact4.doc** located on the data disk.
2. Use newspaper columns and the following information to complete the document.
   a. Make decisions regarding:

      Margins and font size to fit document on one page
      Number of columns
      Spacing between columns
      Line between columns
      Alignment
      Fonts
      Spacing before and after sideheads
      Bold/italic/underline/capitalization of title and sideheads
      Use of bullets or numbering to emphasize the list after the first paragraph
      Hyphenation
3. Correct three spelling errors and two punctuation errors.
4. Use the filename **2pfin4.doc** and save the file.
5. Print the document and close the document.
6. If you have completed your work, exit Word.

Part 3
A Step Up

Create Reports and Special Documents

Chapters 9-12

- Add space between paragraphs
- Indent paragraphs from the left and right margins
- Change vertical line spacing
- Word Count
- Thesaurus
- Grammar-checking
- Standard paragraphs
- Copy text between windows
- Create headers and footers
- Print page numbers
- Control text flow (widow/orphan)
- Create footnotes and endnotes
- Print specific pages
- Create a data source and main document
- Merge a main document and data source
- Edit a data source and main document
- Select data records to be merged
- Create envelope addresses
- Create mailing labels using predefined labels
- Create and sort mailing labels using a new main document and existing data source

CHAPTER

Create a One-Page Document

Features Covered

- Format paragraphs
- Change vertical line spacing
- Word Count
- Thesaurus
- Grammar-Check
- Standard paragraphs
- Copy text between windows

Objectives and Introduction

After successfully completing this chapter, you will be able to use the Paragraph dialog box to change vertical line spacing, spacing between paragraphs, alignment, and paragraph indention. You will learn how to use Word Count, Thesaurus, and grammar-check features to improve a document, and you will learn to assemble personalized documents using standard paragraphs and to copy text between document windows.

A one-page document can be an article, essay, meeting minutes, an agenda, report, or any type of document that describes an event or provides information. Investment, insurance, sales, real estate, and medical documents are examples of one-page business documents.

Create a One-Page Document

Documents have traditionally been created with either vertical line spacing of one (single-spacing) or vertical line spacing of two (double-spacing). With a typewriter, vertical line spacing of two is accomplished by pressing the Return key twice after each sentence or by moving a lever on the typewriter to set the desired vertical spacing. Vertical line spacing in Word can be set at any interval desired (see Change Vertical Line Spacing and Paragraph Format later in this chapter).

When a document is formatted with vertical line spacing of one, generally, paragraphs begin at the left margin with an extra line space between paragraphs (see Figure 9.1). This extra space can be added by pressing the Enter key twice between paragraphs, but it can also be added using the Paragraph dialog box. Usually, no extra spacing is placed between paragraphs when vertical line spacing of two is used, but the first line of each paragraph is indented approximately one-half inch from the left margin (see Figure 9.4). If vertical line spacing will be greater than 1.3 lines, the formatting guidelines (e.g., first line indent and no extra spacing between paragraphs) for line spacing of two should be used.

Either left alignment or justify alignment can be used in a one-page document, depending on the writer's preference and the appearance of the document. Often long quotes or other paragraphs that should be given special attention are indented from both the left and right margins with a vertical line spacing of one.

Format a Document

A standard $8^{1}/_{2}$- by 11-inch sheet of paper using the default 1" top and bottom margins has 9 vertical inches available for printed text. Normally, the default margins will be used when creating a one-page document; however, if desired, the margins can be changed.

The document title is usually centered and often emphasized by using bold, by changing to a different font, or by capitalizing all the letters. If a subtitle is used, one blank line follows the title. A subtitle is usually centered and typed in lowercase letters with the first letter of each main word capitalized. *Initial caps* is the phrase used to indicate words/phrases typed with the first letter of each main word capitalized.

Additional space is added before the first paragraph of a document and before and after each sidehead or subhead in the document. This gives the reader visual clues as to where the document begins and where each important idea is discussed. The additional spacing should equal one to two lines of text and should be consistent throughout the document.

Start-Up Instructions

- Open the file named **9drill1.doc** located on the data disk.
- Place the insertion point to the left of the first character in the body text and press **Enter** twice to add additional space between the subtitle and the first paragraph.
- Center and bold the title and subtitle.
- Nonprinting characters, such as tabs and paragraph markers, should be displayed in the document window. If necessary, select the **Show/Hide** button on the Standard Toolbar.

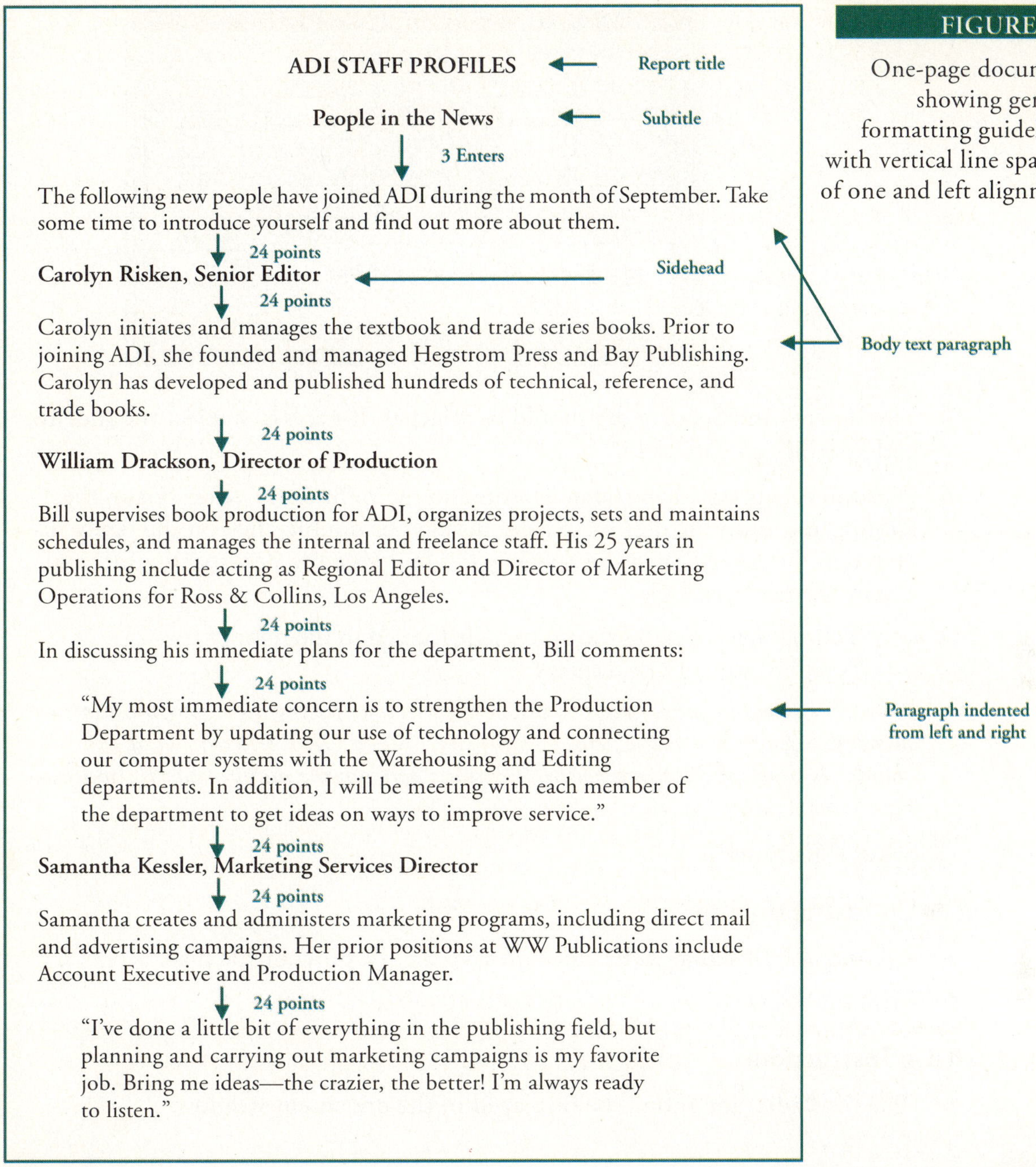

ADI STAFF PROFILES ← Report title

People in the News ← Subtitle

↓ 3 Enters

The following new people have joined ADI during the month of September. Take some time to introduce yourself and find out more about them.

↓ 24 points

Carolyn Risken, Senior Editor ← Sidehead

↓ 24 points

Carolyn initiates and manages the textbook and trade series books. Prior to joining ADI, she founded and managed Hegstrom Press and Bay Publishing. Carolyn has developed and published hundreds of technical, reference, and trade books. ← Body text paragraph

↓ 24 points

William Drackson, Director of Production

↓ 24 points

Bill supervises book production for ADI, organizes projects, sets and maintains schedules, and manages the internal and freelance staff. His 25 years in publishing include acting as Regional Editor and Director of Marketing Operations for Ross & Collins, Los Angeles.

↓ 24 points

In discussing his immediate plans for the department, Bill comments:

↓ 24 points

> "My most immediate concern is to strengthen the Production Department by updating our use of technology and connecting our computer systems with the Warehousing and Editing departments. In addition, I will be meeting with each member of the department to get ideas on ways to improve service." ← Paragraph indented from left and right

↓ 24 points

Samantha Kessler, Marketing Services Director

↓ 24 points

Samantha creates and administers marketing programs, including direct mail and advertising campaigns. Her prior positions at WW Publications include Account Executive and Production Manager.

↓ 24 points

> "I've done a little bit of everything in the publishing field, but planning and carrying out marketing campaigns is my favorite job. Bring me ideas—the crazier, the better! I'm always ready to listen."

FIGURE 9.1

One-page document showing general formatting guidelines with vertical line spacing of one and left alignment

Chapter 9 Create a One-Page Document

Steps to Create a One-Page Document with Additional Space Between Paragraphs

1. Select the text to which the paragraph formatting is to be applied.

   For example, select all the paragraphs and sideheads below the subtitle. (Place the insertion point to the left of the first body text paragraph, hold down the **Shift** key and press **Ctrl** and **End**.)

2. Select **Format, Paragraph** {Alt, o, p}.

   Note: *The Paragraph dialog box displays (see Figure 9.2).*

FIGURE 9.2

Paragraph dialog box

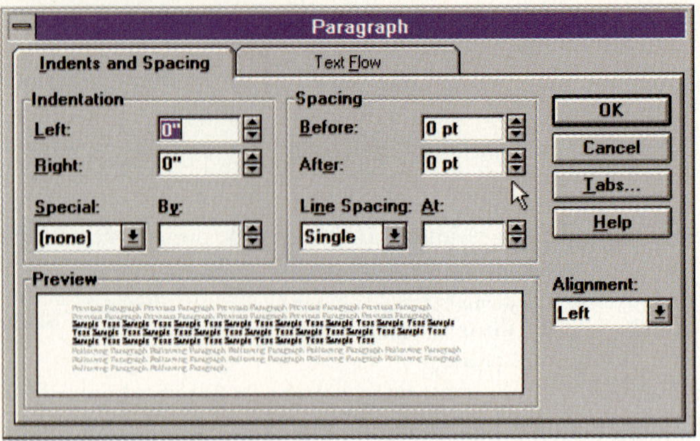

3. The Indents and Spacing tab should be selected. If necessary, select the **Indents and Spacing** tab {Alt and i}.

4. Click on the up or down triangle located to the right of the **After** box in the Spacing area until the desired spacing displays or double-click on the figure displayed in the **After** box in the Spacing area and type the new spacing {Alt and e, type the new spacing}.

   For example, click on the up triangle located to the right of the After box until **12 pt** displays.

   Note: *The following abbreviations can be used in the Spacing area: pi = picas, pt = points, li = lines, in = inches, cm = centimeters. When **OK** is selected, Word will change the measurement into points. The space between the number and the measurement is optional.*

5. Select **OK** {Enter}.

Finish-Up Instructions

- Use the *new* filename **9adi1.doc** and save the file on your file disk.
- Print one copy.

Start-Up Instructions

- The file **9adi1.doc** should be displayed in the document window.

Indent Paragraphs from Both Margins

1. Place the insertion point at any location in the first paragraph to be indented from both margins.

   For example, place the insertion point in the first paragraph beginning with quote marks, i.e., "My most immediate..."

2. Select **Format, Paragraph** {Alt, o, p}.

3. The Indents and Spacing tab should be selected. If necessary, select the **Indents and Spacing** tab {Alt and i}.

4. Click on the up or down triangle located to the right of the desired Indentation box or double-click in the Indentation box to be changed and type the new indentation {Alt and L and Alt and r, type the desired indentation}.

For example, check that the amount in the Left indentation box is highlighted. (If necessary, double-click in the **Left** box.) Type .5. Double-click in the **Right** indentation box and type **.5**.

Note: *The Indentation area shows the measurement in inches. Press the* **Tab** *key once to display the new settings in the Preview box.*

5. Select **OK** {press Enter}.

Note: *The paragraph is indented .5" from both the left and right margins.*

Finish-Up Instructions

- Select the paragraph just changed, then click once on the **Format Painter** button. Move the mouse pointer to the last paragraph in the document and click once. The Format Painter will copy the indentations to this paragraph.
- If desired, bold the first sidehead—Carolyn Risken, Senior Editor—then double-click on the **Format Painter** button. Select each sidehead to apply the copied format. When all sideheads have been formatted, click once on the Format Painter button to turn off the Format Painter feature.
- Use the *new* filename **9adi2.doc** and save the file on your file disk.
- Print one copy.

Change Vertical Line Spacing and Paragraph Formats

Additional space can be created between lines of text by changing the vertical line spacing. The added space can be used, for example, to accommodate handwritten changes to draft letters or reports. Also, a report set for line spacing of two may be easier to read. The line spacing options available in Word are: *Single*, *1.5 Lines*, *Double*, *At Least*, *Exactly*, and *Multiple*. Line spacing options are located on the Indents and Spacing tab of the Paragraph dialog box (see Figure 9.2).

On a typewriter, single spacing traditionally meant that a fixed amount of space (approximately .164") was placed between text lines. Also, the amount of space between text lines did not change if a larger font was used.

When using Word, *Single* line spacing means that the point size of the text plus an amount equal to approximately 20% of the point size is placed between lines of text. For example, if a 12-point font size is selected and single spacing is chosen, the actual amount of line spacing is approximately 14 points (.194"). The actual amount of line spacing changes depending upon the point size of the text (see Figure 9.3).

If the *Double* line spacing option is selected, the amount of line spacing is equal to twice the single line spacing amount. For example, if the single line spacing amount is 14 points, 28 points of line spacing will be inserted when the Double line spacing option is selected.

The *1.5 Lines* option places one and a half times the single line spacing amount between the text lines. For example, if the single line spacing amount is 12 points, 18 points of line spacing will be inserted when the 1.5 Lines option is selected.

FIGURE 9.3

Sample of single line spacing in various point sizes

This is a sample of 12-point text and single line spacing.

This is a sample of 18-point text and single line spacing.

This is a sample of 24-point text and single line spacing.

To increase or decrease the line spacing by an amount other than Double or 1.5 Lines, the *Multiple* option is selected and the desired line spacing increment is typed in the At box. For example, to triple the amount of line spacing, select the Multiple option and type 3 in the At box; to decrease the amount of line spacing by 25%, select the Multiple option and type .75 in the At box.

The *At Least* option sets a minimum amount of line spacing. If necessary, Word will automatically adjust the line spacing to accommodate large fonts or graphic images. When the *Exactly* option is selected, an exact line spacing can be typed in. The line spacing is then fixed at that measurement, regardless of changes in font size.

Line spacing can also be changed by selecting the text and pressing the appropriate shortcut key: **Ctrl and 1** for single line spacing, **Ctrl and 2** for line spacing of two (double), and **Ctrl and 5** for line spacing of 1.5 Lines.

In addition to setting line spacing, the Paragraph dialog box is used to format paragraphs, conforming to standard usage and making the document more attractive. For example, the Paragraph dialog box can be used to set left and right paragraph indents and to create hanging and first line indents. A sample of each indentation type can be found in Figure 7.5 (Chapter 7, page 166)

The Special box in the Indentation area of the Paragraph dialog box contains two options: First Line and Hanging. The *First Line* option applies the indentation only to the first line of a paragraph. The *Hanging* option applies the indentation to the second and following lines of a paragraph (the first line of a hanging indent begins at the left margin).

Start-Up Instructions

- The file **9adi2.doc** should be displayed in the document window.

Change Paragraph Formats

1. Select the paragraph(s) to be changed.

   For example, select the first paragraph in the body text.

2. Select **Format, Paragraph** {Alt, o, p}.

3. Make any formatting changes as desired.

   For example, change all of the following items:

a. Click in the **Line Spacing** box. Select the **Double** option {Alt and n, press the down arrow twice to highlight Double}.

b. Move the mouse pointer to the down triangle located to the right of the After box and click twice to display **0 pt** {Alt and e, press the down arrow key once, type zero (0)}.

c. Click in the **Special** box in the Indentation area. Select the **First Line** option {Alt and s, press the down arrow to highlight First Line}.

Note: The defalut .5 inches displays in the By box.

d. Click in the **Alignment** box. Select the **Justified** option {Alt and g, press the down arrow three times to highlight Justified}.

4. Check that all options are set as desired, select **OK** {press Enter}.

5. Use the **Format Painter** button to copy the paragraph formatting to all other desired paragraphs. When all desired paragraphs have been formatted, click once on **Format Painter** button to turn off the Format Painter feature.

For example, with the first body text paragraph selected, double-click on the **Format Painter** button. Move the mouse pointer to the body text next paragraph and click once. Repeat for all body text paragraphs *except* the quoted paragraphs. Click once on the **Format Painter** button to turn off the **Format Painter** feature.

Finish-Up Instructions

- Format the first sidehead with 6 points of space before and 12 points of space after (select **Format**, **Paragraph**, click on the up or down triangle to display **6 pt** in the Before box and **12 pt** in the After box). Then use the **Format Painter** button to copy the format to the other sidehead.

  ***Note:** Your document should look similar to the one shown in Figure 9.4*

- Optional. Select one of the paragraphs in quotes. Press **Ctrl** and **5** to change the line spacing to 1.5 Lines. Use the **Format Painter** button to copy this format to the other quoted paragraph. Add an extra blank line if needed after the quoted paragraph.
- Use the *new* filename **9adi3.doc** and save the file on your file disk.
- Print one copy.

Chapter 9
Create a One-Page Document

Word Count

Word can compile various statistics for either an entire document or for a selected portion of a document. When **Tools, Word Count** is selected, the number of pages, words, characters, paragraphs, and lines are calculated and displayed in the Word Count dialog box.

When only a portion of a document is selected, the statistics displayed in the dialog box relate only to the selected text. A total word, character, or line count is useful when preparing a document that must meet specific guidelines, for example, a school research paper or an article submitted for publication.

FIGURE 9.4

One-page document showing general formatting guidelines with vertical line spacing of two, and justified alignment

Body text paragraph

The following new people have joined ADI during the month of September. Take some time to introduce yourself and find out more about them.

Carolyn Risken, Senior Editor — Sidehead

Carolyn initiates and manages the textbook and trade series books. Prior to joining ADI, she founded and managed Hegstrom Press and Bay Publishing. Carolyn has developed and published hundreds of technical, reference, and trade books.

William Drackson, Director of Production

Bill supervises book production for ADI, organizes projects, sets and maintains schedules, and manages the internal and freelance staff. His 25 years in publishing include acting as Regional Editor and Director of Marketing Operations for Ross & Collins, Los Angeles.

In discussing his immediate plans for the department, Bill comments:

> "My most immediate concern is to strengthen the Production Department by updating our use of technology and connecting our computer systems with the Warehousing and Editing departments. In addition, I will be meeting with each member of the department to get ideas on ways to improve service."

Samantha Kessler, Marketing Services Director

Samantha creates and administers marketing programs, including direct mail and advertising campaigns. Her prior positions at WW Publications include Account Executive and Production Manager.

> "I've done a little bit of everything in the publishing field, but planning and carrying out marketing campaigns is my favorite job. Bring me ideas—the crazier, the better! I'm always ready to listen."

Start-Up Instructions

- The file named **9adi3.doc** should be displayed in the document window.

Use Word Count

1. Select **Tools, Word Count** {Alt, t, w}.

   Note: The Word Count dialog box, similar to Figure 9.5, displays.

2. Select **Close** to return to the document window {Enter}.

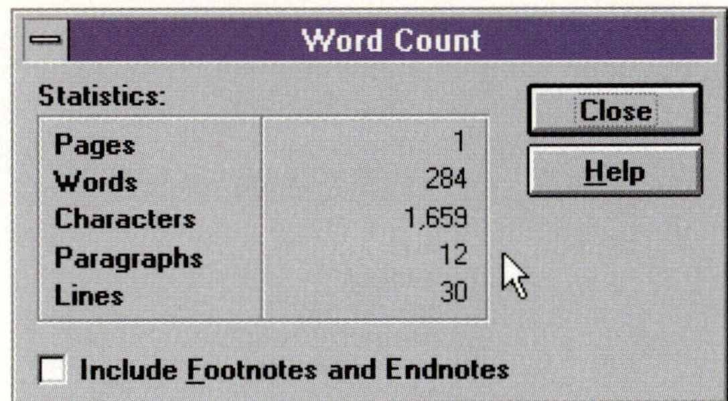

FIGURE 9.5

Word Count dialog box

Finish-Up Instructions

- Optional. Print one copy. At the top of the printed document, handwrite the total number of words and paragraphs.
- If any changes are made to the document, save the file again using the same filename, **9adi3.doc**.
- Close the document.

Chapter 9 Create a One-Page Document

Use the Thesaurus

A list of words that have the same or similar meaning (synonyms) are stored in Word's Thesaurus. A writer attempts to use words that will effectively communicate ideas. A thesaurus assists a writer by providing synonyms to convey his/her message more clearly. Word's Thesaurus can be used during the writing process or after a document has been written.

When the **Thesaurus** command is selected, a dialog box displays containing a list of possible meanings for the selected word, designated as nouns, verbs, and/or adjectives. The synonym(s) for the highlighted word in the Meanings box is displayed in the list located to the right of the Meanings box. When a synonym is highlighted, it also appears in the Replace with Synonym box.

If the word Antonyms displays in the Meanings box, a list of antonyms (words with the opposite meaning) can be viewed by clicking on the word Antonyms. A list of antonyms will then appear in the Meanings box, and they can be highlighted to display other similar words in the list to the right. Also, the Replace with Synonym box will change to a Replace with Antonym box.

In the Thesaurus dialog box, a writer can replace the word with a synonym or antonym, look up another word, or select various meanings of the word to view different lists of synonyms or antonyms. (If the selected word cannot be found, an alphabetical list of words closely resembling the selected word displays.)

After Word replaces the selected word with a different word, the word ending may need to be corrected to match the meaning of the sentence or for verb-subject agreement.

Start-Up Instructions

- Open the file named **9drill4.doc** located on the data disk.

FIGURE 9.6

Thesaurus dialog box

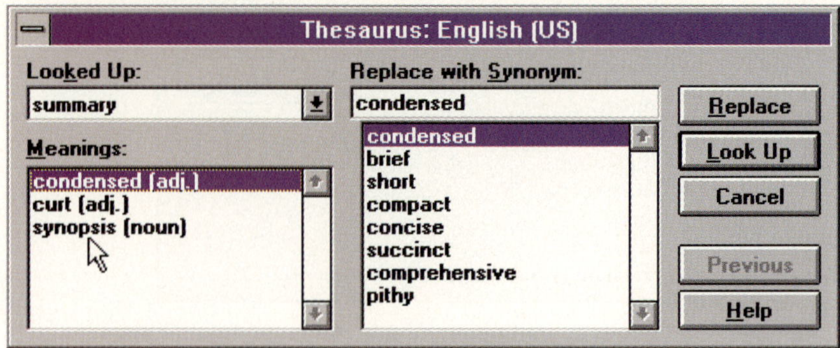

Steps to Select Synonyms From the Thesaurus

1. Place the insertion point in the word to be looked up in the Thesaurus.

   For example, place the insertion point in the word *summary* in the first sentence of the body text.

2. Select **Tools, Thesaurus** {Alt, t, t *or* Shift and F7}.

   Note: The Thesaurus dialog box displays (see Figure 9.6).

3. From the words listed under the heading Meanings, select the word closest to the meaning of the word in the sentence {use the up or down arrow key to highlight the desired word}.

   For example, select the word **synopsis.**

   Note: If there are more meanings than can be displayed at one time, the scroll bar on the right side of the Meanings box will be activated. Scroll through the listed meanings until the desired meaning displays.

4. Select the desired replacement word from the **Replace with Synonym** list {press Tab once, then press the up or down arrow key to highlight the desired word}.

   For example, select the word **outline**.

   Note: The word selected will immediately appear in the Replace with Synonym box at the top of the list.

5. Select **Replace** {Alt and r}.

6. Place the insertion point in the next word to be looked up.

   For example, place the insertion point in the word ***benefit*** in the second sentence of the second body text paragraph.

7. Select **Tools, Thesaurus** {Alt, t, t *or* Shift and F7}.

8. In the Meanings list, select an appropriate meaning. Then scan through the synonyms list and determine if there is a suitable replacement. If no suitable replacement word displays, select **Cancel** {Esc}.

   For example, because there is no suitable replacement for the word ***benefit*** under any of the meanings shown, select **Cancel**.

9. Place the insertion point in the next word to be looked up.

   For example, place the insertion point in the word ***administering*** in the third sentence of the second body text paragraph.

10. Select **Tools, Thesaurus** and scan the listed words. Select the desired synonym and choose **Replace** {Alt and r}.

For example, select the word **managing** in the list of synonyms. Select **Replace.**

Finish-Up Instructions

- Place the insertion point in the word *assets* in the first sentence of the third body text paragraph; select **Tools, Thesaurus** and select **holdings**; select **Replace.**
- Place the insertion point in the word *receive* in the first sentence of the fourth body text paragraph; select **Tools, Thesaurus** and scan the list of words. Select **obtain**; choose **Replace.**
- Use the *new* filename **9the4.doc** and save the file on your file disk.
- Print one copy.
- Close the document.

Chapter 9 Create a One-Page Document

Grammar-Checking

Word's grammar-checking program reviews a document for grammatical, spelling, and writing-style errors. When the grammar-checking program is activated by selecting **Tools, Grammar,** the text is checked against a list of grammar rules, such as passive voice, subject-verb agreement, double negatives, repetitive expressions, and capitalization.

The grammar rules used to check text can be viewed or changed by selecting **Tools, Options, Grammar** or by selecting **Options** in the Grammar dialog box to display the Grammar card (see Figure 9.7). Select a set of grammar and writing style rules, such as those For Business Writing or those For Casual Writing or select one of the Custom sets to create a set that suits your writing needs. To customize any of the writing sets, select the **Customize Settings** button, then review the grammar and writing style rules shown in the Customize Grammar Settings dialog box. If there is an X in the box in front of the rule, the rule is selected and will be applied to the document. The default settings of the rule set For Business Writing are used in the Steps to Use Grammar-Checking.

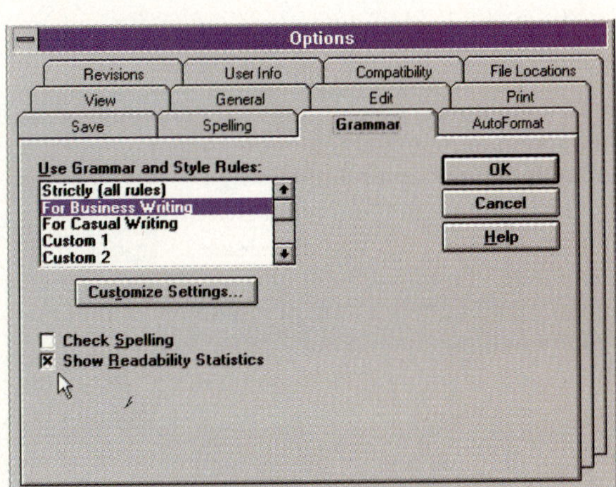

FIGURE 9.7

Grammar Options card

In the Grammar card, the Check Spelling option can be deselected (if the Spelling tool will be used separately). If the Show Readability Statistics option is activated on the Grammar card, the word, character, paragraph, and sentence counts display along with the average number of sentences in a paragraph, words per sentence, and characters per word. Also listed in the statistics is the Flesch Reading Ease readability number. The number displayed by the Flesch Reading Ease option indicates a grade level in school. For example, a number under 30 is considered college level while a number over 90 is considered fourth grade level. Any readability number between 50 and 80 is considered an effective reading level for most individuals.

During the grammar-checking process, suggested changes are displayed. The suggested grammar change can be accepted, ignored, or the sentence may be rewritten. The grammar suggestions provided should be used only as a guide, because the grammar information may or may not be correct according to other grammatical sources or based on the content and context of the sentence. The **Explain** button can be selected at any time to display an explanation of the currently highlighted rule.

Start-Up Instructions

- Open the file named **9drill5.doc** located on the data disk.
- The spell-checking option in the Grammar feature should be turned off, since spelling will be checked separately. (Select **Tools, Options, Grammar.** If there is an X in front of the Check Spelling option, click once on the box to deselect it. Select **OK** to return to the document window.)
- The insertion point should be at the beginning of the document (**Ctrl** and **Home**).

Use Grammar-Checking

1. The document to be grammar-checked must be saved and displayed in the document window.
2. Select **Tools, Grammar** {Alt, t, g}.

   Note: The Grammar dialog box displays. The first potential problem is highlighted in the document window and displays in the Sentence area of the Grammar dialog box. The specific item in question display in red. For example, the first sentence in the first paragraph displays with the words ***different than*** *in red. The Suggestions box displays "Use different from or rephrase using a more specific comparative." (See Figure 9.8.)*

FIGURE 9.8

Grammar dialog box

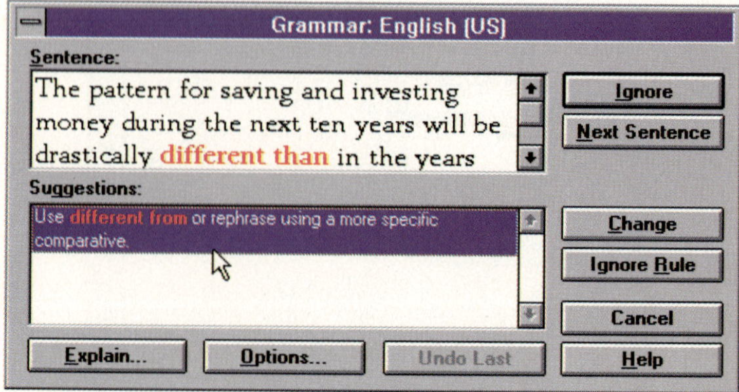

3. Select the **Change** button in to make the change suggested {Alt and c}.

Note: The next potential problem, the word **years** *in the same sentence, is displayed. Neither of the suggestions is correct, but the phrase could be edited to be less awkward.*

4. Move the mouse pointer into the document window to the phrase to be edited. Click in the document window, then use the arrow keys to move to the point where the change is to be made {Ctrl and Tab, use arrow keys}.

Note: If necessary, move the Grammar dialog box by moving the mouse pointer to the dialog box Title bar, pressing and holding the mouse button, and dragging the box down and to the right.

5. Edit the phrase as needed, then select **Start** in the Grammar dialog box to resume grammar checking {Ctrl and Tab, Alt and s}.

For example, delete the phrase "**in the years past**" and type the phrase "**past years.**" Select **Start** to continue.

Note: The next item to be checked is shown in red, e.g., distinct. "Distinct" is the correct word.

6. Select the **Ignore** button {Alt and i}.

Note: The next item to be checked is shown in red, e.g., American attitudes. Two suggestions are shown in the Suggestions box, and the second suggestion is correct.

7. To use one of the alternate suggestions, move the mouse pointer to the desired suggestion and click once to select it, then select the **Change** button {press the up or down arrow until the desired suggestion is highlighted, Alt and c}.

For example, select the second suggestion, then select **Change**.

Note: The next item to be checked is shown in red, e.g., Americans. The program assumes "Americans" is the subject of the sentence. However, the subject is "savings rate" and the singular verb, "was" is correct.

8. Select the **Ignore** button {Alt and i}.

Note: The next item to be checked is highlighted, e.g., the sentence that begins, For example . . . . A careful reading of the sentence shows that the sentence is correct.

9. Select the **Ignore** button{Alt and i}.

Note: The next item to be checked is highlighted, e.g., industry. The second suggestion is correct.

10. Select the correct suggestion, then select the **Change** button {Alt and c}.

Note: The Readability Statistics box may display. Select **OK**.

Finish-Up Instructions

- Use the *new* filename **9gram5.doc** and save the file.
- Print one copy.
- Close the document.

Use Standard Paragraphs to Assemble Personalized Documents

Text that is used repeatedly to personalize documents can be saved and opened when needed. For example, a will created by a lawyer contains many standard paragraphs that are common to all wills. The standard paragraphs are saved in a separate document, and the desired paragraph(s) is retrieved to assemble a document created for a specific individual.

The first part of the process to assemble documents using standard paragraphs is to create and save a document that contains the standard paragraphs. The second part of the process is to open a new document and type the information that is specific to the personalized document, for example, date, name, address, and nonstandard paragraphs.

The final process to assemble documents using standard paragraphs is to copy text from the standard paragraphs document to the personalized document. Each document is placed in a separate document window. For example, the standard paragraphs document and the personalized document are both open and each is in a separate window. With the standard paragraphs document displayed, the desired standard paragraph(s) is copied to the Clipboard (temporary memory). After switching to the personalized document window, the text is pasted in the personalized document at the desired location. The insertion point is located where the copied text is to be inserted.

Create the Standard Paragraphs Document

1. Type the standard paragraphs.

   For example, type the information shown in Figure 9.9.

2. Save the file that contains the standard paragraphs.

   For example, save the file on your file disk; use the filename **9stn6.doc**.

Create the Personalized Document

1. Create a new document by selecting the **New** button on the Standard Toolbar {Alt and f, n *or* Ctrl and n}.

   Note: *A new document window displays on the screen. The file named* ***9stn6.doc*** *is still open in memory but is currently hidden.*

2. Type the information that is specific to the personalized document.

   For example, type the current date, inside address, salutation, and first two paragraphs of the letter shown in Figure 9.10. Press **Enter** twice after the second paragraph.

3. Save the personalized document.

   For example, save the file on your file disk; use the filename **9nelson.doc**.

FIGURE 9.9

Standard paragraphs document (**9stn6.doc**)

Standard Seminar Information

Seminar Locations and Dates

December 5-6, 199x—Airport Marriott, St. Louis, Missouri
December 14-15, 199x—Four Ambassadors, Miami, Florida
December 19-20, 199x—Hyatt Regency, San Francisco, California
December 21-22, 199x—Seattle Hilton, Seattle, Washington

Session Descriptions

Improving Computer Performance—This session covers essential techniques to configure Windows and get the best performance and reliability out of Windows applications, DOS applications, and Windows on networks.

Electronic Distribution—This session discusses the best way to distribute sophisticated print documents in electronic form that can be viewed on a screen, printed out when needed, and updated instantaneously.

Managing Electronic Information—This session will teach you how to control costs and ensure productivity while taking advantage of new technologies such as online databases and CD-ROMs.

Telecommunications for Print Production—This session begins with a summary of the status of high-speed digital communications around the world. Specific user examples illustrating methods in which print publishers are using the technology will be discussed.

Real Uses for Business Multimedia—This session will be a panel discussion on how to make multimedia pay off in training and marketing applications. It includes technical guidelines, tips on estimating costs, and a checklist for implementation.

Steps to Copy Text Between Windows

1. Select **Window** {Alt, w}.
2. Select the filename of the document that contains the standard paragraphs {press the down arrow key to highlight the desired filename, press Enter}.

   For example, click once on the file named **9stn6.doc**.

   Note: *The file containing the standard paragraphs displays on the screen. The file containing the new document is still open in memory but is currently hidden.*

3. Select the desired text to be copied to the personalized document.

   For example, select **December 19-20, 199x—Hyatt Regency, San Francisco, California.**

4. Select the **Copy** button on the Standard Toolbar {Alt, e, c *or* Ctrl and c}.

   Note: *A copy of the selected text has been placed in the Clipboard.*

FIGURE 9.10

Document personalized using standard paragraphs (**9nelson.doc**)

(Use current date)

Mr. Theodore Nelson
8508 Cassy Creek
Fort Worth, TX 76132

Dear Mr. Nelson:

Your registration has been received to attend the upcoming Computers and Communications Conference.

The conference date, location, and description of your selected session(s) are as follows:

> Copy the following paragraphs from the list of Standard Seminar Information (**9stn6.doc**):
>
> December 19-20 conference date and location information
>
> Managing Electronic Information--
>
> Real Uses for Business Multimedia--

If you need additional information about the seminar or hotel accommodations, please call 1-800-555-2100.

Sincerely,

Hazel Walters
Seminar Coordinator

HW/xx
9nelson.doc/disk1

5. Select **Window** {Alt, w}.
6. Choose the filename of the personalized document {press the down arrow key to highlight the desired filename, Enter}.

   For example, click once on the file named **9nelson.doc**.
7. With the insertion point placed at the location where the copied text should be inserted, select the **Paste** button on the Standard Toolbar {Alt, e, p *or* Ctrl and v}.

   For example, with the insertion point located at the left margin one blank line space below the second body text paragraph, select the **Paste** button.

***Note:** The copied text is retrieved from the Clipboard and displays in the document window. The insertion point should be located one blank line below the copied text. If necessary, press the End key to locate the insertion point at the end of the line, and* *press **Enter** one or two times in order to locate the insertion point one blank line space below the copied text.*

8. Select **Window**; choose the filename of the document that contains the standard paragraphs {Alt, w, press the down arrow key to highlight the desired filename, Enter}.

   For example, choose **9stn6.doc**.

9. Select the text to be copied to the personalized document.

   For example, select the paragraph that begins **Managing Electronic Information—**, including the blank line that follows the paragraph.

10. Select the **Copy** button on the Standard Toolbar {Alt, e, c *or* Ctrl and c}.

11. Select **Window**; choose the filename of the personalized document {Alt, w, press the down arrow key to highlight the desired filename, Enter}.

    For example, choose **9nelson.doc**.

12. With the insertion point placed at the location where the copied text should be inserted, select the **Paste** button on the Standard Toolbar {Alt, e, p *or* Ctrl and v}.

    For example, with the insertion point located at the left margin one blank line below the conference date information, select the **Paste** button. If necessary, press **Enter** one or two times so that the insertion point is located one blank line space below the copied paragraph.

Finish-Up Instructions

- Repeat steps 8–12 and copy the paragraph that begins **Real Uses for Business Multimedia—**.
- Type the final paragraph, complimentary closing, typed signature, title, reference initials, and document identification as shown in Figure 9.10.
- Save the personalized document file using the same filename, **9nelson.doc**.
- Print one copy and close both documents.

The Next Step

Chapter Review and Activities

Self-Check Quiz

T F 1. The first line of a paragraph in a document with vertical line spacing of one is always indented.

T F 2. A thesaurus contains synonyms that assist a writer in communicating clearly.

T F 3. A document typed with vertical line spacing of two is always printed with justified alignment.

T F 4. The changes suggested by the grammar-checking program should always be used to correct the grammar in a document.

5. The standard paragraphs file must be ____ before copying text to personalize a document.
   a. open in a document window
   b. created
   c. closed
   d. both a and b

6. If a document is formatted with vertical line spacing of two,
   a. the first line of each paragraph should be indented.
   b. extra space should be added before each paragraph.
   c. the body text should be left aligned.
   d. none of these

7. A document title is often centered and printed in ____.
   a. a different font
   b. italic
   c. uppercase letters
   d. both a and c

8. The text copied from an open document is placed ____________.
   a. in the Clipboard
   b. on the hard disk
   c. in the document window
   d. on a floppy disk

9. List the names of the menu and submenu selected in order to display the Word Count dialog box.

10. State one purpose for using standard paragraphs to assemble personalized documents.

Enriching Language Arts Skills

Spelling/Vocabulary Words

certified to declare a thing true or accurate by formal document.

comprehensive wide in scope; complete; inclusive.
forum an assembly or program for the discussion of public matters.
independent self-governing; not connected with others.
productivity fertile; marked by abundant production.

Speller Hint

The Speller approves words that are correctly spelled; however, a correctly spelled word can be incorrectly used in a sentence. After using the Speller, proofread the document for words used incorrectly.

Examples:

of, off	you, your, you're	is, it, in, if	to, too, two	its, it's
no, not	for, from, form	a, as, an	there, their	used, sued

Activities

Activity 9.1—Change the Paragraph Format, Use Format Painter, and Word Count

1. Open the file named **9act1.doc** located on the data disk.
2. Select the title. Use **14-point**, **bold**, and **center** the title. Press **Enter** twice.
3. Use the Paragraph dialog box to insert a space equal to one blank line (12 points) after each paragraph (select all paragraphs except the title, select **Format**, **Paragraph**, click twice on the up triangle located to the right of the **After** box in the Spacing area to display **12 pt**, select **OK**).
4. Select the first sidehead, **Who to Call**. Use **bold** and **12-point**.
5. Use the **Format Painter** button to copy the formatting of the first sidehead to the other sideheads. (With the first sidehead highlighted, double-click on the **Format Painter** button, then select each of the other sideheads. Click once on the **Format Painter** button to turn off the Format Painter.)
6. Use the *new* filename **9tel1.doc** and save the file on your file disk.
7. Print one copy.
8. Select **Tools, Word Count** to determine the total number of words in the document. Handwrite the number of words at the top of your printed copy. Select **Close**.
9. Close the document.

Activity 9.2—Create Personalized Letters Using Standard Paragraphs

1. Open the file named **9stn6.doc** that was created previously in this chapter or create the standard paragraphs document shown in Figure 9.9.

2. Create a new file and type the following personalized letter. Copy the standard paragraphs from the file named **9stn6.doc** as indicated.

(Use current date)

Ms. Margaret Simpson
519 Vincent Road
W. Lafayette, IN 47906

Dear Ms. Simpson:

Thank you for your interest in attending our Computers and Communications Conferences. Below is a listing of the upcoming conference dates and a description of the two seminars in which you have expressed an interest.

> Copy the following standard paragraphs from the list of seminar information in the file named **9stn6.doc.**
>
> Copy all four seminar locations and dates.
>
> Copy the paragraph that begins "Real Uses for Business Multimedia."
>
> Copy the paragraph that begins "Managing Electronic Information."

If you need additional information about the seminars or hotel accommodations, please call 1-800-555-2100.

Sincerely,

Hazel Walters
Seminar Coordinator

HW/xx
simp.doc/disk3

---

3. Use the filename **9simp.doc** and save the file on your file disk.
4. Print one copy.
5. Create a new file and type the following personalized letter. Copy the paragraphs indicated from the file named **9stn6.doc**.

(Use current date)

Ms. Patricia R. Tompkins
Technology and Development Center
8522 Maple Street
Sacramento, CA 95841

Dear Ms. Tompkins:

We appreciate your request for information regarding our upcoming West Coast seminars. Currently, the following two seminars are scheduled for the western region:

Copy the location and date information for the San Francisco, California, and Seattle, Washington, seminars from the list of standard seminar information in the file named **9stn6.doc**.

With regard to your interest in increasing office productivity, the following seminar is recommended:

Copy the paragraph that begins "Improving Computer Performance" from the list of standard seminar information in the file named **9stn6.doc**.

I hope to see you at one of our western region seminars.

Sincerely,

Hazel Walters
Seminar Coordinator

HW/xx
tomp.doc/disk2

6. Use the filename **9tomp.doc** and save the file on your file disk.
7. Print one copy and close all documents windows (close the personalized letter files and the standard paragraphs file).

Activity 9.3—Change Paragraph Formats and Use the Thesaurus

1. Open the file named **9act3.doc** located on the data disk.
2. Select the entire document except the title and subtitle and use the following information to format the paragraphs:

a. Add space after each paragraph equal to one blank line (12 points). (Select **Format**, **Paragraph**, click on the up triangle located to the right of the After box until **12 pt** displays.)

b. Set the line spacing to **At Least 15 pt** (click in the **Line Spacing** box, click on **At Least**, click on the up triangle located to the right of the At box until **15 pt** displays).

c. Select **OK**.

3. Select the title and subtitle. Change the font size to **14 point** and select **Bold**.
4. Select the sidehead "Condition." Change the font size to **14 point** and select **Bold**.
5. Use the Thesaurus to find synonyms for the underlined words (place the insertion point in an underlined word, select **Tools**, **Thesaurus**). Bold the synonyms and remove the underlining.

   Note: There may not be appropriate synonyms for all underlined words. Also, remember to check word endings after words are replaced.
6. Use the *new* filename **9syn3.doc** and save the file on your file disk.
7. Print one copy and close the document.

Activity 9.4—Use Grammar-Checking and Format Painter

1. Open the file named **9act4.doc** located on the data disk.
2. Format the entire document to have vertical spacing of **1.5 Lines**, a first line indent of .3", and justified alignment. (Select the entire document, select **Format**, **Paragraph**, click in the **Line Spacing** box, and select **1.5 Lines**. Click in the **Special** box and select **First Line**. Click on the down triangle located to the right of the **By** box until **0.3"** displays. Click in the **Alignment** box and select **Justified** alignment. Select **OK**.)
3. Use the *new* filename **9com4.doc** and save the file on your file disk.
4. Use the grammar-checking feature to check the document using the following information:

   a. Select **Tools, Grammar**.

   b. The first possible problem is that **An** should be **A**. Select **Change**.

   c. The phrase "is overlooked" is grammatically correct; select the **Ignore** button.

   d. The first sentence in the second paragraph does not have a verb. Insert the word "**is**" after the word "solution" in the document window. Select **Start** to continue checking the document.

   e. The subject of the sentence is "Computers," which is plural. Select the second suggestion to change to the plural verb "**are**," then select **Change**.

   f. The word "personnel" is correct; select the **Ignore** button.

g. The phrase "is overlooked" may be shown again because the program was restarted. Select **Ignore** again.

   Note: The Readability Statistics box displays.

h. Select **OK**.

5. Use the *new* filename **9gra4.doc** and save the corrected file on your file disk.
6. Print one copy and close the document.

Challenge Your Skills

Skill 9.1—Edit a One-Page Document

1. Open the file named **9skill1.doc** located on the data disk.
2. Make decisions regarding:

   Font
   Margins
   Use of bold
   Spacing after the title

3. Use the Paragraph dialog box to add 12 points of space between the body text paragraphs and to choose an appropriate alignment.
4. Edit the document as follows:

   a. Delete the last sentence of paragraph 2; combine paragraphs 1 and 2 into a single paragraph.

   b. Add the sideheads:

      Add **Technical Training Program** above the current paragraph 2.

      Add **Management Trainee Program** above the current paragraph 3.

      Add **Employee Assistance Program** above the current paragraph 5.

   c. Make decisions regarding the font, spacing, and bolding for the first sidehead. Use **Format Painter** to copy the formatting to the other sideheads.

5. Use the *new* filename **9lex1.doc** and save the file.
6. Print one copy and close the document.

Skill 9.2—Create a One-Page Document and Use the Thesaurus

1. Open the file named **9skill2.doc** located on the data disk.
2. Change the format to vertical line spacing of **Double**.
3. Change the format for the items under the sidehead **Cautions** to a bulleted or numbered list, single-spaced.
4. Make decisions regarding:

Margins
Alignment
Title alignment and capitalization
Bold
Sidehead spacing and capitalization
Indents

Hint: *If First Line indents are to be set for the body text, select the first body text paragraph including the paragraph symbol. Set the First Line indent desired. Then use the* ***Format Painter*** *to apply the formatting to other body text paragraphs.*

5. Use the Thesaurus to make decisions for replacing (or *not* replacing) the bolded words. Bold the substituted words.
6. Use the *new* filename **9drip2.doc** and save the file on your file disk.
7. Print one copy and close the document.

Skill 9.3—Create Standard Paragraphs and Assemble Personalized Documents; Language Arts

Part I

1. Type the following standard list of available support services as shown.
2. Correct four spelling errors, three misused words, and two punctuation errors.

Standard List of Available Support Services

Productivity Enhancement

Dupont Plus is a program offering an increased level off software information, access, service and support to increase knowledge and enhance prodectivity for the serious software user.

Developer Assistance

Dupont Developer is the best source for development-related technical, stratejic, and resource information.

Online Dupont

Online Dupont provides access to they Dupont Knowledge Database, Software Programs Library, and User and Developer forums. Call 800-555-2424 for information on access to Online Dupont.

Hard Copy

Dupont Press offers a variety of books and technical references for computer users and programmers at all levels, including comprehenseeve reference and how-to information.

Point of View

Express your point of view by joining Dupont's registered customer list and by sending in your ideas, comments, or tips. Make suggestions on future Dupont software products. If your suggestion is used a cash bonus of $50-$500 will be yours.

Independent Supporters

Independent Supporters are companies not owned or financed by Dupont that provide consulting, development, technical support, and other services for Dupont products. Call for information or for a Dupont Independent Supporter near you.

Certified Professional Program

The Dupont Certefied Professional Program is a comprehensive certification program for assessing and maintaining software-related skills. It can be used as part of an ongoing employee training program, or it can bee used independently by persons motivated to improve their skills and marketability.

Consulting Services

Dupont Consulting Services help both end-user organizations and third-party software developers worldwide to design and build information technology solutions using Dupont programs.

---

3. Use the filename **9std3.doc** and save the standard list on your file disk.
4. Print one copy.

Part II

1. If necessary, open the file named **9std3.doc**.
2. The standard list of available support services will be used to construct two one-page documents to be posted on bulletin boards to provide employees with information.
3. For each document, make decisions regarding:

   Line spacing (one or two)
   Alignment
   Margins
   Bold
   Fonts
4. Create a new file and type the following personalized document:

WORD PROCESSORS, ASSISTANTS, AND CLERKS
Available Dupont Services

Copy the following paragraphs in the order listed from the standard list of available support services (**9std3.doc**).

Productivity Enhancement
Online Dupont
Hard Copy
Point of View
Certified Professional Program

5. Use the filename **9wdprc3.doc** and save the personalized document on your file disk. Print one copy.
6. Create a new file and type the following personalized document:

PROGRAMMERS AND SYSTEM DESIGNERS
Available Dupont Services

Copy the following paragraphs in the order listed from the standard list of available support services (**9std3.doc**).

Productivity Enhancement
Developer Assistance
Point of View
Certified Professional Program
Consulting Services

7. Use the filename **9prog3.doc** and save the personalized document on your file disk. Print one copy.
8. If you have completed your work, exit Word.

CHAPTER

10

Create a Multiple-Page Document

Features Covered

- Print page numbers
- Create headers and footers
- Control text flow
- Create footnotes and endnotes
- Print specific pages

Objectives and Introduction

After successfully completing this chapter, you will be able to create a multiple-page document, print page numbers on each page, and use the Text Flow feature to control text. You also will be able to create and edit headers, footers, footnotes, and endnotes, as well as print a specific page(s).

A multiple-page document consists of two or more pages and is formatted similar to the format used when creating a one-page document. A multiple-page report can be an article, essay, meeting minutes, an agenda, or any type of document that describes an event or provides information. Examples of multiple-page business documents are investment, insurance, legal, medical, and sales documents.

Create a Multiple-Page Document

Like a one-page document, a multiple-page document can be created with vertical line spacing of one (single-spacing) or two (double-spacing). Pages of a multiple-page document are formatted in the same way as a one-page document, with default margins set at 1 inch top and bottom and 1.25 inches left and right (see Chapter 9, Figures 9.1 and 9.4.)

Each page of a multiple-page document is separated by either an automatic or manual page break. An automatic page break is inserted by Word when the number of available vertical lines on the page is filled. When text is edited, automatic page

FIGURE 10.1

Hard page break in Normal view

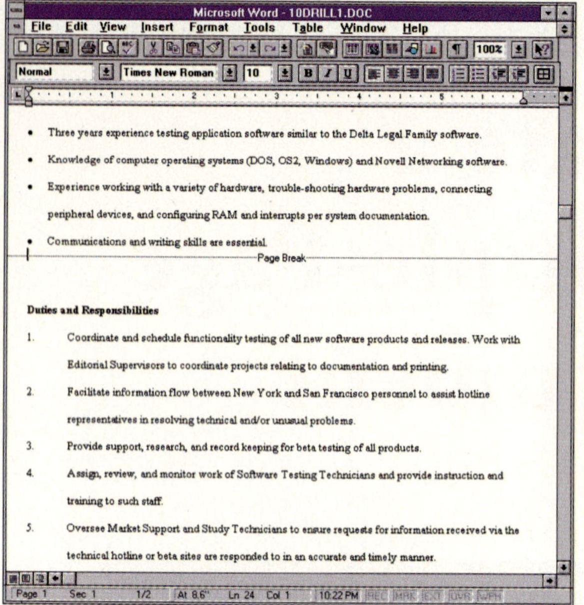

breaks, known as soft page breaks, are automatically adjusted so the maximum number of lines fits on each page.

If a new page is desired before the available lines on the page are filled, a manual page break, also referred to as a hard page break, is inserted by pressing the **Ctrl** and **Enter** keys or by selecting **Insert**, **Break**, **Page Break** (see Figure 10.1). Because a manual page break will always remain at the location where it was inserted, each manual page break should be checked when a document is edited and deleted if necessary.

Pages of a multiple-page document can be viewed on the screen to see the placement of the lines, sideheads, page numbers, headers, and footers. The current page is viewed either by using the Page Layout view then selecting **View, Zoom, Whole Page** or by selecting the **Print Preview** button. In either view, additional pages can be displayed by pressing the **Page Up** and **Page Down** keys or by selecting the **Previous Page** and **Next Page** buttons, which are located at the bottom of the vertical scroll bar (see Figure 10.3). In the Print Preview mode, two to six pages can be displayed on the screen at one time by selecting the **Multiple Pages** button and clicking on the desired number of pages.

Headers and Footers

Generally, a multiple-page document includes headers and/or footers. A header is a title or information that prints in the top margin of the second and following pages (see Figures 10.2 and 10.4). A footer is a title or information that prints in the bottom margin of each page (see Figure 10.4). Headers and footers can consist of more than one line of text. Once created, headers and footers can be edited or deleted.

When headers are used, the header information is not normally printed on the first page of a document but prints at the top of the second and following pages. When footers are used, the title information along with the page number (optional)

FIGURE 10.2

Two samples of header styles

Three-line header for multiple-page memorandum or report

Right Moves Presentation
Page 2
March 25, 199x

This process will not fail if made a part of the presentation format discipline. In addition, remember that no more than three recommended changes should be presented at one time. The recommendations should be presented in a

One-line header for a multiple-page letter

Ms. Holly Pierce Page 2 March 25, 199x

Costs included in this invoice are for final preparation by a Senior Engineer, review by a Principal, geotechnical drafting and typing, and reproduction of the Distress Investigation report. Expenses are for film purchase, developing, and printing.

prints at the bottom of every page. The default position for headers is .5" from the top of the page, and the default position for footers is .5" from the bottom of the page.

A header or footer is created by selecting **View, Header and Footer**. The screen will display a header area with the insertion point in the first space. If the Page Layout view is not active, the view mode will automatically switch to Page Layout view. The document text will be dimmed as a reminder that it cannot be edited until the Header and Footer area is closed. The Header and Footer Toolbar will display in the middle of the page. To create a footer, select the **Switch Between Header and Footer** button on the Header and Footer Toolbar. After the text for the header or footer is typed and formatted, select the **Close** button on the Header and Footer Toolbar to return to the document window.

A header or footer can be viewed by selecting **View, Page Layout** or by choosing the **Print Preview** button. To edit a header or footer, double-click on the header or footer text in the document window or select **View, Header and Footer**. If necessary, select the **Switch Between Header and Footer** button, then select the **Show Next** or **Show Previous** button on the Header and Footer Toolbar until the desired header or footer appears.

Three different headers or footers can be created for each section: one for even pages, one for odd pages, and one for the first page. The footers in this textbook are examples of different even- and odd-page footers. Also, the footer on the first page of each chapter in this textbook is an example of a different first page footer, i.e., only the page number is shown with no accompanying text. Because a header is not usually printed on the first page of a document, a different first page header is used to create a blank or empty header for page 1.

If the format of a document is changed, the format of the header or footer must be changed to match the new document format. For example, if the fonts are changed for the entire document, the fonts of the header and/or footer must also be changed.

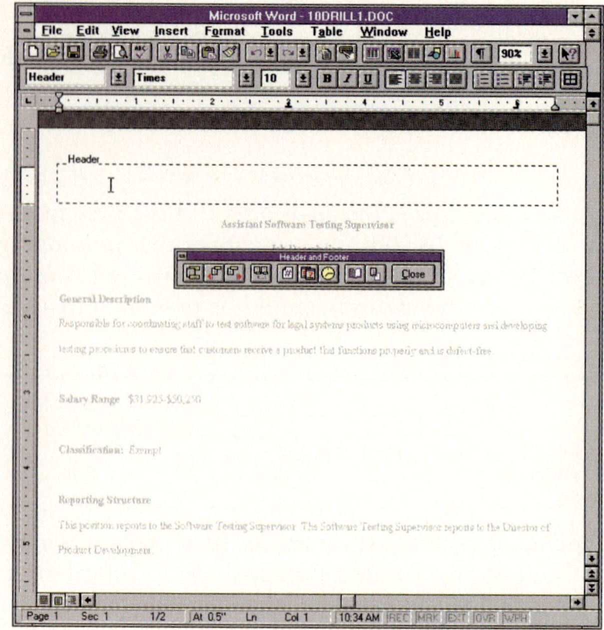

FIGURE 10.3

Header and Footer and Footer Toolbar

To make it easier to align header/footer text in the center of the page and at the right margin, the header and footer areas have a default tab setting with one center tab in the center of the document and one right tab at the default right margin. Another easy way to align text in a header or footer is to create a one-row table with two or three columns. For example, in the one-line header displayed in the second sample in Figure 10.2, Ms. Holly Pierce is left aligned in the first table cell, Page 2 is centered in the middle cell, and the date is right aligned in the right cell.

Start-Up Instructions

- Open the file named **10drill1.doc** located on the data disk.
- Check that the Page Layout view is turned on. If necessary, select **View**, **Page Layout**.

Steps to Create a Blank First Page Header

1. With the insertion point located at any position on page 1, select **View, Header and Footer** {Alt, v, h}.

   Note: The header area appears with the insertion point in the space for the first character, and the Header and Footer Toolbar displays (see Figure 10.3). (If the Header and Footer Toolbar does not appear, move the mouse pointer into the Standard or Formatting Toolbar, click the ***right*** *mouse button once, then select* ***Header and Footer.****)*

2. Select the **Page Setup** button on the Header and Footer Toolbar {Alt, f, u; Alt and L}.

   Note: The Layout tab should be selected. (If necessary, select the ***Layout*** *tab.)*

3. In the Headers and Footers section, choose the desired option.

   For example, select the **Different First Page** option {Alt and f}.

   Note: To toggle the option on or off, click once on the box to display the X. The option is selected when the X displays.

4. Select **OK** to return to the Header area.
5. Type the header information or leave the header blank to create a blank header on the first page.

   For example, to create a blank first page header do not type anything.

Finish-Up Instructions

- ❖ Continue with the following Steps to Create a Second Page Header with a Page Number.

Create a Second Page Header with a Page Number

1. Select the **Show Next** button on the Header and Footer Toolbar {press the down arrow twice to move to the next header area}.
2. Type and format the header information for the second and subsequent pages.

   For example, type **Assistant Software Testing Supervisor**. Press **Tab** twice to move the insertion point to the right tab at the right margin. Type the word **Page**, then press the **Spacebar** once.
3. To insert a Page Number field, select the **Page Numbers** button on the Header and Footer Toolbar {Alt, i, e; Alt and n, press the down arrow to highlight the word Page, press Enter}.

   Note: *The Page Number appears in the Header area where the insertion point is located. This is a field and can be deleted only by selecting the number and then pressing the* ***Delete*** *key.*
4. Select the **Close** button on the Header and Footer Toolbar to return to the document window {Alt and Shift and c}.

Finish-Up Instructions

- ❖ To view the header, select the down arrow next to the **Zoom Control** button, **Two Pages**. After viewing the document, select the down arrow next to the **Zoom Control** button again and select **100%**.
- ❖ Use the new filename **10hdr1.doc** and save the file on your file disk.
- ❖ Print one copy.

Start-Up Instructions

- ❖ The file named **10hdr1.doc** should be displayed in the document window.

Create a Footer and Insert a Date

1. With the insertion point located at any position on page 1, select **View, Header and Footer** {Alt, v, h}.

   Note: *The First Page Header area and the Header and Footer Toolbar display.*
2. Select the **Switch Between Header and Footer** button {press the down arrow once to move to the First Page Footer area}.

Note: A Footer area displays at the bottom of the document window.

3. Type and format the text for the First Page footer.

   For example, press the **Tab** key once to move the insertion point to the center tab, then type **Revision Date:** and press the **Spacebar** once.

4. To insert a date field into the footer, select the **Date** button on the Header and Footer Toolbar {Alt, i, t, highlight the desired date format, press Enter}.

   *Note: When using the **Date** button, the date will be in the format last selected using the **Insert, Date** and Time option. This date is a field and will be updated to the current date whenever the document is printed or saved. If the date should not be automatically updated, select the date field and then press **Ctrl** and **Shift** and **F9**.*

5. To use the same footer on the second and subsequent pages, select the text, then select the **Copy** button on the Standard Toolbar {Ctrl and c}. Select the **Show** Next button on the Header and Footer Toolbar, then select the **Paste** button on the Standard Toolbar {Ctrl and v}.

   For example, select the footer text, select **Copy**, **Show Next** and select **Paste**.

   *Note: If necessary, select the **Center** button to center the footer information.*

6. Select the **Close** button on the Header and Footer Toolbar {Alt and Shift and c}.

   *Note: Select **Print Preview** to view the headers and footers. Select **Close** to return to the document window.*

Finish-Up Instructions

- To view the footer, select the down arrow next to the **Zoom Control** button, **Two Pages**. After viewing, select the down arrow next to the **Zoom Control** button and select **100%**.
- Use the *new* filename **10ftr1.doc** and save the file on your file disk.
- Print one copy.

Edit Headers and Footers

1. Select **View, Header and Footer** {Alt, v, h}.

2. To view another header, select the **Show Next** button repeatedly until the desired header displays {press the down arrow until the desired header displays}.

   For example, select the **Show Next** button to display the header for the second and subsequent pages.

3. Make the desired changes to the header text using the customary editing methods.

   For example, select the word Page and the Page Number field, then type **Job Description**.

   *Note: The text **Job Description** should be aligned flush right (see Figure 10.4).*

4. To edit a footer, select the **Switch Between Header and Footer** button on the Header and Footer Toolbar, then select the **Show Next** button repeatedly

Assistant Software Testing Supervisor Job Description

2. Facilitate information flow between New York and San Francisco personnel to assist hotline representatives in resolving technical and/or unusual problems.
3. Provide support, research, and record keeping for beta testing of all products.
4. Assign, review, and monitor work of Software Testing Technicians and provide instruction and training to such staff.
5. Oversee Market Support and Study Technicians to ensure that requests for information received via the technical hotline or beta sites are responded to in an accurate and timely manner.
6. Communicate results of testing to supervisor and director and recommend further testing if necessary.
7. Organize and coordinate problem-solving reporting process. Verify reported problems and track resolution.
8. Organize data files and test cases to be used for updating future releases. Assist in preparation of test script files to electronically test software.
9. Maintain in-house master and vault copies of all software.
10. Assist Technical Systems Analyst, legal staff, and systems programmers in program development.

Revision Date: (Current date)
Page 2

FIGURE 10.4

A document with a header and footer

until the desired footer displays {press the down arrow until the desired footer displays}.

For example, select the **Switch Between Header and Footer** button to display the second page footer.

5. Make the desired changes to the footer text using the customary editing methods.

For example, press **End** to go to the end of the current line. Press **Enter** once to start a new line. If necessary, press the **Tab** key once to move the insertion point to the center tab. Type the word **Page** and press the **Spacebar** once. Select the **Page Numbers** button to insert the Page Number field.

6. If necessary, make the same revisions to the next or previous footer.

For example, select the **Show Previous** button on the Header and Footer Toolbar, then follow the directions in step 5 to insert the word **Page** and the **Page Number** field.

7. Select **Close** {Alt and Shift and c}.

Shortcut to Select a Header or Footer

1. In the Page Layout or Print Preview mode, scroll through the document until the desired header or footer is displayed.
2. Move the mouse pointer into the header or footer area and double-click.

   Note: The Header and Footer Toolbar will display, and the header or footer can be edited or deleted.

Finish-Up Instructions

- Select the down arrow next to the **Zoom Control** button, **Two Pages** to view the changed header and footer. Page two of your document should look similar to Figure 10.4. Select the down arrow next to the **Zoom Control** button again and **100%**.
- Use the *new* filename **10edi1.doc** and save the file on your file disk.
- Print one copy and close the document.

Delete Headers and Footers

Note: These steps are for your information only.

1. Select **View, Header and Footer** {Alt, v, h}.
2. Use the **Switch Between Header and Footer** and the **Show Next** buttons until the desired header or footer displays {press the down arrow until the desired header or footer displays}.
3. Select all text in the header or footer area, then press the **Delete** key.
4. Select **Close** on the Header and Footer Toolbar {Alt and Shift and c}.

Print Page Numbers

Each page of a multiple-page document should be numbered. Word provides a quick way to create a header or footer containing only the page number. If the pages are numbered at the bottom, number 1 is printed at the bottom of the first page. If pages are numbered at the top, the first page of the document may or may not be numbered.

Page numbers can be set to print at the top or bottom of the page and at the left margin, centered, or at the right margin. The default position for page numbers is .5 inches from the top of the page or .5 inches from the bottom of the page. The Position option in the Page Numbers dialog box is used to specify whether the page number will be placed at the top or bottom of the page, while the **Alignment** option determines whether the page number will be aligned at the Left Margin, Centered or Right Margin. The **Format** button in the Page Numbers dialog box can then be selected to display the Page Number Format dialog box. Page numbers can be set to print as lowercase letters (a, b, c, etc.) or uppercase letters (A, B, C, etc.), lowercase Roman numerals (i, ii, iii, etc.), uppercase Roman numerals (I, II, III, etc.), or numbers (1, 2, 3, etc.).

A different beginning page number can be set by selecting the **Start At** option in the Page Number Format dialog box. For example, to begin numbering pages with page 4, type 4 in the Start At box in the Page Numbering section.

Once the page number has been inserted, it can be edited or deleted. The same methods used to change headers or footers are used to change the page number format, add or delete text, etc. See the Steps to Edit Headers and Footers beginning on page 234.

Start-Up Instructions

❖ Open the file named **10drill1.doc** located on the data disk.

Number Pages

1. With the insertion point located at any position on page 1, select **Insert, Page Numbers** {Alt, i, u}.

   Note: The Page Numbers dialog box displays.

2. Click in the Position box and choose the desired page number position option {Alt and p, press the up or down arrow key until the desired position option is highlighted}.

   For example, check that the **Bottom of Page (Footer)** option displays. (If necessary, click in the Position box and choose the **Bottom of Page (Footer)** option.)

3. Click in the **Alignment** box and select the desired page number alignment option {Alt and a, press the up or down arrow keys until the desired alignment option is highlighted}.

   For example, click in the **Alignment** box and select **Center.**

   Note: A sample of the page number location displays in the Preview box (see Figure 10.5).

4. If the page number is to be in a footer, an X should display in the **Show Number on First Page** box.

   For example, select the **Show Number on First Page** option {Alt and s}.

   Note: An X must display in the Show Number on First Page option box for the number to print on the first page.

5. Select **OK** {press Enter}.

   *Note: Select **Print Preview** to display the page number. Select the **Next Page** button to observe the page number on the second page. Select **Close** to return to the document window.*

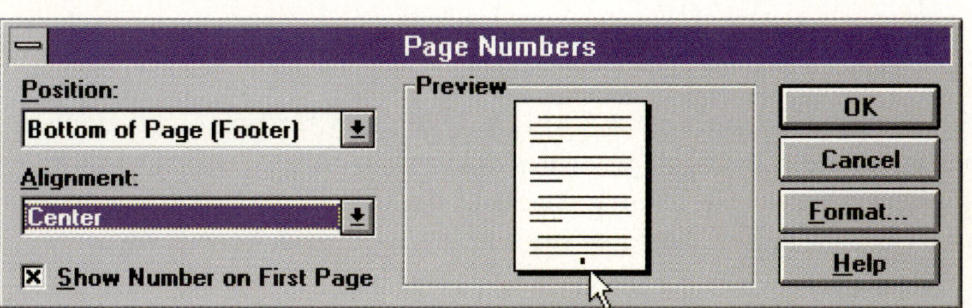

FIGURE 10.5

Page Numbers dialog box

Chapter 10 Create a Multiple-Page Document

FIGURE 10.6

Page Number Format dialog box

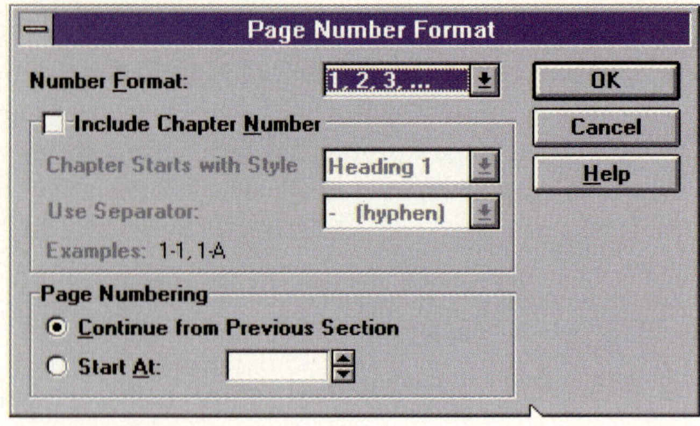

Finish-Up Instructions

- Use the *new* filename **10num2.doc** and save the file on your file disk.
- Print one copy.

Start-Up Instructions

- The file named **10num2.doc** should be displayed in the document window.

Change the Page Numbering Format

1. With the insertion point located at any position on page 1, select **Insert, Page Numbers** {Alt, i, u}.
2. Select **Format** {Alt and f}.

   Note: The Page Number Format dialog box displays (see Figure 10.6).
3. Click in the **Number Format** box, select the desired number type {Alt and f, press the up or down arrow key until the desired option displays}.

   For example, select **Uppercase Roman (I, II, III...)**.
4. Select **OK** to return to the Page Numbers dialog box {press Enter}.
5. Select **OK** to return to the document window {press Enter}.

Finish-Up Instructions

- Select the **Print Preview** button to display the roman numeral page number(s). Select **Close**.
- Use the *new* filename **10rom2.doc** and save the file on your file disk.
- Print one copy.

Control Text Flow

To enhance the document's appearance and to provide easy reading of the document's information, standard typography rules are used to control the minimum number of paragraph lines displayed on a page and the lines of text that should be kept on the same page. Word's Text Flow options are used to designate where text is allowed to flow between pages so that text automatically breaks at the desired line even when text is added or deleted.

There are four standard rules used to determine the flow of text. Word provides options that can be used to follow these rules and to control text flow.

Rule 1: There should be a minimum of two lines of a paragraph at the bottom and/or top of a page. In other words, the first two lines or last two lines of a paragraph will not be separated from one page to another. Separated lines are traditionally called *widows* (one paragraph line displayed on the previous page) and *orphans* (one paragraph line displayed on the next page). Word's default is to have the Widow/Orphan Control option turned on. To check that the Widow/Orphan Control option is on, select the entire document, then select **Format**, **Paragraph**, choose the **Text Flow** tab. The **Widow/Orphan Control** option should be selected. Choose **OK**.

Rule 2: Headings and sideheads should not be separated from the first line of the next paragraph. In other words, the headings or sideheads should not be on one page and first line of the following paragraph displayed on the next page. To control the heading or sidehead and first paragraph line, place the insertion point in the heading/sidehead, then select **Format**, **Paragraph**, choose the **Text Flow** tab, select **Keep with Next**, select **OK**.

Rule 3: Whenever possible, a short paragraph should not be divided. To prevent the lines of a short paragraph from being divided, place the insertion point in the paragraph, then select **Format**, **Paragraph**, choose the **Text Flow** tab, select **Keep Lines Together**, select **OK**.

Rule 4: Chapter titles and sometimes section titles should start at the top of a page. Place the insertion point in the title or other element that is to begin a new page and select **Format**, **Paragraph**, choose the **Text Flow** tab, select **Page Break Before**, select **OK**.

Start-Up Instructions

- The file named **10rom2.doc** should be displayed in the document window.
- The nonprinting symbols should be turned on. (If necessary, select the **Show/Hide** button.)

Steps to Control Text Flow

1. Place the insertion point in the heading or sidehead that may be followed by a page break.

   For example, place the insertion point in the sidehead **Duties and Responsibilities**.

2. Select **Format, Paragraph** {Alt, o, p}.
3. If the Text Flow tab card is not displayed, click on the **Text Flow** tab {Alt and f}.
4. In the Pagination section, select the desired option.

For example, select the **Keep with Next** option to keep the sidehead with the following paragraph {Alt and x}.

Note: An X displays in the box next to the words "Keep with Next."

5. Select **OK** {press Enter once}.

   *Note: A small dark square displays to the left of the sidehead Duties and Responsibilities. Select the **Help** button. Point to the sidehead and click once. The message, "Keep with Next," displays in the Paragraph Formatting box. Click once again on the Help button to remove the Paragraph Formatting box from the document window.*

Finish-Up Instructions

- Check that Widow/Orphan control is turned on (press **Ctrl** and **a** to select the entire document; select **Format**, **Paragraph**, choose the **Text Flow** tab; if necessary, select the **Widow/Orphan Control** option; select **OK**).
- Use the *new* file name **10text2.doc and save the file on your file disk.**
- Print one copy and close the document.

Create Footnotes and Endnotes

A multiple-page document can include footnotes or endnotes. The footnote or endnote reference information provides the name, date, and page number of the source from which the information being discussed was obtained (see Figure 10.7). Footnotes and endnotes are also referred to as reference notes or sources.

Once a footnote or endnote is created, Word automatically places the footnote or endnote reference number in the document text. The reference number is superscripted (i.e., raised slightly above the text line).

The footnote and endnote reference information can be displayed in the document window by selecting **Print Preview** or **Page Layout**.

Footnote reference information is printed at the bottom of the page where the footnote reference number is located. A 2-inch separator line is placed above the footnote reference information. The first line of the footnote reference information is indented, the footnote reference number is superscripted, and the information is printed with vertical line spacing of one. A blank space is placed between footnotes (see Figure 10.7).

Endnotes are automatically placed at the end of the document text. A hard page break (**Ctrl** and **Enter**) is inserted after the last line of text in the document so that endnotes will print on a separate page. A title such as *Notes* is usually placed at the top of the endnote page. Depending on the requested design/style, the first line of the endnote reference information may either begin at the left margin or be indented, and the information may be printed with vertical line spacing of one or two. A blank line is usually placed between endnotes. Word's default is to place a separator line before the endnotes, but this can be deleted when the endnotes are placed on a separate page.

To change the number format and other options for footnotes or endnotes, the **Options** button is chosen in the Footnote and Endnote dialog box. In the Notes Options dialog box, numbers, uppercase or lowercase Roman numerals, letters, or a symbol set can be designated in the Number Format box (see Figure 10.8). The

four-year scholarships have been established for children of firefighters who have died in the line of duty. Other Lieberman Enterprises scholarship programs have been for graduates of West City Community College, city employees, and Norfolk high school teachers. In response to the need for more qualified science teachers, Lieberman Enterprises offers training in computer science to high school teachers. A Science Seminar Program provides science teachers with updated teaching materials and methods.[2]

---

[1]J. Russell Mason, The President's Report to the Board of Directors, Spring 1990, p. 2.

[2]Ibid., p. 3.

FIGURE 10.7

Partial document with footnotes

Chapter 10 Create a Multiple-Page Document

Place At options are used to specify whether footnotes should be printed at the bottom of the page or beneath the text (if the text stops before the end of the page) and whether endnotes should be printed at the end of the document or the end of each section. A different starting number can be entered in the **Start At** box. For footnotes, the **Numbering** options include *Continuous* (throughout the document), *Restart Each Section*, and *Restart Each Page*. Endnote **Numbering** options include *Continuous* and *Restart Each Section*.

Start-Up Instructions

- Open the file named **10drill3.doc** located on the data disk.
- If necessary, select the Normal view mode (select **View**, **Normal**).

Create Footnotes

1. Place the insertion point to the right of the text being referenced.

   For example, place the insertion point after the period in the last sentence of the first paragraph that ends with the word *annually*.

2. Select **Insert, Footnote** {Alt, i, n}.

   Note: *The Footnote and Endnote dialog box will display. A solid dot in the circle next to the word Footnote indicates that the Footnote option is selected. The setting from the last use will display.*

3. Select the desired Insert option.

   For example, check that **Footnote** is selected. (If necessary, select **Footnote** {Alt and f}).

4. Select the desired Numbering option.

   For example, check that **AutoNumber** is selected. (If necessary, select the **AutoNumber** option {Alt and a}).

5. Select **OK** {press Enter}.

Note: In the Normal view, a note pane for the footnote(s) will appear at the bottom of the page. In the Page Layout view, a divider line and footnote number display at the bottom of the current page. The insertion point is located to the right of the footnote number.

6. Type the footnote information.

   For example, type **J. Russell Mason, The President's Report to the Board of Directors, Spring 1990, p. 2.** Press the **Enter** key once.

7. To indent the footnote, place the insertion point to the left of the superscripted character in the footnote and press the **Tab** key once.

8. Select the **Close** button in the note pane {Alt and Shift and c}.

   Note: *The footnote number displays at the location of the insertion point. To display the footnote, select **View, Page Layout** and scroll to the bottom of the page.*

Finish-Up Instructions

- Place the insertion point after the last period in the third paragraph that ends with the word *methods*.
- Repeat steps 2-7 to create the following footnote:

  Ibid., p. 3.
- Place the insertion point after the last period in the final paragraph that ends with the word *centers*.
- Repeat steps 2-7 to create the following footnote:

  Lois Hodges, "Contribution to Community Education," *The Times Crier*, **3 May 1991, p. 10.**
- To keep the sidehead, Education Programs, with the following paragraph, locate the insertion point in the sidehead, select **Format**, **Paragraph**, choose the **Text Flow** tab, select **Keep with Next, OK.**
- Use the *new* filename **10fnt3.doc** and save the file on your file disk.
- Print one copy.

Start-Up Instructions

- The file named **10fnt3.doc** should be displayed in the document window.
- The Page Layout view should be selected. (If necessary, select **View**, **Page Layout**.)

Edit a Footnote or Endnote

Note: *The same method is used to edit footnotes and endnotes. For information on creating endnotes, see the Steps to Create Endnotes on page 243 later in this chapter.*

1. In Page Layout view, scroll to the location of the footnote(s).

   For example, scroll to the bottom of page 2 where footnote 3 is displayed.

2. Make corrections using the customary editing methods.

For example, in footnote 3 change p. 10 to **p. 24.**

Note: *If using Normal view when editing a footnote or endnote, point to the desired footnote/endnote number in the document and double-click. In the Footnote pane, make the desired corrections. Select* ***Close.***

Finish-Up Instructions

- Save the file again using the same filename, **10fnt3.doc**.

Start-Up Instructions

- The file named **10fnt3.doc** should be displayed in the document window.
- The Normal or Page Layout view can be chosen when using the Steps to Delete a Footnote or Endnote.

Delete a Footnote or Endnote

Note: *The same method is used to delete both footnotes and endnotes. For information on creating endnotes, see the Steps to Create Endnotes, which follows.*

1. Select the footnote or endnote reference number in the document.

   For example, select the footnote reference number **2** that displays after the third paragraph.

2. Press the **Delete** key once. The footnote/endnote number and the footnote/endnote information are both deleted.

   Note: *If other footnotes/endnotes follow the deleted footnote or endnote, the remaining footnotes/endnotes are automatically renumbered. Select the* ***Next Page*** *button to display the last footnote, which is now footnote 2.*

Finish-Up Instructions

- Use the *new* filename **10fin3.doc** and save the file.
- Print one copy and close the document.

Start-Up Instructions

- Open the file named **10drill3.doc** located on the data disk.
- The Normal view should be selected (if necessary, select **View, Normal**).

Create Endnotes

1. Place the insertion point to the right of the text being referenced.

   For example, place the insertion point to the right of the period in the last sentence in the first paragraph that ends with the word *annually*.

2. Select **Insert, Footnote** {Alt, i, n}.

   Note: *The Footnote and Endnote dialog box displays.*

FIGURE 10.8

Note Options dialog box

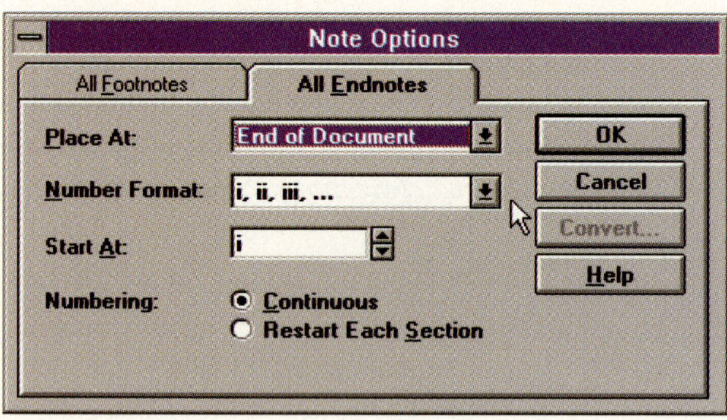

3. Select the **Endnote** option {Alt and e}.
4. If necessary, select the **AutoNumber** option {Alt and a}.
5. Select the **Options** button {Alt and o}.

   Note: *The Note Options dialog box displays (see Figure 10.8). The All Endnotes tab should be selected.*

6. Click once in the **Number Format** box {Alt and n}.
7. Select the desired number format {press the down arrow to highlight the desired number format}.

   For example, select the **1, 2, 3, ...** format.

   Note: *Word's default Number Format for endnotes is lowercase roman numerals; however, it is more common to use Arabic numerals.*

8. Select **OK** twice {press Enter twice}.

   Note: *In the Normal view, a note pane for the endnotes will appear at the bottom of the document window. In the Page Layout view, a divider line and endnote number display at the end of the document. The insertion point is located to the right of the endnote number.*

9. Type the endnote information.

   For example, type **J. Russell Mason, The President's Report to the Board of Directors, Spring 1990, p. 2.** Press **Enter** once.

10. To indent the endnote, place the insertion point to the left of the superscripted characters in the endnote and press the **Tab** key once.

    Note: *If this is the second or following endnote being created, skip to step 13.*

To Delete the Defaulted Separator Line

11. Click on the words **All Endnotes** in the upper left corner of the note pane. Select the item to be changed.

    For example, select **Endnote Separator.**

    Note: *The separator line will appear in the note pane and the endnote text is no longer displayed. There are no keystrokes to accomplish this step.*

12. Edit the line in the note pane to create the type of separator desired.

    For example, select the separator line and press **Delete** to remove it.

13. Select the **Close** button in the note pane {Alt and Shift and c}.

Note: The insertion point returns to the referenced text, and the number 1 displays at the end of the paragraph. In Page Layout view, scroll down to display the last page of the document and view the endnote. A separate page for the endnotes will be created later.

Finish-Up Instructions

- If necessary, select **View, Normal.**
- Place the insertion point after the last period in the third paragraph that ends with the word *methods.*
- Repeat steps 1–13 to create the following endnote:

  Ibid., p. 3.
- Place the insertion point in the document window after the last period in the final paragraph that ends with the word *centers.*
- Repeat steps 1–13 to create the following endnote:

  Lois Hodges, "Contribution to Community Education," ***The Times Crier,*** **3 May 1991, p. 24.**
- To view all endnotes, select **View, Page Layout.** If necessary, scroll down the page to view the Endnotes.
- To place the endnotes on a separate page with a title, locate the insertion point in a blank line above the first endnote and press **Ctrl** and **Enter.** Type **Notes** and press **Enter** once. Center and bold the word **Notes.**
- Use the *new* filename **10end3.doc** and save the file on your file disk.
- Print one copy.

Chapter 10 Create a Multiple-Page Document

Print Specific Pages

After printing a multiple-page document, one or more of the pages may need to be edited and reprinted. To specify the exact pages to print, the **Pages** option is selected in the Print dialog box, and the desired pages are entered as follows:

- Place a comma between nonconsecutive pages, e.g., 1,3 or 2,4,6.
- Place a dash between the beginning and ending page numbers to print a consecutive range of pages, e.g., 5-9.

A combination of these methods can be used, e.g., 4,5, 8-11 *or* 2-4, 6. Page numbers must be typed in numerical order. If, for example, you specified pages 8, 2-5, only page 8 will print.

Also, a single page can be printed by typing the page number in the Page(s) box or by placing the insertion point anywhere on the page, selecting **File, Print,** choosing the **Current Page** option, and selecting **Print.** When the **Current Page** option is selected, only the page where the insertion point is located will print.

FIGURE 10.9

Print dialog box with selected pages entered

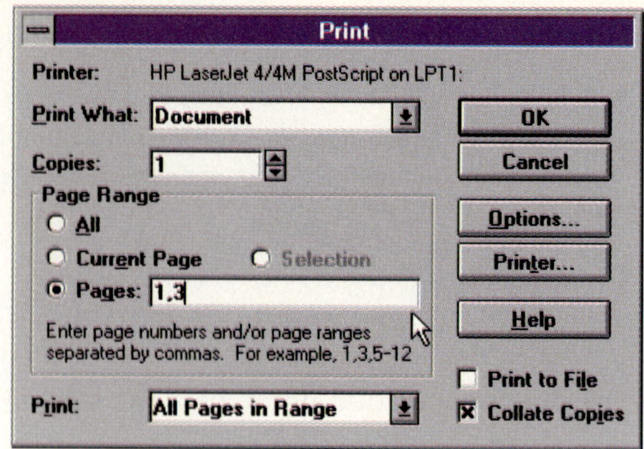

Start-Up Instructions

- The document containing the pages to print should be displayed in the document window. For example, the file named **10end3.doc** should be displayed in the document window.

Print Specific Pages

1. Select **File, Print** {Alt, f, p *or* Ctrl and p}.
2. Select the **Pages** option in the Print dialog box (see Figure 10.9) {Alt and g}.
3. In the Page(s) box, type the page numbers to be printed.

   For example, type **1,3** to print pages 1 and 3 only.
4. Select **OK** {press Enter}.

Finish-Up Instructions

- Close and do not save the document.

The Next Step

Chapter Review and Activities

Self-Check Quiz

T F 1. A multiple-page report is printed with vertical line spacing of one or two.

T F 2. A footer is typed once and can then be printed on all pages of a multiple-page document.

T F 3. A header is normally printed on all pages of a document.

T F 4. Footnotes are consecutively numbered and printed on the page where the information is referenced.

5. Press ______ and **Enter** to place a hard page break in a document.
   a. **Ctrl**
   b. **Alt**
   c. **Shift**
   d. **Home**

6. When page numbers are inserted, the options available in the Page Number Format dialog box are ____________.
   a. lowercase or uppercase letters
   b. lowercase or uppercase Roman numerals
   c. numbers (1, 2, 3, etc.)
   d. all of these

7. The _______ option on the Text Flow card can be used to prevent a heading and the following paragraph from being printed on two separate pages.
   a. **Widow/Orphan Control**
   b. **Keep Lines Together**
   c. **Keep with Next**
   d. none of the above

8. What option must be selected on the Layout card after selecting the **Page Setup** button to create a blank header on the first page and a regular heading on the second and subsequent pages?
   a. **Different Odd and Even**
   b. **Different First Page**
   c. **Blank First Page**
   d. **Show Number on First Page**

9. State the difference between a footnote and a footer.

10. Explain how to remove the endnote separator line.

Enriching Language Arts Skills

Spelling/Vocabulary Words

contagious transmitted by contact; spread from one to another.

knowledge the state of knowing; understanding gained through study or experience.

technological affected by or resulting from scientific and industrial progress.

Quotation Marks with Punctuation

Always place a comma or period inside a closing quotation mark.

Example:

"I wonder," said Joan to herself, "how I got myself into this situation."

Place a question mark or exclamation point inside closing quotation marks if the question or exclamation pertains only to the quoted information. Place a question mark or exclamation point outside the closing quotation marks if the question or exclamation pertains to the entire sentence.

Example:

Jan said, "Help me!" (The exclamation pertains only to the quoted information.)

Was the returned check marked "Insufficient Funds"? (The question pertains to the entire sentence.)

Semicolons and colons are placed outside closing quotation marks.

Example:

The following items were in a package marked "Fragile": an antique bowl, four glasses, and a pitcher.

Activities

Activity 10.1—Create a Multiple-Page Document with Page Numbers and Text Flow Control

1. Type the following report with the spacing and bolding as shown.

The Funds and the Management

The Funds are two of the funds in the Greyhound Family of Funds. The Company was organized as a Washington corporation on January 10, 1992, and currently offers shares of three other series: the Washington Tax-Free Bond Fund, the Ginnie Mae Fund, and the Variable Rate Government Fund. The Board of Directors of the company supervises the Funds' activities and monitors their contractual arrangements with various service providers.

Shareholder Meetings

Although the Company is not required to hold annual shareholder meetings, special meetings may be required for purposes such as electing or removing Directors, approving advisory contracts and distribution plans, and changing the Funds' investment objectives or fundamental investment policies.

Voting Rights

All shares of the Company have equal voting rights and will be voted in the aggregate, rather than by series, unless otherwise required by law (such as when the voting matter affects only one series). As a shareholder of the Funds, you are entitled to one vote for each share you own and fractional votes for fractional shares owned.

Madison Bank Contract

Madison Bank is the Funds' investment adviser, transfer and dividend disbursing agent, and custodian. In addition, Madison Bank is a Shareholder Servicing Agent of the Funds and a Selling Agent under a Selling Agreement with the Funds' distributor. Madison Bank, one of the 15 largest banks in the United States, was founded in 1865 and is the third oldest bank in the western United States.

As of December 31, 1993, various divisions and affiliates of Madison Bank provided investment advisory services for approximately $195 billion of assets of individuals, trusts, estates, and institutions. Madison Bank also serves as the investment adviser to the other separately managed series of the Company and to eight other registered, open-end, management investment companies, which consist of several separately managed investment portfolios. Madison Bank is located at 455 Sansome Street, San Francisco, California 94163.

Williams Contract
Williams is the Funds' sponsor and administrator and distributes the Funds' shares. Williams is a full-service broker/dealer and investment advisory firm located at 1422 Locust Street, St. Louis, Missouri 63101. Williams and its predecessor have been providing securities and investment services for more than 55 years. Additionally, they have been providing discretionary portfolio management services since 1982. Williams currently manages investment portfolios for pension and profit-sharing plans, individual investors, foundations, insurance companies, and university endowments.

---

2. Use the filename **10fund1.doc** and save the file on your file disk.
3. Select the body text including the sideheads and set the vertical line spacing to 2 (**Ctrl** and 2).
4. Bold the first sidehead, **Shareholder Meetings**.
5. With the insertion point in the first sidehead, turn on the **Keep with Next** option (select **Format, Paragraph, Text Flow, Keep with Next, OK**).
6. Use the Format Painter feature to copy the first sidehead format to the remaining three sideheads (select the first sidehead, double-click on the **Format Painter** button, select each of the remaining sideheads, select the **Format Painter** button again to turn off the Format Painter feature).
7. Check that Widow/Orphan Control is turned on (select the entire document; select **Format, Paragraph, Text Flow**; if necessary, click on the **Widow/Orphan Control** box to place an X in the box; select **OK**.)
8. Use page numbering to print numbers at the bottom center of each page (select **Insert**, **Page Numbers**, select the **Position** box, select **Bottom of Page (Footer)**, choose the **Alignment** box, select **Center**, **OK**).
9. In Page Layout view, scroll down to display the page numbers.
10. Use the *new* filename **10fund1r.doc** and save the file on your file disk.
11. Print one copy and close the document.

Activity 10.2—Create a Header for a Two-Page Memorandum

1. Open the memorandum with the filename **10act2.doc** located on the data disk.
2. Create a blank first page header (select **View**, **Header and Footer**, select the **Page Setup** button; select **Different First Page** on the **Layout** tab, **OK**).
3. Create the three-line header for the second and subsequent pages (select the **Show Next** button), then type the following information:

    Rapid River Relocation
    Current Date (select the **Date** button, then select the date and press **Ctrl** and **Shift** and **F9** to convert the date to text)
    Page (press the **Spacebar** once and select the **Page Numbers** button) (Press **Enter** twice.)

4. Select the **Close** button on the Header and Footer Toolbar.
5. In Page Layout view, scroll down to display the second page header.
6. Use the *new* filename **10rapid2.doc** and save the file on your file disk.
7. Print one copy.
8. Close the document.

Activity 10.3—Create a Header and Footer for a Multiple-Page Document

1. Open the report with the filename **10act3.doc** located on the data disk.
2. Select the body text and set the vertical line spacing to two (**Ctrl** and **2**).
3. Create a blank first page header (select **View**, **Header and Footer**, select the **Page Setup** button; select **Different First Page** on the **Layout** tab, **OK**).
4. Create the header for the second and subsequent pages by selecting the **Show Next** button and type the following information with the format shown:

   Book Review (Press **Tab** twice) **The Overview Effect**

5. With the Header and Footer Toolbar still displayed in the document window, create a footer to place page numbers at the bottom center of each page (select the **Switch Between Header and Footer** button, press the **Tab** key once, select the **Page Number** button, select the tab symbol and page number, choose the **Copy** button on the Toolbar, select the **Show Previous** button, choose the **Paste** button, **Close**).
6. In the Page Layout view, scroll down to display the page number and header.
7. Use the *new* filename **10over3.doc** and save the file on your file disk.
8. Print one copy and close the document.

Activity 10.4—Create a Footer and Footnote for a Multiple-Page Document

1. Open the report with the filename **10act4.doc** located on the data disk.
2. Set the **Keep with Next** option for the sideheads (with the insertion point located in the first sidehead, Graphic Design Factors, select **Format**, **Paragraph**, **Text Flow**, **Keep with Next**, **OK**; select the sidehead, click on the **Format Painter** button once, scroll down and select the sidehead, Summary).
3. Create a footer (select **View**, **Header and Footer**, select the **Switch Between Header and Footer** button, then type the following information:

   Desktop Publishing and Graphic Design (**Tab** twice) **Page** (**Page Numbers** button)

4. Select the **Close** button on the Header and Footer Toolbar.
5. Create a footnote using the following information:

a. Place the insertion point after the last character in the document, select **Insert, Footnote.** (If necessary, select the **Footnote** option and the **AutoNumber** option, then select **OK.**)

b. Type the following footnote:

LaVaughn Hart and Katie Layman, "Desktop Publishing and Graphic Design," ***The California Business Teacher*****, Spring 1990, pp. 22–23.**

c. Place the insertion point in front of the footnote number 1 and press the **Tab** key once.

d. Select **Close** on the Footnote pane.

6. To view the multiple-page document with footers and a footnote, select the **Print Preview** button, choose the **Multiple Pages** button, select the top right page.
7. Select **Close** to exit Print Preview.
8. Use the *new* filename **10dtp4.doc** and save the file.
9. Print one copy and close the document.

Challenge Your Skills

Skill 10.1—Create a Header and Format a Two-Page Memorandum and Table

1. Use Memorandum—Style 1 and the following information to complete the memorandum.

a. Make decisions regarding:

Margins
Alignment
Fonts
Table format
Text flow options
Reference initials

b. The memo should be sent to George Grindell, Business Development Manager.

c. The memo is from Janet T. Woodstock, Regional Vice President.

d. The memo should be dated June 22, 199x.

e. The subject of the memo is Northland Transition.

f. Copies of the memo should be sent to:

J.H. Allenson, Ethel Hamrock, Al Long, and Regional Staff.

g. The memorandum body text follows:

The Northland organization continues to experience many changes as they make the transition with their new majority ownership from Germany. We solicit your support in directing your sales organization to aggressively pursue all 8-Midnight outlets to sell the advantages of Health-Wise products. Here are a few of Northland's concerns and our opportunity to address them via our Direct Sale Representatives.

Northland Concerns	Health-Wise Responses
Balanced Inventories	To offer consistent service call frequencies with a 5-unit minimum order; if necessary, maintaining balanced inventories.
Improving Turnover	We offer more category market leaders than any other manufacturer, resulting in faster turnovers.
Introducing New Items	Future plans are to capitalize on our ability to quickly offer more new products into the market.
Meeting Consumer Demands	Conduct market analysis via our representatives on competitive pricing, SKU rankings, and consumer Pull Programs.

Our direct store delivery organization has the ability and the opportunity to uncomplicate their cookie and cracker needs. We must sell each and every franchise operator on our ability to take care of their needs as the dominant category leader. We possess the products and the market share to maximize their sales and profits. It is up to us to SELL this story and to develop those local in-store partnerships that move their/our business forward and upward.

Both the Marketing Support Division and the Direct Account Promotions Division have developed additional incentive plans to be offered to franchise operators. These promotions are based on the overall sales potential of the franchise and the types of promotions that have been successful in the past. Each Direct Sale Representative should create a list of any franchises that seem hesitant. This list should be discussed with the Marketing Support or Direct Account Promotion team leader for the sector to develop an individual plan for thc franchisc.

Keep us posted on your successes!

---

2. Create the following two-line header:

   Note: Remember to create a blank header on the first page.

Northland Transition	**June 22, 199x**
Health-Wise Promotion	**Page** (insert page number)

3. Use the filename **10wise1.doc** and save the file on your file disk.
4. Print one copy.
5. Close the document.

Skill 10.2—Create a Header and Footnotes; Format a Multiple-Page Document with Table

1. Open the multiple-page document named **10skill2.doc** located on the data disk.
2. Make decisions regarding:

   Margins
   Line spacing
   Alignment
   Fonts
   Table format
   Text flow
   Header format and placement
   Spacing before and after, capitalization, and bold for title and sideheads
3. Create the following footnotes in the document.
   a. Place the first footnote reference at the end of the first paragraph. Footnote text: *The Southwest Stock Exchange Bulletin*, p. 6.
   b. Place the second footnote reference at the end of the third paragraph. Footnote text: *EITAK Commodities Annual Report*, p. 2.
   c. Place the third footnote reference at the end of item number 2, ". . . eliminating the order match problem." Footnote text: Ibid.
4. Create an appropriate header including the page number.
5. Use the *new* filename **10stock2.doc** and save the file.
6. Print one copy and close the document.

Chapter 10
Create a Multiple-Page Document

Skill 10.3—Create a Footnote and Page Numbering for a Multiple-Page Document; Language Arts

1. Open the multiple-page document with the filename **10skill3.doc** located on the data disk.
2. Make decisions regarding:

   Margins
   Line spacing
   Fonts and font sizes
   Formatting of title and subtitle
   Alignment
   Hyphenation
   Headers and footers
   Text flow
3. Correct three spelling, two punctuation errors, and one misused word.
4. Create the following footnote in the document.
   a. Place a footnote reference after the exclamation point in the last sentence of the document. Footnote text: Pearce, Bill, "Everyday Magic," *Modern Living Journal*, August 1992, p. 10.
5. Number the document pages at the bottom right corner.

6. Use the *new* filename **10magic.doc** and save the file.
7. Print one copy.
8. If you have completed your work, exit Word.

CHAPTER

Create a Form Letter and Mailing List

Features Covered

- Create a data source for a form letter
- Create a main document for a form letter
- Merge the main document with the data source file
- Edit a data source and a main document
- Select data records to be merged

Objectives and Introduction

After successfully completing this chapter, you will be able to create and merge a data source file and a main document. You will understand fields and records and learn how to use the Mail Merge Helper. In addition, you will be able to edit the data source and form files and to select specific data records to be merged.

A form letter is a standard letter that is sent to many individuals or companies. The same letter can be typed once, merged with a list of names and addresses, and printed. A form letter can be used for collecting overdue accounts, requesting donations, presenting product information, etc. The form letter is referred to as the main document. The list of names and addresses is referred to as the data source.

Create a Data Source File

The *data source* is a group of variables and field names. A variable is information that changes in each form letter and can include names, addresses, dollar amounts, dates, special comments, etc. The variable information is referred to as data. The data source can also be used to print envelope addresses or to create a mailing list (see Chapter 12).

Each set of variable information is referred to as a record. In other words, a record refers to all of the data for one entity, e.g., one company's name, address, city, state, and zip code.

A *field name* is a descriptive name used to identify a variable such as an address or dollar amount. Word suggests field names for variables that are commonly used when creating documents for merging. The field names can be accepted or deleted or a new field name(s) can be added.

Word provides a Mail Merge Helper dialog box to help create the main document and data source, and to merge the data with the main document. First, a choice is made to determine the location where the main document is to be created, i.e., in the active window or in a new main document. Once you have designated the location for the main document, the data source is created. The field names for the variables are suggested by Word in the Create Data Source dialog box. The unneeded field names are selected and removed from the list of available field names. The data source is given a filename and the choice is made to either add new records to the data source (choose **Edit Data Source**) or to add merge fields to the main document (choose **Edit Main Document**).

When the **Edit Data Source** button is selected, a Data Form dialog box displays with the field names listed beside blank boxes where the variable information can be typed. After typing the information for all records, select **View Source** to display the typed data. The data displays in a table. The first table row is called a *header row* and contains the bolded field names. The second and following table rows contain records. The data can be edited and columns and/or rows added or deleted. The data file should be checked and saved. After completing, checking, and saving the data source records, the main document (form letter) is created. See Create a Main Document later in this chapter.

Start-Up Instructions

- A new document window should be displayed. If necessary, select the **New** button on the Standard Toolbar.

Create a Data Source File

1. Select **Tools, Mail Merge** {Alt and t, r}.

   Note: The Mail Merge Helper dialog box displays (see Figure 11.1).

2. Select the **Create** button in the Main Document area {Alt and c}.

FIGURE 11.1

Mail Merge Helper dialog box

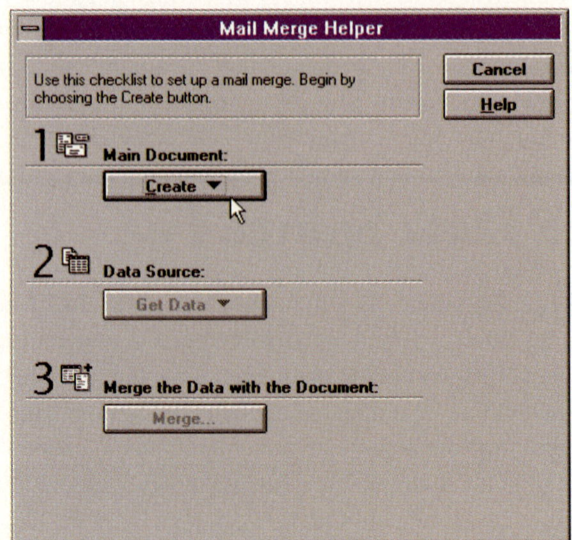

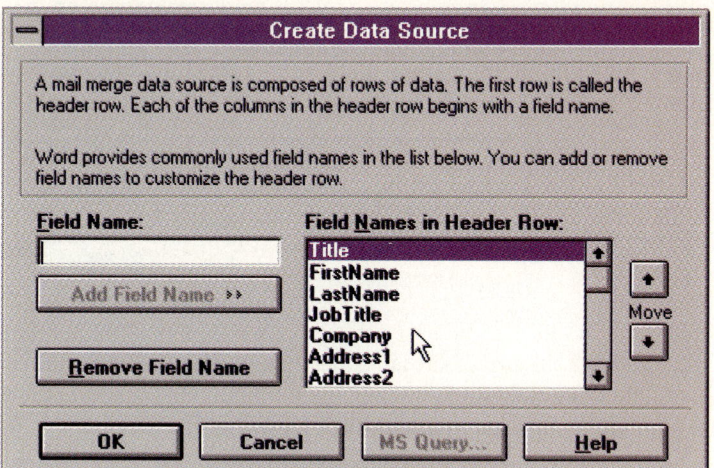

FIGURE 11.2

Create Data Source dialog box

3. Select **Form Letters** {L}.

   Note: A Microsoft Word message box displays.

4. Select the **New Main Document** button {n}.

   Note: The Mail Merge Helper dialog box displays again.

5. Select **Get Data, Create Data Source** {Alt and g, c}.

   Note: The Create Data Source dialog box displays (see Figure 11.2).

6. Remove the unneeded field names by selecting the field name and then selecting the **Remove Field Name** button {Alt and n, press the up or down arrow key to highlight the Field Name, Alt and r}.

   For example, select **Job Title**, then select the **Remove Field Name** button. Repeat for the field names **Address2, Country, HomePhone**, and **WorkPhone**.

   Note: If necessary, scroll down the list of field names to view additional field names.

7. If desired, add new field names by typing the desired field name in the Field Name box and selecting the **Add Field Name** button.

   For example, no new field names are needed at this time. Continue to step 8.

8. Select **OK** {Enter}.

9. In the Save Data Source dialog box, type the filename for the data source. If necessary, select the drive and/or directory where the data source should be stored. Select **OK** {Enter}.

   For example, type the filename **11list1.doc**. If necessary, select the drive where your file disk is located. Select **OK**.

   Note: A Microsoft Word message box displays.

10. Select **Edit Data Source** {Alt and d}.

    Note: The Data Form dialog box displays (see Figure 11.3).

11. Enter the information for each field. Press the **Tab** key to move from field to field. After you have entered the information for the last field of a record, select the **Add New** button to obtain a new data form {Alt and a}.

FIGURE 11.3

Data Form dialog box

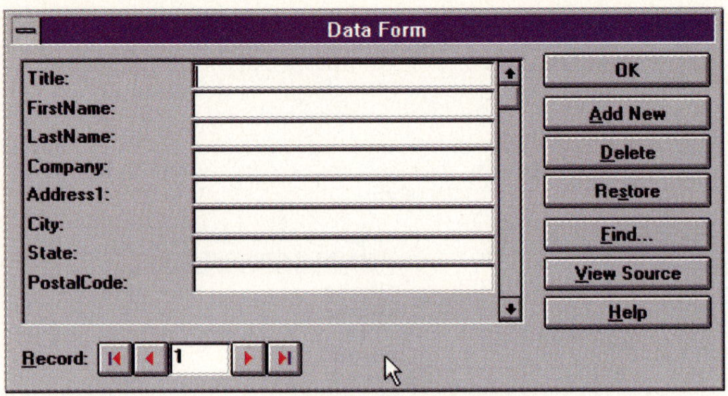

For example, enter the following information into the Data Form.

Mr.	**Tab**
Manuel	**Tab**
Hansen	**Tab**
Hansen Hardware	**Tab**
346 Oakbridge	**Tab**
San Jose	**Tab**
CA	**Tab**
95123	Select **Add New**
Ms.	**Tab**
Sandra	**Tab**
Jacobs	**Tab**
Sandy's Supplies	**Tab**
5524 Elm Ave.	**Tab**
Dallas	**Tab**
TX	**Tab**
75206	Select **Add New**
Mr.	**Tab**
Andrew	**Tab**
Archer	**Tab**
ABC Paints	**Tab**
2286 NW 65th Ave.	**Tab**
Portland	**Tab**
OR	**Tab**
97210	Do **not** select **Add New**

12. When all the records have been completed, select the **View Source** button {Alt and v}.

Note: The Database Toolbar and a table with all records display.

13. Check the accuracy of the data in each table cell. Make any necessary changes to the data in the table.

14. Save the data source file (select the **Save** button).

Finish-Up Instructions

❖ Continue with the Steps to Create a Main Document.

Create a Main Document

A *main document* is the information that remains the same in each letter (see Figure 11.4). The main document also includes the field names that correspond to the variable information that will print in each letter. Field names are placed in the form file to indicate the exact location for each field. The main document is often referred to as a form letter.

Because field information in a data source file can vary, Word has provided special instructions that give the user more control over the varied information. Some fields in the data source can be empty, e.g., a company field may not be needed in all form letters. Blank cells in the data source indicate fields that contain no data. When the data source and main document are prepared for merging, the **Merge** button can be selected to obtain the Merge dialog box. When the default option "Don't print blank lines when data fields are empty" is chosen, the Enter(s) that ordinarily result from a blank field will not be placed in the merged letter.

A form letter can be used over and over again with the date set up to change with each use. The date field is inserted in the form letter at the location at which the current date is to print. To insert a date field, the **Insert as Field** option is selected in the Date and Time dialog box. To check that the date is inserted as a field in the form letter, click on the date. A gray shading will display on a date field.

When a field name is inserted in a document, the field name is displayed between chevrons, e.g., <<Title>>. *Field codes* can also be displayed with the field name. When the field codes display, the word MERGEFIELD is inserted before each field name, e.g., { MERGEFIELD Title }. To display (or hide) field codes, select **Tools**, **Options**, **View** tab, then select **Field Codes** option.

Start-Up Instructions

- The data source file named **11list1.doc** should be displayed in the document window.

Create a Main Document

1. With the data source file displayed in the document window, select the **Mail Merge Main Document** button on the Database Toolbar.

   Note: A new document window and the Mail Merge Toolbar display.

2. If desired, insert the date as a field code.

   For example, select **Insert, Date and Time.** If necessary, select the **Insert as Field** option. Select the fourth date format, **OK.** Press **Enter** five more times.

3. Select the **Insert Merge Field** button in the Mail Merge Toolbar.

   Note: A list of the field names in the data source file displays.

4. Select the desired field name.

   For example, select **Title** and press the **Spacebar** once.

5. Repeat steps 3 and 4 to insert the desired field names. Also, remember to include punctuation and spacing as needed with field names.

FIGURE 11.4

Main document

(Date)

«Title» «FirstName» «LastName»
«Company»
«Address1»
«City», «State» «PostalCode»

Dear «Title» «LastName»:

We are pleased to announce a very special discount offer to all of our friends at «Company». All orders placed during the next month will not only receive our regular low prices but will also receive an additional 15 percent discount.

Our new catalog is enclosed. Please note the new paint supplies and materials that we have recently added to our excellent line of products.

Sincerely,

Ellen Anderson, Sales Manager
Premium Paints, Inc.

EA/xx
11mainlt.doc

Enc.

For example insert the following field names with the indicated spacing and punctuation:

a. Insert the **FirstName** field name and press the **Spacebar**.
b. Insert the **LastName** field name and press **Enter**.
c. Insert the **Company** field name and press **Enter**.
d. Insert the **Address1** field name and press **Enter**.
e. Insert the **City** field name, type a comma, and press the **Spacebar**.
f. Insert the **State** field name and press the **Spacebar**.
g. Insert the **PostalCode** field name and press **Enter** twice.
h. Type **Dear** and press the **Spacebar** once.
i. Insert the **Title** field name and press the **Spacebar** once.
j. Insert the **LastName** field name, type a colon, and press **Enter** twice.
k. Type the remainder of the letter. Notice that the Company field is inserted in the first sentence of the first paragraph.

Note: *Your main document should look similar to Figure 11.4.*

6. Save the main document.

   For example, use the filename **11mainlt.doc** and save the main document.

Finish-Up Instructions

- Continue with the Steps to Merge a Main Document and Data Source File.

Merge a Main Document and Data Source File

Once the main document and data source file are created and saved, the files are combined by selecting the **Merge to New Document**, **Merge to Printer** or the **Mail Merge** button on the Mail Merge Toolbar. If the **Merge to Printer** button is selected, the merged letters are sent directly to the printer. To select specific records to be merged, the **Mail Merge** button is chosen (see Select Data Records to be Merged later in this chapter). When the **Merge to New Document** button is selected, all the merged letters display in a new document window with each letter in a separate section. In Normal view, an End of Section bar displays between each merged letter.

Once the main document and data source file have been merged, check the merged letters for accuracy. If any errors exist, close (but do not save) the merged file and access the main document and/or data source file to make corrections. Once the necessary corrections have been made, the main document and/or data source file is saved, and the main document and data source file are merged again. If desired, the merged letters can be saved; however, saving the merged letters is not recommended because the same information has been saved previously in the main document and data source file.

A copy of each letter is printed using the normal print feature. Because a section break is placed between each letter, each letter will print on a separate page. If only one or two of the merged letters are to be printed, see Steps to Select Data Records to be Merged later in this chapter.

After the main document is merged with the data source file, printed copies both of the main document and the data source file can be very useful for filing or reference purposes. If desired, the data source and structure can be changed to display the information in a more attractive and readable manner. For example, widening the columns, selecting a smaller font, and/or changing the table position to center will help make the table easier to read.

If desired, envelopes and mailing labels can also be created using the merge process (see Chapter 12, page 277).

Start-Up Instructions

- The files named **11list1.doc** and **11mainlt.doc** must have been previously created in this chapter.

Merge a Main Document and Data Source File

1. The main document to be merged and the Mail Merge Toolbar should be displayed in the document window. If necessary, open the main document file.

   For example, the file named **11mainlt.doc** and the Mail Merge Toolbar should be displayed.

2. Select the **Merge to New Document** button on the Mail Merge Toolbar.

   Note: In a moment the merged letters display in the document window. Form Letters # . . . displays in the Title bar. Scroll through the letters and check that each letter and address have merged properly.

Finish-Up Instructions

- Optional. Use the filename **11mergl.doc** and save the merged letters.
- Print one copy of the merged letters.
- Close the merged letters.

Edit a Data Source File and Main Document

Often the information in a data source file or main document must be updated or altered. The data source is changed by adding and/or deleting a record(s) or field(s). The data in any field can be changed also. A main document is changed by deleting or inserting fields and/or by changing the text of the document. The record information in the data source file and the text in the main document can be altered using normal editing procedures.

Records can be added, deleted, or edited by selecting options in the Data Form dialog box, by displaying the data source file and using the **Add Record** or **Delete Record** buttons on the Database Toolbar, and by selecting data in the table and inserting new information. To insert or delete a field(s), display the data source file and select the **Manage Fields** button. Also, if desired, records and fields can be added or deleted using the same procedures as used to edit a table (see Chapter 5 and 6).

An edited main document and/or data source file should be saved again before merging. After a main document or data source file is changed, all or specific data source records can be merged with the main document.

Start-Up Instructions

- The file named **11mainlt.doc** should be displayed in the document window.

Edit a Data Source File

1. With the main document displayed in the document window, select the **Edit Data Source** button on the Mail Merge Toolbar.

   Note: The Data Form dialog box displays.

Insert a New Record

2. Select the **Add New** button.
3. Type the information for the new record into the appropriate field boxes.

   For example, insert the following information:

   Ms.
   Mercedes
   Washington
   Washington Paints
   572 Tiyunga Blvd.
   North Hollywood
   CA
   91600

Edit an Existing Record

4. Locate the desired record by clicking on the left triangle or right triangle button located beside the Record box.

   For example, click on the left triangle button until record 2, **Ms. Sandra Jacobs**, displays.

   Note: *The button displays the first record and the button displays the last record.*
5. Make the desired changes to the record information.

   For example, change the Address1 field to **4140 Regent Drive.**
6. When all changes to the existing records have been made and all new records have been added, select the **View Source** button.

   Note: *When View Source is selected, the data source,* **11list1.doc** *displays in the document window. The new record has been added and the address of Ms. Sandra Jacobs has been changed.*

Add a New Field

7. Select the **Manage Fields** button on the Database Toolbar.

   Note: *The Manage Fields dialog box displays.*
8. Type the name of the new field in the Field Name box.

   For example, type **Percent.**
9. Select the **Add** button.
10. Select **OK** to exit the Manage Fields dialog box.

    Note: *A new column with the heading "Percent" has been added to the table.*
11. Type the desired information into the cells in the new field (column).

    For example, type the following information into the cells of the Percent field (column):

    10 percent
    12 percent

Chapter 11
Create a Form Letter and Mailing List

20 percent
15 percent

12. When all changes have been made, select the **Save** button to save the edited data source file.
13. Select the **Mail Merge Main Document** button to return to the main document.

Finish-Up Instructions

- Continue with the Steps to Edit a Main Document.

Start-Up Instructions

- The file named **11mainlt.doc** should be displayed in the document window. If necessary, open the file named **11mainlt.doc**, or, if the data source file named **11list1.doc** is displayed in the document window, select the **Mail Merge Main Document** button.

Edit a Main Document

1. With the main document displayed in the document window, make the necessary corrections.

   For example, delete **15 percent** in the last sentence of the first paragraph and insert the merge field **Percent** (select the **Insert Merge Field** button on the Mail Merge Toolbar, click on **Percent**).

   Note: Be sure to check spacing before and after the field name.

2. Save the edited main document.

   For example, use the *new* filename **11main2.doc** and save the file.

Finish-Up Instructions

- Select the **Merge to New Document** button and merge the letters again.
- Print the merged letters.
- Close the merged letters (do not save).

Select Data Records to be Merged

If data records to be merged are not sequentially arranged in the data source file, the **Query Option** can be selected from the Merge dialog box and the options on the **Filter Records** tab can be used to specify criteria (rules) to be met when selecting records to be merged. For example, you could choose to merge only those records for people who live in a certain state. The criteria consists of three parts: (1) the field name, (2) the comparison phrase, and (3) the text or numbers with which to compare the contents of the data field. Six criteria can be specified. When more than one criteria is created, the criteria are connected by AND or OR. When AND is used, Word selects only records that match all criteria. When OR is used Word selects records that satisfy at least one of the criteria.

Once the Filter Records tab has been used to select specific records, Word remembers the criteria specified and will continue to select only records that meet that criteria. Select the **Clear All** button on the Filter Records tab to clear the specified criteria. You can then create new criteria or merge all records in the data source file.

If the desired data records to be merged are in sequential order, the range of records can be specified in the **Records to be Merged** area of the Merge dialog box. For example, to merge records 2–5, type **2** in the From box, type **5** in the To box of the Merge dialog box, and select **Merge**.

Start-Up Instructions

- The main document **11main2.doc** should be displayed in the document window. Select the **Edit Data Source** button to display the data source file **11list1.doc**.
- Select the **Add New** button and type the following information into the appropriate field boxes in the Data Form dialog box:

  Mr.
  Brent
  Madison
  Madison Paints
  7822 Main Street
  Seattle
  WA
  98121
  15 percent

- Edit the record of Mr. Andrew Archer using the following information.

  Click on the left triangle button in the Record area to display record 3, Mr. Andrew Archer. Change the Address1 field to **2600 NW 65th Avenue**.

- Select the **View Source** button.
- Select the **Save** button to save the updated data source file.
- Select the **Mail Merge Main Document** button.

Steps to Select Data Records to be Merged

1. Select the **Mail Merge** button on the Mail Merge Toolbar.

   Note: *The Merge dialog box displays.*

2. Select the **Query Options** button.

   Note: *The Query Options dialog box displays.*

3. With the **Filter Records** tab selected, click on the down arrow in the top **Field** box and select the desired field name.

   For example, select **LastName**.

FIGURE 11.5

Query Options dialog box with criteria

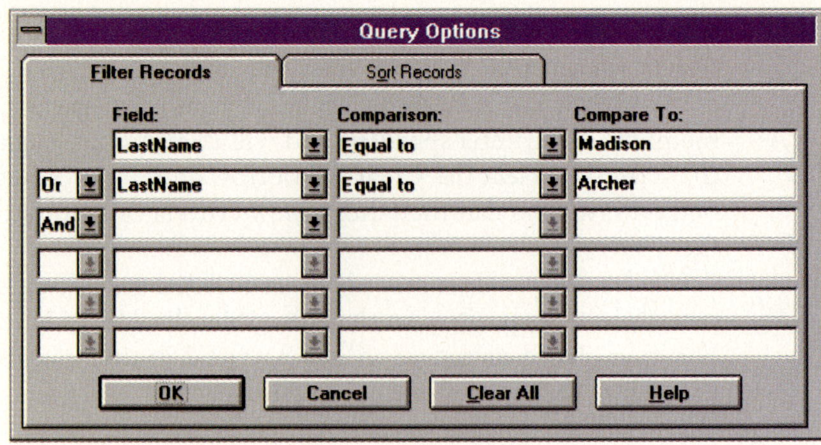

For example, check that **Equal to** displays.

5. Select the **Compare To** box and type the desired criteria.

   For example, type **Madison**.

6. Click in the first column and/or option box and choose the desired option.

   For example, select **Or**.

7. Repeat steps 3 through 5 to create additional criteria.

   For example, create a second criterion using the following information:

Field:	**LastName**
Comparison:	**Equal to**
Compare To:	**Archer**

   Note: *Your Query Options dialog box should look similar to Figure 11.5.*

8. When all needed criteria have been created, select **OK**.

   Note: *The Merge dialog box displays again.*

9. Select the **Merge** button.

   Note: *In a moment, the specified letters display in the document window.*

Finish-Up Instructions

- Print the two letters.
- Close the merged letters. Do not save the file.

The Next Step

Chapter Review and Activities

Self-Check Quiz

T F 1. The form letter is referred to as the data source file.

T F 2. An example of a variable is a company name.

T F 3. A form letter is sent to many individuals and companies.

T F 4. Word provides suggested field names that are listed in the Create Data Source dialog box.

T F 5. Criteria can be specified as a basis for merging nonsequential records.

6. Mail Merge is selected from the _______ menu.
   a. **Tools**
   b. **Insert**
   c. **Edit**
   d. **Format**

7. The _______ is referred to as data.
   a. form letter
   b. field name
   c. variable information
   d. main document

8. The main document contains the letter text, _______, spacing, and any other information that remains the same in each letter.
   a. filenames
   b. data source
   c. field names
   d. both a and b

9. State the difference between a record and a field.

10. State one reason why the date would be inserted as a field in the main document.

Enriching Language Arts Skills

Spelling/Vocabulary Words

apology an expression acknowledging regret for a fault or offense.
hallmark an indication of quality or excellence; a distinctive characteristic.

inconvenience the state of being inconvenient; lack of comfort; difficulty.

Nonrestrictive Clause

A nonrestrictive clause is a clause that is not essential to the meaning of the sentence and, therefore, is set off by a comma or commas.

Example:

We will meet next Thursday for our planning meeting, which was postponed last week.

Activities

Activity 11.1—Create a Data Source File and Main Document and Use Mail Merge

1. Create a data source file using the following information.

   a. In a document window, access the Create Data Source dialog box (select **Tools**, **Mail Merge**, **Create**, select **Form Letters**, **New Main Document**, select **Get Data**, **Create Data Source**).

   b. In the Create Data Source dialog box, highlight and remove the following field names: **JobTitle**, **Company**, **Address2**, **Country**, **HomePhone** and **WorkPhone** (select the desired field name in the Field Names in Header Row list, select the **Remove Field Name** button).

   c. Add the field name **Amount** (if necessary, double-click in the Field Name box, type the desired field name, select **Add Field Name**).

   d. Exit the Create Data Source dialog box. Use the filename, **11data1.doc** and save the file (select **OK**; if necessary, select or type the drive letter where your file disk is located followed by a colon and the filename, select **OK**).

   e. Obtain the Data Form dialog box (in the Microsoft Word message box, select the **Edit Data Source** button).

   f. In the Data Form dialog box, fill in the field name boxes with the following information. Press the **Tab** key to move to the next field. Select **Add New** to begin a new record.

Mr.	Ms.	Mr.
Randy	Janet	Eugene
Allen	Walters	Lewis
145 River Road	Route 6	455 Park Ave.
Chicago	Lancaster	Denver
IL	PA	CO
60656	17603	80239
$4,500	$5,000	$4,000

   ***Note:** Do **not** select **Add New** after the last record.*

   g. View and save the data source records (select **View Source**, make any needed changes, select the **Save** button).

h. Go to the main document window (select the **Mail Merge Main Document** button).

2. Create the main document using the following information:

   a. Create the date field (select **Insert**, **Date and Time**, check that the **Insert as Field** option is selected, choose an appropriate date format, select **OK**; press **Enter** five times).

   b. Type the following letter and insert the merge fields as shown (use the **Insert Merge Field** button to select the field names for the form letter.) Remember to press the **Spacebar** or **Enter** key or type a punctuation mark as needed after each field name).

(Insert Date as a Field)

<<Title>> <<FirstName>> <<LastName>>
<<Address1>>
<<City>>, <<State>> <<PostalCode>>

Dear <<Title>> <<LastName>>:

Because of your outstanding credit record, you have been selected to receive our new Outlet Club credit card.

Your credit limit will be <<Amount>>. You may use your new Outlet Club credit card at all of the Outlet Club stores.

If you take advantage of this special offer within the next 30 days, you will also receive 10 percent off your first Outlet Club credit card purchase. Call our toll-free number today, 1-800-555-6520, to activate your Outlet Club credit card.

Sincerely,

Francine E. Harris
Vice President, Sales

FEH/xx
11club1.doc/disk6

---

3. Use the filename **11club1.doc** and save the file on your file disk.
4. Merge the Main document, **11club1.doc**, and the data source file, **11data1.doc** (select the **Merge to New Main Document** button).
5. Optional. Print one copy of each letter.
6. Close all documents. Do not save the merged letter document.

Activity 11.2—Create a Data Source File and Main Document, Edit the Data Source File, and Select Data Records

1. Create a data source file using the following information:

    a. In a document window, access the Create Data Source dialog box (select **Tools, Mail Merge, Create**, select **Form Letters, New Main Document**, select **Get Data, Create Data Source**).

    b. In the Create Data Source dialog box, highlight and remove all field names with the *exception* of **FirstName** and **LastName** (select the desired field name in the **Field Names in Header Row** list, select the **Remove Field Name** button).

    c. Add the field names **Department, Mailstop, Category, Step,** and **Amount** (if necessary, double-click in the Field Name box, type the desired field name, select **Add Field Name**).

    d. Exit the Create Data Source dialog box. Use the filename **11data2.doc** and save the file (select **OK**; if necessary select or type the drive where your file disk is located followed by a colon and the filename, select **OK**).

    e. Obtain the Data Form dialog box (in the Microsoft Word message box, select the **Edit Data Source** button).

    f. In a the Data Form dialog box, fill in the field name boxes with the following information. Press the **Tab** key to move to the next field. Select **Add New** to begin a new record.

Sam R.	Joyce	Linda M.
Collier	Chong	Kirk
Marketing Department	Finance Department	Shipping Department
Mailstop 260F	Mailstop 228G	Mailstop 163B
Category H	Category J	Category G
Step 7	Step 4	Step 10
$45,000	$48,000	$43,000

    Note: Do not select ***Add New*** *after the last record.*

    g. View and save the data source file (select the **View Source** button, make any needed changes, select the **Save** button).

    h. Go to the main document window (select the **Mail Merge Main Document** button).

2. Create the Main Document using the following information:

    a. Change the top margin to 1.75 inches.

    b. Create the date field (select **Insert, Date and Time**, check that the **Insert as Field** option is selected, choose an appropriate date format, select **OK**; press **Enter** five times).

    c. Type the following letter and insert the merge fields as shown. (Use the **Insert Merge Field** button to select the field names for the form letter.) Remember to press the **Spacebar** or **Enter** key or type a punctuation mark as needed after each field name.

(Insert Date as a Field)

Private and Confidential
<<FirstName>> <<LastName>>
<<Department>>
<<Mailstop>>

CONFIRMATION OF SALARY STATUS

I am pleased to confirm your salary status for the new fiscal year.

On the salary schedule, you are in <<Category>> on <<Step>> with a new annual adjusted salary of <<Amount>>.

If you have any questions, please telephone Betty Jacobson at Extension 3833.

SYDNEY LIDDLE, HUMAN RESOURCES DIRECTOR

SL/xx
11sal2.doc/diskS

---

3. Use the filename, **11sal2.doc**, and save the file.
4. Merge the main document, **11sal2.doc**, and the data source file, **11data2.doc** (select the **Merge to New Main Document** button).
5. Optional. Print one copy of each letter.
6. Close and don't save the merged letters.
7. Edit the data record for Linda Kirk to change her salary to **$48,500** (select the **Edit Data Source** button, click on the right triangle button in the Record box until record **3** displays, make desired changes).
8. Add two new data records (select **Add New** and type in the information).

Valerie	Milton R.
Peters	Foxworthy
Research and Development	Shipping Department
Mailstop 209H	Mailstop 163B
Category J	Category F
Step 5	Step 9
$51,000	$40,500

***Note:** Do **not** select **Add New** after the last record.*

9. View the data source and make any needed changes (select **View Source**, make any needed changes).

10. Save the edited data source (select the **Save** button).

11. Select data records and merge only the added and corrected data records with the salary form letter (select the **Mail Merge Main Document** button, select the **Mail Merge** button, click in the From box, type 3, click in the To box, type 5, select **Merge**).

12. Optional. Print one copy of each letter.

13. Close all documents. Do not save the merge letters.

Challenge Your Skills

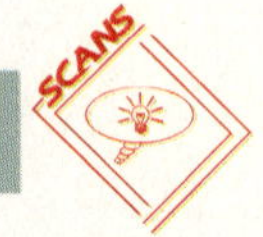

Skill 11.1—Create a Data Source File and Main Document; Edit and Select Specific Data Records

1. Use the following information to create a data source:

    a. In the Create Data Source dialog box, remove the field names that will not be needed, i.e., **Title**, **JobTitle**, **Company**, **Address2**, **Country**, and **WorkPhone**.

    b. Add the Field Names: **BranchName**, **AcctNumber**, and **BranchNumber**.

    c. Use the filename **11skdat1.doc**.

    d. Type the information for each data record as follows:

    Vernon Lackey
    4251 Auburn Rd.
    Texas City, TX 77591
    713-555-4923
    Houston Branch
    HO 23959007
    713-555-6003

    Edward Nichols
    697 S. Whiting St.
    Baytown, TX 77520
    713-555-8321
    Houston Branch
    HO 23956008
    713-555-6003

    Cynthia Prinz
    834 San Pedro
    San Antonio, TX 78212
    210-555-2535
    San Antonio Branch
    SA 46289002
    210-555-9200

    Chappel Ammons
    5233 Greenville Ave.
    Dallas, TX 75206
    214-555-2133
    Dallas Branch
    DA 54328801
    214-555-1010

    Conrad Harbour
    P. O. Box 4275
    Kerrville, TX 78028
    210-555-1824
    San Antonio Branch
    SA 46288001
    210-555-9200

    Cheryl Mears
    2469 Windham Dr.
    Dallas, TX 75243
    214-555-9243
    Dallas Branch
    DA 54326803
    214-555-1010

    Note: The first phone number is the HomePhone. The second phone number is the BranchNumber.

2. Create the main document that follows. Make decisions regarding:

Bold
Margins
Justification
Fonts
Spacing

(Insert Date as a field)

<<FirstName>> <<LastName>>
<<Address1>>
<<City>> <<State>> <<PostalCode>>

ACCOUNT NUMBER: <<AcctNumber>>

As you requested, we recently updated the name and address information we use to print your Templeton One deposit slips and/or checks. The new information is listed below. Please review the changes for accuracy and, if you have any additional changes, call the <<BranchName>>, <<BranchNumber>> for assistance.

<<FirstName>> <<LastName>>
<<Address1>>
<<City>> <<State>> <<PostalCode>>

Thank you for allowing Templeton Financial Group to serve your investment needs. If you have any questions, please contact our <<BranchName>> between 9 a.m. and 4 p.m., Monday through Friday.

TEMPLETON FINANCIAL GROUP

TFG/xx
11update.doc/diskA

---

3. Use the filename **11update.doc** and save the main document file on your file disk.
4. Merge the data source file, **11skdat1.doc**, with the main document, **11update.doc**.
5. Print one copy of each letter.
6. Edit the data source records and change the phone number of the Houston Branch to 713-555-8900.
7. Use the **Query Options** to select only the Houston branch records for merging.

   Hint: *In the Filter Records tab, select the field name* ***BranchName****, check that* ***Equals to*** *displays in the Comparison box, type* ***Houston Branch*** *in the Compare To box.*
8. Merge the specified records and print one copy of the merged letters.

9. Close all documents. Do not save the merged letters

Skill 11.2—Create a Data Source File and Main Document; Language Arts

1. Create a data source file using the following information:
   a. Determine the field names to delete and create any field names needed (see the main document that follows).
   b. Use the filename **11skdat2.doc**.
   c. Type the information for each data record as follows:

Mr. Daniel J. Martin	Ms. Rachel Garcia	Mr. Art R. Jacobs
Financial Officer	Budget Director	Chief Accountant
Norcal Communications	Discount Software	Western Trucking
3823 Wilshire Blvd.	1370 North Ave.	342 Mason Blvd.
Los Angeles, CA 90010	Miami, FL 33139	Arlington, VA 22203
15 percent	20 percent	10 percent

2. Create the main document that follows. Make decisions regarding:

   Bold
   Margins
   Alignment
   Fonts
   Enclosure notation

3. Correct three spelling errors, two misused words, and two punctuation errors.

(Insert Date as a field)

<<Title>> <<FirstName>> <<LastName>>
<<JobTitle>>
<<Company>>
<<Address1>>
<<City>> <<State>> <<PostalCode>>

Dear <<Title>> <<LastName>>:

Please accept my sincere apolgy for the inconvenience you experienced during your stay at the Stagecoach Inn. I apreciate your bringing this matter to our attention.

I have discussed your complaint with our Director of Housekeeping, and steps are being taken to ensure that the problem your experienced does not happen again.

The Vallejo Stagecoach Inn is proud to provide the highest standard in service and quality which has been our hallmark since opening in 1972. We hope on your next visit to our Inn, or any other Stagecoach Inn, that you will experience the high standards of the Stagecoach Inns.

Enclosed is a <<percent>> discount coupon for your use when visiting any Stagecoach Inn.

We are looking forward to your next visit and I again extend my sincere apologies for any inconvenence that occurred during you stay at Stagecoach Inns.

Respectfully,

Charlotte McAllister
General Manager

CM/xx
11guest2.doc/disk03

---

4. Use the filename **11guest2.doc** and save the main document on your file disk.
5. Merge the data source, **11skdat2.doc**, with the main document, **11guest2.doc**.
6. Print one copy of each letter.
7. Close all documents. Do not save the merged letters.
8. If you have completed your work, exit Word.

CHAPTER 12

Create and Print Envelopes and Mailing Labels

Features Covered

- Create envelope addresses
- Create mailing labels using predefined labels
- Create a full page of the same label
- Create mailing labels for different addresses
- Create and sort mailing labels using a new main document and an existing data source
- Create and print a single label

Objectives and Introduction

After successfully completing this chapter, you will be able to create envelope addresses, create a full page of the same label, and create and print a single label. In addition, you will be able to create and sort mailing labels using a new main document and an existing data source.

Once a main document is merged with a data source, envelope addresses or mailing labels can be created for each letter or document. Using existing data source addresses or letter addresses to create envelope addresses or mailing labels can expedite the process of setting up and printing addresses on envelopes or labels.

Create Envelope Addresses

Envelope addresses are easily created by using the **Tools**, **Envelopes and Labels** feature. Word reviews the file in the current document window and automatically identifies the address information, or an address can be typed in the address area of the Envelopes and Labels dialog box.

Once Word has identified the address information and the Envelopes and Labels dialog box is displayed, the **Envelopes** tab should be selected (see Figure 12.1).

The address information displays in the Delivery Address box. If Word has incorrectly identified the address information, the correct address can be typed. If no address information is found in the document displayed in the window, the Delivery Address box will be empty and an address can be typed.

A previously typed return address may display in the Return Address box. If the return address is not to be printed on the envelope, select the **Omit** option. If the Omit option is selected (an X displays in the Omit option box), no return address displays in the Preview box and no return address will be printed on the envelope.

The Envelope Options dialog box is used to change fonts and to select an envelope size and/or mailing options. The font for the return or mailing addresses can be changed easily by selecting the **Font** button located in the Delivery or Return Address areas.

The U.S. Postal Service requests that mailing addresses be typed with vertical line spacing of one and no italic text or indented lines. For a standard, large No. 10 envelope, the address is placed approximately 2 to 2½ inches from the top edge and 4 to 4½ inches from the left edge of the envelope. Word automatically places the address on an envelope at the location suggested by the U.S. Postal Service.

For many years, the Postal Service preferred addresses to be typed in all uppercase letters with no punctuation; however, the main concern of the Postal Service is that the typed address be placed in an area easily read by OCR (optical character recognition) equipment. OCR equipment scans addresses electronically and sorts mail quickly, thus expediting the mail service.

Using uppercase letters and no punctuation or using lowercase letters with initial capitals and punctuation are now both considered acceptable forms for mailing addresses. Typing envelopes or mailing label addresses in uppercase letters with no punctuation is recommended, however, because it is more efficient to type characters in one case and keystrokes are saved when punctuation is omitted.

The position of the return or mailing addresses can be changed by selecting the **Options** button on the Envelopes card. If desired, the From Left and From Top positions can be changed in the Delivery Address area. Word also has the capability of creating the POSTNET (POSTal Numeric Encoding Techniques) bar code for any zip code. Select the **Delivery Point Bar Code** option to print a bar code above the delivery address. (The POSTNET bar code is used by the U.S. Postal Service to expedite the routing of mail.) Also, the FIM (Facing Identification Mark) option can be selected to print a code that identifies the face of a courtesy reply envelope. The FIM is used by the Postal Service during presorting.

Start-Up Instructions

❖ Open the file named **12torres.doc** located on the data disk.

Create an Envelope Address

1. With the insertion point located at any position in the letter, select **Tools, Envelopes and Labels** {Alt, t, e}.

   Note: The Envelopes and Labels dialog box displays (see Figure 12.1). Check that the Envelopes tab is selected. If necessary, select the ***Envelopes*** *tab. The address for the letter displays in the Delivery Address box. If a return address was typed at a prior time, the return address also displays in the Return Address box. If a delivery address is not displayed, you can click in the Delivery Address box and type an address.*

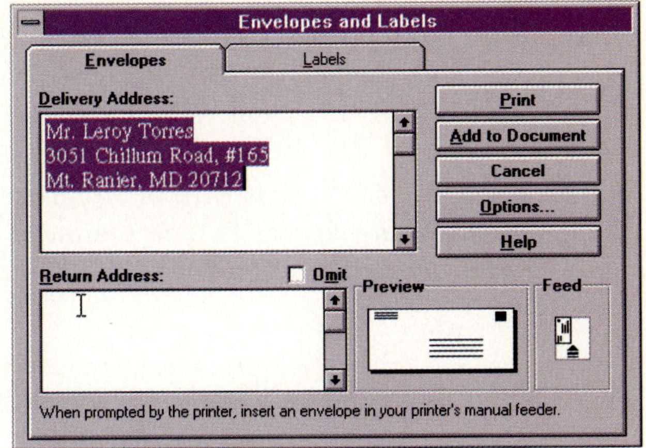

FIGURE 12.1

Envelopes and Labels dialog box

2. If a return address is desired, click in the **Return Address** box or if a return address is displayed, select all lines of the return address. Type the desired return address {Alt and r}.

   For example, click in the **Return Address** box or if a return address is displayed, select all lines of the return address. Type your name and return address information.

3. Select the **Options** button {Alt and o}.

   Note: The Envelope Options dialog box displays.

4. Select the **Delivery Point Bar Code** option {Alt and b}.

   Note: The Bar Code displays above the address lines in the Preview box.

5. Check that an Envelope Size displays. If necessary, click on the down arrow at the right of the Envelope Size box and click once on the desired envelope size {Alt and s, press the up or down arrow key until the desired envelope is highlighted, press Enter}.

   For example, check that **Size 10** ($4^1/_8$ x $9^1/_2$ in) displays in the Envelope Size box or **make a selection of your own.**

6. Select the **Font** button in the Delivery Address area and choose a font and size.

   For example, select **Times New Roman, 14 point** {Alt and f, press the up or down arrow key to highlight the desired font; Alt and s, press the up or down arrow key to highlight the desired size}.

7. Select **OK** twice {Enter, Tab, Enter}.

8. Select the **Add to Document** option {Alt and a}.

   *Note: A message displays "Do you want to save the new return address . . ." Select **No**. The envelope information is placed (added) at the beginning of the letter followed by a section break. To view the letter and/or envelope, select the **Print Preview** button. Choose the **Multiple Pages** button, choose any button on the first row. Select **Close** {Alt and Shift and c}.*

To Print an Envelope from the Document Window

9. The insertion point should be located on the page (section) containing the envelope address and bar code.

10. Select **File, Print** {Ctrl and p}.

11. Select **Current Page** {Alt and e}.

12. Select **OK** {Enter}.

Note: The printer pauses, allowing an envelope to be inserted in the printer or paper tray. Use of plain paper is OK for this practice activity. Press the **Online** *or* **Start** *button on your printer. The address prints on the paper in the appropriate area.*

Finish-Up Instructions

❖ Use the *new* filename **12envel.doc** and save the file. Close the document.

Create Mailing Labels Using Predefined Labels

Mailing labels are short forms on which names and addresses are printed. Mailing labels come in various sizes. Two commonly used sizes are 2⅝" x 1" and 1⅓" x 4". Generally, the labels are self-adhered to paper that is 11 inches in length. The self-adhesive mailing label is removed from this paper and placed on an envelope.

Mailing labels are usually designed with one, two, or three columns per page. Preferably the address is printed two to three spaces from the left edge of the form and starts on the second or third line.

Word provides predefined label options for both dot matrix and laser printers. Various Avery brand label product numbers and sizes are available in the Label Options dialog box. (Avery brand labels are sold in most office supply stores or stationary departments.)

The label information, e.g., height, width, paper size, etc. is listed in the Label Information area of the Label Options dialog box (see Figure 12.2). Select the **Details** button to view the exact location of the label on the backing paper. The top and side margins, label height and width, and number of labels across and down the page are shown. (The details displayed will depend on the printer that is selected.) The vertical and horizontal pitch displays, which is the space between label rows and label columns. The details can be changed if the selected labels do not exactly match the dimensions and layout of your labels. If desired, the **Custom Laser** or **Custom Dot Matrix** option in the Product Number list can be used to custom design a label size.

Mailing labels can also be created by using the Merge feature (see Chapter 11). The data source used to create form letters can be merged with a new main document that has been formatted using a predefined label format to create mailing labels. (See Steps to Create and Sort Mailing Labels Using a New Main Document and an Existing Data Source later in this chapter.)

Start-Up Instructions

❖ A clear document window should be displayed. If necessary, select the **New** button on the Standard Toolbar.

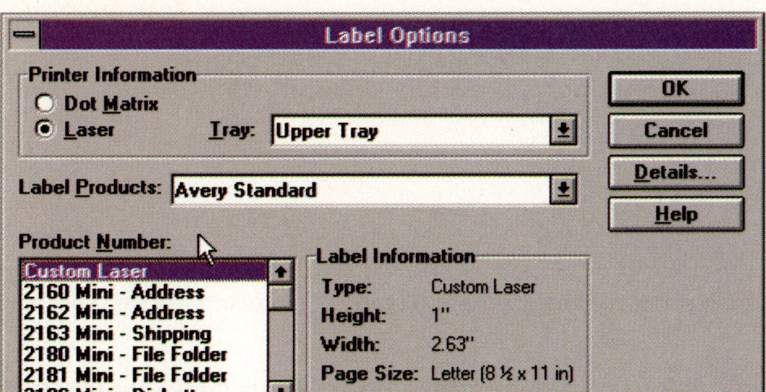

FIGURE 12.2

Label Options dialog box

Steps to Create a Full Page of the Same Mailing Label

1. Select **Tools, Envelopes and Labels** {Alt, t, e}.

   Note: The Envelopes and Labels dialog box displays.

2. If necessary, select the **Labels** tab {Alt and L}.

3. In the Address box, type the desired mailing label address {Alt and a}.

   For example, type the following address:

   Sanchez Plumbing
   5673 East Forest St.
   Helena, MT 59601

4. Choose the desired print option.

   For example, check that the **Full Page of Same Label** option is selected. (If necessary, select the **Full Page of the Same Label** option.)

5. To select the desired label size, select **Options**.

   Note: The Label Options dialog box displays (see Figure 12.2).

6. Choose the desired Printer Information option {Alt and m *or* Alt and L}.

   For example, select your printer, i.e., **Dot Matrix** or **Laser**.

7. In the Product Number box, select the desired product number {Alt and n, press the up or down arrow key to highlight the desired product number}.

   For example, *if using a dot matrix printer,* choose **4144 - Address.** *If using a laser printer,* choose **5160 - Address.**

   Note: Label information including type, height, width, and page size displays in the Label Information area.

8. Select **OK** {Enter}.

9. Select the **Print** or **New Document** option.

   For example, select **New Document** {Alt and d}.

   *Note: The document window displays the labels as they will appear on a page when printed. If desired, select the down arrow next to the **Zoom Control** button and 75% to view more of the labels on the screen.*

Finish-Up Instructions

- Use the filename **12labels.doc** and save the labels on your file disk.
- Print one copy of the labels.
- Close the document.

Start-Up Instructions

- A new document window should be displayed. If necessary, select the **New** button.
- Select the down arrow next to the **Zoom Control** button and choose 75%.
- The nonprinting symbols should be displayed. If necessary, select the **Show/Hide** button.

Create Mailing Labels for Different Addresses

1. Select **Tools, Envelopes and Labels** {Alt, t, e}.

   Note: *The Envelopes and Labels dialog box displays.*

2. If necessary, select the **Labels** tab.
3. Select the **Options** button {Alt and o}.
4. Select the desired Printer Information option {Alt and m *or* Alt and L}.

   For example, *if using a dot matrix printer,* select the **Dot Matrix** option. *If using a laser printer,* select the **Laser** option.

5. Select the desired Product Number {Alt and n, press the up or down arrow key to highlight the desired product number}.

   For example, *if using a dot matrix printer,* **select 4611 - Address.** *If using a laser printer,* select **5662 - Address.**

6. Select **OK** to return to the Labels tab in the Envelopes and Labels dialog box.
7. Choose the **New Document** button {Alt and d}.

   Note: *The label outlines display in the document window.*

8. If desired, select all labels and change the paragraph line spacing.

   For example, press **Ctrl** and **a** to select all labels, choose **Format, Paragraph**; on the Indents and Spacing tab, select the up arrow beside the **Spacing Before** option until **6 pt** displays, select **OK.**

9. Click beside the first paragraph symbol in the first label {press the up arrow key once}.
10. Type the label information; press **Shift** and **Enter** after each line and press the **Tab** key to move to the next label.

    For example, type the following labels:

    JOLENE NOYD (Shift and **Enter)**
    75 MANNAKE ST (Shift and **Enter)**
    ROCKVILLE MD 20850 (press **Tab**)

GWEN L MAYO (Shift and Enter)
106 GRAYSTONE (Shift and Enter)
TEANECK NJ 07666 (press Tab)

J C CAMERON (Shift and Enter)
1200 SPRING GARDEN ST (Shift and Enter)
PHILADELPHIA PA 19130 (press Tab)

JONATHAN T PALAZZO (Shift and Enter)
INDUSTRIAL TRAINING (Shift and Enter)
400 STANTON - CHRISTIANA RD (Shift and Enter)
NEWARK DE 19713

Note: *It is not necessary to press the* ***Tab*** *key after the last zip code.*

Finish-Up Instructions

- Use the filename **12Labm.doc** and save the file on your file disk.
- If desired, select **Print Preview, One Page** to display the labels on a full page. Select **Close.**
- Print one copy. (Plain paper is OK.)

  Note: *The printer may pause waiting for mailing labels to be manually placed in the tray. If necessary, press the printer online button to activate the printer.*
- Close the document.

Create and Sort Mailing Labels Using a Main Document and a Data Source

Mailing labels can be easily created using a new main document and an existing data source. The Mail Merge Helper is used to create the mailing labels for an existing data source. With the assistance of the Mail Merge Helper, a new main document is created, the data source file is opened, the new main document is set up with the desired label product number and merge fields, and the data is merged with the new main document.

If desired, the data for the mailing labels can be arranged in an assigned order by specifying the field name(s) to be sorted. For example, the data source records can be presorted by zip code in order to receive discounts on mail rates.

The new main document file that contains the chosen labels and merge fields can be saved and used again at a later time. If the data source records are changed, the new main document file can be used to merge the changed records. Open the new main document and merge the changed records by selecting the usual merge buttons.

If an addressed envelope is desired for each merged letter, use the Mail Merge Helper. After selecting **Create** in the Main Document area, select **Envelopes.** An envelope size and the desired fields can be selected by following the same steps used to create mailing labels.

Start-Up Instructions

- ❖ The file named **11list1.doc** created in Chapter 11 must be available.
- ❖ A new document window should be displayed. If necessary, select the **New** button.

Create and Sort Mailing Labels Using a New Main Document and an Existing Data Source

1. Select **Tools, Mail Merge** {Alt, t, r}.
2. Select **Create, Mailing Labels** {Alt and c, m}.
3. Select the **New Main Document** button {n}.
4. Select **Get Data, Open Data Source** {Alt and g, o}.
5. Double-click on the desired filename {press Tab, use the up or down arrow key to highlight the desired file, Enter}.

   For example, double-click on **11list1.doc**.
6. Select the **Set Up Main Document** button {s}.

   Note: The Label Options dialog box displays.
7. Select the desired Printer Information option {Alt and m *or* Alt and L}.

   For example, *if using a dot matrix printer,* choose **Dot Matrix.** *If using a laser printer,* choose **Laser.**
8. Select the desired Product Number {Alt and n, press the up or down arrow key to highlight the desired product number}.

   For example, *if using a dot matrix printer,* select **4605 - Address.** *If using a laser printer,* select **5262 - Address.**
9. Select **OK** {Enter}.

   Note: The Create Labels dialog box displays (see Figure 12.3).

FIGURE 12.3

Create Labels dialog box

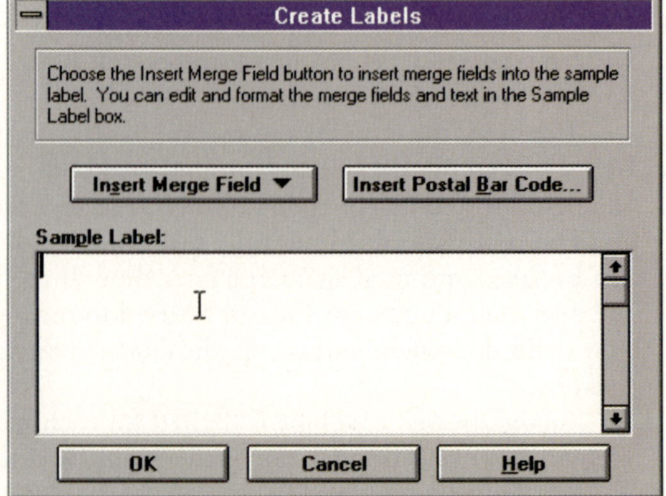

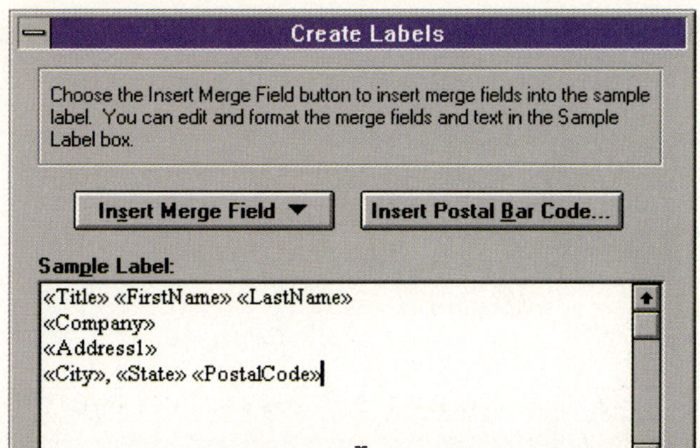

FIGURE 12.4

Create Labels dialog box with field names

10. To display the list of field names, select the **Insert Merge Field** button, choose the desired field names, and use spacing, Enters, and punctuation as desired {Alt and s, press the up or down arrow key to highlight the desired field name, Enter}.

For example, set up the labels with the field codes and format as follows:

<<Title>> <<FirstName>> <<LastName>>
<<Company>>
<<Address1>>
<<City>>, <<State>> <<PostalCode>>

Note: *The field names displayed in the Sample Label box should be arranged in the order that the information is to print on the mailing label (see Figure 12.4).*

11. Select the **Insert Postal Bar Code** button {Alt and b}.

12. Click in the **Merge Field with Zip Code** box {Spacebar}.

13. Select the field name that contains the zip code information {press the down arrow key to highlight the desired field name}.

For example, select **PostalCode.**

14. Select **OK** twice {Enter, press Tab, Enter}.

Note: *The Mail Merge Helper dialog box displays.*

15. To save the new main document containing the chosen labels and field names, select the **Edit** button in the Main Document area and choose **Mailing Label: . . . .**

Note: *The "Zip Code not valid!" message that displays in each label will be replaced by a bar code when the label main document is merged with the data source.*

16. Save the label main document.

For example, use the filename **12newlb.doc** and save the label main document on your file disk.

17. Select the **Mail Merge** button {Alt, t, r}.

Sort Records to be Merged

18. Select the **Query Options** button {Alt and q}.

FIGURE 12.5

Sort Records card in the Query Options dialog box

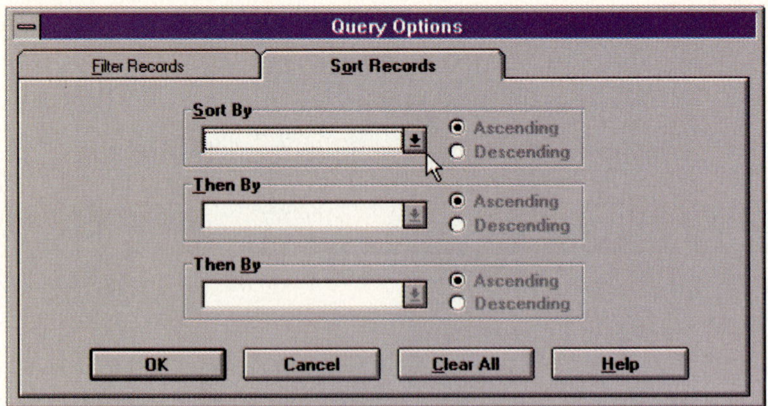

Note: The Query Options dialog box displays.

19. If necessary, select the **Sort Records** tab {Alt and o}.

Note: The Sort Records card displays (see Figure 12.5).

20. Click in the **Sort By** box {Alt and s}.

Note: The list of field names displays.

21. Select the field name to be used for sorting {press the up or down arrow key to highlight the desired field name, press Tab}.

For example, scroll down the list and select **PostalCode.**

22. Select the desired sort order, i.e., **Ascending** or **Descending** {Alt and a *or* Alt and d}.

For example, check that **Ascending** is selected. (If necessary, select **Ascending.**)

23. Select **OK** {Enter}.

Note: The hourglass displays briefly while the data records are being sorted.

24. Select **Merge** twice {Alt and m, Alt and m}.

Note: In a few moments the merged and sorted mailing labels display. Notice the labels (reading from left to right) are arranged in ascending zip code order, i.e., 75206, 91600, 95123, 97210, 98121. Also notice that a bar code has been inserted at the top of each label.

Finish-Up Instructions

- Use the filename **12sorta.doc** and save the label file on your file disk.
- Print one copy. If the printer pauses to allow you to insert labels, press the necessary button(s) on the printer to begin printing. (Plain paper is OK.)
- Close all documents.

Create and Print a Single Label

Word provides the capability of printing one single label. Printing a single label is useful when a mailing label is needed for a large envelope, such as a 5 x 7-inch or 9 x 12-inch size envelope. The single label feature also enables you to create a label at an exact location on the label sheet.

The **Single Label** option is chosen in the Envelopes and labels dialog box on the Labels card. After an address is typed and the **Single Label** option is selected, a choice can be made about row and column location on the label sheet. For example, if the labels in the first two rows and the first column of the third row have been previously used on a 3-column, 10-row label sheet, specify row 3, column 2 for the location at which the next label is to print.

Steps to

Print a Single Label

1. Select **Tools, Envelopes and Labels** {Alt, t, e}.

   Note: *The Labels tab should be displayed. (If necessary, select the* ***Labels*** *tab.)*

2. In the Address box, type the desired mailing address.

   For example, type:

   Mr. Arlie Shannock
   Madigan Entertainment Company
   7001 West Jefferson Blvd.
   Los Angeles, CA 90016

3. Select the **Options** button {Alt and o}.

4. Select the Printer Information and Product Number.

   For example, *if using a dot matrix printer,* select **Dot Matrix** and choose the **4144 - Address** product number. *If using a laser printer,* select **Laser** and choose the **5160 - Address** product number.

5. Select **OK** {Enter}.

6. In the Print area at the bottom of the dialog box, select **Single Label** {Alt and n}.

7. In the Print area, select the desired row location where the label is to be printed on the form {Alt and w, press the up arrow key twice}.

   For example, click on the up arrow beside Row until **3** displays.

8. In the Print area, select the desired column location where the label is to be printed on the form {Alt and c, press the up arrow key}.

   For example, check that **1** displays in the Column box. (If necessary, click on the up or down arrow until the 1 displays.)

9. Select the **Print** button {Alt and p}.

   Note: *Using plain paper is OK. The address prints on the label form in the row and column specified.*

The Next Step

Chapter Review and Activities

Self-Check Quiz

T F 1. Mailing labels are short forms that are self-adhered to paper.

T F 2. When using Envelopes Options, fonts can be changed for the delivery address but cannot be changed for the return address.

T F 3. When typing information in a mailing label using a predefined label, the **Tab** key is pressed to move to the next label.

T F 4. The letter address must be selected before **Tools, Envelopes and Labels** is chosen.

T F 5. The records of a data source can only be sorted by the city name.

6. U.S. Postal Service regulations request that mailing addresses be printed with __________.
   a. line spacing of one
   b. line spacing of two
   c. indented lines
   d. italic characters

7. The ______ button in the Envelopes tab of the Envelopes and Labels dialog box is selected to change the position of the return or delivery address.
   a. **Add to Document**
   b. **Options**
   c. **Print**
   d. none of the above

8. A standard, large business envelope is referred to as a No. ______ envelope.
   a. 6
   b. 8
   c. 10
   d. 12

9. List two occasions when only a single label would need to be printed.

10. List one reason for printing the Delivery Point Bar Code with envelopes or mailing label addresses.

Enriching Language Arts Skills

Spelling/Vocabulary Words

eligibility qualified, suited, desirable.

furnishing providing, giving, supplying.

ensuring making sure, making certain.

adhere to stick fast, to support or be devoted to, to follow without turning away from a specified course.

Subject-Verb Agreement

Verbs must agree in number with their subject. If a subject is singular (one), use a singular verb; if a subject is plural (more than one), use a plural verb.

Examples:

***Laurel** and **Sharee are** co-owners of the condominium.*

*Our **president**, as well as all staff members, **is** looking forward to developing good relationships with new clients.*

To determine if a subject and verb are in agreement, omit the words between the subject and verb.

Examples:

*The **legs** of the chair **were** damaged.*
*(The **legs were** damaged.)*

***Gerald**, together with his two daughters, **is** to arrive on an evening flight.*
*(**Gerald is** to arrive on an evening flight.)*

Activities

Activity 12.1—Create Mailing Labels for Different Addresses

1. Select **Tools, Envelopes and Labels.** The Labels tab should be selected.
2. Use the following information to select the desired label.
   a. On the Labels card, select **Options.**
      If using a dot matrix printer, highlight the **4144 - Address** Product Number.
      If using a laser printer, highlight the **5160 - Address** Product Number.
   b. Select **OK, New Document.**
   c. Select all labels and set the spacing before the paragraphs to **6 pt.** (**Ctrl** and **a**, select **Format, Paragraph,** click on the up arrow beside the Spacing Before box to display **6 pt**, select OK.
3. Click in the first label. Type the following names and addresses in uppercase letters with no punctuation. Press **Shift** and **Enter** after each line as shown and press the **Tab** key after each zip code.

MR WAYNE PIFFERO (**Shift** and **Enter**)
580 AZALEA RD (**Shift** and **Enter**)
BOSTON MA 02154 (**Tab**)

MR YOUNG KOH (**Shift** and **Enter**)
68 BROWNING PL (**Shift** and **Enter**)
DETROIT MI 48220 (**Tab**)

MS BECKY HARBIN (**Shift** and **Enter**)
302 MULFORD RD (**Shift** and **Enter**)
ROCKVILLE IL 61111 (**Tab**)

MS SUSAN SWAIN (**Shift** and **Enter**)
2115 CARL ST #9 (**Shift** and **Enter**)
GARDEN CITY KS 67846 (**Tab**)

MRS NADINE LONG (**Shift** and **Enter**)
400 ROCKWAY DR (**Shift** and **Enter**)
MOREHEAD KY 40351 (**Tab**)

4. Use the filename **12add1.doc** and save the address labels on your file disk.
5. Print the address labels and close the document.

Activity 12.2—Create and Sort Mailing Labels Using a New Main Document and an Existing Data Source

*Note: The file named **11data1.doc** must be completed from Chapter 11, Activity 11.1.*

1. Use the following information to create and sort mailing labels.
   a. Select **Tools, Mail Merge**, choose **Create, Mailing Labels**.
   b. Select **New Main Document**, **Get Data, Open Data Source**.
   c. Double-click on the file named **11data1.doc**.
   d. Select **Set Up Main Document**, choose your printer type, i.e., dot matrix or laser.
   e. Select the Product Number. *If using a dot matrix printer*, choose **4143 - Address**. *If using a laser printer*, choose **5261 - Address**.
   f. Select **OK** and choose the **Insert Merge Field** button; select the desired field names using the following format:

      <<Title>> <<FirstName>> <<LastName>>
      <<Address1>>
      <<City>>, <<State>> <<PostalCode>>

   g. Select **OK**, choose **Edit** in the Main Document area, select **Mailing Label . . .**, save the file using the filename **12form2.doc**.
   h. Choose the **Mail Merge** button; choose **Query Options**.
   i. Select the **Sort Records** tab, select the down arrow beside the **Sort By** box, choose **LastName**, select **OK**.
   j. Merge the main document **12form2.doc** and the data source file **11data1.doc** (select **Merge**).
2. Use the filename **12sort2.doc** and save the labels on your file disk.

3. Print one copy and close all documents.

Activity 12.3—Create an Envelope Address from a Letter

1. Type the following letter:

(Use current date)

Mr. Fred Hampton
832 Middle Road
Ashland, OR 97520

Dear Mr. Hampton:

The probate procedure is now complete in the case of Mr. Mario Claude Hampton. We enclose copies of the final documents for your records.

A check in the amount of $2,500 is enclosed for your fees as the personal representative of this estate.

It has been a pleasure to assist you with this matter. If I can be of additional assistance in the future, please contact me.

Sincerely,

Gloria R. Graham
Attorney at Law

GRG/xx
12hampt3.doc/diskp

Enc.

---

2. Use the filename **12hampt3.doc** and save the file.
3. Create an envelope address (select the **Tools, Envelopes and Labels;** if necessary, select the **Envelopes** tab).
4. Check that the delivery address is correct.
5. Click or select all lines in the Return Address box; type your name and address.
6. Select the **Options** button; select the **Delivery Point Bar Code** option.
7. Check that **Size 10** displays in the Envelope Size box.
8. Change the font size for the delivery address (select the **Delivery Address Font** button; double-click in the Size box, type **13**, select **OK** twice).
9. Place the envelope information at the beginning of the letter (select **Add to Document**). Do not save the new return address as the default return address (select **No**).

10. View the envelope (select the **Print Preview** button, select **Close**).
11. With the insertion point in the page (section) where the envelope appears, print the envelope (select **File**, **Print**, **Current Page**, **OK**).
12. Use the *new* filename **12env3.doc** and save the file on your file disk. Close the document.

Challenge Your Skills

Skill 12.1—Create a Full Page of the Same Label; Create a Single Mailing Label

Part I

1. Create a full page of the same label. Make decisions regarding:

   Printer Information
   Product Number for a two- or three-column label form
2. Type the following address:

   Susan Michele Strand
   Paramount Pictures
   5555 Melrose Avenue
   Hollywood, CA 90038-3197
3. Use the filename **12susan.doc** and save the file on your file disk.
4. Print the page of labels.
5. Close all documents.

Part II

1. Create a single label and make decisions regarding:

   Printer Information
   Product Number for a two- or three-column label form
   Print the label in column 2, row 3
2. Type the following address:

   Mr. Dennis J. Sutter
   Sutter and Cowell Insurance Agency
   1023 Powers Ferry Blvd.
   Marietta, GA 30060
3. Print the single label.

Skill 12.2—Create Mailing Labels for Different Addresses

1. Use the Product Number **4605** (dot matrix) or Product Number **5662** (laser) and create a label file. Set the spacing before paragraphs to **6 pt**. Type the following information.

RAY M HIMMEL
HUMAN RESOURCES
MANAGER
1330 GREENWOOD PLACE
LAKEWOOD CO 80226

R K ADAMSON
INVERNESS INC
6534 75TH AVE
FT COLLINS CO 80525

CARMEN SCOFIELD
HUMAN RESOURCES
DIRECTOR
S & T SYSTEMS
P O BOX 229
LAKE CITY FL 32056

ALMA PRYOR
VICE PRESIDENT
MICROCOMPUTER INC
460 UNIVERSITY AVE
WESTERBURY NY 11590

ROLAND POPKEN
P O BOX 7214
NASHVILLE TN 37221

ORSENDA PEREZ
160-20 91ST STREET
HOWARD BEACH NY 11414

HOA NGUYEN
BUDGET DIRECTOR
WESTERN SALES INC
445 S GRAND AVE
LOS ANGELES CA 90071

JOSH POTTER
123 LONDON TERRACE
NEW CITY NY 10956

MILT KLAUER
55 MARSHALL STREET
ST PAUL MN 55102

2. Select all labels, choose a font of your choice, and use a 12 point size.
3. Use the filename **12skill2.doc** and save the file.
4. Print the mailing labels and close the document.

Skill 12.3—Create a Main Document, Data Source and Mailing Labels; Language Arts

1. Use the Mail Merge Helper to create the data source file and main document. Use an appropriate filename for the data source.
2. In the Create Data Source dialog box, determine the field names needed and remove the field names that are not needed.
3. Use the following addresses to create the data source file.

Mr. Darrell Gray
82 Longman Rd.
Lee Summit MO 64063
Grade 20
$8.50

Ms. Roselyn K. Bangham
408 Violet Lane
St. Louis, MO 63113
Grade 26
$10.80

Mr. Craig Malone, Jr.
1401 Laurel Place, #18
Cape Girardeau, MO 63701
Grade 25
$10.15

Mrs. Marguerite Jakes
One Basin Rd., Apt. 7
Sedalia, MO 65301
Grade 24
$9.90

4. Use the traditional block style letter to create the main document. Make decisions regarding:

    Margins
    Alignment
    Fonts
    Reference initials
    Filename for main document
    Enclosure notation

5. Correct three spelling errors, one misused word, and two punctuation/grammatical errors.

(Insert the date as a field)

{Inside
address
fields}

Dear {salutation field}:

I am pleased to confirm our offer to join Missouri National Bank.

You will be working in the Teleservices Department. Your position will be a Customer Service representative, {gradenumber field}, with an hourly salary of {payrate field}.

In order to comply with the Immigration Reform and Control Act of 1986 you will need to provide documents confirming both your identity and employment elegibility on the first day your report for work. Under this law, your continued employment depends upon your furnishing such documents.

Also enclosed is two documents: *Working at Missouri National Bank* and the *Employment Agreement.* These provide a summary of provisions regarding your employment with Missouri National Bank. Please read both of these documents carefully because they contain important information regarding your employment with our company. On your first day of work, you will be asked to sign the acknowledgment form contained in the *Working at Missouri National Bank* booklet as well as the *Employment Agreement* ensureing that you have received copies and agree to adhear to their terms.

I look forward to your joining our team at Missouri National Bank. If you have questions concerning your employment, please call me at 804-555-8020.

Sincerely,

H. Gail Abler
Human Resources Director

---

6. Merge the main document and data source file to create a personalized letter for each new employee.
7. Optional. Print the merged letters.
8. Create mailing labels for each new employee (create a new main document—you determine an appropriate Product Number to be used with your printer). Save the label main document using an appropriate file name.
9. Merge the data source and new main document to create a mailing label for each new employee.
10. Print the mailing labels.
11. Close all documents
12. If you have completed your work, exit Word.

Part 3
Checking Your Step

Production Skill Builder Activities
Chapters 9-12

Production Activity 3.1—Create Standard Paragraphs and Assemble Personalized Letters

1. Create a document that contains the following standard paragraphs:

Invest WorldWide Fund

The Invest WorldWide Fund provides stability by spreading your investment across international markets. This fund is well structured to respond to changing market conditions. Investors with a long-term investment outlook will benefit from the fund's high degree of stability and current income. This fund provides monthly distribution of dividends.

Tax-Free Bond Fund

This fund provides a tax-free shelter for long-term investments. Although the return is lower, the capital risk is minimal, because all investments are made in municipal bonds.

Environment Series

The Environment Series provides for investment in the securities of companies that meet specific environmental protection criteria. This fund enables investors to support companies that promote environmentally safe products and services. Although earnings tend to be slightly lower than some other funds, the Environmental Series has proven itself as a steady growth investment for environmentally conscious investors.

Current Stock Fund

The Current Stock Fund provides an avenue for the smaller investor to participate in the stock market. Funds can be transferred into and out of this fund without penalty or fee, making this a great short-term investment instrument with high potential return.

---

2. Use the filename **3stand1.doc** and save the standard paragraphs document.

3. Use the following information and the standard paragraphs document to create personalized letters for the following individuals:

   a. Ms. Nichelle Arnold
   4241 West Peace St.
   Raleigh, NC 26703
   Ms. Arnold is interested in investments that provide high current income.

   b. Ms. Kikuko Yamagoto
   3428 Lehigh St.
   Allentown, PA 18103
   Ms. Yamagoto is interested in investing in environmentally conscious companies.

   c. Mr. and Mrs. Gary Edmon
   1536 Old Trenton Rd.
   Trenton, NJ 08690
   Mr. and Mrs. Edmon are interested in investing in a fund that provides a tax shelter for long-term investments.

   d. Ms. Janice VanBriggle
   246 East Ave.
   Marwick, RI 02865
   Ms. VanBriggle is interested in a short-term investment with high potential earnings.

   e. The letters are from Len Cornejo, Investment Planner

   f. Make decisions regarding:

      Letter style
      Margins
      Alignment
      Fonts
      The investment fund description that should be copied into each letter
      Reference initials/document identification/enclosure notation
      Filename for saving each letter

   g. The body of the letter follows:

   Thank you for contacting Cornejo Investment Planning regarding investment programs. Below is a brief description of a program I feel, based on our conversation, will meet your investment needs.

   > Copy the investment fund description that addresses each individual's interest from the file named **3stand1.doc**.

   Please call me after you have reviewed the enclosed brochure about the fund. I will be happy to answer any additional questions you may have and to assist you with your investment strategy.

4. Print one copy of each letter.
5. Close all documents.

Production Activity 3.2—Format a Multiple-Page Report with a Footnote and Page Numbering; Use the Thesaurus

1. Open the report with the filename **3pact2.doc** located on the data disk.
2. Make decisions regarding:

   Margins
   Justification
   Fonts
   Widow/Orphan control
   Spacing before and after sideheads
   Bold/underline/capitalization of title and sideheads
   Possible replacement words from the Thesaurus for double-underlined words
   Page numbering using the page number feature
   Page number position on the page
3. Use the following information to create a footnote:
   a. Place the footnote reference after the period of the last sentence in the document.
   b. Footnote text: **Plan of Cooperative Ownership, Book 1, 1991, pp. 95-96.**
4. Use the *new* filename **3agree2.doc** and save the file.
5. Print one copy.
6. Close the document.

Production Activity 3.3—Create and Merge a Main Document and Data Source File; Create and Sort Mailing Labels

1. Use the Mail Merge Helper to create the data source and main document. Use an appropriate name for the data source file.
2. In the Create Data Source dialog box, determine the field names needed, removing the field names that are not needed.
3. Use the following addresses to create the data source.

Mrs. Marilee Vasquez
Rosewood Terrace
90 E. Spring St., #10
Columbus, OH 43215
Location:
 Clinton Dryden, Inc.
 306 Arlington Blvd.
 Columbus, OH
Phone Inquiry: 614-555-3838

Mr. Dwayne H. Padilla
568 Parkdale St.
Cincinnati, OH 45240
Location:
 Mark Kangas, Inc.
 1010 Westwood Blvd.
 Cincinnati, OH
Phone Inquiry: 513-555-6220

Ms. Frankie S. Botta
3530 Boston Ave.
Tulsa, OK 74119
Location:
Bradley Archer
3066 Fourth St.
Tulsa, OK
Phone Inquiry: 918-555-7500

Mr. Raymond M. Heckman
Canterberry Place
600 Blyon Ct., Apt. 4
Tulsa, OK 74119
Location:
Bradley Archer
3066 Fourth St.
Tulsa, OK
Phone Inquiry: 918-555-7500

4. Use the traditional block style letter to create the main document. Make decisions regarding:

Margins
Justification
Fonts
Reference initials/document identification/enclosure notation

---

(Insert the date as a field)

(Inside address fields)

Dear (salutation fields):

It is our pleasure to inform you that you have been selected to participate in a very special ***Market Test Sale*** to be held next month in (use field names for city and state). The purpose of this special event is to judge the public's acceptance of **One Price Sales**. Over 250 new Dodge, Ford, Cadillac, and Nissan models will be tagged with their suggested retail price and a **Maximum Final Discount** price.

Shopping for a new car or truck will never be easier. Sales personnel have been instructed to assist all shoppers in locating the right vehicle for their needs *without negotiating price.* There will be no surprises.

This **One Price Sale** will last until the end of next week at the following location:

Location: (use field names for location)

Phone Inquiries: (use field name)

In addition to the new models, a large selection of demonstrators, rental returns, and used cars and trucks will be drastically discounted for immediate sale. All vehicles will be specially marked for this sale.

This invitation is being made exclusively to you. Remember, there is absolutely no reason to wait for lower prices.

Sincerely,

H. M. Arceneau
Marketing Research Director

---

5. Use the filename **3pact3md.doc** and save the file.
6. Merge the letter main document and the data source file to create personalized letters.
7. Print one copy of each letter and close all documents.
8. Create a two- or three-column label main document. Select an appropriate label for your printer. The labels should include the Postal Bar Code.
9. Use the filename **3pact3lb.doc** and save the label main document.
10. Merge the label main document and the data source file to create a mailing label for each recipient. Print one copy of the mailing labels.
11. Close all documents.

Production Activity 3.4—Create a Letter and an Envelope; Language Arts

1. Use the traditional block style letter and create the following letter.
   a. Make decisions regarding:
      Margins
      Alignment
      Fonts
      Date of letter
      Salutation
      Text attributes as desired
      Reference initials/document identification/enclosure notation
      Capitalization and punctuation for the letter address
   b. Send the letter to Ms. Lucinda A. Marquez, who resides at 7002 Pacific Drive, Omaha, NE 68114-5400, and should receive an 18 percent One-Day Savings Pass. Ms. Marquez's authorization must be received no later than 25 days after the date of the letter.
   c. Correct two spelling errors, one misused word, and three punctuation/grammatical errors

Dear (provide an appropriate salutation):

Once a year we choose a limited number of pre-qualified people to receive a Bereman Credit Card. You are one of those selected.

Bereman Credit Card rates are among the lowest in the industry. Our rates are 4.4 percent above the prime rate. Our company has eficient and reliable services that is provided through our toll-free number, 24 hours a day, and seven days a week.

To claim your card simply sign and mail the enclosed Armstrong certificate. Because this offer is a special promotion, we need your authorization by (supply the date).

With you new card, you will receive excellent service, a low interest rate, and an (supply percent discount) One-Day Savings Pass. Also you will get a free desktop calculator when you make your first credit card purchase.

Send in your pre-approved certificate today ensurring that a no-annual-fee Bereman Credit Card will be mailed to you within one week.

Sincerely,

M. J. O'Reilly
Special Services Manager

---

2. Print the letter.
3. Create and print an envelope for the letter. (Using a return address is optional.)
4. Use a filename of your choice and save the file.
5. Close the document.
6. If you have completed your work, exit Word.

Part 4
A Step Ahead

Advanced Documents and Features

Chapters 13-16

- Border lines
- Insert a picture (graphic image)
- Create page borders
- Create a graphic with text overlay
- Edit a graphic using the Drawing tools
- Create a frame
- Position and size graphic images
- Create WordArt
- Kerning and Character Spacing
- Set exact line spacing
- AutoText
- The Spike
- Superscripts and subscripts
- Equation Editor
- Sort Text
- Use AutoFormat
- Format document using styles
- Use Templates and Wizards
- Record and play macros
- Tile, cascade, maximize, minimize, move, and size document windows
- Document summary information
- File Find feature
- Convert files
- File security
- Use DOS without exiting Word
- Access Print Manager

CHAPTER 13

Create a Letterhead, Flier, and Newsletter

Features Covered

- Create graphic lines
- Insert a picture (graphic image)
- Create page borders
- Overlay a graphic image with text
- Size a graphic image
- Create a Text Box
- Use the Drawing tools to edit a graphic image
- Copy graphic images
- Place a graphic image in a frame
- Position a frame
- Create WordArt
- Position and size a graphic image using the mouse
- Create a watermark

Objectives and Introduction

After successfully completing this chapter, you will be able to use border lines to create a letterhead; to retrieve, position, and size graphic images (pictures); and to place borders around an entire page. You will also learn how to overlay a graphic image with text and use the Drawing tools to edit a graphic image. In addition, you will be able to use the WordArt feature to create interesting text effects.

Word's graphic features are used to illustrate an idea by means of a picture (graphic image) or to present text or data in an interesting and appealing manner. In addition, horizontal and vertical graphic lines can be used to separate text to create a more pleasing appearance and to assist with easier reading.

Word provides 83 graphic images that can be retrieved into a document. In addition to the graphic images provided by Word, graphic files created by many other graphic programs can also be retrieved into Word documents. Graphic images from other graphic programs must be saved in a format that can be interpreted by Word, such as PCX (PC Paintbrush) or PIC (Lotus 1-2-3).

Create a Letterhead with Border Lines

A letterhead can be created using different fonts, point sizes, and borders. Type the text for the letterhead unformatted. Once the letterhead text is typed, select the fonts, point sizes, graphic lines, and alignment.

To enhance the appearance of letterhead text, use different fonts and point sizes as well as text attributes such as bold and italic. The placement of letterhead text can be changed by using the alignment options. Border lines also can be placed above, below, or around the letterhead text.

Start-Up Instructions

❖ Open the file named **13drill1.doc** located on the data disk.

Create Border Lines

Note: *Using a mouse is the most efficient way to place border lines above and/or below text. A mouse must be used to complete the following steps.*

1. Place the insertion point at the location at which the border line should be inserted.

   For example, check that the insertion point is located in the line that contains the company name.

2. Select the **Borders** button on the Formatting Toolbar.

   Note: *The Borders Toolbar displays below the Formatting Toolbar.*

3. Move the mouse pointer to the down arrow located to the right of the Line Style box and click once. Click on the desired line style.

   For example, click on the **$1^1/_2$ pt** single line style.

4. Select the desired border button on the Borders Toolbar.

   For example, select the **Top Border** button.

   Note: *A border line displays above the text containing the insertion point.*

Finish-Up Instructions

❖ Move the insertion point to the line containing the city, state, and zip.

❖ Move the mouse pointer to the down arrow located to the right of the **Line Style** box on the Borders Toolbar and click once. Click on the **$1^1/_2$ pt** double line style. Select the **Bottom Border** button on the Borders Toolbar.

Disk Exchange and Recovery Systems

1285 Beacon Avenue
Wellesley, Massachusetts 02181

Voice: (617) 555-1622
Fax: (617) 555-3579

FIGURE 13.1

Sample letterhead with border lines

Note: Your letterhead should look similar to Figure 13.1.

- Use the *new* filename **13ltr1.doc** and save the file.
- Print one copy and close the document.
- Click on the **Borders** button on the Formatting Toolbar to turn off the Borders Toolbar.

Create a Flier with a Graphic Image

Creating a flier in Word is similar to creating a flier on a typewriter. The flier, however, can include border lines, graphic images, and text printed in different font styles and point sizes (see Figure 13.3 on page 309).

Once the flier text is typed, the text is formatted with the desired fonts, point sizes, alignment, and appearance. Border lines can be placed above, below, or around selected text or the entire page.

A graphic image (picture) can be inserted into a document to enhance the appearance of the flier. A graphic image can be inserted at the location of the insertion point in the document window, or it can be inserted into a frame. When a graphic image is inserted at the location of the insertion point, the picture is anchored (linked) to the paragraph that contained the insertion point when the graphic image was inserted. If the paragraph is moved, the graphic image will also be moved. If a graphic image is inserted into a frame, the frame can be moved and positioned independently because the frame is not anchored to a specific paragraph or location in text. If a border is to be placed around the entire page, a graphic image should be inserted at the location of the insertion point— not in a frame.

When a graphic image is inserted, a border displays around the image. The border does not print unless a border line style is chosen. Small black handles (boxes), often referred to as sizing handles, display at the edges and corners of the graphic image. These handles can be used to increase or decrease the size of the graphic image (see Steps to Change the Size and Position of a Graphic Image Using the Mouse on page 322).

Start-Up Instructions

- Open the file named **13drill2.doc** located on the data disk.

Insert a Picture (Graphic Image)

1. With the insertion point at the location in the document where the picture (graphic image) should be placed, select **Insert, Picture** {Alt, i, p}.

FIGURE 13.2

Insert Picture dialog box

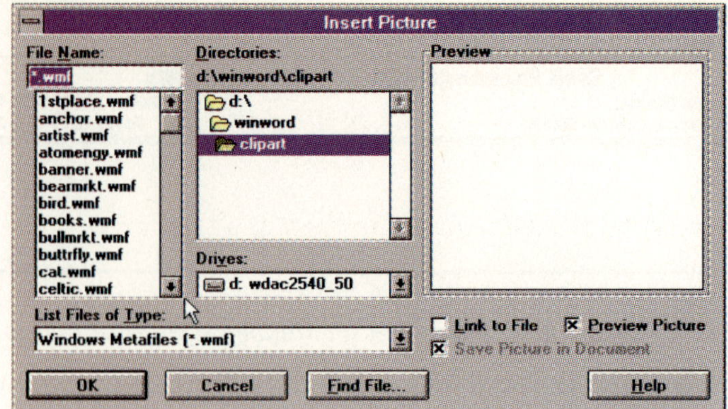

For example, check that the insertion point is located in the blank line at the top of the document. (If necessary, place the insertion point in the blank line at the top of the document.) Select **Insert, Picture**.

*Note: The Insert Picture dialog box displays (see Figure 13.2). A list of graphic files with the filename extension **.wmf** displays. The graphic files are stored in the default Word graphics directory (e.g., d:\winword\clipart).*

2. Scroll through the list of files and click on the desired filename {Alt and n, Tab, press the down arrow key to highlight the desired filename}.

   For example, click once on **dancers.wmf.**

   *Note: The dancers picture should display in the Preview box. If necessary, select the **Preview Picture** button to display the selected graphic image in the Preview box {Alt and p}.*

3. Select **OK** to retrieve the selected graphic image {Enter}.

   Note: The dancers graphic image is placed in the document window.

Finish-Up Instructions

❖ Use the *new* filename **13flier2.doc** and save the file on your file disk.

Start-Up Instructions

❖ The file named **13flier2.doc** should be displayed in the document window.

Create a Page Border

1. Select the text and/or graphic image to be placed in a border.

   For example, select the entire document by pressing **Ctrl** and **a.**

2. Select the **Borders** button on the Formatting Toolbar.

   Note: The Borders Toolbar displays.

3. Move the mouse pointer to the down arrow located to the right of the **Line Style** box and click once. Click on the desired line style {Alt, o, b, y, press the down arrow key to highlight the desired line style}.

   For example, click on the **$1^1/_2$ pt** double line style.

4. Select the desired border button on the Borders Toolbar.

For example, select the **Outside Border** button {Alt and x, Enter}.

*Note: A double line border displays around the entire page. If desired, select the **Print Preview** button to view the full page. Select **Close** to return to the document window.*

Add Space Between the Text and the Border

5. Select **Format, Borders and Shading** {Alt, o, b}.

   *Note: The Borders and Shading dialog box displays. The Borders tab should be selected. If necessary, click on the **Borders** tab.*

6. To increase the amount of space between text and the border lines, move the mouse pointer to the up triangle located to the right of the From Text box and click until the desired amount of space displays {f, type desired space}.

   For example, click on the up triangle until **4 pt** displays in the **From Text** box.

   Note: To decrease the amount of space between text and the border lines, click on the down triangle located to the right of the From Text box.

7. Select **OK** {Enter}.

8. To remove the Borders Toolbar, click on the **Borders** button on the Formatting Toolbar.

Finish-Up Instructions

- Use the same filename, **13flier2.doc**, and save the file.

  Note: Your flier should look similar to the flier shown in Figure 13.3.

- Print one copy and close the document.

Chapter 13 Create a Letterhead, Flier, and Newsletter

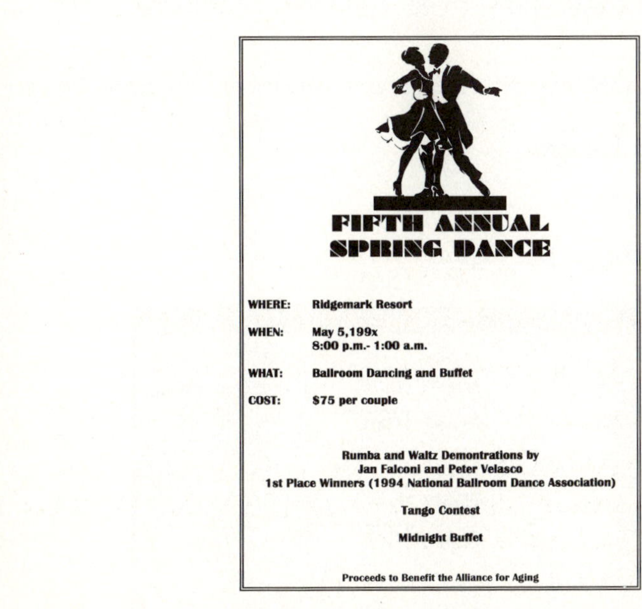

FIGURE 13.3

Flier with a graphic image

Graphic with Text Overlay

Text can be placed over a graphic image to create a text overlay. Word provides several graphic images suitable for creating documents with text overlays (see Figure 13.7 and Appendix C). The Drawing tools can be used to create a Text Box that can be placed on top of (overlay) a graphic image. The Drawing tools can also be used to edit a graphic image, e.g., to change line colors or fill colors.

The Fill Color, Line Color, and Line Style drawing tools are used to edit a graphic image. The Line, Rectangle, Ellipse, Arc, and Freeform drawing tools can be used to create new graphic images or to edit existing images.

When the drawing tools are used to edit or create a graphic image, an anchor displays (if nonprinting characters are turned on) in the document window to the left of the paragraph that is closest to the graphic image. If the graphic image is moved, the anchor will relocate to the paragraph closest to the new location of the graphic image.

Start-Up Instructions

- A new document window should be displayed. If necessary, select the **New** button.
- Change the top, bottom, left, and right margins to .5" (select **File, Page Setup**, type .5 in each margin box, select **OK**).

Create Graphic with Text Overlay

1. Select **Insert, Picture** {Alt, i, p}.
2. Double-click on the desired picture {Alt and n, Tab, press the down arrow key to highlight the desired filename, Enter}.

   For example, double-click on **hdecobox.wmf.**

   Note: The border graphic image displays in the document window.
3. Move the mouse pointer into the graphic image and click once to select the graphic image.

   Note: Small black handles (boxes) display at the edges and corners of the graphic image.

Change the Size of the Graphic Image

4. Select **Format, Picture** {Alt, o, r}.

   Note: The Picture dialog box displays (see Figure 13.4).

FIGURE 13.4

The Format Picture dialog box

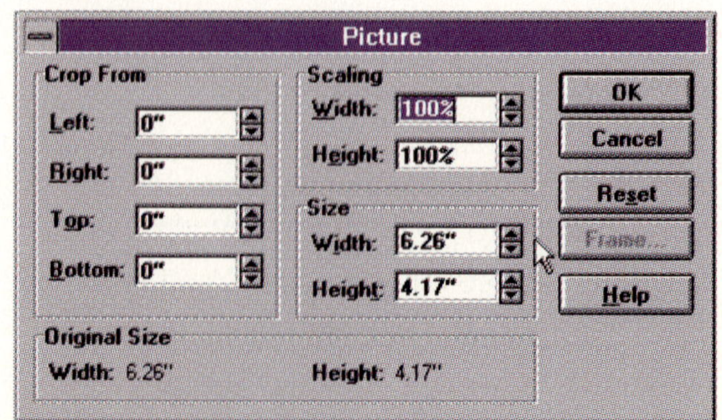

5. In the Size area, double-click in the **Width** box and type the desired width for the graphic image {Alt and i, type desired width}.

    For example, type **6.5**.

6. In the Size area, double-click in the **Height** box and type the desired height for the graphic image {Alt and t, type desired height}.

    For example, type **4.5**.

7. Select **OK** {Enter}.

8. Select the desired horizontal position for the graphic image.

    For example, select the **Center** alignment button on the Formatting Toolbar {Ctrl and e}.

Create a Text Box

Note: A mouse is required to complete the following steps.

9. Select the **Drawing** button on the Standard Toolbar.

    Note: The Drawing Toolbar displays at the bottom of the document window.

10. Select the down arrow next to the **Zoom Control** button on the Standard Toolbar and choose a display size that will enable you to see the entire graphic image in the document window.

    For example, choose **75%**.

11. Select the **Text Box** button on the Drawing Toolbar.

    Note: The mouse pointer changes to a + symbol.

12. Move the mouse pointer to the location where the upper left corner of the Text Box should be placed.

    For example, move the mouse pointer just inside the rounded corner at the upper left of the **hdecobox** graphic image.

13. Press and hold the mouse button and drag down and to the right until the Text Box is the desired size. Release the mouse button.

    For example, press and hold the mouse button and drag down and to the right until the mouse pointer reaches the bottom right corner of the **hdecobox** graphic image just inside the rounded corner. Release the mouse button.

    Note: The Text Box displays with a thin black border and a gray shadow in the graphic image (see Figure 13.5). The insertion point is located in the top left corner of the Text Box.

14. Type or insert the desired text.

    For example, select **Insert, File.** (If necessary, click in the Drives box and click on the drive letter where the data disk is located.) Double-click on the file named **13text3.doc**.

    Note: The text is placed in the Text Box.

FIGURE 13.5

Text Box containing the insertion point

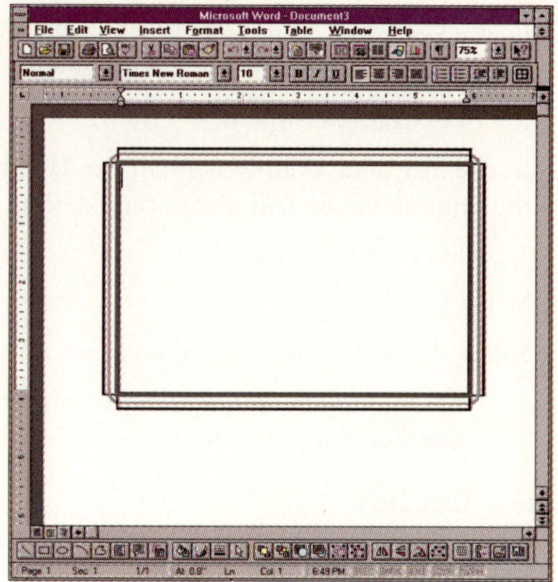

Remove the Border From the Text Box

15. Select the **Line Style** button on the Drawing Toolbar. Select the **More** option.
16. In the Line Area of the Drawing Objects dialog box, select **None**.
17. Select **OK**.

    Note: The border line is removed. However, the gray shadow still displays. That's OK. The gray shadow will not print.

Finish-Up Instructions

- Use the *new* filename **13ovr3.doc** and save the file on your file disk.
- Print one copy.
- Keep the **13ovr3.doc** file in the document window and continue with the Steps to Edit a Graphic Image Using the Drawing Tools.

Edit a Graphic Image Using the Drawing Tools

Note: A mouse is required to complete the following steps.

1. Move the mouse pointer to the desired graphic image and double-click.

   For example, move the mouse pointer to the top two border lines of the **hdecobox** graphic image and double-click.

   Note: The picture editing window displays containing the **hdecobox** *graphic image and the Picture Toolbar (see Figure 13.6).*

2. Move the mouse pointer to the desired drawing object and click once.

   For example, move the mouse pointer to the outside border line of the **hdecobox** graphic image and click once.

   Note: Small black handles display on the outside border line.

3. Select the **Fill Color** button on the Drawing Toolbar.

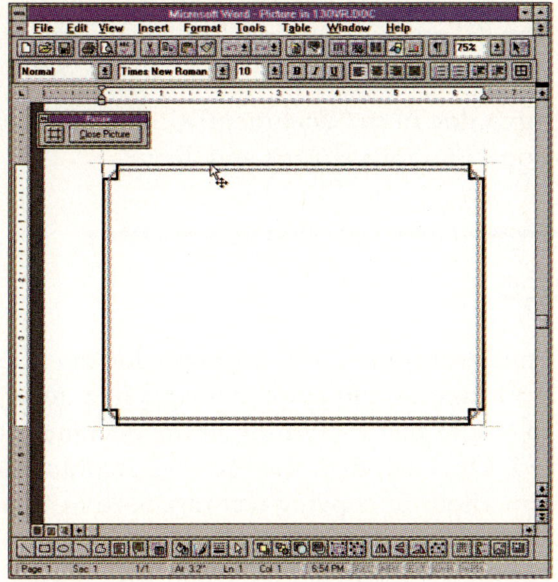

FIGURE 13.6

Picture editing window containing the **hdecobox** graphic image

4. Click on the desired color.

   For example, click on the **dark green** color (seventh row, third button).

5. If desired, change the line color or fill color for other drawing objects.

   For example, click on the inside border of the **hdecobox** graphic image. Select the **Fill Color** button on the Drawing Toolbar and click on the light green color (sixth row, third button).

6. Select the **Close Picture** button on the Picture Toolbar to return to the document window.

Finish-Up Instructions

- Use the *new* filename **13inv3.doc** and save the file on your file disk.

  Note: *Your document should look similar to Figure 13.7.*

- Print one copy.

The Offices of Virginia Diamond, CPA
are pleased to announce the opening of a new office
located at
1904 Sulphur Spring Road
Baltimore, Maryland

Phone Number (410) 555-8510

To celebrate our new office, we are holding an
Open House
on Thursday, May 15, 199x,
from 2:00 - 6:00 p.m.

Please come and help us celebrate!

FIGURE 13.7

Graphic with text overlay

- Select the **Drawing** button on the Standard Toolbar to remove the Drawing Toolbar.
- Keep the file named **13inv3.doc** in the document window and continue with the following Steps to Copy a Graphic Image and Text.

Copy a Graphic Image

A graphic image can be selected and copied into the same document or, if desired, into a different document. If all the text and graphic images in a document are to be copied, press **Ctrl** and **a** to ensure that everything in the document (e.g., text and graphic images) is selected. Once selected, the text and graphic images can be copied by using either of the methods of copying text discussed in Chapter 4, pages 83-85.

Start-Up Instructions

- **The file named** 13inv3.doc should be displayed in the document window.

Copy a Graphic Image and Text

1. Select the graphic image and/or text to be copied.

   For example, press **Ctrl** and **a** to select the entire document.

   Note: *The graphic image is highlighted and the text is hidden. That's OK.*

2. Select the **Copy** button {Alt, e, c *or* Ctrl and c}.
3. Move the mouse pointer into the right margin below the selected graphic image and/or text and click once to deselect {press the down arrow key once}.

   Note: *The insertion point is located at the bottom right edge of the graphic image.*

4. Move the insertion point to the desired location.

   For example, with the insertion point at the bottom right corner of the graphic image, press the **Enter** key six times.

5. Select the **Paste** button {Alt, e, p *or* Ctrl and v}.

   Note: *A copy of the graphic image and text is inserted into the document.*

Finish-Up Instructions

- Select the **Print Preview** button to view both copies of the text and graphic image. Select the **Close** button to return to the document window.
- Use the *new* filename **13copy.doc** and save the file on your file disk.
- Print one copy and close the document.

Create a Newsletter

A typical newsletter includes text columns, graphics, and borders. Different fonts and point sizes can be used for the newsletter text (see Figure 13.11). A newsletter usually contains several sections with different formats. For example, a newsletter may have a section with a one-column format that contains the title, subtitle, and issue date and a second section with a multiple-column format that contains the newsletter text and graphic images.

A border can be placed around the newsletter title, subtitle, and issue date to create a nameplate. Shading can be added to enhance the nameplate.

The **Columns** button on the Standard Toolbar can be used to specify the desired number of columns for the newsletter body text. (See Chapter 8, Steps to Create Newspaper Columns on page 181.)

Graphic images (pictures) can be placed in the document to add visual appeal. Also, graphic images can be placed in frames so that text will flow around the graphic images. When a graphic image is placed in a frame, the image can be positioned relative to the edge of the page or the margins. When a frame is selected and nonprinting symbols are turned on, an anchor displays to the left of the paragraph that is closest to the frame. If the frame is moved, the anchor will relocate to the left of the paragraph closest to the frame's new location.

A mouse can be used to change the position and/or size of a graphic image in a frame. To use the mouse to position or size a graphic image, the graphic image must be selected. To select a graphic image, move the mouse pointer into the graphic image and click once. When selected, a border with small black handles displays around the graphic image. A selected graphic image can be deleted by pressing the **Delete** key.

Start-Up Instructions

❖ Open the file named **13drill4.doc** located on the data disk.

Create a Newsletter Nameplate

1. Type or select the text to be the newsletter nameplate.

   For example, select the first three lines of text.

Add a Border

2. Select the **Borders** button on the Formatting Toolbar.

   Note: The Borders Toolbar displays.

3. To select the desired line style, move the mouse pointer to the **Line Style** box on the Borders Toolbar, click once, and then click on the desired line style {Alt, o, b, y, press the down arrow key to highlight the desired line style}.

   For example, click on the **$1\frac{1}{2}$ pt** double-line style.

4. Select the desired border button on the Borders Toolbar.

   For example, select the **Outside Border** button {Alt and x, Enter}.

   Note: The selected text displays inside a double-line border.

Shade the Nameplate

5. Move the mouse pointer to the **Shading** box (the last box on the Borders Toolbar), click once, and then click on the desired shading option {Alt, o, b, s, Alt and d, press the down arrow key to highlight desired shading, Enter}.

For example, click on the **20%** shading option.

Finish-Up Instructions

- Add space between the text and border (select **Format, Borders and Shading, Borders** tab, click on the up triangle to the right of the **From Text** box until **3 pt** displays, select **OK**).
- Select the **Borders** button ⊞ on the Formatting Toolbar to remove the Borders Toolbar from the screen.
- To format the body text of the newsletter in two columns, select the text beginning with the heading "Improvements that Sell" to the end of the document. Select the **Columns** button on the Standard Toolbar and click on the second column.
- Click once to deselect the text.
- Use the *new* filename **13box4.doc** and save the file on your file disk.

Start-Up Instructions

- The file named **13box4.doc** should be displayed in the document window.
- The Page Layout view should be selected.
- Scroll down so that the first few items in the bulleted lists display. The insertion point can be located at any position on the page.

Create a Frame and Insert a Graphic Image (Picture)

1. Select **Insert, Frame** {Alt, i, f}.

Note: In the document window, the mouse pointer displays as a plus sign (+). A mouse must be used to perform the next step.

2. Move the mouse pointer to the desired frame location. Press and hold the mouse button and drag down and to the right until the frame is the desired size. Release the mouse button.

For example, move the mouse pointer to the approximate center of page 1. Press and hold the mouse button and drag down and to the right until a square approximately 2" by 2" displays. Release the mouse button.

Note: The insertion point displays inside the frame (see Figure 13.8).

Position the Frame

3. Select **Format, Frame** {Alt, o, m}.

Note: The Frame dialog box display.

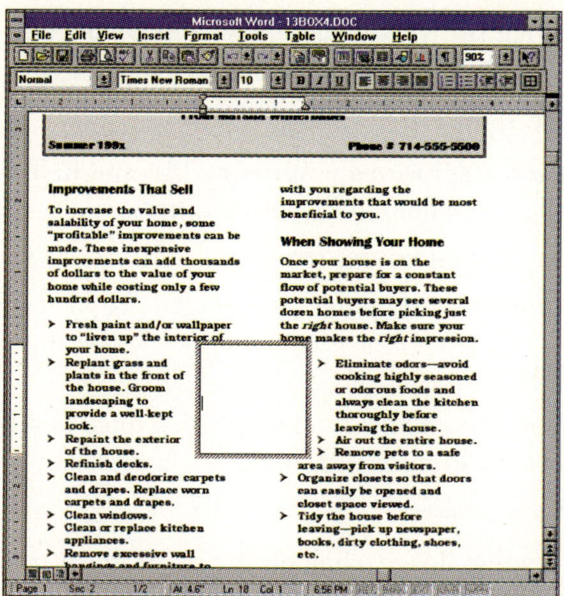

FIGURE 13.8

Frame containing the insertion point

4. In the Horizontal area, click on the down arrow located to the right of the **Position** box and select the desired position {s, press the down arrow key to highlight the desired horizontal position, Tab}.

   For example, select **Center.**

   *Note: Page should display in the Relative To box in the Horizontal area. (If necessary, click on the down arrow to the right of the Relative To box in the Horizontal area and select **Page.**)*

5. To increase the space between the frame and the text located to the left and right of the frame, in the Horizontal area, click on the up triangle located to the right of the **Distance from Text** box or double-click in the **Distance from Text** box and type the desired amount of space {Alt and x, press the up or down arrow key or type the desired distance}.

   For example, click on the up triangle located to the right of the **Distance from Text** box once to display **0.2".**

   Note: To decrease the space between the frame and the text located to the left and right of the frame, click on the down triangle located to the right of the Distance from Text box.

6. In the Vertical area, click on the down arrow located to the right of the **Position** box and select the desired vertical position {Alt and i, press the down arrow key to highlight the desired vertical position, Tab}.

   For example, select **Center.**

   *Note: Margin should display in the Relative To box in the Vertical area. (If necessary, click on the down arrow to the right of the Relative To box in the Vertical area and select **Margin.**)*

7. Select **OK** {Enter}.

Place a Graphic Image in a Frame

8. The frame should be selected (small black handles display at the edges and corners of a selected frame) or the insertion point should be located inside the frame.

For example, check that the frame is selected. (If necessary, move the mouse pointer to any edge of the frame and click once.)

9. Select **Insert, Picture** {Alt, i, p}.

10. Double-click on the desired graphic image filename {Alt and n, Tab, press the down arrow key to highlight the desired filename, Enter}.

    For example, double-click on **houses.wmf**.

    Note: The graphic image displays in the frame.

Change the Size of the Picture

11. Move the mouse pointer to the graphic image and click once to select the graphic image. Select **Format, Picture** {Alt, o, r}.

    Note: The Picture dialog box displays.

12. To set the width of the graphic image, click on the up or down triangle located to the right of the **Width** box in the Size area until the desired width displays or double-click in the width box and type the desired width {Alt and i, type the desired width}.

    For example, click on the up or down triangle until **1.9"** displays.

13. To set the height of the graphic image, click on the up or down triangle located to the right of the **Height** box in the Size area until the desired height displays or double-click in the height box and type the desired height {Alt and t, type the desired height}.

    For example, click on the up or down triangle until **1.6"** displays.

15. Select **OK** {Enter}.

Finish-Up Instructions

- Use the *new* filename **13new4.doc** and save the file on your file disk.
- Continue with the Steps to Create WordArt.

Create WordArt

Word provides a graphics feature called WordArt that is used to create text in special shapes, such as circles, curves, waves, and buttons. Font, justification, fill color, outline color, and shadow effects for WordArt can also be specified. After typing the desired WordArt text, a shape is selected and the desired font, alignment, color, and/or shadow effect is chosen. To return to the document window, the mouse pointer is moved away from the WordArt and the mouse button is clicked.

WordArt is placed in a box. The box is *sized* by moving the mouse pointer to the black handles that display at the edges and corners of the selected box and dragging to resize the box. When the box reaches the desired size, release the mouse button. The **Format**, **Picture** command can also be used to size the WordArt. WordArt is positioned by placing a frame around the WordArt, moving the mouse pointer anywhere inside the frame containing the WordArt, pressing and holding the mouse button, and dragging the frame to the desired location. When the frame is in the desired location, release the mouse button. The **Format, Frame** command can also be used to position the frame containing the WordArt.

WordArt can be edited by moving the mouse pointer to the WordArt and double-clicking to display the WordArt Toolbar. Make changes as desired to the text, such as font, shape, color, or shadow. When the changes are complete, move the mouse pointer away from the WordArt and click once.

Start-Up Instructions

- The file named **13new4.doc** should be displayed in the document window.
- If necessary, turn on nonprinting characters (select the **Show/Hide** button).
- Create a section with a one-column format at the end of the document. Scroll down to view the end of the document. Select the two blank lines (paragraph symbols) located at the end of the document. Select the **Columns** button and click on the first column.
- If desired, turn off nonprinting characters.

Steps to Create WordArt

1. Move the insertion point to the location where the WordArt is to be inserted.

   For example, move the insertion point to the second blank line at the end of the document.

2. Select **Insert, Object** {Alt, i, o}.

   Note: The Object dialog box displays with the ***Create New*** *tab selected (see Figure 13.9).*

3. Scroll down the Object Type list to display **Microsoft WordArt 2.0**. Double-click on **Microsoft WordArt 2.0** {press the down arrow key to highlight Microsoft WordArt 2.0, Enter}.

   Note: The WordArt Toolbar displays. A WordArt text entry box also displays containing the words "Your Text Here" (see Figure 13.10). A box outline displays in the document window above the WordArt text entry box.

4. Type the desired text in the WordArt text entry box.

   For example, type the following:

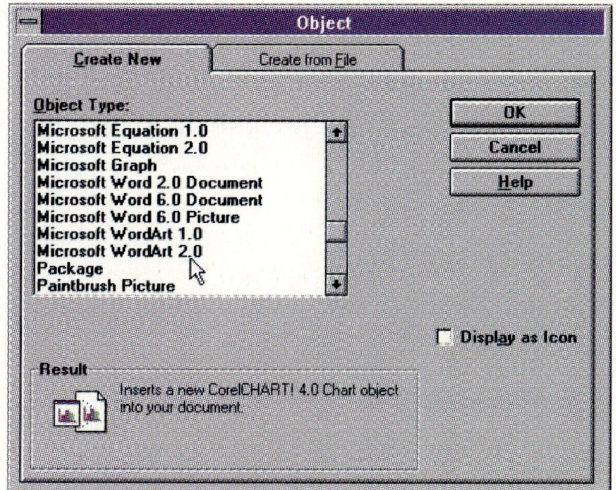

FIGURE 13.9

The Object dialog box

FIGURE 13.10

The WordArt Toolbar and text entry box

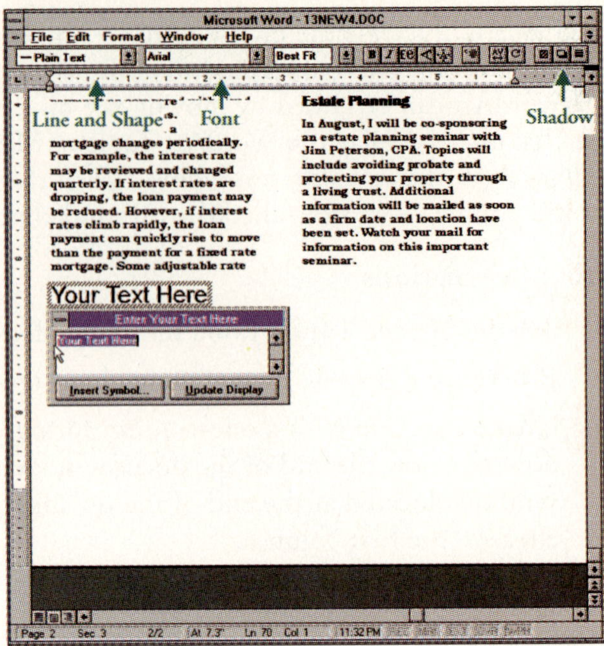

Marsha Winterbauer (press **Enter**)
Creating Moving Experiences (press **Enter**)
For Buyers and Sellers (do not press Enter)

Note: A mouse must be used to complete the following steps.

5. Move the mouse pointer to the down arrow located to the right of the **Font** box (the second button on the WordArt Toolbar) and click once.

6. Scroll through the list of font names and click on the desired font.

   For example, click on **Britannic Bold** or **make a font choice of your own**.

   Note: The WordArt text displays in the selected font in the shaded box located in the document window.

7. Move the mouse pointer to the down arrow located to the right of the **Line and Shape** box (the first button on the WordArt Toolbar) and click once.

   Note: A palette of shapes displays.

8. Click on the desired shape.

   For example, click on the **Deflate** shape (fifth row, second button).

   Note: The shape name, Deflate, displays in the **Line and Shape** *box on the WordArt Toolbar.*

9. To create a shadow effect for the WordArt, click on the **Shadow** button (second button from the right on the WordArt Toolbar).

   Note: A palette of shadow options displays. Additional shadow options can be displayed by selecting the ***More*** *option.*

10. Click on the desired shadow option.

    For example, click on the second shadow option in row 1.

11. To remove the WordArt text entry box and WordArt Toolbar and return to the document window, move the mouse pointer away from the WordArt text entry box and click once.

Note: A border displays around the WordArt in the document window. Small black handles display at the edges and corners of the WordArt indicating that the WordArt is selected. If necessary, move the mouse pointer into the WordArt and click once to select the WordArt.

12. To change the size of the WordArt, select **Format, Picture** {Alt , o, r}.

Note: The Picture dialog box displays.

13. Move the mouse pointer to the **Width** box in the Size area and double-click. Type the desired width for the WordArt {Alt and i, type the desired width}.

For example, type 6.

14. Move the mouse pointer to the **Height** box in the Size area and double-click. Type the desired height for the WordArt {Alt and t, type the desired height}.

For example type 1.8.

15. Select **OK** {Enter}.

Note: In a few moments, the WordArt redraws in the desired width, height, shape, and font in the document window.

Finish-Up Instructions

- Insert page numbers at the bottom center of both pages of the newsletter. (Select **Insert**, **Page Numbers**, click on the down arrow to the right of the Alignment box and select **Center**. Select **OK**.)
- Insert a frame around the WordArt and set the vertical position to Bottom. (With the WordArt selected, choose **Insert**, **Frame**. Select **Format**, **Frame**. In the Vertical area, click on the down arrow to the right of the Position box and select **Bottom**. Select **OK**.) Remember, a frame only displays when a graphic image or WordArt is selected.

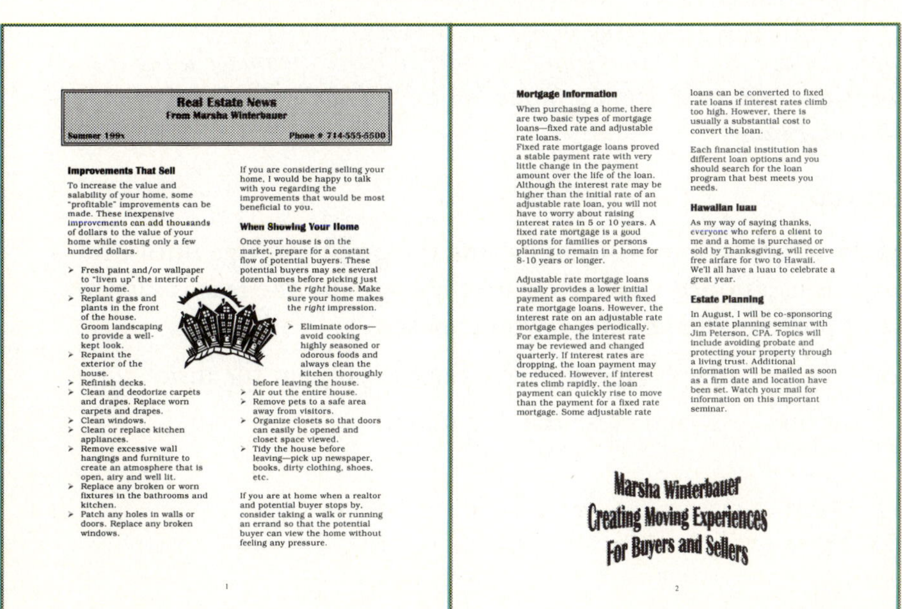

Real Estate News
From Marsha Winterbauer

Summer 199x — Phone # 714-555-5500

Improvements That Sell

To increase the value and salability of your home, some "profitable" improvements can be made. These inexpensive improvements can add thousands of dollars to the value of your home while costing only a few hundred dollars.

- Fresh paint and/or wallpaper to "liven up" the interior of your home.
- Replant grass and plants in the front of the house. Groom landscaping to provide a well-kept look.
- Repaint the exterior of the house.
- Refinish decks.
- Clean and deodorize carpets and drapes. Replace worn carpets and drapes.
- Clean windows.
- Clean or replace kitchen appliances.
- Remove excessive wall hangings and furniture to create an atmosphere that is open, airy and well lit.
- Replace any broken or worn fixtures in the bathrooms and kitchen.
- Patch any holes in walls or doors. Replace any broken windows.

If you are considering selling your home, I would be happy to talk with you regarding the improvements that would be most beneficial to you.

When Showing Your Home

Once your house is on the market, prepare for a constant flow of potential buyers. These potential buyers may see several dozen homes before picking just the *right* house. Make sure your home makes the *right* impression.

- Eliminate odors—avoid cooking highly seasoned or odorous foods and always clean the kitchen thoroughly before leaving the house.
- Air out the entire house.
- Remove pets to a safe area away from visitors.
- Organize closets so that doors can easily be opened and closet space viewed.
- Tidy the house before leaving—pick up newspaper, books, dirty clothing, shoes, etc.

If you are at home when a realtor and potential buyer stops by, consider taking a walk or running an errand so that the potential buyer can view the home without feeling any pressure.

1

Mortgage Information

When purchasing a home, there are two basic types of mortgage loans—fixed rate and adjustable rate loans.
Fixed rate mortgage loans proved a stable payment rate with very little change in the payment amount over the life of the loan. Although the interest rate may be higher than the initial rate of an adjustable rate loan, you will not have to worry about raising interest rates in 5 or 10 years. A fixed rate mortgage is a good options for families or persons planning to remain in a home for 8-10 years or longer.

Adjustable rate mortgage loans usually provides a lower initial payment as compared with fixed rate mortgage loans. However, the interest rate on an adjustable rate mortgage changes periodically. For example, the interest rate may be reviewed and changed quarterly. If interest rates are dropping, the loan payment may be reduced. However, if interest rates climb rapidly, the loan payment can quickly rise to move than the payment for a fixed rate mortgage. Some adjustable rate loans can be converted to fixed rate loans if interest rates climb too high. However, there is usually a substantial cost to convert the loan.

Each financial institution has different loan options and you should search for the loan program that best meets you needs.

Hawaiian luau

As my way of saying thanks, everyone who refers a client to me and a home is purchased or sold by Thanksgiving, will receive free airfare for two to Hawaii. We'll all have a luau to celebrate a great year.

Estate Planning

In August, I will be co-sponsoring an estate planning seminar with Jim Peterson, CPA. Topics will include avoiding probate and protecting your property through a living trust. Additional information will be mailed as soon as a firm date and location have been set. Watch your mail for information on this important seminar.

Marsha Winterbauer
Creating Moving Experiences
For Buyers and Sellers

2

FIGURE 13.11

Final newsletter

Chapter 13
Create a Letterhead, Flier, and Newsletter

Note: Your newsletter should look similar to the newsletter shown in Figure 13.11.

- ❖ Use the same filename, **13new4.doc**, and save the file.
- ❖ Print one copy.

Start-Up Instructions

- ❖ The file named **13new4.doc** should be displayed in the document window.

Change the Size and Position of a Graphic Image Using the Mouse

1. To select the graphic image, move the mouse pointer into the graphic image and click once.

   For example, move the mouse pointer into the **houses.wmf** graphic image and click once.

   Note: *Small black handles display along the edges and at the corners of the graphic image.*

2. *To change the size of the graphic image,* move the mouse pointer to one of the black handles until a double-headed arrow displays. Press and hold the mouse button and drag to size the graphic image.

   For example, place the mouse pointer on the black handle at the bottom right corner of the **houses.wmf** graphic image until a double-headed arrow displays, press and hold the mouse button, and drag up and to the left until the image is approximately 3/4 of an inch square. Release the mouse button.

3. *To change the position of the graphic image,* with the graphic image selected (see step 1 above), move the mouse pointer within the graphic image. A four-headed arrow displays below the mouse pointer. Press and hold the mouse button and drag the graphic image to the new location.

   For example, drag the **houses.wmf** graphic image up and place it below the sidehead "When Showing Your House"; release the mouse button.

   Note: *A graphic image must be in a frame in order to move the image using the mouse. If the graphic image is not in a frame (no shaded border), select the image, then select* ***Insert, Frame.***

Finish-Up Instructions

- ❖ Use the mouse to practice moving and sizing the graphic image until the graphic image is positioned attractively on the page and the text is easy to read. Size and position the graphic as you choose.
- ❖ Use the *new* filename **13rev4.doc** and save the file on your file disk.
- ❖ Optional. Print one copy and close the document.

Create a Watermark

A watermark is text or a graphic image that is repeated on each page of a document. The watermark text or graphic image is printed in a light gray on the page and other text and/or images can be placed on top of the watermark image. In order for the watermark to display on each page of document, the Header and Footer feature is used. By using the Drawing tools, the watermark can be placed at any location on the page. For example, a Text Box can be drawn in the center of the page and a graphic image can be inserted into the Text Box. The **Fill Color** and/or **Line Color** buttons on the Drawing Toolbar can be used to edit the graphic image. For example, the fill color of a graphic image can be changed to a very light gray.

Start-Up Instructions

- Open the file named **13ltr1.doc** created earlier in this chapter.
- The Page Layout view should be selected, If necessary, select **View**, **Page Layout**.
- Move the mouse pointer to the down arrow located to the right of the **Zoom Control** button and click once. Select the **Whole Page** option.

Create a Watermark

Note: A mouse must be used to complete the following steps.

1. Select **View, Header and Footer**.

   Note: The Header and Footer Toolbar displays and the Header and Footer windows display at the top and bottom of the document window.

2. Select the **Drawing** button on the Standard Toolbar.

   Note: The Drawing Toolbar displays at the bottom of the document window.

3. Move the mouse pointer to the Title bar of the Header and Footer Toolbar, press and hold the mouse button, and drag the Header and Footer Toolbar to the bottom left side of the document window above the scroll bar.
4. Select the **Text Box** button on the Drawing Toolbar.
5. Move the mouse pointer to the location where the watermark will be placed.

   For example, move the mouse pointer to the center of the page.

6. Press and hold the mouse button and drag down and to the right until the Text box is the desired size. Release the mouse button.

   For example, drag down and to the right until the Text Box is approximately 3" by 3". Release the mouse button.

   Note: Do not worry about the exact size or placement of the Text Box. If necessary, size and placement of the Text Box can be changed later.

7. If necessary, remove the border around the Text Box:
   a. Select the **Line Style** button on the Drawing Toolbar.
   b. Select the **More** option.

Chapter 13 Create a Letterhead, Flier, and Newsletter

Note: The Drawing Object dialog box displays with the **Line** *tab selected.*

c. In the Line area, select **None**.

d. Select **OK**.

8. Type or insert the desired watermark text or graphic image.

For example, select **Insert, Picture**, and double-click on the file named **disk.wmf**.

Edit the Watermark Graphic Image

9. To access the picture editing window, double-click on the graphic image.

For example, move the mouse pointer to the **disk.wmf** graphic image and double-click.

Note: The picture editing window displays. Only the graphic image displays in the window. A dotted border displays around the graphic image. The Picture Toolbar displays in the upper left corner of the window.

10. Select the **Select Drawing Object(s)** button on the Drawing Toolbar. Move the mouse pointer into the graphic image and click once to select one portion of the graphic image.

For example, move the mouse pointer to the left edge of the graphic image (anywhere in the black area) and click once. (Do not click on any of the white area.)

Note: Small black handles display at the edges of the dotted border that surrounds the graphic image.

11. Select the **Fill Color** button on the Drawing Toolbar.

12. Click on the desired color.

For example, click on the third button in the first row (5% gray).

Note: The selected layer of the graphic image displays in a very light gray. There is still one layer of the graphic image that is black. That's OK.

13. Repeat steps 10–12 to change the color of any other layers of the graphic image.

For example, click on the black rectangle, select the **Fill Color** button and click in the third button on the first row.

14. Select the **Close Picture** button on the Picture Toolbar.

Note: The graphic image displays in a very light gray in the document window.

Position the Watermark

15. Move the mouse pointer into the graphic image and click once.

Note: Small black handles display at the edges and corners of the graphic image.

16. Move the mouse pointer into the graphic image, press and hold the mouse button and drag the graphic image to the desired location on the page.

For example, press and hold the mouse button while dragging the graphic image so that the graphic image is centered vertically and horizontally on the page.

17. Select the **Close** button on the Header and Footer Toolbar.

Note: The watermark does not display in the document window. However, you may see some light gray lines. That's OK. Select the **Print Preview** *button to view the watermark image. Select* **Close** *to return to the document window.*

Finish-Up Instructions

- Use the *new* filename **13water.doc** and save the file on your file disk.
- Print one copy.
- Close the document.

The Next Step

Chapter Review and Activities

Self-Check Quiz

T F 1. A graphic image can be inserted at the location of the insertion point in a document or in a frame.

T F 2. Only a graphic image can be used as a watermark.

T F 3. Border lines can be placed above, below, or around a paragraph.

T F 4. In order for text to overlay a graphic image, the text is placed in a Text Box.

T F 5. The vertical and horizontal position of a graphic image that has been placed in a frame cannot be changed once a graphic image has been inserted into a document.

6. When a graphic image is placed in a frame, ____________________.
   a. the location and size of the graphic image cannot be changed
   b. the frame can be moved to any location on the page
   c. text will flow around the frame
   d. both b and c

7. The small black handles that display on the edges and corners of a graphic image __________.
   a. indicate that the graphic image is selected
   b. can be used to size the graphic image
   c. allow text to flow through a graphic box
   d. both a and b

Chapter 13 Create a Letterhead, Flier, and Newsletter

8. WordArt is used to create text in special shapes such as _____.
   a. curves
   b. circles
   c. buttons
   d. all of the above
9. Write down the name of the directory where Word's graphics files are stored on your system.

10. A frame or graphic image is selected when _________ display at the edges and corners of the frame or graphic image.

Enriching Language Arts Skills

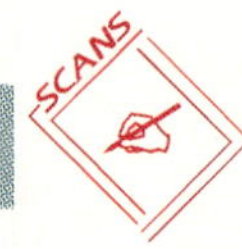

Spelling/Vocabulary Words

anonymously without a name.
complaints an expression of dissatisfaction or discontent.
coordinator a person who manages and arranges tasks in the proper order.

Initials Abbreviated

Periods or spaces are not placed after the letters of an acronym such as IRS (Internal Revenue Service) or TWA (Trans World Airlines).

Examples:

Always remember to mail your tax return to the IRS by April 15.

St. Louis is a hub for TWA.

Activities

Activity 13.1—Create a Flier with a Graphic Image and Borders

1. Open the file named **13act1.doc** located on the data disk.
2. Insert the graphic image named **heart.wmf** at the top of the document (with the insertion point located in the blank line at the top of the document, select **Insert**, **Picture**, double-click on **heart.wmf**).
3. Place a **$1^1/_2$ pt** double-line border around the entire page (select the entire document, click on the **Borders** button to display the Borders Toolbar, click on the **Line Style** box, click on **$1^1/_2$ pt** double-line style, select the **Outside Border** button). Select the **Borders** button again to remove the Borders Toolbar.
4. Move the text and **heart.wmf** graphic image away from the border by **6** points (select **Format**, **Border and Shading**, click on the up triangle located to the right of the From Text box until **6 pt** displays, select **OK**).

5. Use the *new* filename **13heart.doc** and save the file on your file disk.

Note: Your flier will look similar to the flier shown below.

Have a Heart
Be a Blood Donor

Date: Monday, June 6, 199x

Time: 8:00 a.m. - 4:00 p.m.

Location: Tri-Valley Community Center
3334 Market Ave., Canton

Contact: Edith Shenk at 216-555-7738

All those donating blood are automatically entered in the "Have a Heart" drawing!

Prizes include:

☆ Dinner for two at the Siamese Bay Restaurant

☆ Two nights free lodging at the elegant Canton Gardens Hotel

☆ Four passes to the Festival Theatre

☆ Dinner for four at the Cutting Horse Steak House

☆ Brunch for two at the Quail Lodge

Sponsored by the Blood Bank of Canton--216-555-7700 or 1-800-555-BANK.

6. Print one copy and close the document

Activity 13.2—Create a Flier with a Graphic and Text Overlay

1. In a new document window, change the top and bottom margins to .75". Change the left and right margins to 1".
2. Insert the graphic image named **ldiamond.wmf** (select **Insert**, **Picture**, double-click on **ldiamond.wmf**).
3. Change the width of the **ldiamond.wmf** graphic image to 7" and the height to 8.75" (click on the **ldiamond.wmf** graphic image, select **Format**, **Picture**, double-click in the Width box and type 7, double-click in the Height box and type 8.75, select **OK**).
4. Insert a frame around the graphic image (with the graphic image selected, choose **Insert**, **Frame**).

5. Center the **ldiamond.wmf** graphic image horizontally and vertically (with the graphic image selected, choose **Format**, **Frame**, click on the down arrow located to the right of the Position box in the Horizontal area, select **Center**, click on the down arrow located to the right of the Position box in the Vertical area, select **Center**; select **OK**).
6. Create a Text Box in the upper portion of the **ldiamond.wmf** graphic image. (If necessary, click on the **Drawing** button to display the Drawing Toolbar. Select the **Text Box** button on the Drawing Toolbar. Draw a rectangle in the upper portion of the **ldiamond.wmf** graphic image).
7. Type and center the text shown in the Text Box 1 area of the flier shown below.
8. Create a second Text Box in the banner portion of the **ldiamond.wmf** graphic image.
9. Type and center the text shown in the Text Box 2 area of the flier shown below.
10. Create a third Text Box in the lower area of the **ldiamond.wmf** graphic image.

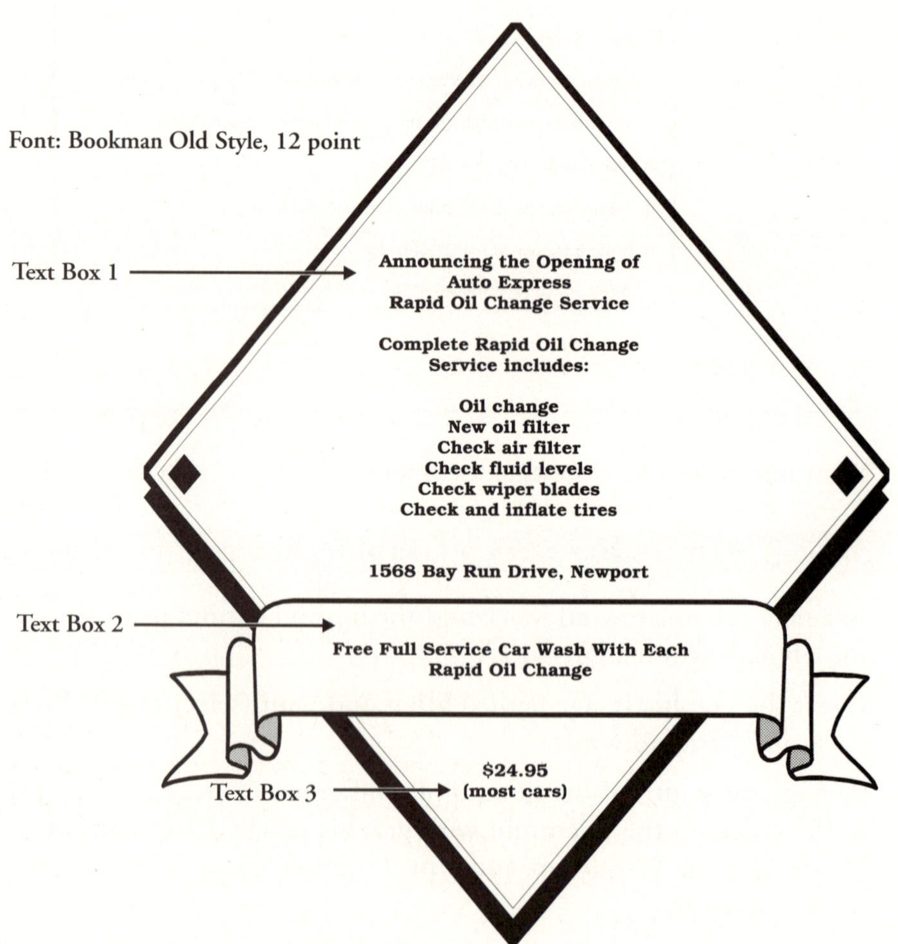

11. Type and center the text shown in the Text Box 3 area of the flier shown on page 328.

12. If necessary, select each Text Box and change the line style to **None**. (Move the mouse pointer to the border of a Text Box, click once, move the mouse pointer to the second Text Box, press and hold the **Shift** key and click once, release the **Shift** key, move the mouse pointer to the third Text Box, press and hold the **Shift** key and click once. Select the **Line Style** button, click on **More**, select **None**, **OK**). Move the mouse pointer away from the selected Text Boxes and click once to deselect.

13. If necessary, adjust the placement of the Text Boxes so that the text is placed attractively within the **ldiamond.wmf** graphic image (see the flier on page 328). (Move the mouse pointer to the Text Box containing the text to be moved. Click once to select the Text Box, move the mouse pointer to the border of the Text Box until a four-headed arrow displays, press and hold the mouse button, and drag the Text Box to the desired location, release the mouse button.)

14. Remove the Drawing Toolbar (select the **Drawing** button on the Standard Toolbar).

15. Use the filename **13act2.doc** and save the file on your file disk.

16. Print one copy and close the document.

Activity 13.3—Create a Watermark

1. Open the file named **13act3.doc** located on the data disk.
2. Create a watermark using the **anchor.wmf** graphic image.
    a. Select **View, Header and Footer.**
    b. Display the Drawing Toolbar (select the **Drawing** button).
    c. Select the **Text Box** button on the Drawing Toolbar.
    d. Draw a 3" by 3" Text Box in the center of the page.
    e. If necessary, remove the line that displays around the Text Box (select the **Line Style** button on the Drawing Toolbar, select the **More** option, choose **None** in the Line area, select **OK**).
    f. Select **Insert, Picture** and double-click on the **anchor.wmf** filename.
    g. In the document window, double-click on the **anchor.wmf** graphic image.
    h. Lighten the color of the graphic image (click on the **Select Drawing Object(s)** button, click on the **anchor.wmf** graphic image, select the **Fill Color** button, and click on the very lightest gray button—third button in the first row, repeat for any remaining black portions of the anchor graphic image).
    i. Select **Close Picture.**
    j. If necessary, reposition the **anchor.wmf** graphic image so that the image appears centered horizontally and vertically on the page.

k. Select **Close** on the Header and Footer Toolbar.

3. Use the *new* filename **13serve.doc** and save the file on your file disk.
4. Use Print Preview to view the document with the watermark. Your document should look similar to the document shown below.

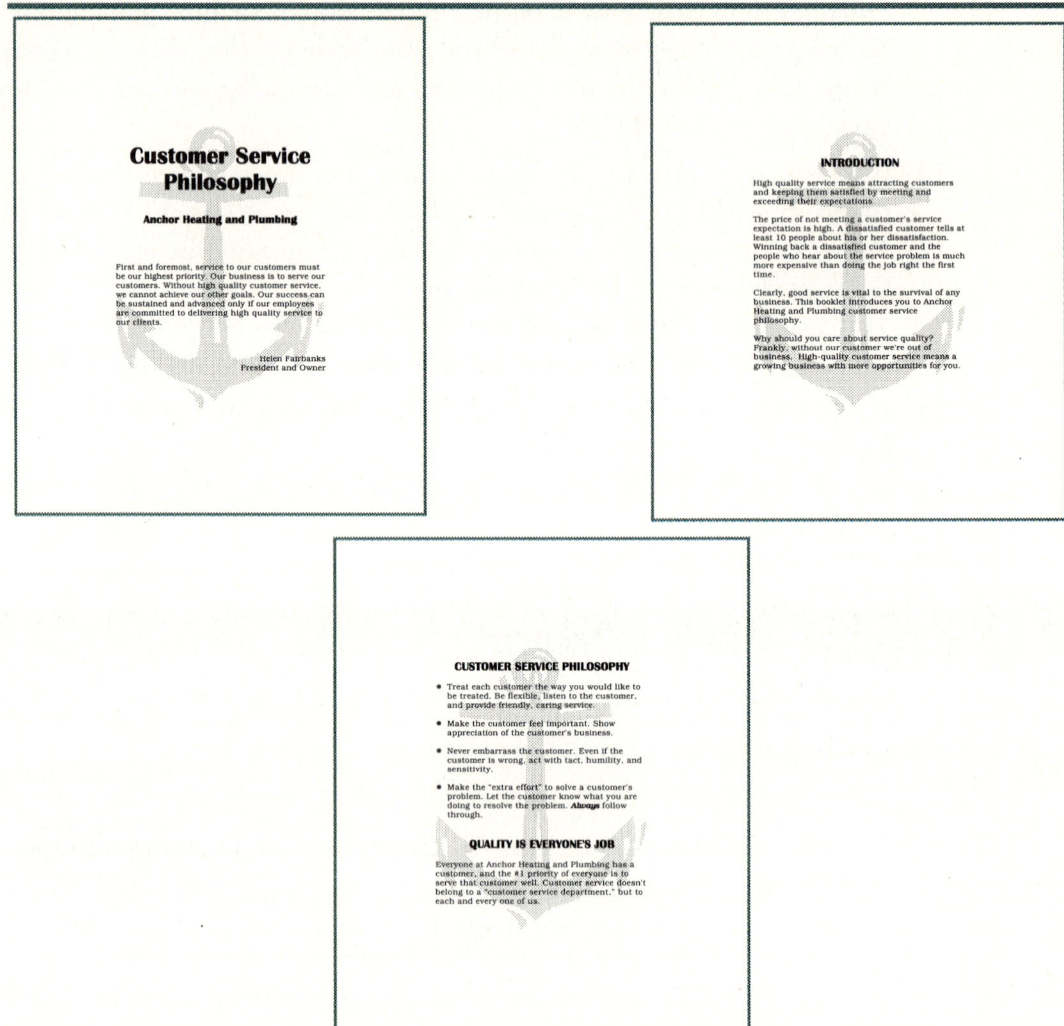

Customer Service Philosophy

Anchor Heating and Plumbing

First and foremost, service to our customers must be our highest priority. Our business is to serve our customers. Without high quality customer service, we cannot achieve our other goals. Our success can be sustained and advanced only if our employees are committed to delivering high quality service to our clients.

Helen Fairbanks
President and Owner

INTRODUCTION

High quality service means attracting customers and keeping them satisfied by meeting and exceeding their expectations.

The price of not meeting a customer's service expectation is high. A dissatisfied customer tells at least 10 people about his or her dissatisfaction. Winning back a dissatisfied customer and the people who hear about the service problem is much more expensive than doing the job right the first time.

Clearly, good service is vital to the survival of any business. This booklet introduces you to Anchor Heating and Plumbing customer service philosophy.

Why should you care about service quality? Frankly, without our customer we're out of business. High-quality customer service means a growing business with more opportunities for you.

CUSTOMER SERVICE PHILOSOPHY

- Treat each customer the way you would like to be treated. Be flexible, listen to the customer, and provide friendly, caring service.
- Make the customer feel important. Show appreciation of the customer's business.
- Never embarrass the customer. Even if the customer is wrong, act with tact, humility, and sensitivity.
- Make the "extra effort" to solve a customer's problem. Let the customer know what you are doing to resolve the problem. ***Always*** follow through.

QUALITY IS EVERYONE'S JOB

Everyone at Anchor Heating and Plumbing has a customer, and the #1 priority of everyone is to serve that customer well. Customer service doesn't belong to a "customer service department," but to each and every one of us.

5. Print one copy and close the document.

Challenge Your Skills

Skill 13.1—Create a Flier with Graphics

1. Use the following information and create a flier for the Summer Fishing Derby.
   a. The Fishing Derby will be held on June 30 in Vancouver, British Columbia.

b. Prizes will be awarded for the largest fish caught. First Place Prize is $1,000; Second Place Prize is $500; and Third Place Prize is $250.

c. The entry fee is $150.

d. The contact person is Lisbeth St. Clair (604) 555-2400. The Summer Fishing Derby is sponsored by the Vancouver Fishing Association.

e. Create appropriate WordArt or insert any *two* of the following graphic images:

anchor.wmf	**sail.wmf**
1stplace.wmf	**fishrman.pcx** (located on the data disk)

Note: To use the ***fishrman.pcx*** *graphic image, select the List Files of Type box in the Insert Picture dialog box and choose PC Paintbrush (*.pcx).*

f. Make decisions regarding:

Fonts and point sizes for flier text
Position and size of graphic images
Hint: *Place the graphic image in a frame in order to move the image on the page.*

2. Use the filename **13skill1.doc** and save the file on your file disk.
3. Print one copy and close the document.

Skill 13.2—Create a Newsletter with a Graphic Image and a Table; Language Arts

1. Open the file named **13skill2.doc**. Use a two-column style similar to the one shown in Figure 13.11 to create the newsletter.

a. Make decisions regarding:

Fonts and point sizes (a 10- to 12-point size is recommended for the newsletter body text)
Borders and shading for the newsletter nameplate
Spacing between the border and nameplate text
Alignment
Hyphenation
Widow/Orphan control

b. Insert several graphic images to illustrate the information in the newsletter. (Suggested graphic images are **lightblb.wmf** and **mail.wmf** located in the Word clipart directory and **hndwrtng.wmf** located on the data disk.)

c. If desired, create WordArt to enhance the newsletter.

2. Correct three spelling errors, two punctuation/grammatical errors, and one misused word.
3. Use the filename **13open2.doc** and save the file on your file disk.
4. Print one copy.
5. If you have completed your work, exit Word.

CHAPTER 14

Create Documents with Special Features

Features Covered

- Kern text and change character spacing
- Set an exact amount of line spacing
- Use AutoText
- Use the Spike
- Create superscripts and subscripts
- Use the Equation Editor

Objectives and Introduction

After successfully completing this chapter, you will be able to enhance the appearance of documents by using typesetting features such as kerning, character spacing, and setting an exact line spacing amount. You also will be able to use the AutoText and Spike features to eliminate repetitious typing. In addition, you will learn how to create superscript and subscript text and how to create equations/formulas using the Equation Editor.

After a document is typed, the document can be enhanced to present information in a more attractive way that is easier to read. For example, the space between letters and paragraph lines can be precisely controlled. With the AutoText feature, frequently typed text can be saved and then used repeatedly to eliminate repetitious typing, reducing the opportunity for errors. Using the Spike feature, documents can be developed by copying sections from existing documents, thereby eliminating the need to rekey information. Scientific/mathematical documents can be enhanced with the insertion of superscripts and subscripts, and the Equation Editor can be used to create complex formulas and equations.

Use Typesetting Features

Word provides advanced typesetting features to enhance the appearance of documents. These typesetting features include kerning and character spacing. The amount of space between lines of text in a paragraph also can be set to a fixed (exact) amount.

Kerning is used to improve the readability of text. After a document is typed, the manual kerning feature is used to adjust the space between two characters. With manual kerning, the space between the letters AV can be reduced, e.g., AV. In addition, the automatic kerning feature can be used to kern specific pairs of letters. The automatic kerning feature is turned on by selecting **Format, Font, Character Spacing, Kerning for Fonts, OK**. The automatic kerning feature adjusts the spacing for all occurrences of predefined pairs of letters. The Word program defines which pairs of letters are to be kerned depending on the font in use. In other words, kerned pairs of letters will vary depending on the font.

The character spacing feature (also known as tracking) is used to increase or decrease the amount of space between letters in selected text or in an entire document. Condensing character spacing allows more text to be compressed into the same amount of space. By expanding the character spacing, words can be stretched out to create a special effect (see Figure 14.2).

Word automatically adjusts the line spacing to accommodate the largest point size in each line. At times, however, it is desirable to control the exact amount of spacing between lines of a paragraph, especially if different font sizes are used in the same paragraph. In order to make the line spacing uniform, an exact amount of line spacing can be specified.

Start-Up Instructions

- Open the file named **14drill1.doc** located on the data disk.
- If desired, use a 75% zoom view (select the down arrow next to **Zoom Control** button, choose 75%).
- The space between the lines of the indented paragraphs is not equal because two different point sizes have been set. For example, you may notice that in the document on the screen, there is more spacing between the first and second lines than between the second and third lines in the paragraph that begins "With interest rates finally . . ." The section Steps to Set Exact Line Spacing will be used to correct this problem. (Because additional changes will be made to the text, do not be concerned about the spacing and alignment at this time.)

Manually Kern Text

1. Select the two letters to be kerned.

   For example, select the "om" in the word "Common" located in the title.

2. Select **Format, Font** {Alt, o, f}.
3. Select the **Character Spacing** tab {Alt and r}.

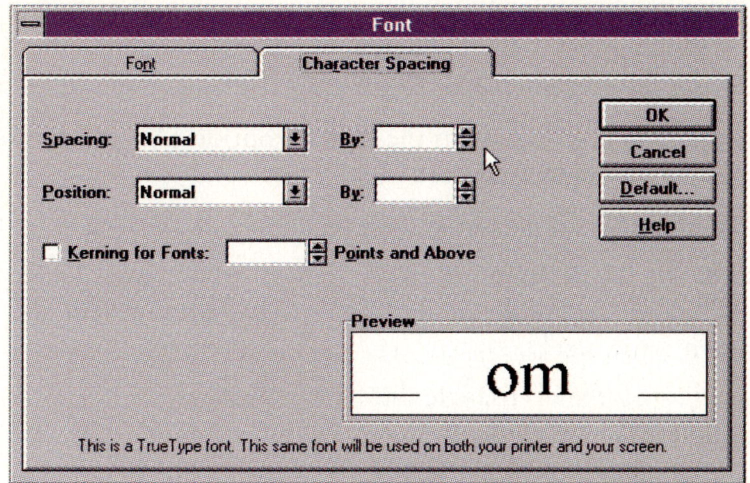

FIGURE 14.1

Character Spacing options

Note: The Character Spacing options display (see Figure 14.1).

4. *To decrease the amount of space between the letters,* click on the down triangle located to the right of the By box in the Spacing area until the desired amount of kerning displays {Alt and b, press the down arrow key}.

   For example, click on the down triangle located to the right of the **By** box in the Spacing area until **1 pt** displays.

   Note: *While clicking on the down triangle, look in the Preview box. The two letters will have moved slightly closer to each other.*

   To increase the amount of space between the letters, click on the up triangle located to the right of the **By** box in the Spacing area until the desired amount of kerning displays {Alt and b, press the up arrow key}.

5. When the characters are the desired distance apart, select **OK** {Enter}.

Finish-Up Instructions

- Select the letters **mo** in the word "Common."
- Repeat steps 2–5 and decrease the amount of space between the letters by 1 pt.
- Select the letters **ue** in the word "Question."
- Repeat steps 2–5 and decrease the amount of space between the letters by .5 pt.
- Select the letters **io** in the word "Question."
- Repeat steps 2–5 and decrease the amount of space between the letters by 1 pt.
- Use the *new* filename **14kern1.doc** and save the file.
- Optional. Print one copy.

Start-Up Instructions

- The file named **14kern1.doc** should be displayed in the document window.

Set Exact Line Spacing

1. Select the text where the line spacing is to be set.

   For example, select all paragraphs except the title.

2. Select **Format, Paragraph** {Alt, o, p}.

   Note: The ***Indents and Spacing*** *tab should be selected.*

3. Click in the **Line Spacing** box and select the **Exactly** option {Alt and n, press the down arrow key to highlight Exactly}.

   Note: 12 pt displays in the At box located to the right of the Line Spacing box.

4. Click on the up triangle (to increase) or down triangle (to decrease) located to the right of the At box to display the desired line spacing amount {Alt and a, press the up or down arrow key}.

   For example, click on the up triangle until **24 pt** displays.

5. Select **OK** {Enter}.

   Note: Additional spacing has been placed between the paragraph lines. Notice that the spacing between the lines of a paragraph are the same even though there are different font sizes within a paragraph. For example, the space between the lines is now the same in the paragraph that begins "With interest rates finally . . ."

Finish-Up Instructions

- Click once to deselect the text.
- Use the same filename, **14kern1.doc**, and save the file again.

Start-Up Instructions

- The file named **14kern1.doc** should be displayed in the document window.

Change Character Spacing

1. Select the desired word(s) where character spacing is to be changed.

   For example, select the first lead word, **Question**.

2. Select **Format, Font** {Alt, o, f}.
3. If necessary, select the **Character Spacing** tab {Alt and r}.
4. *To expand (increase) the space between each character*, click on the up triangle located to the right of the By box in the Spacing area {Alt and b, press the up arrow key}.

   For example, click on the up triangle until **2.5 pt** displays.

   If the space between each character is to be condensed (decreased), click on the down triangle located to the right of the By box in the Spacing area {Alt and b, press the down arrow key}.

5. Select **OK** {Enter}.

   Note: Additional space has been placed between each letter in the selected word.

Finish-Up Instructions

- Use the **Format Painter** to copy the expanded character spacing to each lead word (with the word "Question" selected, double-click on the **Format Painter**

Common Questions

Question With interest rates finally going up after a long period at near-record lows, how has this affected the Money Market Series?

Answer Shareholders in money market funds have been the "winners" in the fixed-income markets during the first half of 1995. The dividend portion of their total return increased while the principal value remained constant.

Question What changes did you make in the portfolio during the first half of the year to take advantage of the rising rates?

Answer We shortened the average maturity of the holdings in the portfolio from approximately 40 days at the end of 1994 to the current 30-day average maturity.

Question How has the Series performed over the first half of the year?

Answer Although the first six months of the year were extremely difficult, the Series experienced a modest growth rate of 5.62 percent.

FIGURE 14.2

Document created using exact line spacing, kerning, and character spacing

button. Select each lead word. When all lead words have been formatted, click on the **Format Painter** button once.)

- Check the alignment of the indented paragraphs. If necessary, add or delete indents in order to align all the paragraphs.
- Use the *new* filename **14space.doc** and save the file on your file disk.

  Note: Your document should look similar to Figure 14.2.
- Print one copy.
- Close the document.

AutoText

AutoText entries are shortcut abbreviations that can be typed in place of a longer word or group of words. When the AutoText entry name is typed and the **Insert AutoText** button is selected, the expanded word or group of words displays in the document window. For example, an AutoText entry named "closing" could contain a standard closing paragraph, signature line, and reference initials for a business letter. When the word "closing" is typed and the **Insert AutoText** button is selected, the text of the closing paragraph, the signature line, and the reference initials are instantly placed in the document window.

When AutoText entries are created, Word also remembers text format, e.g., font and point size. To include paragraph formatting, e.g., alignment, indents, line spacing, be sure to include the paragraph mark (hard return) when the text to be an AutoText entry is selected.

AutoText entries are stored in the *normal.dot* template. The *normal.dot* template is usually active unless another template has been selected (see Chapter 15 for information regarding templates). Once an AutoText entry has been created, the entry is available and can be used in any document. If an AutoText entry is no longer needed, the entry can be deleted.

To edit an AutoText entry, insert the AutoText entry into a document window, edit the text as desired, select the text, choose the **Edit AutoText** button, select the original AutoText entry name in the Name List, and select **Add**. Select **Yes** to replace the existing entry with the new (edited) entry.

Start-Up Instructions

- Open the file named **14drill2.doc** located on the data disk. The file contains a closing paragraph, signature line, reference initials, and an enclosure notation. These will be used to create an AutoText entry named "**close.**"
- Select the typist's initials and insert your own initials.

Create an AutoText Entry

1. Select the text that will be an AutoText entry.

   For example, select all of the text.

2. Select the **Edit AutoText** button on the Standard Toolbar {Alt, e, x}.

   ***Note:** The AutoText dialog box displays. Word proposes the first few characters of the selected text as the AutoText name. This name can be accepted or a different name can be typed.*

3. If desired, type a name for the AutoText entry in the Name box.

   For example, type **close**.

4. Select **Add** {Alt and a}.

   ***Note:** The AutoText entry **close** is created, and the AutoText dialog box is exited automatically.*

Finish-Up Instructions

- ❖ Close the document named **14drill2.doc**. Do not save any changes.
- ❖ Continue with the Steps to Insert an AutoText Entry.

Start-Up Instructions

- ❖ Open the file named **14gordon.doc** located on the data disk.

Insert an AutoText Entry

1. Place the insertion point at the location in the document where the AutoText entry should be inserted.

   For example, place the insertion point in the second blank line below the last paragraph in the letter.

2. Type the AutoText name and then select the **Insert AutoText** button (same as the **Edit AutoText** button) {type AutoText name and press F3}.

   For example, type close and select the **Insert AutoText** button.

   Note: *If you forget an AutoText entry name, select the* **Edit** *menu, choose* ***AutoText,*** *and double-click on the desired AutoText entry name.*

Finish-Up Instructions

- ❖ Use the *new* filename **14auto.doc** and save the file on your file disk.
- ❖ Print one copy and close the document.
- ❖ If necessary, select the **New** button to display a document window.
- ❖ Continue with the Steps to Delete an AutoText Entry.

Delete an AutoText Entry

1. Select the **Edit** menu and choose **AutoText** {Alt, e, x}.
2. Highlight the name of the AutoText entry to be deleted {press the down arrow key to highlight the AutoText entry name}.

   For example, check that **close** is selected.

3. Select the **Delete** button {Alt and d}.
4. Select **Close** {Enter}.

Chapter 14 Create Document with Special Features

Use the Spike

The Spike is a special AutoText entry that allows you to cut items located in different areas of a document and to insert all the items into another document as a group. Text or graphics can be accumulated in the Spike and then transferred to a new location. The Spike feature is useful in creating new documents without having to rekey information. For example, the Spike feature can be used to accumulate the main points from a report document and to make a new report file listing these main points. Once all items are accumulated in the Spike, the information is retrieved to an existing document or in a new document by typing the word **Spike** and pressing **F3**. The information placed in the Spike can be retrieved to as many different locations as needed. The information remains in the Spike until the contents of the Spike are retrieved and the Spike is emptied by pressing **Ctrl** and **Shift** and **F3**.

Start-Up Instructions

- Open the file named **14drill3.doc** located on the data disk.

Use the Spike

1. Select the text to be accumulated in the Spike.

    For example, select the first two lines containing the title, date, and time of the first seminar (i.e., Introduction to Publishing Hardware and Software).

2. Press **Ctrl** and **F3**.

    Note: The selected text is removed from the document window and placed in the Spike.

3. Select the next text to be accumulated in the Spike.

    For example, select the second seminar title, date, and time (i.e., Publishing with Interactive Media).

4. Press **Ctrl** and **F3**.

5. Repeat steps 3 and 4 and accumulate any other desired text in the Spike.

    For example, place the remaining seminar titles, dates, and times in the Spike.

6. When all desired text has been selected and accumulated in the Spike, close the document and **do not** save the changes.

7. Open an existing file or select the **New** button to create a new file.

    For example, select the **New** button. Change the top margin to 2" and the left and right margins to .75". Press the **Enter** key three times.

8. *To insert the contents of the Spike,* type **Spike** and press the **F3** key.

    To insert the contents of the Spike and empty the Spike, press **Ctrl** and **Shift** and **F3**.

    For example, insert the contents of the Spike and empty the Spike by pressing **Ctrl** and **Shift** and **F3**.

    Note: The contents of the Spike are placed in the document window.

Finish-Up Instructions

- Place the insertion point at the top of the document and type the title **Upcoming Seminars**. Select the title and change the font to **Bookman Old Style, 18 point**. Center the title.
- Use the filename **14spike.doc** and save the file on your file disk.
- Print one copy and close the document.

Create Superscripts and Subscripts

Superscripts are characters that are printed a fraction above the text line, and subscripts are characters that are printed a fraction below the text line (see Figure 14.3). Superscripts and subscripts are used, for example, when printing chemical formulas, algebraic equations, or degrees of temperature.

Start-Up Instructions

- An empty document window should be displayed. (If necessary, select the **New** button.)
- Use a **150%** view (select the down arrow next to the **Zoom Control** button, choose **150%**).
- The nonprinting symbols should be displayed. If necessary, select the **Show/Hide** button.

Create a Superscript

1. Type the desired text.

   For example, type **x(a + b)3** and press the **Tab** key twice.

   *Note: Pressing the **Tab, Spacebar,** or **Enter** key after the character to be a superscript makes it easier to insert additional text later.*

2. Select the character to be a superscript.

   For example, select the **3**.

3. Select **Format, Font**. On the Font tab, select the **Superscript** option in the Effects area. Select **OK** {Alt, o, f; Alt and p, Enter *or* Ctrl and Shift and =}

   ***Note:** The selected character displays as a superscript in the document window.*

4. Before continuing to type, locate the insertion point at the position where the next typing will take place.

   For example, click to the right of the second tab symbol.

Create a Subscript

1. Type the desired text.

   For example, type **NaNH2** and press the **Enter** key twice.

2. Select the character to be a subscript.

   For example, select the **2**.

3. Select **Format, Font**. On the Font tab, select the Subscript option in the Effects area. Select OK {Alt, o, f; Alt and b, Enter *or* Ctrl and =}.

   ***Note:** The selected character displays as a subscript in the document window.*

$x(a + b)^3$	$NaNH_2$
$a^2 - b^3$	$Na_2S_2O_4$

FIGURE 14.3

Superscripts and subscripts

Chapter 14 Create Document with Special Features

4. Before continuing to type, locate the insertion point at the position where the next typing will take place.

   For example, place the insertion point in the second blank line below the text.

Finish-Up Instructions

- Using the Steps to Create a Superscript and Steps to Create a Subscript, type the equation and formula in the second line of Figure 14.3.
- Use the filename **14super.doc** and save the file on your file disk.
- Print one copy and close the document.

Use the Equation Editor

The Equation Editor is used to build scientific and mathematical equations and formulas. The Equation Editor can be used to create and format equations/formulas but cannot solve the equation/formula. As an equation/formula is being built, a zoom view such as 150% or 200% can be used to make the equation/formula easier to read on the screen. The desired zoom view must be selected before the Equation Editor is accessed. The Equation Editor is accessed by selecting **Insert**, **Object**, and choosing **Microsoft Equation 2.0**. Once the Equation Editor is accessed, the Equation Editor Toolbar and Menu bar display in the document window.

The Equation Editor Toolbar contains two rows of buttons (see Figure 14.4). The top row of buttons on the Equation Editor Toolbar contains symbols such as operators (±, ÷) and Greek letters (Φ, Ω). The bottom row of the Equation Editor Toolbar contains templates that are used to create fractions (▯/▯), square roots ($\sqrt{\ }$), and superscripts (▮▫). When a button on the Equation Editor Toolbar is selected, a palette of symbols or templates displays. To build an equation or formula, select the desired symbol(s) and template(s) and type numbers and/or letters into the template slots. For example, when the ▯/▯ template is selected, text and/or numbers can be typed into the numerator and denominator slots, $\frac{2x}{4y}$. The arrow keys and **Tab** key are used to move the insertion point while creating an equation/formula.

When building equations/formulas, the Equation Editor automatically inserts the spacing needed in the equation/formula. For example, when a plus (+) is typed, spacing is automatically inserted before and after the symbol. If desired, additional spacing can be inserted by selecting the **Spaces and Ellipses** button on the Equation Editor Toolbar and selecting the desired spacing symbol.

The font of the equation/formula can be changed by selecting the **Styles** menu and choosing the **Define** option. The size of text, symbols, and superscripts/subscripts can be changed by selecting the **Size** menu and choosing the **Define** option.

Once the equation/formula is complete, move the mouse pointer away from the equation/formula and click once. The Equation Editor Toolbar and Menu bar are removed from the screen. Small black handles (boxes) display at the edges and corners of the equation/formula. The equation/formula can be positioned, sized, and framed using the same procedures that are used to position, size, and frame graphic images (see Chapter 13). For example, the equation/formula can be sized by moving the mouse pointer to a small black handle, pressing and holding the mouse button, and then dragging to enlarge or reduce the equation size.

To edit the equation/formula, double-click on the equation/formula. The Equation Editor Toolbar and the Menu bar display. Make the desired changes using normal editing procedures. When changes are complete, move the mouse pointer away from the equation/formula and click once.

Start-Up Instructions

- An empty document window should be displayed. If necessary, select the **New** button.
- Use a 150% view (select the down arrow next to the **Zoom Control** button and click on **150%**).
- The following steps will be used to create the equation shown in Figure 14.5. A mouse is required to complete the following steps.

Create an Equation/Formula Using the Equation Editor

Note: The insertion point should be located in the document at the place where the equation/formula will be inserted.

1. Select **Insert, Object**.

   Note: The Object dialog box displays. The ***Create New*** *tab should be selected.*

2. In the Object Type box, double-click on **Microsoft Equation 2.0**.

   Note: The Equation Editor Toolbar and Menu bar display. A small frame containing a template slot and the insertion point displays in the document window (see Figure 14.4).

3. Select or type the desired symbol, template, or text.

   For example, type **t=**. (Do not type the period). Select the **Operators** button and click on the ± operator (first row, first column symbol).

4. Select or type the desired symbol, template, or text.

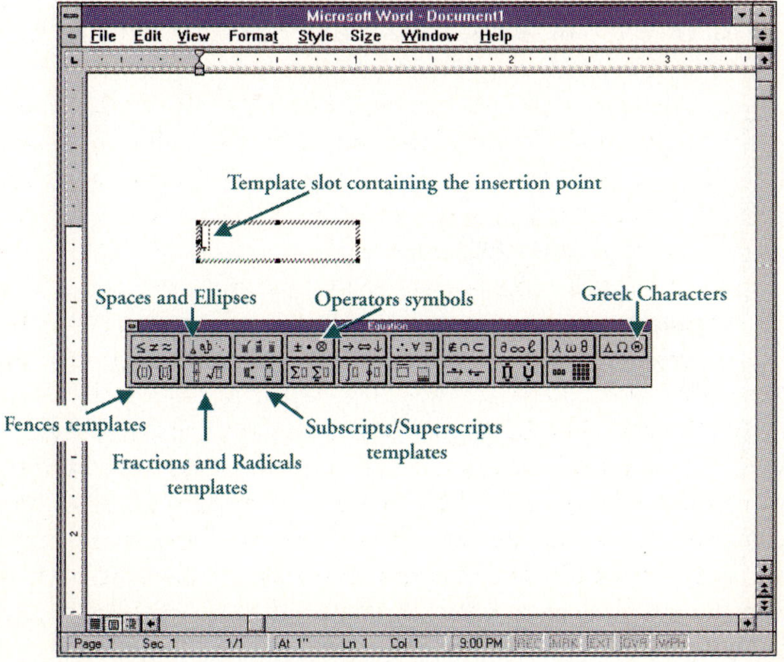

FIGURE 14.4

Equation Editor window

Chapter 14 Create Document with Special Features

For example, select the **Fractions and Radicals** button and click on the **Square Root** template.

5. Select or type the desired symbol, template, or text.

   For example, select the **Fractions and Radicals** button and click on the **Fraction** template.

6. Select or type the desired symbol, template, or text.

   For example, type a **2**. (Do not type the period.)

7. Select or type the desired symbol, template, or text.

   For example, select the **Fences** button and click on the **Parentheses** template.

8. Select or type the desired symbol, template, or text.

   For example, type **x+3y**. (Do not type the period.)

9. Select or type the desired symbol, template, or text.

   For example, select the **Subscripts/Superscripts** button and click on the **Superscript** template.

10. Select or type the desired symbol, template, or text.

    For example, type **2**. (Do not type the period.)

11. Select or type the desired symbol, template, or text.

    For example, press the **Tab** key three times to move the insertion point to the template slot in the denominator. Type **9y**. (Do not type the period.)

***Note:** The equation should look similar to the equation shown in Figure 14.5.*

12. To return to the document window, move the mouse pointer away from the equation/formula and click once.

FIGURE 14.5

Equation Editor with completed equation

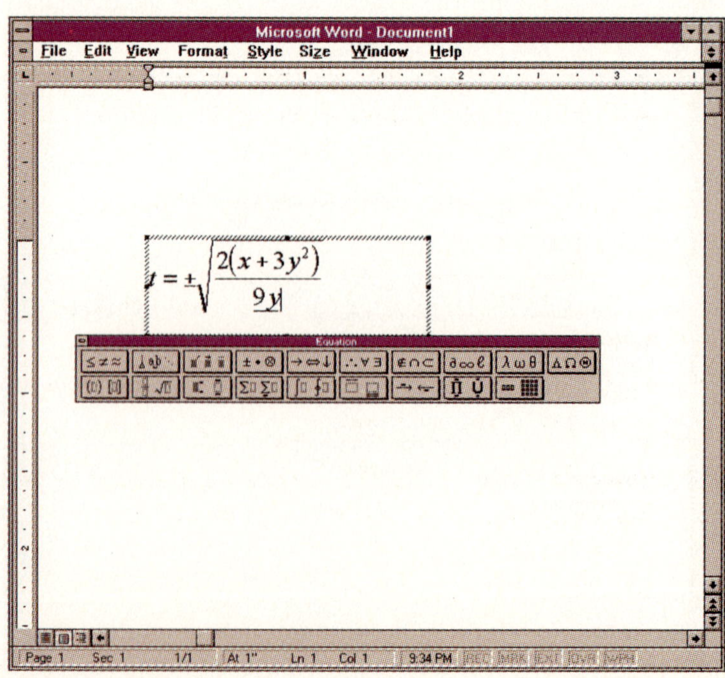

Finish-Up Instructions

- Use the filename **14equat.doc** and save the file.
- Print one copy and close the document.

Edit an Equation/Formula

Note: The following steps are for your information only.

1. Move the mouse pointer into the equation/formula in the document window and double-click.

   Note: The Equation Editor Toolbar and Menu bar display.

2. Make the desired changes.
3. Move the mouse pointer away from the equation/formula and click once.

The Next Step

Chapter Review and Activities

Self-Check Quiz

T F 1. To set an exact amount of line spacing, select the text to be affected, select **Format**, **Paragraph**, click in the **Line Spacing** box, choose **Exactly**, change the amount of spacing in the **At** box, and select **OK**.

T F 2. Information can be accumulated in the Spike and retrieved in a new or existing document.

T F 3. Once an equation/formula has been created using the Equation Editor, the equation/formula cannot be edited.

T F 4. Character spacing (tracking) is used to expand or condense the amount of space between letters in selected text.

T F 5. An AutoText entry is inserted into a document by typing the AutoText entry name and selecting the **Insert AutoText** button.

6. Select the ____________ button on the Equation Editor Toolbar to access the square root template.
   a. **Greek Characters**
   b. **Operators**
   c. **Fractions and Radicals**
   d. **Fences**

7. To manually kern two characters, use the ________ option in the Format menu.
   a. Font
   b. Character
   c. Paragraph
   d. Tab

8. A subscript is a character that prints a fraction ____ the text line.
   a. above
   b. below
   c. on
   d. either a or c

9. List two items that can be created (built) using the Equation Editor. Can the Equation Editor be used to solve mathematical equations?

10. Write one example in which you personally might use the AutoText or Spike feature.

Enriching Language Arts Skills

Spelling/Vocabulary Words

simplify to make easier or less complicated.
unique different, standing alone in quality, unequaled.
withdrawal to take away or take back.

Independent Adjectives

Two consecutive adjectives that modify the same noun are separated by a comma.

Example:

Orlando performs his job duties in an effective, diligent manner.

Activities

Activity 14.1—Change Character Spacing and Set Exact Line Spacing

1. Open the file named **14act1.doc** located on the data disk.
2. Select the title and increase the character spacing by 2 points (select **Format**, **Font**, **Character Spacing**, click on the up triangle located to the right of the **By** box in the Spacing area until **2 pt** displays, select **OK**).
3. Select the first lead word, **Attendance**, and increase the character spacing by 1.5 points (select **Format**, **Font**, **Character Spacing**, click on the up triangle located to the right of the **By** box in the Spacing area until **1.5 pt** displays, select **OK**).

4. Use the **Format Painter** to copy the character spacing of the lead word "Attendance" to the other lead words, **Deadline**, **Cooperation**, **Professionalism**, and **Flexibility** (if necessary, select the word **Attendance**; double-click on the **Format Painter** button; select each lead word; when all lead words have been formatted, click on the **Format Painter** button again).
5. Select all paragraphs except the title and set exact line spacing of 18 points (select **Format**, **Paragraph**; click in the **Line Spacing** box, select **Exactly**; click on the up triangle located to the right of the At box until **18 pt** displays; select **OK**).
6. Use the *new* filename **14hint1.doc** and save the file on your file disk.
7. Print one copy and close the document.

Activity 14.2—Use the Spike to Create an Overhead Transparency

1. Open the file named **14act2.doc** located on the data disk.
2. Select the title **Accounting Terms** and the following two blank lines.
3. Press **Ctrl** and **F3** to place the selected text in the Spike.
4. Select the first heading, **Accrued Expense**, and the following blank line.
5. Press Ctrl and **F3** to place the selected text in the Spike.
6. Select the next heading and the following blank line.
7. Press **Ctrl** and **F3**.
8. Repeat steps 6 and 7 to accumulate the remaining headings in the Spike.
9. When all of the remaining headings have been accumulated in the Spike, close the file named **14act2.doc** and **do not** save the changes.
10. Select the **New** button.
11. Press **Ctrl** and **Shift** and **F3** to retrieve the contents of the Spike and empty the Spike.
12. Format the text for use as an overhead transparency (e.g., use a large font size).
13. Use the filename **14overhd.doc** and save the file on your file disk.
14. Print one copy and close document.

Activity 14.3—Use the Equation Editor

1. Use the Equation Editor (select **Insert, Object,** double-click on **Microsoft Equation 2.0**) to create the following equations:

$\frac{6y-5}{8x}$ (Select the **Fractions and Radicals** button, click on the **Fractions** template, type **6y-5**, press the **Tab** key once, type **8x**. Move the mouse pointer away from the equation and click once. Click once to deselect the equation, press **Enter** three times.)

$$\frac{\sqrt{a^2 - b^2}}{c^2}$$

(Access the Equation Editor. Select the **Fractions and Radicals** button, click on the **Square Root** template, select the **Fractions and Radicals** button again and click on the **Fractions** template, type **a**, select the **Subscripts/Superscripts** button and click on the **Superscript** template, type **2**, press **Tab**, type **b**, select the **Subscripts/Superscripts** button and click on the **Superscript** template, type **2**, press **Tab** twice, type **c**, select the **Subscripts/Superscripts** button and click on the **Superscript** template, type **2**. Move the mouse pointer away from the equation and click once. Click once to deselect the equation. Place the insertion point to the right of the second equation and press **Enter** three times.)

$$v = \frac{5^2 h}{3}$$

(Access the Equation Editor. Type **v=**, select the **Fractions and Radicals** button, click on the **Fractions** template, type **5**, select the **Subscripts/Superscripts** button and click on the **Superscript** template, type **2**, press **Tab**, type **h**, press the **Tab** key, type **3**. Move the mouse pointer away from the equation and click once. Click once to deselect the equation.)

---

2. Use the filename **14equ3.doc** and save the file on your file disk.
3. Print one copy and close the document.

Activity 14.4—Create Subscripts

1. In a new document window, type and center the following text using subscripts as shown (select the character to be a subscript, choose **Format**, **Font**, select **Subscript** on the Font tab, select **OK**).

CHEMICAL FORMULAS--Potassium

Potassium Carbonate: K_2CO_3
Potassium Oxalate: $K_2C_2O_4H_2O$
Potassium Sulfate: K_2SO_4
Potassium Xanthate: $KS_2COC_2H_5$

---

2. Use the filename **14sub4.doc** and save the file on your file disk.
3. Print one copy and close the document.

Activity 14.5—Use Superscripts

1. In a new document window, type and center the following text using superscripts as shown. A lowercase letter *o* is used to represent the degree symbol (select the character to be superscripted, choose **Format**, **Font**, select **Superscript** on the Font tab, select **OK**).

DEGREES OF TEMPERATURE

Celsius vs. Fahrenheit

0°C = 32°F
10°C = 50°F
20°C = 68°F
35°C = 95°F
100°C = 212°F

2. Use the filename **14super5.doc** and save the file.
3. Print one copy and close the document.

Challenge Your Skills

Skill 14.1—Create and Use AutoText

1. Create an AutoText entry named **final** using the following information:
   a. Type the following text:

If the foregoing meets with your approval, please indicate your agreement by signing the original copy hereof and returning it to the undersigned.

Sincerely,

Megan A. Patterson

ACCEPTED and AGREED TO:

____

By: ______________________

Date: ______________________

cc: Standards and Practices Department

   b. Select all the text and create an AutoText entry named **final**.
   c. Close the document. Do not save the file.

2. Type the following letter. Insert the **final** AutoText entry at the end of the letter as shown.

(Use current date)

Ms. Roselle Withrow
24363 NW 17th Avenue
Miami, FL 33169

Dear Ms. Withrow:

This will serve to confirm our agreement regarding the merchandise to be supplied by you for use on the *Today/Tomorrow* program.

1. You will provide, without charge or expense, the following merchandise for such performers as may be designated by Worthington Pictures for use by such performers solely on the above-mentioned program: **Janet Westley's Wardrobe.**

2. You understand and agree that Worthington Pictures shall have the right to disclose the receipt of this consideration in the form of an announcement similar to the following: **Janet Westley's Wardrobe Furnished by Roselle Withrow.**

3. Said announcement shall be made upon each broadcast or rebroadcast of the specific program upon which the merchandise furnished by you is used, but you shall not make any claim or be entitled to any damages in the event such announcement is inadvertently omitted.

4. This letter when signed by both parties shall constitute the entire agreement between the parties, supersede any prior oral or written understanding, and may not be modified or amended except in writing.

(insert the AutoText entry named **final**).

---

3. Change the left and right margins to **1"**. Select the entire document and change the font to **Times New Roman, 11 point.**
4. Use the filename **14withrw.doc** and save the file on your file disk.
5. Print one copy and close the document.
6. Optional. Open the file named **14gordon.doc** located on the data disk. Insert the AutoText entry named **final** after the last paragraph. Use the *new* filename **14gord2.doc** and save the file on your file disk. Print one copy and close the file.
7. Delete the AutoText entry named **final** (in a document window, select **Edit, AutoText**, select **final, Delete, Close**).

Skill 14.2—Use the Equation Editor

1. Create the following equations.

Note: Place each equation on a separate line.

$$\left(\frac{m_1}{m_2} = \frac{n_2}{n_1}\right) \qquad \pm\sqrt{\frac{3y^2 - 3m}{5y^3}} \qquad \sqrt[3]{\frac{2(m^2 - n^2)}{m^3}}$$

2. Use the filename **14skequ2.doc** and save the file on your file disk.
3. Print one copy and close the document.

Skill 14.3—Change Character Spacing, Superscripts, Subscripts; Use the Spike; Language Arts

1. Open the file named **14skill3.doc** located on the data disk. Make decisions regarding:

   Margins
   Fonts and sizes for title, sideheads, and body text
   Alignment
   Widow/Orphan control
   Text attributes for the title and sideheads
   Character spacing for title and sideheads
   Use of the Format Painter
   Superscripts or subscripts for service names (e.g., Interest Checking$^+$ or Interest Checking$_+$)
   Alignment of paragraphs
   Header or footer text and placement

2. Correct five spelling errors and three punctuation errors.
3. Use the *new* filename **14bank.doc** and save the file.
4. Print one copy.
5. Once the document is formatted and saved, use the Spike to create a new document that contains the title and sideheads.
6. Format the new document as a flier announcing Savanna National Bank's services. Make decisions regarding:

   Font and point sizes
   Margins
   Alignment
   Borders
   Graphic images

7. Use the filename **14bkfli.doc** and save the file on your file disk.
8. Print one copy and close the document.
9. If you have completed your work, exit Word.

CHAPTER 15

Create Documents Using Special Functions

Features Covered

- Sort table rows, paragraphs, and lines
- Use AutoFormat
- Edit, create, and apply styles
- Use Wizards
- Record and play macros

Objectives and Introduction

After successfully completing this chapter, you will know how to use the Sort feature to sort table rows and text numerically, alphabetically, and by date. You will also learn how to use the AutoFormat feature to instantly format documents. You will be able to edit, create, and apply styles to quickly format documents and to create documents using a Wizard. In addition, you will learn to record and play macros to expedite your work.

Word provides many special functions to expedite document production and to eliminate repetitious tasks. The Sort function makes alphabetical and numerical sorting easy and quick. Macros can be created to perform quickly and efficiently tasks that must be repeated on a regular basis. Styles, templates, and the AutoFormat functions make it easy to develop and apply a custom look to your document(s).

Create Alphabetically and Numerically Sorted Text

The Sort function is used to arrange paragraphs, table rows, and words in alphabetical, numerical, or date order. A list of names can be sorted alphabetically, and a list of numbers can be sorted numerically. Text can be selected to sort in alphabetical (Text), numerical (Number) or date order. Text can also be sorted either in descending or ascending order. Ascending order begins with letter A through Z or the lowest number to the highest number; descending order begins with letter Z through A or the highest number to the lowest number.

For the purpose of sorting, a paragraph is defined as any text that ends with a single hard return. When sorting words that begin with the same character, Word uses the character(s) that follows to determine the correct order. For example, if there are two last names that begin with the same letter, the second (then the third, fourth, etc.) character in the names is used to determine the alphabetical order.

Before sorting a document, all text to be sorted is selected. The Sort dialog box is used to choose the Sort By option (Column, Field, Word, or Paragraph) and to define criteria. A sort criteria identifies the type of sort (Text, Number, or Date), the order of the sort (ascending or descending), and the portion of text to sort (column, field, word, or paragraph).

When a sort is performed, Word reorders the text in accordance with the Sort By criteria and then uses any additional sort criteria to refine the sort. For example, if a list of names is to be sorted by last name and several individuals have the same last name, the first sort criteria is the last name (the primary sort criteria). A second sort criteria would specify that the first name is the "secondary" sort criteria.

Start-Up Instructions

- Open the file named **15drill1.doc** located on the data disk.

Sort Table Rows Numerically

1. Select the rows of the table to be sorted.

   For example, select all table cells except the first two rows, which contain the table title and column headings.

2. Select **Table, Sort** {Alt, a, t}.

   Note: The Sort dialog box displays (see Figure 15.1).

3. To change the Sort By option, click on the down arrow located to the right of the Sort By box and click on the desired option {press the down arrow key to highlight the desired option}.

   For example, click on the down arrow located to the right of the Sort By box and click on **Column 3** to sort the table by the third column.

FIGURE 15.1

Sort dialog box

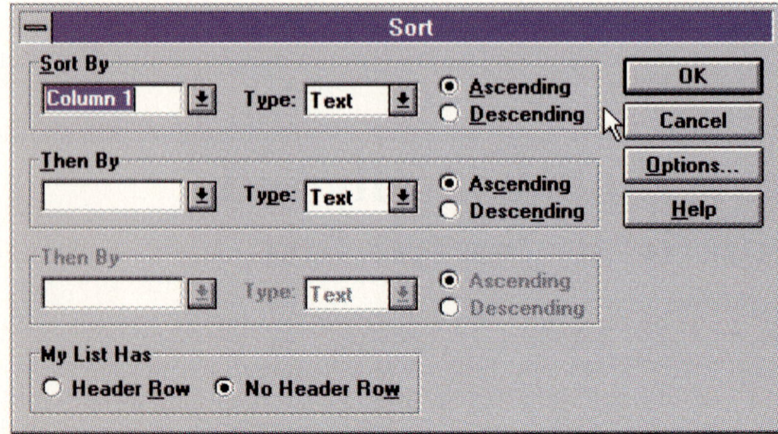

4. To select a different type of sort, i.e., **Text, Number,** or **Date**, click on the down arrow located to the right of the Type box and select the desired type {Alt and y, press the up or down arrow key to highlight the desired type}.

   For example, check that **Number** displays. (If necessary, select **Number**.)

5. Select the sort order, i.e., **Ascending** or **Descending** {Alt and a *or* Alt and d}.

   For example, select **Descending** {Alt and d}.

6. Select **OK** {Enter}.

   ***Note:** After a moment, the sorted table displays. The table rows have been sorted using the information in column three.*

Finish-Up Instructions

❖ Use the *new* filename **15numsrt.doc** and save the file on your file disk. Print one copy and close the document.

Start-Up Instructions

❖ Open the file named **15drill1.doc** located on the data disk.

Sort Table Rows Alphabetically

1. Select the rows of the table to be sorted.

   For example, select all table cells except the first two rows, which contain the table title and column headings.

2. Select **Table, Sort** {Alt, a, t}.

3. To change the Sort By option, click on the down arrow located to the right of the Sort By box and click on the desired option {press the down arrow key to highlight the desired option}.

   For example, click on the down arrow located to the right of the Sort By box and click on Column 1 to sort the table by the first column.

4. To select a different type of sort, i.e., **Text, Number,** or **Date**, click on the down arrow located to the right of the Type box and select the desired type {Alt and y, press the up or down arrow key to highlight the desired type}.

   For example, select **Text**.

5. Select the sort order, i.e., **Ascending** or **Descending** {Alt and a *or* Alt and d}.

   For example, select **Ascending** {Alt and a}.

6. Select **OK** {Enter}.

   ***Note:** The salespeople's names are listed alphabetically. Notice that the first names were used to sort the rows that contained individuals with the same last name.*

Finish-Up Instructions

❖ Use the *new* filename **15txtsrt.doc** and save the file on your file disk. Print one copy and close the document.

Start-Up Instructions

- Open the file named **15drill2.doc** located on the data disk.
- To sort text by words, the field separator must be set as a space. Select **Table, Sort Text, Options, Other**, press the **Spacebar** once, **OK, Cancel**.

Sort by Word or Paragraph

1. Select the text to be sorted.

   For example, scroll to the bottom of the document or press **Ctrl** and **End** and select all the names in the distribution list.

2. Select **Table, Sort Text** {Alt, a, t}.
3. To change the Sort By option, click on the down arrow located to the right of the Sort By box and click on the desired option {press the down arrow key to highlight the desired option}.

   For example, to sort the distribution list by last name, select **Word 2**.

4. To select a different type of sort, i.e., **Text, Number,** or **Date**, click on the down arrow located to the right of the Type box and select the desired type {Alt and y, press the up or down arrow key to highlight the desired type}.

   For example, if necessary, select **Text**.

5. Select the Sort Order, i.e., **Ascending** or **Descending** {Alt and a *or* Alt and d}.

   For example, if necessary, select **Ascending** {Alt and a}.

Create a Secondary Sort Criteria

6. Select the down arrow located to the right of the **Then By** box and click on the desired option {Alt and t, press the down arrow key to highlight the desired options}.

   For example, click on **Word 1**.

7. Select the desired sort type and sort order.

   For example, check that **Text** is selected in the Type box and that **Ascending** is selected as the sort order.

8. Select **OK** {Enter}.

   Note: *The distribution list is sorted by last name (Word 2). When the last names were identical, the first initial (Word 1) was used to sort the list.*

Finish-Up Instructions

- Use the *new* filename **15list3.doc** and save the file on your file disk. Print one copy and close the document.

Start-Up Instructions

- Open the file named **15drill3.doc** located on the data disk.

Sort by Date

1. Select the lines of text to be sorted.

   For example, select the entire table.

2. Select **Table, Sort** {Alt, a, t}.

   *Note: Word proposes a sort criteria. This criteria can be accepted or changed. Also, Word has determined that the first row of the table is a "header" row and should not be considered when the table is sorted. Therefore, the **Header Row** option is selected in the **My List Has** area.*

3. To change the Sort By option, click on the down arrow located to the right of the Sort By box and click on the desired option {press the down arrow key to highlighted the desired option}.

   For example, select **Release Date**.

   *Note: Word automatically changes the sort Type to **Date**.*

4. Select the Sort Order, i.e., **Ascending** or **Descending** {Alt and a *or* Alt and d}.

   For example, select **Descending** {Alt and d}.

5. Select **OK** {Enter}.

Finish-Up Instructions

- Use the *new* filename **15date.doc** and save the file on your file disk. Print one copy and close the document.

Chapter 15 Create Documents Using Special Functions

Use AutoFormat

The AutoFormat feature quickly formats a document using Word's built-in styles. (For more information on the built-in styles, see the following section, Use Styles to Format Documents.) The AutoFormat feature can be accessed by selecting the **AutoFormat** button on the Standard Toolbar or by selecting **Format, AutoFormat.** When the AutoFormat feature is accessed by selecting the **AutoFormat** button, the document or selected text is immediately formatted. If the AutoFormat feature is accessed by selecting **Format, AutoFormat**, the formatting can be reviewed and accepted or rejected.

Start-Up Instructions

- Open the file named **15drill4.doc** located on the data disk.

Use AutoFormat

1. With the insertion point located at any position in the document or with the desired text selected, select the **AutoFormat** button on the Standard Toolbar.

   For example, place the insertion point at any location in the document and select the **AutoFormat** button.

   Note: The document is formatted using Word's built-in styles.

Finish-Up Instructions

- Select the **Print Preview** button to view the formatted document. Select **Close** to return to the document window.
- Use the *new* filename **15auto.doc** and save the file on your file disk. Print one copy.

Use Styles to Format Documents

A *style* is a group of formatting instructions that can be applied to related sections of text and that can be saved and used in other documents. For example, a style can be used to format the sideheads of a report to print in 16-point Bookman Old Style. Use of styles saves time and ensures consistency throughout a document. Applying the same style repeatedly to related sections saves time because many formatting changes can be made instantly. Also, if a style is changed, the new format is automatically assigned to all text in the current document where the style has been previously applied.

There are two types of styles: *Paragraph* and *Character*. A Paragraph style is used to affect the appearance of an entire paragraph. For example, a Paragraph style could change the font and point size, set center justification, and bold the title of a report. A Character style is used to apply font and text attributes to selected text. For example, a Character style might apply the bold and italic text attributes to text. To apply a Paragraph style, locate the insertion point anywhere in the paragraph to be affected. To apply a Character style, select the text to be affected.

Word has several built-in styles that can be used to format body text, headings, headers/footers, footnotes/endnotes, bulleted lists, etc. When the **Style** button is selected, a list of available styles displays. If no new styles have been created, the Style box will contain only built-in styles, e.g., *Normal, Heading 1,* and *Heading 2.*

New styles can be created "by example" or by choosing formatting options in the New Style dialog box. The "by example" method is used to create styles based on previously formatted text. To create a style "from scratch," the options in the New Style dialog box are used.

Styles are edited by selecting **Format**, **Style**, highlighting the desired style name, and selecting **Modify**. The options in the Modify Style dialog box are then used to change the existing style format. When a style is edited, any text in the current document that was previously formatted with the edited style is changed to reflect the new format specifications.

When a document containing styles is saved, the edited or new styles are also saved. These styles can then be used to format other documents by copying the style information from the existing document into another document.

Start-Up Instructions

- The file named **15auto.doc** should be displayed in the document window.

Edit a Style

1. Select **Format, Style** {Alt, o s}.

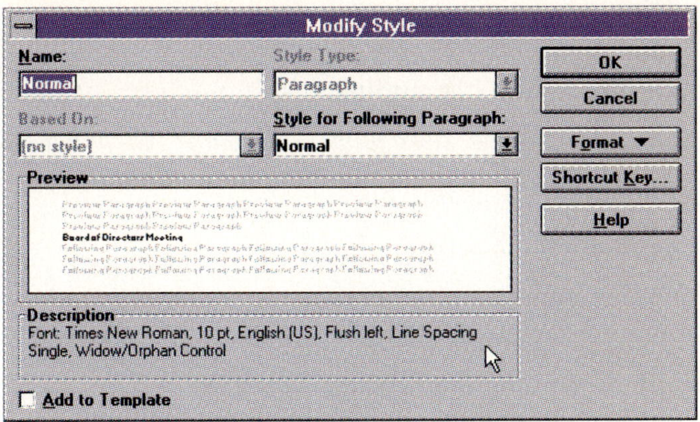

FIGURE 15.2

Modify Styles dialog box

Note: The Style dialog box displays containing a list of existing styles. The styles listed are the "built-in"styles that are available for formatting all documents.

2. Click on the style to be edited {press the up or down arrow key to highlight desired style}.

   For example, click on the style named **Normal**.

3. Select **Modify** {Alt and m}.

   Note: The Modify Style dialog box displays. A description of the format of the style displays in the Description box (see Figure 15.2).

4. Use the options in the Modify Style dialog box to make the desired changes to the style.

   For example, select the **Format** button and click on **Font** and change the font to **Footlight MT Light, 11 point, or make a font choice of your own**. Select **OK**.

   Note: As formatting options are selected, the description of the style is changed in the Description area.

5. Select **OK** to exit the Modify Style dialog box.

6. Select **Close** to exit the Style dialog box.

   Note: The font for the document body text will have been changed.

Finish-Up Instructions

- Select **Format**, **Style**, click on the style name **Title**, and select **Modify**. Select **Format**, **Font**, and change the font size to **14 point**. Select **OK** twice, **Close**.
- Use the *new* filename **15style.doc** and save the file on your file disk.

Start-Up Instructions

- The file named **15style.doc** should be displayed in the document window.

Create a New Style

1. Place the insertion point in the paragraph that will be formatted with the new style.

   For example, place the insertion point in the text "Board of Directors Meeting."

Chapter 15 Create Documents Using Special Functions

2. Select **Format, Style** {Alt, o, s}.
3. Select **New** in the Style dialog box {Alt and n}.

   Note: The New Style dialog box displays. Word proposes the name Style1 in the Name box.
4. Type the desired style name in the Name box.

   For example, type **Centered Subtitle**.
5. Click in the **Based On** box and select a style that most closely matches the new style {Alt and b, press the up or down arrow key to highlight the desired style}.

   For example, scroll down the list and select **Subtitle.**

   Note: A sample of the style format displays in the Preview box, and a description of the style format is shown in the Description box.
6. If necessary, click in the **Style Type** box and select the desired style type, i.e., **Character** or **Paragraph** {Alt and t, press the up or down arrow key to highlight the desired type}.

   For example, check that **Paragraph** displays in the **Style Type** box.
7. Use the options in the New Style dialog box to create the desired format for the new style.

   For example, select the **Format** button and click on **Font**, and change the font to **Footlight MT Light, Bold Italic, 12 point**, or **make a font choice of your own**. Select **OK**.
8. Select **OK** and choose **Apply**.

   Note: *The words "Board of Directors Meeting" are centered and display bold and italic.*

Finish-Up Instructions

- Use the same filename, **15style.doc**, and save the file. (The newly created style will also be saved.)
- Continue with the Steps to Create a Paragraph Style By Example.

Start-Up Instructions

- The file named **15style.doc** should be displayed in the document window.

Create a Paragraph Style By Example

1. Select and format a paragraph as desired.

   For example, select the first bulleted item "Own a home . . ." Select the **Increase Indent** button twice. Select the **Numbering** button to change the bullet character to a number.
2. Move the mouse pointer to the **Style** box in the Formatting Toolbar and click once to highlight the current style name.

   For example, click once to highlight the **List Bullet** style name.
3. Type the new style name and press Enter.

   For example, type **Numbered List** and press **Enter**.

Finish-Up Instructions

- Use the same filename, **15style.doc**, and save the document. (The newly created style will also be saved.)
- Continue with the Steps to Apply Styles.

Start-Up Instructions

- The file named **15style.doc** should be displayed in the document window.

Apply Styles

1. *To apply a Paragraph style*, place the insertion point between any two characters in the paragraph or select the paragraphs to be affected. Click on the down arrow located to the right of the **Style** box. Click on the desired Paragraph style name.

   For example, place the insertion point between any two characters in the date, **September 4, 199x.** Click on the down arrow located to the right of the **Style** box and click on the **Centered Subtitle** style name.

2. *To apply a Character style*, select the text to be affected. Click on the down arrow located to the right of the Styles box. Click on the desired Character style name.

   For example, no character styles need to be applied at this time.

Finish-Up Instructions

- Select the two remaining bulleted items and change the style to Numbered List (click on the down arrow located to the right of the Style box, click on **Numbered List**).
- Use the same filename, **15style.doc**, and save the file on your file disk. Print one copy and close the document.

Start-Up Instructions

- Open the file named **15min.doc** located on the data disk.
- Use the *new* filename **15minfmt.doc** and save the file on your file disk.

Copy Styles to Format Another Document

1. Select **Format, Styles** {Alt, o, s}.
2. Select the **Organizer** button {Alt and o}.

   Note: The Organizer dialog box displays and the Styles tab should be selected.

3. Select the **Close File** button located below the first column {Alt and f}.

   Note: The name of the button changes to Open File.

4. Select the **Close File** button located below the second column {Alt and e}.
5. Select the **Open File** button located below the first column and double-click on the name of the file that contains the desired styles {Alt and f, Tab, press the down arrow key to highlight desired filename, Enter}.

FIGURE 15.3

Organizer dialog box

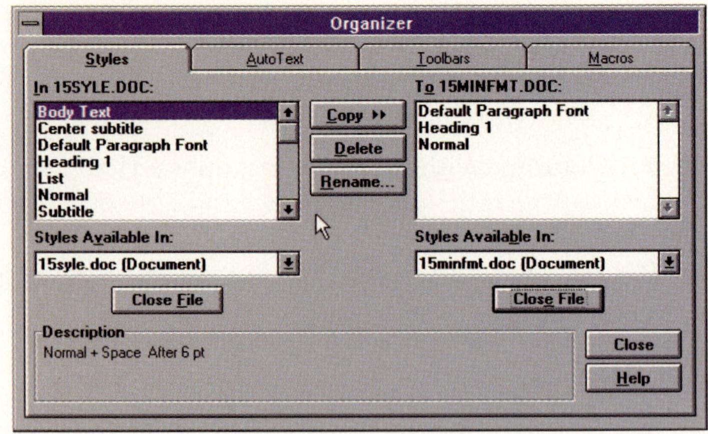

For example, double-click on **15style.doc** located on your file disk.

Note: *The words "In 15STYLE.DOC" displays above the column and the column contains a list of the styles in the document.*

6. Select the Open File button located below the second column and double-click on the file to which the style are to be copied {Alt and e, Tab, press the down arrow key to highlight the desired filename}.

   For example, double-click on **15minfmt.doc** located on your file disk.

   Note: *The words "To 15MINFMT.DOC" display above the second column. Your Organizer dialog box should look similar to Figure 15.3.*

7. Select the style(s) to be copied.

   For example, scroll down to the bottom of the list of styles in the first column. Press and hold the **Shift** key and click once on the last style name to select all the styles.

8. Select the **Copy** button located between the columns {Alt and c}.

   Note: *A message box displays asking "Do you wish to overwrite . . . "*

9. Select **Yes to All** to overwrite all existing built-in styles with the edited styles {Alt and a}.

   Note: *The selected styles are copied to the* **15minfmt.doc** *document.*

10. Select **Close** {Tab twice, Enter}.

11. If the message "Do you want to save changes to . . ." displays, select **Yes** {y}.

Finish-Up Instructions

- Select the **AutoFormat** button.
- Select the two subtitle paragraphs (Board of Directors Meeting and the date). Apply the Centered Subtitle style. (If necessary, see step 1 of the Steps to Apply the Styles.)
- Select the bulleted list and apply the Numbered List style (If necessary, see step 1 of the Steps to Apply the Styles.)
- Use the same filename, **15minfmt.doc**, and save the file. Print one copy and close the document.

Use Templates

A template is a model for a document. A template stores information on how a document is to be formatted, e.g., margins, and styles. Templates also can contain elements such as border lines, graphics, AutoText entries, and macros. Unless another template is selected, the *normal.dot* template is attached when a new document is created. Word provides other templates for many common types of document such as memos, letters, and reports (see Appendix C for examples of supplied templates).

A template can be attached to a new document by selecting **File**, **New**, and double-clicking on the desired template name. A different template can be attached to an existing document by selecting **File**, **Template**, **Attach**, and double-clicking on the desired template name.

Once a template is attached to a document, the styles associated with the template can be applied to the document text by selecting the **AutoFormat** button or by using the **Style** box on the Formatting Toolbar. Existing styles can be edited and new styles created using the Steps to Edit a Style on page 358 and Steps to Create a New Style on page 359.

Start-Up Instructions

❖ Open the file named **15drill4.doc** located on the data disk.

Attach a Different Template to an Existing Document

1. Select **File, Templates** {Alt, f, t}.

   Note: *The Templates and Add-ins dialog box displays.*

2. Select **Attach** {Alt and a}.

3. Select the drive and/or directory that contains the Word template files (e.g., c:\winword\template).

   Note: *Check with your instructor or instructional assistant to determine the location of the template files on your system.*

4. Double-click on the desire template name {Tab, press the down arrow key to highlight the desired template name}.

   For example, double-click on **report2.dot**.

5. If necessary, select the **Automatically Update Document Styles** option {Alt and u.}

   Note: *An X should display in the box located beside the Automatically Update Document Styles option.*

6. Select **OK** {Enter}.

   Note: *The font of the text has been changed to reflect the "normal" font for the Report2 template.*

7. Apply the styles contained in the template as desired.

   For example, select the **AutoFormat** button to apply the built-in styles contained in the Report2 template.

Finish-Up Instructions

- Review the document and apply different styles as desired. For example:
  a. Select the two lines of text below the document title (Board of Directors Meeting and September 4, 199x) and apply the **Subtitle** style (click on the down arrow located to the right of the **Style** box and click on **Subtitle**).
  b. Place the insertion point in the paragraph that follows the bulleted list and apply the **Body Text Indent** style (click on the down arrow located to the right of the **Style** box and click on **Body Text Indent**).
  c. Select the final three lines of text in the document and apply the **Attention Line** style (click on the down arrow located to the right of the Style box and click on **Attention Line**).
- Use the *new* filename **15rept.doc** and save the file on your file disk.
- Print one copy and close the document.

Create a Document Using a Template

1. Select **File, New** {Alt, f, n}.

Note: Do not select the New button.

2. In the New dialog box, double-click on the desired template name {press the up or down arrow key to highlight the desired template name, Enter}.

For example, double-click on **Memo2**.

Note: In a moment, the top portion of a memorandum displays in the document window (see Figure 15.4). The current date has been inserted to the right of the lead word DATE. Beside the lead words TO, FROM, and CC, the bracketed word [Names] has been inserted. The bracketed word [Subject] has been inserted beside the lead word RE. To create the memorandum, delete the bracketed word and type the appropriate text.

3. Select the first bracketed word and insert the desired text.

FIGURE 15.4

Top portion of a memorandum created using Memo2 template

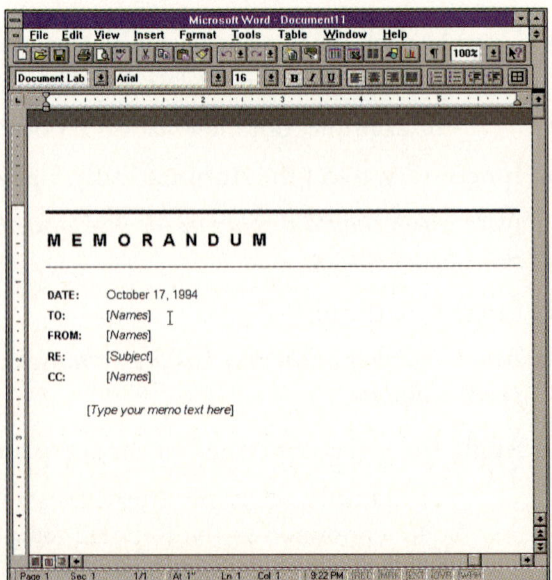

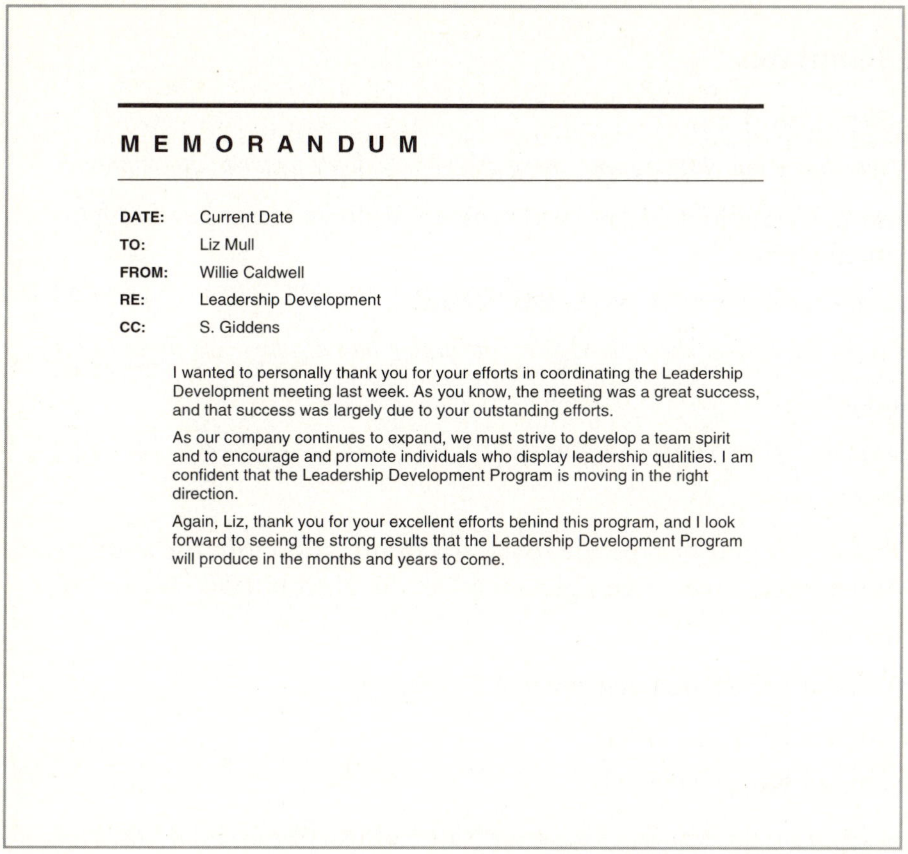

MEMORANDUM

DATE:	Current Date
TO:	Liz Mull
FROM:	Willie Caldwell
RE:	Leadership Development
CC:	S. Giddens

I wanted to personally thank you for your efforts in coordinating the Leadership Development meeting last week. As you know, the meeting was a great success, and that success was largely due to your outstanding efforts.

As our company continues to expand, we must strive to develop a team spirit and to encourage and promote individuals who display leadership qualities. I am confident that the Leadership Development Program is moving in the right direction.

Again, Liz, thank you for your excellent efforts behind this program, and I look forward to seeing the strong results that the Leadership Development Program will produce in the months and years to come.

FIGURE 15.5

Memorandum created using the Memo2 template

For example, select [**Names**] beside the lead word TO: and type **Liz Mull**.

4. Continue to select the bracketed words and insert the appropriate text.

   For example, continue to deleted the bracketed words and create the memorandum shown in Figure 15.5.

Finish-Up Instructions

- Use the filename **15memo2.doc** and save the file on your file disk. Print one copy and close the document.

Use Wizard Templates

The wizards are one of the new features of Word 6.0 for Windows. Wizards are templates that contain prompts to guide the user when entering information into predefined forms. Word provides nine Wizards to assist you in creating documents such as an agenda, award, letter, newsletter, and résumé.

Each Wizard provides questions that guide you step by step through the process of creating the chosen document type. By answering these questions, you specify how the document is to appear. For example, if the Award Wizard is selected, the first question to answer is "Which style would you like?" You can select a Formal, Modern, Decorative, or Jazzy style. Other answered questions provide Word with the specific information to display in the form. Using Wizard templates is one of the easiest methods for creating documents.

Use Wizard Templates

1. Select **File, New** {Alt, f, n}.

   Note: *The New dialog box displays containing a list of available wizards and templates.*

2. Double-click on the desired wizard {press the up or down arrow key to highlight the desired wizard}.

   For example, double-click on **Award Wizard.**

   Note: *After a few moments, the Award Wizard dialog box displays (see Figure 15.6).*

3. Select the desired style.

   For example, select **Jazzy** {Alt and j}.

4. Select **Next** {Alt and n}.

5. Select the desired options or type the requested information into the appropriate boxes. When each screen is completed, select the **Next** button {Alt and n}.

   For example,

   a. Select the desired orientation, **Landscape**.

   b. Select **No.**

   c. Select **Next.**

   d. Double-click in the "Type the name of the person who will receive the award" box and type your name.

   e. Highlight the information in the Title box and type **Microsoft Word Training.**

   f. Select **Next.**

   g. Type your instructor's name in the "Type the names of the people who will sign the award" box.

   h. Select **Add.** Your instructor's name displays in the "These are the people who will sign" box. (If other names are displayed in the "These are the people who will sign" box, click on the names and select the **Remove** button.)

FIGURE 15.6

Award Wizard dialog box

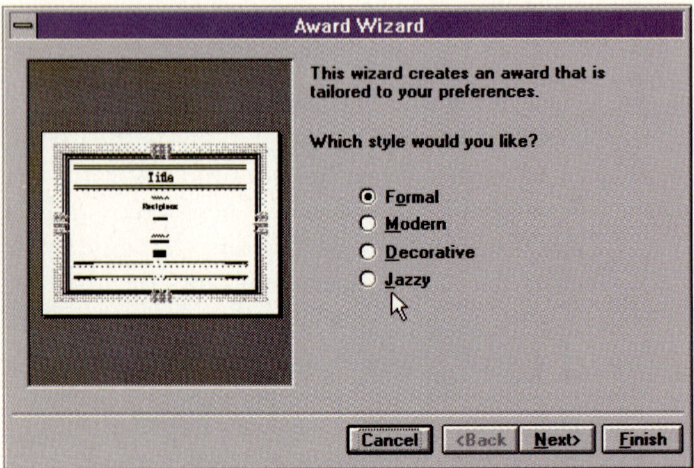

i. Select **Next**.

j. If necessary, select the **Presented by** option. Delete any information in the Presented by box and type your school's name.

k. Select **Next**.

l. If necessary, type the current date.

m. Insert the words **and dedication** after the words "For extraordinary work in the "Type any additional text that you want on the award" box.

n. Select **Next**.

Note: A checkered flag displays in the dialog box to indicate that you have completed the information needed for the wizard.

6. Select **Finish** {Alt and f}.

*Note: In a few moments, the completed award certificate displays in the document window. If desired, select the **Print Preview** button to view the entire certificate. Select the **Close** button to return to the document window.*

Finish-Up Instructions

- Use the filename **15award.doc** and save the file on your file disk.
- Print one copy and close the document.

Use Macros

Macros are shortcuts that eliminate repetitious action. Macros are especially useful when your actions involve selecting several menus or making changes in dialog boxes. Macros are created by recording keystrokes and mouse selections. Because Word remembers each keystroke and mouse selection when a macro is being recorded, the macro should be planned before the recording process is started. Write down each step needed to create the macro.

To begin recording a macro, **Tools, Macro** is selected, and the macro is given a name. If desired, a description of the purpose of the macro can be typed. When the **Record** button is selected, the Record Macro dialog box displays. At this point, the macro can be assigned to a Toolbar, menu, or keyboard shortcut, if desired. The macro can be made available to all documents by placing the macro in the *normal.dot* (global) template, or the macro can be made available only to documents created using a specific template. To make a macro available only to documents created using a specific template, select the desired template before selecting **Tools**, **Macro**.

Once the macro has been named and a decision has been made regarding assigning the macro to a Toolbar, menu or keyboard shortcut, the Record mode becomes active. A Macro Record Toolbar containing **Stop** and **Pause** buttons will display in the document window, and the mouse pointer will change to a pointer arrow with a cassette tape icon to indicate that the Record mode is on.

Word remembers each keystroke and mouse selection made while the Record mode is on. When recording a macro, the mouse can be used to select buttons, commands, and options. However, the mouse cannot be used to select text or to move the insertion point in the document window. Selecting text and moving the insertion point must be accomplished using keystrokes. When all the desired keystrokes and mouse selections have been completed, the **Stop** button is selected on the Macro Record Toolbar.

The **Pause** button on the Macro Record Toolbar can be selected while the Record mode is on to allow you to perform steps that should not be recorded. To resume recording, select the **Pause** button again.

To save a macro, the **File, Save All** command is selected. If **File, Exit** is selected and the macro has not been saved, a message displays asking if you wish to save the changes to the template, usually *normal.dot*. Select **Yes** if the macro is to be saved.

Once a macro is recorded, the macro can be played as often as needed by selecting **Tools, Macro** and double-clicking on the desired macro name, by pressing the assigned shortcut keys, or by selecting the macro from a Toolbar or menu. The macro performs each recorded step. When all the recorded steps have been completed, you can edit, save, print, or close the file by using normal procedures. Changes to a document created by a macro do not alter the macro. The macro can be used again and again.

Start-Up Instructions

- A new document window should be displayed. (If necessary, select the **New** button.)

Record a Macro

1. In a clear document window, select **Tools, Macro** {Alt, t, m}.

   Note: The Macro dialog box displays. The insertion point is located in the Name box.

2. In the Name box, type the name of the macro.

   For example, type **mylabels**. (Do not type the period.)

3. Click in the Description box, and type a description of the purpose of the macro {Alt and i, type a description}.

   For example, type **creates a sheet of labels with my address**.

4. Select **Record** {Alt and o}.

   Note: The Record Macro dialog box displays. If desired, a macro can be assigned to a Toolbar, Menu, or a keystroke shortcut (Keyboard).

5. To assign the macro to a Toolbar, menu or keyboard shortcut, select the **Toolbars, Menus,** or **Keyboard** button in the Assign Macro To area.

   For example, to assign a keyboard shortcut for the **mylabels** macro, select the **Keyboard** button. With the insertion point located in the Press New Shortcut Key box, press **Ctrl** and **F1**. Select **Assign**. Select **Close**.

   *Note: The Macro Record Toolbar displays with Stop and Pause buttons. From now on, every keystroke or mouse selection you make will be remembered by Word until you select the **Stop** button.*

6. Perform the actions to be recorded.

   For example, perform the following steps:

a. Select **Tools, Envelopes and Labels.**

b. Select the **Labels** tab.

c. In the Address box, type:
   Your name (press **Enter**)
   Your address (press **Enter**)
   Your City, State Zip

d. Select **Options.**

e. In the Product number box, select **5260 address** (if using a laser printer) or **4144 Address** (if using a dot matrix printer).

f. Select **OK.**

g. Check that the **Full Page of the Same Label** option is selected in the Print area.

h. Select **New Document.**

i. When the page of labels displays, select all the labels by pressing **Ctrl** and **a.**

j. Change the font to **Bookman Old Style, 11 point.**

k. To deselect the text, press the up arrow key once.

7. When all actions to be recorded have been performed, select the **Stop** button on the Macro Record Toolbar.

   For example, the **mylabels** macro is complete. Select the **Stop** button.

Finish-Up Instructions

- Close the document (do not save the file).
- Continue with the Steps to Play a Macro.

Start-Up Instructions

- The macro named mylabels must have been created using the previous Steps to Record a Macro.

Play a Macro

1. Press the keyboard shortcut keys assigned to the macro or select **Tools, Macro** and double-click on the desired macro name.

   For example, press **Ctrl** and **F1**.

   ***Note:** In a few moments, the labels containing your name and address display in the document window. The document can now be edited, saved, printed, etc., as any other document.*

Finish-Up Instructions

- Use the *new* filename **15label.doc** and save the file. Print one copy and close the document.

❖ Continue with the Steps to Delete a Macro.

Steps to Delete a Macro

1. Select **Tools, Macro** {Alt, t, m}.
2. Click on the macro name to be deleted {press the down arrow key to highlight the desired macro name}.

   For example, click on **mylabels**.
3. Select **Delete** {Alt and d}.
4. Select Yes to the message "Do you want to delete macro . . ." {y}.
5. Select Close to exit the Macro dialog box {Esc}.

The Next Step

Chapter Review and Activities

Self-Check Quiz

T F 1. Before a character style is applied, the desired text must be selected.

T F 2. Text can be sorted in alphabetical or numerical order.

T F 3. Descending sort order is A through Z, or lowest to highest.

T F 4. The Macro dialog box can be used to run a macro.

T F 5. A macro can be run by selecting **Tools, Macro** and double-clicking on the macro name, by pressing the keyboard shortcut keys, or by selecting the macro from a Toolbar or Menu.

6. A template can contain ________________.
   a. formatting instructions
   b. graphic lines
   c. text
   d. all of the above

7. When the **AutoFormat** button is selected, ____________________.
   a. the document is formatted using built-in styles
   b. the document is spell-checked
   c. you can review and accept or reject format changes

8. Two types of styles are ___________ and Character.
   a. Document
   b. Paragraph
   c. Page
   d. Column

9. Define a style and state two advantages of using styles.

10. Explain why a macro should be planned before you begin to record a macro.

Enriching Language Arts Skills

Spelling/Vocabulary Words

exempt not subject to an obligation or a liability.

prohibit to forbid; to prevent.

sole the only one; one of a kind.

Apostrophe Used to Show Possession

If a noun is singular and used to show possession, add an apostrophe (') and an s. If the noun is plural or the final letter in the noun is an s, add only an apostrophe after the *s*.

Examples:

The secretary's table was misplaced.
The brothers' houses and the Lexis' garage are on the corner of Piedmont and High streets.

Chapter 15 Create Documents Using Special Functions

Activities

Activity 15.1—Attach a Template and Use AutoFormat

1. Open the file named **15act1.doc** located on the data disk.
2. Attach the template named **presrel2** (select **File**, **Templates**, **Attach**; select the drive and/or directory where the template files are located; double-click on **presrel2.dot**; check that the **Automatically Update Document Styles** option is selected; OK).
3. Apply the built-in styles by selecting the **AutoFormat** button.
4. Insert page numbers at the bottom center of all pages (select **Insert**, **Page Numbers**, **Alignment**, **Center**, **OK**).
5. Use the new filename **15bank.doc** and save the formatted report on your file disk.
6. Print one copy and close the document.

Activity 15.2—Sort Table Columns

Part I

1. Open the file named **15act2.doc** located on the data disk and use the following instructions to sort the clients alphabetically.
2. Select all table cells except the table title and column heads.
3. Select **Table, Sort.** Make the following selections in the Sort By area:

   Sort By: Column 1
   Type: Text
   Sort Order: Ascending

4. Select **OK.**
5. Click once to deselect the table cells.
6. Use the filename **15vendor.doc** and save the file on your file disk. Print one copy.

Part II

Note: *Use the following instructions to sort the clients by fourth quarter sales from the highest to lowest amounts.*

1. Select all table cells except the title and the column heads.
2. Select **Table, Sort.** Make the following selections in the Sort By area:

   Sort By: Column 5
   Type: Number
   Sort Order: Descending

3. Select **OK.**
4. Use the *new* filename **15sales.doc** and save the file on your file disk.
5. Print one copy and close the document.

Activity 15.3—Sort Lines

1. Create the memorandum shown below.

Memorandum

To: See Distribution Below

From: Gayle Marlow

Date: (Use current date)

Subject: Reprint Procedures Meeting

A meeting has been scheduled for Monday in the East Conference Room on the third floor to discuss the proposed changes in the reprint procedures for all documents. Your input would be greatly appreciated.

Please call me at Extension 5246 to confirm your attendance.

Distribution:

A. Myer
T. Dake
P. Jones
S. Thomas
B. Lee
J. Bray
L. Thomas

---

2. Use the filename **15memo.doc** and save the file on your file disk. Print one copy.
3. Use the following information to sort the distribution list in ascending order by last name (Word 2). Create a secondary sort criteria to sort the distribution list by first initial when last names are the same.
    a. Select the names in the distribution list.
    b. Select **Table, Sort Text.**
    c. In the Sort By box, select **Word 2**. If necessary, select **Ascending.**
    d. In the Then By box, select **Word 1**. If necessary, select **Ascending.**
    e. Select **OK.**
4. Save the file again using the same filename, **15memo.doc**. Print one copy and close the document.

Activity 15.4—Use the Agenda Wizard

1. Create an agenda using the following information.
    a. Select **File, New** and double-click on **Agenda Wizard.**
    b. Select the **Modern** style. Select **Next.**
    c. In the date box, type a date one week from the current date.
    d. The meeting starts at **10:00 a.m**. Select **Next.**
    e. The title of the meeting is **Monthly Sales Meeting.**
    f. The location of the meeting is **Conference Room 303**. Select **Next.**
    g. Deselect all the headings. Select **Next.**
    h. Deselect all the names. Select **Next.**
    i. Insert the following information into the appropriate columns in the Agenda Wizard dialog box. Press the **Tab** key to move from cell to cell.

Agenda topic	Person responsible	Minutes allocated
Review of Monthly Sales Report	Insert your name	15

Marketing Plans for New Products	Insert a friend's name	15
Update on Product Development	Irene Sherman	20
Marketing Budget Review	Henry Nelson	10

j. Select **Next.**

k. If desired, change the order of the agenda items. Select **Next.**

l. Select **Yes** to create a form for recording the minutes. Select **Next.**

m. Select **Finish.**

2. Use the filename **15agenda.doc** and save the file on your file disk.
3. Print one copy and close the document.

Challenge Your Skills

Skill 15.1—Create and Apply Styles

1. Type the following unformatted presentation text.

WORD 6.0 FOR WINDOWS
Features Presentation

1. MENU BAR
a. File
b. Edit
c. View
d. Insert
e. Format
f. Tools
g. Table
h. Window
i. Help

2. TOOLBARS
a. Standard
b. Formatting
c. Borders
d. Mail Merge
e. Database
f. Forms
g. Drawing
h. Macro
j. Word for Windows 2.0

---

2. Use the filename **15skill1.doc** and save the unformatted file on your file disk.

3. Edit the *normal* style as follows:

   Font: **Footlight MT Light, 16 point**, or make a choice of your own.

4. Create the following new styles.

   Name: P-Title
   Type: Paragraph
   Based on: Title
   Font: Arial, Bold, 24 point
   Paragraph: Spacing After—24 pt

   Name: P-Subtitle
   Type: Paragraph
   Based on: P-Title
   Font: Arial, Bold, 20 point

   Name: P-Level 1
   Type: Paragraph
   Based on: Normal
   Font: Footlight MT Light, 18 point, or make your own choice
   Paragraph: Spacing After—18 pt

   Name: P-Level 2
   Type: Paragraph
   Based on: P-Level 1
   Font: Footlight MT Light, 16 point, or make your own choice
   Paragraph: Left indent of .5"

5. Apply the new styles to the document paragraphs.

   Hint: *Apply the P-Level 1 style to items numbered 1 and 2. Apply the P-Level 2 style to the items listed with lowercase letters. A style can be applied to multiple paragraphs by selecting the desired paragraphs before choosing the* ***Styles*** *box.*

6. Use the filename **15format.doc** and save the formatted presentation. Print one copy and close the document.

Chapter 15 Create Documents Using Special Functions

Skill 15.2—Create a Macro to Select, Copy, Paste and Sort a Table

1. Open the file named **15skill2.doc** located on the data disk.

2. Use the following information to create a macro that selects, copies, pastes the copy, and sorts the table by salesperson and sales volume.

   a. Place the insertion point to the left of the "C" in the word "Client" in the first cell of the table.

   b. The macro name is to be **revenue**. If desired, the macro can be assigned to the keystrokes **Alt** and **1**.

   c. Select and copy the table.

      Hint: *Place the insertion point in the first table cell, press* ***F8*** *and use the arrow keys to select all the table cells.* ***The mouse cannot be used to select text or to move the insertion point when a macro is being recorded.***

d. Paste a copy of the table below the heading *Monthly Revenue Report by Salesperson.*

e. Select the copied table and sort the table by salesperson in ascending order.

f. Copy the table. Paste the copy of the table below the heading *Monthly Revenue Report by Sales Volume.*

g. Select the copied table and sort the table by sales volume in descending order.

h. Deselect the table.

i. Stop recording.

3. Close the document. Do not save the changes.
4. Open the file named **15rev3.doc** located on the data disk.
5. Place the insertion point in the first table cell and play the **revenue** macro.
6. Use the *new* filename **15revst.doc** and save the file on your file disk.
7. Print one copy and close the document.
8. Delete the revenue macro.

Skill 15.3—Sort Paragraphs; Language Arts

1. Open the file named **15skill3.doc** located on the data disk.
2. Make decisions regarding bolding and fonts for the title, ballot measure numbers and names.
3. Correct one number format error, three spelling, and three punctuation/grammatical errors.
4. Select all paragraphs except the title.
5. Sort the paragraphs numerically in descending order by the ballot measure number.
6. Use the *new* filename **15ballot.doc** and save the sorted file on your file disk.
7. Print one copy.
8. Select all paragraphs except the title.
9. Sort the paragraphs alphabetically in ascending order by the second word in each paragraph.
10. Use the new filename **15measur.doc** and save the sorted file on your file disk.
11. Print one copy and close the document.
12. If you have completed your work, exit Word.

CHAPTER 16

Managing Document Windows and Files

Features Covered

- Arrange, maximize, minimize, move, restore, and resize document windows
- Create, revise, and print the summary information for a document
- Use the Find File feature to print, find, copy, move, and delete files and to create directories
- Convert files to and from other word processing formats
- Assign a password
- Use DOS without exiting Word
- Cancel the printing of a document

Objectives and Introduction

After successfully completing this chapter, you will be able to arrange, maximize, minimize, move, restore, and resize document windows as well as create, revise, and print document summary information. You will also learn how to use Word's Find File feature to open, delete, rename, move, and locate files, and to create and delete directories and subdirectories. In addition, you will learn to use Word's file conversion and password features. You will learn to access DOS without exiting Word in order to perform tasks such as checking your hard disk or formatting a new disk. Finally, you will learn to cancel the printing of a document.

Word provides tools to arrange, access, and secure files. Files can be arranged or managed by using Window, Find File, and Summary Info features. Passwords can be created and used to secure files. Also, files from other word processing programs can be converted to or from the Word format. If desired, Word can be temporarily exited to accomplish tasks at the DOS prompt or to cancel the printing of a document.

The Windows in Word

The Word document window displays after the Word program is launched. When a new file is created or an existing file is opened, a new window displays. Word keeps track of the most recent documents you have worked on and lists them at the bottom of the **File** menu. To open one of these files, simply click on the filename. Up to nine documents can be listed at the bottom of the **File** menu. To change the number of files listed at the bottom of the **File** menu, select **Tools, Option, General**, increase or decrease the number in the **Recently Used File List** box, select **OK**.

As each new file is created, Word sequentially numbers each document window; for example, Document1, Document2, etc. The document number displays in the Title bar. After a file is saved, the filename displays in the Title bar. Any document window can be arranged, maximized, minimized, moved, restored, resized, or closed.

Start-Up Instructions

- Create five files as follows:
    a. In a new document window, type **This is file 1.**; press **Enter** twice.
    b. Use the filename **16file1.doc** and save the file on your file disk.
    Note: Do not close the file.
    c. Select the **New** button on the Standard Toolbar; type **This is file 2.**; press **Enter** twice.
    d. Use the filename **16file2.doc** and save the file on your file disk.
    Note: Do not close the file.
    e. Select the **New** button on the Standard Toolbar; type **This is file 3.**; press **Enter** twice.
    f. Use the filename **16file3.doc** and save the file on your file disk.
    Note: Do not close the file.
    g. Select the **New** button on the Standard Toolbar; type **This is file 4.**; press **Enter** twice.
    h. Use the filename **16file4.doc** and save the file on your file disk.
    Note: Do not close the file.
    i. Select the **New** button on the Standard Toolbar; type **This is file 5.**; press **Enter** twice.
    j. Use the filename **16file5.doc** and save the file on your file disk.
    Note: Do not close the file.

Arrange All Document Windows

1. Select **Window, Arrange All** {Alt, w, a}.

   *Note: When **Arrange All** is selected, all opened document windows are visible. The **active window** displays at the top or top left of the screen with the Title bar highlighted (see Figure 16.1).*

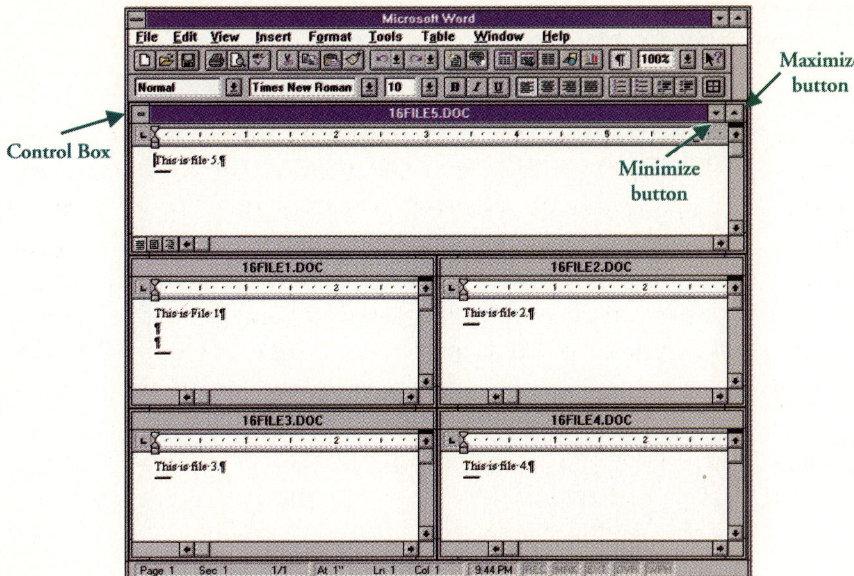

FIGURE 16.1

Arranged document windows with maximize, minimize buttons, and control box

Activate/Change the Active Window

1. Place the mouse pointer in the desired window and click once to activate the window {Alt, w, type the number of the desired window *or* Ctrl and F6 until the desired window is activated}.

   For example, move the mouse pointer to the various open windows and click.

   Note: Remember, a window is active when its Title bar is highlighted or displayed in a different color.

Maximize a Window

1. If more than one window is displayed on the screen, activate the desired window and select the **Maximize** button (up triangle) to view the window in full size {activate the desired window, Alt and hyphen, x}.

   For example, activate and maximize the window containing the file named **16file4.doc**.

   *Note: The document window containing the file named **16file4.doc** displays in full size on the screen.*

Restore a Window

Note: Restoring a document window is the process of returning the document window to its previously determined size.

1. With the document window maximized on the screen, return the window to its previous size by selecting the **Restore** button ⬍ located at the right end of the Menu bar {Alt and hyphen, r}.

   For example, select the **Restore** button in the window containing the file named **16file4.doc**.

FIGURE 16.2

Minimized document window

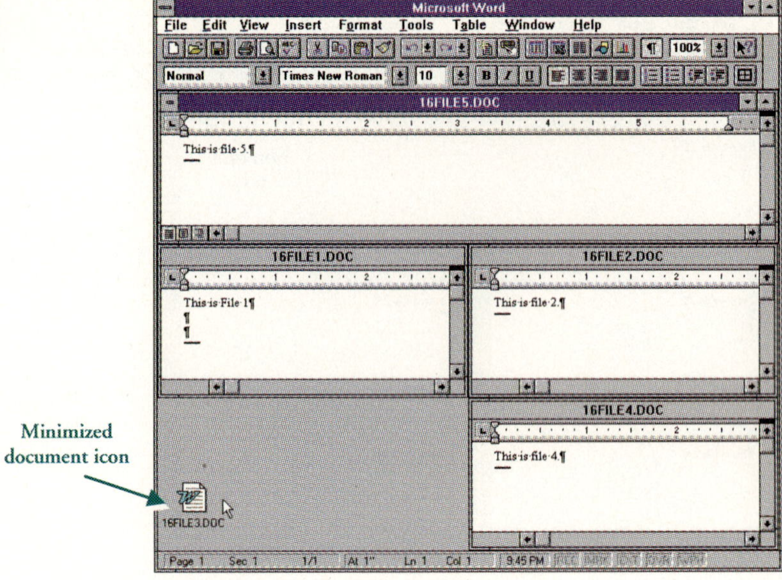

Note: The file is returned to its previous size (before it was maximized).

Minimize a Window

Note: Minimizing a document window reduces the document window to a small icon (see Figure 16.2).

1. Activate the desired window, select the **Minimize** button located in the Title bar of the document window {Alt and hyphen, n}.

   For example, activate and minimize the window containing the file named **16file3.doc**.

   Note: The document window is changed to a small icon and displays in the bottom left corner of the screen. The document name displays below the icon. (See Figure 16.2.)

Restore a Minimized Window

1. Double-click on the icon that represents the desired window {Alt, w, type the number of the window to be restored}.

   For example, double-click on the icon that represents the file named **16file3.doc**.

Move a Window

Note: The window to be moved must be smaller than the full, maximized size.

1. Locate the mouse pointer in the Title bar of the desired document window; press and hold the mouse button {activate the desired window, press Alt and hyphen, m *or* Ctrl and F7}.

   For example, move the mouse pointer to the Title bar of the document window containing the file named **16file3.doc**; press and hold the mouse button.

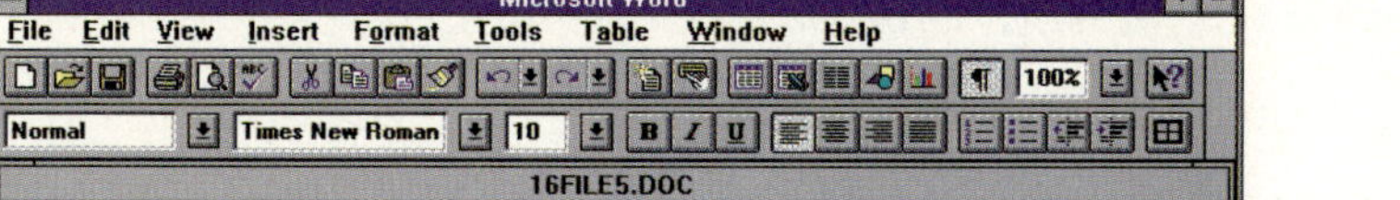

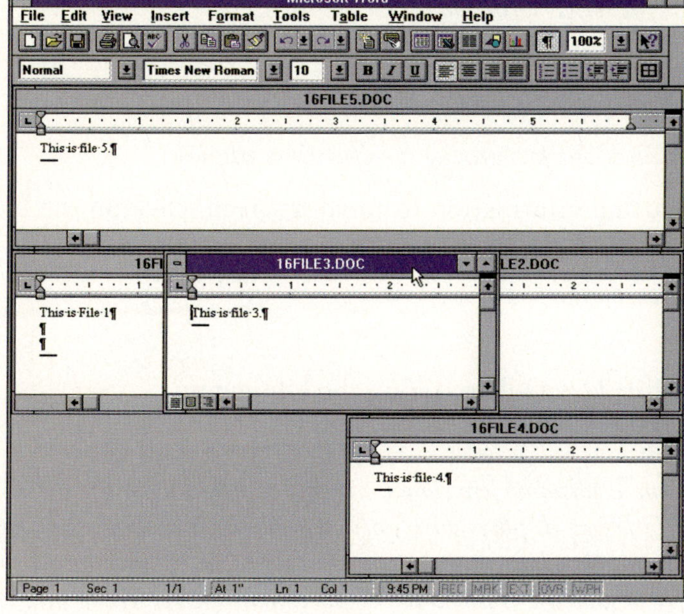

FIGURE 16.3

Moved document window

Note: A dashed outline appears around the document window and the color surrounding that document window may change.

2. Drag the dashed window to the desired position and release the mouse button {press the up, down, left, or right arrow keys to move the window to the desired location, press Enter}.

   For example, drag the dashed outline for the document window containing the file named **16file3.doc** to approximately the center of the screen (see Figure 16.3).

Resize a Window

Note: The window must be smaller than the full, maximized size.

1. Locate the mouse pointer on the document window's left, right, or bottom edge until a double-headed arrow displays. Press and hold the mouse button and drag the dashed outline to the desired size, release the mouse button {activate the desired window, Alt and hyphen, s, press the left, right, up, or down arrow keys to obtain the double-headed arrow at the desired document window's edge; press the chosen arrow key repeatedly until the desired size displays, press Enter. Repeat to change the window size at any edge}.

   For example, activate the window that contains the file named **16file2.doc**. Move the mouse pointer to the bottom edge of the document window and increase the window height.

Start-Up Instructions

- Maximize the file named **16file5.doc**.

Use Help and the Mouse to Display Formatting Information

1. Select the **Help** button on the Standard Toolbar.

Note: A question mark displays with the mouse pointer.

2. Click on the desired text.

   For example, click on the text **This is file 5**.

   Note: The paragraph and font formatting specifications display.

3. To remove the formatting information from your screen, click on the **Help** button again.

Close All Windows

1. Press and hold the **Shift** key while selecting the **File** menu.
2. Select **Close All**.

   *Note: When all document window are closed, an empty screen with the words "Microsoft Word" in the Title bar displays with only two menus, i.e., File and Help. If a file has been changed and the changes have not been saved, a message box displays asking whether you want to save the changes to the document. Select **Yes** to save the changes or select **No** to close the document without saving the changes.*

Document Summary Information

Summary Information can be created for a document to provide specific information about a file, such as the title of the document, subject, and the name of the author. Also keywords can be included that can be used later to search for a document. In addition, in the Comments box you can type information you may want to refer to later; however, you cannot use the Find File command to search for comments. The summary information is created by selecting **File, Summary Info** and typing the desired information into the option boxes in the Summary Info dialog box (see Figure 16.4). If desired, Word can prompt you for summary information when you first save a document.

Once the summary information is typed, the information can be changed (updated) and saved. If desired, you can print a document's summary information along with the document, or the summary information can be printed separately.

Start-Up Instructions

- Open the file named **16file5.doc** located on your file disk.

Create Summary Information After a Document Is Saved

1. Select **File, Summary Info** {Alt, f, i}.

   Note: The Summary Info dialog box displays (see Figure 16.4). The filename and directory automatically display.

2. Select the **Statistics** button {Alt and i}.

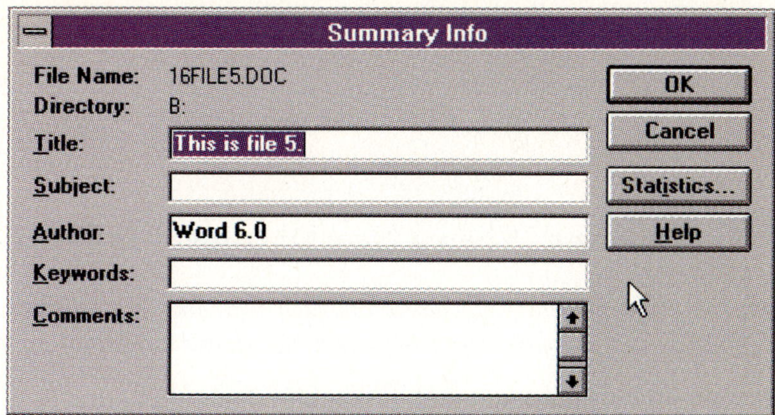

FIGURE 16.4

Summary Info dialog box

Note: The Last Saved date and the Revision Number are displayed. The Created date and the Last Saved date are saved and updated by Word and cannot be changed by the user.

3. Select **Close**.
4. Check that the insertion point is located in the Title box and type the title of the file {press Tab to locate the insertion point in the desired box, type the title}.

   For example, type **This is a sample file.**
5. Click in the **Subject** box and type the words that identify the document's subject {press the Tab key once}.

   For example, type **Sample.**
6. Click in the **Author** box and type the name of the author {press the Tab key once}.

   For example, type your name.

   Note: If desired, type any additional information you wish to place in the Keywords and Comments boxes.
7. Select **OK** {press Enter}.

Chapter 16 Managing Document Windows and Files

Steps to Revise Summary Information

1. Select **File, Summary Info** {Alt, f, i}.
2. Select the option(s) to be changed and type the updated information.

   For example, in the Author's box, select your name and type the name of a friend.
3. Select **OK** to save the updated summary information {Enter}.

Steps to Print Summary Information

1. Select **File, Print** {Alt f, p}.
2. Click in the **Print What** box and select **Summary Info, OK** {Alt and p, press the up or down arrow key to highlight Summary Info}.
3. Select **OK** {Enter}.

Note: The Summary Info prints; the document does not print.

Finish-Up Instructions

- Close the document window. It is not necessary to save the file.

Create Summary Information When a New Document Is Saved

Note: The following steps are for your information only. If these steps are followed, the Summary Info dialog box will display every time a new document is saved or exited.

1. With a document window displayed, select Tools, Options {Alt, t, o}.
2. Click on the **Save** tab {press Ctrl and Tab until a dotted outline displays on the Save tab}.
3. Click in the **Prompt for Summary Info** box {Alt and i}.
4. Select **OK** {Enter}.

Use the Find File Feature

The Find File feature is used to perform the usual disk maintenance tasks of copying, moving, renaming, and deleting files. Additional options include printing all or specified pages of a file, printing multiple files, creating directories/subdirectories, removing directories, and searching for a specific filename or text contained in a file. The Find File feature is accessed by selecting **File**, **Find File** or by choosing the **Find File** button in the Open or Save As dialog box.

The Find File feature is also used to quickly locate a file by finding a filename, partial filename, or even by searching for text that is contained in the file. For example, if there is a file named *jfoxltr1.doc* on your disk but you cannot remember the entire filename, the file can be located by typing *jfox*.doc* in the File Name box of the Search dialog box and selecting the drive letter where the file is located. Word will search for any filename that begins *jfox* and ends with the extension *doc.* To locate a document by searching for a specific word(s) contained in the document, the **Advanced Search** button is selected in the Search dialog box and the drive and directory location of the file is specified in the **Location** tab. Then the Summary tab is selected, and the desired word(s) is typed in the **Containing Text** box. Word will locate any files on the selected drive and/or directory that contain the specified word(s).

In the Find File dialog box, the **View** option is used to specify the type of information that will display in the Find File dialog box. Three View options are available: *Preview*, *Summary*, and *File Info*. The Preview option is selected to view the contents of a file. The Summary option is selected to display the document summary information. The File Info option is selected to display file information such as file size and the date the document was last saved.

Start-Up Instructions

- The files **16file1.doc**, **16file2.doc**, **16file3.doc**, **16file4.doc**, and **16file5.doc** must be available on your file disk.

Note: A mouse is the most efficient method for performing actions when using Find File options and commands. A mouse must be used to perform the Find File options and commands that follow.

Print Multiple Files

1. Select **File, Find File**.

   *Note: The Find File or Search dialog box displays. The first time you use Find File, Word displays the Search dialog box. If Find File has been used previously, Word uses the last search criteria specified and displays the list of files in the Find File dialog box. If the Find File dialog box displays, select the **Search** button to access the Search dialog box.*

2. Click on the down arrow located to the right of the Location box in the Search dialog box and select the desired drive letter.

   For example, click on the drive letter where your file disk is located.

3. If the selected drive contains subdirectories, select the **Include Subdirectories** option.

   For example, your file disk does not contain subdirectories at this time, so you do not need to select the Include Subdirectories option.

4. Select **OK**.

   Note: The Find File dialog box displays. The files stored on your file disk are displayed in the Listed Files box.

5. Click on the first file that you wish to print.

   For example, click on the filename **16file1.doc**.

6. *To select a list of consecutive files,* press and hold the **Shift** key while you click on the last file you wish to print.

   For example, press and hold the **Shift** key and click on the filename **16file5.doc**

   To select a list of nonconsecutive files, press and hold the **Ctrl** key while you click on each desired filename.

7. Select the **Commands** button in the Find File dialog box.

8. Select **Print**.

   Note: The Print dialog box displays.

9. Check that the desired options are chosen in the Print dialog box.

   For example, check that **All** is select in the Print Range area.

10. Select **OK**.

Start-Up Instructions

- The files named **16file1.doc**, **16file2.doc**, **16file3.doc**, **16file4.doc**, and **16file5.doc** should be available on your file disk.

Find Files by Filename

1. Select **File, Find File.**

   *Note: The Find File or Search dialog box displays. If the Find File dialog box displays, select the **Search** button to access the Search dialog box.*

2. In the File Name box of the Search dialog box, type the name or partial name of the file(s) to be found.

   For example, type **16fi*.doc.**

   *Note: The asterisk is a DOS "wildcard" character. The asterisk is a substitute for multiple characters. In this example, **16fi*.doc** instructs the search to find all filenames that begin with the characters **16fi** and have the extension **.doc**.*

3. If necessary, click on the down arrow located to the right of the **Location** box and select the desired drive letter.

   For example, if necessary, click on the down arrow located to the right of the **Location** box and select the drive letter where your file disk is located.

   *Note: If the search is to include looking for a file(s) in subdirectories, select the **Include Subdirectories** option.*

4. Select **OK**.

   *Note: A Building File List message box displays briefly. Then the Find File dialog box displays containing a list of files that match the specified filename or partial filename. If desired, the name of a file(s) can be selected and the **Open** button chosen to open the document(s).*

5. Select **Close** to exit the Find File dialog box.

Create a Directory

1. Select **File, Find File**.

   *Note: The Find File or Search dialog box displays. If the Find File dialog box displays, select the **Search** button to access the Search dialog box.*

2. Click on the down arrow located to the right of the Location box in the Search dialog box and select the desired drive letter.

   For example, select the drive letter where your file disk is located.

3. Select **OK**.

   Note: The Find File dialog box displays containing a list of the files on your file disk.

4. Select the **Commands** button in the Find File dialog box.

5. Select **Copy**.

6. If necessary, click in the Drives box and select the drive letter where the new directory is to be located.

For example, if necessary, click in the Drives box and select the drive letter where your file disk is located.

7. Select the **New** button to display the **Create Directory** dialog box.

8. Type the new directory name in the Name box.

   For example, type your last name (up to eight characters).

9. Select **OK** to exit the Create Directory dialog box.

   Note: *The directory name displays beneath the disk drive letter shown in the Directories box. Notice the file folder icon displaying next to the directory name.*

Create a Subdirectory

10. Repeat step 9.

11. Type the new subdirectory name.

    For example, type your first name (up to eight characters).

12. Select **OK** to exit the Create Directory dialog box.

13. Select **Close** to exit the Copy dialog box.

    Note: *The new directory and subdirectory will not display in the Listed Files area. Empty directories and subdirectories are not displayed in the Listed Files area.*

14. Select **Close** to exit the Find File dialog box.

Copy a File(s)

1. Select **File, Find File.**

   Note: *The Find File or Search dialog box displays. If the Find File dialog box displays containing the list of files on your file disk, proceed to step 2. If the Search dialog box displays, click on the down arrow located to the right of the Location box and select the drive letter where your file disk is located. Select* ***OK.***

2. In the Find File dialog box, select the file(s) to be copied.

   For example, to select the files named **16file1.doc, 16file2.doc, 16file3.doc, 16file4.doc,** and **16file5.doc,** click once on the file named **16file1.doc,** move the mouse pointer to the file named **16file5.doc,** press and hold the **Shift** key and click once.

   Note: *All files between* ***16file1.doc*** *and* ***16file5.doc*** *are selected.*

3. Select the **Commands** button in the Find File dialog box.

4. Select **Copy**.

5. In the Directories box, click on the directory or subdirectory where the files are to be copied.

   For example, click on your last name directory.

6. Select **OK**.

   Note: *The Copy message box displays briefly. When the Copy message box no longer displays, the copy process is complete.*

Finish-Up Instructions

- When the copy process is completed, click on the **Close** button in the Find File dialog box.
- Select **File, Find File**. In the Find File dialog box, select the **Search** button. The **Include Subdirectories** option should be selected. If necessary, click on **Include Subdirectories**. Select **OK**.
- In the Find File dialog box, scroll down the list of files on your file disk until you see your last name directory.
- Use steps 2–6 of the Steps to Copy a File(s) and copy the files named **16file2.doc** and **16file4.doc** from your last name directory to your first name subdirectory.

  *Note: To select nonconsecutive files, select the first filename, move the mouse pointer to the next filename, and press the **Ctrl** key and click once.*
- To view the copied files, select the **Search** button and select **OK**. Word redisplays the files in the Listed Files box of the Find File dialog box. Scroll down the list of files to view your first name subdirectory.
- Select **Close** to exit the Find File dialog box.

Delete a File(s)

Note: All files to be deleted must be closed.

1. Select **File, Find File**.

   *Note: The Find File or Search dialog box displays. If the Find File dialog box displays containing the list of files on your file disk, proceed to step 2. If the Search dialog box displays, click on the down arrow located to the right of the Location box and select the drive letter where your file disk is located. Check that the **Include Subdirectories** option is selected. Select **OK**.*
2. In the Find File dialog box, select the files to be deleted.

   For example, select the files named **16file2.doc** and **16file4.doc** located in your first name subdirectory.
3. Select the **Commands** button and then choose **Delete**.
4. When Word displays a message to confirm that you want to delete the document(s), select **Yes**.

   *Note: The files are deleted. Because the files named **16file2.doc** and **16file4.doc** were the only files in your first name subdirectory, Word has removed the subdirectory from the Listed Files box. Although the subdirectory still exists, Word does not display empty directories or subdirectories.*
5. Select **Close**.

Open Multiple Files

*Note: Multiple files can also be opened by selecting the desired files in the Find File dialog box and by choosing the **Open** button.*

1. If necessary, select the **Open** button. Click on the first file to be opened.

   For example, click on the file named **16file1.doc**.

2. Press and hold the **Ctrl** key while selecting the next file to be opened.

   For example, select the file named **16file2.doc**.

3. Repeat step 2 and highlight any additional file(s) to be opened.

   For example, highlight the file named **16file4.doc**.

4. Select **OK**.

   Note: Word opens each file in a separate document window. The last file opened displays in the document window. Multiple files can be open at the same time. The number of files that can be opened depends on the amount of memory available.

Finish-Up Instructions

- Select **Window, Arrange All** to display all opened document windows.
- Press **Shift** and select **File, Close All**.

Convert File Formats

Word for Windows provides a method to change the file format of a document. A document can be saved to another file format or converted from a different file format. For example, a document originally saved in WordPerfect for Windows can be converted to a Word file format. Also, a Word document can be saved in another format, such as Microsoft Excel.

Chapter 16 Managing Document Windows and Files

Start-Up Instructions

- Open the file named **16file1.doc** located on your file disk.

Save a File in a Different Format

1. Select **File, Save As** {Alt, f, a}.
2. Type the desired filename in the File Name box.

   For example, type **16conver.doc**. (Do not type the final period.)

3. Select the down arrow button next to the **Save File as Type** box {Alt and t, press up or the down arrow key to highlight the desired file format}.

   For example, select **WordPerfect 5.1 for MS-DOS**.

4. Select **OK** {Enter}.

   *Note: The file named **16conver.doc** is now saved in the WordPerfect 5.1 for DOS file format. The file named **16file1.doc** is still available on your file disk and is saved in the Word for Windows 6.0 file format.*

Finish-Up Instructions

- ❖ Close the document. If a message displays asking if you want to save the changes to **16convert.doc**, select **No** because no changes have been made.

Open a File Created in a Different Program and Save as a Word File

1. Select **File, Open** and double-click on the desired file {Alt, f, o, Tab, press the down arrow key to highlight the filename, Enter}.

   For example, double-click on **16conver.doc**.

2. If necessary, select the file format in the Convert File box.

   For example, check that the file format is **WordPerfect**.

3. Select **File, Save As** {Alt, f, a}.
4. Select the down arrow button next to the **Save File as Type** box {Alt and t, press the up or down arrow key to highlight desired file format}.

   For example, select **Word Document**.

5. Select **OK** {Enter}.

   *Note: The file named **16conver.doc** is now saved in the Word for Windows 6.0 file format.*

Finish-Up Instructions

- ❖ Close the document.

File Security

Once a file is created, the file can be saved and given a password. Each time the saved file is opened, the password is requested. The password must be remembered by the user because there is no method available for finding a forgotten password. A password can be removed or changed at any time (but only if you remember the current password).

Passwords are case sensitive (an uppercase W and a lowercase w are considered two different characters) and can contain as many as 15 characters made up of numbers, letters, symbols, and spaces. Word provides two protection options: Write Reservation Password and Protection Password. When the **Write Reservation Password** option has been selected for a document, anyone can open the document as a read-only file. The document can be edited, but a new filename must be used in order to save the changed file. The original file can only be edited and saved by someone who knows the password. When the **Protection Password** option has been selected for a document, only a person who knows the password can open the document.

Start-Up Instructions

- ❖ Select the **New** button on the Standard Toolbar.
- ❖ Type the following sentence:

  This is a very secret file that no one but me should ever see.

Create or Change a Password

1. Select **File, Save As** {Alt, f, a}.
2. Type the desired filename.

   For example, type **16secret.doc**. (Do not type the final period.)
3. Select **Options** {Alt and o}.

   Note: *The Options dialog box appears with the* ***Save*** *tab selected.*
4. Click in the **Protection Password** box located in the lower left corner of the dialog box {Alt and p}.
5. Type the desired password in the Protection Password box.

   For example, type **007**. (Do not type the final period.)

   Note: *To ensure privacy, the typed characters are displayed as asterisks (*) on the screen. Remember, passwords are case sensitive and can contain as many as 15 characters made up of numbers, letters, symbols, and spaces.*
6. Select **OK** {Enter}.

   Note: *The Confirm Password dialog box appears.*
7. Type the password again in the Confirm Password box.
8. Select **OK** {Enter}.
9. Select **OK** in the Save As dialog box {Enter}.

   Note: *You will be returned to the document window.*

Finish-Up Instructions

❖ Close the document.

Open a File That Has Been Protected with a Password

1. Select the **Open** button (Alt, f, o}.
2. Select the desired filename {Tab, press the down arrow key to highlight the desired filename, Enter}.

   For example, double-click on **16secret.doc**.

   Note: *The Password dialog box displays.*
3. Type the password exactly as typed when the password was created.

   For example, type **007**. (Do not type the final period.)

   Note: *As the password is typed, asterisks display on the screen.*
4. Select **OK** {Enter}.

Remove a Password

1. With the password-required document open, select **File, Save As** {Alt, f, a}.
2. Select **Options** {Alt and o}.

Note: The Options dialog box displays with the Save tab selected.

3. Double-click in the **Protection Password** box {Alt and p}.
4. Press **Delete**.
5. Select **OK** {Enter}.
6. Select **OK** to save the file without the password {Enter}.

Finish-Up Instructions

- Close the document window.

Use DOS Without Exiting Word

DOS commands such as format, chkdsk (check disk), dir (directory), date, erase, and diskcopy can be accessed without exiting the Word program. Windows allows multiple programs to run at the same time. The names of the programs that are currently running can be viewed by pressing and holding the **Alt** key while tapping the **Tab** key repeatedly to display the program names. When the desired program name displays, release the **Alt** key to switch to the program.

Use DOS Without Exiting Word

1. Press and hold the **Alt** key while tapping the **Tab** key until the **Program Manager** option displays. Release the **Alt** key.
2. If necessary, double-click on the **Main** group icon.
3. Double-click on the **MS-DOS** prompt icon.

   Note: After a few moments, the DOS prompt displays.
4. Type and execute the desired DOS command.

   For example, type **ver** and press **Enter**.

   *Note: After typing **ver**, the number of the DOS version in use displays.*
5. If desired, type another DOS command or type **exit** to return to the Program Manager and close the DOS window.

   For example, type **exit** and press **Enter**.
6. Press and hold the **Alt** key while tapping the **Tab** key until the **Microsoft Word** option displays. Release the **Alt** key.

   Note: The Word screen displays.

Cancel the Printing of a Document

Once a document has been sent to print, the printing may be stopped or canceled. Word gives you the option in **Tools**, **Options**, **Print** to set the Print feature to allow background printing. This feature allows you to print one document while working in another document. If background printing is turned on in **Tools, Options, Print**, a print command can be canceled in one of two ways: double-click on the printer flag in the Status bar (the printer flag only displays when a file is printing) or select **File, Print, Stop Print.** If background printing is not turned on, press **ESC** to stop a print command. Windows Print Manager can also be used to cancel the printing of a document.

If you are having trouble printing a document, check that the printer is turned on and that the printer cables are securely connected. Also, if a printer is shared, check the switch box or Local Area Network (LAN) connection (see your instructor). Before resending a print job, check Windows Print Manager for any filenames of documents waiting to print. If necessary, delete the filenames of the documents that should not be printed.

Steps to Access Print Manager

***Note:** The following steps are for your information only.*

1. After a document has been sent to print, press and hold the **Alt** key while tapping the **Tab** key repeatedly until Print Manager displays. Release the **Alt** key.

   ***Note:** The Print Manager dialog box displays.*

2. *To delete a file from the print* queue, highlight the name of the desired document and select the **Delete** button.

   ***Note:** If the document is in the process of printing, a message displays "Do you want to quit printing the document . . .?". Select OK.*

3. *To resume the printing of a document,* select the printer name and select **Resume**.

4. *To exit Print* Manager, select **View, Exit.**

5. *To return to Word without exiting the Print Manager*, press and hold the **Alt** key while tapping the **Tab** key until Microsoft Word displays. Release the **Alt** key.

The Next Step

Chapter Review and Activities

Self-Check Quiz

T F 1. When multiple document windows are open, select **Window**, **Arrange All** to display all the documents on the screen.

T F 2. The **Maximize** button can be selected to reduce the size of a document window.

T F 3. All open document windows can be closed at once by holding down the **Shift** key and selecting **File**, **Close All**.

T F 4. You can print a document's summary information without printing the document.

T F 5. The number of files that can be open at one time depends on the amount of available memory.

6. The maximum number of characters that can be used as a password is ________.
   a. 19
   b. 16
   c. 23
   d. 15

7. A file can be previewed before it is opened in the _____ ________ dialog box.
   a. Print Manager
   b. Find File
   c. Window, Split
   d. Format Paragraph

8. Using the **Help** button with the mouse allows you to see ________________.
   a. paragraph formatting
   b. font formatting
   c. Help demos
   d. both a and b

9. List five tasks that can be accomplished using the Find File feature.

10. List the steps to access DOS without exiting Word.

Enriching Language Arts Skills

Proofreading Hints

When proofreading a document, read the document twice: once for content and meaning and once to check grammar, spelling, and punctuation. When proofreading your own work, place the original document/draft beside the screen and read across comparing line by line. Read aloud with a second person to compare the printed copy with the original document/draft.

Examples of errors to look for when proofreading:

Repeated words	The wedding reception will be held *on on* Sunday at the Palmer Country Club.
Misused or missing words	The transaction is *not* legal. The transaction is *now* legal.
Missing punctuation	The cost was *$2516.* (should be $25.16)
Misspelled names	Kathryn or Catherine
Transposed letters/numbers	The *item* is 10:00 a.m. (should be time) The report is due October *21.* (should be October 12)

Activities

Activity 16.1—Arrange and Maximize Document Windows

1. Open four files of your choice from your file disk.
2. Arrange all windows (select **Window**, **Arrange All**).
3. Maximize one of the document windows (double-click on the **Maximize** button in the desired document's Title bar).
4. Close all document windows {press and hold the **Shift** key and select **File**, **Close All**}.

Activity 16.2—Print a List of Files

1. Select **File**, **Find File**.

   Note: *If a list of the files on your file disk displays, skip to step 3.*
2. In the Search dialog box, click on the down arrow located to the right of the Location box and choose the drive letter where your file disk is located.
3. Select two or three consecutive files located on your file disk.
4. Print the selected files (select the **Commands** button, select **Print**, **OK**).

Activity 16.3—Create and Print Document Summary Information

1. Open one of the files from your file disk and review the document to determine the subject of the document.
2. Create a Summary Info for your chosen file. Fill in the title, subject, author, and keywords boxes with the appropriate information (select **File**, **Summary Info**, type the desired information in the appropriate boxes, select **OK**.)
3. Print the Summary Info (select **File**, **Print**, click in the **Print What** box, choose **Summary Info**, select **OK**).
4. Save and close the document.

Challenge Your Skills

Skill 16.1—Create Directories and Copy and Delete Files

1. Create two directories on your file disk using the directory names **dir1** and **dir2**.
2. Select and copy four graphic image (**.wmf**) files from the clipart subdirectory to **dir1**. (If necessary, check with your instructor or instructional assistant for the drive and/or directory in which the graphic image files are located.
3. Copy two of the files from **dir1** to **dir2**.
4. In the **dir1** directory, delete one of the graphic image files.
5. If you have completed your work, exit Word.

Part 4
Checking Your Step

Production Skill Builder Activities
Chapters 13-16

Production Activity 4.1—Create a Flier with Graphic Image(s); Use Character Spacing

1. Use the following information to create a flier:
   a. A safari to Africa is scheduled for May 15–30, 199x. The safari is being coordinated by Francene Engdahl of Safaris Unlimited. Francene can be contacted at 319-555-2550.
   b. The safari package includes airfare, accommodations, sightseeing tours, and daily breakfast.
   c. The cost of the safari package is $4,495 per person.
   d. Use one or two graphic images to enhance the appearance of the flier. Suggested graphic images are **elephant.wmf**, **jet.wmf**, **luggage.wmf**, and **continen.wmf**.
   e. Use WordArt, borders, and spacing as desired.
   f. Make decisions on appropriate fonts and sizes for the text.
   g. Use character spacing to adjust the spacing between words and letters as desired.
2. Use the filename **4pflier.doc** and save the file.
3. Print one copy and close the document.

Production Activity 4.2—Use Superscripts, Subscripts, and Equations

1. Create the following document using superscripts, subscripts, and equations.

SUPERSCRIPTS, SUBSCRIPTS, AND EQUATIONS

COMPLEMENTARY ANGLES		SUPPLEMENTARY ANGLES	
20° 70°	30° 60°	75° 105°	60° 120°

CHEMICAL FORMULAS

Barium Stearate = $Ba(C_{18}H_{35}O_2)_2$

Magnesium Hydroxide = $Mg(OH)_2$

Sulfapyridine = $NH_2C_6H_4SO_2NHC_5H_4N$

Thiopental = $C_{11}H_{18}N_2O_2S$

ALGEBRAIC EQUATIONS

$$\frac{\sqrt{5}-4}{2\sqrt{5}-2} \qquad \frac{-8a^3}{15x} \le \frac{-4a}{3x} \qquad A = \frac{1}{4}\prod d^2$$

---

2. Use the filename **4p2sse.doc** and save the file.
3. Print one copy and close the document.

Production Activity 4.3—Use the Spike to Accumulate Text and to Create an Overhead Transparency

1. Open the file named **4pact3.doc** located on the data disk.
2. Use the Spike feature to create an overhead transparency consisting of the document title and the sideheads contained in the file named **4pact3.doc**.
3. When the title and sideheads have been accumulated in the Spike, create a new document and insert the text in the Spike and empty the Spike.
4. Format the new document as an overhead transparency. Make decisions regarding:

   Fonts and point sizes
   Alignment
   Spacing between paragraphs
5. If desired, insert the **mail.wmf** graphic image.
6. Use the *new* filename **4ovrhd3.doc** and save the overhead transparency file.
7. Print one copy and close the documents.

Production Activity 4.4—Create and Modify Styles; Language Arts

1. Open the file named **4pact4.doc** located on the data disk.
2. Use AutoFormat to apply the built-in styles to the document.
3. Edit the built-in styles as follows:

Style name:	Normal
Font:	Arial, Regular, 11 point, or make a choice of your own
Style name:	Title
Font:	Britannic Bold, 16 point, or make a choice of your own
Paragraph:	Spacing After–18 pt
Style name:	Heading 1
Font:	Britannic Bold, 14 point, or make a choice of your own
Paragraph:	Spacing Before–12 pt; Spacing After–6 pt

4. Create the following new Character style:

Style name:	TV Prog Name
Style type:	Character
Font:	Arial, Bold Italic, 11 point, or make a choice of your own

5. Review the document and apply styles as necessary. For example, find each occurrence of the program name "Unresolved Investigations" and apply the TV Prog Name character style. Check that all the sideheads have been formatted with the Heading 1 style.
6. Correct three spelling errors, two punctuation errors, and one repeated word error.
7. Use the *new* filename **4desc4.doc** and save the formatted document.
8. If you have completed your work, exit Word.

Part 5
A Giant Step

Use Desktop Publishing

Chapters 17–19

- Use the brochure template
- Insert previously created text into a document or frame
- Shadow boxes
- Insert a PCX file into a frame
- Create a caption
- Rotated text and reversed text
- Shadow text attribute
- Create unequal column width
- Create odd and even page headers/footers
- Create a drop cap
- Indent the first line of all paragraphs automatically
- Use correct typography symbols for quote marks and em dashes
- Use a form template
- Create a form template
- Edit a form template
- Create a calculation field
- Create a macro that updates a calculation field

CHAPTER 17

Special Desktop Publishing Features

Features Covered

- Use the brochure template
- Insert previously created text into a document or frame
- Create a shadow border
- Insert a PCX file into a document or frame
- Create a caption
- Rotate text
- Reverse text

Objectives and Introduction

After successfully completing this chapter, you will be able to use the brochure template, multiple columns, and frames to create a two-sided, tri-fold mailer brochure. You will also learn how to create special effects using shadow borders, rotated text, and reversed text.

Brochures come in all shapes and sizes. One of the most common brochures is the tri-fold mailer. Information is printed on both sides of the page. Generally, a three-column format is used and the pages are printed in landscape orientation (i.e., 11 inches by 8.5 inches) as shown in Figures 17.1 and 17.2. Often a tri-fold mailer will include graphic images, border lines, and special effects such as shadow boxes, rotated text, and reversed text. The features presented in this chapter will be used to develop the tri-fold mailer brochure shown on page 414.

Format a Brochure

Before beginning to create a brochure in Word, it is a good idea to create a mock-up—a hand-drawn representation of how the final brochure will look. From the

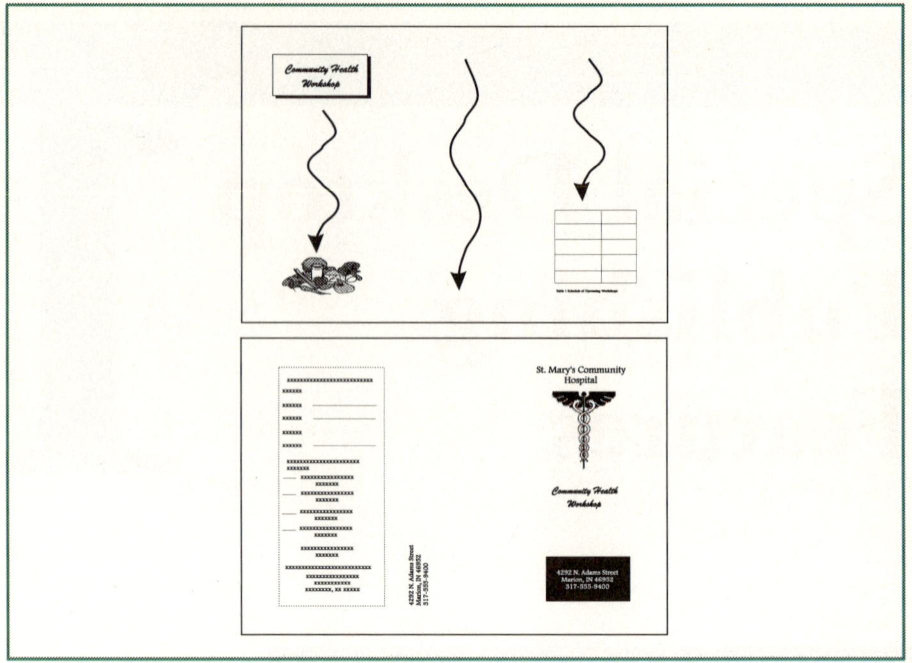

FIGURE 17.1

Mock-up of a tri-fold mailer brochure

mock-up you can decide on the page orientation (landscape or portrait), number of columns, margins, types of borders to be used, where graphic images will be placed, and what special effects will be used. The mock-up can also show where text will be placed in each column (see Figure 17.1).

One of the first decisions that must be made is what paper orientation will be used—portrait or landscape. Until now, all of the documents that have been created in this book have used portrait orientation (i.e., 8.5 inches by 11 inches). Word can also be used to create documents using landscape orientation (see Figure 17.2). When landscape orientation is selected, Word automatically rotates text when the document is printed so that the text prints horizontally in relation to the long (11-inch) side of the page. The orientation of a page can be changed by selecting **File**, **Page Setup**. On the Paper Size tab, select **Landscape** and choose **OK**.

Once paper orientation has been decided, the number of columns can be set. For example, if a tri-fold mailer is to be created, three columns usually are set. Margins are also set. Small margins generally are used so that as much information as possible can be placed on the page. If a laser printer will be used to print the brochure, margins greater than .25 inches are used because the printer cannot place text closer than about .25 inches from the edges of the page. (Note: Although the area that cannot be printed varies from printer to printer, a .25-inch margin generally can be used.)

To enhance the appearance of a brochure, the color of borders and text can be changed. If a color printer is available, Word can print text, graphic images, and borders in the specified colors. Any Windows-supported color printer can be used (e.g., HP Deskjet 500C Series, IBM Color Printer, and HP Paintjet XL).

To make the task of creating brochures easier, Word provides a brochure template (*brochur1*), which changes the orientation of the paper to landscape and sets the left and right margins to .5". The brochure template also contains styles for formatting the brochure text. If desired, the styles can be modified (see Chapter 15, page 359 for information on modifying styles).

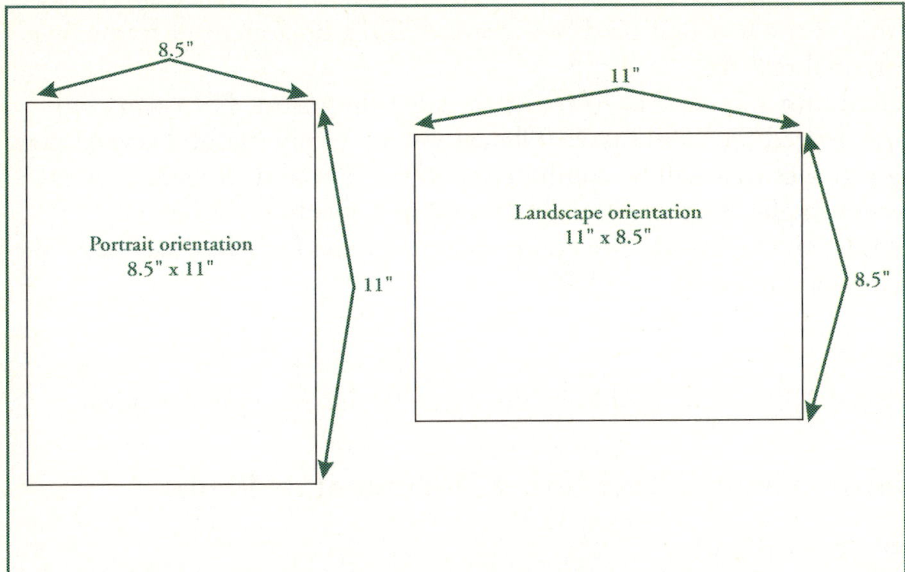

FIGURE 17.2

Portrait and landscape orientation

Start-Up Instructions

- The Page Layout view should be used. (If necessary, select the **Page Layout** button or choose **View**, **Page Layout**.)

Use the Brochure Template

1. Select File, New {Alt, f, n}.

   Note: Do not select the New button.

2. Double-click on Brochur1 {press the up or down arrow key to highlight Brochur1, Enter}.

   *Note: No change displays on the screen. However, if the down arrow beside the Zoom Control button is selected and **Whole Page** is chosen, you will notice that the horizontal Ruler displays 11" along the top of the page and the vertical Ruler displays $8^1/_2$" along the left edge of the page. The left and right margins are .5", and the top and bottom margins are 1".*

Finish-Up Instructions

- Select **Format**, **Columns**, select **Three** in the Presets area. Change the Spacing in the Width and Spacing area to **.9**". Select **OK**.
- Use the filename **17land.doc** and save the file on your file disk.

Insert Previously Created Text Into a Document or Frame

Text that has been previously created and saved can be inserted into a document or frame. When a previously saved file is inserted into a document or frame, the original text file remains untouched and a copy of the text is placed into the document or frame. The copy of the text can be formatted and changed as desired. Any formatting or editing of the text that has been inserted into a document or frame does not affect the original text file.

Text is inserted into a document or frame by using the **Insert, File** command and choosing the desired file. The **Insert, File** command is very useful if several people are creating text files that will be combined to create a final document. For example, each person might create a different portion of a brochure. When all sections are completed, the **Insert, File** command can be used to place each text file into the brochure document.

Start-Up Instructions

- The file named 17**land.doc** should be displayed in the document window.

Insert Previously Created Text Into a Document or Frame

1. Select **Insert, File** {Alt, i, L}.
2. Type or select the location and name of the desired file.

   For example, select the file named **17dtxt1.doc** located on the data disk.
3. Select **OK** {Enter}.

   *Note: The text contained in the file named **17dtxt1.doc** displays in the document window.*

Finish-Up Instructions

- Use the same filename 17**land.doc** and save the file.

Create a Shadow Border

The shadow border (box) special effect is created by choosing the **Shadow** option on the Borders tab in the Paragraph Borders and Shading dialog box. The color of the border can be changed, if desired; however, the color of the shadow will remain black.

Start-Up Instructions

- The file named 17**land.doc** should be displayed in the document window.

Create a Shadow Box

1. Type or select the text to be enclosed in the Shadow box.

   For example, select the words **Community Health Workshops** at the top of the first page.
2. Select **Format, Borders and Shading** {Alt, o, b}.
3. On the Borders tab, select the **Shadow** option in the Presets area {a}.
4. Select the desired line style {y, press the down arrow to highlight desired line style}.

For example, select the **3 pt** line style.

Change the Color of the Border

5. Select the down arrow located to the right of the **Color** box {Alt and c}.
6. Click on the desired color {press the down arrow to highlight the desired color}.

   For example, select **Blue**.

   Note: Although the color of the border line changes, the shadow remains black.
7. Select **OK** {Enter}.

Finish-Up Instructions

- Change the font of the selected text, **Community Health Workshops**, to **BrushScript MT, 28 point**. Select **Center** justification.
- Use the *new* filename **17shadow.doc** and save the file on your file disk.

Insert a PCX File Into a Document or Frame

Graphic images created in many different programs can be retrieved into a Word document or frame. For example, a graph created in Lotus 1-2-3 (filename extension *.pic*) or a drawing created in PC Paintbrush (filename extension *.pcx*) can be retrieved into a Word document or frame. Below is a list of some of the popular graphic file formats that can be inserted into a Word document.

Computer graphics metafile (*.cgm*)	Tag image file format (*.tif*)
Encapsulated PostScript files (*.eps*)	WordPerfect graphics files (*.wpg*)
HP graphics language files (*.hpg*)	PC Paintbrush files (*.pcx*)
Lotus 1-2-3 graphics files (*.pic*)	Corel Draw files (*.cdr*)
Micrografx Designer/Draw files (*.drw*)	Macintosh PICT files (*.pct*)
Windows bitmaps (*.bmp*)	Windows metafiles (*.wmf*)

After a graphic image has been inserted into a document or frame, the graphic image can be edited by double-clicking on the graphic image to access the picture editing window (see Chapter 13, page 312, for information on editing a graphic image using the drawing tools).

Start-Up Instructions

- The file named **17shadow.doc** should be displayed in the document window.
- Scroll down so that the bottom of the first column on page 1 is displayed.
- The Page Layout view should be used. (If necessary, select the **Page Layout** button or choose **View, Page Layout**.)

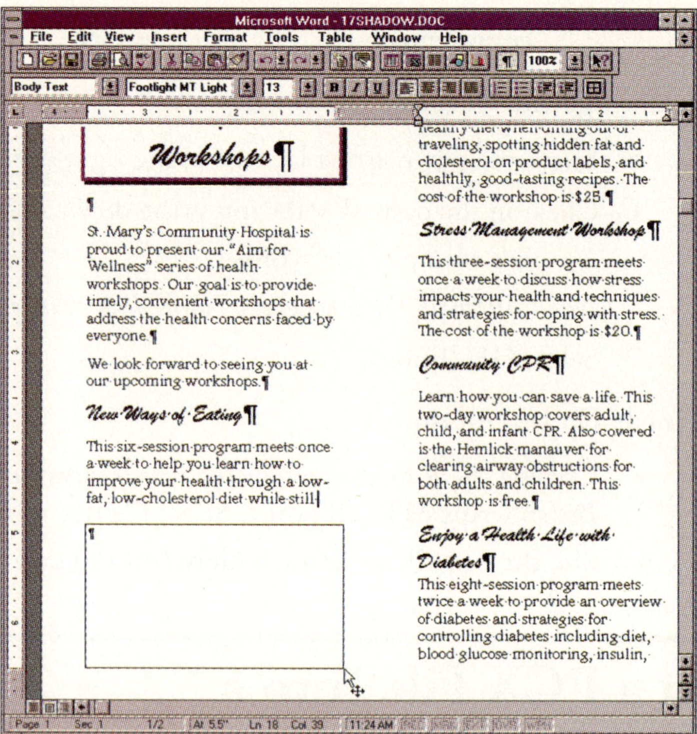

FIGURE 17.3

Tri-fold mailer brochure with a frame that will contain a graphic image

Insert a PCX File Into a Frame

1. Select **Insert, Frame** {Alt, i, f}.

   Note: The mouse pointer changes to a cross-hair (+).

2. Draw a frame at the desired location.

   For example, draw a frame in column 1 that begins at 5" on the vertical Ruler, extends to approximately 6½" on the vertical Ruler and is the width of the first column (see Figure 17.3).

3. Select **Insert, Picture** {Alt, i, p}.

4. Click on the down arrow located to the right of the **List Files of Type** box {Alt and t}.

   Note: A list of graphic file formats displays.

5. Select the desired graphic file format {press the up or down arrow to highlight the desired file type, Enter}.

   For example. scroll down the list of file types and click on **PC Paintbrush (*.pcx)**.

6. If necessary, click in the Drives box and click on the drive letter where the desired file is located.

   For example, if necessary, click in the Drives box and click on the drive letter where the data disk is located.

7. Double-click on the desired filename {press the up or down arrow key to highlight the desired filename, Enter}.

   For example, double-click on the file named **food.pcx**.

Size the Graphic Image

8. If desired, size the graphic image by moving the mouse pointer onto the graphic image and clicking once. Move the mouse pointer to a black box at the edge or corner of the graphic image until a double-headed arrow displays. Press and hold the mouse button and drag until the graphic image is the desired size. Release the mouse button.

   For example, click on the **food.pcx** graphic image. Move the mouse pointer to the black box at the bottom center of the graphic image, press and hold the mouse button and drag up until the graphic image is approximately 1.5" in height.

Position the Frame

9. Select **Format, Frame** {Alt, o, m}.

10. Select the desired horizontal and vertical position for the frame.

    For example, set the horizontal position to **Left**, Relative To **Margin**. Set the vertical position to **Bottom**, Relative To **Margin**. Also, double-click in the **Distance from Text** box in the Vertical area and type **.15**.

11. Select **OK**.

Finish-Up Instructions

❖ Use the same filename **17shadow.doc** and save the file.

Create a Caption

Captions can be created for pictures, frames, tables, equations, etc. A caption always contains a label such as Figure or Table and a number. If desired, additional text can be added to the caption. For example, a caption might read, *Table 1 Upcoming Workshops*. The Position option in the Caption dialog box is used to place a caption above or below a selected item.

Word automatically numbers each caption. For example, when a caption is created for the first table in a document, the label "Table 1" is inserted. When a caption is added to another table in the document, the label "Table 2" is automatically inserted. Each type of label (Figure, Table, Equation, etc.) will have its own numbering sequence. For example, if your document contains captions *Table 1* and *Table 2* and you then insert a picture and create a caption using the *Figure* label, the new caption label will be *Figure 1*. Caption numbers are automatically updated as additional captions are inserted. If captioned items are moved or deleted, the remaining caption numbers will be updated when you select the entire document and press **F9** or when you print the document.

If desired, a new label can be created by selecting the **New Label** button in the Caption dialog box (see Figure 17.4) and by typing the desired label name. The numbering format for captions can be changed by selecting the **Numbering** button and choosing the desired numbering format, e.g., 1, 2, 3, or a, b, c.

The AutoCaption option in the Caption dialog box is used to tell Word to automatically create a caption for a specific type of object. For example, you can tell

Word to insert a caption as each table in a document is created. When the **Auto-Caption** option is selected, the AutoCaption dialog box displays. Select the type of object for which captions are to be automatically created and specify the label and number format.

Each time a caption is inserted, Word automatically applies the Caption style to the caption label, number, and any additional text that you insert. If desired, the caption style can be modified (see Chapter 15, page 359 for information on modifying styles).

Start-Up Instructions

- The file named **17shadow.doc** should be displayed in the document window.

Create a Caption

1. Select the item for which a caption is to be made.

   For example, select the table in column three on page 1.

2. Select **Insert, Caption** {Alt, i, i}.

   Note: The Caption dialog box displays. The label "Table 1" displays in the Caption box (See Figure 17.4).

3. Type the desired caption that will display with the label.

   For example, press the **Spacebar** once and type **Schedule of Upcoming Workshops**.

4. Click on the down arrow located to the right of the **Position** box and select the desired position for the caption.

   For example, select **Below Selected Item**.

5. Select **OK** {Enter}.

Finish-Up Instructions

- Select the label (i.e., Table 1) and the caption text. Change the font to **Footlight MT Light, 11 point**.
- Use the *new* filename **17page1.doc** and save the file on your file disk.
- If desired, print a copy of page 1 (select **File, Print**; in the Page Range area, select **Current Page**; select **OK**}.

FIGURE 17.4

Caption dialog box

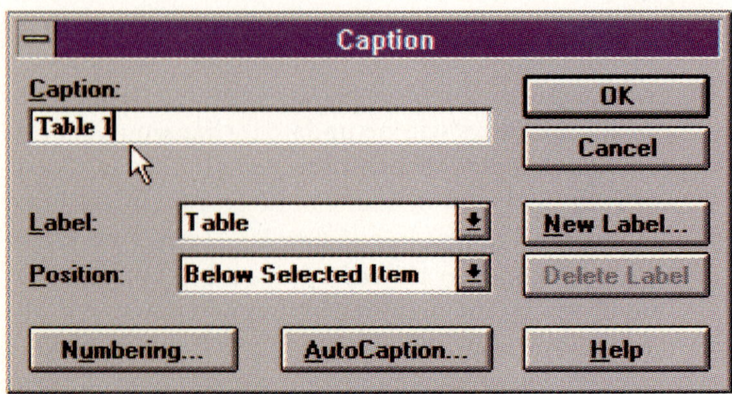

Start-Up Instructions

- ❖ The file named **17page1.doc** should be displayed in the document window.

Create a Dashed Border for a Tear Sheet

1. Select the text to be enclosed in the dashed box.

   For example, select all the text in column one on page 2.

2. Click on the **Borders** button to display the Borders Toolbar.
3. Click on the down arrow beside the Line Style box and select the **¾ pt dashed** line style.
4. Select the desired border button(s).

   For example, select the **Outside Border** button.

5. Select the **Borders** button again to remove the Borders Toolbar from the screen.

Finish-Up Instructions

- ❖ Move the mouse pointer away from the selected text and click once to deselect the text.
- ❖ Use the same filename **17page1.doc** and save the file.

Rotate Text and Reverse Text

Two special effects that can be created using Word are rotated text and reversed text. The WordArt program is used to rotate text. Text can be rotated in 1-degree increments between –360 and 360 degrees. After the rotated text has been created, a frame can be inserted around the text to position the text at the desired location on the page.

Reversed text (white text on a dark background) is accomplished by choosing a dark shading for a paragraph(s), frame, table, cell(s), or picture and then changing the color of the text to white. If the default foreground shading color, black, and the default background shading color, white, are used, Word automatically changes the color of the text in the selected paragraph(s), frame, table, or cell(s) to white. If a different foreground and/or background color is selected for the shading, the color of the text must be manually changed to white.

If desired, the color of the shading can be customized by specifying the foreground and background colors and choosing the desired percentage option on the Shading tab in the Paragraph, Frame, Cell, or Picture Borders and Shading dialog box. For example, to create a dark purple shading, select **Blue** as the Foreground color, select **Red** as the Background color, and choose the **70%** option.

Start-Up Instructions

- ❖ The file named **17page1.doc** should be displayed in the document window.
- ❖ Nonprinting characters should be displayed. If necessary, select the **Show/Hide** button.

❖ The insertion point should be located at the second blank line in column two on page 2.

Create Rotated Text Using WordArt

1. Select **Insert, Object** and double-click on **Microsoft WordArt 2.0**.

Note: The WordArt Toolbar and text box display.

2. Type the text to be rotated.

For example, type:

St. Mary's Community Hospital
4292 N. Adams St.
Marion, IN 46952

3. Select the **Special Effects** button on the WordArt Toolbar

Note: The Special Effects dialog box displays.

4. Type the desired rotation amount in the Rotation box.

For example, type **90**.

5. Select **OK**.

6. If desired, change the font of the text.

For example, select the down arrow beside the **Font** box and click on **Footlight MT Light**.

7. To remove the WordArt Toolbar and the text box, move the mouse pointer away from the WordArt and click once.

Note: The WordArt is selected (small boxes display at the corner and edges of the WordArt).

Position the WordArt

8. Select **Insert, Frame**.

9. Select **Format, Frame** and choose the desired horizontal and vertical position.

For example, set the Horizontal position to **Left**, Relative To **Column**. Set the Vertical position to **Bottom**, Relative To **Margin**.

10. Select **OK**.

Finish-Up Instructions

❖ Use the *new* filename **17page2.doc** and save the file on your file disk.

Start-Up Instructions

❖ The file named **17page2.doc** should be displayed in the document window.

❖ Place the insertion point to the left of the "S" in "St. Mary's" (column two, page 2).

❖ Insert a column break by selecting **Insert**, **Break**, **Column Break**, **OK**.

❖ Place the insertion point on the blank line below the words "St. Mary's Community Hospital."

- Insert the **medstaff.wmf** graphic image by selecting **Insert**, **Picture**. If necessary, select the drive and/or directory where the Word clipart files are stored. Double-click on **medstaff.wmf**.

Create Reversed Text

1. Select the text to be reversed.

   For example, in the third column on page 2, select the blank line above the address and the address, phone number, and the blank line below the phone number.

2. Select the **Borders** button ⊞ to display the Borders Toolbar.

3. Select the down arrow beside the **Shading** box and click on the desired shading option.

   For example, select **Solid (100%)**.

Change the Color of the Shading

4. Select **Format, Borders and Shading**.

5. Select the **Shading** tab.

6. Select the desired Foreground and/or Background color and click on the desired color.

   For example, select the down arrow located to the right of the **Foreground** box and click on **Blue**.

7. Select **OK**.

Change the Color of the Text

8. Select **Format, Font**.

9. Click in the **Color** box and click on the desired color.

   For example, click on **White**.

10. Select **OK**.

Finish-Up Instructions

- Change the color of the brochure title and sideheads to blue (select the desired text, select **Format, Font**, click in the **Color** box, click on **Blue**, select **OK**).
- Use the *new* filename **17final.doc** and save the file on your file disk.
- Print one copy of the tri-fold mailer brochure. Your final brochure should look similar to the tri-fold mailer brochure shown on page 414.

Community Health Workshops

St. Mary's Community Hospital is proud to present our "Aim for Wellness" series of health workshops. Our goal is to provide timely, convenient workshops that address the health concerns faced by everyone.

We look forward to seeing you at our upcoming workshops.

New Ways of Eating

This six-session program meets once a week to help you learn how to improve your health through a low-fat, low-cholesterol diet while still enjoying your food. Discussions will include tips on maintaining a healthy diet when dining out or traveling, spotting hidden fat and cholesterol on product labels, and healthy, good-tasting recipes. The cost of the workshop is $25.

Stress Management

This three-session program meets once a week to discuss how stress impacts your health and techniques and strategies for coping with stress. The cost of the workshop is $20.

Community CPR

Learn how you can save a life. This two-day workshop covers adult, child, and infant CPR. Also covered is the Heimlich maneuver for clearing airway obstructions for both adults and children. This workshop is free.

Enjoy a Health Life With Diabetes

This eight-session program meets twice a week to provide an overview of diabetes and strategies for controlling diabetes including diet, blood glucose monitoring, insulin, and medications. A personal diabetes management plan is developed for each participant. This workshop is free.

Fresh Start: Quit Smoking

Learn how to stop smoking and remain smoke-free. This eight-session program meets once a week to assist you to stop smoking and to resist the urge to begin again. Also covered are strategies for handling relapses. The cost of the workshop is $25.

Workshop	Starting Date
New Ways of Eating	April 16
Stress Management	May 1
Community CPR	June 5
Enjoy a Healthy Life With Diabetes	June 15
Fresh Start: Quit Smoking	June 30

Table 1 Schedule of Upcoming Workshops

Community Health Workshops

Name ____________________

Address ____________________

City ____________________

State/ZIP ____________________

Phone ____________________

Please sign me up for the following workshop(s):

___ New Ways of Eating
$25/person

___ Stress Management
$20/person

___ Community CPR
Free

___ Enjoy a Healthy Life With Diabetes
Free

___ Fresh Start: Quit Smoking
$25/person

Please return this form and payment to:

St. Mary's Community Hospital
4292 N. Adams St.
Marion, IN 46952

St. Mary's Community Hospital
4292 N. Adams St.
Marion, IN 46952

St. Mary's Community Hospital

Community Health Workshops

4292 N. Adams St.
Marion, IN 46952
317-555-9400

The Next Step

Chapter Review and Activities

Self-Check Quiz

T F 1. Information is printed on both sides of a tri-fold mailer brochure.

T F 2. When text is printed in landscape orientation, the top of the page is the 11-inch side.

T F 3. Previously created text cannot be inserted into a document.

T F 4. The horizontal position of a frame can be specified; however, the vertical position cannot be changed.

T F 5. Graphic images created using PC Paintbrush cannot be inserted into a Word document.

6. To update the remaining caption numbers when a captioned item is moved or deleted, select the entire document and press _____.
   a. **F9**
   b. **F1**
   c. **Enter**
   d. **Tab**

7. To insert existing text into a document, select ________, **File**, type or select the location and the name of the desired file, choose **OK**.
   a. **Open**
   b. **Insert**
   c. **Window**
   d. **File**

8. Using WordArt, text can be rotated in __________.
   a. 15-degree increments
   b. 90-degree increments
   c. 1-degree increments
   d. 45-degree increments

9. List the steps to create a caption for a table or frame.

10. The color of the shading for a paragraph, frame, table, cell, or picture can be customized by specifying the __________ and _________ colors and choosing the desired _________ option.

Chapter 17 Special Desktop Publishing Features

Enriching Language Arts Skills

Spelling/Vocabulary Words

demonstrate to prove; to display or operate.

techniques procedures by which a task is accomplished.

tuition a fee for instruction.

Parentheses

Parentheses can be used to set off nonessential expressions that might otherwise confuse the reader. The information within the parentheses provides supplemental information that has no direct bearing on the main idea of the sentence or paragraph. Words, phrases, or clauses can be enclosed within parentheses. Unless a comma, colon, or semicolon is necessary to the text within parentheses, place the punctuation outside the closing parenthesis. If the text within the parentheses is a complete sentence, the final period is placed within the parentheses.

Examples:

The actual gross sales for the quarter were $1,050,000 (compared with projected sales of $795,000).

If you are planning to attend the next sales conference (March 5), please contact the travel department immediately.

Several staff members will attend the sales conference next month. (The conference will be held in Hawaii.)

Activities

Activity 17.1—Create a Tri-Fold Mailer Brochure

1. Use the skills learned in this chapter and the following information to create the tri-fold mailer brochure shown on page 417.
   a. Use the *brochur1* template (select **File**, **New**, double-click on **Brochur1**).
   b. Set the number of columns to three and the spacing between columns to .9" (select **Format, Columns**; select **Three** in the Presets area; click on the up triangle beside the Spacing box until **.9** displays; select **OK**).
   c. Change the font for the Body Text style to **Footlight MT Light, 14 point** (select **Format**, **Style**; with the Body Text style name selected, choose **Modify**; select **Format, Font**; choose the desired font and size; select **OK** twice).
   d. Change the font for the Heading 1 style to **Britannic Bold, 16 point**. Change the spacing before the paragraph to **9 points**. (In the Style dialog box, select the **Heading 1** style, choose **Modify**; select **Format, Font**, choose the desired font and size, select **OK**; select **Format, Para-**

Safety Guidelines

Introduction

The Royal Equestrian Center is committed to the safety of our employees. Each year many employees are injured while on the job.

Most on-the-job injuries can be prevented or minimized by observing the safety practices outlined in this brochure. Two of the most common safety hazards are falls, trips, and slips and back injuries. If you find a safety hazard, inform your supervisor immediately. A safe work area benefits everyone.

Review these safety guidelines and apply them to your everyday activities, both on and off the job.

Falls, Trips, and Slips

Falls, trips, and slips are the most common types of accidents. Be aware of your surroundings and remember the following:

- ➔ Wipe up spills immediately.
- ➔ Pick up debris around your work area.
- ➔ Keep boxes, low-level cards, etc., out of doorways and away from traffic areas.
- ➔ Make sure that telephone and electrical cords are under desks or along walls.
- ➔ Open doors slowly. Watch for oncoming traffic.
- ➔ Report torn carpets, cracked tiles, etc.

Back Injuries

Back sprains usually result from improper lifting, bending, standing, or sitting. Your back is a complex mechanism that needs respectful handling.

- ➔ Practice good posture.
- ➔ Lift with your legs, not your back.
- ➔ Don't turn, twist, or bend to pick up objects even if they are light.
- ➔ Avoid slouching or slumping. Sit firmly against the back of chairs.
- ➔ Don't carry anything heavier than you can manage with ease.

Be Prepared

All accidents and emergencies cannot be eliminated. Therefore, it is important to be prepared for any accidents or emergencies.

- ➔ Keep emergency telephone numbers in a convenient location near your telephone.
- ➔ Know the location of the nearest emergency exit.
- ➔ Know where fire extinguishers are located and how to use them.
- ➔ Learn CPR, the Heimlich maneuver, and other first aid.

What to do if

There is a FIRE

- ♦ Report the fire to the fire department immediately.
- ♦ If possible, extinguish small fires using a fire extinguisher.
- ♦ Calmly evacuate the building. Make your way quickly and safely to the nearest emergency exit.
- ♦ If the room fills with smoke, get as close as possible to the floor.

There is an EARTHQUAKE

- ♦ Move away from windows and loose objects.
- ♦ Stand in a doorway or seek shelter under sturdy furniture.
- ♦ Do not use elevators or escalators.

There is an INJURY

- ♦ Call 911 for professional help immediately.
- ♦ Do not move the injured person unless there is danger of further injury.
- ♦ If you are trained, administer CPR or other first aid.

Using a Fire Extinguisher

Most of the fire extinguishers at the Royal Equestrian Center are type ABC all-purpose and can be operated using these instructions. Only fight fires if it is safe to do so and only after alerting the fire department of the situation. To operate a fire extinguisher, remember the following simple steps:

- ➔ Pull the pin or plastic loop.
- ➔ Aim the extinguisher so that it discharges at the base of the fire. Grip the handle and neck area for better control. Some units have a hose or horn.
- ➔ Squeeze the handles together.
- ➔ Sweep the base of the fire using a side-to-side motion. The sweeping motion pushes the flames away from you.

Royal Equestrian Center

1424 Equestrian Way
Athen, GA 30602
706-555-1242

Chapter 17 Special Desktop Publishing Features

graph, type **9 pt** in the **Spacing Before** box; select **OK** twice; select **Close**).

e. Make decisions regarding color for borders, shading, and text.

f. The text for the brochure is saved on the data disk under the filename **17act1.doc**.

g. The graphic file in the third column of the second page is named **horse.wmf** and is usually located in the Word *clipart* directory.

h. Enlarge the size of the graphic image. (Place the mouse pointer on the sizing handle at the bottom right corner of the graphic image until a double-headed arrow displays. Press and hold the mouse button while dragging down and to the right until the graphic image is approximately 2 1/2" tall and 1 3/4" wide. Release the mouse button.)

i. Select the address, city, state, zip, and phone number and create reversed text with a shaded background. [Select the text, select the **Borders** button, select the down arrow beside the **Shading** box and select **Solid (100%)**.]

j. Optional. Change the color of the shading for the reversed text. You choose the color. (Select **Format**, **Borders and Shading**. On the Shading tab, select the down arrow beside the **Foreground** box and choose the desired color. Select the down arrow beside the **Background** box and choose the desired color. Select the desired percentage option in the Shading area. Select **OK**. Select **Format**, **Font**. Select the down arrow beside the **Color** box and select **White**, select **OK**.)

2. Optional. Use the Drawing tools to turn the **horse.wmf** to face the opposite direction.

   a. Double-click on the **horse.wmf** graphic image.

   b. Select the **Select Drawing Objects** button and draw a rectangle around the entire graphic image to select all graphic objects that make up the **horse.wmf graphic** image.

   c. Select the **Flip Horizontal** button.

   d. Select **Close Picture** on the Picture Toolbar to return to the document window.

3. Use the filename **17actfin.doc** and save the file on your file disk.

4. Print one copy.

5. Close the document.

Challenge Your Skills

Skill 17.1—Create a Tri-Fold Mailer Brochure; Language Arts

1. Use the following information to create the tri-fold mailer brochure shown on page 419.

   a. Make decisions regarding:

      Margins
      Space between columns
      Colors for borders, shading, and text
      Font for title, headings, and brochure text
      Modifying styles
      Rotated and reversed text

   b. Suggested graphic images are **computer.wmf** and **1stplace.wmf**. These graphic images are usually stored in the Word *clipart* directory.

   c. The text for the brochure is saved on the data disk under the filename **17skill1.doc**.

   d. Create the following caption for the table located in the third column on page 1.

      Table 1 Upcoming Seminars

2. Correct three spelling errors and one parentheses error.
3. Use the filename **17skfin.doc** and save the file on your file disk.
4. Print one copy.
5. If you have completed your work in Word, exit the program.

Learn How to Create the Ultimate Newsletter

This two-day seminar for marketing professionals, salespeople, fundraisers, and writers will introduce you to techniques for designing and producing newsletters with impact.

Imagine going back to the office with powerful techniques to assist you in quickly and effortlessly putting together your next newsletter. You'll have all the skills you need to produce a visually attractive newsletter that will grab the attention of all your readers (without breaking your budget.)

Learn to Write Like a Pro

Learn proven copywriting tips that will assist you in writing informative and interesting articles. The seminar will also cover how to create effective, attention-grabbing headlines that draw readers to your newsletter. You will also learn how to stretch (or shrink) copy to fit and to overcome "writer's" block in order to meet the deadline.

The seminar will also introduce you to resources for "filler" articles and art and provide specific guidelines on how to hire freelance writers to assist you with articles.

Once the Articles Are Written

Anyone that produces a newsletter knows that having the articles is only half the battle. On day two of this seminar, we will discuss editing techniques, design concerns, and obtaining the necessary approvals before publication. We will also explore the computer equipment and software needed to produce a professional-looking newsletter.

We will also demonstrate the effective use of photographs, graphs, and charts in newsletters and discuss affordable sources of artwork and clipart.

Baltimore	June 15-16
Minneapolis	August 1-2
Pittsburgh	September 3-4
St. Louis	October 14-15

Table 1 Upcoming Seminars

Register Today

Seminar Tuition
$225 per person

Name: ________________

Address: ________________

City: ________________

State/ZIP: ________________

Phone: ________________

Please sign me up for the following seminar:

___ Baltimore June 15-16
___ Minneapolis August 1-2
___ Pittsburgh September 3-4
___ St. Louis October 14-15

Please return this form with payment to:

Design Associates
4692 Lafayette St.
Salem, MA 01970

Design Associates
4692 Lafayette St.
Salem, MA 01970

Design Associates

Create the Ultimate Newsletter

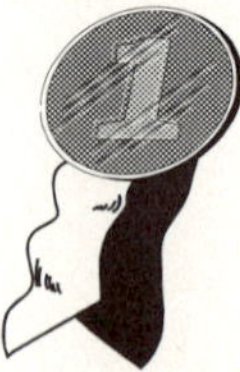

Learn Proven Ways to Make Your Newsletter Better

4692 Lafayette St.
Salem, MA 01970
508-555-1399

CHAPTER 18

Create a Magazine Article

Features Covered

- Create a pull quote
- Create unequal column widths
- Create odd and even page headers/footers
- Create drop caps
- Automatically indent the first line of paragraphs
- Use correct typographic symbols for quote marks and em dashes

Objectives and Introduction

After successfully completing this chapter, you will be able to create columns of unequal widths, different footers for odd and even pages, and drop caps. In addition, you will learn how to automatically indent each paragraph in a document, create frames for and format pull quotes and sidebar text, and use typographic symbols for quotation marks and em dashes.

Word 6.0 for Windows has continued to incorporate and enhance many of the functions that have traditionally been accomplished through the use of typesetting or desktop publishing programs. In this chapter, you will perform many desktop publishing functions that are used to enhance publications such as magazine articles.

Create a Magazine Article

Before beginning to create a magazine article, decisions need to be made regarding the graphic images to be included, the number of columns, and the widths of columns. Also, decisions will be made concerning the use of special fonts and other effects such as borders and shading.

Many articles also include pull quotes and sidebars. A pull quote is a small portion of the article text that is excerpted from the article and placed in a separate frame. The purpose of a pull quote is to attract attention to the article. Therefore, the font of the pull quote text is often changed and/or enlarged. Also, borders are usually placed above, below, or around the text to set the quote off from the article text.

A sidebar is a box or area that contains information that is related to the article text. The purpose of a sidebar is to further explain a subject covered in the article or to provide additional statistics or information that may interest the reader.

One of the main purposes of a magazine article's format is to entice people to read the article. Therefore, special text effects (created using WordArt) and drop caps are used to add visual interest. Also, graphic images or pictures are often included in a magazine article to enhance page appearance or to illustrate the article's key points.

Start-Up Instructions

- Open the file named **18drill1.doc** located on the data disk.
- The Page Layout view should be used. (If necessary, select the **Page Layout** button or choose **View**, **Page Layout**.)
- Select the down arrow beside the **Zoom Control** box and choose **Whole Page**.

Create a Frame for Pull Quote Text

1. Select **Insert, Frame.**
2. Move the mouse pointer to the location where the frame containing the pull quote text should be placed. Press and hold the mouse button while dragging down and to the right to draw a rectangle. Release the mouse button when the rectangle is the desired size.

    For example, move the mouse pointer to approximately the center of the page, press and hold the mouse button and drag down and to the right to draw a rectangle approximately $2\frac{1}{4}$" wide and 1"deep. Release the mouse button.

3. If necessary, click on an edge of the frame to select the frame.

    Note: *Sizing handles (small black boxes) display at the corners and edges of the frame.*

4. Select **Format, Frame.**
5. Select the desired horizontal and vertical position for the frame.

    For example:

    a. In the Horizontal area, select **Center** in the Position box and select **Margin** in the Relative To box.

    b. In the Vertical area, double-click in the **Position** box and type **6.2**. Select **Page** in the Relative To box.

6. If desired, set the space between the frame and text by specifying the Distance from Text in the Horizontal and/or Vertical area.

    For example, **0.13**" should display in the Distance from Text in the Horizontal area. In the Vertical area, double-click in the Distance from Text box and type **.1**.

7. If desired, set the width and height for the frame.

For example:

a. To set an exact width for the pull quote frame, double-click in the **At** box located to the right of the Width box and type **2.35**.

b. To set the minimum (At Least) height for the pull quote frame, double-click in the **At** box located to the right of the Height box and type .75.

8. Select **OK**.

Place a Border Above and Below a Frame

9. With the frame selected, click on the **Border** button to display the Borders Toolbar.

10. Select the **No Border** button to clear any existing border.

11. Click in the **Line Style** box and select the desired line style.

For example, select the **2¼ pt** single line style.

12. Select the desired border button(s).

For example, select the **Top Border** and **Bottom Border** buttons.

13. If desired, shade the frame by selecting the down arrow beside the Shading box and choosing a shading option.

For example, in the **Shading** box, select the **10%** shading option.

14. Type, copy, or insert the desired text for the pull quote.

For example, select the down arrow beside the **Zoom Control** box and choose **100%**. Select and copy the first sentence (i.e., How much . . .) below the heading The Consumer's Challenge . . . located on page 2. Click in the pull quote frame on page 1 and select the **Paste** button.

15. Format the pull quote text.

For example, select the pull quote text and change the font to **Bold, 14 point**. Change the alignment to **Center**.

Note: *The height of the pull quote frame will increase if necessary to accommodate the text.*

Finish-Up Instructions

- Use the *new* filename **18pull.doc** and save the file on your file disk.
- Continue with the Steps to Create Unequal Column Widths.

Create Unequal Column Widths

Until now, only equal width newspaper columns have been created. However, it is also possible to create columns with different widths. When creating columns with different widths, it is important to remember that the total of the widths of all columns and the space between columns should equal the width of the page minus the margins. For example, if the default 1.25" left and right margins are used, the total of all columns and the space between columns should equal 6 inches.

In the Columns dialog box, Word has two preset options for creating unequal column widths, i.e., **Left** and **Right**. When the **Left** or **Right** preset option is selected, Word automatically creates a two-column layout with one wide column and one narrow column and .5" of space between the columns. If desired, the number of columns, widths of the columns, and the space between the columns can be changed. When the number of columns, the width of a column(s), or the space between columns is changed Word automatically recalculates the width of the other column(s).

Also, after the number of columns has been selected, the width of each column can be changed using the horizontal Ruler. To adjust the width of a column using the Ruler, move the mouse pointer to middle of the column marker between the columns, press and hold the mouse button, drag to the desired width, and release the mouse button. To change the space between two columns, place the mouse pointer on the left or right edge of the column marker, press and hold the mouse button and drag left or right to increase or decrease the space between the two columns.

Start-Up Instructions

- The file named **18pull.doc** should be displayed in the document window.
- The Page Layout view should be used. (If necessary, select the **Page Layout** button or choose **View**, **Page Layout**.)

Create Unequal Column Widths

1. Select the text to be placed in columns

   For example, select all of the article text beginning with the first sentence "Multimedia. Probably no . . ."

2. Select **Format, Columns** {Alt, o, c}.
3. Select the desired number of columns in the Presets area.

   For example, select the **Right** option in the Presets area to create two columns, with the left column wider than the right column {Alt and r}.

Note: In the Preview area, Word displays a wide left column and a narrow right column (see Figure 18.1).

FIGURE 18.1

Columns dialog box

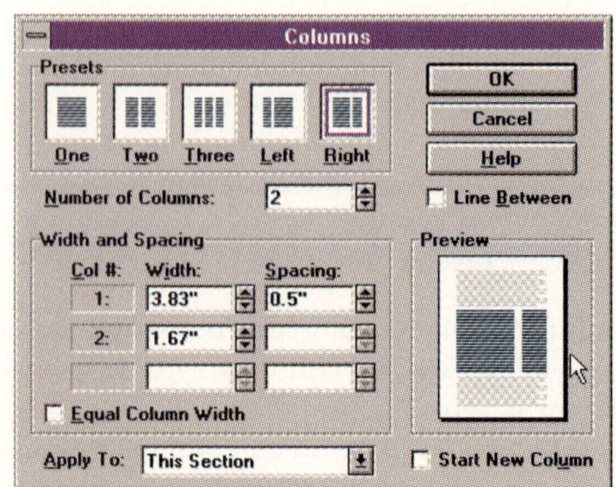

Change the Preset Column Widths

4. Click on the up or down triangle beside the Col # 1 Width box, or double-click in the Col # 1 Width box and type the desired width {press the Tab key until the figure in the Col # 1 Width box is highlighted, type the desired column width}.

   For example, click on the down triangle twice to display **3.7"**.

5. To change the amount of space between column 1 and column 2, click on the up or down triangle located to the right of the **Spacing** box until the desired spacing displays, or double-click in the **Spacing** box and type the desired spacing {Alt and s, press the up or down arrow key to display the desired spacing amount}.

   For example, click on the down triangle twice to display **0.3"**.

   Note: *As the space between columns is changed, Word automatically recalculates the width of column 2. Column 2 should have a width of 2".*

6. When all column widths have been set, select **OK** {Enter}.

   Note: *To view the columns, select the down arrow beside the* ***Zoom Control*** *box and choose* ***Whole Page****. Select the down arrow beside the* ***Zoom Control*** *box again and choose* ***100%****.*

Finish-Up Instructions

- Use the same filename **18pull.doc** and save the file.

Create Headers/Footers for Odd and Even Pages

If desired, different headers and/or footers can be created for odd and even pages of a document. Different headers/footers are often created when the pages of a document will be printed on both sides of the paper (back to back). For example, different footers have been created for the even and odd pages of this book. As you look at the footers of this book, notice that the page numbers are printed at the left margin on even-numbered pages and at the right margin on odd-numbered pages.

Start-Up Instructions

- The file named **18pull.doc** should be displayed in the document window.
- The insertion point should be located at the beginning of the document (**Ctrl** and **Home**).

Create Headers/Footers for Odd and Even Pages

1. Select **View, Header and Footer** {Alt, v, h}.
2. Select the **Page Setup** button on the Header and Footer Toolbar {Alt, f, u}.

   Note: *The Layout tab of the Page Setup dialog box displays.*

3. Select **Different Odd and Even** in the Headers and Footers area {Alt and o}.
4. Select **OK** {Enter}.
5. If necessary, select the **Switch Between Header and Footer** button on the Header and Footer Toolbar to switch to the footer pane {press the down arrow key until the desired pane displays}.

   For example, select the **Switch Between Header and Footer** button to display the Odd Page Footer pane.

6. Type and format the header/footer text.

   For example:

   a. Type **Applications of Information Technology**. (Do not type the period.)

   b. Press the **Tab** key twice to move the insertion point to the right margin.

   c. Select the **Page Numbers** button on the Header and Footer Toolbar {Alt, i, e; Alt and n, press the down arrow key to highlight the word Page, Enter}.

   d. Select the footer text and change the font size to **10 point**.

7. Select the **Show Next** button to move the insertion point to the Even Page Footer pane {press the down arrow key until the desired pane displays}.
8. Type and format the desired header/footer text.

   a. Select the **Page Numbers** button {Alt, i, e; Alt and n, press the down arrow to highlight the word Page, Enter}.

   b. Press the **Tab** key twice.

   c. Type **Multimedia: Teaching the Computer to Sing and Dance**. (Do not type the period.)

   Note: *The text may extend beyond the right margin. That's OK.*

   d. Select the footer text and change the font size to **10 point**.

   Note: *The footer text should now display within the footer pane.*

9. Select **Close** on the Header and Footer Toolbar {Alt and Shift and c}.

Finish-Up Instructions

- Use the *new* filename **18footer.doc** and save the file on your file disk.
- Continue with the Steps to Create a Drop Cap.

Create a Drop Cap

A drop cap is a special effect that is often used in the first paragraph of an article or at the beginning of key sections in a document. The first character of the first word in a paragraph is enlarged and the remaining text is indented to allow space for the enlarged character. Word provides two positions for drop cap characters: **Dropped** and **In Margin**. The **Dropped** position option places the character within the margin, and the **In Margin** position option places the drop cap character in the left margin.

When a drop cap is created, the character is placed in a frame. The amount of space between the frame and the paragraph text can be set by typing the desired amount in the **Distance from Text** box in the Drop Cap dialog box. Often the font for the drop cap character is changed to provide a contrast between the drop cap character and the paragraph text. The font of the drop cap character can be specified in the Drop Cap dialog box. The size of the drop cap character is automatically determined by Word based on the number of lines the character is to be dropped. For example, if a large drop cap character is desired, increase the number of lines that the character is to be dropped in the Lines to Drop box.

Start-Up Instructions

- The file named **18footer.doc** should be displayed in the document window.

Create a Drop Cap

1. Select the character that will become a drop cap.

   For example, select the **M** in the word Multimedia in the first sentence of the body text.

2. Select **Format, Drop Cap** {Alt, o, d}.

   Note: *The Drop Cap dialog box displays (see Figure 18.2).*

3. Select the desired Position for the drop cap letter.

   For example, select **Dropped** {d}.

4. Select the desired font for the drop cap letter.

   For example, select **Colonna MT**.

5. Type or select the number of lines the letter should be dropped.

   For example, select the down triangle next to the **Lines to Drop** box once to display **2**.

6. If desired, specify a distance between the drop cap letter and the other letters.

   For example, double-click in the **Distance from Text** box and type **.05**.

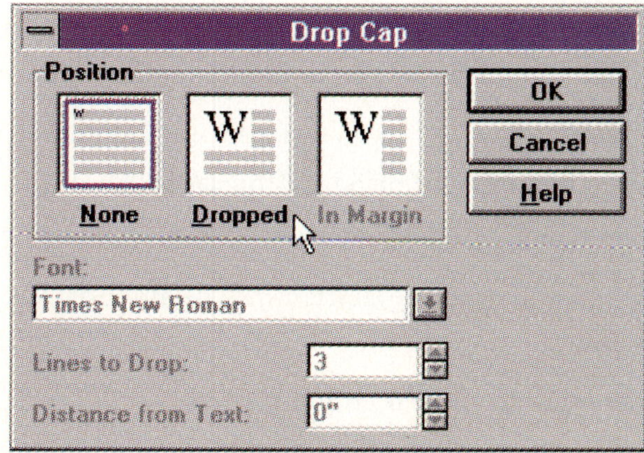

FIGURE 18.2

Drop Cap dialog box

Chapter 18 Create a Magazine Article

7. Select **OK**.

Note: The drop cap letter displays in the document window. The drop cap letter has been automatically placed in a frame.

Finish-Up Instructions

- Use the same filename **18footer.doc** and save the file.
- Continue with the Steps to Automatically Indent the First Line of Paragraphs.

Automatically Indent the First Line of Paragraphs

To save space, the first line of each paragraph is indented so that an extra blank line is not needed between paragraphs. The first line of each paragraph can be indented manually by moving the insertion point to the beginning of each paragraph and pressing the **Tab** key. However, the first line of each paragraph can be automatically indented by changing the style that was used to format the paragraphs. For example, the Body Text style can be modified to indent the first line of each body text paragraph .25" and to delete the space after the paragraphs. Once the Body Text style has been modified, all the paragraphs that are formatted with the Body Text style will be indented automatically.

Start-Up Instructions

- The file named **18footer.doc** should be displayed in the document window.

Automatically Indent the First Line of Paragraphs

1. Place the insertion point in a paragraph that is currently formatted with the desired style.

   For example, place the insertion point in the first paragraph below the heading **Multimedia--A Definition**.

   Note: The Body Text style has been applied to this paragraph and other paragraphs of the article.

2. Select **Format, Style** {Alt, o, s}.
3. If necessary, click on the name of the style to be modified.

   For example, the style name **Body Text** should be highlighted.

4. Select **Modify** {Alt and m}.
5. In the Modify Style dialog box, select **Format, Paragraph** {Alt o, p}.
6. On the Indents and Spacing tab, click in the **Special** box and select **First Line**.
7. Double-click in the **By** box and type the desired indent amount.

   For example, type **.25**.

8. If desired, make other changes to the paragraph format.

For example, set the Spacing After to **0** pt (zero).

9. Select **OK** twice. Select **Close**.

   ***Note:** The first line of all paragraphs in the article that had been formatted with the Body Text style are now indented.*

Finish-Up Instructions

- Use the *new* filename **18indent.doc** and save the file on your file disk.
- Continue with the Steps to Create a Sidebar Frame and to Insert Text.

Start-Up Instructions

- The file named **18indent.doc** should be displayed in the document window.
- The Page Layout view should be used. (If necessary, select the **Page Layout** button or choose **View, Page Layout.**)

Create a Sidebar Frame and to Insert Text

1. Display the page on which the frame will be placed and click once to place the insertion point anywhere on the page.

   For example, select the down arrow beside the **Zoom Control** box and choose **Whole Page**. Scroll down to display page 2. Click once to place the insertion point on page 2.

2. Select **Insert, Frame.**

3. Draw a frame at the desired location on the page.

   For example, draw a frame at the bottom of the page that extends from the left margin to the right margin and is approximately 3.75' tall (see Figure 18.3).

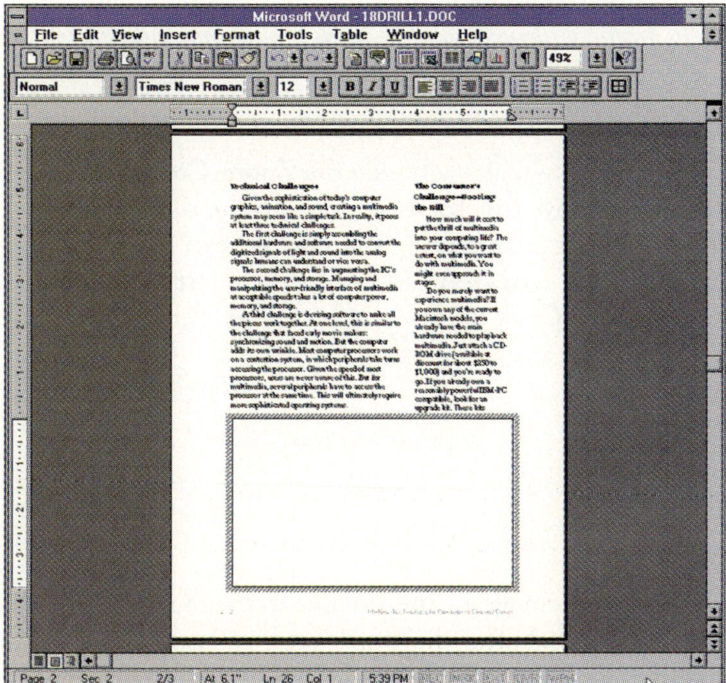

FIGURE 18.3

Sidebar frame

4. If necessary, click on the edge of the frame to select the frame. Select **Format, Frame** and set the horizontal and vertical position and the distance from text for the frame.

   For example:

   a. In the Horizontal area, select **Center** in the Position box and select **Margin** in the Relative To box.

   b. In the Vertical area, select **Bottom** in the Position box and select **Margin** in the Relative To box. Also, double-click in the **Distance from Text** box and type **.1**.

5. Set the width and height of the frame.

   For example:

   a. Double-click in the **At** box located to the right of the Width box and type **5.75**. (Exactly should display in the Width box.)

   b. Double-click in the **At** box located to the right of the Height box and type **3.75**. (At Least should display in the Height box.)

6. Select **OK**.

7. If desired, place a border around the frame.

   For example, select **Format, Borders and Shading**. Select **Shadow** in the Presets area. Choose the **3 pt** line style in the Style area. Click on the up triangle beside the **From Text** box until **6 pt** displays. Select **OK**.

8. Type or insert the desired information in the frame.

   For example, insert the file named **18side1.doc** located on the data disk by selecting **Insert, File**. (If necessary, select the drive/directory where the data disk is located.) Double-click on the file named **18side1.doc**.

   Note: *The height of the frame will increase if necessary to accommodate the inserted text.*

9. Format the text within the frame and insert a graphic image if desired.

   For example, select the down arrow beside the **Zoom Control** box and select **100%**. Move the insertion point to the right of the final period in the last paragraph of the sidebar text. Insert the graphic image named **notes.wmf** (select **Insert, Picture**, double-click on **notes.wmf**). Click on the graphic image. Select **Format, Picture**. Change the size as follows:

   Width: .6"
   Height: .15"

10. Select **OK**.

Finish-Up Instructions

❖ Select the **notes.wmf** graphic image in the sidebar frame. Select the **Copy** button. Click to right of the period after the word "studios" at the end of the article text. Select the **Paste** button to insert a copy of the graphic image at the end of the article text.

- Use the *new* filename **18sidebr.doc** and save the file on your file disk.

Use Correct Typographic Symbols for Quote Marks and Em Dashes

In the past when using a typewriter, the quotation mark (") has been used in place of the correct opening (“) and closing (”) quotation marks. Also, two hyphens (--) have been used to indicate a dash in place of the correct em dash (—). Because these (“, ”), and — characters are not available on keyboards, often " and -- are still used when creating text on the computer.

The Smart Quotes feature can be used to convert straight single or double quotation marks ' or " to paired quotation marks (‘ ’ or “ ”). If the Smart Quotes feature is enabled before typing text, the quotation marks are automatically converted as text is typed. If the Smart Quotes feature is enabled after text has been typed, the Replace feature can be used to search for straight quotation marks (either ' or ") and insert the appropriate opening or closing quotation marks. To determine if the Smart Quotes feature is enabled, select **Tools, AutoCorrect**. If an X displays beside the **Change 'Straight Quotes' to ‘Smart Quotes’** option, the Smart Quotes feature is enabled.

The Replace feature can also be used to search for double hyphens (--) and insert the em dash (—) character. By selecting the **Special** button in the Replace dialog box special characters such as em dashes can be inserted into either the Find What or Replace With boxes in the Replace dialog box.

Start-Up Instructions

- The file named **18sidebr.doc** should be displayed in the document window.

Enable “Smart Quotes” and Use Replace to Insert Correct Typographic Symbols

1. Select **Tools, AutoCorrect** {Alt, t, a}.
2. Check that the **Change 'Straight Quotes' to ‘Smart Quotes’** option is selected. (If necessary, select the **Change 'Straight Quotes' to ‘Smart Quotes'** option.)
3. Select **OK**.
4. Place the insertion point at the beginning of the text to be searched.

   For example, press **Ctrl** and **Home** to place the insertion point at the beginning of the document.
5. Select **Edit, Replace** {Alt, e, e}.
6. In the Find What box, type a quotation mark (").
7. In the Replace With box, type a quotation mark (").
8. Select **Replace All**.

Note: When all straight quotation marks have been converted to opening (") and closing (") quotation marks, a message box displays indicating that the document has been searched and showing the number of replacements made.

9. Select **OK**.
10. Select **Close** to remove the Replace dialog box from the screen.

Finish-Up Instructions

- ❖ Use the same filename **18sidebr.doc** and save the file.

Start-Up Instructions

- ❖ The file named **18sidebr.doc** should be displayed in the document window.

Convert Typed Characters to Correct Typographic Symbols

1. Place the insertion point at the beginning of the text to be searched.

   For example, if necessary, press **Ctrl** and **Home** to place the insertion point at the beginning of the document.

2. Select **Edit, Replace** {Alt, e, e}.
3. In the Find What box, type the character(s) to be replaced.

   For example, type -- (two hyphens).

4. Double-click in the **Replace With** box.
5. Select the **Special** button at the bottom of the Replace dialog box.

   Note: A list of special characters displays.

6. Select the desired character.

   For example, select **Em Dash**.

   Note: A special code ^+, which represents an em dash (—), displays in the Replace With box.

7. Select **Replace All**.

   Note: When all double hyphens have been changed to em dashes (—), a message box displays indicating that the document has been searched and the number of replacements made.

8. Select **OK**.
9. Select **Close** to remove the Replace dialog box from the screen.

Finish-Up Instructions

- ❖ Use the *new* filename **18fin1.doc** and save the file on your file disk.

  Note: Your final document should look similar to the magazine article shown on page 433.

- ❖ Print one copy.
- ❖ Close the document.

Multimedia

Teaching the Computer to Sing and Dance

Multimedia. Probably no other "buzzword" is causing as much excitement today. To understand the excitement, just consider the "show biz" appeal of these few examples.

- *Microsoft Bookshelf for Windows*, a single CD-ROM disk contains seven reference works, including a "talking" dictionary that demonstrates correct pronunciations and a book of quotations that includes digitized recordings of such luminaries as John F. Kennedy, an atlas that plays every country's national anthem, and a concise encyclopedia illustrated with high-resolution graphics and narrated animations showing how certain processes work. And, like any computer file, the CD-ROM can be searched by key word or phrase, taking a lot of the tedium out of research. *Bookshelf* is just one of a growing list of multimedia software titles that merge entertainment and education.
- A computerized information kiosk at the Montreux Jazz Festival allowed users to call up biographies, photos, and performance videos of all the performers.
- Thousands of workers are now learning Microsoft Word, Lotus 1-2-3, and other popular applications via interactive multimedia tutorials that are enlivened with music, graphics, and motion. A 1990 Department of Defense study concluded that such tutorials take about a third less time, cost about a third less, and are more effective than traditional training methods.

How much will it cost to put the thrill of multimedia into your computing life?

The lure and range of such applications have sparked predictions that a multimedia revolution is just over the horizon. The revolution is still in the making, though, in part because multimedia generates almost as much confusion as excitement.

Multimedia—A Definition

One source of confusion is the misuse of the term multimedia itself. You may see it used to describe everything from an animated, talking, and singing children's book on CD-ROM to a high-resolution monitor. Although there's no official definition, most computer experts agree that Multimedia refers to a computer system that lets users access and interact with computerized text, high-resolution still graphics, motion visuals, and sound. Three elements in particular distinguish multimedia—sound, motion, and the opportunity for interaction.

Technical Challenges

Given the sophistication of today's computer graphics, animation, and sound, creating a multimedia system may seem like a simple task. In reality, it poses at least three technical challenges.

The first challenge is simply assembling the additional hardware and software needed to convert the digitized signals of light and sound into the analog signals humans can understand or vice versa.

The second challenge lies in augmenting the PC's processor, memory, and storage. Managing and manipulating the user-friendly interface of multimedia at acceptable speeds takes a lot of computer power, memory, and storage.

A third challenge is devising software to make all the pieces work together. At one level, this is similar to the challenge that faced early movie makers: synchronizing sound and motion. But the computer adds its own wrinkle. Most computer processor work on a contention system, in which peripherals take turns accessing the processor. Given the speed of most processors, users are never aware of this. But for multimedia, several peripherals have to access the processor at the same time. This will ultimately require more sophisticated operating systems.

The Consumer's Challenge—Footing the Bill

How much will it cost to put the thrill of multimedia into your computing life? The answer depends, to a great extent, on what you want to do with multimedia. You might even approach it in stages.

Do you merely want to experience multimedia? If you own any of the current Macintosh models, you already have the main hardware needed to play back multimedia. Just attach a CD-ROM drive (available at discount for about $400 to $1,000) and you're ready to go. If you already own a reasonably powerful IBM-PC compatible, look for an

A Confusion of Standards

Both consumers and software developers are confused by the lack of standards for multimedia. To a great extent, computer standards are forged in the marketplace: the companies the garner the largest market share set a de facto standard that others follow. The IBM PC and Microsoft MS-DOS are good examples. At this point a number of players are set to battle it out.

Apple Computer maintains that its Macintosh modes are multimedia-ready. With the bundled authoring system of HyperCard, many users are already developing their own multimedia applications. Macintosh multimedia applications have an especially strong presence in education. Another highly publicized standard has been proposed by Multimedia PC Marketing Council, a trade organization made up of Microsoft and a numbers of major hardware vendors. Like the VHS logo on a videotape, the MPC logo is meant to reassure consumers and establish a multimedia platform.

IBM, the industry giant, is pursuing its own course. Its first multimedia PC users both Windows and OS/2 in tandem, and the company is currently developing a number of multimedia configurations that will target a variety of business and educational customers.

upgrade kit. These kits contain a CD-ROM drive an audio board (and sometimes external speakers or headphones) and Microsoft Windows with Multimedia Extensions, which provides a software-based method of playing back motion. Such kits average about $1,000. Or, if you need to upgrade your computer anyway, consider paying 10% to 30% more for one of the emerging multimedia computers, which comes with multimedia hardware already built in. At this point, you will probably still be playing multimedia titles, which cost from $70 to $600 each.

The next stage comes when you decide to develop multimedia applications—either your own multimedia title, a computer-based tutorial, or a business presentation. At this point, you many need to invest in additional hardware, such as a microphone, tape cassette player, CD-audio player, or music synthesizer (for inputting sound); a color scanner, video camera, videocassette recorder, and video board (for inputting and manipulating still and motion graphics, including input to and output from a television set); plus software for creating graphics and animation, as well as an authoring system. An authoring system is software that lets nonprogrammers use English-like commands to create interactive computer programs. One popular authoring system is HyperCard; it is bundled with all Macintosh computers. Similar, relatively inexpensive authoring and presentation software is available for IBM-PC compatibles. More sophisticated authoring software costs as much as $8,000. Some multimedia developers have invested more than $50,000 in their studios.

Reprinted with permission from Introduction to Computers and Information Systems by Larry Long, Prentice Hall, 1994.

The Next Step

Chapter Review and Activities

Self-Check Quiz

T F 1. When the number of columns, the width of a column(s), or the space between columns is changed, Word automatically recalculates the width of the other column(s).

T F 2. Once the number of unequal width columns is selected, the width of each column can be changed by using the horizontal Ruler.

T F 3. When a drop cap letter is created, the character is placed in a frame.

T F 4. When "Smart Quotes" is enabled, straight double quotation marks (") can be changed to typographically correct opening (") and closing (") quotation marks by using the Replace feature.

5. The Presets option(s) for creating unequal width columns is/are________.
   a. Left
   b. Right
   c. Top
   d. both a and b

6. Different headers and footers are often created when the pages of a document are printed on ________________.
   a. both sides of the paper
   b. one side of the paper
   c. neither of these

7. Word provides two positions for drop cap characters. The two positions are__________.
   a. Dropped and In Margin
   b. Dropped and Out of Margin
   c. Dropped and Above Margin

8. The ______________ command is used to automate the process of creating drop cap letters.
   a. **File, Drop Cap**
   b. **Format, Drop Cap**
   c. **Tools, Drop Cap**

9. List one purpose for indenting the first lines of each paragraph.

10. A pull quote is a small portion of text excerpted from an article and placed in a separate ______________.

Enriching Language Arts Skills

Spelling/Vocabulary Words

repetitive repeated action; redundant; continual; unending.

symptoms an indication of change in bodily sensation or function that indicates a disorder or abnormality.

trauma a bodily injury that has a lasting mental or physical effect; breakdown; wound.

Em and En Dashes

The em dash (—), a typographic symbol about the width of the character m, is often used in place of a comma. Press the hyphen key twice (--) to create a dash on a typewriter or computer keyboard. Many software programs provide a method to create typographically correct em dashes (see page 432). The en dash (–), a typographic symbol about the width of the character n, is used as a hyphen or as a substitute for the word "to," e.g., July–September. The correct typographic symbols for em and en dashes have traditionally been used for books, newspapers, and advertisements, and are recommended for use when creating a professional-looking document.

Examples:

em dash *Our notebook sales have increased 20 percent since last year—from $50,000 to $60,000.*

en dash *The annual report for fiscal year 1995–96 will be available at the end of April.*

Activities

Activity 18.1—Create a Magazine Article

1. Open the file named **18act1.doc** located on the data disk.
2. With the insertion point located at the top of the document, insert the graphic image named **atomengy.wmf** located in the Word clipart directory (select **Insert**, **Picture**, double-click on **atomengy.wmf**).
3. Place a frame around the graphic image (click on the graphic image and select **Insert**, **Frame**).
4. Select **Format**, **Frame**. In the Text Wrapping area, select **None**. Select **OK**.
5. Create the article title using WordArt and the following information:
    a. Place the insertion point on the blank line below the graphic image.
    b. Select **Insert**, **Object** and double-click on **Microsoft WordArt 2.0**.
    c. Type **Weekend Astronauts**. Change the font to **Britannic Bold**.
    d. Click in the **Line and Shape** box (the first button on the WordArt Toolbar) and select the **Inflate (Top)** shape.
    e. Click in the **Size** box (next to the Font box) and select **30**.
    f. Select the **Shadow** button and select the second shadow option in row 1.

g. Click away from the WordArt to return to the document window.

h. With the WordArt selected in the document windows, select **Insert, Frame** to place a frame around the WordArt.

i. Select **Format, Frame.** In the Horizontal area, select **Right** in the Position box. Select **Margin** in the Relative To box. In the Vertical area, select **Top** in the Position box. Select **Margin** in the Relative To box. Select **OK.**

6. Select the article text beginning "Are you ready . . ." to the end of the document.

7. Select **Format, Columns** and create two columns using the **Left** option in the Presets box. Change the width of Col # 1 to **2.25"** and the spacing between columns to **.4"**. Select **OK.**

8. Create footers for odd and even pages using the following information:

   a. Select **View, Header and Footer.**

   b. Select the **Page Setup** button and choose **Different Odd and Even.** Select **OK.**

   c. Select the **Switch Between Header and Footer** button to display the Odd Page Footer pane.

   d. In the Odd Page Footer pane, type **Spacefarers Monthly**. Press the **Tab** key twice and select the **Page Numbers** button. Select the footer text and change the font to **Britannic Bold, 10 point.**

   e. Select the **Show Next** button.

   f. In the Even Page Footer pane, select the **Page Numbers** button. Press the **Tab** key twice and type **Weekend Astronauts**. Select the footer text and change the font to **Britannic Bold, 10 point.**

   g. Select **Close** on the Header and Footer Toolbar.

9. Insert a frame for the pull quote text.

   a. Select **Insert, Frame.**

   b. Move the mouse pointer to the center of page 1 and draw a rectangle approximately **2.75"** in width and **1"** in height.

   c. Select and copy the text **Who is made of the "right stuff"? Everyone.** located in the first paragraph in column 2 on page 1.

   d. Click in the pull quote frame and select the **Paste** button.

   e. Change the font of the pull quote text to **Britannic Bold, 24 point.** Change the alignment of the pull quote text to **Center.**

   f. Select the pull quote frame. If necessary, click on the **Borders** button to display the Borders Toolbar. Click on the **No Border** button.

   g. Click in the **Line Style** box and select the **1½ pt** double-line style. Click on the **Top Border** and **Bottom Border** buttons.

   h. Select **Format, Frame.** In the Horizontal area, select **Center** in the Position box and select **Page** in the Relative To box. In the Vertical area, select **Center** in the Position box, select **Margin** in the Relative To box, and double-click in the **Distance from Text** box and type **.05**. Select **OK.**

10. Create a drop cap for the first character of the first paragraph. (Select the first character in the first paragraph of the article text. Select **Format**, **Drop Cap**. Select the **Dropped** option. Change the font to **Britannic Bold**. Double-click in the **Distance from Text** box and type **.05**. Select **OK.**)

11. Modify the Body Text style so that the first lines of the Body Text paragraphs are indented .35" and there is no spacing after the paragraphs.
    a. Place the insertion point in a paragraph that has been formatted with the Body Text style.
    b. Select **Format**, **Style**. With the Body Text style highlighted in the Styles list, select **Modify**.
    c. Select **Format**, **Paragraph**. Click in the **Special** box and select **First Line**. Double-click in the **By** box and type **.35**. Click on the down triangle beside the Spacing After box until **0** displays. Select **OK** twice. Select **Close**.

12. Create a frame that will contain the sidebar text. The sidebar text is contained in the file named **18side2.doc** located on the data disk.
    a. Select the **Whole Page** view and scroll down to view page 2.
    b. Select **Insert**, **Frame**. Draw a rectangle that is approximately **3.5"** in width and **8.5"** in length.
    c. Select **Format**, **Frame**. In the Horizontal area, select **Right** in the Position box and select **Margin** in the Relative To box. In the Vertical area, select **Top** in the Position box and select **Margin** in the Relative To box. Double-click in the **Width** box and type **3.5**. Select **OK**.
    d. Select **Format**, **Borders and Shading**. Choose the **Shadow** option and a **1½ pt** double-line style. Set the From Text option to **6 pt**. Select **OK**.
    e. Select **Insert**, **File** and insert the file named **18side2.doc** located on the data disk.

13. If necessary, enable "Smart Quotes." (Select **Tools**, **AutoCorrect**, check that an X displays beside the **Change 'Straight Quotes' to 'Smart Quotes'** option, select **OK**).

14. Use the Replace feature to convert straight quotation marks (") to opening and closing quotation marks. (Place the insertion point at the top of the document, select **Edit**, **Replace**, type a " in the Find What box, type a " in the Replace With box, select **Replace All**, **OK**, **Close**.)

15. Use the Replace feature to convert two hyphens (--) to an em dash (—). (With the insertion point at the top of the document, select **Edit**, **Replace**, type -- in the Find What box, click in the Replace With box, select the **Special** button and click on **Em Dash**, select **Replace All**, **OK**, **Close**.)

16. Use the *new* filename **18actfin.doc** and save the file on your file disk.

Note: Your final document should look similar to the magazine article shown below.

Weekend Astronauts

Are you ready to be a Weekend Astronaut? "This is launch control with a preflight audio test. Flight director, how do you read me? Mission Director, you are go for air to ground audio check. All other positions begin pre-launch check lists."

Is this really mission control preparing to launch a Space Shuttle? Yes, if you are participating in a simulated Space Shuttle mission at the Alabama U.S. Space Academy.

It is raining outside, but inside the tent-shaped three-domed Space Camp building "space cadets" are learning the basic principles of propulsion, receiving flight assignments, and training for tomorrow's Space Shuttle mission.

Dodging the raindrops, the space cadets skip over to the Marriott for a quick lunch. After lunch, huddled under a sheet ready for laundry, the cadets dash over to the 67-foot domed theater to watch a film. The theater screen and audio system engulf the audience in the large screen and surround sound system while astronauts practiced maneuvers, emergency procedures, and orbited the earth.

Outside the theater and inside the museum, cadets experience the multi-axis maneuvering pod that turns 60 revolutions per minute and never revolves in any one specific direction more than two times. Who is made of the "right stuff?" Everyone. Dizziness and stomach somersaults are not experienced because there is not enough time for the brain to register the equilibrium change.

Who is made of the "right stuff?" Everyone.

A new day begins at 5:00 a.m. when an alarm clock rings in the dormitory—both mission crews are awake. The mission pilot and commander must review the launch and landing procedures and mission maneuvers in order to prepare for the late afternoon shuttle launch.

At 3:00 p.m. the air is filled with excitement as the Atlantic Crew enters the Space Shuttle simulator ready for the two-hour shuttle mission. "This is Mission Directory. All positions report satisfactory audio and air to ground wind check is complete." The countdown begins and there is lift-off! The shuttle clears the tower.

Mission specialists prepare to exit the space shuttle. Mission scientists begin laboratory experiments inside the space lab module. Mission Control's launch directory, flight directory, and mission director are busy communicating—via radio controlled headsets—to each crew member. A remote control camera takes pictures of the EVAs (Extra Vehicular Activities) and the video is displayed on a screen at Mission Control.

The shuttle has completed its mission and will be landing soon. "The landing convoy is along the runway," reports Mission Control's public relations announcer. The pilot announces that the descent has begun, the air force base is in sight, and we have touchdown.

Preparing for a Change

A 19-year old student slides out of bed and, still asleep, slides into his Introduction to Business class at the Highland Park Community College. When his eyes focus on the instructor at the front of the room, he squints and shakes his head. She is wearing a blue jumpsuit with NASA and American flag patches. And she is saying, "Just imagine what it would be like to live in the space station. You'll probably be working on that kind of project someday. What kind of job do you see for yourself there?"

The instructor is Sarah Weber, teaching her business class as usual. "It's my duty to prepare people for change," she says. "That may mean retraining at the age of 40. I try to introduce it in subtle ways—like having a word processing class create a letter inviting people to become members of the National Space Society or assigning an accounting class to develop a budget for a space colony."

About five years ago at an air show at NASA-Ames, Weber saw a National Space Society (NSS) booth. "I knew I was interested in exploring space, so when I saw the NSS booth, I picked up a membership form. I became a member immediately."

Weber see the NSS as a way to fulfill her dream of using her computer skills working in a space module. The vision took on focus last month when she attended Space Camp in Huntsville, Alabama. "The gear is so heavy, I could hardly stand up. You have a pair of surgical gloves, then a thick pair of gloves on top of those. Then they strap you into this chair and tell your to build a tetrahedron (a pyramid-shaped structure). It seems simple, but it was really difficult," Weber said. Yet, when the four-day camp was over, she said "I didn't want to leave. I wanted to do it all over again."

Spacefarers Monthly 1

2 Weekend Astronauts

17. Print one copy and close the document.

Challenge Your Skills

Skill 18.1—Create a Magazine Article

1. Open the file named **18skill1.doc** located on the data disk. Review the text and determine an appropriate pull quote.
2. Make decisions regarding the placement and size of a graphic image(s). Suggested graphic images are **computer.wmf**, **disk.wmf**, and **lightblb.wmf**, which are located in the Word clipart directory.
3. The article title is **Smart Tips for the Workplace**. Make decisions regarding using WordArt, a special font, shadows, etc., to format the article title.
4. Make decisions regarding:

   Number and widths of columns and spacing between columns
   Placement and text for pull quote
   Use of a drop cap
   Indentation of paragraphs
   Placement and format of sidebar information
   Footers for odd and even pages of the article
   Use of em dashes to replace double hyphens (--)

5. The sidebar text is contained in a file named **18side3.doc** located on the data disk.
6. Correct three spelling errors, two punctuation errors, and one parentheses error.
7. Use the *new* filename **18skfin.doc** and save the document on your file disk.

   Note: *An example of the final article is shown on page 440. Your document does not need to match this example.*
8. Print one copy.
9. If you have completed your work in Word, exit the program.

Computers are becoming an essential part of the workplace and increasingly popular at home. Workers who regularly use computers often complain of headaches, back and muscle aches, blurred vision, stress, and wrist pain. When designing a computer workstation, it is important to consider the individual(s) who will use the workstation and the type of work that will be performed at the station.

One of the most common problems for people working at computer workstations is physical strain. The most common simptoms include headaches and aches and pains of the neck, shoulder, back, arm, wrist, and hand. These complaints stem from several problems. Constant upper body movement may result in the various neck, wrist, and back discomforts. Constant sitting at a keyboard staring at the computer monitor without frequent breaks increases muscle tension. Inadequate workplace design and furnishings may aggravate the various muscle aches. Improper chair size and poor back support are the most common causes of back pain. One of the most common problems is carpal tunnel syndrome.

Review the document and determine an appropriate pull quote.

What Is Carpal Tunnel Syndrome

Carpal tunnel syndrome is a painful hand disorder caused by stressful and repetitive motions of the hand. Although the site of the injury is the wrist, pain is usually felt in the hand. Excessive movement of the wrists or holding the wrists in static positions for long periods of time can irritate the nerves, tendons, and arteries inside a narrow formation of ligament and bone at the wrist--the carpal tunnel. In the early stages of carpal tunnel syndrome, symptoms can include numbness and tingling in the hand, pain in your hands and wrists, and the dropping objects. Initially, the symptoms occur at night; however, the symptoms soon appear during the day and intensify.

Modern Office Monthly 1

Carpal tunnel syndrome is preventable. Preventing carpal tunnel syndrome depends on many factors including good posture, work environment, and exercise. If your work includes using a computer or other keyboard machine be sure to practice proper posture and good keyboarding techniques. When typing, move only the fingers and always maintain a straight-wrist position. If your keyboard has a pad, use it to rest your wrists during breaks. Stretching and strengthening exercises to build up the muscles in the wrists and forearms are very important. (See the Carpal Tunnel Exercises in the sidebar for further information. However, if you have advanced carpal tunnel syndrome, do not perform the listed exercises.

In the case of advanced carpal tunnel syndrome, wrist splints, and injections of anti-inflammatory medications may reduce swelling and decrease the compression on the nerve. If these measures fail to provide relief, surgery may be necessary. After surgery, it is important to exercise as soon as possible in order to regain full function and mobility in your hands and wrists.

Carpal tunnel syndrome often occurs in people who do repetative tasks--housewives, secretaries, meat cutters, assembly line workers, carpenters, musicians, etc. Women are five times more likely than men to develop carpal tunnel syndrome. Carpal tunnel syndrome is also referred to as repetitive truama disorder or overuse syndrome.

Carpal Tunnel Exercises

Before beginning a typing job and during breaks throughout the day, perform the following stretching exercises. None of these exercises should cause discomfort.

Wrist Bends

- With your forearm resting on the edge of a table, grasp the fingers of one hand with the other hand and gently bend back the wrist, stretching the hand and wrist. Hold for five seconds. Repeat for other wrist.
- Place your hand palm down with fingers spread on a table. Gently press the hand against the table, stretching the fingers and wrist. Hold for five seconds. Repeat for other hand.

Wrist Stretches

- Press both palms together at chest level. Slowly lift your elbows up and away from the sides of your body as far as they can comfortably go. Hold for five seconds. Repeat three or four times.

Finger Stretches

- Clench your hands into tight fists. Release and stretch the fingers as far as they will go.
- Flex each finger against the palm to touch the tip of the thumb.
- Raise your arms over your head and stretch out the fingers as if you were attempting to touch the ceiling.

Wrist Strengtheners

- With your arm resting on a table, make a loose fist with one hand palm up.
- Use the other hand to gently press down and against the clenched hand. Resist the force with the closed hand for five seconds. Keep wrist straight.
- Turn the clenched hand palm down and use the other hand to gently press down and against the clenched hand. Resist the force with the clenched hand for five seconds. Keep wrist straight.
- Turn the clenched hand sideways with your thumb facing up and use the other hand to gently press down and against the clenched hand. Resist the force with the clenched hand for five seconds. Keep wrist straight.
- Turn the clenched hand palm down. Place your other hand against the knuckles of the clenched hand and use the other hand to gently press against the clenched hand. Resist the force with the closed hand for five seconds. Keep wrist straight.
- Repeat the sequence five times. Repeat for other hand.

2 Smart Tips for the Workplace

Minimizing Physical Strain

To minimize physical strain, a computer workstation should provide the worker with a comfortable sitting position, sufficiently flexible to reach, use, and see the computer monitor, keyboard, and documents. When designing a workstation, keep the following guidelines in mind.

1. The chair should have an easily adjustable seat height and backrest position. The chair height should be adjusted so that the worker's feet rest firmly on the floor and his/her thighs are parallel to the floor.
2. Adjust the screen height so that the top of the screen is at or below eye level. Adjust the screen angle to reduce glare.
3. If the worker will be viewing a document and the screen, adjust the document to the same height, distance, and orientation as the screen.
4. Place the keyboard so that the wrists remain straight when typing. Provide a wrist rest.
5. Adjust lighting to reduce glare on the screen, but still provide adequate lighting for normal paperwork.

Physical stress can also be reduced by taking regular breaks, varying tasks, and performing simple exercises.

Modern Office Monthly 3

CHAPTER 19

Create Fill-in Forms

Features Covered

- Use a form template
- Create a form template
- Edit a form template
- Create a calculation field
- Create a macro that updates a calculation field

Objectives and Introduction

After successfully completing this chapter, you will be able to use a form template to create a document, as well as create a form template containing text fields, check box fields, and drop-down fields. In additional, you will learn how to edit a form template, create a field that calculates the total of the values in other fields, and create a macro that automatically updates the calculated field.

Word's form field features can be used to create online forms. These forms are stored as templates. The form templates contains form fields and the text to appear in each document that is created using the template. Word provides several form templates to help you create invoices, purchase orders, and weekly time sheets. In addition, new form templates can be created as needed.

Use a Form Template

A form template is a model for a document. A form template can contain text fields, check box fields, and drop-down fields. When a new document is created using a form template, a copy of the form structure, fields, and text displays in the document window. Data is entered into text fields, check boxes are selected, and items are selected from drop-down lists to fill out (complete) the form document. The form document is then saved and printed.

A form document is protected so that the structure, text, and fields cannot be accidentally changed. If desired, the form's structure, text, and fields can be changed. To edit a form, the form document must be unprotected. After the desired changes have been made to the form's structure, text, or fields, protect the form document and enter the data needed to complete the form. Removing the protection from the form document and making changes does not change the original form template. For information on editing a form template, see the Steps to Edit a Form Template on page 451.

Use a Fill-in Form Template

1. Select **File, New** {Alt, f, n}.

Note: The New dialog box displays containing a list of templates.

2. Double-click on the desired template name, or type the location and name of the desired template file in the Template box.

For example, scroll down and double-click on **Weektime.**

Note: A weekly time sheet form displays in the document window. Gray areas display at the location of the fields to be filled in. The first field in the form (located beside the words Employee Name) is selected. A Help message displays in the Status Bar describing the information to be entered into the selected field.

Edit the Form

3. Select **Tools, Unprotect Document** {Alt, t, p}.

4. Make the desired changes to the preprinted form text.

For example,

a. Select the words "Your Company Name" and type **Countrywide Trucking Company.**

b. Select the words "Your Company Slogan" and type **Moving Your Freight from Here to There.**

c. Select the words "Your Company Street Address" and type **4843 Kenwood Circle.**

d. Select the words "City, State ZIP" and type **Mansfield, OH 44906.**

e. Select the "000.000.0000" and type **419-555-2400.** Select the "000.000.0000" that follows the word "Fax" and type **419-555-2432.**

5. Select **Tools, Protect Document** {Alt, t p}.

Note: The Protect Document dialog box displays.

6. Select **Forms** in the Protect Document For area. Select **OK** {Alt, f, Enter}.

Enter Data Into Form Fields

7. Type the desired information into the fields of the form. Press the **Tab** key to move from field to field.

For example,

a. In the Employee Name field, type your name. Press the **Tab** key.

Note: *The field next to the word "Title" is selected.*

b. In the Title field, type **Administrative Assistant**. Press the **Tab** key.

c. In the Employee Number field, type **11211**. Press the **Tab** key.

Note: *The Status field contains a drop-down list of options. The first option, Full-time, currently displays in the field.*

d. To select a different status, move the mouse pointer to the words "Full-time" and click once. Click on **Part-time**. Press the **Tab** key.

e. In the Department field, type **Human Resources**. Press the **Tab** key.

f. In the Supervisor field, type **Anna Ringel**. Press the **Tab** key.

g. In the first field below the word "Date," enter last Monday's date in the **m/d/yy** format. Press the **Tab** key.

h. In the first field below the words "Start Time," type **9:30 am**. Press the **Tab** key.

i. In the first field below the words "End Time," type **3:30 pm**. Press the **Tab** key.

j. In the first field below the words "Regular Hrs.," type **6**. Press the **Tab** key.

Note: *6 is placed in the first field below the words "Total Hrs."*

k. Press the **Tab** key to move to the second field in the Date column.

l. Continue to enter the information in the fields of the weekly time sheet as shown in Figure 19.1

Countrywide Trucking Company

Moving Your Freight from Here to There

4843 Kenwood Circle

Mansfield, OH 44906

419-555-2400 Fax 419-555-2432

Employee Name: Your Name — Title: Administrative Assistant

Employee Number: 11211 — Status: Part-time

Department: Human Resources — Supervisor: Anna Ringel

Date	Start Time	End Time	Regular Hrs.	Overtime Hrs.	Total Hrs.
Monday's date	9:30 AM	3:30 PM	6		6
Tuesday's date	7:30 AM	5:30 PM	8	2	10
Wednesday's date	9:00 AM	12:30 PM	3.5		3.5
Thursday's date	9:30 AM	12:30 PM	3		3
Friday's date	9:00 AM	1:00 PM	4		4
					0
					0
		WEEKLY TOTALS	24.5	2	26.5

Employee Signature: — Date:

Supervisor Signature: — Date:

FIGURE 19.1

Weekly time sheet created using the *Weektime* form template

Finish-Up Instructions

- Use the filename **19wktime.doc** and save the file on your file disk.
- Print one copy and close the document.

Create a Form Template

To create a new form, a template must be created. A new template can be based on the *normal.dot* template or on an existing template that closely matches the structure of the new form. Form templates can contain three different types of form fields: text fields, check box fields, and drop-down fields. Each type of form field can be customized. For example, a text form field can be customized to accept only numbers and to display the numbers in a specific format.

Before beginning to create a form template, develop a mock-up or illustration of how the final form should look. Determine the types of form fields that will be used to enter data and the structure that best meets the needs of the people who will be using the form. Form fields can be placed in table cells or inserted into text. See Figure 19.2 for examples of form templates.

A Forms Toolbar is available to assist you in developing a form template. The Forms Toolbar contains a **Text Form Field** button, **Check Box Form Field** button, **Drop-Down Form Field** button, and a **Form Field Options** button. These buttons are used to insert and customize fields when creating a form. (If your form contains only a few fields, the **Insert**, **Form Field** command can be used to insert form fields instead of displaying and using the Forms Toolbar.) As form fields are inserted, Word automatically creates a bookmark name for each field, e.g., Text1, Dropdown1, Check1. These bookmark names can be used when creating formulas and macros (see Steps to Create a Macro That Updates a Calculation Field and Assign the Macro to a Form Field on page 452).

To assist users in filling out a form, Help messages can be created for the form fields. Help text is added by selecting the **Add Help Text** button in the Form Field Options dialog box. In the Form Field Help Text dialog box, the **Status Bar** tab or **Help Key (F1)** tab is selected and the desired Help text is typed in the **Type Your Own** box, or an AutoText Entry name is selected. A Help message of up to 138 characters can be displayed in the Status Bar. If the **Help Key (F1)** tab is selected, Word creates a message box that will display when the **F1** key is pressed by the user. The message box can contain a Help message of up to 255 characters.

Once the form template is complete, the form is protected by selecting the **Protect Form** button. When the **Protect Form** button is selected, the form template cannot be edited. (For information on editing a form template, see the section Edit a Form Template later in this chapter.) The form template is then saved. By default, Word saves template files in the directory specified on the File Locations tab, User Templates setting of the Options dialog box. If desired, the template can be saved in a different location by typing a drive and/or directory in the File Name box in the Save As dialog box.

Create a Fill-in Form Template

1. Select **File, New** {Alt, f, n}.

FIGURE 19.2
Examples of form templates

Form template with form fields in table cells

Printing Quote

Customer Name:	Contact:	Phone Number:	Date of Quote:
Quantity:	Finish Size:	Description:	
Paper Stock:	Ink: Black	Number of Pages:	☐ Camera Ready
Self-Cover: ☐	Separate Cover: ☐	Cover Stock:	Cover Ink: Black
Typesetting Services:	☐ Desktop Publishing	☐ Lino Output	☐ Paste-up
	☐ Paper	☐ Film	
Binding:	☐ Saddle Stitch	☐ Perfect binding	☐ Spiral
	☐ Pad	☐ NCR Pad	☐ Stapled
☐ 3-hole Drill	☐ 2-hold Drill	☐ Folded	☐ Cut
Printing Quote:	Typesetting Quote:	Binding Quote:	Total Printing Quote: $ 0.00

Form template with form fields in text

Gateway Resort

March 11, 1995

Dear :

Thank you for choosing Gateway Resort for your lodging accommodations. We are please to confirm your reservation for the following:

Arrival Date:
Departure Date:
Room Rate:
Number of Rooms:
Non-smoking Room: ☐ Yes ☐ No
Guarantee Method: Visa

To avoid any charges to your account, cancellations must be made within 24 hours of your arrival date. Check in time is and check out time is .

If you have any questions or need further assistance, please contact the Lodging Department at (800)555-9250.

Sincerely,

Lodging Department

Note: The New dialog box displays.

2. In the New area, select the **Template** option {Alt and e}.
3. Select **OK** {Enter}.

   Note: Template1 displays in the Title Bar.

4. Format the template as needed.

FIGURE 19.3

Forms Toolbar

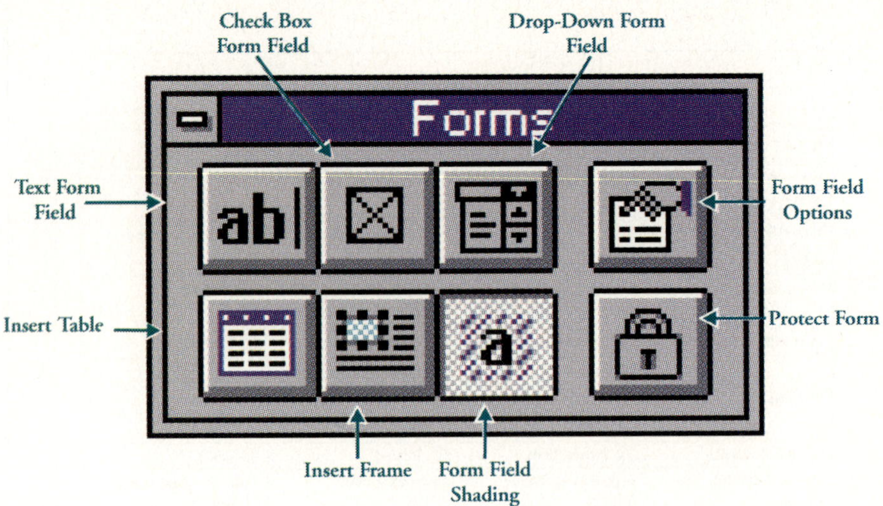

For example,

a. Change the top and bottom margins to .75". Change the left and right margins to .5".

b. Type **COUNTRYWIDE TRUCKING COMPANY**. Press **Enter** and type **Employee Evaluation Form**. Press **Enter** twice.

c. Select **COUNTRYWIDE TRUCKING COMPANY** and **Employee Evaluation Form**. Change the alignment to **Center** and the font to **Arial, 12 point, Bold**.

d. Place the insertion point on the second blank line below the words Employee Evaluation Form and create a table with **3 rows** and **5 columns**.

5. To display the Forms Toolbar, move the mouse pointer into the Standard or Formatting Toolbar in the gray area between two buttons and click the *right* mouse button once. Select **Forms** on the drop-down menu.

Note: *The Forms Toolbar displays in the upper right corner of the document window (see Figure 19.3).*

6. Type text and select Forms Toolbar buttons to create the desired form.

For example,

a. In the first cell of the table, type **Social Security:** and press **Enter**.

b. On the Forms Toolbar, select the **Text Form Field** button ab|.

Note: *A gray area indicating that a field has been inserted displays in the table.*

c. Select the **Form Field Options** button.

Note: *The Text Form Field Options dialog box displays (see Figure 19.4).*

d. Double-click in the **Maximum Length** box and type **11**. Select **OK**.

e. Press the **Tab** key to move the insertion point to the first cell in column 2. Type **Name (Last):** and press **Enter**. Select the **Text Form Field** button ab|.

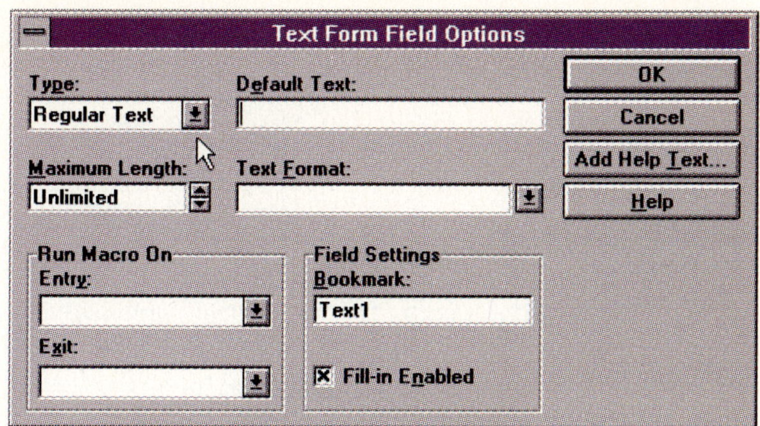

FIGURE 19.4

Text Form Field Options dialog box

f. Press the **Tab** key to move the insertion point to the first cell in column 3. Type **First:** and press **Enter**. Select the **Text Form Field** button.

g. Press the **Tab** key to move the insertion point to the first cell in column 4. Type **Middle:** and press **Enter**. Select the **Text Form Field** button.

h. Press the **Tab** key to move the insertion point to the first cell in column 5. Type **Employee No.:** and press **Enter**. Select the **Text Form Field** button.

i. Select the **Form Field Options** button.

j. Click in the **Type** box and select **Number**.

k. Double-click in the **Maximum Length** box and type **5**.

l. Click on the down arrow located to the right of the **Number Format** box and select **0** (whole numbers).

m. Select the **Add Help Text** button. On the Status Bar tab, select the **Type Your Own** option. Type **Enter the employee's five digit identification number** (see Figure 19.5). Select **OK** to exit the Form Field Help Text dialog box.

n. Select **OK** to exit the Text Form Field Options dialog box.

o. Press the **Tab** key to move the insertion point to the first cell of row 2. Type **Department:** and press **Enter**.

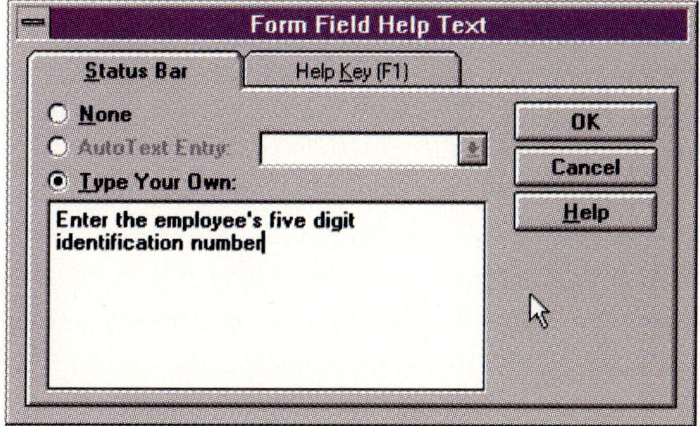

FIGURE 19.5

Form Field Help Text dialog box

FIGURE 19.6

Drop-Down Form Field Options dialog box

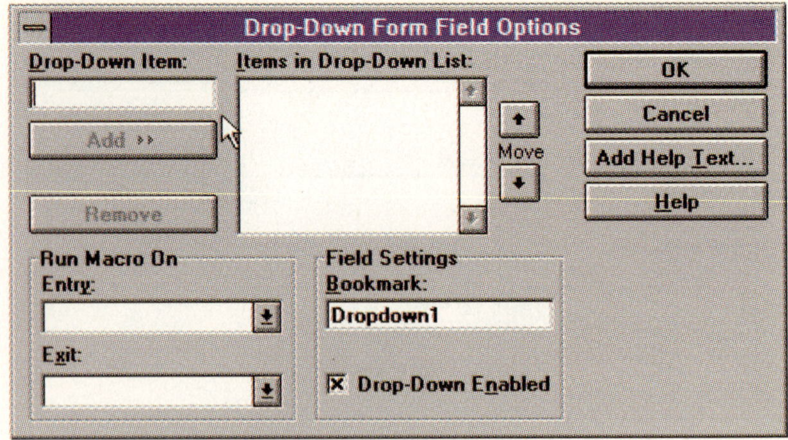

p. Select the **Drop-Down Form Field** button.

q. Select the **Form Field Options** button.

Note: *The Drop-Down Form Field Options dialog box displays (see Figure 19.6).*

r. In the Drop-Down Item box, type **Accounting**. Select **Add**. Type the following item names in the Drop-Down Item box. Select **Add** after each item.

Delivery	(select **Add**)
Human Resources	(select **Add**)
Warehouse	(select **Add**)
Sales	(select **Add**)

s. Select **OK**.

Note: *The first item in the drop-down list (Accounting) displays in the drop-down form field.*

t. Press the **Tab** key to move the insertion point to row 2, column 2. Type **Position:** and press **Enter**. Select the **Text Form Field** button.

u. Press the **Tab** key to move the insertion point to row 2, column 3. Type **Date of Evaluation:** and press **Enter**. Select the **Text Form Field** button. Select the **Form Field Options** button. In the Type box, select **Date**. In the Date Format box, select **M/d/yy**. Select **OK**.

v. Press the **Tab** key to move the insertion point to row 2, column 4. Type **Date in Position:** and press **Enter**. Select the **Text Form Field** button. Select the **Form Field Options** button. In the Type box, select **Date**. In the Date Format box, select **M/d/yy**. Select **OK**.

w. Press the **Tab** key to move the insertion point to row 2, column 5. Type **Date of Last Review:** and press **Enter**. Select the **Text Form Field** button. Select the **Form Field Options** button. In the Type box, select **Date**. In the Date Format box, select **M/d/yy**. Select **OK**.

x. Press the **Tab** key to move the insertion point to row 3, column 1. Type **Type of Evaluation:** and press the **Tab** key once to move the insertion point to row 3, column 2.

y. Select the **Check Box Form Field** button ☒. Press the **Spacebar** twice. Type **Probationary review.**

z. Press the **Tab** key to move the insertion point to row 3, column 3. Select the **Check Box Form Field** button ☒. Press the **Spacebar** twice. Type **6-month review.** Press the **Tab** key once to move the insertion point to row 3, column 4. Select the **Check Box Form Field** button ☒. Press the **Spacebar** twice. Type **Annual review.** Press the **Tab** key to move the insertion point to row 3, column 5. Select the **Check Box Form Field** button ☒. Press the **Spacebar** twice. Type **Salary increase.**

7. Format the form as needed.

For example,

a. Select all the text in the table and change the font to **Arial, 9** point.

b. Select **Format, Paragraph,** type **3 pt** in the Spacing Before and Spacing After boxes on the Indents and Spacing tab. Select **OK.**

c. Select the **Borders** button on the Formatting Toolbar. Choose a **3/4 pt double-line** style for the Outside border and a **3/4 pt single-line** style for the Inside border. Select the **Borders** button again to remove the Borders Toolbar from the screen.

d. Place the insertion point below the table and press the **Enter** key once. Continue to create the form by inserting the file named **19evaltx.doc** located on the data disk (select **Insert, File;** if necessary, select the drive where the data disk is located; double-click on **19evaltx.doc**).

Note: *The form should look similar to the form shown in Figure 19.7.*

8. When the form is complete, select the **Protect Form** button on the Forms Toolbar.

9. To remove the Forms Toolbar, move the mouse pointer into the Standard or Formatting Toolbar in the gray area between two buttons and click the *right* mouse button once. Select **Forms** on the drop-down menu.

10. Save the form template.

For example, select the **Save** button. In the File Name box, type the drive letter where your file disk is located followed by a colon and the name **evaluate** (*a:evaluate*).

Note: *Word will automatically add the extension* ***.dot*** *to the template file. If a drive location is not typed in the File Name box, Word saves the template file to the default template directory specified on the File Locations tab in the Options dialog box.*

11. Close the document.

FIGURE 19.7

Fill-in form template with text fields, drop-down fields, and check box fields

COUNTRYWIDE TRUCKING COMPANY
Employee Evaluation Form

Social Security:	Name (Last):	First:	Middle:	Employee No.:
Department: Accounting	Position:	Date of Evaulation:	Date in Position:	Date of Last Review:
Type of Evaluation:	☐ Probationary review	☐ 6-month review	☐ Annual review	☐ Salary increase

	Needs Improvement	Meets Requirement	Exceeds Requirement	Comments
Customer Service	☐	☐	☐	
Completeness of Paperwork	☐	☐	☐	
Driving Record (Safety)	☐	☐	☐	
Follows Company Policies	☐	☐	☐	
Dependability	☐	☐	☐	
Cooperation with Others	☐	☐	☐	
Job Responsibility	☐	☐	☐	
Job Attitude	☐	☐	☐	
Overall Rating	☐	☐	☐	

Strong Areas of Performance

Areas Needing Improvement

Action Plan

Supervisor's Comments

Employee Comments

I acknowledge that the above evaluation has been discussed with me.	Employee Signature:	Date:

Finish-Up Instructions

- ❖ Continue with the Steps to Use a Fill-in Form Template.

Use a Fill-in Form Template

1. Select **File, New** {Alt, f, n}.
2. In the New dialog box, double-click on the desired template name, or type the location and name of the template file in the Template box and select **OK**.

   For example, in the Template box, type the drive letter where your file disk is located followed by a colon and the filename **evaluate** (*a:evaluate*). Select **OK**.
3. Enter the needed information into the form fields. Press the **Tab** key to move from field to field.

   For example, enter the information shown in Figure 19.8.
4. When the information has been entered into the necessary fields, save and print the document using the normal procedures.

   For example, use the filename **19darden.doc** and save the file on your file disk. Print one copy and close the document.

COUNTRYWIDE TRUCKING COMPANY
Employee Evaluation Form

Social Security: 555-12-3456	Name (Last): Darden	First: Martha	Middle: P.	Employee No.: 14468
Department: Delivery	Position: Driver (Local)	Date of Evaulation: (insert current date)	Date in Position: 3/12/95	Date of Last Review: 3/12/95
Type of Evaluation:	☐ Probationary review	☒ 6-month review	☒ Annual review	☐ Salary increase

	Needs Improvement	Meets Requirement	Exceeds Requirement	Comments
Customer Service	☐	☐	☒	Several letters of commendation have been received from customers
Completeness of Paperwork	☐	☒	☐	
Driving Record (Safety)	☐	☐	☒	
Follows Company Policies	☐	☒	☐	
Dependability	☐	☐	☒	
Cooperation with Others	☒	☐	☐	
Job Responsibility	☐	☐	☒	
Job Attitude	☐	☐	☒	
Overall Rating	☐	☐	☒	

Strong Areas of Performance
Martha excels in customer service. She is always ready to meet the customer's needs.
Areas Needing Improvement
Communication and cooperation with co-workers needs to be improved to avoid misunderstandings.
Action Plan
Bi-weekly meetings will be held to review progress in the areas of communication and cooperation with co-workers.
Supervisor's Comments
Martha has proven to be a very dependable and hard-working employee. She has shown her ability to address customer needs effectively. She has a positive, "get the job done" attitude.
Employee Comments

I acknowledge that the above evaluation has been discussed with me.	**Employee Signature:**	**Date:**

FIGURE 19.8

Completed fill-in form created using the *evaluate.dot* template

Edit a Form Template

To edit a form template, open template file and turn protection off. Once the form template is unprotected, changes can be made to existing fields, text can be edited, and new fields can be added. After the form template has been edited, protect and save the form template.

Start-Up Instructions

❖ To complete the following drill, copy the file named **quote.dot** located on the data disk to your file disk. For information on copying files, see Chapter 16, page 387.

Edit a Form Template and Create a Calculated Field

1. Select **File, Open**. Click in the **List Files of Type** box and select **Document Templates (*.dot)**.

Chapter 19
Create Fill-in Forms

2. Select the desired drive and/or directory where the template file is located.

   For example, select the drive where your file disk is located.

3. Double-click on the desired template name.

   For example, double-click on **quote.dot**.

4. To display the Forms Toolbar, move the mouse pointer into the Standard or Formatting Toolbar in the gray area between two buttons and click the *right* mouse button once. Select **Forms** on the drop-down menu.

5. Select the **Protect Form** button to turn off the protect feature so that the form can be edited.

6. Edit the form as desired.

   For example, add the following fields:

   a. Click below the words "Printing Quote". Select the **Text Form Field** button. Select the **Form Field Options** button. Set the Type to **Number** and the Number Format to **$#,##0.00;($#,##0.00)**. Select **OK.**

   b. Click below the words "Typesetting Quote." Select the **Text Form Field** button. Select the **Form Field Options** button. Set the Type to **Number** and the Number Format to **$#,##0.00;($#,##0.00)**. Select **OK.**

   c. Click below the words "Binding Quote." Select the **Text Form Field** button. Select the **Form Field Options** button. Set the Type to **Number** and the Number Format to **$#,##0.00;($#,##0.00)**. Select **OK.**

Create a Calculation Field

7. Place the insertion point at the location where the calculated value is to be displayed.

   For example, click below the word "Total Printing Quote."

8. Select the **Text Form Field** button.

9. Select the **Form Field Options** button.

10. Click in the **Type** box and select **Calculation**.

    Note: *An equals sign (=) displays in the Expression box.*

11. In the **Expression** box, type the desired formula.

    For example, move the mouse pointer to the right of the equals sign and click. Type the formula **SUM(A10:C10)**. (Do not type the period.)

12. If desired, click on the down arrow beside the **Number Format** box and select a number format.

    For example, select the **$#,##0.00;($#,##0.00)** number type.

13. Make a note of the Bookmark name that displays in the Field Settings area.

For example, the Bookmark name **Text14** displays in the Field Settings area.

14. Select **OK**.

Finish-Up Instructions

- Select **File, Save** to save the form template.
- Continue with the Steps to Create a Macro That Updates a Calculation Field.

Assign a Macro to a Form Field

Macros can be assigned to form fields. The macros can be set to run when a field is entered or exited. For example, a macro that updates a calculation field can be assigned to a field and will automatically run when the field is exited. The bookmark names assigned to form fields are used in macros to reference the fields. Macros that are assigned to form fields should be stored in the form template to ensure that the macro is available each time the form template is used.

Start-Up Instructions

- The template named **quote.dot** should be displayed in the document window.

Create a Macro That Updates a Calculation Field and Assign the Macro to a Form Field

1. Select **Tools, Macro**.
2. In the Macro Name box, type the desired macro name.

   For example, type **Total**.
3. Click in the **Macros Available In** box and select the name of the template where the macro should be stored.

   For example, click on **Quote.dot** (Template).
4. Select **Create**.

   Note: *The words QUOTE.DOT:Total displays in the Title Bar and the words Sub MAIN and End Sub display in the document window.*
5. Type the desired macro commands.

   For example,

   a. type **SetFormResult** (do not insert any spaces within the command).

   b. Press the **Spacebar** once.

   c. Type **"text14"** (the bookmark name for the field containing the formula).

   Note: *Quotation marks must be placed around the bookmark name.*
6. Select **File, Close**.

Chapter 19
Create Fill-in Forms

FIGURE 19.9

Completed fill-in form created using the *quote.dot* template

Printing Quote

Customer Name: Searfoss and Blount, Inc.	**Contact:** Eunice	**Phone Number:** 714-555-1242	**Date of Quote:** (insert current date)
Quantity: 500	**Finish Size:** 8.5 x 11	**Description:** Tri-fold brochure	
Paper Stock: 67 lb card stock	**Ink:** Custom	**Number of Pages:** 2	☐ **Camera Ready**
Self-Cover: ☐	**Separate Cover:** ☐	**Cover Stock:**	**Cover Ink:** none
Typesetting Services:	☐ **Desktop Publishing**	☒ **Lino Output**	☐ **Paste-up**
	☐ **Paper**	☐ **Film**	
Binding:	☐ **Saddle Stitch**	☐ **Perfect binding**	☐ **Spiral**
	☐ **Pad**	☐ **NCR Pad**	☐ **Stapled**
☐ **3-hole Drill**	☐ **2-hold Drill**	☒ **Folded**	☐ **Cut**
Printing Quote: $ 395.59	**Typesetting Quote:** $ 14.00	**Binding Quote:** $ 25.00	**Total Printing Quote:** **$ 434.59**

7. Select **Yes** to the message "Do you want to keep changes . . . ?"
8. Double-click on the field where the macro should be linked.

   For example, double-click on the text form field below the words Binding Quote.
9. In the Run Macro On area, click in the **Entry** or **Exit** box.

   For example, click in the **Exit** box.
10. Select the desired macro name.

    For example, click on **Total.**
11. Select **OK.**
12. Select the **Protect Form** button on the Forms Toolbar.
13. Save the template.

Finish-Up Instructions

- Remove the Forms Toolbar from the screen.
- Close the template.
- Select **File, New**. Type the drive letter where your file disk is located followed by a colon and the filename **quote** (e.g., **a:quote**). Select **OK.**
- Enter the information shown in Figure 19.9 into the Printing Quote form.
- Use the filename **19prnqt.doc** and save the form on your file disk.
- Print one copy and close the document.

Print and Save Form Data Only

If desired, the data entered into a form can be printed without printing the form structure. This feature can be used to print the form data onto preprinted forms. Also, the data entered into a form can be saved without saving the structure of the form. When only the data is saved, Word creates a Text Only file that can be imported into other programs such as a database program.

Print Data on a Preprinted Form

Note: *The following steps are for your information only.*

1. Insert the preprinted form into your printer.
2. With the completed form displayed in the document window, select **File, Print**.
3. Select **Options**.
4. On the Print tab of the Options dialog box, select the **Print Data Only** option.
5. Select **OK** to exit the Options dialog box.
6. Select **OK** to print the data.

Save Data Only

Note: *The following steps are for your information only.*

1. Select **File, Save**.
2. Select **Options**.
3. On the Save tab of the Options dialog box, select **Save Data Only for Forms**.
4. Select **OK** to exit the Options dialog box.
5. Type the desired filename in the File Name box and select **OK**.

The Next Step

Chapter Review and Activities

Self-Check Quiz

T F 1. A form template can contain text fields, check box fields, and drop-down fields.

T F 2. If the structure, text, or fields of a document created using a form template are edited, the original form template is also changed.

T F 3. A form template must be unprotected before the template can be edited.

T F 4. A drop-down form field can be customized; however, a text form field cannot be customized.

T F 5. Help text can be added to form fields to assist the user when the form is being filled out.

6. After a form template is completed, the __________ button is selected to protect the form.
   a. **Lock Form**
   b. **Protect Form**
   c. **Lock Document**
   d. **Save**

7. The ________ ______ is used in a macro to reference a field.
   a. cell address
   b. field type
   c. bookmark name
   d. any of the above

8. A Help message that will display in the Status Bar can contain up to _____ characters.
   a. 100
   b. 255
   c. 53
   d. 138

9. There are six types of text form fields. Use the Text Form Field Options dialog box and list the six types available.

10. List two actions that should be taken before beginning to create a form template.

Enriching Language Arts Skills

Spelling/Vocabulary Words

arbitration the hearing and determination of a dispute or grievance between parties by a person or persons appointed by mutual consent or statutory provision.

grievance a complaint or the grounds for a complaint against a situation viewed as unjust.

interpretation the act or process of explaining or clarifying.

Colons, Capitalization, and Punctuation for Bulleted and Enumerated Lists

Place a colon after an independent clause that introduces a bulleted or enumerated (numbered) list. An introductory clause frequently includes words such as "the following" and "as follows." When creating a bulleted or enumerated list, capitalize the first word and insert a final punctuation mark (period, question mark, or exclamation point) after each item that is a complete sentence or phrase. Do not capitalize the first word or insert final punctuation when bulleted or enumerated list items are not complete thoughts.

Example:

The following qualifications are suggested for an air-conditioning mechanic applicant:

1. *high school diploma or equivalent, plus three years' experience*
2. *hold a valid driver's license*
3. *successful compliance with job-related medical standards*
4. *proof of U.S. citizenship or valid work permit*

Activities

Activity 19.1—Create a Form Template

1. Use the following information to create the form template shown on page 458.
    a. Select **File**, **New**, **Template**, **OK**.
    b. Set the top margin to 2".
    c. Display the Forms Toolbar (move the mouse pointer into the Standard or Formatting Toolbar in the gray area between buttons and click the *right* mouse button once; select **Forms**).
    d. Create a text form field that automatically inserts the current date. (Select the **Text Form Field** button. Select the **Form Field Options** button. In the Type box, select **Current Date**. In the Date Format box, select **MMMM d, yyyy**. Select **OK**.) Deselect the field and press **Enter** twice.
    e. Create a text form field for the guest's name. Create the Help message "Enter guest's name" to display in the Status Bar. (Select the **Text Form Field** button. Select the **Form Field Options** button. Select the **Add Help Text** button. On the Status Bar tab, select the **Type Your Own** option. Type **Enter guest's name**. Select **OK** twice.
    f. Deselect the field and press **Enter** once.
    g. Select the **Text Form Field** button to create a field for the guest's address. (If desired, create the Help message "Enter guest's street address" to be displayed in the Status Bar.)
    h. Deselect the field and press **Enter** once.
    i. Select the **Text Form Field** button to create a field for the guest's city, state, and zip code. (If desired, create the Help message "Enter guest's city, state and zip code" to be displayed in the Status Bar.)
    j. Deselect the field and press **Enter** twice. Type the word **Dear** and press the **Spacebar** once.
    k. Select the **Text Form Field** button to create a field for the salutation. (If desired, create the help message "Enter guest's name for the salutation" to be displayed in the Status Bar.)
    l. Type a colon (:) and press **Enter** twice. Type the following paragraph.

Thank you for choosing Gateway Resort for your lodging accommodations. We are pleased to confirm your reservation for the following:

m. Press **Enter** twice after the last character in the paragraph.

n. Press the **Tab** key once. Type **Arrival Date:** and press the **Tab** key twice. Select the **Text Form Field** button. Select the **Form Field Options** button. Change the Type to **Date** and the Date Format to **MMMM d, yyyy**. Select **OK**.

o. Deselect the field and press the **Enter** key once. Press the **Tab** key once. Type **Departure Date:** and press the **Tab** key once. Select the **Text Form Field** button. Select the **Form Field Options** button. Change the Type to **Date** and the Date Format to **MMMM d, yyyy**. Select **OK**.

p. Deselect the field and press the **Enter** key once. Press the **Tab** key once. Type **Room Rate:** and press the **Tab** key twice. Select the **Text Form Field** button. Select the **Form Field Options** button. Change

Current date

Dear :

Thank you for choosing Gateway Resort for your lodging accommodations. We are pleased to confirm your reservation for the following:

Arrival Date:
Departure Date:
Room Rate:
Number of Rooms:
Non-smoking Room: ☐ Yes ☐ No
Guarantee Method: Visa

To avoid any charges to your account, cancellations must be made at least 24 hours before your arrival date. Check-in time is and check-out time is .

If you have any questions or need further assistance, please contact the Lodging Department at (800)555-9250.

Sincerely,

Lodging Department

the Type to **Number** and the Number Format to **$#,##0.00; ($#,##0.00)**. Select **OK**.

q. Deselect the field and press the **Enter** key once. Press the **Tab** key once. Type **Number of Rooms:** and press the **Tab** key once. Select the **Text Form Field** button. Select the **Form Field Options** button. Change the Type to **Number** and the Number Format to **0**.

r. Deselect the field and press the **Enter** key once. Press the **Tab** key once. Type **Non-smoking Room:** and press the **Tab** key once. Select the **Check Box Form Field** button. Press the **Spacebar** once and type **Yes**. Press the **Tab** key once. Select the **Check Box Form Field** button. Press the **Spacebar** once and type **No**.

s. Deselect the field and press the **Enter** key once. Press the **Tab** key once. Type **Guarantee Method:** and press the **Tab** key once. Select the **Drop-Down Form Field** button. Select the **Form Field Options** button. In the Drop-Down Item box, add the following items:

Visa
MasterCard
American Express
Check

t. Select **OK**.

u. Deselect the field and press the **Enter** key twice and type the following text, inserting the text form fields as indicated:

To avoid any charges to your account, cancellations must be made at least 24 hours before your arrival date. Check-in time is *(insert a Text Form Field; set the Type to Date and the Date Format to h:mm AM/PM)* **and check-out time is** *(insert a Text Form Field; set the Type to Date and the Date Format to h:mm AM/PM).*

If you have any questions or need further assistance, please contact the Lodging Department at (800)555-9250.

Sincerely,

Lodging Department

2. Spell check and proofread the form.
3. Protect the form template (select the **Protect Form** button).
4. Remove the Forms Toolbar (move the mouse pointer into the Standard or Formatting Toolbar in the gray area between two buttons and click the *right* mouse button once; select **Forms**).
5. Use the filename **reserve.dot** and save the form template to your file disk (select **File, Save**; in the File Name box, type the drive letter where your file disk is located followed by a colon and the filename **reserve.dot**; select **OK**).

6. Print a copy of the form.
7. Close the document.
8. Use the **reserve** form template to create the document shown below (select **File**, **New**; type the drive letter where your file disk is located followed by a colon and the filename **reserve**; select **OK**). Press the **Tab** key to move from field to field.

Current date

Ms. Crystal Filla
13651 Smoketown Rd.
Woodbridge, VA 22191

Dear Ms. Filla:

Thank you for choosing Gateway Resort for your lodging accommodations. We are pleased to confirm your reservation for the following:

Arrival Date:	(Insert a date three weeks from the current date)
Departure Date:	(Insert a date two days after the arrival date)
Room Rate:	$ 125.95
Number of Rooms:	2
Non-smoking Room:	☒ Yes ☐ No
Guarantee Method:	American Express

To avoid any charges to your account, cancellations must be made at least 24 hours of your arrival date. Check-in time is 2:00 PM and check-out time is 11:30 AM.

If you have any questions or need further assistance, please contact the Lodging Department at (800)555-9250.

Sincerely,

Lodging Department

9. Use the filename **19filla.doc** and save the completed form.
10. Print one copy.
11. Close the document.

Activity 19.2—Edit a Form Template, Create Calculation Fields, and Create Macros to Update Calculation Fields

1. Copy the file named **invoice2.dot** located on the data disk to your file disk.
2. Open the form template named **invoice2.dot** [select **File**, **Open**; in the List Files of Type box select **Document Templates** (*.dot); select the drive where your file disk is located; double-click on **invoice2.dot**].

3. Display the Forms Toolbar (move the mouse pointer into the Standard or Formatting Toolbar in the gray area between two buttons and click the *right* mouse button once; select **Forms**).
4. Unprotect the form (select the **Protect Form** button).
5. Edit the form text as follows:
    a. Select the words "Company Name" and type **Derexon Consulting.**
    b. Select the words "Company address" and type **2956 Greene Street.**
    c. Select the words "Phone number" and type **509-555-3246.**
    d. Select the words "City, State, Zip" and type **Spokane, WA 99207.**
    e. Place the insertion point in the blank line at the top of the document and insert the graphic image named **computer.wmf** that is located in the Word clipart subdirectory (select **Insert, Picture**, double-click on **computer.wmf**).
    f. Select the *computer.wmf* graphic image and insert a frame (click on the *computer.wmf* graphic image; select **Insert, Frame**; if necessary, select **Yes** to switch to the Page Layout view).
    g. Set the Horizontal position of the frame containing the *computer.wmf* graphic image to **Center** and set the Vertical position to **Top.** Set the Text Wrapping to **None.** (Select **Format, Frame.** In the Horizontal area, set the Position to **Center.** In the Vertical area, set the Position to **Top.** Select **None** in the Text Wrapping area. Select **OK.**)
    h. Select **File, Save** to save the edited form template.
6. Place the insertion point in the first cell below the column heading Rate/Hour (do not select the cell). Select the **Text Form Field** button. Select the **Form Field Options** button. Set the Type to **Number** and the Number Format to **$#,##0.00;($#,##0.00)**.
7. Place the insertion point in the first cell below the column heading Total. Select the **Text Form Field** button. Select the **Form Field Options** button. Set the Type to **Calculation.** In the Expression box, type =(**B2*D2**) to multiply the number of hours by the rate. Set the Number Format to **#,##0.00**. Change the Bookmark name to **Total1**.
8. Place the insertion point in the second cell below the column heading Rate/Hour. Create a **Text Form Field.** Set the Type to **Number** and the Number format to **#,##0.00**.
9. Place the insertion point in the second cell below the column heading Total. Create a **Text Form Field.** Set the Type to **Calculation.** In the Expression box, type =(**B3*D3**). Set the Number Format to **#,##0.00**. Change the Bookmark name to **Total2**.
10. Place the insertion point in the third cell below the column heading Rate/Hour. Create a **Text Form Field.** Set the Type to **Number** and the Number Format to **#,##0.00**.

11. Place the insertion point in the third cell below the column heading Total. Create a **Text Form Field**. Set the Type to **Calculation**. In the Expression box, type **=(B4*D4)**. Set the Number Format to **#,##0.00**. Change the Bookmark name to **Total3**.

12. Place the insertion point in the fourth cell below the column heading Rate/Hour. Create a **Text Form Field**. Set the Type to **Number** and the Number Format to **#,##0.00**.

13. Place the insertion point in the fourth cell below the column heading Total. Create a **Text Form Field**. Set the Type to **Calculation**. In the Expression box, type **=(B5*D5)**. Set the Number Format to **#,##0.00**. Change the Bookmark name to **Total4**.

14. Place the insertion point in the fifth cell below the column heading Rate/Hour. Create a **Text Form Field**. Set the Type to **Number** and the Number Format to **#,##0.00**.

15. Place the insertion point in the fifth cell below the column heading Total. Create a **Text Form Field**. Set the Type to **Calculation**. In the Expression box, type **=(B6*D6)**. Set the Number Format to **#,##0.00**. Change the Bookmark name to **Total5**.

16. Place the insertion point in the sixth cell below the column heading Total. Create a **Text Form Field**. Set the Type to **Calculation**. In the Expression box, type **=SUM(ABOVE)**. Set the Number Format to **$#,##0.00;($#,##0.00)**. Change the Bookmark name to **Total6**.

17. Save the template before continuing (select **File**, **Save**).

18. Use the following information to create five macros that will be used to update the calculation fields.

    Note: *Each macro will update two calculation fields. For example, the first macro will update the calculation field identified with the Bookmark name Total1 and the calculation field identified with the Bookmark name Total6. The second macro will update the calculation field identified with the Bookmark name Total2 and the calculation field identified with the Bookmark name Total6 and so on.*

    a. Select **Tools**, **Macro**.

    b. In the Macro Name box, type **Update1**.

    c. In the Macros Available In box, select **Invoice2.dot (Template)**.

    d. Select **Create**.

    e. Type the following two lines between the Sub MAIN and End Sub lines:

    ```
    SetFormResult "total1"
    SetFormResult "total6"
    ```

    f. Select **File**, **Save Template**, **Yes**.

    g. Select **File**, **Close**.

    h. Select **Tools**, **Macro**. In the Macro Name box, type **Update2**. Select **Create**.

    i. Type the following two lines between the Sub MAIN and End Sub lines:

SetFormResult "total2"
SetFormResult "total6"

j. Select **File, Save Template, Yes**. Select **File, Close**.

k. Select **Tools, Macro**. In the Macro Name box, type **Update3**. Select **Create**.

l. Type the following two lines between the Sub MAIN and End Sub lines:

   SetFormResult "total3"
   SetFormResult "total6"

m. Select **File, Save Template, Yes**. Select **File, Close**.

n. Select **Tools, Macro**. In the Macro Name box, type **Update4**. Select **Create**.

o. Type the following two lines between the Sub MAIN and End Sub lines:

   SetFormResult "total4"
   SetFormResult "total6"

p. Select **File, Save Template, Yes**. Select **File, Close**.

q. Select **Tools, Macro**. In the Macro Name box, type **Update5**. Select **Create**.

r. Type the following two lines between the Sub MAIN and End Sub lines:

   SetFormResult "total5"
   SetFormResult "total6"

s. Select **File, Save Template, Yes**. Select **File, Close**.

19. Use the following information to assign the macros to the appropriate form fields.

a. Double-click on the form field in the first cell below the column heading Rate/Hour. Click in the **Exit** box in the Run Macro On area and select **Update1**. Select **OK**.

b. Double-click on the form field in the second cell below the column heading Rate/Hour. Click in the **Exit** box in the Run Macro On area and select **Update2**. Select **OK**.

c. Double-click on the form field in the third cell below the column heading Rate/Hour. Click in the **Exit** box in the Run Macro On area and select **Update3**. Select **OK**.

d. Double-click on the form field in the fourth cell below the column heading Rate/Hour. Click in the **Exit** box in the Run Macro On area and select **Update4**. Select **OK**.

e. Double-click on the form field in the fifth cell below the column heading Rate/Hour. Click in the **Exit** box in the Run Macro On area and select **Update5**. Select **OK**.

20. Protect the form (select the **Protect Form** button).

21. Save the template (select **File, Save**).

22. Close the template.

23. Select **File**, **New**. Type the drive letter where your file disk is located followed by a colon and the filename **invoice2**. Select **OK**.

24. Use the information shown below to complete the form. Press the **Tab** key to move from field to field.

Derexon Consulting
509-555-3246

2956 Greene Street
Spokane, WA 99207

Consulting Services Invoice

Invoice Date:	Current Date
Client Name:	Baird & Associates
Contact Person:	Nina Weever
Address:	P.O. Box 2254
City, State Zip	Spokane, WA 99210

Date	No. of Hours	Description of Services	Rate/Hour	Total
Insert the date for last Tuesday	4	Consultation on implementation of the Microsoft Office as the company standard	$ 65.00	260.00
Insert the date for last Thursday	2	Meeting to schedule staff training on Microsoft Office programs	45.00	90.00
Insert the date for last Friday	4	Assessment of conversion of existing database to Microsoft Access	65.00	260.00
			Invoice Total	$ 610.00

25. Use the filename **19inv.doc** and save the document.

26. Print one copy.

27. Close the document.

Challenge Your Skills

Skill 19.1—Create a Form Template; Use the Form Template; Language Arts

1. Create the form template shown below.
2. Correct three spelling errors and two punctuation/grammar errors.
3. When the form template is completed, protect and save the template to your file disk using the filename **19griev1.dot**.
4. Print one copy of the template.

AUL Workers of America
District 3
14241 Pleasant Valley Road
Columbus, Ohio 44130
(614) 555-2400 — FAX (614) 555-2421

Current Date ← Insert a Text Form Field, Current Date type, Date Format—MMMM d, yyyy

Create a Drop-Down Form Feld containing the following items:
Russell Gehris, President, AULWA, Local 1210
Shelia McClendon, President, AULWA, Local 1220
Matthew Siskind, President, AULWA, Local 1230
Pam Messer, President, AULWA, Local 1240

To: Russell Gehris, President, AULWA, Local 1210

From: Karen P. Rutledge, AULWA Representative

Subject: Arbitation Case No. ← Insert a Text Form Field, Number type, maximum length 6
Grievence No. ← Insert a Text Form Field, Number type
Grievant Name ← Insert a Text Form Field
Issue ← Insert a Text Form Field
Note: If desired, create Help text for each of these fields.

This is to advise you that the following action has been taken on the above grievance:

☐ initial claim has been received and the time limits protected

☐ has been accepted for further processing.

☐ Is continuing to be processed

Remarks:

This case is being forwarded to the District Legal Department for further processing. Future contacts should be made with, and received from, the District Legal staff. In accordance with District policy the Legal Department handles contract interpetation cases such as this.

Please be advised that the Union discussed the above pending arbitration case with ______ (Insert a Text Form Field) representative(s) on ______. (Insert a Text Form Field, Date type, Date Format—MMMM d, yyyy)

You are requested to inform the Grievant of this action.

KPR/xx

cc: J. Brenning

Chapter 19 Create Fill-in Forms

5. Close the document.
6. Use the **19griev1.dot** template to create the form shown below.
7. Use the filename **19skill1.doc** and save the file on your file disk.
8. Print one copy.
9. If you have completed your work, exit Word.

AUL Workers of America
District 3
14241 Pleasant Valley Road
Columbus, Ohio 44130
(614) 555-2400 — FAX (614) 555-2421

Current Date

To: Matthew Siskind, President, Local 1230

From: Karen P. Rutledge, AULWA Representative

Subject:	Arbitration Case No.	854217
	Grievence No.	123004458
	Grievant Name	Destefano, Jack
	Issue	Employment Status

This is to advise you that the following action has been taken on the above grievance:

☐ initial claim has been received and the time limits protected

☒ has been accepted for further processing.

☐ Is continuing to be processed

Remarks:

This case is being forwarded to the District Legal Department for further processing. Future contacts should be made with, and received from, the District Legal staff. In accordance with District policy the Legal Department handles contract interpetation cases such as this.

Please be advised that the Union discussed the above pending arbitration case with Columbus Cement representative(s) on (insert last Tuesday's date).

You are requested to inform the Grievant of this action.

KPR/xx

cc: J. Brenning

Part 5 Checking Your Step

Production Skill Builder Activities Chapters 17-19

Production Activity 5.1—Create a Tri-Fold Brochure

1. Create a tri-fold brochure using the following information:
    a. The brochure describes the mini vacation packages offered by Villa Padilla Resort and Golf.
    b. The brochure text is contained in the file named **5pact1.doc** located on the data disk.
    c. Make decisions regarding:
        Use of the **brochur1** template
        Margins
        Font, point size and justification for text
        Use of shadow boxes
        Colors for borders and text
        Appropriate graphic image(s)
        (Suggested graphic images: **golf.wmf**, **tennis.wmf**, **spring.wmf** **dinner1.wmf**, or **dinner2.wmf**)
        Rotated text for second column of page 2 (return address)
        Use of graphic image(s), reversed text, and borders for the third column of page 2 (the cover of the brochure)
2. Use the filename **5golf.doc** and save the file.
3. Print one copy.
4. Close the document.

Production Activity 5.2—Create a Magazine Article (Group Project)

1. In groups of 3–5 people, write a magazine article that contains pull quote(s), sidebar information, different left and right page footers, columns with different widths, and graphic images.
2. Suggested article topics:

   Favorite features in Word 6.0 for Windows
   Word 6.0 for Windows vs. WordPerfect 6.0 for Windows
   Incorporating sound and/or animation in documents
   Desktop publishing features in Word 6.0 for Windows
3. Make decisions regarding:

   Margins
   Use of WordArt for article title
   Font and point size for article text
   Use of drop cap(s)
   Column widths
   Pull quote information, format, and placement
   Appropriate graphic image(s)
   Sidebar information, format, and placement
   Use of shadow box, reversed text and/or rotated text
   Indentation for first line of paragraphs
   Footer text
4. Save the final magazine article using the filename **5pact2.doc**.
5. Print one copy and close the document.

Production Activity 5.3—Create and Use a Form Template

1. Create the form template shown on page 469. Make decisions regarding:

   Types of form fields to be created
   Adding Help text
   Justification of text within the table
   Table borders
   Fonts and point sizes

   Hint: *To indent text within a table cell, press **Ctrl** and **Tab**.*
2. When the form template is completed, protect and save the template to your file disk using the filename **checklst.dot**.
3. Print one copy of the template.
4. Close the template.

PC RENTAL CHECKLIST

Customer Name:	Phone Number:	
Date Out: Current Date	Date In:	
Model Number: 486-66	Serial Number:	
Accessories Included:	Yes	No
Power Supply	☐	☐
A/C Cable	☐	☐
VGA Cable	☐	☐
Mac Cables	☐	☐
Mouse/Trackball	☐	☐
Pen/Tablet	☐	☐
Speakers	☐	☐
Fax/Modem (PCMCIA Card)	☐	☐
Additional Supplies:		
Received By:	Returned By:	
Date:	Date:	

Text Form Field, Current Date type, Date Format M/d/yy

Text Form Field, Date type, Date Format M/d/yy

Drop-Down Form Field with the following items:
486-100
486-75
486-66
386-40
386-33
Laptop 486-66

5. Use the **checklst** template and create the form document shown on page 470.
6. Use the *new* filename **5chklst.doc** and save the file.
7. Print one copy
8. Close the document.

PC RENTAL CHECKLIST

<table>
<tr><td>Customer Name:
Augustine Occhipinti</td><td colspan="2">Phone Number:
504-555-1342</td></tr>
<tr><td>Date Out: Current Date</td><td colspan="2">Date In: (insert a date one week from current date)</td></tr>
<tr><td>Model Number: Laptop 486</td><td colspan="2">Serial Number: P24623</td></tr>
<tr><td>Accessories Included:</td><td>Yes</td><td>No</td></tr>
<tr><td>Power Supply</td><td>☐</td><td>☒</td></tr>
<tr><td>A/C Cable</td><td>☒</td><td>☐</td></tr>
<tr><td>VGA Cable</td><td>☐</td><td>☒</td></tr>
<tr><td>Mac Cables</td><td>☐</td><td>☒</td></tr>
<tr><td>Mouse/Trackball</td><td>☐</td><td>☒</td></tr>
<tr><td>Pen/Tablet</td><td>☐</td><td>☒</td></tr>
<tr><td>Speakers</td><td>☒</td><td>☐</td></tr>
<tr><td>Fax/Modem (PCMCIA Card)</td><td>☒</td><td>☐</td></tr>
<tr><td colspan="3">Additional Supplies:
Carrying case, 1 extra battery, 1 recharger</td></tr>
<tr><td>Received By:</td><td colspan="2">Returned By:</td></tr>
<tr><td>Date:</td><td colspan="2">Date:</td></tr>
</table>

Part 6
Step Right Up

Create Special Documents

Chapters 20-22

- Use Line Numbering
- Use the Revisions feature
- Use the Compare Versions feature
- Mark hidden text
- Insert annotations
- Create bookmarks
- Create outlines
- Create a table of contents
- Create an index
- Create a table of authorities
- Create paragraph styles containing borders
- Create a style containing a special symbol
- Designate one style to follow another
- Use the Style Gallery
- Create cross-references
- Create master documents

CHAPTER 20

Advanced Editing Techniques

Features Covered

- Turn on line numbering
- Use the Revisions feature
- Use the Compare Versions feature
- Mark hidden text
- Insert annotations
- Create bookmarks

Objectives and Introduction

After successfully completing this chapter, you will be able to turn on line numbering, use the Revisions feature to mark inserted and deleted text, and use the Compare Versions feature to mark the differences between two documents. You will also be able to use the Annotations and Hidden Text features to insert notes into a document and to electronically mark a specific portion of text by using the Bookmark feature.

Word's line numbering feature can be turned on to print a line number beside each line of text in a document. This feature is often used when creating legal documents. The Revisions feature can be used to mark inserted and deleted text as a document is edited. The Compare Versions feature is used to mark the differences between two documents. The Revisions and Compare Versions features are used to help track the changes made to a document. The Annotations and Hidden Text features are used to insert notes into a document. These features are often used when a document is reviewed by more than one person. Each person reviewing the document inserts hidden text or annotations that suggest changes, ask additional questions, or add remarks about the document's contents. The author of the document can then review the annotations or hidden text and determine the changes that need to be made to the document. Bookmarks are used to mark text and enable you to quickly go to different portions of a document.

Turn On Line Numbering

A number can be placed beside each line of text in a document. Line numbering is often used for legal documents and other documents in which text needs to be referenced by line number.

The Line Numbers dialog box is used to turn on line numbering and to control how line numbers are printed (see Figure 20.1). The **Start At** option is used to change the number of the first line. For example, instead of beginning the line numbers at number 1, line numbers can be set to begin at number 100. The **Count By** option is used to specify the interval at which numbers will be printed. For example, Word can be instructed to print line numbers every fifth line.

Lines numbers are placed in the left margin. The default (Auto) position for line numbers is .25 inches to the left of text in a single column layout and .13 inches to the left of text in a multiple-column layout. If desired, the distance between the line numbers and text can be increased or decreased by specifying the desired amount of space in the **From Text** box in the Line Numbers dialog box.

When the **Restart Each Page** option is selected in the Line Numbers dialog box, the line numbers on each page begin counting again from the number designated in the Start At box. If the **Restart Each Section** option is selected, the line numbers begin counting again at the beginning of each section from the number designated in the Start At box. If the **Continuous** option is selected, the lines on all pages of a document will be numbered consecutively.

The font, color, or text attributes (bold, italic, etc.) for the line numbers can be changed by modifying the Line Number style. Select **Format**, **Style**, choose the **Line Number** style name, choose **Modify**, and make the desired change(s) in the Modify Style dialog box.

After line numbers have been turned on, the numbers can be viewed in the document window; however, it may be necessary to use the horizontal scroll bar to view the left margin of the page. Also, the **Page Width** or **Whole Page Zoom Control** option can be selected to view the placement of the line numbers on the page. The line numbers can also be viewed by selecting the **Print Preview** button.

If desired, line numbers can be suppressed by selecting the paragraph(s) for which you want to suppress the line numbers and choosing **Format**, **Paragraph**. On the Text Flow tab, select **Suppress Line Numbers** and choose **OK**. Line numbers can be turned off for specific paragraphs or for a section of a document by selecting the desired paragraphs or section and choosing **File**, **Page Setup**. On the Layout tab, select the **Line Numbers** button. Click on **Add Line Numbering** to deselect the option and select **OK** twice.

Start-Up Instructions

- Open the file named **20drill1.doc** located on the data disk.

Turn On Line Numbering

1. Place the insertion point at the location at which the line numbering should begin.

   For example, place the insertion point at the beginning of the document.

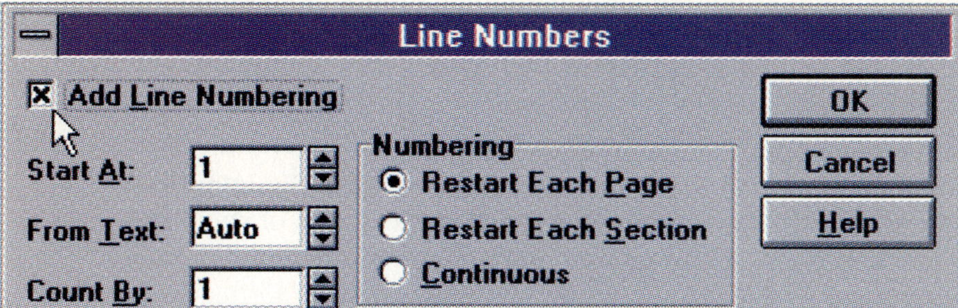

FIGURE 20.1

Line Numbers dialog box

2. Select **File, Page Setup** {Alt, f, u}.
3. Select the **Layout** tab {Alt and L}.
4. Select the **Line Numbers** button {Alt and n}.

   Note: *The Line Numbers dialog box displays.*
5. Select **Add Line Numbering** {L}.
6. Select or change any desired option(s).

   For example, check that the option settings in the Line Numbers dialog box match the settings shown in Figure 20.1.
7. Select **OK** to exit the Line Numbers dialog box {Enter}.
8. Select **OK** to exit the Page Setup dialog box {Enter}.

   Note: *If necessary, use the horizontal scroll bar to scroll to the left to view the line numbers. Line numbers can also be viewed by selecting the down arrow beside the* ***Zoom Control*** *box and choosing the* ***Page Width*** *or* ***Whole Page*** *option.*

Finish-Up Instructions

- Use the *new* filename **20num1.doc** and save the file on your file disk.
- Print one copy and close the document.

Use the Revisions Feature

The Revisions feature can be used to automatically mark editing changes in a document. When the Revisions feature is turned on, inserted text is underlined, the strikethrough text attribute is applied to deleted text, and a revision bar displays in the margin next to lines that contain inserted or deleted text. All editing changes display in a color.

If more than one person edits a document, different colors are used to distinguish the revisions of each reviewer. Word has eight colors available for marking revisions. If more than eight individuals review a document, the same color will be used for more than one reviewer. Word uses the information stored on the User Info tab of the Options dialog box to determine the name of the person editing a document. Each piece of inserted or deleted text is marked with the date, time, and reviewer's name. This information can be viewed by placing the insertion point in the edited text and selecting **Tools**, **Revisions**, **Review**. The Review Revisions dialog box displays, showing the name of the person who made the change and the date and time the change was made. The revision can be accepted or rejected. Other revisions can be located by selecting the **Find** buttons.

When multiple reviewers receive copies of the document, the suggested revisions of each reviewer can be merged into the original document. To merge the revisions into the original document, open the file containing the revisions, select **Tools, Revisions, Merge Revisions.** Type or select the name of the original document and select **OK.** Repeat this process until the revisions for all copies of the document have been merged into the original document.

The method and color used to mark revised text can be changed. By default inserted text is underlined. If desired, the method of marking inserted text can be changed to bold by selecting the **Options** button in the Revisions dialog box and making the desired changes to the options on the Revisions tab. (See the Steps to Change the Method of Marking Revisions on page 477.)

After revisions have been made, the Revisions dialog box can be used to **Accept All** changes, to **Reject All** changes, or to **Review** each change and make a decision to accept or reject each change individually. If a change(s) is accepted, Word removes deleted text and removes the color and underline (or other selected attribute) from inserted text. If a change(s) is rejected, Word deletes inserted text and removes the strikethrough attribute from deleted text.

Start-Up Instructions

- Open the file named **20drill2.doc** located on the data disk.

Steps to Use the Revisions Feature

1. Select **Tools, Revisions** {Alt, t, v}.

   Note: The Revisions dialog box displays (see Figure 20.2).

2. Select the desired option(s).

   For example, in the Document Revisions area, select **Mark Revisions While Editing.** The Show Revisions on Screen and Show Revisions in Printed Document options should also be selected.

3. Select **OK** {Enter}.

4. Make the desired changes.

   For example, select the word "**completely**" in the first sentence of the first paragraph and type the word "**fully.**"

   *Note: When the word "**fully**" is typed, the letters display in a color and are underlined and the word "**completely**" has been formatted as strikethrough (e.g., ~~completely~~).*

FIGURE 20.2

Revisions dialog box

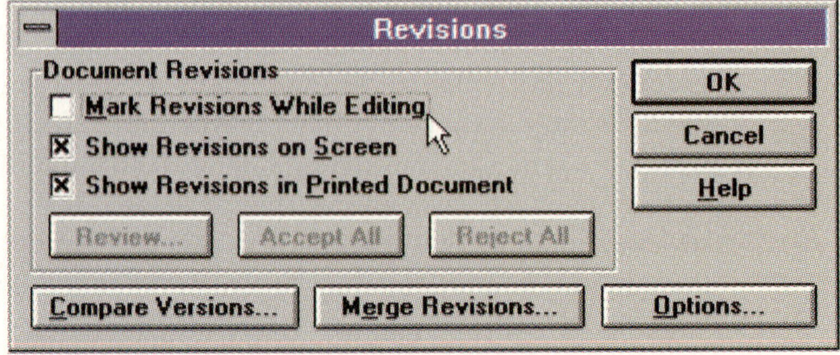

FIGURE 20.3

Revision text

Membership and Voting Rights

Section 1

Every owner of a lot that is subject to assessment shall be a member of the Association. Each owner is obligated to promptly, fully ~~completely~~, and faithfully comply and conform to the Articles, Bylaws, Covenants, Conditions, and Restrictions. # Membership in the Association shall not be transferred, pledged, or alienated in any way except upon the sale of the lot. Any attempt to make a prohibited transfer is void.

Section 2

The Association will have ~~a single~~ one class of voting membership that shall be all owners who are entitled to one vote for each lot owned. When more than one person owns an interest in any lot, all such persons shall be members. The vote for such lot will be exercised as they determine, but in no event shall more than one vote be cast with respect to any lot.

Section 3

Any provision calling for membership approval of action to be taken by the Association shall require the assent of the prescribed percentage of Association members existing at the time of such action. If the proposed action is favored by a majority of the votes cast at the membership meeting, but such vote is less than the required percentage of members, the approval of members who are not present in person must be given in writing ~~sixty~~ thirty (~~60~~ 30) days prior to such action being implemented.

Finish-Up Instructions

- Make the changes shown in Figure 20.3.
- Use the *new* filename **20revis2.doc** and save the file on your file disk.
- Print one copy

Start-Up Instructions

- The file named **20revis2.doc** should be displayed in the document window.

Change the Method of Marking Revisions

1. With the insertion point located anywhere in the document, select **Tools, Revisions** {Alt, t, v}.
2. In the Revisions dialog box, select the **Options** button {o}.

   Note: *The Options dialog box displays with the Revisions tab selected.*
3. Select the desired option(s) for the display of Inserted Text, Deleted Text, and Revised Lines.

   For example, in the Inserted Text area, click in the **Mark** box and select **Bold.**
4. Select **OK** twice {Enter}.

Note: The inserted text in the document now displays in bold (instead of underlined).

Remove Revision Marks

1. Place the insertion point at the top of the document (**Ctrl** and **Home**).
2. Select **Tools, Revisions** {Alt, t, v}.
3. Select the **Review, Accept All,** or **Reject All** option.

   For example, to accept the revisions, select **Accept All.** Select **Yes** to the message "Do you want to accept all revisions in 20revis2.doc?"

4. Select **OK** to close the Revisions dialog box.

   Note: The color and bolding for the inserted text has been removed and the deleted (strikethrough) text has been removed from the document.

Finish-Up Instructions

- Use the same filename **20revis2.doc** and save the file again.
- Print one copy.
- To return to the default method for marking revisions, select **Tools**, **Revisions**, **Options**. In the Inserted Text area, click in the **Mark** box and select **Underline**. Select **OK** twice.
- Close the document.

Use the Compare Versions Feature

The Compare Versions feature is used to identify the differences between the text in two files. When documents are compared, Word uses revision marks to identify inserted and deleted text. Inserted text is underlined, deleted text is formatted with the strikethrough attribute and all editing changes are marked in color also. After the documents have been compared, revision marks can be removed using the Steps to Remove Revision Marks.

Start-Up Instructions

- Open the file named **20drill3.doc** located on the data disk.

Use Compare Versions

1. Make desired revisions.

   For example, make the revisions shown in Figure 20.4. Use the *new* filename **20comp3.doc** and save the file on your file disk.

2. Select **Tools, Revisions** {Alt, t, v}.
3. Select **Compare Versions** {c}.
4. Type or select the filename of the original version of the document.

FIGURE 20.4

Revised text

Tuition Assistance Program

Steller Systems ~~recognizes~~ acknowledges that continuing education is important to the development of motivated and informed employees. Therefore, the company's Tuition Assistance Program reimburses hourly employees who work at least ~~20~~ 25 hours per week and salaried employee for expenses related to degree programs and/or courses at accredited colleges and universities. To be eligible for tuition assistance, employees must have been employed by Steller Systems for a period of one year.

The maximum reimbursement for covered expenses and tuition is $~~725~~ 1,000 per year.

For example, select the file named **20drill3.doc** located on the data disk.

Note: *In a moment, the document displays with revision marks showing the inserted and deleted text.*

Finish-Up Instructions

- Use the same filename **20comp3.doc** and save the file again.
- Print one copy.
- Close the document.

Mark Hidden Text

The Hidden Text feature is useful for creating notes, questions, messages, or confidential information that can display (be visible on the screen) or be hidden (not displayed on the screen). By using hidden text, a single document can be used for more than one purpose. For example, a list of employee names, departments, business phone numbers, home phone numbers, and home addresses can be created, marking the home phone numbers and home addresses as hidden text. The complete document, including the hidden text, can then be printed for managers while a second document containing only the employee names, departments, and business phone numbers can be printed for everyone else.

Hidden text *displays* in the document window when nonprinting characters are turned on or if the **Hidden Text** option is selected on the View tab of the Options dialog box. Text that has been formatted as hidden will *print* if the **Hidden Text** option is selected on the Print tab of the Options dialog box.

Start-Up Instructions

- Open the file named **20drill4.doc** located on the data disk.

Steps to Use the Hidden Text Effect

1. If necessary, select the **Show/Hide** button to display the nonprinting characters.
2. Select the text to be hidden.

   For example, move the mouse pointer above the column heading **Salary** until a down arrow displays and click once to select the entire column.
3. Select **Format, Font** {Alt, o, f}.
4. Select **Hidden** in the Effects area {Alt and i}.
5. Select **OK** {Enter}.
6. Click once to deselect the text.

   Note: A dotted underline displays below the text formatted as hidden.
7. Select the **Show/Hide** button to turn off the display of nonprinting characters.

   Note: When nonprinting characters are turned off, the hidden text will not display; however, the table gridlines for the hidden column will continue to display.

Finish-Up Instructions

- Use the *new* filename **20hide4.doc** and save the file on your file disk.
- Print one copy.

  *Note: The hidden text should not print. However, if the hidden text does print, the **Hidden Text** option has been selected on the Print tab in the Options dialog box (see Steps to Print Hidden Text).*

Start-Up Instructions

- The file named **20hide4.doc** should be displayed in the document window.

Print Hidden Text

1. Once text has been marked as hidden, select **File, Print** {Alt, f, p}.
2. Select the **Options** button {Alt and o}.

   Note: The Options dialog box displays with the Print tab selected.
3. Select the **Hidden Text** option in the Include with Document area {Alt and i}.
4. Select **OK** twice.

Finish-Up Instructions

- To turn off the printing of hidden text, select **File, Print, Options,** click on the **Hidden Text** option in the Include with Document area, select **OK, Close.**
- Close the document.

Insert Annotations

Notes (annotations) can be placed within a document using the Annotations feature. Annotations can remind you of special formatting or printing requirements, or other tasks that need to be accomplished. For example, an annotation might remind you to load letterhead paper into the printer before printing the document or to call to verify the title of the addressee before sending a letter. The Annotations feature can also be used to collect the responses of people who review a document. For example, a proposal can be sent via e-mail (electronic mail) to several people asking for their input. The reviewers can insert their annotations into the document and return the document to the originator of the document.

When an annotation is created, an annotation mark is placed in the document at the location of the insertion point or after selected text. The annotation mark is formatted as hidden text and displays only if nonprinting characters are turned on or if the **Hidden Text** option is selected on the View tab of the Options dialog box.

The annotation mark contains the initials of the reviewer (as stored in the User Info tab of the Options dialog box) and the annotation number. Annotations are numbered sequentially throughout a document. If an annotation is added or deleted, Word automatically renumbers the annotations as needed.

When creating or viewing annotations, the Annotation pane displays at the bottom of the document window. The annotation mark(s) and annotation text display in the Annotation pane. If desired, annotations from a single reviewer or from all reviewers can be displayed by clicking in the **From** box on the Annotation pane and selecting the desired reviewer's name or selecting **All Reviewers**. If sound equipment is installed on your system, the **Insert Sound Object** button can be used to record a voice annotation.

Annotations can be located in a document by selecting **Edit**, **Go To**, choosing **Annotation** in the Go to What box and selecting the **Next** or **Previous** button. To delete an annotation, highlight the annotation mark in the document window and press the **Delete** key. If desired, annotation text can be moved from the Annotation pane into the document by selecting the desired annotation text and dragging the text to the desired location in the document.

If copies of a document are distributed to several reviewers, the annotations from each reviewer can be merged into the original document so that all the annotations can be reviewed at one time. To merge the annotations into the original document, open the document containing the annotation(s), select **Tools**, **Revisions**, **Merge Revisions**, type or select the name of the original document, and select **OK**. Repeat this process until the annotations in each copy of the document have been merged into the original document.

Printing annotations can be accomplished by selecting the **Options** button in the Print dialog box, choosing the **Annotations** option in the Include with Document area, and select **OK** twice. When the **Annotations** option is selected, Word automatically selects the **Hidden Text** option. When the document is printed, the annotation mark(s) is printed in the document, and the annotation text is printed on a separate page. A page reference is included with the annotation text. If you wish to print only the annotation text (without the document), select **File**, **Print**, select **Annotations** in the Print What box, and choose **OK**.

Start-Up Instructions

- Open the file named **20drill5.doc** located on the data disk.

View an Annotation(s)

1. If necessary, turn on nonprinting characters by selecting the **Show/Hide** button.
2. Move the mouse pointer to the annotation mark and click once.

   For example, move the mouse pointer to the annotation mark [km1] located at the end of the subject line and double-click.

   Note: The Annotation pane displays at the bottom of the document window, showing the annotation text.

3. To close the Annotation pane and return to the document, select the **Close** button on the Annotation pane.

Insert an Annotation(s)

1. Select the text for which the annotation is to be made, or place the insertion point at the location at which the annotation mark should be inserted into the document.

   For example, place the insertion point after the final period in the paragraph the begins Excellent—. . . .

2. Select **Insert, Annotation** {Alt, i, a}.

   Note: An annotation mark is placed in the document. The annotation mark is formatted as hidden text. The annotation mark contains the initials stored in the User Info

FIGURE 20.5

Document window containing annotation marks and the Annotation pane

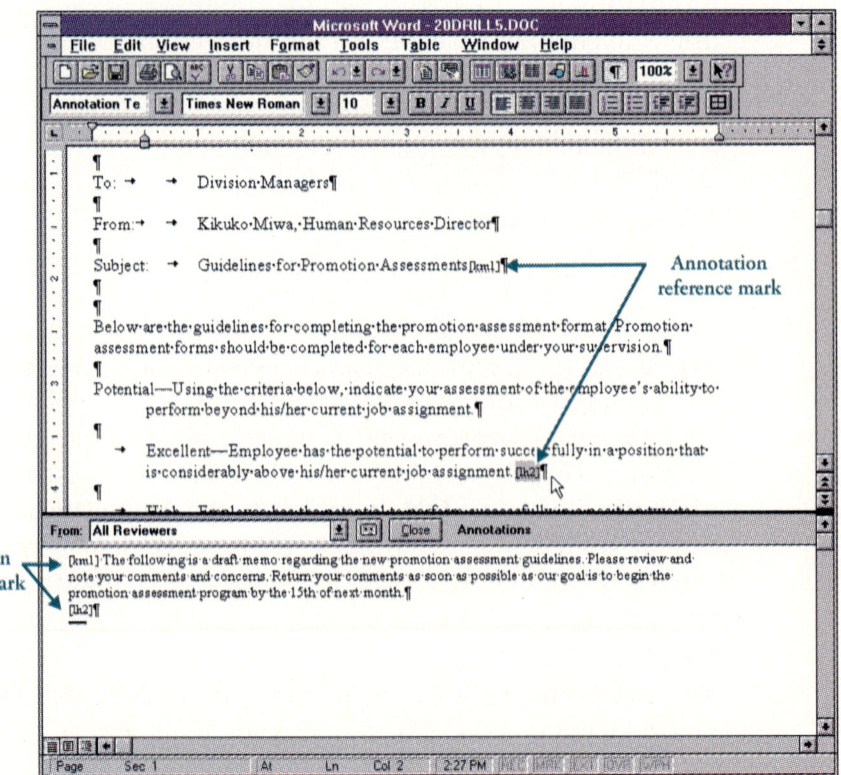

tab of the Options dialog box and the annotation number (see Figure 20.5). The annotation mark is also placed in the Annotation pane displayed at the bottom of the document window.

3. Type the annotation text.

   For example, press the **Spacebar** once and type the following:
   I suggest that the following sentence be added to this paragraph: This designation should be reserved for employees who have the potential for top-level management. (Insert your initials.)

4. Select the **Close** button on the Annotation pane.

Finish-Up Instructions

- Place the insertion point in the blank line below the last paragraph in the document.
- Repeat steps 2–4 and create the following annotation:

  I suggest the following scale:
  Now--Employee is ready for promotion.
  6-18--Employee will be ready for promotion in 6 to 18 months.
  18-36--Employee will be ready for promotion in 18 to 36 months.
  36-60--Employee will be ready for promotion in 36 to 60 months.

- Use the *new* filename **20annot5.doc** and save the file.
- Continue with the Steps to Print Annotations.

Start-Up Instructions

- The file named **20annot5.doc** should be displayed in the document window.

Print Annotations

1. Select **File, Print** {Alt, f, p}.
2. Select the **Options** button {Alt and o}.

   Note: *The Options dialog box displays with the Print tab selected.*

3. Select **Annotations** in the Include with Document area {a}.

   Note: *The Hidden Text option is automatically selected when the Annotations option is chosen.*

4. Select **OK** twice.

   Note: *When the document is printed, the annotation marks, which are formatted as hidden text, are printed in the document and a separate page(s) containing the annotation text is printed.*

Finish-Up Instructions

- To turn off the printing of annotations, select **File, Print, Options**, deselect **Annotations** and **Hidden Text** in the Include with Document area, select **OK, Close**.

- Close the document.

Create Bookmarks

The Bookmark feature enables you to electronically mark a specific portion of text in a document in a manner similar to placing a paper bookmark within a book to mark a reference or page. Several bookmarks can be placed in a document. Each bookmark is given a unique name. A bookmark name can contain up to 40 characters including letters, numbers, hyphens, and underscores. However, the bookmark name cannot contain any spaces.

By default, the location of bookmarks do not display in a document. If desired, bookmark indicators can be displayed by selecting **Tools**, **Options**, choosing the View tab, selecting **Bookmarks** in the Show area, and choosing **OK**. The bookmark indicator displays as a very large I-beam.

Bookmarks can also be used when creating cross-references in a document (see Chapter 22), naming cells and performing calculations in a table or text (see Chapter 23), and inserting information in a mail merge document (see Chapter 24).

Start-Up Instructions

- Open the file named **20drill6.doc** located on the data disk.

Create a Bookmark

1. Place the insertion point at the location where the bookmark will be inserted.

   For example, place the insertion point at the beginning of the heading **Shopping Malls** on page 2 of the document.

2. Select **Edit, Bookmark** {Alt, e, b}.

   Note: *The Bookmark dialog box displays.*

3. Type the desired bookmark name.

   For example, type **shopping_malls**. (Do not type the period.)

   Note: *A bookmark name can be up to 40 characters (letters, numbers, hyphens, and underscores) with no spaces.*

4. Select **Add**.

   Note: *No change displays in the document window. To view the bookmark indicator, select* ***Tools, Options****. On the View tab, select the* ***Bookmarks*** *option in the Show area. Select* ***OK****. A large I-beam displays at the location where the bookmark was created.*

Finish-Up Instructions

- Place the insertion point at the beginning of the heading **Apartment Complexes** on page 3 of the document.
- Repeat steps 2–4 to create a bookmark named **apartment**.
- Place the insertion point at the beginning of the heading **Warehouse/Distribution Properties** on page 4.

Steps to Number an Outline

1. To number an outline, select the lines to be numbered.

   For example, select all lines of the outline.

2. Select **Format, Heading Numbering** {Alt, o, h}.
3. Select the desired numbering style.

   For example, check that the top left outline Heading Numbering sample is selected. (If necessary, click in the top left Heading Numbering sample.)

   Note: *The selected Heading Numbering sample displays with a colored border or outline.*

4. Select **OK**.

Finish-Up Instructions

- Use the same filename **21pout1.doc** and save the file.
- Continue with the Steps to View the Formatted Outline.

Start-Up Instructions

- The file named **21pout1.doc** should be displayed in the document window.

Steps to View the Formatted Outline

1. Select the **Normal View** button located at the left of the horizontal scroll bar {Alt, v, n}.

   Note: *The outline displays with extra space between lines and will print as displayed in the document window.*

Finish-Up Instructions

- Optional. Place the insertion point in front of the first word "This" in the body text. Select the **Increase Indent** button repeatedly to place the body text under Level four.
- Use the same filename **21pout1.doc** and save the file.
- Optional. Print one copy.

Start-Up Instructions

- The file named **21pout1.doc** should be displayed in the document window.

Steps to Insert a New Item(s) in an Outline

Note: *The Outline view should be displayed. (If necessary, select the* ***Outline View*** *button.)*

1. Place the insertion point to the right of the final character in the item that will precede the new item.

For example, place the insertion point to the right of the "r" in four (i.e., Level four).

2. Press **Enter** once to obtain the next outline number.

   Note: *The level letter b) and the Heading 4 style display.*

3. Type the desired outline item.

   For example, type **Second idea at level four**. (Do not type the period.)

Finish-Up Instructions

- Use the *new* filename **21poutl r.doc** and save the file.
- Continue with the Steps to Collapse (Hide) or Expand (Show) an Outline Family.

Start-Up Instructions

- The file named **21poutl r.doc** should be displayed in the document window.

Collapse (Hide) or Expand (Show) an Outline Family

Note: *The Outline view should be displayed. (If necessary, select the **Outline View** button.)*

1. Place the insertion point in the first item of the family to be collapsed (hidden).

   For example, place the insertion point in Level five.

2. Select the **Collapse** button on the Outlining Toolbar repeatedly until the desired outline family is hidden {press Alt and Shift and hyphen repeatedly until the desired family is hidden}.

   For example, select the **Collapse** button four times.

   Note: *The indented items below Level five are hidden and no longer display in the document window.*

3. To expand a collapsed family, place the insertion point in the level item above the item to be expanded; select the **Expand** button on the Outlining Toolbar repeatedly until the desired outline family is expanded {press Alt and Shift and plus repeatedly until the desired family is expanded}.

   For example, place the insertion point in Level five; select the **Expand** button four times.

   Note: *The indented outline family displays in the document window.*

Finish-Up Instructions

- Continue with the Steps to Show Outline Headings.

Start-Up Instructions

- The file named **21poutl r.doc** should be displayed in the document window.

Show Outline Headings

*Note: The Outline view should be displayed. (If necessary, select the **Outline View** button.)*

1. Place the insertion point in the desired outline heading.

   For example, place the insertion point in Level one.

2. Select the desired **Show Heading** number button on the Outlining Toolbar {Alt and Shift and 2}.

   For example, select the **Show Heading 2** button.

   Note: Only the Level one and two items display. Levels three through nine are removed temporarily (hidden) from the document window.

3. Show all hidden levels.

   For example, select the **All** button on the Outlining Toolbar {Alt and Shift and a}.

Finish-Up Instructions

❖ Continue with the Steps to Move an Outline Family.

Start-Up Instructions

❖ The file named **21pout1r.doc** should be displayed in the document window.

❖ The Outline view should be displayed. (If necessary, select the **Outline View** button.)

❖ Hide outline items below Level seven. (Place the insertion point in the Level seven item and select the **Collapse** button twice on the Outlining Toolbar.)

Move an Outline Family

1. Move the mouse pointer to the plus icon beside the desired level item until a four-headed arrow displays; press and hold the mouse button and drag the thin horizontal line to the desired location.

   For example, move the mouse pointer to the plus icon beside the Level seven item until a four-headed arrow displays; press and hold the mouse button and drag the thin horizontal line *straight up* until the line displays between the second idea at Level two and the Level three item. Release the mouse button.

   Note: Level seven displays highlighted between Level two and Level three. The family is still collapsed—that's OK.

2. To renumber the moved family, click once to dehighlight the item and locate the insertion point in the desired line. Select the **Demote** or **Promote** button until the desired level displays.

   For example, click on the Level seven item to locate the insertion point in the moved Level seven item. Click on the **Promote** button four times until Heading 3 displays in the Style box.

Note: The Level seven item is automatically renumbered.

3. To display the moved family, select the **Expand** ⊞ button on the Outlining Toolbar.

   For example, select the **Expand** button twice.

Finish-Up Instructions

- Use the *new* filename **21revis1.doc** and save the file.
- Optional. Print one copy.
- Close the document.

Start-Up Instructions

- The Normal view should be displayed. (If necessary, select the **Normal View** button.)
- Display a new document window. (If necessary, select the **New** button.)

Steps to Create an Outline Using the Indent Buttons and the Multilevel Numbering Feature

Note: You will be creating the outline from the text shown in Figure 21.3.

1. Type and center the title followed by three **Enters**.

   For example, type and center **VENTURA PUBLISHER SEMINAR** in uppercase letters, press **Enter** three times. (If necessary, select the **Left** alignment button to return the insertion point to the left margin.)

   Note: You will choose the outline numbering style later.

2. Type the text for the first major point.

   For example, type **Overview of Ventura Publisher** and press **Enter** once.

FIGURE 21.3

Unnumbered outline

VENTURA PUBLISHER SEMINAR

Overview of Ventura Publisher
    Description of features
        Word processing
        Graphics
        Page layout
    Required equipment
        Hard disk
        Memory requirements
    Printers

Word processing capabilities
    Entering text directly into Ventura Publisher
    Importing text from word processing programs
        Supported word processing programs
        Limitations

Graphics capabilities
    Creating graphics in Ventura Publisher
    Importing graphics from other programs

3. Select the desired **Indent** button on the Formatting Toolbar and type the next-level text.

   For example, select the **Increase Indent** button and type **Description of features**; press **Enter** once.

4. Select the desired **Indent** button on the Formatting Toolbar and type the next entry.

   For example, select the **Increase Indent** button and type the following entries. Press **Enter** once after each entry.

   Word processing (Press **Enter**.)
   Graphics (Press **Enter**.)
   Page layout (Press **Enter**.)

5. Select the desired **Indent** button on the Formatting Toolbar and type the next entry.

   For example, select the **Decrease Indent** button and type **Required equipment**; press **Enter** once.

6. Repeat Step 4 and type the next entries.

   For example, select the **Increase Indent** button and type the following third-level entries:

   Hard disk (Press **Enter**.)
   Memory requirements (Press **Enter**.)

7. Repeat step 5 and type the next entry.

   For example, select the **Decrease Indent** button and type **Printers**. Press **Enter** twice.

8. Repeat step 5 and type the next entry.

   For example, select the **Decrease Indent** button and type **Word processing capabilities**; press **Enter** once.

9. Repeat steps 4 and 5 as needed to enter the remaining outline entries.

   For example, repeat steps 4 and 5 to create the outline shown in Figure 21.3. (Press **Enter** twice after the word "Limitations.")

Numbering an Outline Using the Multilevel Numbering Feature

10. Select all outline entries except the title.

11. Select **Format, Bullets and Numbering** {Alt, o, n}.

12. Select the desired Bullets and Numbering tab.

    For example, select the **Multilevel** tab {Alt and u}.

13. Select the desired Multilevel numbering style.

    For example, click in the middle top row sample to select the style with uppercase Roman numerals, uppercase letters, and Arabic numbers (i.e., I., A., and 1.).

14. Select **OK**.

FIGURE 21.4

An outline created using the Indent buttons and the Multilevel Numbering feature

VENTURA PUBLISHER SEMINAR

I. Overview of Ventura Publisher
  A. Description of features
    1. Word processing
    2. Graphics
    3. Page layout
  B. Required equipment
    1. Hard disk
    2. Memory requirements
  C. Printers

II. Word processing capabilities
  A. Entering text directly into Ventura Publisher
  B. Importing text from word processing programs
    1. Supported word processing programs
    2. Limitations

III. Graphics capabilities
  A. Creating graphics in Ventura Publisher
  B. Importing graphics from other programs

Finish-Up Instructions

- Click once to deselect the text.
- Your document should look similar to Figure 21.4.
- Use the filename **21pout2.doc** and save the file.
- Print one copy.
- Close the document.

Create a Table of Contents

A table of contents lists the main topics that are written in a report, newspaper, book, etc. Many different formats can be used when a table of contents is created. For example, a border line can be placed below main topics and the page number where the topic is located placed at the right margin (see Figure 21.5).

Creating a table of contents is a three-part process:

1. The document is typed.
2. The table of contents entries are marked or the heading styles are applied.
3. The table of contents is formatted and compiled.

The simplest method for creating a table of contents is to use the built-in heading styles to format the headings that will appear in the table of contents. Word' default heading styles, Heading 1 through Heading 9 can be applied to the document headings and subheadings. The Heading 1 style is used to format the text that will be a level 1 entry in the table of contents; the Heading 2 style is used to from the text that will be a level 2 entry in the table of contents, etc.

Once the heading styles have been applied to the desired headings and subheadings, the table of contents is formatted and compiled. Before the table of contents is compiled, a predefined format can be selected in the Formats area of the Table of Contents tab (Index and Tables dialog box). Other formatting options also can be

Contents	
PRESIDENT'S ANNOUNCEMENT	1
OPERATION CHANGES	1
A JOINT VENTURE	1
MARKET CONDITIONS	1
RAW LAND	2
RAW LAND/JOINT VENTURES	2

FIGURE 21.5

Sample of a table of contents

chosen, such as right aligned page numbers, leaders, etc. When the table of contents is compiled, the entries are placed at the location of the insertion point.

The table of contents is usually placed on a separate page at the beginning of the document. Lowercase roman numeral page numbers are used for numbering the table of contents page(s). The title "Contents" is placed at the beginning of the table of contents and is centered and often boldfaced. A section break is placed after the table of contents entries, and the page number on page 2 is changed to begin numbering as page 1.

A table of contents can also be created by placing a Table of Contents field code (TC) after the text to be listed in the table of contents. The TC field is inserted by pressing **Ctrl** and **F9**, and typing TC followed by the table of contents entry text in quotes, e.g., {TC "PRESIDENT'S ANNOUNCEMENT"}. The Table of Contents field code is automatically formatted as hidden text. (Hidden text is visible on the screen when nonprinting symbols are turned on but does not print.) In order to mark second-level entries (subheadings) for the table of contents, \L2 is added to the Table of Contents field code, e.g., {TC "Operation Changes"\L2}. To create a third-level entry, \L3 is added; adding \L4 would create a fourth-level entry, etc. Up to nine levels can be identified.

Start-Up Instructions

- Open the file named **21drill2.doc** located on the data disk.

Create a Table of Contents Using Built-in Heading Styles

1. Place the insertion point at any position in the heading that is to be listed as a first-level entry in the table of contents.

   For example, place the insertion point in the heading **President's Announcement**.

2. Select the desired style in the Style box on the Formatting Toolbar.

   For example, select the down arrow next to the **Style** box. Scroll up and select **Heading 1**.

   Note: The heading displays with the Heading 1 style.

3. Place the insertion point at any position in the heading that is to be listed as a second-level entry in the table of contents.

For example, place the insertion point in the heading **Operation Changes.**

4. Select the desired style.

   For example, select the down arrow next to the Style box. Scroll up and select **Heading 2.**

5. Repeat steps 1 and 2 and apply the Heading 1 style to the desired headings.

   For example apply the **Heading 1** style to the following table of contents entries:

   A Joint Venture (located on page 1)

   Raw Land (located on page 2)

6. Repeat steps 3 and 4 and apply the Heading 2 style to the desired headings.

   For example, apply the **Heading 2** style to the following table of contents entries:

   Market Conditions (located on page 1)

   Raw Land/Joint Ventures (located on page 2)

7. After the styles have been applied to the headings, place the insertion point at the location in the document where the table of contents is to be displayed.

   For example, place the insertion point to the left of the first character in the document (**Ctrl** and **Home**).

Format and Compile a Table of Contents

8. Select **Insert, Index and Tables** {Alt, i, x}.

   Note: *The Index and Tables dialog box displays (see Figure 21.6).*

9. Select the desired tab.

   For example select the **Table of Contents** tab {Alt and c}.

10. Select the desired format in the Formats box.

    For example, select **Fancy** {Alt and t and the down arrow}.

    Note: *The options Show Page Numbers and Right Align Page Numbers should be selected. Also, the Show Levels option should be set for 2 or greater.*

11. Select **OK** to compile the table of contents {Enter}.

FIGURE 21.6

Index and Tables dialog box with Table of Contents tab selected

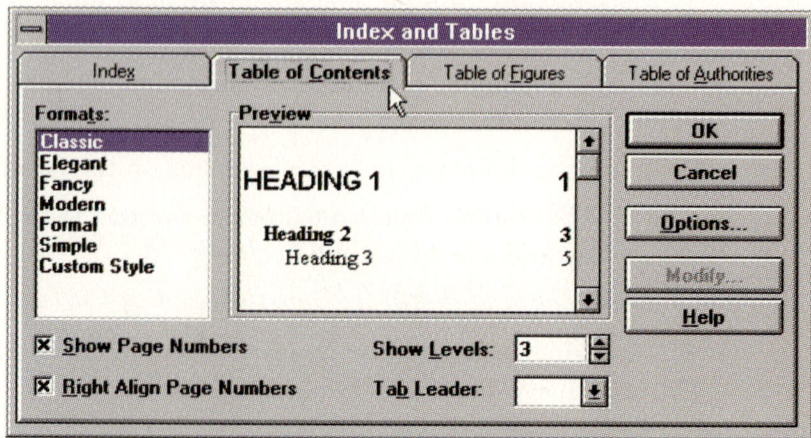

Note: The table of contents displays above the report title LAND MANAGEMENT INVESTMENT.

12. Insert a section break after the table of contents.

For example, with the insertion point to the left of the L in "LAND," select **Insert, Break, Next Page, OK** {Alt, i, b, n, Enter}.

13. Place a title above the table of contents.

For example, press **Ctrl** and **Home**, press **Enter** once, press the up arrow key once and type the title **Contents**. Select **Normal** in the Style box. (If necessary, capitalize the C in Contents.) Select the title **Contents**. Choose **Times New Roman, Bold, 16 point** and select the **Center** alignment button.

14. Change the page number(s) to lowercase roman numerals for the table of contents page(s).

For example, with the insertion point located on the page containing the table of contents, select **Insert, Page Numbers**, select **Format**, select the **Number Format** box. Choose lowercase roman numerals, i.e., i, ii, iii. Select **OK** twice.

15. Change the page number on page 2 to begin numbering starting with 1.

For example, locate the insertion point on page 2 of the report. Select **Insert, Page Numbers**. Choose **Format**, select the up arrow beside the **Start At** option in the Page Numbering area until 1 displays. Choose **OK** twice.

Note: If desired, select the Print Preview button and select 50% to see the page numbers.

Finish-Up Instructions

- Use the *new* filename **21toc2.doc** and save the file on your file disk.
- Print one copy and close the document.

Update or Replace a Table of Contents

Note: The following steps are for your information only.

1. Place the insertion point at any location in the document containing the Table of Contents to be updated/replaced.
2. Select **Insert, Index and Tables** {Alt, i, x}. If necessary select the **Tables of Contents** tab {Alt and c}.
3. Select **OK** {Enter}.

   Note: The message displays "Do you want to replace the selected table of contents?" The highlighted table of contents displays behind the message box. (It is highlighted in a dark gray because it is a field code.)

4. Select **Yes** {y}.

Shortcut

1. Place the insertion point in the table of contents, press **F9**; select your desired choice, e.g., select **Update Page Numbers only**, or select **Update Entire Table.**
2. Select **OK**.

Create an Index

An index is an alphabetical listing of topics contained in a document. Entries in the index usually include a page number to indicate the location of the topic. Once a document is typed, main index entries and subentries can be marked, the index type and form chosen, and the index compiled.

Index entries can be marked automatically by using a concordance file. (A concordance is an index of subjects or topics.) The concordance file is an ordinary file that contains a two column table. In the first column the words to be indexed are typed exactly (matching the upper/lowercase letters) as displayed in the document to be indexed. The second column contains the main entry words (topics) that are to be listed in the index. The second column can also contain the subentry word(s). A colon separates the main entry and subentry. One row is used for each index entry (see Figure 21.7)

Also, index entries can be marked individually. Select the word(s) to be indexed. Select **Insert**, **Index and Tables** and choose the **Index** tab. Select the **Mark Entry** button. In the Mark Index Entry dialog box, choose the **Mark** button. Index subentries and cross-reference entries can also be marked in the Mark Index Entry dialog box. An index can have up to seven levels of subentries.

After all entries have been marked, the Index format is chosen in the Formats area of the Index tab (in the Index and Tables dialog box). Once the index format has been chosen, the index is compiled. The compiled index organizes all topics alphabetically and lists the page numbers where the entries are located in the document.

An index is usually placed on a separate page at the end of the document. A hard page break is inserted at the end of the document to provide a separate page for the index.

If a document is modified after the index has been compiled, the index can be updated to show new page numbers. In addition, new main index entries and subentries can be marked. When all changes to the document have been made, the index is updated by clicking on any index line, pressing the *right* mouse button, and then choosing the **Update Field** option. (Pressing **F9** will also update the modified index.)

Create a Concordance File

Create a Main Entry

1. In a new document, create a table with one row and two columns.

   For example, select the **Insert Table** button and choose one row and two columns.

Words that are to be indexed typed exactly as they appear in the document	Main entries and subentries that will be placed in the index
limited partnership	Limited partnership
raw land	Joint venture:raw land
joint venture	Joint venture
Market Conditions	Maket conditions
form of partnership	Joint venture:form of partnership

FIGURE 21.7

Concordance file

2. In the first column, type the text to be indexed exactly (including upper/lowercase) as it displays in the document.

   For example, type **limited partnership**; press **Tab** to move the insertion point to column 2.

3. In the second column, type the main entry as it will display in the index.

   For example, type **Limited partnership**. (Do not type the period.)

   Note: *If you are continuing to type index entries, press the* ***Tab*** *key to create a new row and move the insertion point to column 1.*

Create a Subentry

4. In column 1, type the text to be indexed exactly (including upper/lowercase) as it displays in the document.

   For example, type **raw land**; press **Tab** to move the insertion point to column 2.

5. Type the main entry followed by a colon and the subentry.

   For example, type **Joint venture:raw land** (do not press the Spacebar before or after the colon).

Finish-Up Instructions

- Repeat steps 2 and 3 and type the following main entries.

joint venture	Joint venture
Market Conditions	Market conditions

- Repeat steps 4 and 5 and type the following subentry.

form of partnership	Joint venture:form of partnership

- Use the filename **21index.doc** and save the index concordance file.

  Note: *If desired, the index concordance file can be closed.*

- Continue with the Steps to Mark Index Entries Using AutoMark.

Start-Up Instructions

- Open the file named **21drill2.doc** located on the data disk.

Mark Index Entries Using AutoMark

1. With the document to be indexed displayed in the document window, select **Insert, Index and Tables** {Alt, i, x}.

   Note: The Index and Tables dialog box displays.

2. Select the **Index** tab {Alt and x}.
3. Select the **AutoMark** button {Alt and u}.

   Note: The Open Index AutoMark File dialog box displays.

4. Select the desired index concordance filename.

   For example, double-click on the file named **21index.doc**.

   Note: *Each index entry is marked. The entries display between braces, e.g., {XE "Limited partnership"}.*

Format and Compile an Index

1. Place the insertion point at the location in the document where the index is to be compiled.

   For example, press **Ctrl** and **End** to locate the insertion point at the end of the document.

2. Type, center, and bold the index title.

   For example, type, center, and bold the word **Index**. Press **Enter** twice.

   *Note: If necessary, select the **Align Left** button to locate the insertion point at the left margin.*

3. With the insertion point two blank lines below the index title, select **Insert, Index and Tables** {Alt, i, x}.
4. The Index tab should be displayed.

   For example, if necessary, select the **Index** tab.

5. Select the desired Type.

   For example, check that **Indented** is selected. (If necessary, select **Indented** in the Type area.)

6. Select the desired Format.

   For example, scroll down in the Formats box and select **Formal**.

   Note: A sample of the selected format displays in the Preview box.

7. Deselect the **Right Align Page Numbers** option.

   Note: No X should display next to the Right Align Page Numbers option.

8. Select the desired number of columns for the index in the Columns option.

   For example, select the up or down triangle in the Columns option until **1** displays.

9. Select **OK** to compile the index {Enter}.

Note: The index's main entries and subentries along with page number locations display. An End of Section mark displays beside the last index entry.

10. To place the Index on a separate page, locate the insertion point to the left of the "I" in the title Index. Press **Ctrl** and **Enter**.

Finish-Up Instructions

- Use the *new* filename **21d3ind.doc** and save the file on your file disk.
- Print one copy of the index page. Printing all pages of the document is optional.
- Close all document windows.

Table of Authorities

A table of authorities is a list of the specific sources that are used to substantiate a statement or statements in a legal document. A source can include information such as a case name, volume, reporter, page, court and jurisdiction, and date. The source information is referred to as a citation. The most common sources cited are statutes and cases. Headings are used to group the listed sources, e.g., Statutes, Cases, Other Authorities (see Figure 21.8). A table of authorities is predominately used for cases being heard at an upper level court.

Creating a table of authorities is similar to creating a table of contents, i.e., the document is typed, the table of authorities entries are created (marked), the citation formats are chosen, and the table of authorities is compiled.

When a table of authorities entry is marked, the Mark Citation dialog box is used. In the Mark Citation dialog box, the selected text appears in both the Selected Text and Short Citation boxes. The selected text can be edited, if necessary, in the Selected Text box. In the Short Citation box, the complete information is usually deleted and the short form of the citation is typed. For example, the short form "Sandler" is typed to represent the long citation that begins "Sandler v. Casale (1981) 125 . . . ."

The Category box is used to indicate the category in the table of authorities where the source information (citation) will be listed. For example, "Sandler v. Casale . . ." is a case source and is listed under the heading "Cases" (see Figure 21.8).

Once the selected text and short citation text is prepared and the category is chosen, the **Mark All** button is selected. All long and short citations that match those listed in the Mark Citation dialog box are marked with a TA (table of authorities) field code. The table of authorities field code displays between braces and follows the citation in the document, i.e., {TA \l "Sandler v. Casale (1981) 125 CA 3d 707, 178 CR265"\s "Sandler" \c1}. If a TA field code is not displayed, select the **Show/Hide** button.

Once table of authority entries are created, an entry can be edited by placing the insertion point in the field and making the desired changes. If necessary, select the **Show/Hide** button on the Standard Toolbar to display the table of authorities field code (TA).

Before the table of authorities is compiled, the insertion point is placed at the location in the document where the citations are to be listed, which is usually the

FIGURE 21.8

Sample table of authorities

TABLE OF AUTHORITIES

CASES

FDIC v. Air Florida System, Inc. 822 F 2d 833, 843 2
Jannis v. Ellis (1957) 308 P 2d 750, 149 CA 2d 751 CCP 1287 .... 2, 3
Sandler v. Casale (1981) 125 CA 3d 707, 178 CR 265 2

OTHER AUTHORITIES

CP 86 (a)(10) 3

beginning of the document. On the Table of Authorities tab, the format for the table of authorities is chosen. For example, the format can include the text, leaders, and page numbers, or the format can include only the text and page number. The default (Classic) numbering format is text with dot leaders and a page number (see Figure 21.8).

The default table of authorities options displayed at the bottom of the Table of Authorities tab are on and include: Use Passim, Keep Original Formatting, Category All, and Tab Leader. The Use Passim option instructs Word to substitute the word Passim for the page numbers when the citation is noted on more than five pages in the document. (Passim means throughout or frequently.)

After the format is chosen, the defaults are checked and the table of authorities is compiled. A title is typed at the beginning of the compiled table of authorities and a section break is placed after the listed citations. A lowercase roman numeral page number(s) is inserted on the table of authorities page(s) and the page number is changed on page 2 to begin numbering as page 1.

Start-Up Instructions

- Open the file named **21legal4.doc** located on the data disk.

Create Long and Short Citation Table of Authorities Entries

1. Locate and select the desired citation.

   For example, select the citation **Sandler v. Casale . . . CR 265** on page 2 in the first paragraph under III, Law and Argument.

2. Select **Insert, Index and Tables** {Alt, i, x}.

   Note: The Index and Tables dialog box displays.

3. If necessary, select the **Table of Authorities** tab {a}.

4. Select the **Mark Citation** button {Alt and k}.

   Note: The Mark Citation dialog box displays. The selected text displays in both the Selected Text and Short Citation boxes.

5. Click in the **Selected Text** box and make any editing changes needed for the long citation {Alt and t}.

   For example, if necessary, delete the comma at the end of the citation.

   *Note: If desired, the text can be selected and character formatting such as bold (**Ctrl and b**) can be used.*

6. Select the desired category in the Category box {Alt and g, press the up or down arrow key to highlight the desired category, Enter}.

   For example, check that Cases displays. (If necessary, select **Cases.**)

7. Edit the text in the Short Citation box so that it matches the short citation you want Word to search for in the document {Alt and s}.

   For example, check that the text in the Short Citation box is highlighted. (If necessary, select the text in the Short Citation box.) Type the short citation, i.e., **Sandler.**

8. Select the **Mark All** button {Alt and a}.

   Note: *The marked table of authorities entry code displays in the document window between braces, e.g., {TA\l "Sandler v. Casale . . .}. The Mark Citation dialog box remains open in the document window.*

9. Select the **Next Citation** button {Alt and n}.

   Note: *The next citation containing a "v." is located. After the* ***Next Citation*** *button is selected, Word searches through the document for the next occurrence of text commonly found in citations such as "in re" or "v.".*

10. Click once above the Mark Citation dialog box to locate the insertion point in the document window; select the desired citation.

    For example, select the citation **FDIC v. Air Florida System . . . 843.**

11. Click once in the Selected Text area of the Mark Citation dialog box.

    Note: *The selected text now displays in the Selected Text and Short Citation boxes of the Mark Citation dialog box.*

12. Repeat steps 5–8.

    For example, use the Cases category and type **FDIC** in the Short Citation box. Select **Mark All.**

13. Select the **Next Citation** button {Alt and n}.

    Note: *The short citation "FDIC" is highlighted. Since this abbreviation is contained in the same paragraph as the previously marked long citation, it is unnecessary to mark this citation. Continue with the next step.*

14. Select the **Next Citation** button {Alt and n} and repeat steps 10–12.

    For example, select the citation **Jannis v. Ellis . . . CCP 1287,** use the **Cases** category, and type **Jannis** in the Short Citation box. Select **Mark All.**

15. Select the **Next Citation** button {Alt and n}.

    Note: *The short citation "Jannis" is highlighted and marked with the Table of Authorities code. The Jannis citation was marked automatically when the long citation for Jannis v. Ellis . . . was created in step 14. Since no changes need to be made, continue with the next step.*

16. Select the **Next Citation** button {Alt and n}.

Note: The message displays, "Word has reached the end of the document. Do you want to continue searching at the beginning?".

17. Select **No** {n}.

Note: The previously marked Jannis v. Ellis citation displays highlighted and the Mark Citation dialog box remains on the screen. There is another citation that is not found automatically because it does not contain a "v." or "in re," etc. However, this citation should be marked and listed in the table of authorities.

18. Scroll to the desired location where the next citation is to be marked.

For example, scroll to page 3 and select the citation **CP 86 (a) (10)** that is located at the end of the paragraph that starts with the words "Jurisdiction remains . . . " The Category is **Other Authorities.** The short citation name is **CP 86.** Repeat steps 5–8.

19. Select **Close**.

Finish-Up Instructions

- Use the *new* filename **21markd4.doc** and save the file on your file disk.
- Continue with the Steps to Format and Compile a Table of Authorities.

Start-Up Instructions

- The file named **21markd4.doc** should be displayed in the document window with marked citations.

Format and Compile a Table of Authorities

1. Place the insertion point at the location in the document where the table of authorities is to be compiled.

For example, press **Ctrl and Home** to place the insertion point to the left of the nonprinting paragraph symbol at the beginning of the document.

2. Select **Insert, Index and Tables** {Alt, i, x}.

3. Select the Table of Authorities tab.

4. Select the desired format.

For example, check that the **Classic** format is highlighted.

Note: A sample of the Classic format displays in the Preview box.

5. Select **OK** to compile the table of authorities {Enter}.

Note: The Table of Authorities displays with the citations alphabetized in each category. Also, the page(s) for each citation displays.

6. With the insertion point located to the left of the nonprinting paragraph symbol that displays below the table of authorities, create a section break by selecting **Insert, Break, Next Page, OK** {Alt, i, n, Enter}.

7. With the insertion point located on page 2, restart the page numbering to begin numbering at page 1 (select **Insert, Page Numbers**, choose **Format**, choose **Start At**, **1**, select **OK** twice).

8. Type a title for the table of authorities.

    For example, locate the insertion point at the top of the table of authorities (press **Ctrl** and **Home**). Press **Enter** once, press the up arrow key once, type **Table of Authorities**, select the **Center** alignment button).

9. Change the page numbering for the Table of Authorities page to lowercase roman numerals (select **Insert, Page Numbers**, select **Format**, choose the down arrow beside the Number Format box and highlight the lowercase roman numerals **i, ii, iii**; select **OK** twice).

Finish-Up Instructions

- Optional. In the Page Layout view, scroll down the page to display the page numbers.
- Use the *new* filename **21toa4.doc** and save the file on your file disk.
- Print one copy of the table of authorities page. Printing all pages of the document is optional.
- Close the document.

Update or Replace a Table of Authorities

Note: The following instructions are for your information only.

1. Select **Insert, Index and Tables** {Alt, i, x}.
2. With the Table of Authorities tab selected, choose **OK** {Enter}.

    Note: A message displays, "Do you want to replace the selected category of the table of authorities?" The first category of the table of authorities is selected and displays behind the message box.

3. Select **Yes** to update or replace the table of authorities.

    Note: The table of authorities is updated or replaced and the next category of the table of authorities is highlighted.

4. If the next category is to be updated/replaced, repeat steps 1–3.

Shortcut

1. Place the insertion point in the table of authorities or table of authorities field code, press **F9**.

Delete a Table of Authorities

1. Select all lines in the table of authorities.
2. Press the **Delete** key.

The Next Step

Chapter Review and Activities

Self-Check Quiz

T F 1. Word can number nine outline levels automatically.

T F 2. Select Tools, Outline to begin creating an outline.

T F 3. When using the Outlining Toolbar, select the **Demote** button to obtain the next lower outline level.

T F 4. When a table of contents is compiled, the entries are placed where the insertion point is located.

T F 5. All items in a numbered outline, including body text, are numbered.

6. A compiled index is usually placed on a separate page at the _____ of a document.
   a. beginning
   b. end
   c. middle
   d. none of these

7. The __________ box is used to indicate the category in the table of authorities where the source information (citation) will be placed.
   a. Section
   b. Area
   c. Statute
   d. Category

8. An outline family can include _____.
   a. an idea
   b. indented related ideas
   c. body text
   d. all of these

9. Creating a table of contents in Word is a three-part process. List the three processes.

10. The most common sources cited in a table of authorities are _____ and _____.

Enriching Language Arts Skills

Spelling/Vocabulary Words

exclusive not shared with others, restricting most people, as from membership.

entitled to be furnished with a right; allowed.

render to give; to make available.
diversity difference; variety.

Percentage Amounts

Use figures for numbers that are followed by the word percent. Spell out the word percent unless the percentage amount is used in a table that contains statistical information or in a headline/title.

Examples:

Salaries are 30 percent of the total budget. (Percent spelled out)

Percentage of Males and Females		
Age Group	Male	Female
20-29	68.0%	65.0%
30-39	18.5%	19.5%
40-49	13.5%	15.5%

(Statistical information in a table)

PRICES ARE SLASHED 40% STOREWIDE!!! (Headline information)

Activities

Activity 21.1—Create an Outline Using the Indent Buttons and Multilevel Numbering Feature

1. Use the following information to create an outline. (If necessary, see the Steps to Create an Outline Using the Indent Buttons and Multilevel Numbering Feature on pages 498.)
    a. Type the following outline title followed by three **Enters**.

        Computer Systems

    b. Select and center the title.
2. Type the following unnumbered outline with the indents shown. (Use the **Increase Indent** button on the Formatting Toolbar to move the insertion point to the right and indent (demote) the outline levels. Use the **Decrease Indent** button on the Formatting Toolbar to move the insertion point to the left and promote the outline levels.)

The Computer (Hardware)
    CPU
    Keyboard
        101 keyboard with trackball
        Ergonomic keyboard
    Monitor
        Full screen
        VGA

        - Multiscan
    - Disk Drives
        - Hard disk drive
        - Floppy disk drive
        - Syquest disk drive
    - Printers
        - Laser
        - Inkjet
            - Full color
            - Monochrome
        - Dot matrix

- Application Programs (Software)
    - Word processing
        - Microsoft Word
        - WordPerfect
        - Ami Pro
    - Spreadsheet
        - Microsoft Excel
        - Lotus 1-2-3
        - Quattro Pro
    - Database
        - Microsoft Access
        - Paradox
    - Desktop Publishing
        - Corel Ventura
        - FrameMaker
        - PageMaker
        - QuarkXpress

- Other Hardware
    - CD ROM
    - Fax/Modem
    - Scanner
        - Hand-held
        - Flatbed
        - Color
        - Grayscale
    - Sound board
    - Tape backup
        - External
        - Internal

---

3. Number the outline (select all the outline entries except the title, choose **Format, Bullets and Numbering** and select the **Multilevel** tab; select the middle top row numbering sample).
4. Use the filename **21act1.doc** and save the file.
5. Print one copy.
6. Optional. Fax the outline to a local fax machine, or send the outline via e-mail to a fellow student or to your teacher using the network.
7. Close the document.

Activity 21.2—Create a Table of Contents and Index

1. Open the file named **21act2.doc** located on the data disk.
2. Apply the Heading 1 style to the sideheads with all uppercase letters, i.e., **MEMBER MEETINGS** on page 1 and **MEMBER BINDER** on page 2 (place the insertion point in the sidehead, select the down arrow beside the Style box, scroll up and click on **Heading 1**).
3. Apply the Heading 2 style to the following sideheads, which display with upper- and lowercase letters (place the insertion point in the sidehead, select the down arrow beside the Style box, scroll up and select **Heading 2**):

   Annual Meetings
   Special Meetings
   Notice of Meetings
   Place of Meetings
   Proxies
   Quorum
4. Format and compile the table of contents.
   a. Place the insertion point at the top of the document (**Ctrl** and **Home**).
   b. Select **Insert**, **Index and Tables**, choose the **Table of Contents** tab.
   c. Choose the desired format (select **Fancy** in the Formats box).
   d. Check that the following options are chosen, or change the following options if needed:

      Show Page Numbers
      Right Align Page Numbers
      Show Levels: 2
      Tab Leader: None
   e. Select **OK**.
   f. Place a section break between the table of contents and the document (with the insertion point located to the left of the B in BYLAWS, select **Insert**, **Break**, **Next Page**, **OK**).
   g. Place a title above the table of contents (press **Ctrl** and **Home**, press **Enter** once, press the up arrow key once, and type the title **Contents**; choose the **Normal** style; select the title, choose **Times New Roman**, **bold** and **16 point**; select the **Center** alignment button).
   h. Change the table of contents page number to lowercase roman numerals (select **Insert**, **Page Numbers**, select **Format**; in the Number Format box, select lowercase roman numerals, i.e., **i, ii, iii**; select **OK** twice).
   i. Change the page number on page 2 to begin numbering starting with 1. (Locate the insertion point on page 2, select **Insert**, **Page Numbers**, **Format**; select the up arrow beside the **Start At** option until **1** displays. Choose **OK** twice).
5. Use the *new* filename **21acttoc.doc** and save the file on your file disk.

6. To develop an index, create a concordance file using the following information:

   a. In a new document window, create a table with one row and two columns.

   b. Type the following index entries using the ***exact*** upper/lowercase letters as shown. Remember to press **Tab** to move to the next column and to obtain a new row.

member meetings	Member meetings
annual meeting	Member meetings:annual meetings
Special meetings	Member meetings:special meetings
Executive Committee	Executive committee
proxies	Proxies
quorum	Quorum

7. Use the filename **21actind.doc** and save the index concordance file on your file disk.

8. With the file named **21acttoc.doc** on the screen, mark the index entries using the concordance file named **21actind.doc** that was created in step 6 above (select **Insert**, **Index and Tables**, **Index** tab, **AutoMark**, type the drive letter where your file disk is located followed by a colon and filename **21actind.doc**, select **OK**).

9. Format and compile the index (press **Ctrl** and **End**, type **Index**, press **Enter** twice, center and bold the title, place the insertion point below the title, select **Insert**, **Index and Tables**, **Index** tab, select **Formal** in the Formats box, deselect the **Right Align Page Numbers** option, select **1** column, **OK**).

10. Place the index on a separate page (locate the insertion point to the left of the "I" in Index, press **Ctrl** and **Enter**).

11. Use the *new* filename **21fin2.doc** and save the file on your file disk.

12. Print one copy.

13. Optional. Using a communications program, upload the file named **21fin2.doc** to a fellow student or to your teacher, or send the document to a local fax machine.

14. Close all document windows.

Activity 21.3—Create a Table of Authorities

1. Open the file named **21act3.doc** located on the data disk.

2. Create long and short Table of Authorities entries using the following information. (Select the desired citation, select **Insert**, **Index and Tables**, choose **Table of Authorities** tab, choose **Mark Citation**; make any editing changes desired in the Selected Text box; select the desired category in the Category box; type the short citation in the Short Citation box; select **Mark All**; scroll in the document to locate the next citation to be marked. Repeat the process until all citations are created; choose **Close** when finished).

Note: The following description of the location of text is based on the Times New Roman font, 12 pt. If your font differs in type or size, you may need to look in the next paragraph or page.

a. Select the citation **Civil Code section 1354** located on page 1, the second paragraph, first sentence. The category is **Statutes**. The short citation name is **CC 1354**.

b. Select the citation **Civil Code section 1355** located on page 2, the last paragraph, first sentence. The category is **Statutes**. The short citation name is **CC 1355**.

c. Select the citation **Civil Code section 1351, et seq** located on page 2, the last paragraph, third sentence. The category is **Statutes**. The short citation name is **CC 1351**.

d. Select the citation that begins **B. Emerson, Condominium and Homeowner . . .(1988 2d ed)** on page 3 at the end of the first partial paragraph. The category is **Statutes**. The short citation name is **B. Emerson**.

e. Select the citation that begins **Marina Imperial Owners . . . 681-682 (1981)** located on page 3 in the second sentence of paragraph two. The category is **Cases**. The short citation name is **Marina Imperial**.

f. Select the citation that begins **Carmel Cove Estates . . . App 1975)** located on page 3 at the end of second paragraph. The category is **Cases**. The short citation name is **Carmel Cove**.

g. Select the citation that begins **Cypress v. Thorsen . . .(1989)** located on page 4 in the first complete paragraph. The category is **Cases**. The short citation name is **Cypress**.

3. Create a table of authorities using the following information:

a. Format and compile the table of authorities (press **Ctrl** and **Home**, select **Insert**, **Index and Tables**, choose the **Table of Authorities** tab, choose **Classic** in the Formats box, select **All** in the Category box, select **OK**).

b. Create the table of authorities page (with the insertion point to the left of the "S" in the title Statement, select **Insert**, **Break**, **Next Page**, **OK**).

c. Check on page 2 that the page numbering is set to begin page numbering as page 1 (if necessary, place the insertion point on page 2, select **Insert**, **Page Numbers**, choose **Format**, **Start At 1**, select **OK** twice).

d. Type a title for the table of authorities (press **Ctrl** and **Home**, press **Enter** once, press the up arrow key once, type **TABLE OF AUTHORITIES**, select the **Center** alignment button, select the title and choose **Bold**). Remember, the Caps lock key does not need to be pressed; the title automatically displays in uppercase letters.

e. Change the page number on the table of authorities page to lowercase roman numerals (select **Insert**, **Page Numbers**, **Format**, select **Number Format**, choose **i, ii, iii**, select **OK** twice).

4. Use the *new* filename **21acttoa.doc** and save the file to your file disk.
5. Print one copy and close the document.

Challenge Your Skills

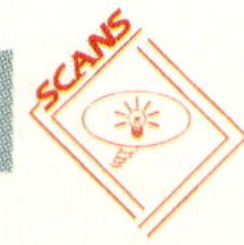

Skill 21.1—Create and Edit an Outline

1. Use the Outlining Toolbar or the **Increase/Decrease Indent** buttons to create the following outline. The paragraphs have been indented to show the levels for outline numbering. *(Hint: If the Outline feature places letters or numbers where you want a blank line, select the unwanted number or letter and select **Normal** in the Style box.)*
2. Make decisions regarding:

    Margins
    Alignment
    Fonts
    Outline numbering and spacing

Nickel Plating
Procedure to Load/Unload Substrates in Plating

Purpose

Operator training
    On-the-floor training
    Monitor during trainee's first shift

Safety

Housekeeping

Handling procedure
    Loading trays
        Handle one caddie per hand
        Use the radial grasp
    Loading the plating fixture
        Hold end tightly
        Use only designated caddie

Load/unload substrates
    Loading procedure
        Place caddie on workbench
        Remove discs
        Transfer to plating line

Unloading the fixture
    Wear latex gloves
        Visually inspect discs placed in new baths
        Label each caddie
    Place full caddie on transfer cart
    Wrap transfer cart in plastic foil

---

3. Use the filename **21skill1.doc** and save the file. (Optional: Print one copy.)
4. Edit the outline as follows:
    a. Insert the following items under item III (Safety)
        A. Carefully remove mandrels
        B. Set mandrel correctly in place
    b. Insert the following second- and third-level items between item a and b under Handling procedure
        Unloading the mandrel
            Set disc straight in correct slot
            Avoid damaging the inside diameter of the discs
            Remove discs from tray
    c. Use your choice of any numbering style.
5. Once changes are made, use the *new* filename **21skfin1.doc** and save the file again.
6. Print one copy.
7. Optional. Fax the outline to a local fax machine or send the outline via e-mail to a fellow student or to your teacher using the network.
8. Close the document.

Skill 21.2—Create an Index and a Table of Contents; Language Arts

1. Open the file named **21skill2.doc** located on the data disk. Make decisions regarding:
    Margins
    Alignment
    Fonts
    Text flow, i.e. Keep text together, Widow/Orphan
    Bold, capitalization of titles, headings, and subheads
    Format of table of contents
    Format of index
    Page numbering
    Section break(s)

    Hint: *Make a printed copy of 21skill2.doc to use as a guide when creating the index and table of contents.*
2. Correct three spelling errors, two misused words, one percent error, and two punctuation errors.

3. The title of the document is **Black Hawk College Agreement**.
4. Create a table of contents using built-in heading styles. Apply the Heading 1 and Heading 2 styles to the appropriate headings in the document.
5. Format and compile the table of contents and create a separate page for the table of contents at the top of the document.

   Hint: *Remember to reset the page number for the first page of the document (after the table of contents page) to 1.*
6. Create an index using a concordance file and mark all occurrences of the following main index entries and subentries. Remember, the entries in the first column of the concordance file must exactly match the case (upper and lower) of the words in the document. The following are the main entries and subentries:

   Preamble
   Recognition
   Leaves
      Sick leave
      Industrial accident or illness leave
      Jury duty
   Transfers and Reassignments
   Professional Education Program
      Multicultural Program
      Learning Styles Program
   Layoffs
   Performance Evaluation Procedures
      Contract employees
      Regular employees
7. Use the filename **21skind.doc** and save the concordance file on your file disk.
8. Format and compile the index. Create a separate page for the index at the end of the document.
9. Use the *new* filename **21skifin.doc** and save the file on your file disk.
10. Print one copy and close the document.
11. If you have completed your work, exit Word.

CHAPTER

Advanced Features and Master Documents

Features Covered

- Create a paragraph style containing a border
- Create a style containing a special symbol
- Designate one style to follow another
- Use the Style Gallery
- Create cross-references
- Create a master document by inserting subdocuments
- Create a cross-reference in a master document

Objectives and Introduction

After successfully completing this chapter, you will be able to create a paragraph style containing a border and a graphic image. You will also be able to specify one style to follow another. You will learn to create cross-references and master documents. In addition, you will use cross references in a master document.

In addition to formatting codes (see Chapter 15), text and graphic symbols can be included in styles. Using styles can assist you in creating documents with a consistent and professional appearance.

Advanced Styles

In Chapter 15, basic styles that contain formatting such as margins, font changes, and justification were created. In addition, many other formatting elements, such as borders and special symbols, can also be incorporated into a style. Also, if desired, text that is used often can be inserted into a style. For example, a letterhead style can be created that contains text, font changes, and borders. The letterhead style can be saved and used each time a letter is created.

Word also has an extensive Style Gallery that can be used to select the format for various documents such as letters, brochures, fax cover sheets, and invoices. To use the Style Gallery, built-in styles (Heading 1, Heading 2, etc.) or the AutoFormat command must have been used to apply styles in the original document. In the Style Gallery dialog box, a supplied template can be selected. An illustration of each template can be viewed in the Preview of box.

If the Document option is selected in the Preview area of the Style Gallery dialog box, the file in the document window (current document) displays in the Preview of box with the template styles applied. Also, in the Preview box, the Example and Style Samples options are used to view the template styles. The Example option displays a model document with styles from the highlighted template. The Style Samples option displays sample text with a list of styles from the highlighted template.

A style can be automatically followed by another style. When one style is specified to follow another, the first style is in effect until the **Enter** key is pressed. When the **Enter** key is pressed, the first style is turned off and the next style is turned on.

Start-Up Instructions

❖ Open the file named **22drill1.doc** located on the data disk.

Note: A mouse must be used to complete the activities in this chapter.

Create a Paragraph Style Containing a Border

1. Place the insertion point in the paragraph where the new style will be applied.

   For example, place the insertion point in the first sidehead, **Always Ask Questions.**

2. Select **Format, Style.**

   Note: The Style dialog box displays.

3. Select **New.**

   Note: The New Style dialog box displays.

4. In the **Name** box, type a name for the new style.

   For example, type **sidehead.**

5. In the Style Type box, choose the desired style type.

   For example, check that the **Paragraph** style displays in the Style Type box. (If necessary, select the **Style Type** box and choose **Paragraph.**)

6. To change the font, appearance, or size, select **Format, Font,** make the desired changes, and select **OK.**

   For example, change the font to **Century Gothic, Bold, 14 point,** and select **OK.**

   Note: The format information, i.e., Normal + Font: Century Gothic..., displays in the Description area of the New Style dialog box. Also, an example of the style displays in the Preview box.

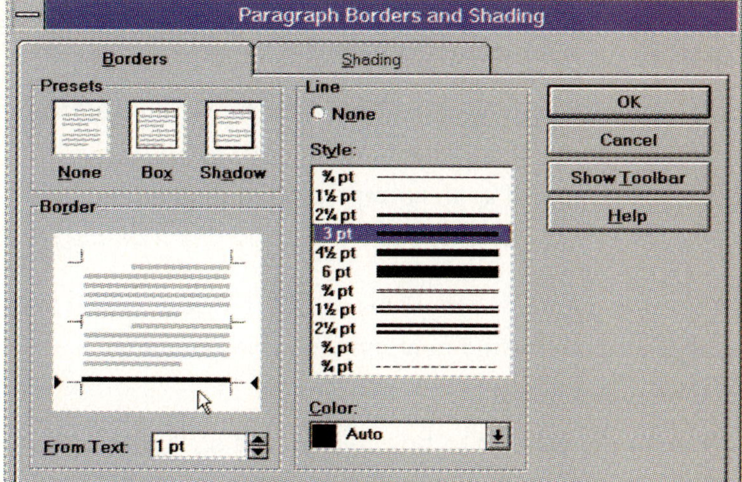

FIGURE 22.1

Paragraph Borders and Shading dialog box with the border area and line style selected

Place a Border Below the Paragraph

7. Select **Format, Border.**

Note: The Paragraph Borders and Shading dialog box displays.

8. Choose the desired line style in the Line Style area.

For example, click on the **3 pt** line.

9. Choose the desired border area and select **OK.**

For example, click on the bottom middle of the border box to display the border line between the left and right triangles (see Figure 22.1). Select **OK.**

Note: The New Style dialog box with the additional format information displays in the Description box, i.e., Border: Bottom(Thick, 3 pt Line Width). Also, the Preview box displays with the Border line below the heading.

10. When all the style formats have been specified, select **OK.**

For example, select **OK.**

11. Select the **Apply** button to apply the new style to the paragraph containing the insertion point.

Note: The sidehead displays with the new style applied, i.e., a bottom border and Century Gothic Bold font, 14 pt. Also, the new style, "sidehead," displays in the Style box in the Formatting Toolbar.

Finish-Up Instructions

- ❖ Apply the style to the next two sideheads that begin Listen to Advice . . . and There are No . . . (place the insertion point in the desired sidehead, select the down arrow next to the Style box, choose the style named **sidehead**).
- ❖ Use the *new* filename **22pstyle.doc** and save the file.

Start-Up Instructions

- ❖ The file named **22pstyle.doc** should be displayed in the document window.

Create a Style Containing a Special Symbol

1. Place the insertion point in the paragraph where the new style is to be applied.

   For example, place the insertion point in the first body text paragraph that begins "To succeed as an entrepreneur . . .".

2. Select **Format, Style.**

3. Select **New.**

4. In the **Name** box, type a name for the new style.

   For example, type **para symbol.**

5. Select the down arrow in the **Based On** box and select a style that is similar to the style being created.

   For example, scroll up and select **List Bullet.**

6. Select **Format, Numbering.**

7. Select **Modify, Bullet.**

8. Click on the down arrow beside the **Symbol From** box and select the desired symbol font.

   For example, select **Wingdings.**

9. Choose the desired symbol from the selected font.

   For example, double-click on the ➢ symbol in row 7, column 17.

10. Make additional selections to modify the new style.

    For example, in the **Distance from Indent to Text** box, select the down triangle until zero (**0**) displays; select the **Color** box and select **Blue**; double-click in the Point Size box; type **14**; select **OK** twice.

11. Select **Apply**.

    Note: *The symbol displays blue on your screen and will print in blue if you have a color printer.*

Finish-Up Instructions

- Apply the **para symbol** style to the other body text paragraphs (place the insertion point in the desired paragraph, click on the down arrow beside the **Style** box, choose the **para symbol** style).
- Use the *new* filename **22symbol.doc** and save the file.
- Continue with the Steps to Designate One Style to Follow Another.

Designate One Style to Follow Another

1. Select **Format, Style.**

2. In the Styles box, select the style for which you want to specify a following style.

   For example, click once on the style named **Presentation title.**

3. Select **Modify**.

Note: The Modify Style dialog box displays.

4. In the **Style for Following Paragraph** box, select the style you want to specify as the following style.

   For example, click once on the style named **Presentation subtitle**.

5. Select **OK**.

6. Select **Close** to close the Style dialog box.

Finish-Up Instructions

- ❖ Press **Ctrl** and **Home** to locate the insertion point at the top of the document. Type the following text:

  Becoming a Successful Entrepreneur (do not press Enter).

- ❖ Click on the down arrow located beside the **Style** box. Click on the style named **Presentation title**.
- ❖ Press **Enter** to activate the style specified to follow the Presentation title style.
- ❖ Type the following text:

  Key Points to Remember

- ❖ Use the *new* filename **22pfinal.doc** and save the file.
- ❖ Print one copy and close the document.

Start-Up Instructions

- ❖ Open the file named **22drill2.doc** located on the data disk.
- ❖ Apply the **Heading 1** style to the title, **Saving and Investing Trends** (place the insertion point in the title, select the down arrow beside the **Style** box, click on **Heading 1**).
- ❖ Apply the **Heading 2** style to the following headings (place the insertion point in the desired heading, select the down arrow beside the **Style** box, click on **Heading 2**, repeat for all headings).

  Healthy Savings Attitudes
  Demographics
  Products
  Demand for Change
  Financial Institutions

Use the Style Gallery

1. With the insertion point at any position in the document, select **Format, Style Gallery**.

   *Note: The Style Gallery dialog box displays with a preview of the current document. Notice that **Document** is selected in the Preview area at the bottom left of the Style Gallery dialog box (see Figure 22.2).*

2. Select the desired template.

   For example, scroll down the Template list and select **Report2**.

FIGURE 22.2

Style Gallery dialog box

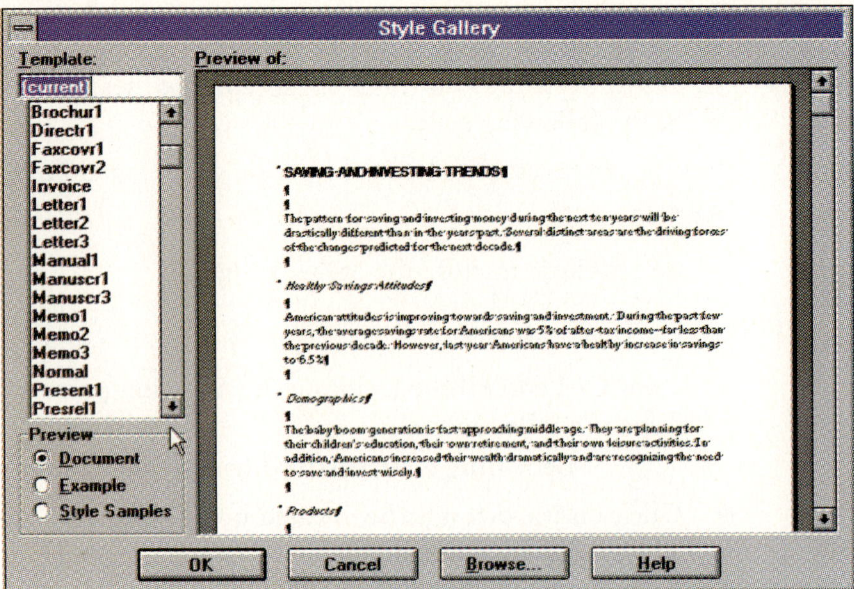

Note: The Preview of box displays the current document with the style for the Report2 template. If desired, other templates can be selected and viewed.

3. Select **OK**.

   Note: The document is formatted immediately with the Report2 template style and displays in the document window. If desired, scroll through the document to view the formatted document headings.

Finish-Up Instructions

- Use the *new* filename **22gstyle.doc** and save the file.
- Print one copy.
- Close the file.

Create Cross-references

The Cross-reference feature is used to direct readers from one area of a document to another area of a document. For example, in this textbook, cross-references are often used to direct readers from the text to a related figure. Cross-references can also be linked to headings, figures, tables, bookmarks, etc.

An easy method for creating cross-references is to identify the item to be cross-referenced by creating a bookmark (see Create Bookmarks in Chapter 20). Once the item to be cross-referenced is bookmarked, use the Cross-reference dialog box to identify the **Reference Type** (e.g., Bookmark), select the **Insert Reference To** item (e.g., Page Number), and choose the **For Which . . .** item (e.g., Figure1_1). Update the cross-reference pages by printing the document or by selecting the entire document and pressing **F9**.

A cross-reference can contain more than one type of reference information. For example, both the bookmark name and page number can be inserted as the cross-reference. If the document containing the cross-reference is changed, the cross-reference may need to be updated in order to reflect new page numbers. To cross-reference items in different documents, the documents must be part of a master document. See Steps to Create a Cross-reference in a Master Document later in this chapter.

Start-Up Instructions

- ❖ To complete the drills, activities, and skills in this chapter, copy the following files located on the data disk to your file disk. For information on copying files, see Chapter 16, page 387.

22subch1.doc	**22sbsk1.doc**
22subch2.doc	**22sbact2.doc**
22subch3.doc	**22sbsk2.doc**
22subch4.doc	**22sbact3.doc**
22subch5.doc	**22sbsk3.doc**
22skill1.doc	**22sbact4.doc**
22sbact1.doc	**22sbsk4.doc**

- ❖ Open the file named **22subch1.doc** located on your file disk.
- ❖ Use Normal view. If necessary, select **View**, **Normal**.

Create a Cross-reference Using Bookmarks

1. Place the insertion point where the reference is to be located in the document.

For example place the insertion point in the second paragraph between the words "page" and "for."

2. Select **Insert, Cross-reference**.

Note: *The Cross-reference dialog box displays (see Figure 22.3).*

3. Select the desired reference in the **Reference Type** box.

For example, select **Bookmark**.

Note: *The Bookmark has been previously created in the file.*

4. Choose the desired **Insert Reference To** item.

For example, click on **Page Number**.

5. In the **For Which . . .** box, select desired item.

For example, check that **Figure1_1** is highlighted.

6. Choose the **Insert** button.

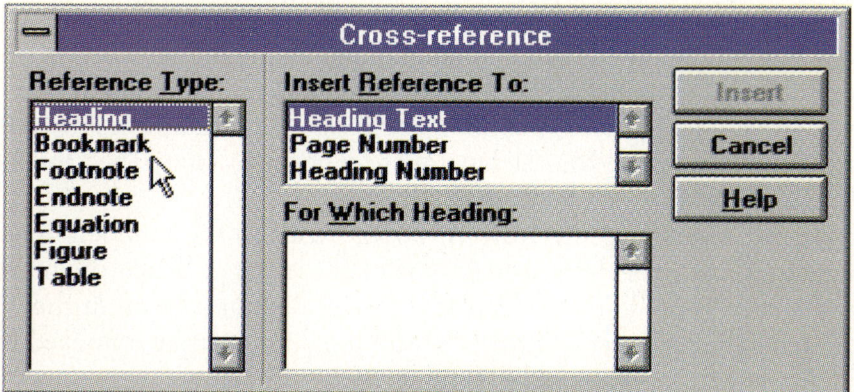

FIGURE 22.3

Cross-reference dialog box

Note: The page number is placed in the document at the location of the insertion point.

7. Select **Close**.

   Note: The cross-reference page number is a field code and can only be deleted by first selecting the page number and then pressing the Delete key.

Finish-Up Instructions

- Save the file using the same filename, **22subch1.doc**.
- Open the file named **22subch2.doc** located on your file disk.
- Create a cross-reference using the following information:
  a. Place the insertion point in the second paragraph between the words "page" and "for."
  b. Repeat steps 2–7 in the Steps to Create a Cross-reference Using Bookmarks. In step 5, check that **Figure2_1** is highlighted.
- Save the file using the same filename, **22subch2.doc**.
- Close all document windows.

Create a Master Document

The Master Document feature in Word for Windows is useful for managing large documents such as a book with chapters. The master document is a file containing information that links other files (called subdocuments) to the master document file. The master document file also includes any formatting choices that will apply to the entire document. Subdocuments are files that are saved separately and when desired are assembled together into one master file (document). Any Word document can be a master document or a subdocument. One of the major advantages of creating a master document is that many individuals can then work on different sections of a project at the same time. The Master Document feature is then used to combine all the sections into one document.

To create a master document, use the Master Document view. The Master Document view contains the Outlining/Master Document Toolbar (see Figure 22.4). Use the **Insert Subdocument** button to access the Word files that will be placed in the master document. Once the subdocuments are inserted in the master document, the formatting that is to be applied to the entire document is set up.

Once the master document containing subdocuments has been created and saved, information in a subdocument can be edited either in the master document or by opening the subdocument and making the desired changes. A subdocument can be opened by double-clicking on the subdocument icon (located in the top left of the subdocument section) in the Master Document view or by using the **Open** button on the Standard Toolbar.

To make it easier for several users to work simultaneously on the subdocuments in a master document, Word provides a special type of file locking. When the master document is opened, a lock icon appears below the subdocument icon in the top left corner of each subdocument section. The subdocument can be unlocked by placing the insertion point in the desired subdocument and selecting the **Lock Document** button on the Outlining/Master Document Toolbar.

When a master document is opened, the subdocuments that you own are available as read-write files, which means the subdocument can be viewed, edited, and saved. The subdocuments that you do not own, are opened as read-only files. The read-only file(s) can be changed after the subdocument(s) is unlocked and then saved with a new filename.

To determine who owns a subdocument, Word checks the name displayed in the Author field of the document summary information against the name stored on the User Info tab of the Options dialog box. The name in the document summary is displayed by selecting **File**, **Summary Info**. The name stored on the User Info tab of the options dialog box can be viewed by selecting **Tools**, **Options**, and selecting the **User Info** tab.

A large document can be converted to a master document and divided into subdocuments. The headings in each section of the original document must be formatted with the built-in heading styles. Select the headings and text that are to be divided into subdocuments, making sure that the first item selected is the heading level that indicates the beginning of a new document. On the Master Document Toolbar, select the **Split Subdocument** button. Word separates each subdocument into an individual section and places a subdocument icon in the upper left corner of each section. When saving the master document, Word automatically creates a name for each subdocument. To see the filename, double-click on the subdocument icon. The subdocument name is located in the title bar, and the full path can be displayed by selecting **File, Save As**. Select **Close** to return to the master document, or select **Window** and choose the desired master document filename.

When a subdocument is inserted in the Master Document view, the heading/outline symbols (✥ ▭ ▫) display beside the subdocument information. Note that when Word's heading styles are used to format the subdocuments, the plus and minus symbols display. When Word's heading styles are not used, a small square box displays (see Figure 22.4). The heading/outline symbols are used to move the headings and subordinate text to another location in the master document. Also, by clicking on the subdocument icon, all of the subdocument text is highlighted and can be deleted or relocated. If a lock icon displays below the subdocument icon, this indicates that the subdocument is open in a separate window.

In the Master Document view, each subdocument is placed in a separate section. An End Of Section mark displays above and below each subdocument. The majority of the formatting does not display in the Master Document view. Formatting such as bold, however, can be displayed by selecting the **Show Formatting** button on the Master Document Toolbar.

Formatting that applies to the entire document, such as page numbering, margins, and font type and size, is placed in the master document. If a subdocument contains formatting applied in the original subdocument, this formatting has precedence over the formatting applied in the master document. If a title page is desired, the title information is typed. Since each subdocument is a section of the master document, you can change section formatting, such as headers, footers, page numbers, and margins, at the beginning of each subdocument if you wish.

Start-Up Instructions

- Open a new document window.

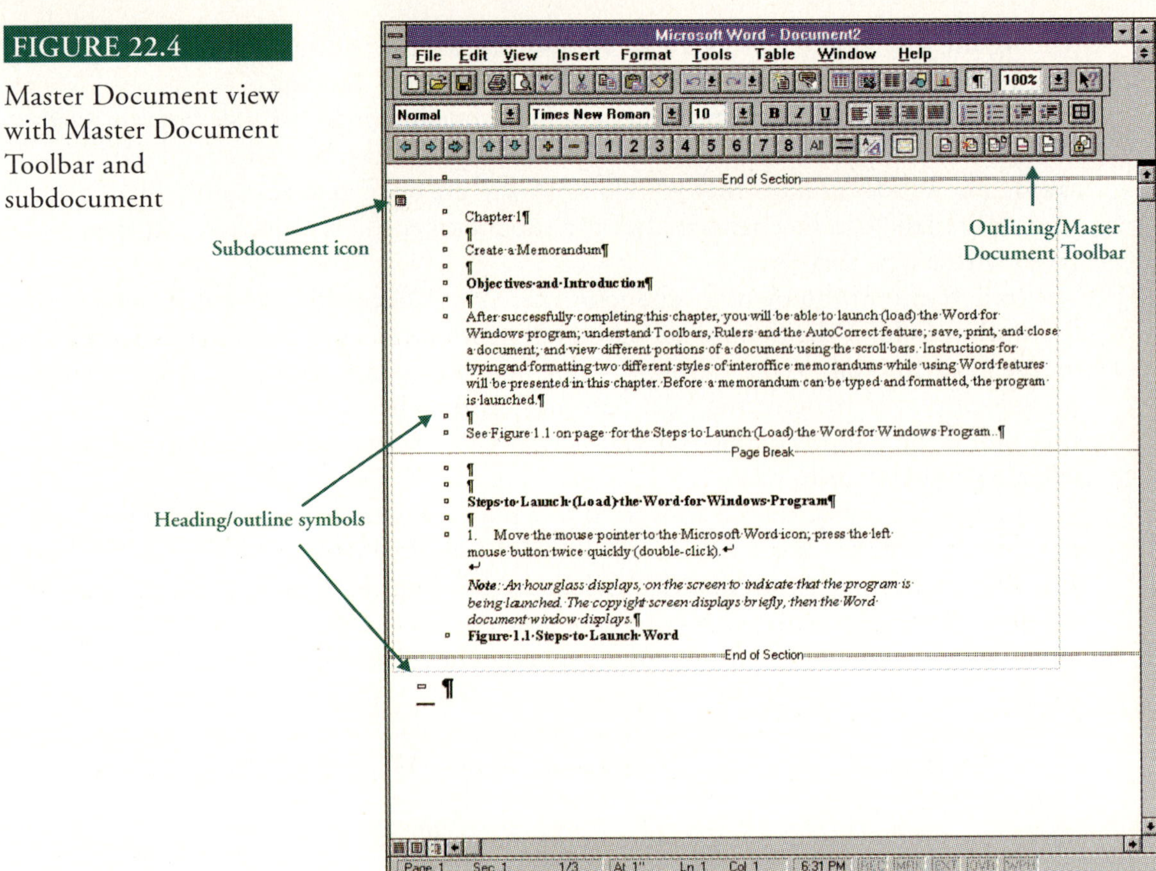

FIGURE 22.4

Master Document view with Master Document Toolbar and subdocument

Steps to Create a New Master Document by Inserting Subdocuments

1. Select **View, Master Document.**

   Note: The Outlining/Master Document Toolbar displays.

2. Select the **Insert Subdocument** button on the Outlining/Master Document Toolbar.

   Note: The Insert Subdocument dialog box displays.

3. Select the desired drive/directory where the subdocuments are located and double-click on the desired filename.

   For example, select the drive where your subdocument files are located; double-click on the file named **22subch1.doc**.

   Note: The subdocument displays in the Master Document view. The heading/outline symbols display in front of each document level. Also, a light gray line displays around the subdocument. If desired, scroll down the screen to see the bottom of the subdocument (see Figure 22.4).

4. Place the insertion point at the end of the subdocument.

   For example, press **Ctrl** and **End** to locate the insertion point at the end of the subdocument.

5. Repeat steps 2–4 and insert the following subdocuments.

   22subch2.doc
   22subch3.doc

22subch4.doc
22subch5.doc

Note: Scroll through the master document. Each subdocument is contained within a box; no formatting displays in the Master Document view.

Finish-Up Instructions

- Use the filename **22master.doc** and save the file on your file disk.

  Note: Saving the master document may take a few minutes because each subdocument is also being saved.

- Continue with the Steps to Show First Line Only.

Start-Up Instructions

- The file named **22master.doc** should be displayed in the document window.
- The Outlining/Master Document Toolbar should be displayed. If necessary, select **View**, **Master Document**.

Show First Line Only

1. Select the **Show First Line Only** button on the Outlining/Master Document Toolbar.

   Note: Scroll through the subdocuments, noting that only the first line of each paragraph is displayed.

2. To display all lines in the document window, select the **Show First Line Only** button again.

   For example, select the **Show First Line Only** button again.

Finish-Up Instructions

- Continue with the Steps to Create a Cross-reference in a Master Document.

Cross-referencing in a Master Document

Using a master document is the only way in Word to create cross-references to particular items in different documents. To create a cross-reference to information in different documents, simply open the master document in Normal view and create the cross-references just as if you were working in a single document. (Refer back to Create Cross-references on page 526 if necessary.)

To update cross-references to items in different documents, the master document must be used. Select the master document and press **F9**.

Start-Up Instructions

- The master document named **22master.doc** should be displayed in the document window.

- Use the Normal view. If necessary, select **View**, **Normal**.

Steps to Create a Cross-reference in a Master Document

*Note: The Master Document, Normal, or Page Layout view can be used when creating cross-references in the master document. If the Master Document view is used, all lines should be displayed. (If necessary, select the **Show First Line Only** button on the Outlining/Master Document Toolbar.)*

1. Place the insertion point at the desired location where the reference is to be inserted in the master document.

   For example, in **Chapter 3** place the insertion point to the left of the last period in the final paragraph.

2. Select **Insert, Cross-reference**.
3. Choose the desired **Reference Type, Insert Reference To,** and **For Which . . .** options.

   For example, check that the following options are highlighted or select the following options: **Bookmark** in Reference Type, **Page Number** in Insert Reference To, and **Chapter4** in For Which Bookmark.

4. Select the **Insert** button.

   Note: The page number is automatically inserted in the document and the Cross-reference dialog box remains open in the document window.

5. Select **Close** to exit the Cross-reference dialog box .

Finish-Up Instructions

- Use the Normal view. If necessary, select **View**, **Normal**.
- Type and format a title (press **Ctrl** and **Home**, type **Word 6.0 for Windows**, press **Enter** twice, type **compiled by** followed by your name; select the title lines, change the font size to **20 point**, and choose **Center** alignment; select **File**, **Page Setup**, **Layout**, **Vertical Alignment**, **Center**, **OK**).
- If necessary, click to deselect text. With the insertion point located in the title page, create a blank (different) first page footer and create a second page footer (select **View**, **Header and Footer**, select the **Switch Between Header and Footer** button, select the **Page Setup** button, select **Different First Page**, **OK**; choose the **Show Next** button, type **Word 6.0 for Windows**, press **Tab** twice, select the **Page Numbers** button, choose **Close**).
- Change the page number on page 2 to begin numbering at page 1 (locate the insertion point in page 2, select **Insert**, **Page Numbers**, **Format**; select the up triangle next to the **Start At** box until **1** displays; select **OK** twice).
- Use the same filename **22master.doc** and save the file on your file disk.
- If desired, select **Print Preview** and scroll through the master document.
- Optional. Print the master document.
- Close the document.

The Next Step

Chapter Review and Activities

Self-Check Quiz

T F 1. When one style is specified to follow another, the second style is in effect after the Enter key is pressed.

T F 2. Using a master document is the only way to create cross-references that point to items in different documents.

T F 3. Cross-references can be linked to figures, headings, tables, and bookmarks.

T F 4. The Style Gallery can be used to select a format for letters, brochures, fax cover sheets, and invoices.

T F 5. In a master document, each subdocument is placed in a separate section.

6. The _________ is used to set up a master document.
   a. Cross-reference feature
   b. Outlining/Master Document Toolbar
   c. Borders Toolbar
   d. Bookmark feature

7. A style can contain __________.
   a. borders
   b. special symbols
   c. formatting changes
   d. all of the above

8. List one major advantage of creating a master document.

9. Define a subdocument.

10. State the main purpose of using a cross-reference.

Enriching Language Arts Skills

Spelling/Vocabulary Words

cuisine a style of cooking or preparing food.

exception the act of leaving out, excluding; a case not conforming to the general rule.

clients customers, buyers; person who seeks the professional services of another.

minimal least possible, smallest.

savor taste or smell of something; to taste with enjoyment.

Basic Rules for Numbers

Generally, numbers one through ten when used in writing are spelled out. Also, numbers used in approximation and numbers at the beginning of a sentence are usually spelled out. Use figures when a number is followed by the word percent. Omit the colon and zeros when writing an even clock time.

Examples:

Thirty-one people are enrolled in the television course on Real Estate Appraisals. (Spell out a number at the beginning of a sentence.)

We will pick up eight additional passengers at the next bus stop. (Spell out numbers one through ten.)

Donald reported that around sixty people attended the luncheon. (Spell out a number used in approximation.)

We decreased our use of electricity by 12 percent this month. (Use a figure when the number is followed by the word percent.)

We will arrive in Houston at 3 p.m. (Colons and zeros are omitted when the clock time is even.)

Activities

Activity 22.1—Master Document and Cross-reference

1. Open a new document window.
2. Select the Master Document view (select **View**, **Master Document**).
3. Create a master document by inserting the following subdocuments that are located on the data disk (select the **Insert Subdocument** button, double-click on the desired subdocument filename, press **Ctrl** and **End**. Repeat for each subdocument).

   22sbact1.doc
   22sbact2.doc
   22sbact3.doc
   22sbact4.doc

4. With the master document open, use the following information to create cross-references:

   a. In the last paragraph of Chapter 1, place the insertion point one space to the right of the word "pages."

   b. Select **Insert**, **Cross-reference.** Choose the desired Reference Type, Insert Reference To, and For Which Bookmark options (check that the following options are highlighted or select the following options: **Bookmark**, **Page Number**, and **Chapter_3**).

c. Select **Insert.** Click in the document window to the right of the cross-reference number. Press the **Spacebar** once, type the word **and** and press the **Spacebar** once.

d. With the Cross-reference dialog box displayed in the document window, place the insertion point to the left of the period in the last paragraph of Chapter 1 and repeat the instructions in step 4b. Select **Chapter_4** in the For Which Bookmark box.

e. With the Cross-reference dialog box displayed, scroll down and locate the insertion point in the last paragraph of Chapter 4 to the left of the period. Repeat the instructions in step 4b and choose **Figure4_1** in the For Which Bookmark box.

f. Exit the Cross-reference dialog box (select **Cancel**).

5. Change to Normal view (select **View, Normal**).
6. Type and format a title (press **Ctrl** and **Home**, type **Free the Environment**, press **Enter** twice, type **compiled by** followed by your name; select the title lines, choose **Britannic Bold, 20 point, Center** alignment; select **File, Page Setup, Layout, Vertical Alignment, Center, OK**).
7. Click to deselect. With the insertion point located in the title page, create a blank (different) first page footer and create a second page footer (select **View, Header and Footer**, select the **Switch Between Header and Footer** button, choose the **Page Setup** button, select **Different First Page, OK**; choose the **Show Next** button, type **Free the Environment**, press **Tab** twice, select the **Page Numbers** button, choose **Close**).
8. Change the page number on page 2 to begin numbering at page 1 (locate the insertion point in page 2, select **Insert, Page Numbers, Format**; select the up triangle next to the **Start At** box until **1** displays; select **OK** twice).
9. Use the filename **22act1m.doc** and save the file on your file disk. If desired, select **Print Preview** and scroll through the document to check the page numbers.
10. Optional. Fax the printed copy of the master document to another fax machine.
11. Close the document.

Activity 22.2—Create Advanced Styles in a Master Document

1. Open the file named **22act1m.doc** that was created in Activity 22.1.
2. Create a chapter heading style using the following instructions:

   a. Place the insertion point at any position in the title, Chapter 1—Save Energy.

   b. Select **Format, Style, New.**

   c. In the Name box, type **chapter head.**

   d. Check that **Paragraph** displays in the Style Type box. (If necessary, choose **Paragraph** in the Style Type box.)

e. Change the font to **Century Gothic, 14 point, Bold** (select **Format, Font**, choose the desired font, size, and appearance, select **OK**).

f. Select **Format, Paragraph, Indents and Spacing** tab, **Alignment, Centered, OK.**

g. Create a paragraph border (select **Format, Border**, select the **$1\frac{1}{2}$ pt** line style, click in the bottom of the **Border** box to display the border line between the left and right triangles, select **OK**).

h. Select **OK** and choose **Apply.**

3. Create a paragraph style that contains a symbol.

   a. Place the insertion point at any location in the first paragraph of Chapter 1.

   b. Select **Format, Style, New** and type the name for the new style, **graphic para.**

   c. Select **Based On** and scroll up and select **List Bullet.**

   d. Select **Format, Numbering.**

   e. Select **Modify, Bullet**, choose **Wingdings** in the Symbols From box.

   f. Choose the ✸ symbol (row 6, column 2).

   g. Select **OK** three times.

4. Select **Apply.**
5. Apply the **graphic para** and **chapter head** styles to Chapters 2, 3, and 4 paragraph heads and paragraphs (place the insertion point in the desired title or paragraph, select the **Style** button, choose the desired style name).
6. Use the *new* filename **22amast1.doc** and save the edited master document on your file disk.
7. Print one copy of the master document.
8. Close the document.

Challenge Your Skills

Skill 22.1—Create a Master Document, Cross-references, and Advanced Styles; Language Arts

1. Open the file named **22skill1.doc** located on your file disk.
2. With the insertion point on page two, use the **Master Document** view and create a master document. Insert the following subdocuments located on your file disk.

   22sbsk1.doc
   22sbsk2.doc
   22sbsk3.doc
   22sbsk4.doc

3. Correct three spelling, two punctuation, and three number rule errors.
4. Use the filename **22skmast.doc** and save the file on your file disk.
5. Create cross-references for the four sentences on the title page and for the cross reference in Section 3.
6. In Normal View, create a section title style. Make decisions for the style name, font type, size, alignment, and paragraph borders. Apply the title style to each of the four section titles.
7. Create a style that contains a symbol of your choice. Make decisions for the style name, font type, size, alignment, and paragraph borders. Apply this style to each of the four section paragraphs.
8. Use the same filename **22skmast.doc** and save the file on your file disk.
9. Optional. Fax the printed copy of the master document to another Fax machine.
10. Print one copy.
11. If you have completed your work, exit Word.

Part 6
Checking Your Step

Production Skill Builder Activities
Chapters 20-22

Production Activity 6.1—Create a Multiple-Page Outline

1. Create the following outline. The paragraphs have been indented to show levels for outline numbering. Make decisions regarding:

    Margins
    Fonts
    Header/footer text and placement
    Outline numbering and spacing

Health care benefits
- Eligibility and coverage
  - Who is eligible
  - When coverage begins
    - Employee coverage
    - Dependent coverage
  - When to enroll
    - Upon employment
    - Annual open enrollment
    - Dependents
    - At retirement
  - Changing coverage
    - Adding dependents
    - Deleting dependents
  - Contributions
    - Employer's contribution
    - Employee's contribution
    - Retiree's contribution
    - During a personal leave
  - When coverage ends
  - Other rules
  - Continuation coverage
    - COBRA
    - Converting to an individual plan

- Medical Plan
    - Overview
    - Definitions
        - Doctor
        - Medically necessary treatment
        - Deductible and copayment
        - Allowable fee
    - How to file claims
        - Claims administrator
        - How and when to file
        - Appeal process for denied claims
    - Inpatient hospital and surgery benefits
    - Extended medical care
        - Hospice
        - Home health
        - Skilled nursing facility care
    - Outpatient facility and surgery benefits
    - Other medical benefits
        - Limited surgical procedures
        - Maternity and family planning
        - Psychiatric benefits
        - Chiropractic treatment
- Exclusions from coverage
- Payment of benefits
- Dental Plan
    - Diagnostic and preventative care
    - Deductible
    - Basic dental services
    - Dental maximum

Time Off Benefits
- Vacation
    - Eligibility
    - Accrual
- Holidays
- Personal choice days
    - Eligibility
    - Accrual
- Sick leave
    - Eligibility
    - Accrual

Retirements benefits
- Employee Retirement Income Security Act
- ERISA-covered plans
    - 401K plans
    - Defined contribution plans
    - Defined benefit plans
- Claiming benefits

---

2. Use the filename **6pout1.doc** and save the outline.
3. Print one copy.
4. Close the document.

Production Activity 6.2—Use the Revision Features; Annotations

1. Open the file named **6pact2.doc** located on the data disk.
2. Turn on the Revisions feature.
3. Locate each annotation mark in the document. View the annotation text and make the necessary changes to the document.
4. Use the *new* filename **6pminut.doc** and save the file on your file disk.
5. Print one copy of the document with the revision marks.
6. Accept all the revisions and save the document using the same filename.
7. Turn off the Revisions feature.
8. Make decisions regarding:

   Margins
   Fonts
   Header text
   Page number
9. Print the final document.
10. Close the document.

Production Activity 6.3—Create Cross-References and an Index; Language Arts

1. Open the file named **6pact3.doc** located on the data disk.
2. Make decision regarding:

   Margins
   Header/footer text
   Page numbering
3. Correct one spelling error, one number error, one percent error, and two punctuation errors.
4. Create bookmarks for the two figures (tables) and each of the four funds described on pages 3–6 of the document.
5. Review the document and create the needed cross-references. The cross-reference locations have been marked in the text with an asterisk (*). Delete the asterisk and insert the appropriate cross-reference created in step 4.
6. Use the filename **6palden.doc** and save the file on your file disk.
7. Develop a concordance file to use for indexing the document. Remember, the entries in the first column of the concordance file must exactly match the case (upper and lower) of the words in the document. The following are the main index heading entries:

   Capital Accumulation Program
   Risk
   Return
   Growth Stock Fund

General Stock Fund
Real Estate Fund
Principal Fund

8. Use the filename **6pcon3.doc** and save the concordance file.
9. Use the concordance file and mark all occurrences of the main index headings in the file named **6palden.doc**. Format and compile the index on a separate page at the end of the document.
10. Save the file.
11. Print one copy.
12. If you have completed your work, exit Word.

Part 7
A Final Step

Advanced Techniques

Chapters 23-25

- Number cells
- Split cells
- Create a formula to multiple two cells
- Set cell height
- Name cells using a bookmark
- Create a formula using bookmarks
- Toggle field codes and/or update a field
- Create a table using the Table Wizard
- Create a chart using Microsoft Graph 3.0b or 5.0
- Insert a spreadsheet file
- Create repeated table headings
- Link a graphic image to a document
- Use Find Record
- Use IF fields
- Output merged letters directly to a printer
- Open a data source from another application
- Request user input in a merged letter
- Create a header source and open (import) data into a data source
- Use the Set Bookmark field
- Edit and correct (debug) macros
- Record mouse actions and keystrokes while editing a macro
- Use variables and request input in a macro
- Use a conditional statement in a macro

CHAPTER

23

Advanced Tables and Microsoft Graph

Features Covered

- Number cells automatically
- Split cells
- Create a formula to multiply two cells
- Set cell height
- Name cells by using a bookmark
- Create a formula by pasting a bookmark
- Toggle field codes and/or update a field
- Insert a graphic image into a table
- Create a table using the Table Wizard feature
- Create a chart using Microsoft Graph 3.0b or 5.0
- Insert a spreadsheet file
- Create repeated table headings
- Create a spreadsheet link

Objectives and Introduction

After successfully completing this chapter, you will be able to create a form using the Table feature. While creating the table form, you will learn to number cells, split cells, create a formula to multiply two cells, name cells by using a bookmark, and create a formula by pasting a bookmark. You will learn to create a table using the Table Wizard, and learn to place a graphic image in a table. You will also learn to insert and link a spreadsheet, and create repeated table headings for a multiple-page table. Finally, using a Word table, you will learn to create a chart using Microsoft Graph.

In addition to the basic table features discussed in Chapters 5 and 6, other functions are available to create formulas and arrange information in table rows and cells. Also, a table can be enhanced by using any of the available Word clipart images. The Table Wizard and AutoFormat feature are used to quickly create and format tables. The Table Wizard also provides automatic data for row or column heads such as days of the week and months of the year.

Create a Form Using the Table Feature

Business forms, such as expense reports and invoices, can be created easily using the Table feature. Also, six predesigned table styles are available when the Table Wizard feature is used (see the section Create a Table Using the Table Wizard on page 553).

Often a cell row and column address is used to create formulas. To assist in identifying a table row, the rows can be quickly numbered by using the **Numbering** button on the Formatting Toolbar. After the table formulas are created and the row numbers are no longer needed, the numbers can be removed from the rows.

Table cells can be divided into additional columns. A single table cell can be split up into 31 columns if space is available. To split a cell, use the **Table**, **Split Cell** option.

Formulas are created in cells in which the result of calculations are desired. The formulas created in Word include symbols that indicate various math functions known as arithmetic operators. The arithmetic operator symbols used in formulas are as follows:

+ (addition)	- (subtraction or negative number)
* (multiplication)	/ (division)

When a column of numbers is added, a formula is used to avoid typing each cell address to be added. For example, if cells B1 through B8 are to be added, the formula =Sum(b1:b8) can be used. The cells shown within the parentheses will be added and the result placed in the cell where the formula is located. The equals sign indicates the beginning of a formula; the word *Sum* is used to signify addition; the colon is used to indicate a range of cells, and the parentheses are used to enclose the cell addresses. If a formula contains cell addresses that are not consecutive, a comma is used to separate the individual cell references, e.g., =Sum(c6,c9,d11).

A bookmark name can be created to identify a cell. The bookmark name is used to more easily describe a cell address when creating a formula. The bookmark name is used in a formula in place of a cell address. For example, if cell b6 is named quantity and cell b8 is named amount, a formula could be created to multiply the two cells, i.e., =quantity*amount.

Once a formula is placed in a cell, the formula result is displayed. To view the formula components, select **Tools**, **Options**, and choose the **Field Codes** option in the View tab. The formula field code displays between braces e.g., {=Sum(b3:b4)}. (If the code is selected, it displays with a gray shading.) If changes are made to any cell amounts and/or formulas, the recalculated results are displayed by using the Update Field feature. A formula is updated by clicking on the field and pressing **F9**, or by pressing the *right* mouse button and selecting the **Update Field** option.

When the table row height is increased, the cell text or numbers are defaulted to display at the top of the cell. Use the **Format**, **Paragraph**, **Spacing Above** option to change the location of text or numbers in a cell. The alignment buttons on the

Formatting Toolbar are used to display numbers at the left, right, or center of the cell.

A table form can be enhanced by placing a graphic image in a table cell. After placing a graphic image in a table, the image can be resized to fit by clicking once on the graphic and using the handles to resize it. Remember, a graphic's original proportions can be retained by dragging a corner handle.

Start-Up Instructions

❖ Open the file named **23tform0.doc** located on the data disk.

Number Cells Automatically

Note: All table rows will be automatically numbered to assist in creating table formulas. The numbers will be removed after the final form of the table is set up.

1. Select the cells to be numbered.

   For example, place the mouse pointer in the first row, click and hold while dragging down column 1 to the last row.

   Note: Only column 1 should be highlighted.

2. Select the **Numbering** button in the Formatting Toolbar.

   Note: The Table Numbering dialog box displays (see Figure 23.1).

3. Choose the desired Table Numbering options.

   For example, select the **Number Down Columns** and the **Number Each Cell Only Once** options.

4. Select **OK**.

   Note: All table rows are numbered.

Finish-Up Instructions

❖ Continue with the Steps to Split a Cell.

Start-Up Instructions

❖ The file named **23tform0.doc** should be displayed in the document window.

Split a Cell

Note: A mouse must be used to complete the following instructions.

1. Place the insertion point in the cell to be split.

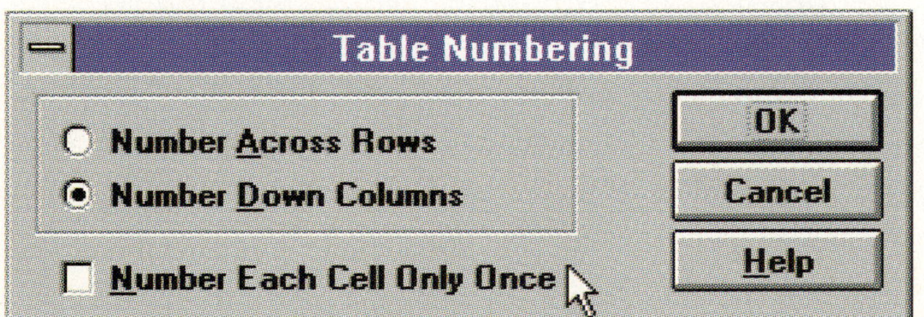

FIGURE 23.1

Table Numbering dialog box

FIGURE 23.2

Split Cells dialog box

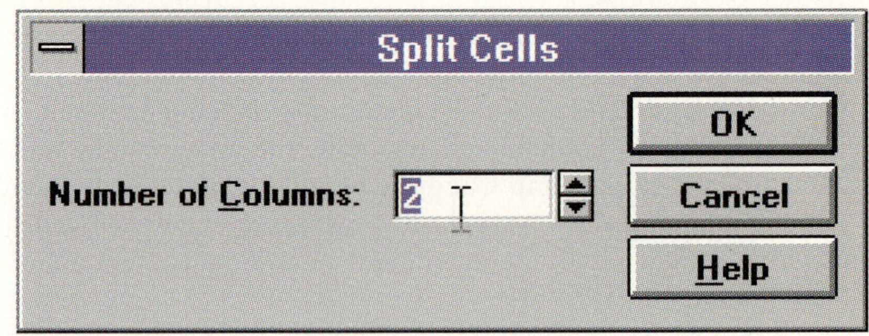

For example, place the insertion point in row 9, column 1 (Mileage).

2. Select **Table, Split Cells.**

   Note: The Split Cells dialog box displays (see Figure 23.2).

3. Point to the up or down triangle beside the Number of Columns box to increase or decrease the number displayed.

   For example, select the up triangle beside the Number of Columns box until **3** displays.

4. Select **OK.**

   Note: The cell is divided into 3 columns. The new cells are each numbered 1. That's OK.

Finish-Up Instructions

- Type the mileage rate **.32** in row 9, column 2.
- Type the number of miles **739** in row 9, column 3.
- Use figures and type the current date in row 2, column 3, e.g., 3/16/9x.
- Use the *new* filename **23tform1.doc** and save the file on your file disk.

Start-Up Instructions

The file named **23tform1.doc** should be displayed in the document window.

Steps to Create a Formula to Multiply Two Cells

1. Locate the insertion point in the cell where the results of the formula are to be displayed.

   For example, locate the insertion point in row 9, column 4, i.e., the word Mileage displays in the first column.

2. Select **Table, Formula** {Alt, a, o}.

   Note: The Formula dialog box displays.

3. Double-click in the Formula box and type the desired formula.

   For example, to multiply the number of miles (739) by the mileage rate (.32), type **=b9*c9**. (Do not type the period.)

4. Select **OK.**

*Note: The result 236.48 displays. If a field code displays, select **Tools, Options,*** View *tab, deselect **Field Codes, OK**.*

Finish-Up Instructions

- Create a formula to add the transportation costs (place the insertion point in row 10, column 3, select **Table**, **Formula**, delete the word **ABOVE** and type **b6:b8,d9** within the parentheses, choose **OK**).

  Note: The total transportation cost is 1168.03. If necessary, check that the formula reads: =sum(b6:b8,d9).
- Use the same filename **23tform1.doc** and save the file on your file disk.
- Continue with the Steps to Set Cell Height.

Start-Up Instructions

- The file named **23tform1.doc** should be displayed in the document window.

Steps to Set Cell Height

1. Place the insertion point in the desired cell(s).

   For example, select all cells in row 2.
2. Select **Table, Cell Height and Width**.

   Note: The Cell Height and Width dialog box displays.
3. If necessary, select the **Row** tab.
4. Select the desired option.

   For example, click on the arrow beside the **Height of Row 2** box; choose **Exactly**.
5. Set the desired amount in the the **At** box.

   For example, select the up triangle repeatedly until **24 pt** displays.
6. Select **OK**.

   Note: Click to deselect the row. The column heads are located at the top of the cell. Continue with the Finish-Up Instructions to place the column heads at the bottom of the cell.

Finish-Up Instructions

- Select row 2 and place space above the column heads (select **Format**, **Paragraph**, **Indents and Spacing** tab, select the up triangle in the **Spacing Before** box until **6 pt** displays, choose **OK**).
- Use the *new* filename **23tform2.doc** and save the file.
- Continue with the Steps to Name Cells Using a Bookmark.

Start-Up Instructions

The file named **23tform2.doc** should be displayed in the document window.

Steps to Name Cells Using a Bookmark

1. Highlight the ENTIRE cell to be named.

   For example, highlight the cell at row 5, column 3.

2. Select **Edit, Bookmark** {Alt, e, b}.

   Note: The Bookmark dialog box displays.

3. Type the desired name in the Bookmark Name box.

   For example, with the insertion point blinking in the Bookmark Name box, type **hotel**.

4. Select **Add** {Enter}.

   *Note: To see the Bookmark indicator, select **Tools, Options, View** tab, **Bookmarks, OK**. A beginning brace displays to the left of the cell amount. A right brace is located to the right of the cell amount, but is hidden behind the table border. The bookmark braces do not print.*

Finish-Up Instructions

- Create a cell name by using a bookmark for the following cells:

  row 10, column 3 **transp**
  row 17, column 3 **misc**

  Note: Be sure to select the entire cell when creating the bookmarks.

- Continue with the Steps to Create a Formula by Pasting a Bookmark.

Start-Up Instructions

- The file named **23tform2.doc** should be displayed in the document window.

Create a Formula by Pasting a Bookmark

1. Locate the insertion point in the cell where the bookmark is to be placed.

   For example, locate the insertion point in row 18, column 3.

2. Select **Table, Formula** {Alt, a, o}.

3. Select and delete the word **ABOVE** in the Formula box.

4. Choose the desired bookmark name from the Paste Bookmark box.

   For example, click in the **Paste Bookmark** box; choose **hotel**, type a comma.

5. Repeat step 4 and select the desired bookmark name(s).

   For example, select the **misc** bookmark; type a comma. Select the **transp** bookmark.

   Note: The formula in the Formula box should display as follows: =SUM(hotel,misc,transp).

6. Select **OK**.

Note: The formula result (1,885.43) displays in the cell where the insertion point is located.

Finish-Up Instructions

- Create a formula in row 20, column 3 to subtract the Advance Received amount from the Grand Total amount (place the insertion point in the desired cell, select **Table**, **Formula**, double-click on the Formula box and type **=c18-c19**. (Do not type the period.)

  Note: Since the Advance Received total was greater than the Grand Total amount, the result is a minus amount (i.e., -14.57).

- Use the *new* filename **23tform3.doc** and save the file.

Start-Up Instructions

- The file named **23tform3.doc** should be displayed in the document window.

Toggle Field Codes and/or Update a Field

Note: The Toggle Field Codes option is used to display a formula in a cell. The Update Field option is used to recalculate a formula after a figure(s) or a formula(s) has been changed.

1. Place the mouse pointer (I-beam) on the desired cell amount.

   For example, place the mouse pointer on row 20, column 3 where the Total Payment/Reimbursement figure is located.

2. Press the *right* mouse button.
3. Choose the desired option.

   For example, to display field codes, select the **Toggle Field Codes** option. To recalculate a formula, select the **Update Field** option.

Shortcut:

1. Place the mouse pointer (I-beam) on the desired cell amount, or select the entire table.
2. Press **F9** to update a field(s).

Finish-Up Instructions

- Remove the numbers from column 1 (place the mouse pointer in the first row, click and hold while dragging down column 1 to the last row, select the **Numbering** button in the Formatting Toolbar). Repeat and remove the numbers from row 9, columns 2 and 3.
- Use the same filename **23tform3.doc** and save the file.
- Continue with the Steps to Place a Graphic Image in a Table.

Start-Up Instructions

- The file named **23tform3.doc** should be displayed in the document window.

Place a Graphic Image in a Table

1. Place the insertion point at the location where the graphic image is to be placed.

   For example, place the insertion point to the left of the "B" in the word "Best" in row 1.

2. Select **Insert, Picture.**

3. Double-click on the desired graphic.

   For example, scroll down and double-click on **party.wmf.**

   Note: *If necessary, select the directory where the graphic image is located—usually in the Winword clipart subdirectory (e.g., c:\winword\clipart).*

Finish-Up Instructions

- Size and position the graphic (select the graphic; use the sizing handles to resize the graphic to approximately $^{3}/_{4}$ inch by $^{3}/_{4}$ inch).
- Place a copy of the graphic on the right side of the title (select the graphic, choose the **Copy** button, locate the insertion point to the right of the "t" in the word "West," select the **Paste** button).
- Select row 2 and change the shading to 10% (use the **Shading** box on the Borders Toolbar).

FIGURE 23.3

Final expense report form

Best in the West
Party Supplies and Services
Sales Representative Expense Report

Item			Week Ending:	1/24/95
Hotel			495.90	
Meals			147.35	
Total Hotel and Meals				643.25
Taxi			44.00	
Airfare			855.00	
Parking and Tolls			32.55	
Mileage	.32	739	236.48	
Total Transportation				1168.03
Miscellaneous			14.90	
Shipping (FedEx)			25.50	
Mailing			3.85	
Telephone			15.00	
Copying			6.90	
Faxing			8.00	
Total Miscellaneous				74.15
Grand Total				1885.43
Advance Received				1900.00
Total Payment/Reimbursement				-14.57
Printed Name:			Signature:	Date:
Note: Receipts are required for every expense				

- Select the cell that contains the Total Payment/Reimbursement figure and use **10%** shading.
- Use the *new* filename **23exform.doc** and save the file.

  ***Note:** Your form should look similar to Figure 23.3.*
- Print one copy and close the document.

Create a Table Using the Table Wizard

Six predesigned table styles are available when the Table Wizard feature is used. A Table Wizard provides table layout choices, column/row heading options, and cell alignment selections. The direction a table is to print (i.e., portrait or landscape) can also be specified when creating a table using a Table Wizard. When selecting Table Wizard column and row headings, choices include months of the year, quarters (i.e., Q1, Q2, Q3, Q4), days of the week, specified numbers, or designated years. Once the Table Wizard options are selected, the Table AutoFormat selections are automatically displayed. A table format can be chosen or the **Cancel** button can be selected to bypass the predefined table formats.

Start-Up Instructions

- Select the **New** button on the Standard Toolbar.

Create a Table Using the Table Wizard

1. Select **Table, Insert Table** {Alt, a, i}.
2. Select the **Wizard** button {Alt and z}.

   ***Note:** The Table Wizard dialog box displays (see Figure 23.4).*

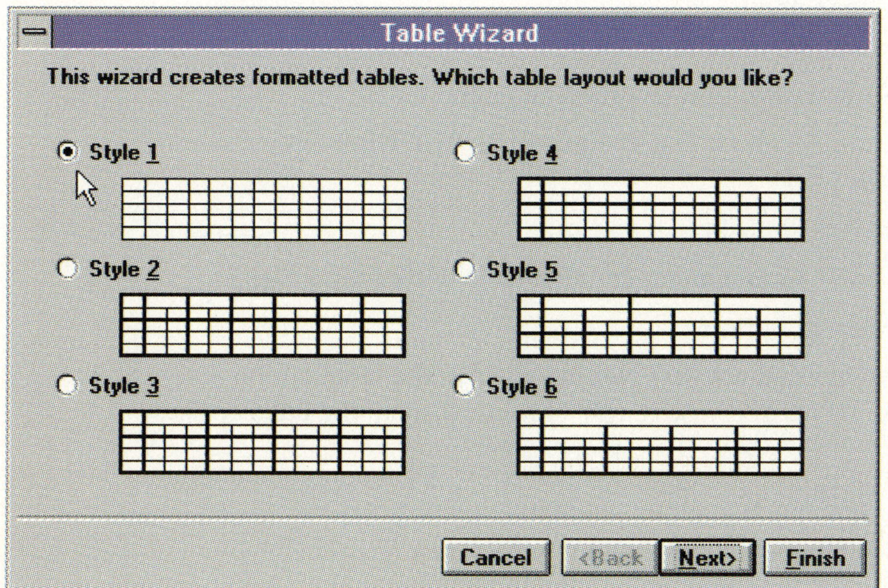

FIGURE 23.4

Table Wizard dialog box

3. Select the desired table layout.

   For example, check that Style 1 is selected. (If necessary, select **Style 1**.)

4. Select the **Next** button {Alt and n}.

   Note: A Table Wizard dialog box displays.

5. Choose the column headings desired and type the number of rows desired {Alt and o, Tab}.

   For example, check that the **No headings** option is selected and **3** displays in the **just columns** box. (If necessary, select the **No Headings** option; double-click in the **just columns** box and type **3**.)

6. Select the **Next** button {Alt and n}.

7. Choose the desired row headings and enter the desired from and to years {Alt and y, Tab twice}.

   For example, check that the **Years, from . . .** option is selected and that **1985** displays in the **from** box and **1994** appears in the **to** box. (If necessary, choose the **Years, from . . .** option; double-click in the **from** box and type **1985**; double-click in the **to** box and type **1994**.)

8. Select the **Next** button {Alt and n}.

9. Select the alignment option for the row headings {L}.

   For example, check that **Left align** is selected. (If necessary, select **Left align**.)

10. Select the **Next** button {Alt and n}.

11. Choose a table cell alignment option {d}.

    For example, check that the **Numbers: aligned on decimal** option is selected. (If necessary, choose the **Numbers: aligned on decimal** option.)

12. Select the **Next** button {Alt and n}.

13. Choose the desired option to print the table.

    For example, check that **Portrait** is selected. (If necessary, select **Portrait** {p}.)

14. Choose the **Next** button {Alt and n}.

    Note: The Table Wizard dialog box displays with the Finish Flag.

15. Select the desired option.

    For example, check that **No, just display the table** option is selected. (If necessary, select the **No, just display the table** option {o}.)

16. Select the **Finish** button {f}.

    Note: The Table AutoFormat dialog box displays.

17. Choose a format from the Formats list. Double-click on the desired format.

For example, scroll down and double-click on the **List8** format.

Note: *The table with the selected specifications and autoformat displays.*

Finish-Up Instructions

- Insert two rows at the top of the table (with the insertion point in any row 1 cell, select **Table**, **Insert Rows**; repeat to insert another row).
- Merge the cells in row 1 (select row 1, choose **Table**, **Merge Cells**).
- Select **Center** alignment and type the title and subtitle in row 1.

  Associated Growth Fund Record

  Based on Fiscal Year Ended July 31
- Type the following column headings in row 2:

  Year **Growth of Capital** **Dividend Return** **Total Return**
- Bold the title, subtitle, and column headings.
- Type the following information into the cells as shown:

Growth of Capital	Dividend Return	Total Return
+13.9%	+7.4	+21.3
+22.6%	+6.5	+29.1
-0.2%	+5.6	+5.4
+12.5%	+6.5	+19.0
+30.2%	+6.2	+36.4
-2.1%	+4.9	+2.8
+6.9%	+5.3	+12.2
+12.8%	+5.2	+18.0
-12.0%	+4.4	-7.6
+23.1%	+4.9	+28.0

- Select the **Growth of Capital** column. Click on the **Tab** alignment button at the left of the Ruler until the **decimal tab** symbol displays. Move the mouse pointer to approximately **2.25"** on the Ruler and click once to set a decimal-aligned tab.
- Place space below the subtitle (with the insertion point at any location in the subtitle, select **Format**, **Paragraph**; click on the up arrow beside the **Spacing After box** until **6 pt** displays, **OK**).
- Use the filename **23wizard.doc** and save the file on your file disk.
- Print one copy.
- Close the document.

Create a Chart Using Microsoft Graph

Data from a Word table can be visually displayed in a chart by using Microsoft Graph or a chart can be created by using new data. Also, data from a spreadsheet program such as Excel, Works, Lotus 1-2-3, and Symphony can be imported and used to create charts. Charts such as bar, pie, line, and column can be created from the table or datasheet data.

There are two different versions of Graph that are commonly provided with the Word 6.0 program. If you have Excel Version 5.0 or have purchased the Microsoft Office package, the Graph version 5.0 will most likely be on your computer. Otherwise, Graph 3.0b is shipped with Word 6.0 and will most likely be available on your computer.

To create a chart using the data from a Word table, select the table cells that contain the data from which the chart will be constructed. When the **Insert Chart** button is selected, the table data is placed in a datasheet window and a sample chart displays in the Chart and document window. To create a chart in the Chart window, click on the datasheet and type the desired information into the cells. The type of chart can be changed if desired. After the desired chart type is selected, a dialog box containing sample charts of the specified type displays.

The chart provides information along the x- and y-axis. The *x-axis* is the bottom horizontal line of a Graph chart. The *y-axis* is the left vertical line of a Graph chart. Information from column one of a table or datasheet is placed in the chart legend. Information from row one or the first highlighted row is placed on the x-axis of the chart except for the first row cell which is used for the chart title. The Data Series option can be used, however, to set up the "Series in Columns" to display the first column data in the x-axis and the row one data in the legend. The numbers in the table/datasheet cells are used to determine the values displayed on the y-axis. The bars in the sample chart visually represent the value of each item in relation to the numbers shown on the y-axis.

Using the **Format**, **Legend** option, the chart legend can be relocated to the top, bottom, right, left, or corner of the chart. Also, the legend font size, style, etc., can be changed.

In the datasheet, the data can be formatted but it cannot be calculated. In other words, column heights and widths can be changed, but a formula cannot be entered to add the figures in a column.

The data in a chart, however, can be edited in Microsoft Graph. When data are edited in the datasheet, the chart is automatically updated each time the data changes. However, if a Word table was used to create the chart, the table and chart will not be automatically updated unless you select the changed table in the document window, copy it to the Clipboard, double-click on the chart to enter Microsoft Graph, and paste the new table over the original table in the datasheet.

A shortcut menu can be used to edit, move, or apply formats such as a border to a chart. Place the mouse pointer on the chart object and click the *right* mouse button. Make any selections you wish from the shortcut menu. For example, select caption. Type a new label or use the defaulted caption, i.e., Figure 1. If desired, you can quickly return to Microsoft Graph by pointing to the chart in the document window and double-clicking.

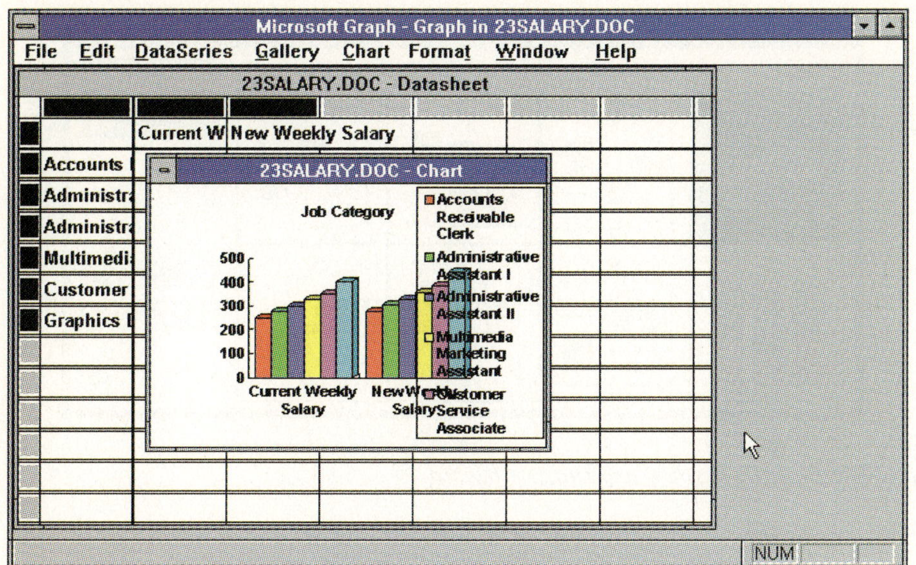

FIGURE 23.5

Microsoft Graph window with the unformatted sample chart

Start-Up Instructions

❖ Open the file named **23salary.doc** located on the data disk.

Create a Chart Using Microsoft Graph 3.0b

Note: A mouse must be used to complete the following instructions.

1. Select the cells that contain the data from which the chart will be created.

   For example, place the insertion point in column 1, row 3 and select all cells in rows 3 through 9 (columns 1, 2, and 3).

2. Select the **Insert Chart** button on the Standard Toolbar.

   Note: In a moment, if the Microsoft Graph window that is shown in Figure 23.5 displays, continue with step 3. If a ChartWizard . . . dialog box displays, go to page 559 and continue with step 3 in the Steps to Create a Chart Using Microsoft Graph 5.0.

   Note: A chart window containing a suggested chart for the selected cells displays in the foreground. A datasheet window displays in the background. The chart legend overlaps the chart. This problem will be corrected by following the next steps.

3. Enlarge the chart window.

   For example, move the mouse pointer to the bottom of the chart window until the double-headed arrow displays, press and hold the mouse button while dragging downward. Release the mouse button. Also, move the mouse pointer to the right side of the chart window until the double-headed arrow displays, press and hold the mouse button while dragging to the right. Release the mouse button. Continue to enlarge the chart window until the chart is easier to view.

4. Select the chart legend.

   For example, click on the chart legend, i.e., the box that begins with the item Accounts Receivable Clerk.

FIGURE 23.6

Chart Gallery (for Columns) dialog box

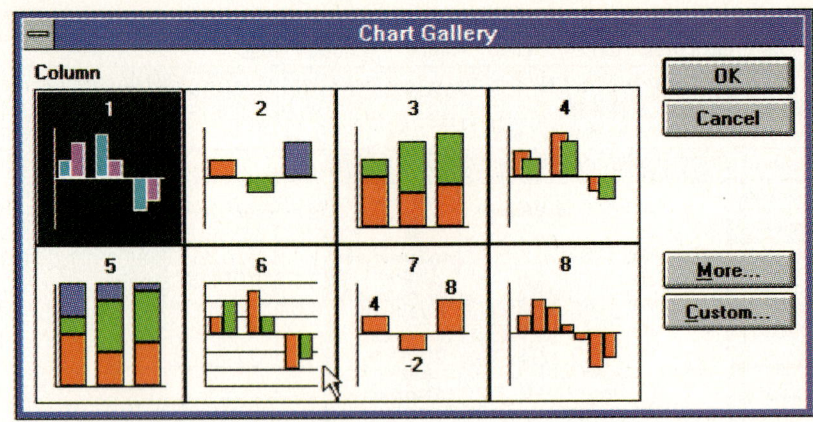

Note: The sizing handles display around the legend.

5. Select **Format, Legend.**

Note: The Legend dialog box displays.

6. Select the desired Type option; choose **OK.**

For example, select **Right**; choose **OK.**

Note: The legend displays on the right side of the chart.

7. Select **Gallery, Column.**

Note: The Chart Gallery (for columns) dialog box displays (see Figure 23.6).

8. Select the desired chart style; choose **OK.**

For example, click on the number **6** option; choose **OK.**

9. If necessary, enlarge the chart window until the column information (located at the bottom of the chart) displays on two lines.

For example, if necessary, move the mouse pointer to the right edge of the chart window until a double-headed arrow displays and drag to the right about 1".

10. Select the title and type a new title.

For example, select the title, **Job Category**. Type **Salary Increases** and click once with the mouse to see both words.

11. Enlarge the font for the title.

For example, with the title selected, choose **Format, Font**; select size **14, OK.**

12. To insert the chart below the table in the current document, select **File, Exit and Return to . . ..**

Note: A Microsoft Graph question box displays.

13. Select **Yes** to Update Graph in . . .

Note: If necessary, scroll up to display the table.

Note: When the Chart data has been obtained from a Word table and No is selected to the update message, the sample chart remains in the document window and is not updated. When the chart data was created in the Graph datasheet and No is selected to the update message, the graph is not transferred to the document window.

Finish-Up Instructions

- Select and center the chart (click on the chart once; select the **Center** button on the Formatting Toolbar).

  *Note: If desired, place additional space between the table and chart. Select **Print Preview** to view the full page. Select **Close** to return to the document window.*
- Use the *new* filename **23salar2.doc** and save the file on your file disk.
- Print one copy and close the document.

Start-Up Instructions

- Open the file named **23salary.doc** located on the data disk.

Steps to Create a Chart Using Microsoft Graph 5.0

1. Select the cells that contain the data from which the chart will be created.

   For example, place the insertion point in column 1 row 3 and select all cells in rows 3 through 9 (columns 1, 2, and 3).
2. Select the **Insert Chart** button on the Standard Toolbar.

   Note: The ChartWizard - Step 1 of 4 dialog box displays in the foreground with the 23SALARY...-Datasheet underneath it.
3. In the ChartWizard dialog box, select a chart type option; select **Next**.

   For example, select **Column**; select **Next**.
4. Select a format for the Column chart; select **Next**.

   For example, click in the number **6** option; select **Next**.
5. Choose the desired Data Series in, Use first row for, and Use first column for options.

   For example, check that **Rows** is selected for the Data Series in option, **Category (X) Axis Labels** is selected for the Use first row for option, and **Legend Text** is selected for the Use first column for option. If necessary, select the options as stated here.
6. Select the **Next** button.
7. In the Add a Legend section, select **Yes** or **No**.

   For example, make sure that **Yes** is selected for the Add a Legend option. If necessary, select **Yes**.
8. Click in the Chart Title box and type the desired title; select **Finish**.

   For example, type **Salary Increases**; select **Finish**.
9. To remove the datasheet from the screen, double-click on the Control box in the Datasheet window.

   For example, double-click on the **Control box** in the 23SALARY...-Datasheet window.
10. Select the chart legend.

For example, click once on the chart legend, i.e., the box that begins with the listed item Accounts Receivable Clerk.

Note: *The sizing handles display around the legend.*

11. Change the size of the legend using the sizing handles.

    For example, move the mouse pointer to the upper left corner of the legend until a double-headed diagonal arrow displays; drag downward and slightly to the right (about 1/8") to reduce the height and width of the legend box.

12. Select the chart title.

    For example, click once on the title **Salary Increases**.

    Note: *The sizing handles display around the title.*

13. Enlarge the font for the title.

    For example, select **Format**, **Selected Chart Title**, click on the **Font** tab, size 12, choose **OK**.

14. Enlarge the chart window.

    For example, place the mouse pointer at the bottom right corner of the chart window until a double-headed diagonal arrow displays, press and hold the mouse button and drag downward and to the right to enlarge the chart window to the approximate width of the table.

15. Click once in an empty area of the window to remove the Chart Toolbar and return to the document window.

Finish-Up Instructions

- Click once in an empty area of the window to deselect the chart.
- Select **Print Preview** to view the full page. Select **Close** to return to the document window.
- Use the *new* filename **23graph5.doc** and save the file on your file disk.
- Print one copy and close the document.

Insert a Spreadsheet File

A spreadsheet file can be inserted easily into a Word document window. Word can open spreadsheet files from programs such as Microsoft Excel and Works, Multiplan, Lotus 1-2-3, and Symphony. Inserting a spreadsheet into Word from a different program is often referred to as *importing*.

When a spreadsheet file is inserted, all of the file information is copied into a new or existing Word file. However, if only a portion of a spreadsheet file is to be inserted, a range (block of cells) is typed to indicate the exact rows and columns to be imported.

To insert a file from another application, select **File**, **Open**. Select **All Files** (*.*) in the List Files of Type box. All files on the disk in the selected drive are listed in the File Name box. Double-click on the document to be opened. In the Open

Worksheet dialog box, select **OK** to open the spreadsheet file. If the **Confirm Conversions** option is selected in the Open dialog box, a prompt displays requesting confirmation of the program where the document originated.

Once a spreadsheet file is inserted, any formatting features available for Word tables can be used. For example, the column widths can be increased or decreased or cells can be merged or split.

Start-Up Instructions

- ❖ Open the file named **23oliver.doc** located on the data disk.

Insert a Spreadsheet File

1. Place the insertion point at the location where the spreadsheet file is to be inserted.

   For example, place the insertion point to the left of the first character in the second body text paragraph, i.e., to the left of the word "If."

2. Select **Insert, File.**
3. Click in the **List Files of Type** box and select **All Files** (*.*).
4. Double-click on the desired filename.

   For example, double-click on the file named **23expns.xls.**

   Note: The Open Worksheet dialog box displays.

5. Type the desired range in the Name or Cell Range box.

   For example, type **a1:h15**. (Do not type the period.)

6. Select **OK**.

   Note: The Microsoft Excel worksheet file displays in the document.

Finish-Up Instructions

- ❖ Scroll up to display the top of the worksheet.
- ❖ Use the following information to format the inserted spreadsheet:
   a. Select and merge the cells in row 1 (select row 1, choose **Table**, **Merge Cells**).
   b. Center the title in row 1 (click on the **Center** alignment button).
   c. Delete the blank spaces in row 1 (with the nonprinting symbols turned on, use the **Backspace** and/or **Delete** key to delete the spaces).
   d. Center the column heads in row 2 (select row 2, select the **Center** alignment button).
   e. Bold the title and column heads (select rows 1 and 2, select the **Bold** button).
   f. Use 10% shading for each column that contains the "Cost" column head, including the column head "Cost" and the last cell of each column (select the column cells, click in the **Shading** box on the Borders

Toolbar, select **10%**). Repeat shading for each column that contains the column head "Cost."

g. Select the entire table and change the font and table borders. (With the insertion point in any table cell, choose **Table, Select Table**; select **Times New Roman, 11 pt**. In the Borders Toolbar, select the 1½ pt single line style; click on the **Outside Border** button; select the ¾ pt single line style, click on the **Inside Border** button.)

h. Replace the reference initials (xx) above the Enclosure notation with your initials.

i. Decrease the widths of columns 4 through 8 until the table fits more evenly between margins. (Place the insertion point on the column line until the double-headed arrow displays; drag left. Repeat for each desired column. Use Print Preview to view the entire document.)

- Use the *new* filename **23olivex.doc** and save the file on your file disk.
- Print one copy and close the document.

Repeat Table Headings In a Multiple-Page Table

The second and following pages of a multiple-page table or spreadsheet should contain header information that identifies the table. A row or consecutive rows from the first page of a multiple-page table can be selected and repeated on the following page(s) by using the **Headings** option in the **Table** menu. Once the Headings option is selected, a check mark displays beside the option in the **Table** menu. To turn off the Headings option, select **Table, Headings** again.

If the Headings option is selected, Word automatically repeats the table headings when a table extends beyond one page. When changes are made to the heading on the first page of the table, the changes will automatically be updated on succeeding pages. However, Word will not repeat or update headings if a hard page break is inserted in the table.

Start-Up Instructions

- Open the file named **23tennis.doc** located on the data disk.

Create Repeated Table Headings

1. Select the row or rows to be used as a table heading.

   For example, select rows 1 and 2.

2. Select **Table, Headings** {Alt, a, h}.

   Note: *The selected text will be the table heading on each page. Select the* ***Print Preview*** *button to display the first two table rows that are repeated on the second page of the table. Select* ***Close*** *to exit Print Preview.*

Finish-Up Instructions

- Insert page numbers (select **Insert, Page Numbers, Position, Bottom of Page (Footer), Alignment, Center, OK**).
- Use the *new* filename **23repeat.doc** and save the file on your disk.
- Print one copy and close the document.

Create a Spreadsheet Link

A spreadsheet file created in another program such as Excel can be inserted and linked to a Word document. When a spreadsheet is linked to a Word document, any changes made in the spreadsheet will be reflected in the Word file. The **Links** function in the **Edit** menu provides a connection between the Word document and the original spreadsheet file.

A link is created by opening the source file in the application in which it was created (for example, Lotus 1-2-3 or Excel), selecting the file, and choosing **Edit, Copy**. Switch to the Word document window (**Ctrl** and **Esc**, select **Microsoft Word**) and place the insertion point where the linked information is to be displayed. Select **Edit**, **Paste Special**, and choose the **Paste Link** option. To transfer the linked data, choose the desired option in the As box, e.g., Excel Worksheet Object, then select **OK**.

A linked spreadsheet is updated automatically each time the document is opened in Word or each time the data in the source file changes. If updates are to occur only at specified times, select the **Manual Update** option in the Links dialog box. If the manual update option is chosen, the linked file is updated only after the **Update Now** button is selected in the Links dialog box (Edit menu).

To create a link to another file or Word document without leaving Word, choose **Insert**, **Object**. Select the **Create from File** tab in the Object dialog box and select the name of the file to be linked. Choose the **Link to File** option and then select **OK**. This procedure to link files can only be used to link entire files. When a file is linked using the Insert Object method, the linked file is updated when the original file is changed and saved.

A link can be broken by selecting the **Links** option from the **Edit** menu. Choose the desired filename from the Source File list, then select **Break Link**. Once the link is broken, the link cannot be reconnected.

The Next Step

Chapter Review and Activities

Self-Check Quiz

T F 1. A table cell can be split into columns but not rows.

T F 2. The asterisk (*) in the cell formula D8*E8 indicates multiplication.

T F 3. Microsoft Graph can be used to create a chart that represents data from a Word table.

T F 4. After the table row height is increased, text or numbers can be repositioned in the cell by using the **Format**, **Columns** option.

T F 5. When a spreadsheet is inserted into a Word document window, all or a portion of the spreadsheet can be inserted.

6. To display the Formula dialog box, select __________, ______________ .
   a. **Edit, Table**
   b. **Table, Formula**
   c. **Insert, Formula**
   d. **Table, Insert**

7. The Table Wizard can fill table column or row headings with ______________ .
   a. months of the year
   b. days of the week
   c. numbers
   d. all of these

8. To view the components of a formula, select **Tools**, **Options**, the **View** tab and ___________
   a. **Field Codes**
   b. **Bookmarks**
   c. **Picture placeholders**
   d. **Hidden text**

9. Write a formula to add the following cells in a Word table: c9, c11, and c15.

10. List one reason for naming a cell using a bookmark.

Enriching Language Arts Skills

Spelling/Vocabulary Words

quarterly occurring at three-month intervals.

reflect to form an image of; to mirror.

surpassed to have gone beyond the limit; exceeded; excelled.

Abbreviations in Table Column Headings

When creating tables and forms, abbreviations are often used in subtitles and column headings because of limited space. However, abbreviations should be used sparingly. If you are unsure of an abbreviation, consult a dictionary.

Common abbreviations:

account	*acct.*	*incorporated*	*inc.*
amount	*amt.*	*miscellaneous*	*misc.*
attention	*attn.*	*number*	*No.*
department	*dept.*	*quarter*	*Q or qtr.*
dozen	*dz. or doz.*	*received*	*recd.*

Activities

Activity 23.1—Create an Invoice Using the Table Feature; Create Formulas

1. Create a table with five columns and ten rows.
2. Use the following information to format the table similar to the Invoice table shown on page 566.
    a. Merge the cells in row 1 (select row 1, choose **Table, Merge Cells**).
    b. Increase the cell height of row 1 to Exactly **84** pt (with the desired cell selected, select **Table, Cell Height and Width, Row** tab, Height of Row 1, **Exactly,** click on the up triangle in the At box repeatedly until the desired number displays, **OK**).
    c. Select and merge columns 1 through 4 in row 2 (select the desired cells, select **Table, Merge Cells**).
    d. Increase the cell height for the merged cells in row 2 and use At Least **48** pt (follow the instructions in step 2b).
    e. Type the unformatted information (text and numbers) as shown.

<table>
<tr><td colspan="5">INVOICE

Cut and Dried Flowers
1832 Geranium Lane
Charleston, SC 29407</td></tr>
<tr><td colspan="4">To:
Buckley County School District
1789 Revolution Avenue
Moncks Corner, SC 29461</td><td>Date:
(use current date)</td></tr>
<tr><td>Quantity</td><td>Stock No.</td><td>Description</td><td>Unit Price</td><td>Total Price</td></tr>
<tr><td>7</td><td>8724</td><td>Floral Spray</td><td>12.00</td><td></td></tr>
<tr><td>5</td><td>8745</td><td>Floral Swag</td><td>15.50</td><td></td></tr>
<tr><td>10</td><td>8773</td><td>Ikebana</td><td>20.00</td><td></td></tr>
<tr><td></td><td></td><td></td><td></td><td></td></tr>
<tr><td></td><td></td><td>Subtotal</td><td></td><td></td></tr>
<tr><td></td><td></td><td>Sales Tax
(8.5%)</td><td></td><td></td></tr>
<tr><td></td><td></td><td>Total</td><td></td><td></td></tr>
</table>

3. Use the following information to format the table.
   a. Select and center the word **INVOICE** in row 1; change to **18 pt**.
   b. Locate the insertion point in the blank line after INVOICE and insert a special symbol (select **Insert**, **Symbol**, **Wingdings**; choose the scissors in row 1, column 3, select **Insert**, **Close**).
   c. Select the symbol and change the point size to **18**.
   d. Select row 3 (where the column heads are located); choose **Center** alignment.
   e. Select rows 4 through 10 and columns 1 through 5 and choose **Right** alignment.
4. Create formulas for column 5, rows 4, 5, and 6 to multiply the Quantity by the Unit Price (with the insertion point in the desired cell, select **Table**, **Formula**, delete the displayed formula and use the following information).

   Column 5, row 4: type **=a4*d4**, select the **$#,##0.00** number format
   Column 5, row 5: type **=a5*d5**, select the **#,##0.00** number format
   Column 5, row 6: type **=a6*d6**, select the **#,##0.00** number format
5. Create a formula in row 8, column 5 to add rows 4, 5, and 6 in column 5 (select **Table**, **Formula**, =SUM[ABOVE], select the **#,##0.00** number format, **OK**).
6. Create a formula in row 9 to multiply row 8, column 5 by the Sales Tax (select **Table**, **Formula**, delete the formula and type **=e8*.085**, select the **#,#00.00** number format, **OK**).

7. Create a formula in row 10 to add rows 8 and 9, column 5 (select **Table, Formula,** delete the formula and type **=e8+e9**, select the **$#,#00.00** number format, **OK**).

8. Select the entire table and place **3/4 pt** single line border around the form and the cells (choose **Table, Select Table**; on the Borders Toolbar, check that **3/4 pt** displays in the Line Style box; choose the **Outside Border** button and the **Inside Border** button).

9. Select and use **10%** shading in rows 3 and 10 (select the row, click in the **Shading** box in the Borders Toolbar, select **10%**). Remove the Borders Toolbar by selecting the **Borders** button.

   Note: *Your form should look similar to the form shown below.*

Invoice ✂ Cut and Dried Flowers 1832 Geranium Lane Charleston, SC 29407				
To: Buckley County School District 1789 Revolution Avenue Moncks Corner, SC 29461				Date: (current date)
Quantity	Stock No.	Description	Unit Price	Total Price
7	8724	Floral Spray	12.00	$ 84.00
5	8745	Floral Swag	15.50	77.50
10	8773	Ikebana	20.00	200.00
		Subtotal		361.50
		Sales Tax (8.5%)		30.73
		Total		$ 392.23

10. Use the filename **23invoic.doc** and save the file.

11. Print one copy of the form.

12. Close the document.

Activity 23.2—Revise a Table Form, Insert a Graphic, Name a Cell, Split a Cell and Update Formulas

1. Open the file named **23invoic.doc** that was created in Activity 23.1.

2. Select and delete the scissors symbol. Change the alignment of the word **INVOICE** to **Left**. Change the font size of the word INVOICE to **26**.

3. Insert the graphic image named **ornamnt1.wmf** (with the insertion point located to the right of the word **INVOICE**, press and hold the **Ctrl** key while tapping the **Tab** key five times, select **Insert, Picture**, double-click on **ornamnt1.wmf**).

4. Select and size the graphic image. (Click on the graphic image, move the mouse pointer to the black box on the center right edge of the graphic image until a double-headed arrow displays, press and hold the mouse button while dragging right until the width of the graphic image is approximately 2½", release the mouse button. Move the mouse pointer to the black box on the bottom center of the graphic image until a double-headed arrow displays, press and hold the mouse button while dragging down until the height of the graphic image is approximately 1½".)
5. Split the cell that contains the date into two columns (with the insertion point located in the desired cell, select **Table**, **Split Cells**, Number of Columns **2**, **OK**).
6. Delete the date in row 2, column 3. Move the word "Date:" in row 2, column 2 to row 2, column 3. Click after the colon in the word "Date:" and press **Enter** twice. Type the current date.
7. Enlarge the split cells by moving the mouse pointer to the border between column 1 and column 2 in row 2 until a double-headed line displays. Press and hold the mouse button and drag to the left approximately ⅛".
8. In row 2, column 2, type the words **Invoice No.** and press the **Enter** key once. Type **3284**.
9. Change the quantity of Floral Swag to **8**.
10. Update all table formulas (choose **Table**, **Select Table**, press **F9**).
11. Use a bookmark to name the cell containing the total amount. (Select the entire cell that contains the total amount, select **Edit**, **Bookmark**. In the Bookmark Name box, type **total**, select **Add**.)
12. Use the following information to type a note below the table and insert a formula using the "total" bookmark.
    a. Press **Ctrl** and **End**. Press **Enter** once.
    b. Type the following:

       Please send your check in the amount of

    c. Press the **Spacebar** once and select **Table**, **Formula**, click in the **Paste Bookmark** box, select **total**, and select **OK**.
    d. Press the **Spacebar** once and type the following:

       to the attention of Duane at the following address: Accounts Receivable, P.O. Box 39421, Charleston, SC 29407-9421.
13. Enhance the table by using bold for the words **To**, **Invoice No.**, and **Date**. Also bold the column headings.
14. Use the *new* filename **23act2.doc** and save the file on your file disk.

    Note: Your form should look similar to the form shown on page 569.
15. Print one copy and close the document.
16. Optional. Fax the printed copy of the invoice to a local Fax machine.

Invoice

Cut and Dried Flowers
1832 Geranium Lane
Charleston, SC 29407

To: Buckley County School District 1789 Revolution Avenue Moncks Corner, SC 29461				Invoice No. 3284	Date: (current date)
Quantity	**Stock No.**	**Description**	**Unit Price**	**Total Price**	
7	8724	Floral Spray	12.00	$ 84.00	
8	8745	Floral Swag	15.50	124.00	
10	8773	Ikebana	20.00	200.00	
		Subtotal		408.00	
		Sales Tax (8.5%)		34.68	
		Total		$ 442.68	

Please send your check in the amount of $442.68 to the attention of Duane at the following address: Accounts Receivable, P.O. Box 39421, Charleston, SC 29407-9421.

Activity 23.3—Create a Table Using a Table Wizard; Create a Chart

1. Use the following information to create a table using a Table Wizard.
    a. In a new document window, select **Table, Insert Table, Wizard.**
    b. Check that **Style 1** is selected or choose **Style 1**; select **Next.**
    c. Select the **Quarters** option for column headings; select **Next.**
    d. Select the **Repeat headings** and **Center** options; select **Next.**
    e. Choose the **No headings . . .** option and type 5 in the rows box; select **Next.**
    f. Select the **Numbers: aligned on decimal** option; select **Next.**
    g. If necessary, select **Portrait**; select **Next.**
    h. If necessary, select the **No, just display the table** option; select **Finish.**
    i. Select the **Grid 1** format in the Table AutoFormat dialog box; select **OK.**
2. Insert a new column to the left of column 1 (select column 1, select the **Insert Columns** button).
3. Change the size of the table columns (choose **Table, Select Table**; choose **Table, Cell Height and Width**; on the **Columns** tab, double-click in the **Width of Columns** box, type **1.25**, select **OK**).

4. Type the following information into each cell.

   Note: Column 1 information will be formatted later.

Receipts	Q 1	Q 2	Q 3	Q 4
Dues	2,560	2,560	3,400	3,400
Assessments	110	180	1,100	590
Penalties	210	150	200	300
Interest	290	450	545	660
Clubhouse	540	654	780	1,550

5. Change the alignment for column 1, rows 2–6 to **Left** (select rows 2–6 in column 1; on the Ruler, move the mouse pointer to the decimal tab above column 1, press and hold the mouse button and drag the tab symbol off the Ruler; release the mouse button).
6. Insert and merge a new first row (with the insertion point located in row 1, select the **Insert Rows** button; select **Table, Merge Cells**).
7. In row 1, type and center the following title and subtitle.

   Fredkins Recreation Center
   Quarterly Cash Receipts
   for Fiscal Year Ended 199x
8. Use the filename **23cash3.doc** and save the file on your file disk.
9. Insert a chart below the table (press **Ctrl** and **End**, select all rows of the table except row 1, select the **Insert Chart** button).
10. Use the following information to format the chart:
    a. Enlarge the chart window (place the mouse pointer at the bottom right corner of the chart window until a double-headed diagonal arrow displays; press and hold the mouse button and drag down and to the right to enlarge the chart window; if necessary, repeat on the various window edges until the chart is easy to read).
    b. Select the 3-D Column chart type (select **Gallery, 3-D Columns**, select the number 2 option, **OK**).
    c. Position the legend at the right of the chart (click on the legend, select **Format, Legend, Right, OK**).
    d. Change the title of the chart to **Cash Receipts** (click on the word "Receipts," type **Cash Receipts**; click to the right of the title, select **Format, Font, 12, OK**).
11. Return to the document window (select **File, Exit and Return to . . .**, select **Yes**).
12. Center the chart below the table (click on the chart, select the **Center** button).
13. Use the same filename, **23cash3.doc** and save the file.
14. Print one copy and close the document.

15. Optional. Fax the printed table and chart to a local Fax machine or send the document to a fellow student or to your instructor using the e-mail feature on the network.

Challenge Your Skills

Skill 23.1—Create Formulas; Use a Bookmark

1. Open the file named **23skill1.doc** located on the data disk.
2. Make decisions regarding the following:
   a. Formulas to calculate the results for column totals (row 6) and the Net Pay column. Choose an appropriate number format.
   Hint: *The formula in column 6, row 3 may be written =b3-(c3+d3+e3).*
   b. Create a bookmark for the result in column 6, row 6.
   Hint: *Be sure to select the entire cell when creating the bookmark.*
   c. Place the insertion point in the first paragraph, second sentence between the words *of* and *are*. Insert the Total Net Pay amount by creating a formula using the bookmark name created in step 2b.
3. Make decisions regarding the fonts and placement of the memorandum text.
4. Use the *new* filename **23skfin.doc** and save the file on your file disk.
5. Print one copy and close the document.
6. Optional. Fax the printed memorandum to a local Fax machine or send the document via e-mail to a fellow student or to your instructor using the network.

Skill 23.2—Create a Chart; Language Arts

1. Open the file named **23skill2.doc** located on the data disk.
2. Correct two spelling errors, two punctuation errors, and one abbreviation error.
3. Choose an appropriate table format by using the Table AutoFormat feature.
   Note: *The table may need to be centered after the Table AutoFormat is chosen.*
4. Create a chart for the table using Microsoft Graph. Make decisions regarding:
   a. An appropriate 3-D Bar or 3-D Column chart.
   b. Position of the legend.
   c. An appropriate title for the chart. If desired, select a different font and/or size for the title.
   d. Placement of the chart in the document.
5. Use the *new* filename **23skfin2.doc** and save the file on your file disk.
6. Print one copy of the document.

7. Optional. Fax the memorandum to a local Fax machine or send the document via e-mail to a fellow student or to your instructor using the network.
8. If you have completed your work, exit Word.

CHAPTER 24

Advanced Merging

Features Covered

- Link a graphic image to a document
- Use an IF field
- Output merged letters directly to a printer
- Use Find Record
- Open a data source from another application
- Request user input in a merged letter
- Create a header source and open (import) data into a data source
- Use the Set Bookmark field

Objectives and Introduction

After successfully completing this chapter, you will be able to use the IF field when merging a main document and data source. Also, you will learn to link a graphic image to a document, output merged letters to a printer, use Find Record and open (import) data into a data source. In addition, you will learn to place a Fill-in field (a special command) in a form letter to allow users to input text from the keyboard as letters are merged.

The basic structure of Word's merge feature, which combines main documents and data sources to produce individualized letters and mailing labels, was introduced in Chapters 11 and 12. In addition to the basics, the merge feature has options and commands that can make merged documents look more professional, make the merge process more flexible and efficient, and allow Word to use data from other applications and open data files from other sources.

Link a Graphic Image to a Main Document

If a graphic image will be printed in merged letters, the merge operation will need less memory and less storage space if the graphic image is linked to the main document. When the **Link to File** option is chosen in the Insert Picture dialog box, each merged letter references the graphic file on the disk instead of saving a copy of the graphic within each letter.

Start-Up Instructions

- Open the main document named **24its1.doc** located on the data disk.

Link a Graphic Image to a Main Document

1. Place the insertion point at the location where the graphic image is to display or select the desired frame.

   For example, move the mouse pointer to the edge of the frame located next to the letterhead information and click once.

   Note: Sizing handles display around the frame.

2. Select **Insert, Picture.**
3. Select the desired graphic image.

   For example, click once on the file named **ornamnt2.wmf.**

4. Select the **Link to File** option.

   Note: An X should display in the Link to File option box.

5. Deselect the **Save Picture in Document** option.

   *Note: An X should **not** display in the Save Picture in Document option box.*

6. Select **OK.**

   *Note: The linked graphic image displays next to the letterhead information. If **Field Codes** are selected in the **Tools, Options, View** tab, a field code displays in place of the graphic image.*

Finish-Up Instructions

- Position the graphic image (with the graphic image selected, choose **Format, Frame, None,** select **Horizontal Position, Left,** select **Relative To, Margin, OK**).
- Use the *new* filename **24its2.doc** and save the file.
- Continue with the Steps to Use an IF Field.

Use IF Fields

An *IF field* allows you to define criteria that data must meet and to specify a different course of action depending on whether the condition is met. For example, a let-

Insert Word Field: IF

IF
Field Name: Address1
Comparison: Less than or Equal
Compare To: 999

OK
Cancel
Help

Insert this Text:
5:30 a.m.

Otherwise Insert this Text:
5:45 a.m.

Text to be inserted in a merged document when the IF statement is met (THEN).

Text to be inserted in a merged document when the IF statement is not met (ELSE).

FIGURE 24.1

Example Insert Word Field: IF dialog box

ter is to be sent to customers informing them of a new time for refuse pickup. Customers with street addresses that are 999 or less must have their refuse at the curb by 5:30 a.m. All other customers must have their refuse at the curb by 5:45 a.m.

In the Insert Word Field: IF dialog box, there are three main sections: *IF*, *Insert this Text*, and *Otherwise Insert this Text*. These sections are comparable to the **If...Then...Else...** option in the Insert Word Field drop-down list.

The IF section defines the criteria for evaluating data in a specific field. It contains three elements: *Field Name*, *Comparison*, and *Compare To*.

The Comparison box is used to specify how the data is to be evaluated, such as equal to, not equal to, less than, or greater than. The Compare To box is used to specify the text or value that the data should meet (or not meet, depending on the comparison phrase selected in the Comparison box).

The Insert this Text section (Then) of the Insert Word Field: IF dialog box contains the information to print if the criteria specified in the IF section *is* met. The Otherwise Insert this Text (Else) section of the Insert Word Field: IF dialog box contains the information to print if the criteria specified in the IF section *is not* met (see Figure 24.1).

Sometimes a data source record will contain fields that are empty. For example, the Title field may be empty. The inside address in the form letter places the Title field on the same line as the FirstName and LastName fields; therefore, some letters will print with a blank space before the first name as shown in Figure 24.2. Since the Title field leaves a blank *horizontal* space, the *IF field* can be used to eliminate the blank horizontal space when a field is empty.

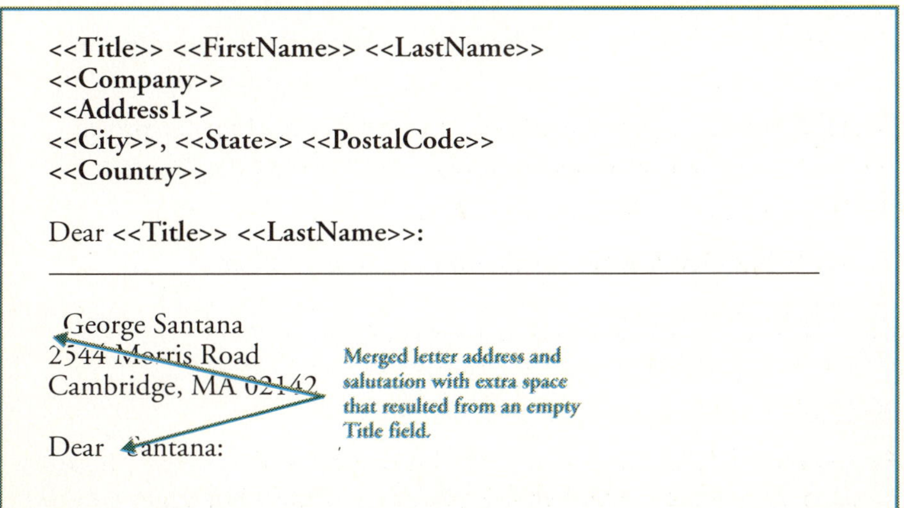

<<Title>> <<FirstName>> <<LastName>>
<<Company>>
<<Address1>>
<<City>>, <<State>> <<PostalCode>>
<<Country>>

Dear **<<Title>> <<LastName>>**:

George Santana
2544 Morris Road
Cambridge, MA 02142

Dear Santana:

FIGURE 24.2

Main document without the IF fields

FIGURE 24.3

Checking and Reporting Errors dialog box

Checking and Reporting Errors

- ○ Simulate the merge and report errors in a new document.
- ◉ Complete the merge, pausing to report each error as it occurs.
- ○ Complete the merge without pausing. Report errors in a new document.

OK | Cancel | Help

Checking for errors before merging can save time and/or prepare the main document and data source for merging at a later time. Before a main document and data source are merged, Word can assist in identifying various merge errors. For example, if a field name in the main document does not match a field name in the data source, Word displays an Invalid Merge Field dialog box, so you can remove or replace the mismatched field.

After the **Check for Errors** button is selected in the Mail Merge Toolbar, the Checking and Reporting Errors dialog box displays with three options: **Simulate the merge and report errors in a new document, Complete the merge pausing to report each error as it occurs**, and **Complete the merge without pausing. Report errors in a new document.** (See Figure 24.3.)

Start-Up Instructions

- The file named **24its2.doc** should be displayed in the document window. (If necessary, open the document named **24its2.doc**.)
- Select the **Mail Merge Helper** button.
- Choose the **Get Data** button.
- Select the **Open Data Source** option.
- Choose the drive/directory and filename desired.

  For example, choose the drive/directory where your file disk is located and double-click on the file named **24data1.doc**.
- Choose **Edit Main Document**.
- Turn on Field Codes (select **Tools**, **Options**, choose **Field Codes** in the **View** tab, select **OK**).

  Note: The field codes for the linked graphic image and date code display.
- Locate the insertion point in front of the third paragraph symbol after the date code. If necessary, turn on the nonprinting symbols (select the **Show/Hide** button).

Use an IF Field

1. Select the **Insert Word Field** button in the Mail Merge Toolbar.
2. Select the **If...Then...Else** option.

   Note: The Insert Word Field: IF dialog box displays (see Figure 24.4).
3. To begin the IF field, select the desired field name.

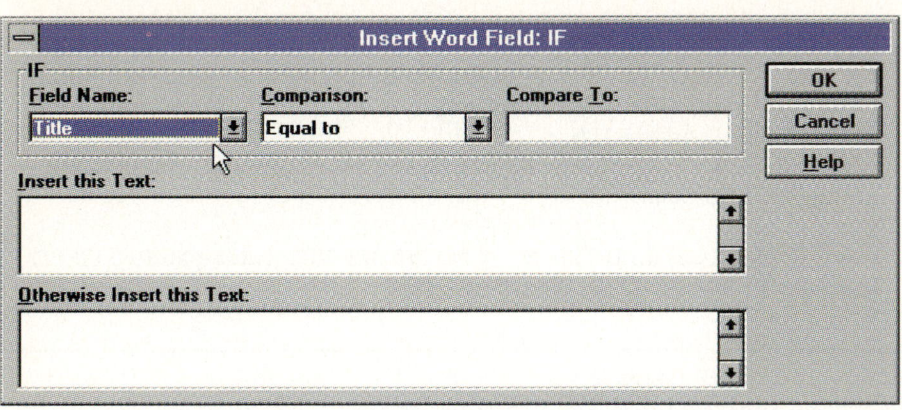

FIGURE 24.4

Insert Word Field: IF dialog box

For example, check that **Title** displays in the Field Name box. (If necessary, select the down arrow next to the Field Name box and choose **Title**.)

4. Select the desired comparison in the Comparison box.

   For example, select the down arrow next to the Comparison box, scroll down and choose **is not Blank**.

5. Type the desired information in the Compare To box.

   For example, the Compare To box will be empty because there is nothing to be compared.

   *Note: The Compare To box is used when any Comparison box option is used except for the **is Blank** or **is Not Blank** options.*

6. Type the desired text or merge field code(s) in the **Insert this Text** box.

   For example, click in the Insert this Text box; press **Ctrl** and **F9**; type **MERGEFIELD Title**; press the **right arrow** key twice, and press the **Spacebar** once.

7. Select **OK**.

   Note: The IF field code containing the field information displays in the document window, i.e., { IF { MERGEFIELD Title }<> "" "{ MERGEFIELD Title } " "" }.

Finish-Up Instructions

- Locate the insertion point at the end of the IF field code. The field code will no longer be highlighted.

  Note: Do not press the Spacebar.

- Continue to insert the desired merge fields, spaces, and punctuation using the following information:

  a. With the insertion point at the end of the IF field code, select the **Insert Merge Field** button; choose **FirstName**; press the **Spacebar** once.

  b. Select the **Insert Merge Field** button; choose **LastName**; press **Enter** once.

  c. Select the **Insert Merge Field** button; choose **Address1**; press **Enter** once.

FIGURE 24.5

Main document address and salutation with IF fields

```
¶
{·IF·{·MERGEFIELD·Title·}<>·"".·"{·MERGEFIELD·Title·}·"·""·}·{·MERGEFIELD·
FirstName·}·{·MERGEFIELD·LastName·}¶
{·MERGEFIELD·Address1·}¶
{·MERGEFIELD·City·},·{·MERGEFIELD·State·}·{·MERGEFIELD·PostalCode·}¶
{·MERGEFIELD·Country·}¶
¶
Dear·{·IF·{·MERGEFIELD·Title·}<>·"".·"{·MERGEFIELD·Title·}·{·MERGEFIELD·
LastName·}"·"{·MERGEFIELD·FirstName·}"·}¶
¶
```

d. Select the **Insert Merge Field** button; choose **City**, type a comma; press the **Spacebar** once.

e. Select the **Insert Merge Field** button; choose **State**; press the **Spacebar** once.

f. Select the **Insert Merge Field** button; choose **PostalCode**; press **Enter** once.

g. Select the **Insert Merge Field** button; choose **Country**; press **Enter** twice.

❖ Type **Dear** followed by a space; select the **Insert Word Field** button; choose the **If...Then...Else...** option.

❖ Use the following instructions to enter information into the Insert Word Field: IF dialog box:

a. Check that **Title** displays in the Field Name box.

b. In the Comparison box, scroll down and select **is Not Blank.**

c. Click in the **Insert this Text** box and press **Ctrl** and **F9**; type **MERGEFIELD Title,** press the **right arrow** key twice; press the **Spacebar** once; press **Ctrl** and **F9**, type **MERGEFIELD LastName.**

d. Click in the **Otherwise Insert this Text** box, press **Ctrl** and **F9**; type **MERGEFIELD FirstName**, select **OK.**

Note: The main document containing the address and salutation with the IF fields should look similar to Figure 24.5.

e. Locate the insertion point at the end of the IF field code and type a colon.

f. Scroll down the file and replace the x's in the reference notation with your initials. Replace the filename **24its1.doc** with **24main1.doc.**

g. Use the *new* filename **24main1.doc** and save the main document.

Note: If desired, turn off field codes (select ***Tools****,* ***Options****, select* ***Field Codes*** *in the* ***View*** *tab,* ***OK****).*

h. Select the **Check for Errors** button. Choose **Complete the merge, pausing to report each error as it occurs.** Select **OK.**

Note: If merging mistakes are found, compare the merge fields to the information shown in Figure 24.5. Make any necessary corrections in the main document.

i. Close but do not save the form letter document that was created when checking for errors.

j. Select the **Merge to New Document** button.

Note: Scroll through the letters and check that the merged information is correct.

- Save the merged letters. Use the filename **24merge1.doc**.
- Close the merged form letters file; do not close the file named 24main1.doc.
- Continue with the Steps to Output Merged Letters Directly to a Printer.

Output Merged Letters Directly to a Printer

One problem that can occur with large data files is that the computer may not have enough memory to store all the merged letters at one time. This can cause the merge process to stop before it has merged all the letters. Using the **Records to Be Merged** option in the Merge dialog box to limit the number of records to be merged may be helpful, or it may be more efficient to use the **Merge to Printer** option and output the information directly to the printer to avoid an out-of-memory error.

The Merge to Printer option can be used to reduce the memory needed during the merge operation. Sending merged letters directly to the printer can avoid some memory problems, but should be used only with a data source and main document that have been merged and checked previously for errors. Otherwise, a lot of paper can be wasted!

Start-Up Instructions

- The file named **24main1.doc** should be displayed in the document window. (If necessary, open the file named **24main1.doc**.)

Output Merged Letters Directly to a Printer

1. With the main document containing the merge field codes in the document window, select the **Merge to Printer** button located on the Mail Merge Toolbar.

   Note: The Print dialog box displays.

2. Select **OK**.

   Note: The Printing message box displays briefly in the document window with the message, "Now printing Page 1...". The printing message disappears when the merge is complete and the letters are sent to the printer.

Finish-Up Instructions

- Check the printed letters for accuracy.
- Continue with the Steps to Use Find Record to Locate a Data Record.

Use Find Record

Modifying information in a data source is necessary when a record is to be added, deleted, or changed. A record is easily viewed and changed by using the **Edit Data Source** button in the Mail Merge Toolbar (see Chapter 11).

If a data source is large, however, quickly accessing an individual record to be changed can save time. A record can be quickly located using the **Find Record** button in the Mail Merge Toolbar or the Data Form dialog box. Type the desired text in the Find What box, then select the desired field in the In Field box. When the **Find First** button is chosen, the record containing the typed text and specified field name is found. After the record is found, close the Find in Field dialog box. If the Data Form dialog box is displayed, the found record appears immediately. If the main document window is open, select the **Edit Data Source** button to display the found record.

Start-Up Instructions

- The document named **24main1.doc** should be displayed. (If necessary, open the document named **24main1.doc**.)

Use Find Record to Locate a Data Record

1. Select the **Find Record** button in the Mail Merge Toolbar.

   Note: The Find in Field dialog box displays.

2. Type the desired text in the Find What box.

   For example, type **Wilshire.** (Do not type the period.)

3. In the In Field box, choose the desired field.

   For example, click in the **In Field** box, and choose **Address1**.

4. Select the **Find First** button.

   Note: After the record is found, the Find in Field dialog box remains in the document window.

5. Select **Close**.

Finish-Up Instructions

- Select the **Edit Data Source** button in the Mail Merge Toolbar.
- To edit the record, click in the **Address1** box and change the Suite number to **209**.
- Select **OK**.
- To merge and print the changed record, select the **Mail Merge** button; in the **From**, type **4**; in the **To** box, type **4**; choose **Merge**.
- Select the **Print** button.
- Close the document but do not save the merged letter.
- Close the document named **24main1.doc** and select **Yes** to save the data source named **24data1.doc**. Select **No** to save changes to **24main1.doc**.

Use a Data Source from a Different Application

A data source from a different application such as Microsoft Access or Microsoft Excel can be merged with a Word main document. The data source is opened as usual by using the Open Data Source option from the **Get Data Source** button in the Mail Merge Helper dialog box.

However, in the Open Data Source dialog box, the **Confirm Conversions** option is selected. Also, to view all filenames, the **All Files** option in the **List Files of Type** box is chosen. After the data source document name to be opened is selected, the Confirm Data Source dialog box displays.

The Confirm Data Source dialog box contains the conversion options available for converting files from different data sources. Select the **Show All** option to display a complete list of converter options that are provided by Word.

When an Excel worksheet file is opened, the entire spreadsheet or a range of cells can be specified. In order to know which range of cells to open from a spreadsheet, you would need to have access to a spreadsheet program where the data could be displayed. In this book, the range information is provided for you when needed.

Start-Up Instructions

- Open the file named **24gmain.doc** located on the data disk.

Open a Data Source From a Different Application

1. Select the **Mail Merge Helper** button.
2. Select the **Get Data** button.
3. Choose **Open Data Source**.
4. Choose the **List Files of Type** box.

   For example, check that **All Files** (*.*) displays. If necessary, select **All Files** (*.*).
5. Select the **Confirm Conversions** option.

   For example, check that the **Confirm Conversions** option is selected. (If necessary, select the **Confirm Conversions** option.)
6. Choose the drive/directory and double-click on the desired filename.

   For example, double-click on the filename **24sheet1.xls**.

   Note: The Confirm Data Source dialog box displays.
7. Choose the desired Open Data Source option.

   For example, choose **Microsoft Excel Worksheet via Converter....**
8. Select **OK**.

   Note: The Open Worksheet dialog box displays.
9. Type the desired range or select **Open the Entire Worksheet** and select the **Format for Mail Merge** option.

For example, in the Name or Cell Range box, type **a2:h5**; select the **Format for Mail Merge** option.

10. Select **OK**.

Note: The path and filename for the data source are displayed below the Get Data button, e.g., a:24SHEET1.XLS.

11. Close the Mail Merge Helper dialog box.

Finish-Up Instructions

- Choose the **Check for Errors** button and select **Complete the merge, pausing to report each error as it occurs**. Select **OK**.
- Scroll through the merged letters and observe the names and addresses that were obtained from the Excel spreadsheet file, e.g., Kelly Ybarra, Yohannes Wohlenberg, and T. J. Carvalho. Close but do not save the merged letters. If necessary, make corrections to the main document.
- To complete the mail merge fields in the body of the main document, continue with the Steps to Create and Edit a Fill-in Field.

Request User Input in a Merged Letter

Special data that may be used only once in a document is often not saved in a data source. A special field, **Fill-in**, can be inserted in the main document to instruct the program to pause and request the user to type the needed information. The Fill-in field is placed in the main document at the position where the specific information will be entered.

When the main document containing the Fill-in field is merged with a data source, the program will pause during the merging of each letter to allow the user to type the specific information. If the **Ask Once** option was selected when the Fill-in field was created, Word will stop at the Fill-in field for the first record only. The information typed at that time will be used for all merged letters. When all letters have been merged and the special information is entered, the insertion point displays at the bottom of the final merged letter.

Start-Up Instructions

- The file named **24gmain.doc** should be displayed. (If necessary, open the file named **24gmain.doc**.)
- The field codes option should be turned on. (If necessary, select **Tools, Options**, select **Field Codes** in the **View** tab, **OK**.)

Create and Edit a Fill-in Field

Note: A mouse must be used to perform the following steps.

1. Place the insertion point at the position where the Fill-in field is to be located.

For example, in the second body text paragraph, sentence one, place the insertion point between the words **for** and **at**.

2. Select the **Insert Word Field** button.
3. Choose the **Fill-in** option.

   Note: *The Insert Word Field: Fill-in dialog box displays.*
4. In the Prompt box, type the desired information.

   For example, type **Enter scheduled interview date for:**. (Do not type the period.)
5. Click in the Default Fill-in Text box and type the desired information.

   For example, type **next Tuesday**. (Do not type the period.)
6. To instruct Word to only ask for the information once, select the **Ask Once** option.

   For example, select the **Ask Once** option so that you will only be asked to enter the date once when the letters are merged.
7. Select **OK**.

   Note: *A Microsoft Word message box displays with the prompt and default text. If a typographical error is noticed, complete step 8 and then make the correction(s) in the document window.*
8. Select **OK**.

   Note: *The FILLIN field code displays in the document, i.e., { FILLIN "Enter scheduled interview date for:" \d "next Tuesday" \o }.*
9. To edit the fill-in field, place the insertion point at the desired location and choose the **Insert Merge Field** button.

   For example, to display the information in the LastName field in the Fill-in Prompt box, place the insertion point between the word for and the colon (:) in the **FILLIN** code, press the **Spacebar** once, select the **Insert Merge Field** button; click on **LastName**.

   Note: *The Microsoft Word message box displays with the last name of the person listed in the first data source record, i.e., Ybarra.*
10. Select **OK**.

    Note: *The LastName merge field is displayed in the FILLIN field.*

Finish-Up Instructions

- Use steps 1–7 and the following information to create another Fill-in field.
  a. In the second body text paragraph, first sentence, place the insertion point to the left of the period.
  b. In the Prompt box, type **Enter interview time:**. (Do not type the period.)
  c. In the default box, type **1:30**. (Do not type the period.)
  d. The Ask Once option should not be selected. (Check that no X displays next to the Ask Once option.)

e. Edit the Fill-in field. Place the insertion point between the word **time** and the colon (:), press the **Spacebar** once, type **for**, and press the **Spacebar** once; insert the LastName merge field.

f. Change the x's in the reference initials to your initials.

g. Change the filename below the reference initials to **24gmainf.doc**.

h. Use the *new* filename **24gmainf.doc** and save the file on your file disk.

i. Continue with the Steps to Merge a Document with User Input.

Start-Up Instructions

- The main document **24gmainf.doc** should be displayed in the document window.

Merge a Document with User Input

1. Select the **Merge to New Document** button.

Note: The Microsoft Word message box displays with the prompt to Enter scheduled interview date for Ybarra. (Ybarra is the last name of the first person listed in the data source.)

2. Accept the default text or type new text; choose **OK**.

For example, type the date for next Tuesday followed by a comma, i.e., **February 21, 1996,**: choose **OK**.

Note: The Microsoft Word message box displays with the prompt to Enter interview time for Ybarra and the default time of 1:30.

3. Accept the default text or type new text; choose **OK**.

For example, choose **OK** to accept the default text.

Finish-Up Instructions

- Repeat step 3 and enter the following times for the remaining records:

  Wohlenberg 2:30
  Carvalho 3:30

  Note: When the user input is complete, the merged documents with field codes display. The codes do not print; if desired, turn off the field codes.

- When all letters have been merged, the insertion point displays at the top of the first merged letter.
- Print one copy of each merged letter.
- Optional. Use the filename **24gmerge.doc** and save the merged letter file.
- Close all document windows.

  Note: It is not necessary to save changes to 24gmainf.doc.

"Mr.","Ben A.","Carrillo","receptionist","7060 Birview Avenue","Malibu","CA",
"90265-7022"
"Mr.","Elvin","Butz","legal clerk","434 Calle Juno, #58","San Clemente",
"CA","92673-3461"
"Ms.","Jodi","Palacio","legal intern","16750 LaGrange Avenue","Los
Angeles","CA","90025-1205"
"Ms.","Darlene","Simmons","senior assistant","3442 Riverside Drive,
#82","Burbank","CA","91505-2391"

FIGURE 24.6

Sample ASCII text file

Create a Header Source and Open (Import) Data into a Data Source

A data source created in a mail merge contains field names for each data field in row 1 of the data table. Row 1 is referred to as a header record. The field names can be listed in a separate header source file, if desired.

Having the capability of creating a separate header source file is useful when the data source used from another application does not contain a header row or the field names do not match the merge field names in the main document. Also, the same header row and field names could be used to merge data from various sources without having to repeat or change the header row in each data source.

Use the **Get Data** button in the Mail Merge Helper dialog box to specify the location of the data source and header source files. When a separate header source is used, both the data source and header source files must be displayed in the Mail Merge Helper dialog box before the main document can be merged with the data source.

In addition to opening a data source from another application such as Excel, a data source can be opened from other sources. Often a data file has been created in the ASCII (DOS) text format in which commas are used to separate fields, Enters are used to separate records, and text is enclosed in quotation marks (see Figure 24.6).

Similar to opening a data source from Excel, the ASCII data source can easily be opened using the Open Data Source option in the Mail Merge Helper dialog box. The Confirm Data Source dialog box and Convert File From options are used to identify the data source and the file format for the data to be opened. Opening a data file from another source is often referred to as *importing* data.

Start-Up Instructions

❖ Open the file named **24job.doc** located on the data disk.

Create a Header Source

1. Select the **Mail Merge Helper** button.
2. Select **Get Data, Header Options.**

   Note: The Header Options dialog box displays.
3. Choose **Create.**
4. Select and remove the field names that will not be used in the header row.

For example, select and remove the following field names: **Company, Address2, Country, HomePhone,** and **WorkPhone**

Note: The following field names should be listed in the Field Names in Header Row box: Title, FirstName, LastName, Job Title, Address1, City, State, and PostalCode.

5. Select **OK.**

   Note: The Save Header Source dialog box displays.

6. Type or select the directory/drive location and type a name for the header source file.

   For example, type or select the drive where your file disk is located; type the filename **24header.doc.**

7. Select **OK.**

   Note: The location and name of the header file displays below the Get Data button, i.e., Header: a:\24HEADER.DOC.

Open (Import) Data into a Data Source

8. Select the **Get Data** button.
9. Select the **Open Data Source** option.
10. The **Confirm Conversions** option should be selected. (If necessary, select the **Confirm Conversions** option.)
11. Double-click on the desired filename.

    For example, double-click on **24text1.doc.**

    Note: The Confirm Data Source dialog box displays.

12. Highlight the desired Open Data Source option.

    For example, check that **Word Documents** [***.doc**] is highlighted.

13. Select **OK.**

    Note: The Convert File dialog box displays (see Figure 24.7).

14. Highlight the desired Convert File From option.

    For example, check that the **Text Only** option is highlighted.

15. Select **OK.**

    *Note: The data source filename **24text1.doc** displays below the **Get Data** button and above the Header location and filename.*

FIGURE 24.7

Convert File dialog box

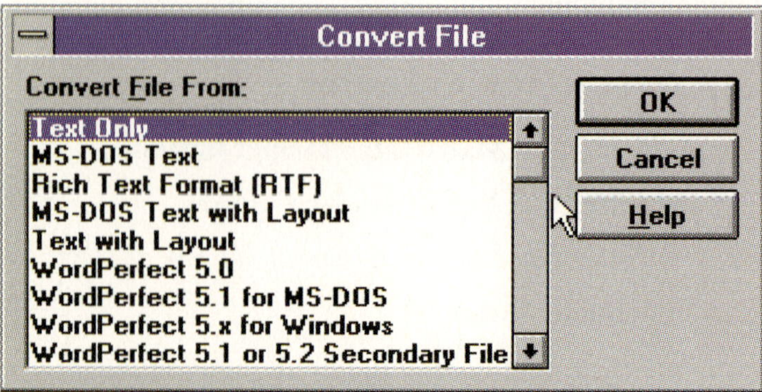

16. Select **Close**.

Finish-Up Instructions

- Use the *new* filename **24jobm.doc** and save the main document on your file disk
- Continue with the Steps to Use the Set Bookmark Field.

Use the Set Bookmark Field in a Mail Merge

Similar to a Fill-in field, the Set Bookmark field is used to print information in a merged document that is not saved in the data source. The Set Bookmark field, however, is used to print the same information in all the resulting merged documents. The Fill-in field on the other hand is used to print information that is different in each merged document.

The Insert Word Field: Set dialog box is used to create the bookmark name and to assign a value (or text). The bookmark field can be used over and over in the main document. Once the bookmark name and value are created, the bookmark field is inserted into the main document using the Cross-reference feature (see Chapter 22).

Start-Up Instructions

- The file named **24jobm.doc** should be displayed in the document window.
- Turn on Field Codes and Bookmarks (select **Tools**, **Options**, **Field Codes** and **Bookmarks** in the View tab, **OK**).

Use the Set Bookmark Field

1. Place the insertion point at the location where the Set Bookmark field is to be inserted.

   For example, place the insertion point on the third blank line after the letterhead.

2. Select the **Insert Word Field** button.
3. Choose the **Set Bookmark** option.

   Note: The Insert Word Field: Set dialog box displays (see Figure 24.8).

4. Type the desired information in the Bookmark box.

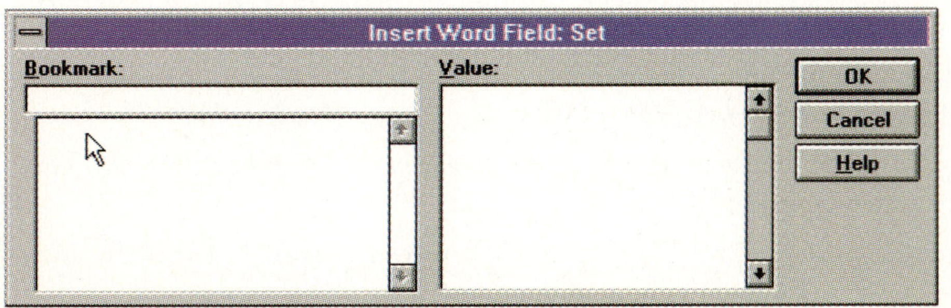

FIGURE 24.8

Insert Word Field: Set dialog box

For example, type **department** in the Bookmark box.

5. Click in the **Value** box and type the desired information.

   For example, type **Foreign Investment**.

6. Select **OK**.

   Note: *The Set Bookmark field displays in the document, e.g., { SET department "Foreign Investment" I} displays. Notice the I-beam (bookmark indicator) that displays before the final brace.*

Insert the Bookmark Using the Cross-reference Feature

7. Place the insertion point where the bookmark is to be located.

   For example, place the insertion point in the first body text paragraph between the words "the" and "Department."

8. Select **Insert, Cross-reference**.

9. Choose the desired Reference Type, Insert Reference To, and For Which Bookmark options.

   For example, select **Bookmark** in the Reference Type box, check that **Bookmark Text** is highlighted in the Insert Reference To box, and that **department** displays in the For Which Bookmark box.

10. Select **Insert**.

    Note: *The Cross-reference field code displays, i.e., { REF department * MERGEFORMAT }, and the Cross-reference dialog box remains in the document window.*

Finish-Up Instructions

- Use steps 7–10 and the following information to place another bookmark in the document.
  a. Scroll down until the first line of the second body text paragraph displays.
  b. Place the insertion point between the first two words, i.e., The and Department.
  c. Check that **Bookmark** is highlighted in the Reference Type box,that **Bookmark Text** is highlighted in the Insert Reference To box, and that **department** is highlighted in the For Which Bookmark box.
  d. Select **Insert**.
- Select **Close** to exit the Cross-reference dialog box.
- Use the same filename **24jobm.doc** and save the file.
- Select the **Check for Errors** button, select **Complete the merge, pausing to report each error as it occurs.** Select **OK**.

  Note: *Scroll through the letters and notice the results of the Set Bookmark fields. Also, check for any possible errors.*
- Close the merged letters but do not save. Correct any errors in the main document.

- Optional. Select the **Merge to New Document** button; print one copy of each letter.
- Optional. Save the merged letters; use the filename **24jmerge.doc**.
- Close all document windows.

The Next Step

Chapter Review and Activities

Self-Check Quiz

T F 1. The IF field can be used in the main document to control extra horizontal spacing when fields are empty.

T F 2. A header source can be created separately from a data source.

T F 3. Data from a different application can be opened and used to merge with a main document.

T F 4. One reason for using a Set Bookmark field is to print information that is not saved in the data source.

T F 5. The Find Record feature is used to reduce the memory needed during the merge operation.

6. A data source from a different application such as _______ can be merged with a Word document.
   a. Microsoft Access
   b. Microsoft Excel
   c. both a and b
   d. none of these

7. The three main sections in the Insert WordL IF dialog box are: IF, Insert this Text, and _____.
   a. Otherwise Insert this Text
   b. Never Insert this Text
   c. Constantly Insert this Text
   d. none of the above

8. The _____ button is used to identify a mistake(s) when the main document and data source are merged.
   a. **Merge to New Document**
   b. **Merge to Printer**
   c. **Find Record**
   d. **Check for Errors**

9. Give one example of why you would use the Fill-in field in a main document.

10. List one option that could be used if the merge operation stopped because there was not enough memory to hold all the merged letters.

Enriching Language Arts Skills

Spelling/Vocabulary Words

vital of or pertaining to life; necessary to the continuance or well being of something.
refuse trash, garbage, something discarded.
initially first; happening at the beginning.

Abbreviations for Time

Type a.m. and p.m. with lowercase letters and no spaces. Only one period is used if the abbreviation is the last element in a sentence. *Note: If Word's Insert, Date and Time command or a Date type Text Form Field are used, the time will be formatted AM or PM regardless of how the abbreviations are typed.*

Example: The planning meeting will begin at 9:00 a.m. and adjourn at 3:00 p.m.

Activities

Activity 24.1—Create a Main Document; Use IF and Fill-in Fields; Link a Graphic Image

1. Open the file named **24act1.doc** located on the data disk.
2. Use the following guidelines to link a graphic image to the main document and insert If...Then...Else... and Fill-in fields:
   a. Point to the edge of the frame located next to the letterhead and click.
   b. Insert the graphic image and link it to the file (select **Insert**, **Picture**, choose **Link to File**, deselect the **Save Picture in Document** option, double-click on the file named **cityscpe.wmf**).
   c. Position the graphic image (select the graphic image, select **Format**, **Frame**, **None**, **Horizontal Position**, **Left**, **Relative to**, **Margin**, **OK**).
   d. Attach the data source **24act1d.doc**. (Select the **Mail Merge Helper** button, **Get Data**, **Open Data Source**. Select the drive where the data disk is located and double-click on **24act1d.doc**. Select **Close**.)
   e. Turn on Field Codes (select **Tools**, **Options**, choose **Field Codes** in the **View** tab, select **OK**).
   f. Insert an IF field (locate the insertion point to the left of the {MERGEFIELD FirstName} field, select the **Insert Word Field** button, select **If...Then...Else...**, click in the **Comparison** box, scroll down and

select **is Not Blank**, click in the **Insert this Text** box, press **Ctrl** and **F9**, type **MERGEFIELD Title**, press the **right arrow** key twice, press the **Spacebar** once, select **OK**).

g. Locate the insertion point to the left of the colon in the salutation and insert an IF field (select the **Insert Word Field** button, select **If...Then...Else...**, click in the **Comparison** box, scroll down, select **is Not Blank**, click in the **Insert this Text** box, press **Ctrl** and **F9**, type **MERGEFIELD Title**, press the **right arrow** key twice, press the **Spacebar** once, press **Ctrl** and **F9**, type **MERGEFIELD LastName**, click in the **Otherwise Insert this Text** box, press **Ctrl** and **F9**, type **MERGEFIELD FirstName**, select **OK**).

h. Insert a Fill-in field (locate the insertion point in the second body text paragraph to the left of the period in the first sentence; select the **Insert Word Field** button, choose **Fill-in**; in the Prompt box, type **Enter new credit line amount for:**, choose **OK** twice).

i. Edit the Fill-in field (locate the insertion point between the word for and the colon in the Fill-in code, press the **Spacebar** once, select the **Insert Merge Field** button, select **LastName**, **OK**).

3. Change the x's in the reference initials to your initials.
4. Change the filename below the reference initials to **24act1m.doc**.
5. Use the *new* filename **24act1m.doc** and save the file on your file disk.
6. Merge the document with user input and use the following information (select the **Merge To New Document** button, type the desired amount, choose **OK**).

Marcus	$8,500
Dalzell	$7,800
Eckles	$10,000
Honea	$9,000

7. Scroll through the letters and check for accuracy.
8. Print one copy of the merged letters.
9. Optional. Use the filename **24act1mr.doc** and save the merged letters.
10. Optional. Fax one of the printed letters to a local fax number.
11. Close all documents.

Note: It is not necessary to save changes to 24act1m.doc.

Challenge Your Skills

Skill 24.1—Create a Header Source, Set Bookmark and IF fields; Insert Data into a Data Source; Language Arts

1. Open the file named **24skillm.doc** located on the data disk.

2. Create a header source file for the data file by using Header Options in the Data Source area of the Mail Merge Helper dialog box. Remove the following Field Names that will not be needed for the data file: **Job Title**, **Company**, **Country**, **HomePhone**, and **WorkPhone**.
3. Use the file name **24skhdr.doc** and save the header source file.
4. Open the data file named **24sktext.doc** into a data source. Use the **Get Data** button, **Open Data Source** option in the Mail Merge Helper dialog box.
5. Create a Set Bookmark field using the following information:
    a. Place the Set Bookmark field one line space after the letter date.
    b. Use the bookmark name **area_name**.
    c. In the Value box, type **East Hartford**.
    d. Use the Cross-reference feature to insert the bookmark between the words **in** and **are** in the first sentence of the body text.
6. Insert the following paragraph between the two body text paragraphs. Correct three spelling and two punctuation errors. Place an IF field in the last sentence between the words **than** and **in** (create an IF field that will print 5:30 a.m. if the street address (Address1) is less than or equal to 999, otherwise print 5:45 a.m.).

    Your new collection route will go into effect the first Monday of next month. Therefore it is vitel that all residents make sure their household refuse is out for rear yard collection by 6:00 A.M. on their scheduled collection day. The day of collection will not change, but pickup time may vary to earlier or later than the current times. However, initialy we request that your reffuse be out no later than (place IF...Then...Else... field here) in order to avoid missed collections.
7. Make decisions regarding reference initials and the document identification notation.
8. Use the *new* filename **24skfin.doc** and save the main document.
9. Merge the main document **24skfin1.doc** with the data file **24sktext.doc**.
10. Optional. Use the filename **24skmerg.doc** and save the merged letters.
11. Print one copy of each merged letter.
12. Close all documents.
13. If you have completed your work, exit Word.

CHAPTER 25

Advanced Macros

Features Covered

- Edit macros
- Correct (debug) macros
- Look up Word macro commands
- Record mouse actions and keystrokes while editing a macro
- Use variables and request input in a macro
- Use a conditional statement in a macro
- Test a macro
- Auto macros

Objectives and Introduction

After successfully completing this chapter, you will be able to better understand macro terminology, edit a macro by recording mouse actions and keystrokes. You will also learn how to find the correct syntax and arguments for macro commands and how to use input, variables, and a conditional statement while editing a macro. In addition, you will learn to debug (correct) macro errors and learn to "test" a macro. Also, discussed will be auto macros.

Macros can be a useful tool to avoid repetitious keystrokes, to ensure that work is accurate, and to set up tasks to be accomplished automatically. In addition to recording simple macros (see Chapter 15), a macro can be created using a combination of *direct* editing and recording.

Useful Terminology

Word uses a macro language called WordBasic that is based on commands. The commands are used to direct and control the running of a macro in Word and other applications. For example, when a macro is being played, the *FileOpen* command will display the Open dialog box.

FIGURE 25.1

Macro terminology

Macro Terminology

COMMAND	A macro command tells the program to take a certain action. The command must be typed with the correct spelling, spacing, and with a combination of upper and lowercase letters as shown in the Help screen, i.e., FileCloseAll.
ARGUMENT	If there are two or more actions that can be directed by one command, the command must have an argument to specify which action to take. The argument may be in parentheses after the command, e.g., InputBox$ (Prompt$ [, Title$] [, Default]).
OPERATOR	A symbol or word that performs a function on one or more items in a command statement. For example, the equals sign (=) is used in many statements to compare two items and asks "Are they equal?".
VARIABLE	A variable represents a named place in memory where information is stored. Variables are often used to keep track of words, numbers, and measurements that change while the macro plays. If a variable ends with a dollar sign ($), the program stores a character or group of characters. If a variable does not end with a dollar sign ($), the program stores a number (value).
CHARACTER STRING	Any text that is not a command or an argument must be enclosed in quotation marks so that the program will recognize it as text.

An explanation of macro terms is found in the Programming with Microsoft Word section of the Word Help Contents box. Select **Help**, **Contents**, **Programming with Microsoft Word**, choose the **Index** button to display a list of WordBasic Statements and Functions (commands). Also, an explanation of key macro terms is shown in Figure 25.1.

Suggestions for Writing and Editing Macros

Use spaces, tabs, indents, and enters to make the macro easier to read. "White space" is ignored by the macro, which sees spacing commands only when they are in character strings and enclosed in quotation marks. DO NOT put spacing codes or characters in the middle of command names.

Many times macros printed in magazines or books will have numbered lines. These numbers are for reference only and are not typed in the macro.

Remarks (comments) are explanations about a macro and should be used liberally when creating or editing a macro. Inserting remarks will make it much easier to change or update the macro, and are very helpful if someone else must figure out how the macro works. To place a remark in the macro, start the line with the abbreviation REM or type an apostrophe at the beginning of a line. The remark will end the next time the Enter key is pressed.

Editing a Macro

Many times macros must be changed after they have been created. For instance, you might have a macro that prints your name and return address to create personal stationery. When you move or change your name, the macro must be changed. While you could re-record the macro (saving it under the same filename), editing the macro is often easier, particularly if the change is small and the macro is complex.

Macros are stored (associated) in templates. To edit the macro, you can do one of the two following things: open a new document that is based on the template that contains the macro you want to edit or open an existing document that was created using the template that contains the desired macro.

Start-Up Instructions

- To complete the following Steps to Edit a Macro, copy the file named **macro.dot** from the data disk to your file disk. (For instructions on copying files, see Chapter 16.)
- Close all documents (press and hold the **Shift** key while selecting **File**, choose **Close All**).

Edit a Macro

1. Select **File, New**.
2. Type the drive letter where your file disk is located followed by a colon and the name of the desired template.

   For example, type **a:macro**.
3. Select **OK**.

   Note: *A new document window displays with the macro.dot template attached. To check that the macro.dot template is attached, select* ***File, Templates****. The template named* ***macro.dot*** *will display in the Document Template box. Select* ***OK****.*
4. Select **Tools, Macro**.
5. Select the desired macro name.

   For example, select **namehd**.
6. Choose the **Edit** button.

   Note: *The macro and the Macro Toolbar display in the document window. Each keystroke that was recorded when the macro was created has been translated into a Word macro command to be performed or a character to be typed. The characters in the name and address are in quotation marks to tell Word to type these characters and not to interpret them as commands.*
7. Make the desired changes to the macro.

   For example, replace the name and address shown in lines 2, 4, and 6 with your name and address being careful not to delete the quotation marks.

8. To save the edited macro, select the **Save** button; choose **Yes** to keep changes to the **MACRO.DOT:namehd** file.

   Note: *If a mistake has been made, the macro can be corrected using the Steps to Correct (Debug) Macro Errors.*

9. Select **File, Close.**

Finish-Up Instructions

❖ Continue with the Steps to Correct and Debug Macro Errors.

Correcting (Debugging) Macros

When the macro is run some errors are identified by Word automatically. For example, if the command *Insert* is keyed as *Incert* or if the beginning quotation mark is missing after the command Insert, the macro will stop and tell you that an error has occurred.

When an error is identified, the macro can be corrected. Correcting a macro is often referred to as "debugging." There are some types of errors the program cannot recognize, such as the following:

a. Logic errors—for instance, forgetting to select a needed menu item.

b. Typographical or grammatical errors in text to be entered or displayed on the screen.

c. Errors that cause the program to do something unintended but are perfectly valid from the program's viewpoint. For example, many options toggle on/off, so a macro that selects the option the first time it is played will deselect it on the second run.

Start-Up Instructions

❖ An empty document window should be displayed with the **macro.dot** template attached. Check that the **macro.dot** template is attached (choose **File, Templates**; the macro.dot name should display in the Document Template box; select **OK**.

  Note: *If the* **macro.dot** *template is not attached, close all files (press* ***Shift*** *and select* ***File, Close All****), select* ***File, New****, type the drive letter where your file disk is located followed by a colon and the template name macro; select* ***OK****.*

❖ Select **Tools**, **Macro**, select **namehd**, choose the **Edit** button.

❖ Make two errors in the macro (in line 2, delete the quotation mark to the left of your first name and in line 7, delete the word *All* at the end of the *EditSelectAll* command.

Correct and Debug Macro Errors

1. Select **Window, Arrange All.**

   Note: *The macro.dot:namehead displays in one window and an empty document window displays.*

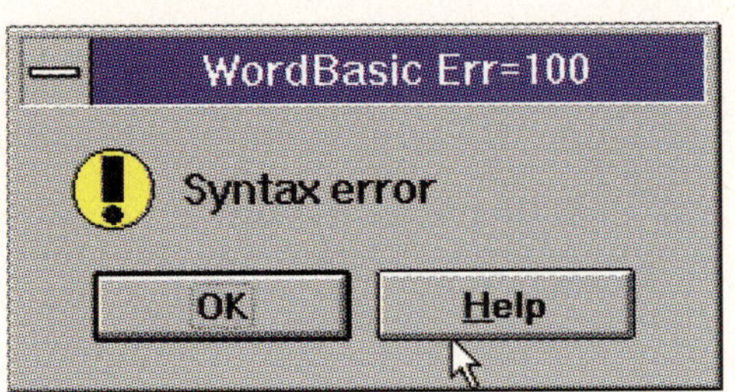

FIGURE 25.2

WordBasic Error dialog box

2. Click in the empty document window.
3. Select the **Step** button on the Macro Toolbar.

   Note: The WordBasic Error dialog box displays with the message "Syntax error" (see Figure 25.2)
4. Select the **Help** button.

   Note: The WordBasic Help dialog box displays with an explanation that the Syntax error may be a missing quotation mark. If the WordBasic Help information is not available on your computer, a message displays stating that Help is not available; select **OK**.
5. To exit Help, select **File, Exit**.
6. To exit the WordBasic Error dialog box, select **OK**.

   Note: The line in the macro containing the error is displayed in color.
7. To correct the error, click once on the line containing the error and make the necessary corrections.

   For example, click to the left of the first character in your first name and type a quotation mark.
8. Click once in the empty document window.
9. Select the **Step** button repeatedly until an error message displays.

   For example, select the **Step** button seven times.

   Note: When the **Step** *button is selected, the next macro line is highlighted; when the* **Step** *button is selected again, the macro line is run (activated) and in this macro the result displays in the empty document window. The WordBasic Error dialog box displays with the message "Unknown Command, Subroutine, or Function."*
10. If WordBasic Help is available on your computer, select the **Help** button; otherwise skip to step 12.

    Note: The WordBasic Help dialog box displays with the statement "This error usually occurs when a function or statement name is misspelled."
11. To exit Help, select **File, Exit**.
12. Select **OK**.
13. Click on the line displayed in color that is located in the window containing the macro.

    For example, click on the line in the window containing the **MACRO.DOT:namehd** file.
14. Click at the location where the correction is to be made and make the correction.

For example, click to the right of the last character and type **All**.

15. Click once in the document window containing the macro results.

    For example, click after the last character in your zip code, in the window containing your name and address.

16. Select the **Step** button.

    Note: The second line of the macro is highlighted to indicate that all macro instructions have been checked and performed and that, if desired, the Step process can be used to perform all macro steps again.

Finish-Up Instructions

- Click in the window containing the macro named MACRO.DOT:namehd and select the **Save** button; choose **Yes** to keep the changes to the macro.
- Close the window containing the MACRO.DOT:namehd macro (select **File**, **Close**).
- Close the window containing the macro results and do not save the file.

Look Up Word Macro Commands

Each macro command tells the program to perform some action. Some commands, such as Enter have only one possible action. Other commands have several possible actions; therefore an argument or several arguments must be included with the macro command to specify which of the possible actions is intended. For example, *CharRight* has two possible actions: Count and Select. If the CharRight command is placed in a macro without either of these arguments, the program will either use defaults or an error will occur.

The arguments must be separated by commas. The macro command must be typed in an exact format so that the program recognizes the command. This is called the *syntax* of the command. Capitalization is usually not important, but may be used to make it easier to spot commands when the macro is being created, edited, or corrected. However, spelling and the parentheses around the arguments are very important. The CharRight command must be typed just as it is shown, without spaces separating the words, and in that exact order. The program will not recognize Char Right or RightChar.

Start-up Instructions

- A new document window should be displayed. If necessary, select **File**, **New**.

Find a Command's Description, Syntax and Argument

Note: To perform the following Steps to Find a Command's Description, the WordBasic Help information must be available on your computer.

1. Select **Help, Contents**.

   Note: The Word Help dialog box displays.

2. Select the icon to the left of the Programming with Microsoft Word option.

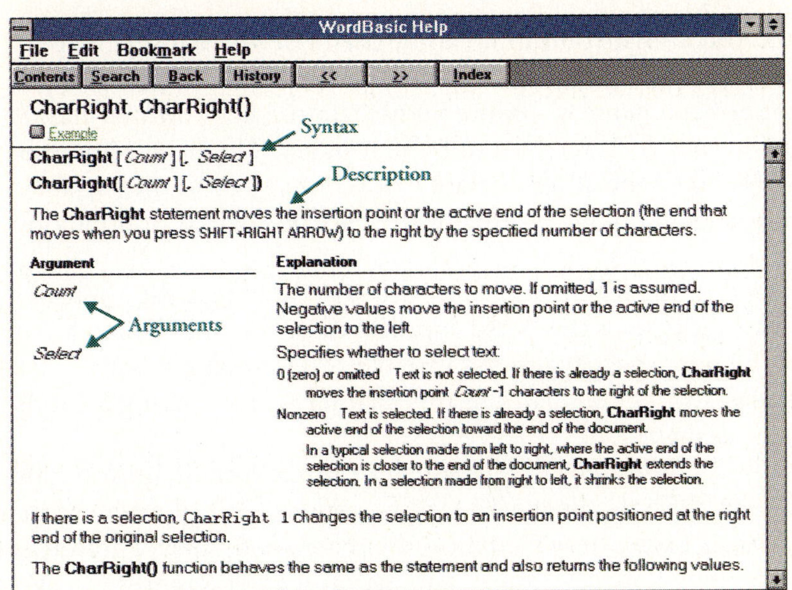

FIGURE 25.3

WordBasic Help Window

3. Select the **Index** button.
4. Select the letter **C** button.
5. Choose the **CharRight, CharRight()** command.

   Note: The help window showing an explanation of the command, correct syntax, and possible arguments for the command displays (see Figure 25.3).

Finish-Up Instructions

- To exit the Help dialog box, select **File**, **Exit**.
- If necessary, close the document window.

Additional Editing Techniques for Macros

Some techniques that can be used to edit macros are using variables, requesting user input, and recording individual steps for use in a different macro. A variable is information that is stored in a designated name and used later by the macro. A macro that requests user input, pauses and indicates to the user that information is to be typed from the keyboard. Additional macro instructions can be recorded in a separate macro and then copied into an existing macro.

Use Variables and Request User Input in a Macro

Storing small pieces of information to be used within the same macro is done through the use of variables. A variable is a small portion of memory that Word sets aside to hold a piece of information. Once information has been stored in a variable, the variable and the information in it can be used elsewhere in the macro. Think of a variable as a scratch pad that the computer uses to hold information, just as you might jot down a name or phone number to use in a few minutes. A variable is given a name and then referred to by that name. The name should be something easy to remember and should relate to what is stored in the variable. When variable names are used in an argument, they are not placed in quotation marks.

The command used in the following Steps to Use a Variable is the "WhatTheUserTyped$." The variable in the Word InputBox$ command "WhatTheUserTyped$" is the name we gave to the variable. The variable named "WhatTheUserTyped$" will be used later in this chapter when creating a conditional If, Then, Else statement.

In many macros, it is convenient to have the user input specific information. This can be the name of a file to open, a Yes or No response to a question to determine what the user wants to do, or what action the macro is to take. There are several macro commands that allow user input, and act on it in different ways. We will use one of the macro commands: *InputBox$*.

Start-up Instructions

Note: By using the following instructions, you will record the first part of a macro that will open a main document, open a data source, and prepare the data source for editing.

- All document windows should be closed. If necessary, press and hold the **Shift** key while selecting **File**, choose **Close All**; select **File**, **New**, type the drive letter where your file disk is located followed by a colon and the template name **macro**, i.e., **a:macro**; select **OK**.
- Select **Tools**, **Macro**.
- Type the macro name **macro25**, click in the Macros Available In box, select the template named **Macro.dot (Template)**; in the Description box, type **Opens a merge document and inserts new records.**
- Select the **Record** button, choose **Keyboard.** With the insertion point in the Press New Shortcut Key box, press **Ctrl** and **9**, choose **Assign,** select **Close.**

  Note: The Macro Record Toolbar displays.
- Select the **Open** button. If necessary, select the drive and/or directory where the file named **25welcom.doc** is located; double-click on the file named **25welcom.doc**.
- Select the **Mail Merge Helper** button, select **Get Data**, choose **Open Data Source**, select the desired filename. Double-click on the file named **25mdata.doc**.
- Select **Close**.
- Select the **Edit Data Source** button, select **OK**.
- Select the **Stop** button in the Macro Record Toolbar.
- Close the merge documents (select **File**, **Close**, choose **Yes** twice to save changes to the **25welcom.doc** file).

- To edit the macro, select **Tools**, **Macro**, choose the macro named **macro25**, select the **Edit** button.
- Place the insertion point in the macro at the desired location (place the insertion point to the left of the "E" in End Sub—last line of the macro and press **Enter** once, press the up arrow key once).

Use a Variable

1. Type the variable command.

   For example, type **WhatTheUserTyped$ = InputBox$ ("Do you want to create new client letters now (Y/N)", "New Client Letters")**. (Do not type the period.)

2. Select the **Save** button and choose **Yes** to keep changes to the template macro file.

   For example, select the **Save** button and choose **Yes** to keep changes to the template macro named **MACRO.DOT macro25.**

Use a Remark Statement

1. Type a remark statement at the desired location in the macro.

   Fore example, place the insertion point to the right of the "N" in the Sub MAIN command--first line of the macro, press **Enter** once and type: **REM This macro opens a merge document and inserts new records into a data file.**

Finish-Up Instructions

- Save the changed macro (select the **Save** button, choose **Yes** to keep changes).
- Continue with the Steps to Create an If, Then, Else, Statement.

Use a Conditional Statement in a Macro

A conditional statement is one that allows the macro to take different actions based on some condition. There are several types of conditional statements, but the most common one is generally referred to as an If statement, If, Then statement, or If, Then, Else statement.

An If statement in a Word macro can consist of three or four parts:

If...Then
ElseIf (optional)
Else
End If

The If portion sets up some type of condition. In our sample, we will evaluate the information stored in the variable named "WhatTheUserTyped$" to determine what action the macro should perform. The program will evaluate this If statement, and if it finds the If statement to be true, it will continue to read the command(s) under the If statement.

The Else or ElseIf portion of the macro tells the program what to do when it evaluates the If statement and finds that it is false. If, for example, the user presses N or any other key except Y and y, the If statement will be false. When the statement is false, the program skips to the next statement in the macro and reads the command(s) under it. The program reads commands until a true or else statement is encountered.

The End If command tells the macro that the If statement is finished, and that it should resume reading the following command(s) and acting upon it.

Start-Up Instructions

- The window containing the MACRO.DOT:macro25 file should be displayed. If necessary, close all files (press and hold the **Shift** key while selecting **File**, **Close All**, select **File**, **New**, type the drive letter where your file disk is located followed by a colon and the template name **macro**, i.e., **a:macro**; select **OK**. Choose **Tools**, **Macro**, select the macro named **macro25**, choose the **Edit** button).
- Place the insertion point in the macro at the desired location (place the insertion point to the left of the "E" in End Sub—last line of the macro, press **Enter** once, press the up arrow key once).

Create an If, Then, Else Statement in a Macro

1. Type the desired If statement lines.

   For example, type:

   If WhatTheUserTyped$ = "Y" Then (press **Enter**)
   (press **Tab**) **Goto LETTERS**
   ElseIf WhatTheUserTyped$ = "y" Then (press **Enter**)
   (press **Tab**) **Goto LETTERS**
   ElseIf WhatTheUserTyped$ = "yes" Then (press **Enter**)
   (press **Tab**) **Goto LETTERS** (press **Enter**)
   Else (press **Enter**)
   (press **Tab**) **Goto FINISH** (press **Enter**)
   End If

2. Select the **Save** button and choose **Yes** to keep changes to the template macro file.

   For example, select the **Save** button and choose **Yes** to keep changes to the template macro named **MACRO.DOT: macro25**.

Finish-Up Instructions

- Close all windows (press and hold the **Shift** key while clicking on **File**, choose **Close All**, select **Yes** to save changes to the **macro.dot** template. Select **Yes** to save changes to the document.
- Continue with the Steps to Record Keystrokes While Editing a Macro.

Record Mouse Actions and Keystrokes While Editing a Macro

The steps of a macro can be recorded and those steps pasted into an already-existing macro. This is very helpful because recording commands, particularly infrequently used commands, is often faster and more accurate than typing the commands. However, there are some commands that must be typed, such as a label to tell the program where to find a specific command.

Start-Up Instructions

- All document windows should be closed. If necessary, press and hold the **Shift** key while selecting **File**, choose **Close All**.
- Create a new macro that will be used to record keystrokes. The recorded keystrokes will be copied later to the already-existing macro.
    a. Choose **File**, **New**, type the drive letter where your file disk is located followed by a colon and the template filename **macro**, i.e., **a:macro**, choose **OK**.
    b. Select **Tools**, **Macro**.
    c. In the Macro Name box, type **copymacro**.
    d. Check that Macro.dot (Template) displays in the Macros Available In box. If necessary, select the Macros Available In box and choose **Macro.dot** (**Template**).
    e. In the description box, type **Recorded keystrokes to be copied to an existing macro.**
    f. Select **Record**, choose **OK**, choose **Assign**, **Close**. (The Macro Record Toolbar displays in the document window.)

Record Keystrokes While Editing a Macro

1. Perform the actions to be recorded.

For example,

a. Select the **Open** button.
b. Double-click on the file named **25welcom.doc.**
c. Select the **Mail Merge Helper** button.
d. Select **Get Data**, choose **Open Data Source.**
e. Double-click on the file named **25mdata.doc.**
f. Choose the **Query Options** button.
g. Select the **Field** box, scroll down and choose **New.**
h. Click in the **Compare To** box, type **y**, choose **OK.**
i. Select **OK** to respond to the message that Word could not merge the main document...

j. Select **Merge**, select **Merge** again.

2. Select the **Stop** button in the Macro Record Toolbar.

Finish-Up Instructions

- Close the merged letters (select **File**, **Close**, choose **No** to save changes).
- Close the main document named **25welcom.doc** (select **File**, **Close**, choose **No** to save changes).
- Choose **Tools**, **Marco**, select the macro named **copymacro**, choose the **Edit** button.
- Locate the insertion point to the left of the "F" in FileOpen in the second line of the macro; press **Enter** once, press the up arrow key once, type **LETTERS** followed by a colon, i.e., **LETTERS:**.
- Select the **Save** button, choose **Yes** to save changes.
- Select the lines to be copied (select all lines after the Sub MAIN command and before the End Sub command).
- Select the **Copy** button.
- Select **Tools**, **Macro**, choose the macro named **Macro25**, select the **Edit** button.
- Scroll down and locate the insertion point to the left of the "E" in the End Sub command—last line of the macro.
- Select the **Paste** button.
- With the insertion point located to the left of the "E" in the End Sub command, type the following commands:

  FileSave (press **Enter**)
  Goto FINISH (press **Enter**)
  FINISH: (press **Enter**)
  FileCloseAll (press **Enter**)
- Choose the **Save** button, select **Yes** to keep changes.
- Print one copy of the macro. (Optional.)
- Close all document windows (press and hold the **Shift** key while selecting **File**, **Close All**).

  Note: *If a message displays asking if you want to "Save changes to document . . . ," choose* ***No.***
- Run the macro (select **File, New**, type the drive letter followed by a colon where your file disk is located and type the template name **macro**, i.e., **a:macro**, choose **OK**, press **Ctrl** and **9**, add the two new records:

Ms. Andrea Morris	Mr. Alfred McCoy
945 Thornton Pl.	253 University Ave.
Dallas, TX 75041-3266	Austin, TX 78713-1001
214-555-6511	512-555-1393
y	y

- After the new records are entered, exit the Data Form dialog box (select **OK**).

- Type y, to respond to the prompt requesting to create new client letters, and then select **OK**.
- Select **Yes** to save the file named **25mdata.doc**.
- In the Save As dialog box, type the filename, **25client**. If necessary, select the drive where your file disk is located. Select **OK**.
- Select **Yes** to save changes to **25welcom.doc**.
- Open the new client letters (select the **Open** button, double-click on the filename **25client**, scroll through the letters and notice that two letters are addressed to the new clients, Andrea Morris and Alfred McCoy.
- Optional. Print the merged letters; close the document window.
- Close the document (select **File**, **Close**).

Test the Macro

Although the macro is stepped through or the macro runs without an error message, errors may still exist in the macro. Always test a macro by running it under all the conditions that you can imagine a user will select. For example, in the macro just created, you would want to test the following:

Scenario A:	The user responds "Y" to merge the new letters.
Scenario B:	The user responds "y" to merge the new letters.
Scenario C:	The user responds "N" to leave the macro without merging the letters.
Scenario D:	The user responds "n" to leave the macro without merging the letters.
Scenario E:	The user accidentally presses any other key on the keyboard. The macro should respond as though the user had pressed N.

As the macro becomes more complex, testing to make sure it will work under most normal conditions also becomes more complex. The amount of time spent developing and testing a complex macro must be weighed against the time saved or the increased accuracy or efficiency possible when the macro is available.

Auto Macros

Word includes five macros that run automatically at certain times. In order to run the macro(s) automatically use the designated name as listed below:

AutoExec runs when Word is loaded (started).
AutoNew runs each time a new document is created.
AutoOpen runs when an existing document is opened
AutoClose runs when a document is closed.
AutoExit runs when Word is exited.

By using the auto macros, tasks that are performed when you create, open, or close a document can be automated. For example, an instruction message can display for new users when the AutoNew macro is run or all fields that are part of the macro's template can be updated when the AutoNew macro is run. Also, an auto macro can be used to set up a macro to run when Word is exited.

The AutoNew, AutoOpen, and AutoClose macros are available in both the global and specific template macros. Each time you create, open, or close any document, the global macro runs (activates) automatically. A specific template macro runs when a document based on that template is created or when a document is opened or closed with the template macro attached to it.

An auto macro can be prevented from running, by holding down the **Shift** key when performing the action to start the macro. For example, hold down the **Shift** key while choosing the **OK** button from the File, Open command

The Next Step

Chapter Review and Activities

Self-Check Quiz

T F 1. Word uses a macro language called WordBasic.

T F 2. Macros are stored in templates.

T F 3. Some macro commands have two possible actions; therefore, an argument(s) is included with the macro command to specify which action(s) to take.

T F 4. A conditional statement allows a macro to take different actions based on a condition.

T F 5. The If part of a conditional If statement, sets up a condition, e.g. If WhatTheUserTyped$.

T F 6. After a macro has been run without an error message, the macro can be run correctly under all conditions.

7. Correcting a macro is often referred to as _____ a macro.
   a. bugging
   b. debugging
   c. changing
   d. correcting

8. List the five Word auto macros and give a brief description of each auto macro.

9. Use two sentences to define a variable.

10. List two types of macro errors that cannot be recognized by the Word program.

Activities

Activity 25.1—Create a macro with User Input and If-ElseIf Statement

1. Use the following information to create a macro that will ask a question and "type" a letter closing:
   a. Mr. Barry Ortega, Facilities Manager, and Ms. Renee Kidwell, Systems Engineer, share an assistant, Marvin J. Churchill who is responsible for both of their word processing needs. Create a macro for Marvin to use that will ask him who will sign the letter, then place an appropriate complementary closing, signature line, and reference initials in the document.
   b. Select **File**, **New**, type the drive letter where your file disk is located followed by a colon and the template name **macro.dot**. Select **OK**.
   c. Use the macro name **25act1**. Make the macro available in the **macro.dot (template)**. If desired, assign a keystroke to the macro.
   d. Make the user input as short as possible (Y/N or one initial of the person's name). Longer input is more likely to be mistyped.
   e. Use an If statement.
   f. Record the keystrokes for the closing, i.e., the text and spacing between lines.
2. Print one copy of the macro.

Challenge Your Skills

Skill 25.1—Create a Macro

1. Use the following information to create a macro that prints and formats the company name using the company format policy.
   a. Your supervisor gives you a document written by several different people. Each person has spelled the company name in a different way. In addition, the company policy is to bold and italicize the name. Moreover, this is going to be a monthly project. Create a macro that will put in the correct company name (Gauthier Pallavicini) and format it

according to company policy. The document is saved on the data disk with the filename **25skill1.doc**.

b. Open the file named **25skill1.doc**.

c. Attach the **macro.dot** template located on your file disk to the file named **25skill1.doc**. After the macro.dot template has been attached, save the file on your file disk using the *new* filename **25skmac.doc**.

   Hint: *Select* **File, Templates, Attach,** *and choose the desired template name.*

d. Use Edit, Find to locate the first occurrence of text to be replaced.

   Hint: *In the Find What box, type the first two letters of the name. Check that* **Match Case** *is selected. Select the* **Find Next** *button, then choose* **Cancel** *to exit out of the Find dialog box. Then start the recording of the macro.*

e. Use the macro name **25skill1**. Make the macro available in the **macro.dot (template)**. If desired, assign a keystroke to the macro.

2. Record the macro to select the name, type the name correctly, bold and italicize the name.
3. Print one copy of the macro.
4. If you have completed your work, exit Word.

Part 7
Checking Your Step

Production Skill Builder Activities
Chapters 23-25

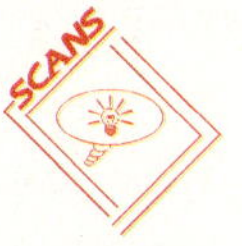

Production Activity 7.1—Create a Macro with a Table and Formulas

1. Use the following information to create a macro that produces the sales report memorandum shown on page 610 when played. Remember, always write down each step *before* beginning to record the macro.

   a. Open a new document using the **macro.dot** template located on your file disk.

   b. Use the macro name **salesrpt**. Make the macro available in the Macro.dot template. If desired, assign a keystroke to the macro.

   c. Create the top portion of the memorandum. Use **Insert**, **Date** to insert the current date as a field. Make a decision on an appropriate date format.

   d. Create a table with six rows and two columns.

   e. Decrease the width of column 2 so that the column displays in approximately the same size as is shown.

      Hint: *Place the insertion point in the first cell of column 2 and select Table, Cell Height and Width, on the Columns tab, type the desired width.*

   f. Join the cells in row 1.

      Hint: *To select a row, place the insertion point in any cell in the row and select* **Table**, **Select Row**.

   g. Type and format the text shown in row 1 and column 1 of the sales report on page 610. (Do not type any text in column 2. Formulas will be created for cells B4 and B5 using the information in step 1i.)

   h. Use Right justification for cells B2-B6.

      Hint: *To select a column, place the insertion point in any cell in the column and select* **Table**, **Select Column**.

   i. A formula should be placed in cell B4 that subtracts the projected sales from the actual sales (B2-B3). Set the number format to #,##0.

MEMORANDUM

Date: (Current date)

To: See Distribution List

From: Your Name, Trak Lighting Product Manager

Subject: Monthly Sales Report

Monthly Sales Report--Trak Lighting Department	
Total Actual Sales	
Total Projected Sales	
Total Amount Over/Under Projected Sales	**!Error at B3**
% Increase/Decrease of Projected Sales	**!Error at B4**
Next Month's Projected Sales	

Formula =B2-B3
Number Format #,##0

Formula = (B4/B3*100)
Number Format 0.00%

Distribution:
Carl Obrist
Kathleen Elkin
Linda Hinkle
Norm Buxton
Leslie Moore
Theresa Williams

A formula that calculates the percentage increase or decrease of actual sales over projected sales (B4/B3*100) should be placed in cell B5. Set the number format to 0.00%.

Note: *An error message, !Error at . . ., displays in the table cells; that's* ***OK****. When the form is used, numbers will be inserted into cells B2, B3, B5 and the error messages will be eliminated when the formulas are updated.*

j. Select the entire table and set the inside table border to **3/4 pt single-line** and the outside table border to **3/4 pt double-line.**

k. With the entire table selected, set **2 pt** of space before and after each paragraph.

Hint: *With the table selected, choose* ***Format, Paragraph.***

l. Center the table horizontally.

m. Place the insertion point several lines below the table and type the distribution list.

n. Stop the macro recording.

2. After the macro recording is stopped, clear the screen. Save the changes to **macro.dot** but do not save the current document.
3. Open a new document based on the **macro.dot** template.
4. Run the **salesrpt** macro. Use the following information to complete the memorandum:

   a. In the blank space between the top portion of the memordum and the table, type the following paragraph.

      Below are the (insert name of last month) monthly sales figures for the Trak Lighting Department. As you will notice, sales have been very strong and have greatly exceeded projected sales. We anticipate that sales will continue to be strong for the next two months and have adjusted our projected sales figures accordingly.

   b. Complete the table using the following information. To update a formula, highlight the error message and press **F9**.

Actual Sales	**$82,583**
Projected Sales	**69,400**
Next Month's Projected Sales	**$78,300**

5. Use the filename **7preptl.doc** and save the report on your file disk.
6. Print one copy.
7. Close the document.

Production Activity 7.2—Create a Form Using the Tables Feature

1. Use the Tables feature to create a form similar to the form shown on page 612. Make decisions regarding:

   Margins
   Number of rows and columns
   Font and size for text
   Formulas
   Merging and splitting cells
   Table borders and shading for cells
   Use of graphic images
   Centering the table vertically and/or horizontally on the page

   Note: *When the formulas are created, error messages will display in the cells containing the formulas. When information is typed into the table cells and the formulas are updated, the error messages will be eliminated.*

2. Use the filename **7pwork.doc** and save the form.
3. Print one copy.
4. Use the following information to fill in the form.

   a. Use your name and address for the Job Name, Address, City/State/Zip, Phone Number, and Bill To information.

   b. In the Description of Work section, type **Repair leaks caused by storm.**

Flynn Roofing Company
46574 Greenwood Avenue
Seattle, WA 98122
206-555-ROOF

JOB WORK ORDER			
Job Name:		Bill To:	
Address:		Address:	
City/State/Zip		City/State/Zip	
Phone:		Phone:	

Description of Work	Estimated Cost

Order Date:		Actual Labor	
Order Taken By:		Actual Materials	
Start Date:		Total Labor & Materials	
Contractor:		Tax (6.25%)	
Date Completed:		Total Price	
I hereby acknowledge the satisfactory completion of the above described work:		**Customer's Signature**	**Date:**

Create a formula to add actual labor and actual materials

Create a formula to multiple total labor and materials by .0625

Create a formula to add total labor and materials and tax

c. In the Estimate Cost section type **$695**.

d. Enter last Monday's date as the Order Date. The order was taken by **Janine**. Enter last Tuesday's date as the Start Date. The Contractor is **E. Niven**. Enter yesterday's date as the Date Completed.

e. The Actual Labor was **$425.59**. The Actual Materials were **$275.74**.

4. To update a formula, highlight the error message and press **F9**.
5. Use the *new* filename **7pwork1.doc** and save the file on your file disk.
6. Print one copy of the completed form.
7. If you have completed your work, exit Word.

Appendices

- Appendix A—Customizing Word
- Appendix B—Summary of Enriching Language Arts
- Appendix C—Sample Word Graphic Images, Templates, and Wizards
- Appendix D—Answers to Self-Check Quizzes
- Appendix E—Integrating the Microsoft Office
- Appendix F—Sound Boards

APPENDIX

Customizing Word

Word Options

Word options assist the user in changing settings for the Word program, such as the Viewing, Saving, Editing, and Spelling settings and file locations. Word creates default settings that are suitable for most word processing users. However, by using options, the settings are easily changed to accommodate each users' specific needs. Once an option is changed, it is in effect each time you launch (load) Word. To obtain specific details for changing any option, use the Help feature.

The **Options** choice is selected from the **Tools** menu. The different software options that are displayed on individual tabs are View, General, Edit, Print, File Locations, Compatibility, User Information, Revisions, Save, Spelling, Grammar and AutoFormat options (see Figure A.1). Each tab contains additional options. When an X displays in the box beside an option item, the option is in effect and remains in effect until the option is deselected. No X displays in the box beside an option

FIGURE A.1

Options dialog box

when the option is not on. To obtain an explanation of each individual option listed in a tab, select the **Help** button that is displayed in each tab.

The *View* tab contains options for displaying various items in the document window. For example, the horizontal or vertical scroll bar can be selected to display in the document window. In Figure A.1 all Window options are selected on, i.e., Status Bar, Horizontal Scroll Bar, Vertical Scroll Bar, and Vertical Ruler. The Picture Placeholder option may be useful to assist when scrolling quickly through a document. Placeholders are displayed to represent the graphic(s) rather than displaying the graphic itself.

The *General* tab contains options used to change settings for various Word Features such as changing the document window to display a blue background with white text. Also, help and navigation keys for WordPerfect users can be selected. The measurement units can be set for inches, centimeters, points or picas and the number (amount) for the most recently used files can be changed.

The *Print* tab contains options for printing documents. The draft output option provides for faster printing on some printers. Also, when the field code option is selected, the field code—not the results—print. For example, the field code for a table formula displays; the result of the formula does not display.

The *Revisions* tab contains the text attributes, color and marking options that can be assigned to inserted, deleted, or revised text. For example, revised lines can be marked by left, right, or outside marks that are placed in the document margins.

The *User Info* tab contains information regarding the name, envelope return address, and annotation initials that identify the primary user of the Word program. The name displayed in the Name box is used in the document summary information. The name and address displayed in the Mailing Address box was originally typed in the Return Address area of the Envelope dialog box. The name, envelope return address and/or initials can be changed if desired.

The *Compatibility* tab options are used to determine how Word displays documents created in earlier versions of Word or other word processors, such as Word for the MacIntosh or WordPerfect so that the document more closely matches the behavior of the original document. For example, when a Word 2.0 document is opened, Word 6.0 will not add an extra space before and after the superscripted or subscripted character(s).

The File Locations tab contains the drive and/or directory name where files are located for documents, clipart, pictures, templates, user options, autosave files, dictionaries, tutorial and startup file(s).

The *Save* tab contains options for customizing how and when documents are saved. Some of the save options are: Always Create a Backup Copy, Allow Fast Saves, Prompt for Summary Information, and Automatic Save with number of minutes specified.

The *Spelling* tab contains options used with the spell check feature. The only two options that can be set are: Always Suggest a Correct Spelling Word and Make Suggestions from the Main Dictionary.

The *Grammar* tab options are used to set up the grammar and style rules that will be used when the grammar check is performed.

The *AutoFormat* tab contains options that control how Word formats text with the built-in styles. For example, if the **Enter** key was pressed at the end of each line and word wrap was not used, the unneeded paragraph mark can be automatically deleted from the document.

Customizing the Toolbars, Menus, and Shortcut Keys

The Word Toolbars can be customized to provide for individual preferences. To customize Toolbars, Menus, or Shortcut Keys, select the **Customize** option from the Tools menu. The Toolbars, Menus, and Keyboard tabs in the Customize dialog box are used to specify your desired setup (see Figure A.3)

A new Toolbar can be created and/or any of the buttons on a Toolbar can be changed. Also, a Toolbar can be rearranged, relocated, and/or displayed differently in the document window. A newly created Toolbar can be deleted. Buttons on a Toolbar can be used to access commands and macros.

Word provides many different Toolbars, such as, Standard, Formatting, Borders, Database, Drawing, Forms, and Microsoft. The list of Toolbars is displayed by pointing to a Toolbar and pressing the *right* mouse button or by selecting **View, Toolbars**.

Similar to the process of customizing Toolbars, menus and the keyboard are customized. To customize a menu, select the **Menus** tab in the Customize dialog box. Select the desired category from the Categories list and select the desired command from the Commands list. Select the Menu to be changed by choosing the Menu listed in the Change What menu box. Also, a separator line can be added between groups of commands.

A menu can be created (added), deleted, or renamed by selecting the **Menu Bar** button and typing the desired name in the Name on Menu Bar box. Also, the location of the menu can be selected. For example, if the First option is selected in the Position on Menu Bar box, the menu name will be displayed in the document window to the left of the File command on the Menu Bar.

Use the Keyboard tab in the Customize dialog box to change Shortcut Key assignments for commands, macros, fonts, autotext entries, styles, and symbols. To assign a new shortcut key, choose the Category and Command desired. If a Shortcut keystroke is currently assigned to the command, the Current Keys box displays the Shortcut Keys. For example, if the File category and the File Exit command are both highlighted, the keys Alt + F4 display in the current keys box. Click in the **Press New Shortcut Key** box and press the new keys: press Alt and e. A message below the **Press New Shortcut Key** box shows that the keys pressed are currently unassigned. Select the assign button to list the new keystrokes in the Current Keys box. In this example, either set of keystrokes (Alt + F4 or Alt + e) activate the File Exit command.

If the changed menus or shortcut keys are to be returned to the default, choose the **Reset All** button. This will restore all menus or shortcut keys to their original Word Settings.

After making the desired changes in the Customize dialog box, the modified Toolbars, Menus, or Keyboard Shortcut Key(s) can be saved in the chosen template. Select the desired template in the Save Changes In box located at the bottom right of any tab card, i.e., Toolbars, Menus, or Keyboard. If the changes are saved in the *normal* document template, the changes will be available to any document based on the *normal* template.

FIGURE A-2

Toolbar dialog box

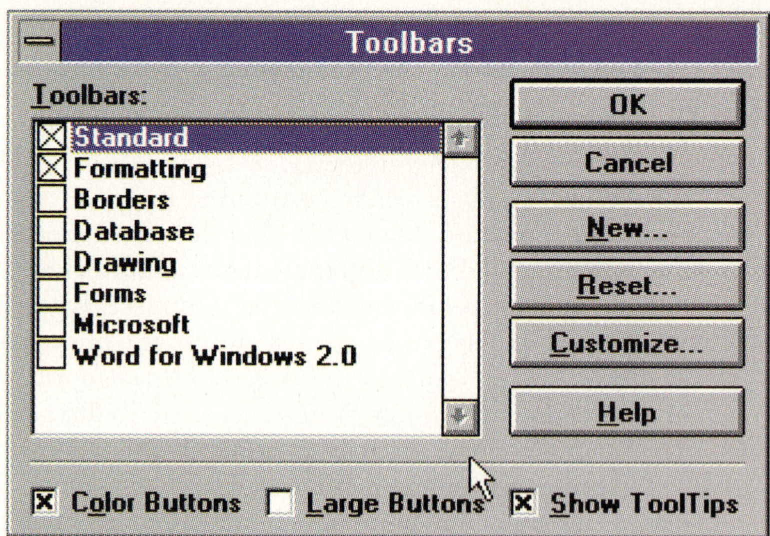

Steps to Display a Different Toolbar

1. Point to any location on the displayed Toolbar, press the *right* mouse button; select Toolbars to display the list of Toolbars or select **View, Toolbars** (see Figure A.2).

   Note: If a Toolbar is not displayed below the Menu bar, select View, **Toolbars**.

2. Select the desired Toolbar. *If the Toolbars dialog box is displayed*, select the desired **Toolbar** and then select **OK**.

Steps to Add a Button to a Toolbar

1. Point anywhere on the displayed Toolbar and press the *right* mouse button; select Toolbars to display the list of Toolbars or select **View, Toolbars**.

   Note: The Toolbars dialog box with a list of the Toolbars displays (see Figure A.2).

2. Select or deselect the desired Toolbar.
3. Select the **Customize** button.

   Note: The Toolbars tab should be selected. A list of Categories displays. Also, available buttons are shown in the Button area for the category option that is highlighted.

4. Select the desired category in the Categories list.

   Note: If desired, click on a button to display the button description.

5. Select the desired template in the Save Changes In box.
6. Point to the desired button, click and hold while dragging the button to the desired location on the displayed Toolbar or Formatting bar.

   Note: The new button surrounded by a dotted (dimmed) line displays.

7. Repeat steps 5-7 to add other buttons.
8. Select **Close**.

Delete a Button on the Toolbar

Note: *If necessary point anywhere on the Toolbar and press the right mouse button; select Toolbars to display the list of Toolbars. Select the desired Toolbar.*

1. Select **View, Toolbars, Customize.**
2. Select the desired template in the Save Changes box where the changes are to be effective.
3. Point to the button on the Toolbar to be deleted. Press and hold the mouse button and drag the button off the Toolbar. Release the mouse button.
4. Select the **Close** button to exit the Customize dialog box.

Move or Copy a Button on a Toolbar

Note: A button can be moved to a new location on the same Toolbar.

1. Select **View, Toolbars, Customize** or move the mouse pointer to a Toolbar, click the right mouse button, select Customize.
2. *To move a button*, point to the desired button, press the left mouse button while holding and dragging the button to the desired location. Release the mouse button.

   To copy a button, point to the desired button, press *and* hold the left mouse button and the **Ctrl** key while dragging a copy of the button outline to the new location. Release the mouse button.
3. Select **Close** to exit the Customize dialog box.

Relocate a Toolbar in the Document Window

1. Point to the top, bottom or side edge of the desired Toolbar, click and hold the mouse button while dragging the Toolbar to the new location. Release the mouse button.

Steps to Create a New Custom Toolbar

1. Select **View, Toolbars** *or* move the mouse pointer to a Toolbar, click the right mouse button, and select **Toolbars**.
2. Select the **New** button.
3. Type a name for the new Toolbar.
4. Select **OK**.

   Note: The Customize dialog box displays (see Figure A.3). The Toolbars tab should be selected. In the Customize dialog box, a list of categories is shown. Beside the categories list, a box containing built-in buttons displays. When different categories are selected, different buttons display. Also a new, small Toolbar displays in the upper left corner of the document window.
5. Select the desired Category.

FIGURE A-3

Customize dialog box

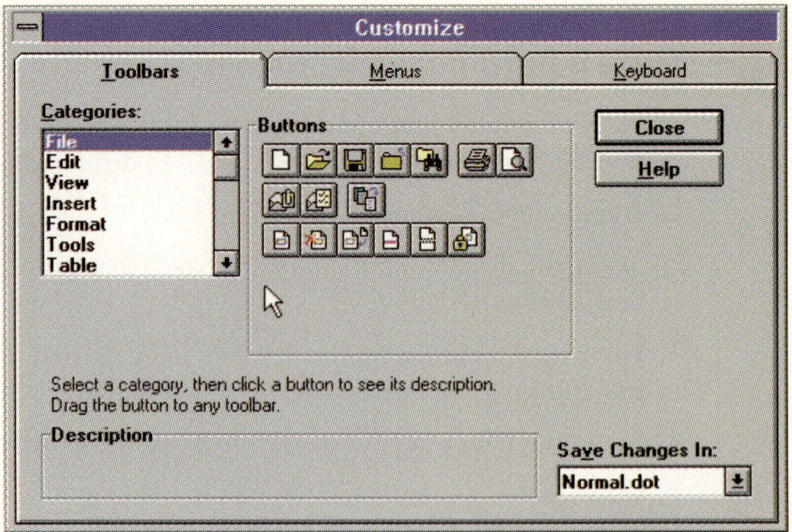

6. Move the mouse pointer to the desired button in the Buttons area and click once.

   Note: A description of the button displays in the Description box.

7. To place a button on the Toolbar, move the mouse pointer to the desired button, press and hold the mouse button while dragging the button to the new Toolbar. Release the mouse button.

8. If desired, select a different category and place a button(s) from a different category on the new Toolbar.

9. When all desired buttons have been placed on the new Toolbar, select **Close**.

10. Point to the Toolbar title bar, press and hold the mouse button while moving the Toolbar to the desired location in the document window.

Steps to Delete a New Custom Toolbar

1. Select **View, Toolbars** or move the mouse pointer to the Toolbar, click the right mouse button and select Toolbars.
2. Highlight the name of the Toolbar to be deleted.
3. Select the **Delete** button.
4. Select **Yes** to the message "Do you wish to delete . . ."
5. Select **OK** or **Close** to exit the Toolbar dialog box.

Steps to Assign a New Customized Button to a Toolbar

Note: *Assigning a new button to a Toolbar is necessary for items that do not have a built-in button. If necessary, point anywhere on the Toolbar and press the right mouse button to display the list of Toolbars. Select the desired Toolbar.*

1. Select **Tools, Customize** or point to a Toolbar, click the right mouse button and select Customize.

   Note: The Customize dialog box displays (see Figure A.3).

2. With the Toolbars tab selected, scroll down the Categories list and choose the desired Category, i.e., **Macros, Fonts, AutoText,** or **Styles**.

   Note: In the Categories list, the items listed below the dotted line do not have built-in buttons.

3. Point to the desired item listed in the box to the right of the Categories list. Click and hold the mouse button to display a button outline. Drag the button outline to the Toolbar, release the mouse button.

   Note: The Custom Button dialog box displays with an outline around the "Text Button." The name of the text button displays in a box at the bottom of the dialog box. If desired, a different text button name can be typed.

4. *To assign the Text Button Name*, select the **Assign** button *or* select one of the available icons displayed in the Button area and then select **Assign**.

   To edit the button, choose an icon, select the **Edit** button; choose the desired color. Select the desired box(es) in the Picture box to create the desired form (shape). When finished, select OK.

   Note: The new button displays in the Toolbar.

5. Select **Close** to exit the Customize box.

Word Technical Support

If you encounter difficulties installing, changing preferences, or using any Word feature, Word's no-charge technical support is available to assist you 6:00 a.m. to 6:00 p.m., Pacific Time, Monday through Friday excluding holidays.

You can contact Technical Support for Microsoft Word for Windows via a toll call at **206-462-9673**. Microsoft distribution and sales can be contacted at 800-426-9400.

APPENDIX

Summary of Enriching Language Arts

Chapter	Vocabulary Words	Grammar/Punctuation Rule
1	comply, efficient, recipient	Introductory Adverbs and Phrases—A comma often follows an introductory adverb or phrase, because the word or phrase provides a transition from the previous sentence.
2	compliance, environment, passive	Introductory (Dependent) Clauses—A comma should follow a dependent clause. An introductory dependent clause often begins with *if, in, when, since,* or *as*.
3	in accordance with, minimum, prospectus, redeem	Appositives—Appositives are words that immediately follow a noun and further identify the noun but usually are not necessary to the meaning of the sentence.
4	appreciate, legislation, qualify	Compound Adjectives and Coordinating Conjunctions—Hyphenate two words that precede and describe a noun and function as a single adjective. A comma is placed before a coordinating conjunction (e.g., and, or, because) that joins two independent clauses.
5	alliances, initiative, strategic	Dollar Amounts Formats—Use a comma to separate the number digits into groups of thousands. No space is placed between a number and the dollar sign. If even numbers are used in the body of a document or if a column of numbers has even dollar amounts, the zeros are omitted.

Chapter	Vocabulary Words	Grammar/Punctuation Rule
6	adversely, per diem, reimbursement	Single and Double Underlines for Dollar Amounts—Place a single underline between the last column amount and the total amount. In a table without lines or borders, a total amount is usually emphasized by placing double underlines beneath the total amount.
7	ecology, journalism, specifically	Commas Used in a Series—Words and/or ideas listed in a series are separated by commas.
8	opportunity, seminar, thoroughly	Using the Abbreviations *e.g.* and *i.e.*—The abbreviation *e.g.* is used in place of "for example" and is often used when one or more of many examples are listed. The abbreviation *i.e.* is used in place of "that is" and is used when all potential conditions are listed.
9	certified, comprehensive, forum, independent, productivity	Speller Hint—The Speller approves words that are correctly spelled; however, a correctly spelled word can be incorrectly used in a sentence.
10	contagious, knowledge, technological	Quotation Marks with Punctuation—Always place a comma or period inside a closing quotation mark. Place a question mark or exclamation point inside closing quotation marks if the question or exclamation pertains only to the quoted information. Place a question mark or exclamation point outside the closing quotation marks if the question or exclamation pertains to the entire sentence.
11	apology, hallmark, inconvenience	Nonrestrictive Clause—A nonrestrictive clause is a clause that is not essential to the meaning of the sentence and is, therefore, set off by a comma or commas.
12	adhere, eligibility, ensuring, furnishing	Subject-Verb Agreement—Verbs must agree in number with their subject. If a subject is singular, use a singular verb; if a subject is plural, use a plural verb.
13	anonymously, complaint, coordinator	Initials Abbreviated—Periods or spaces are not placed after the letters of an acronym such as IRS (Internal Revenue Service) or TWA (Trans World Airlines).
14	simplify, unique, withdrawal	Independent Adjectives—Two adjectives that modify the same noun are separated by a comma.

Chapter	Vocabulary Words	Grammar/Punctuation Rule
15	exempt, prohibit, sole	Apostrophe Used to Show Possession—If a noun is singular and used to show possession, add an apostrophe (') and an s. If the noun is plural or the final letter in the noun is an s, add only an apostrophe after the s.
16	(No vocabulary words)	Proofreading Hints—When proofreading a document, read the document twice: once for content and meaning and once to check grammar, spelling, and punctuation.
17	demonstrate, techniques, tuition	Parentheses—Parentheses can be used to set off nonessential expressions that might otherwise confuse the reader. The information within the parentheses provides supplemental information that has no direct bearing on the main idea of the sentence or paragraph. Words, phrases, or clauses can be enclosed within parentheses. Unless a comma, colon, or semicolon is necessary to the text within parentheses, place the punctuation outside the closing parenthesis. If the text within the parentheses is a complete sentence, the final punctuation is placed within the parentheses
18	repetitive, symptoms, trauma	Em and En Dashes—The em dash (—), a typographic symbol about the width of the character m, is often used in place of a comma. The en dash (–), a typographic symbol about the width of the character n, is used as a hyphen or as a substitute for the word "to," e.g., July–September. The correct typographic symbols for em and en dashes have traditionally been used for books, newspapers, and advertisements, and are recommended for use when creating a professional-looking document.
19	arbitration, grievance, interpretation	Colons, Capitalization, and Punctuation of Bulleted and Enumerated Lists—Place a colon after an independent clause that introduces a bulleted or enumerated (numbered) list. An introductory clauses frequently includes words such as "the following" and "as follows." When creating a bulleted or enumerated list, capitalize the first word and insert a final punctuation mark (period, question mark, or exclamation point) after each item that is a complete sentence or phrase. Do not capitalize the first word or insert final punctuation when bulleted or enumerated lists are not completed thoughts.

Chapter	Vocabulary Words	Grammar/Punctuation Rule
20	deductible, prosthesis, routine	Contractions—An apostrophe is used to indicate where a letter(s) has been omitted when two words are combined to form a verb contraction. Generally contractions are not used in formal business writing. contractions can be used in personal letters or informal business documents.
21	diversity, entitled, exclusive, render	Percentage Amounts—Use figures for numbers that are followed by the word percent. Spell out the word percent unless the percentage amount is used in a table that contains statistical information or in a headline/title.
22	clients, cuisine, exception, minimal, savor	Basic Rulers for Numbers—Generally, numbers one through ten when used in writing are spelled out. Also, numbers used in approximation and numbers at the beginning of a sentence are usually spelled out. Use figures when a number if followed by the word percent. Omit the colon and zeros when writing an even clock time.
23	quarterly, reflect, surpassed	Abbreviations in Table Column Headings—When create tables and forms, abbreviations are often used in subtitles and column headings because of limited space. However, abbreviations should be used sparingly. If you are unsure of an abbreviation, consult a dictionary.
24	initially, refuse, vital	Abbreviations for Time—Type a.m. and p.m. with lowercase letters and no space between. Only one period is used if the abbreviation is the last element in a sentence. *(Note: Word's Insert, Date and Time command or a Date type Text Form Field, format the time as AM or PM regardless of how the abbreviation(s) is typed.)*

APPENDIX

Sample Word Graphic Images, Templates, and Wizards

1stplace.wmf

anchor.wmf

atomengy.wmf

books.wmf

buttrfly.wmf

cat.wmf

celtic.wmf

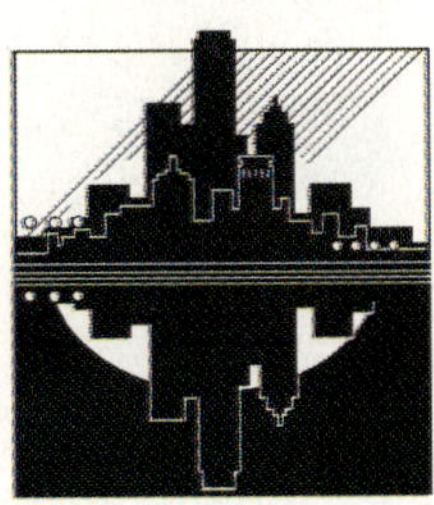

cityscpe.wmf

coffee.wmf

compass.wmf

computer.wmf

continen.wmf

dancer.wmf

deco.wmf

dinner1.wmf

dinner2.wmf

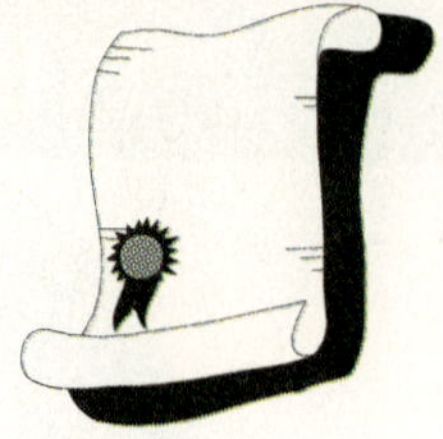

diploma.wmf

disk.wmf

elephant.wmf

fall.wmf

golf.wmf

hcorner.wmf

hdecobox.wmf

heart.wmf

horse.wmf

houses.wmf

hplaque.wmf

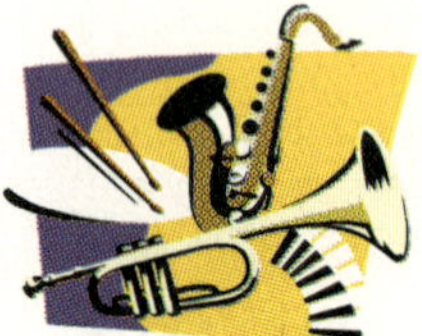

jazz.wmf

jet.wmf

label1.wmf

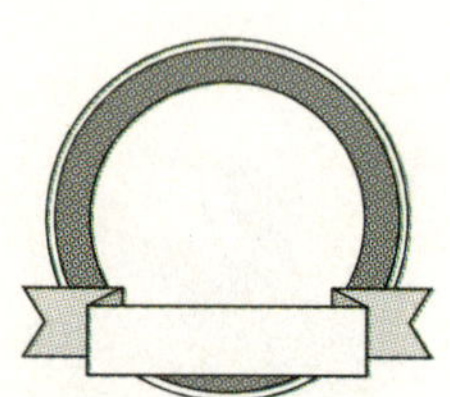

label2.wmf

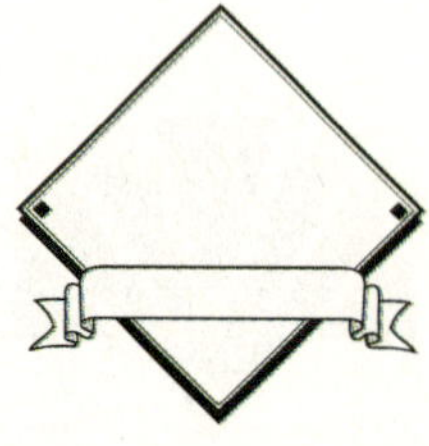

ldiamond.wmf

leaf,wmf

lightblb.wmf

luggage.wmf

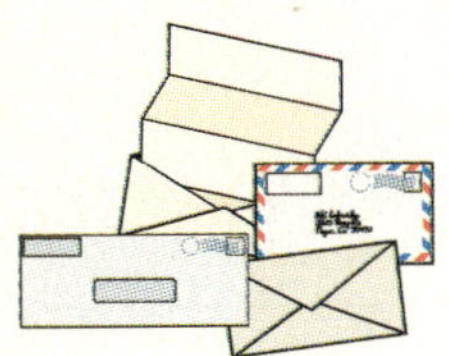

mail.wmf

math.wmf

medstaff.wmf

movie.wmf

nosmoke.wmf

notes.wmf

nouveau2.wmf

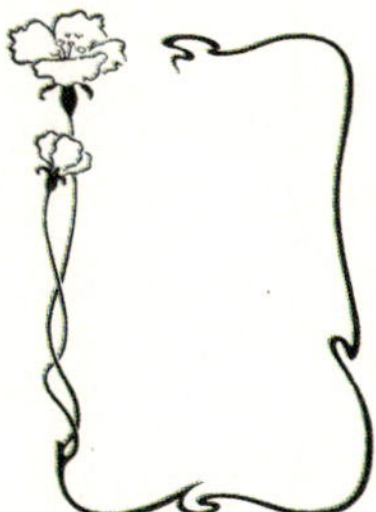

nouvflwr.wmf

office.wmf

ornamnt2.wmf

party.wmf

realest.wmf

scales.wmf

server.wmf

speaker.wmf

sports.wmf

spring.wmf

summer.wmf

tennis.wmf

theatre.wmf

Sample Templates

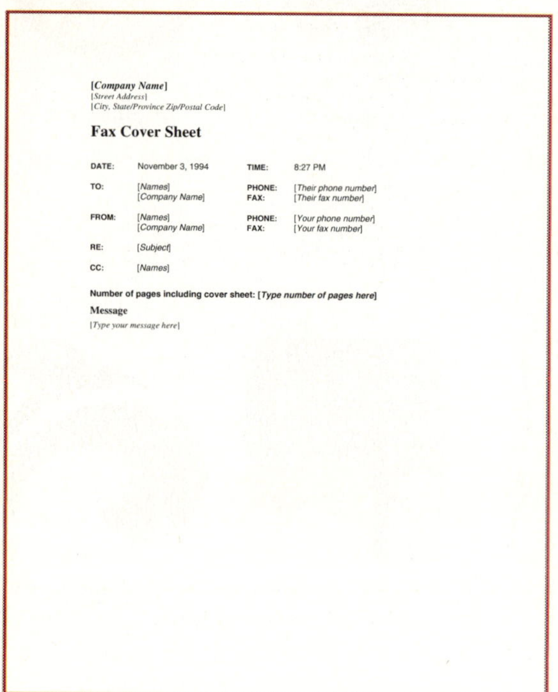

[Company Name]
[Street Address]
[City, State/Province Zip/Postal Code]

Fax Cover Sheet

DATE:	November 3, 1994	TIME:	8:27 PM
TO:	[Names] [Company Name]	PHONE: FAX:	[Their phone number] [Their fax number]
FROM:	[Names] [Company Name]	PHONE: FAX:	[Your phone number] [Your fax number]
RE:	[Subject]		
CC:	[Names]		

Number of pages including cover sheet: [*Type number of pages here*]

Message

[Type your message here]

Faxcovr1—classic fax cover sheet

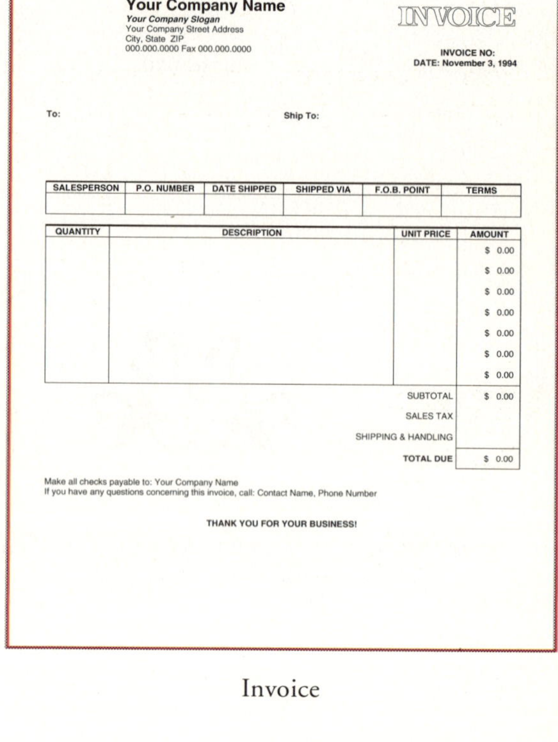

Your Company Name
Your Company Slogan
Your Company Street Address
City, State ZIP
000.000.0000 Fax 000.000.0000

INVOICE

INVOICE NO:
DATE: November 3, 1994

To: **Ship To:**

SALESPERSON	P.O. NUMBER	DATE SHIPPED	SHIPPED VIA	F.O.B. POINT	TERMS

QUANTITY	DESCRIPTION	UNIT PRICE	AMOUNT
			$ 0.00
			$ 0.00
			$ 0.00
			$ 0.00
			$ 0.00
			$ 0.00
			$ 0.00
		SUBTOTAL	$ 0.00
		SALES TAX	
		SHIPPING & HANDLING	
		TOTAL DUE	$ 0.00

Make all checks payable to: Your Company Name
If you have any questions concerning this invoice, call: Contact Name, Phone Number

THANK YOU FOR YOUR BUSINESS!

Invoice

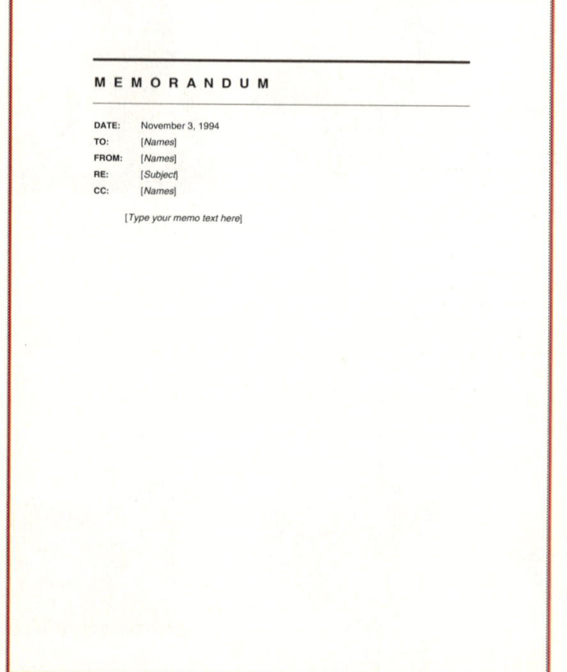

M E M O R A N D U M

DATE:	November 3, 1994
TO:	[Names]
FROM:	[Names]
RE:	[Subject]
CC:	[Names]

[Type your memo text here]

Memo2—contemporary memo

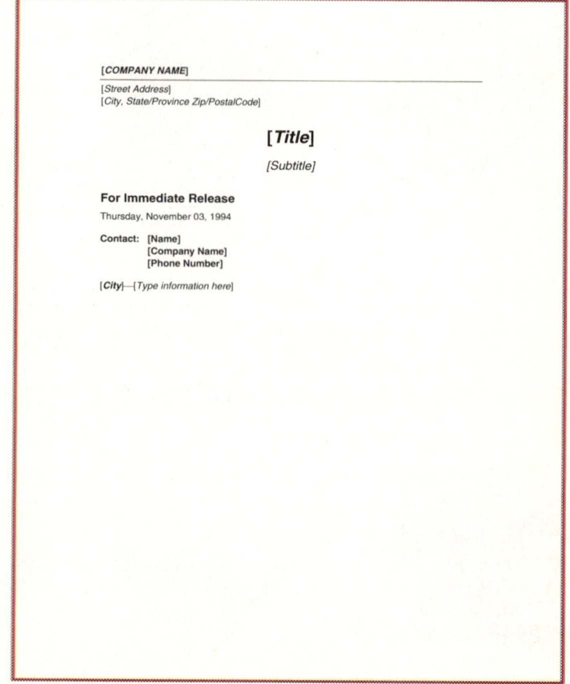

[COMPANY NAME]
[Street Address]
[City, State/Province Zip/PostalCode]

[*Title*]

[Subtitle]

For Immediate Release
Thursday, November 03, 1994

Contact: [Name]
[Company Name]
[Phone Number]

[***City***]—[*Type information here*]

Presrel2—contemporary press release

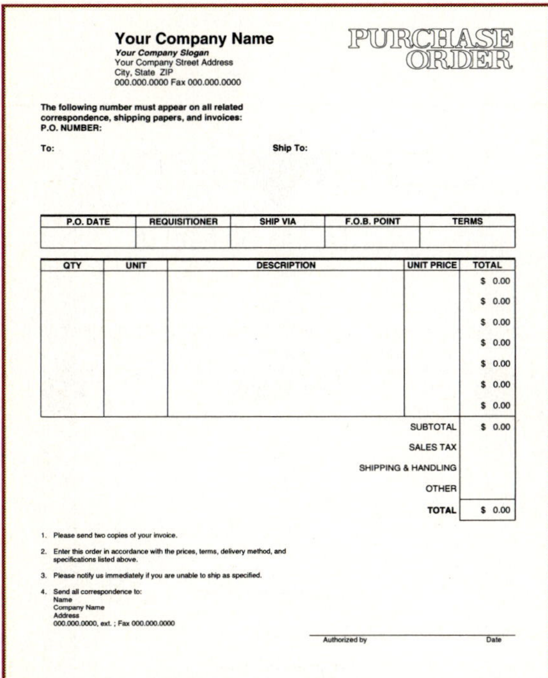

Your Company Name
Your Company Slogan
Your Company Street Address
City, State ZIP
000.000.0000 Fax 000.000.0000

PURCHASE ORDER

The following number must appear on all related correspondence, shipping papers, and invoices:
P.O. NUMBER:

To: **Ship To:**

P.O. DATE	REQUISITIONER	SHIP VIA	F.O.B. POINT	TERMS

QTY	UNIT	DESCRIPTION	UNIT PRICE	TOTAL
				$ 0.00
				$ 0.00
				$ 0.00
				$ 0.00
				$ 0.00
				$ 0.00
				$ 0.00
			SUBTOTAL	$ 0.00
			SALES TAX	
			SHIPPING & HANDLING	
			OTHER	
			TOTAL	$ 0.00

1. Please send two copies of your invoice.
2. Enter this order in accordance with the prices, terms, delivery method, and specifications listed above.
3. Please notify us immediately if you are unable to ship as specified.
4. Send all correspondence to:
   Name
   Company Name
   Address
   000.000.0000, ext. ; Fax 000.000.0000

Authorized by Date

Purchord—purchase order

[*Name*]
[*Street Address*]
[*City, State/Province Zip/Postal Code*]
(###) ###-#### (W) (###) ###-#### (H)

Objective: [Type in your Objective here.]

Professional Experience

Month, 19XX to Present
[*Company Name*]
[City, State/Province]
[Position Held]. [*Details of Position*]

Month, 19XX to Month, 19XX
[*Company Name*]
[City, State/Province]
[Position Held]. [*Details of Position*]

Education

19XX to 19XX
[*Institution Name*]
[City, State/Province]
[*Degree/Achievement*]

Organizations

19XX
[*Company/Institution Name*]
[City, State/Province]
[Position Held]

Resume1—classic résumé

Your Company Name
Your Company Slogan
Your Company Street Address
City, State ZIP
000.000.0000 Fax 000.000.0000

WEEKLY TIME SHEET

Employee Name: Title:
Employee Number: Status: Full-time
Department: Supervisor:

Date	Start Time	End Time	Regular Hrs.	Overtime Hrs.	Total Hrs.
					0
					0
					0
					0
					0
					0
					0
		WEEKLY TOTALS	0	0	0

Employee Signature: Date:
Supervisor Signature: Date:

Weektime—weekly time sheet

Sample Wizards

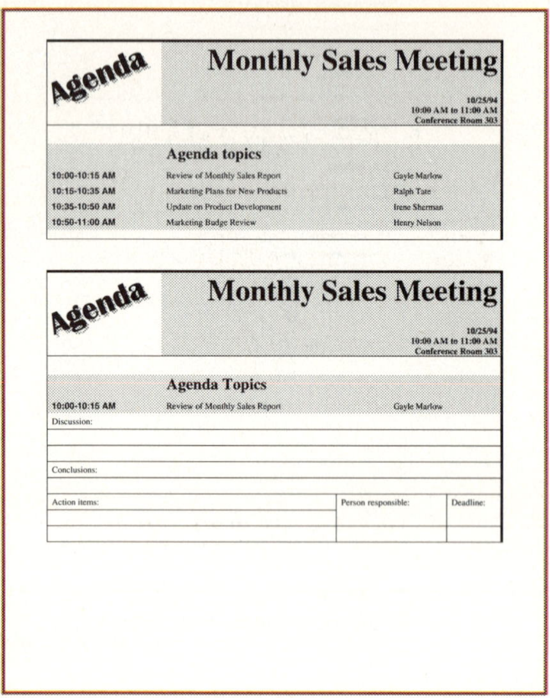

Agenda wizard—Modern
(page 1 and 2)

Award wizard—Jazzy

Calendar wizard—Banner

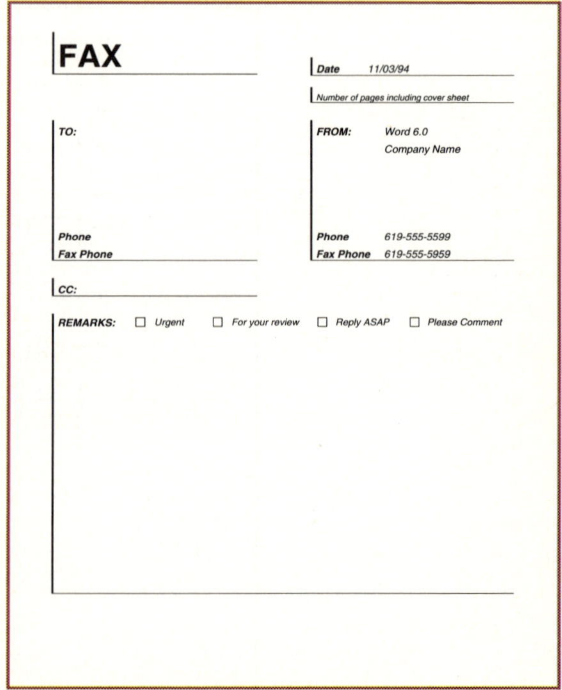

Faz wizard—Contemporary

MEMO

Date: Current date
To: [Names]
From: Your Name
Subject: [Subject]

[Type your memo text here]

lh
Enc. 2

CONFIDENTIAL

Memo wizard—Contemporary

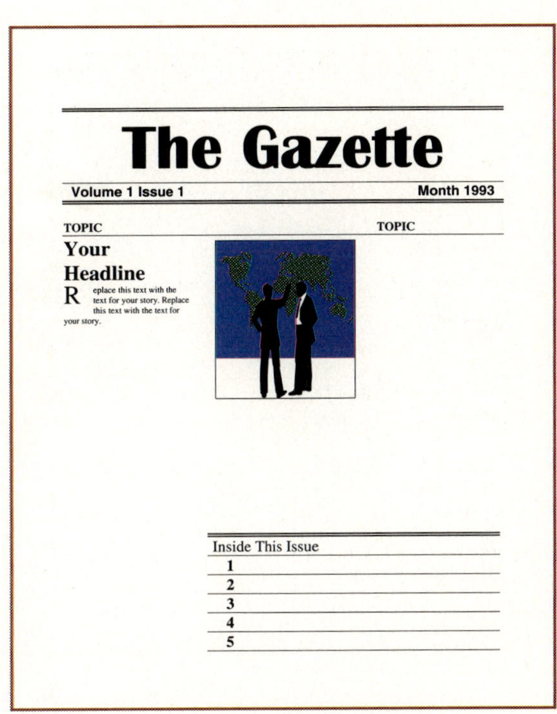

The Gazette

Volume 1 Issue 1 **Month 1993**

TOPIC

Your Headline

Replace this text with the text for your story. Replace this text with the text for your story.

TOPIC

Inside This Issue

1
2
3
4
5

Newsletter wizard—classic

Attorney Name
Company Name
Street Address
City, State/Province Zip/Postal Code
Telephone: (###)###-####
Fax:(###)###-####

Attorney for: Client's name

UNITED STATES DISTRICT COURT

CENTRAL DISTRICT OF CALIFORNIA

PLAINTIFF'S NAME,	No. 12-3-456/89-1
Plaintiff,	
vs.	PLEADING TITLE
DEFENDANT'S NAME,	
Defendant	

Page 1

Pleading wizard

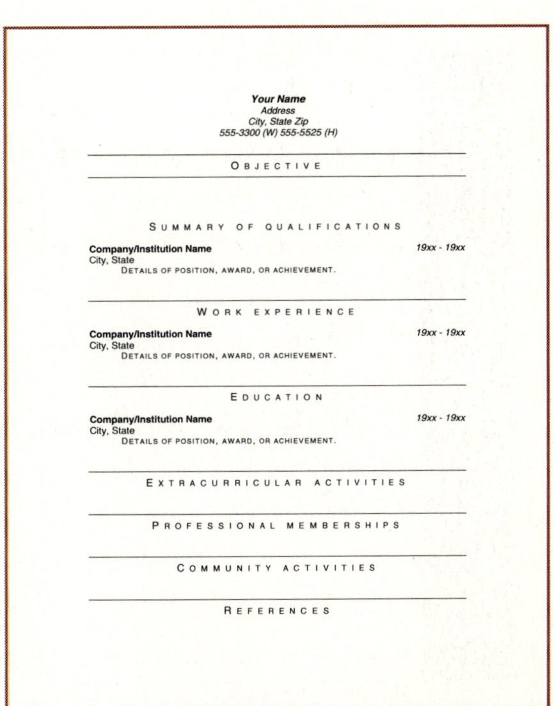

Your Name
Address
City, State Zip
555-3300 (W) 555-5525 (H)

OBJECTIVE

SUMMARY OF QUALIFICATIONS

Company/Institution Name *19xx - 19xx*
City, State
DETAILS OF POSITION, AWARD, OR ACHIEVEMENT.

WORK EXPERIENCE

Company/Institution Name *19xx - 19xx*
City, State
DETAILS OF POSITION, AWARD, OR ACHIEVEMENT.

EDUCATION

Company/Institution Name *19xx - 19xx*
City, State
DETAILS OF POSITION, AWARD, OR ACHIEVEMENT.

EXTRACURRICULAR ACTIVITIES

PROFESSIONAL MEMBERSHIPS

COMMUNITY ACTIVITIES

REFERENCES

Résumé chronological—Contemporary

APPENDIX

Answers to Self-Check Quizzes

Chapter 1	*Chapter 2*	*Chapter 3*	*Chapter 4*	*Chapter 5*	*Chapter 6*
1. T	1. F	1. T	1. T	1. T	1. T
2. T	2. T	2. T	2. F	2. T	2. F
3. T	3. T	3. F	3. T	3. F	3. T
4. F	4. T	4. F	4. T	4. T	4. F
5. F	5. T	5. b	5. F	5. T	5. b
6. a	6. d	6. a	6. a	6. b	6. c
7. b	7. a	7. c	7. d	7. d	7. c
8. c	8. d		8. c	8. c	8. d

Chapter 7	*Chapter 8*	*Chapter 9*	*Chapter 10*	*Chapter 11*	*Chapter 12*
1. F	1. T	1. F	1. T	1. F	1. T
2. T	2. F	2. T	2. T	2. T	2. F
3. T	3. T	3. F	3. F	3. T	3. T
4. T	4. F	4. F	4. T	4. T	4. F
5. d	5. T	5. d	5. a	5. T	5. F
6. d	6. b	6. a	6. d	6. a	6. a
7. d	7. d	7. d	7. c	7. c	7. b
8. d		8. a	8. b	8. c	8. c

Chapter 13	Chapter 14	*Chapter 15*	*Chapter 16*	Chapter 17	Chapter 18
1. T	1. T	1. T	1. T	1. T	1. T
2. F	2. T	2. T	2. F	2. T	2. T
3. T	3. F	3. F	3. T	3. F	3. T
4. T	4. T	4. T	4. T	4. F	4. T
5. F	5. T	5. T	5. T	5. F	5. d
6. d	6. c	6. d	6. d	6. a	6. a
7. d	7. a	7. b	7. b	7. b	7. a
8. d	8. b	8. a	8. d	8. c	8. b

Chapter 19	*Chapter 20*	*Chapter 21*	*Chapter 22*	*Chapter 23*	*Chapter 24*	*Chapter 25*
1. T	1. F	1. T	1. T	1. T	1. T	1. T
2. F	2. T	2. F	2. T	2. T	2. T	2. T
3. T	3. T	3. T	3. T	3. T	3. T	3. T
4. F	4. T	4. T	4. T	4. F	4. T	4. T
5. T	5. b	5. F	5. T	5. T	5. F	5. T
6. b	6. a	6. b	6. b	6. b	6. c	6. F
7. c	7. d	7. d	7. d	7. d	7. a	7. b
8. d	8. d	8. d		8. a	8. d	

APPENDIX

Integrating the Microsoft Office

Windows Multitasking

Word 6.0 for Windows is designed to take full advantage of Windows' ability to run multiple programs and makes it easy to set up a Toolbar to launch other Microsoft products and transfer data and files between programs. Updating a spreadsheet and inserting it in a document, sending faxes and electronic mail (E-Mail), and even merging a form letter directly to the fax or E-Mail system are just a few of the many possibilities to make your workday more productive.

Launching a Program Within Word

The first step to launching a program within Word is to display the Microsoft Toolbar or add buttons for other Microsoft programs to the Toolbar most likely to be in use when the program is needed. Use the Steps to Display a Different Toolbar on page A-4 to select the Microsoft Toolbar. To add a Microsoft program button to the current Toolbar, follow steps 1-3 in the Steps to Add a Button to a Toolbar on page A-4. In step 5, select **Tools** as the desired category, then continue with steps 6-8 to add the desired programs to the Toolbar.

Fax Technology

Fax technology allows an exact copy of a document to be transmitted over the telephone system from one fax device to another. Fax, which was originally called facsimile, made its debut at the beginning of the 1930s.

The first fax devices were machines that sent copies of the documents using analog signals. The analog method was very slow. In the 1980s, digital signals replaced analog signals for the transmission of faxes. Digital fax transmission is much faster than analog transmission and is one of the fastest-growing communications tools available.

A stand-alone fax machine works by scanning a hard copy of the document to be faxed and digitizing it so that it can be transmitted electronically. Many computers now contain fax boards or fax/modem boards. These boards function both as a regular data modem for communicating with other computers and for sending documents as faxes to distant fax machines and other fax/modem boards.

All fax boards require software to control their operation, and such software is usually included with the fax board and installed on the computer when the fax board is installed. In addition, several popular software faxing programs are available, which may offer additional features. To use fax technology within Word 6.0 for Windows, the fax board or fax machine must be connected to the computer and a Windows fax program must be installed on the computer.

Using the Fax Within Word 6.0

One way to use the fax within Word is to install the fax board or fax machine as a printer. If this is possible, the fax manual will explain how to do it, using the Windows Control Panel, or will do it automatically as part of the fax software installation program. Once the fax board or machine is listed in the Windows Control Panel as a Printer, it can be designated in Word as the current printer by selecting **File**, **Select Printer**, highlighting the fax board or machine name, and choosing **Select**. Any document can now be sent to the fax board or machine using the same options as if the document were being sent to a printer. Even a document that is not open in Word can be sent to the fax machine using the File, Find File function to display the file, then selecting **Commands**, **Print**. (See pages 386-387 for more information on the File, Find File function.)

In addition, if Microsoft Mail is installed on your system, a new command, **Send**, will appear on the File menu. Selecting **File**, **Send** will open the Microsoft Mail program and automatically attach the current document (see Figure E.1). Follow the instructions in the Microsoft Mail manual to address and send the document to the fax.

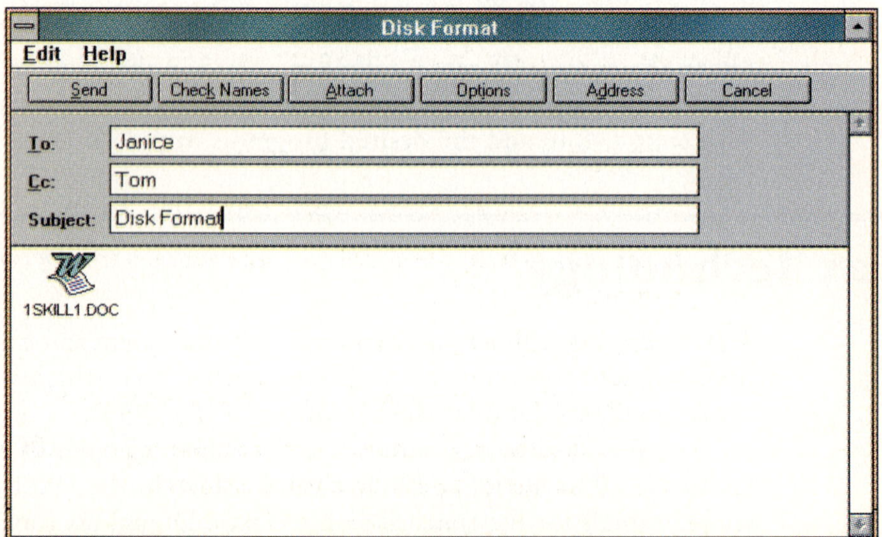

FIGURE E.1

Microsoft Mail program with current document attached

E-Mail

Electronic mail or E-Mail has become a popular way to communicate with work colleagues and friends. Many offices provide network hardware and software so that all computers in the company are connected. When E-Mail software is added, workers can send messages to one another and often work together on projects, depending on the features provided in the E-Mail package. If Microsoft Mail is installed on your system, and the Microsoft Mail package has been installed on your network, you can send documents into the E-Mail system by selecting **File**, **Send**. The Mail program will open with the current document attached (see Figure E.1). Follow the instructions in the Microsoft Mail manual to address and send the document to co-workers on the network.

You can also open the Microsoft Mail program by selecting the **Microsoft Mail** button on the Microsoft Toolbar. With both programs open, information can be copied to the Clipboard and transferred easily between the programs.

Merging to Fax or Mail Programs

When Microsoft Mail has been installed on the system, two new options appear in the Merge dialog box to allow the merged letters to be sent directly to the Mail program, either to the fax or the E-Mail system. The field containing the E-Mail or fax address must be designated. For E-Mail, a subject line can be added. If the fax has been set up in the Mail program to automatically generate a fax cover sheet, the current document can be added as an attachment to this cover sheet. Before these options can be used, the following conditions must be met:

- The fax or E-Mail address must be available in the data source file (the address does not need to be used in the merged letters).
- For faxes, the fax must be connected to the computer and the appropriate set-up options selected in the Mail program.
- For E-Mail, the computer must be connected to a network and the Mail system must be functioning.

Merge to Fax or Mail Programs

1. Create the data source file and main document following the steps in Chapter 11, pages 257-261. Do not merge the files yet.
2. With the main document open, select the **Mail Merge** button.
3. If the data source file contains some records that do not have the fax or E-Mail address:

   a. Select **Query Options**.

   b. Select the **Filter Records** tab if necessary.

   c. Click on the down arrow in the top **Field** box and select the field containing the fax or E-Mail address.

FIGURE E.2

Merge to Setup dialog box

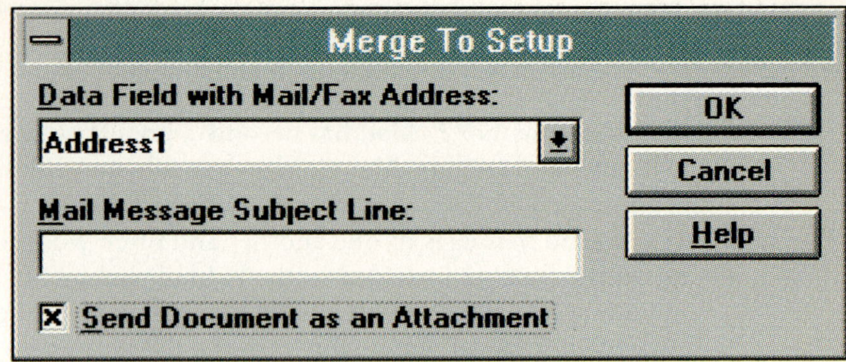

d. Click on the down arrow in the top Comparison box and select the **is Not Blank** option.

e. Select **OK** to return to the Merge dialog box.

4. Click on the down arrow next to the Merge To box.
5. Click once on the desired option.

   For example, click once on **Electronic Mail** or **Electronic Fax.**
6. Click on the **Setup** button.

   Note: The Merge To Setup Dialog box displays (see Figure E.2).
7. Click on the down arrow next to the **Data Field with Mail/Fax Address** and select the appropriate field name from the list.
8. To add a Subject Line to an E-Mail message, click once in the **Mail Message Subject Line** box, then type the desired subject line.
9. To send the merged documents as attachments to an automatically generated fax cover sheet, click once in the **Send Document as an Attachment** box.
10. Select **OK** to return to the Merge dialog box.
11. Select **Merge** to begin the merge process.

APPENDIX

Sound Boards

A sound board converts the computer's discrete digital signals to continuous analog signals. This process uses circuitry called a Digital Analog Converter (DAC). The quality of the sound depends on the digital input, the design of the board, and the audio amplifiers. Better sound usually means more bytes (megabytes) of digital data (larger files) and more expensive cards and amplifiers.

Sound is converted into digital signals from analog signals through software using circuitry called an Analog Digital Converter (ADC). Not all sound boards can perform this function, although most boards today do so. The choice of which sound board to buy will depend on your current and future uses of the board as well as how much money you want to invest.

Sound boards may interface with a Musical Instrument Digital Interface (MIDI). This is a standard interface that was initially created by Kawai, Korg, Roland, Sequential Circuits, and Yamaha. The MIDI interface allows the computer to generate music in a manner similar to earlier analog synthesizers, but at much less expense. Since MIDI files do not actually store the sound (they store instructions that enable the computer to re-create the sound), they are smaller than other sound files.

Sound clip libraries are available with a wide range of sounds, music, and prerecorded phrases (similar to clip art libraries). Sound clips are commonly available in two formats, MIDI (.mid) and digital audio (.wav). Some boards can only read one type of file, but many boards can handle both. Digital audio files work much like an audio tape. The sounds are digitized and stored on a disk or on the hard drive. The files are usually much larger and require more disk space than MIDI files.

Many sound boards have a joystick port because it was the support of sound in games that provided the market that brought about the proliferation of less expensive, more capable sound boards.

Many sound boards also provide support for CD-ROMs. This allows music and other sound sources to be integrated into programs and attached to data files in the computer. CDs with libraries of sound and sound effects are available.

Install and Configure the Sound Board

The first step in installing a sound board is to follow the instructions from the maker of the board. If two sets of connector fingers are on the bottom of the sound board, the board should be placed into a motherboard slot with two openings (a 16-bit slot). In general, the default values that the manufacturer has set up are used. The IRQ (interrupt request) value is often 5 or 7. The base I/O address is often 220H or 240H. The DMA (direct memory access) is usually 1. Generally, the sound board has accompanying diagnostic software to help set the correct values if conflicts are experienced. If the sound board has a DOS program, try using several of the board capabilities with its own software before trying to access the board through Windows.

Once the sound board is installed, you must configure Windows to work with the sound board. Software drivers (files) are usually provided with the sound board. Follow the manufacturer's instructions to copy the Windows software driver to the hard disk and to identify the sound board in the Windows Control Panel.

Note: The following instructions are generic. If there are differences between these instructions and those in the manufacturer's instruction manual for the sound board, follow the manufacturer's instructions.

Start-Up Instructions

- Place the disk containing the sound board drivers into drive A or B.

Identify the Board for Windows

1. Start Windows by typing **win** at the system prompt.
2. Double-click on the **Control Panel** icon in the Main group.
3. Double-click on the **Drivers** icon in the Control Panel.
4. Select **Add**.

   Note: The Add window appears. The box to the left of the Add window lists all of the current sound device drivers installed in Windows.

5. Highlight the item **Unlisted or Updated Driver**, which should be the first item on the list.
6. Select **OK**.

   Note: The Install Driver window will appear. This window asks you to insert the disk containing the Unlisted or Updated Driver into drive A:\.

7. If you are using drive B, substitute the letter B for the letter A in the field. When the drive letter is correct, select **OK**.

   Note: The name of the sound driver will appear in the Add Unlisted or Updated Driver window.

8. Make sure the name of the driver is highlighted, then select **OK**.

9. Follow the manufacturer's instructions to select the appropriate options for the sound board. These will depend on the individual sound board.
10. When the installation process is complete, select **Close** to return to the Control Panel window, then close the Control Panel by double-clicking on the Control button. Exit Windows, then restart it so that the new driver will be included in the Windows program.

Test the Sound Board in Windows

1. Double-click on the **Control Panel** icon in the Main group.
2. Double-click on the **Sound** icon.
3. To play a sound clip, double-click on any of the **.wav** or **.mid** files in the File List. If sound clip files have been installed but do not appear on the list, select the **Browse** button to access the list of directories and find the directory where the files are installed.
4. When you are satisfied that the sound board is working with Windows, select **OK** to close the Sound window, then close the Control Panel by double-clicking on the Control button.

Record Sounds or Voice in a Word 6.0 Document File

Plug the microphone into the phone input jack. Check that the on/off switch is in the On position. Because the proper microphone is vital, many manufacturers include a microphone with their sound board. To record sound, Word for Windows launches the Windows Sound Recorder. With the WIndows Sound Records sound can be saved in a separate file or in the current document. Options are available adjust the volume and to create special effects, such as echos.

Record Sounds or Voice

1. Select **Insert, Object** {Alt, i, o}.

   Note: The Object dialog box will appear.
2. If necessary, select the **Create New** tab {Alt and c}.
3. Scroll down the list of programs and highlight **Sound** {use the down arrow to highlight Sound}.
4. Select **OK**.

   Note: The Windows Sound Recorder is launched (see Figure F-1). Make sure your microphone is turned on.
5. Select the **Record** button (the button with the microphone on it).

   Note: Sound Recorder will display the amount of available memory and the maximum recording time. Wait until the arrow pointer returns before starting to speak.

FIGURE F.1

Sound Recorder dialog box

6. To record your voice, speak into the microphone while holding it 6–10 inches from your mouth. To record sounds, hold the microphone 6–10 inches from the source of the sound. You may need to experiment to find the right range.
7. When you are finished, select the **Stop** button (the button with the square in the middle).
8. Use the Rewind, Play, and Forward buttons to evaluate the recording and make changes, just as you would using a standard tape recorder. For additional options and special effects, refer to the Windows reference manual for information about using Sound Recorder or select **Help** from the Sound Recorder Menu bar.
9. When the recording is complete, return to the document in one of the following ways:

To save the recording in a separate file to be used in other documents:

a. Select **File, Save As**.

b. Type a name for the sound clip, then select **OK**.

Note: The message "Update embedded object before saving to another file?" will appear.

c. Select **Yes** if the recording is to be used in the current document as well as in other documents. If the recording is only to be used in other documents, select **No**.

*Note: When **Yes** is selected, the sound recorder icon (a microphone, shown in Figure F.2) will appear in the current document.*

To save the recording only in the current document:

a. Select **File, Exit**.

Note: The message "The command you have chosen will close the connection of this embedded object. Update Sound in [filename] before proceeding?" will appear.

b. Select **Yes** to save the recording and return to the document. Select **No** to return to the document without saving the recording. Select **Cancel** to return to the Sound Recorder window.

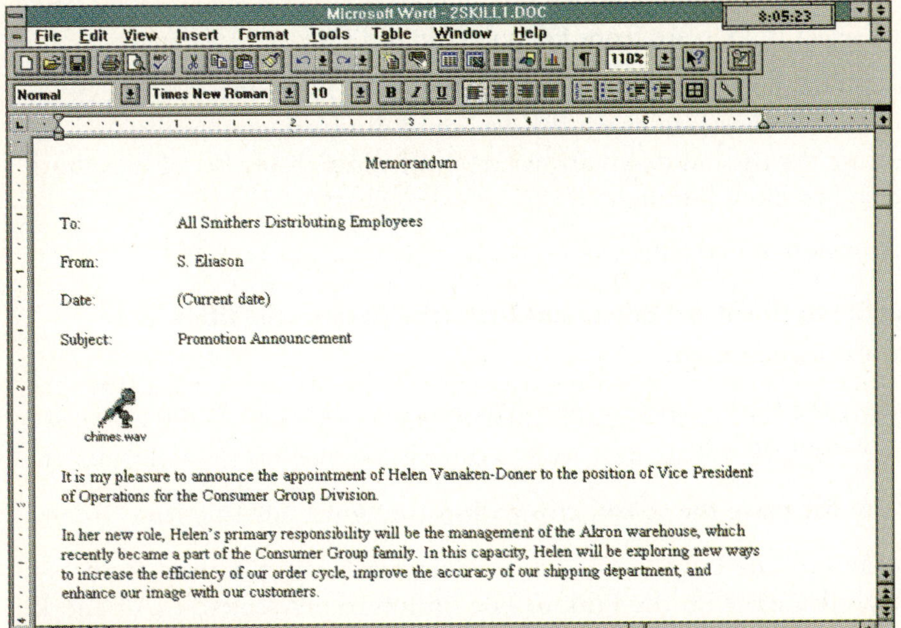

FIGURE F.2

Sound icon in Word 6.0 for Windows document

Use an Existing Sound File in a Word 6.0 Document File

After a recording has been made, it can be inserted into a document. Also, sound clips from other sources can be used by copying them to the hard drive.

A sound clip can be inserted as either a linked file or an embedded object. Using a separate sound file linked to the document is an efficient method because the size of the document file is minimized. It also allows easy reuse of the sound file in other documents. A directory holding a library of sound clips is similar to the directory of graphic images.

The disadvantage of an external sound clip file is that, as with all linked files, moving either the document file or the sound clip file can cause the link to be broken because the path information is no longer correct. This can be a problem on networks even if the files are not moved because people may change directory-to-drive letter mappings. When the sound clip file is inserted as an embedded object, the clip is saved and moved within the document, just as the text of the document is saved. The document file is much larger, but the need to remember to move the sound file when the document file is moved and/or reset the path information is eliminated.

When you insert or link a sound file into the document, a sound clip icon will appear in the document, even if the Display as Icon option is not selected. The default icon is similar to that shown in Figure F.2, or other icons can be substituted.

Embed or Link a Sound Clip

1. Place the insertion point at the location in the document where the sound clip is desired.
2. Select **Insert, Object** {Alt, i, o}.

3. If necessary, select the **Create from File** tab {Alt and f}.
4. Scroll through the list of file names and highlight the file containing the desired sound clip. If necessary, select the drive and directory containing the sound files {use the up and down arrows to scroll through the list of files until the desired sound file is highlighted.
5. Set the link option as desired:

To link the file to the Word document (only the path to the file will be saved within the document):

a. Select the **Link to File** option {Alt and k}, so that an X appears next to the option.

To embed the file (save the sound clip within the Word document):

a. Make sure the Link to File option does not have an X in it. If necessary, click once on the **Link to File** option to deselected it {Alt and k}.

6. To change to a different icon, select the **Display as Icon** option {Alt and a}, then select the **Change Icon** button {Alt and i}.

   Note: The Change Icon dialog box will display.
7. Select **Browse** {Alt and b}. Highlight a file containing icons, such as the progman.exe file, changing the drive and directory if necessary. Select **OK** {Enter} to return to the Change Icon dialog box.
8. To change the text associated with the icon, double-click in the Caption box and type the desired text {Alt and c, type the desired text}. Select **OK** to return to the Object dialog box.
9. Select **OK** to return to the document window.

   Note: The icon representing the linked or embedded file will appear in the document.

Steps to Play the Sound Clip

1. Move the mouse pointer to the sound icon in the document and click once to select it {move the insertion point directly to the left of the sound icon, hold down the Shift key and press the right arrow key once}.
2. Double-click on the sound icon to play it {Alt and e, o, p}.

Steps to Edit a Sound Clip in a Document

1. Move the mouse pointer to the sound icon in the document and click once to select it {move the insertion point directly to the left of the sound icon, hold down the Shift key and press the right arrow key once}.

To delete the sound clip:

a. Select **Edit, Cut** {press Delete}.

To edit the sound recording:

a. Click the right mouse button once, select **Edit Sound Link** or **Edit Sound** {Alt and e, o, e}.

b. When all editing changes have been made, select **File, Save As** to save the changes to a separate file or select **File, Update** to return to the document window and save the changes only in the current document {Alt and f, a or Alt and f, u}. Respond **Yes** to the prompt.

Sound File Storage Information

Sound files may use much of your storage resources, both memory and disk space. Digital audio files (sound converted to a digital format) are usually stored in the way that the board generated the bytes representing the sound. Two common voice file formats are .wav and .voc, which basically differ in their headers (initial sectors). The headers indicate the characteristics of the recorded data—voice or wave, stereo or mono—for the particular file format.

Sampling sizes (8- or 16-bit) and rates help to determine the quality of the recorded sound as well as the size of the files. Eight-bit cards can produce a 1-byte (8-bit) sample. Sixteen-bit cards store 2-byte samples. An 8-bit card can generate 256 discrete steps. Four bits (a nibble) can represent 16 possibilities; 8 bits can represent two 16-possibility groups (16 x 16 = 256). A 16-bit card can represent 65,536 (256 x 256) possibilities or steps in the sound range. If the sampling rate is 6,000 Hertz (Hz), 6,000 samples are taken per second. This restricts the recording of upper frequency limits. High-quality boards are now sampling at the rate of 44,100 samples per second to provide 22,050 sample rates for each of the two stereo channels. At 6,000 Hz, a 60-second recording uses an entire 360K floppy disk. A 20MB hard disk is filled with 7.7 minutes of stereo at 22,050 Hz.

Sound files can be compressed so that they need less disk space. Generally, compressed files degrade the sound quality. Compressed files cannot be converted to other formats and are not easily edited. Compression techniques, somewhat similar to the methods of data compression used to store larger files or to increase effective disk space, are also used. Although LHARC, PKZIP, STACKER, DOUBLESPACE and other programs can make great reductions in data files, they are not as useful with voice files. The speed needed for sound files requires rapid file decompression, and the complex algorithms of extreme data compression have not been able to provide this speed.

INDEX

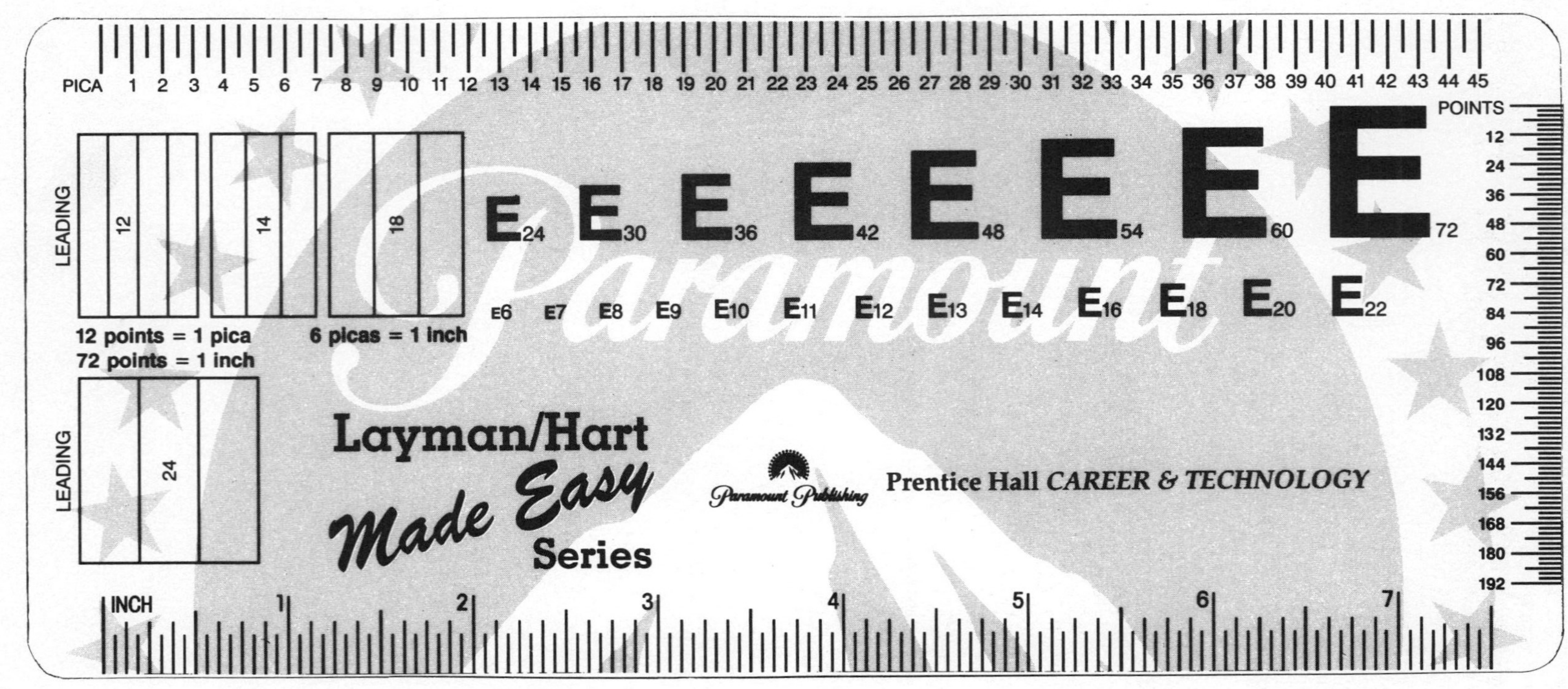
PICA 1 2 3 4 5 6 7 8 9 10 11 12 13 14 15 16 17 18 19 20 21 22 23 24 25 26 27 28 29 30 31 32 33 34 35 36 37 38 39 40 41 42 43 44 45
POINTS 12 24 36 48 60 72 84 96 108 120 132 144 156 168 180 192
LEADING 12 14 18
E24 E30 E36 E42 E48 E54 E60 E72
E6 E7 E8 E9 E10 E11 E12 E13 E14 E16 E18 E20 E22
12 points = 1 pica
72 points = 1 inch
6 picas = 1 inch
LEADING 24
Paramount
Layman/Hart
Made Easy
Series
Paramount Publishing
Prentice Hall CAREER & TECHNOLOGY
INCH 1 2 3 4 5 6 7